BARRON'S

ESSENTIAL WORDS FOR THE

IELTS

with Audio CD

Lin Lougheed
Ed.D., Teachers College
Columbia University

BARRON'S

ACKNOWLEDGMENT

The author would like to thank all the teachers and students around the world who have helped form the content of this book. The author is especially grateful to Daniel Norman for his contribution on the history of the circus and to Kristen Girardi, the editor, for her generous and careful attention to every single detail in the book.

All inquiries should be addressed to:
Barron's Educational Series, Inc.
250 Wireless Boulevard
Hauppauge, NY 11788
www.barronseduc.com

ISBN: 978-1-4380-7071-1

Library of Congress Catalog Card No.: 2010043858

Library of Congress Cataloging-in-Publication Data
Lougheed, Lin, 1946–
    Essential words for the IELTS with audio cd / Lin Lougheed.
      p. cm.
    ISBN 978-1-4380-7071-1
  1. English language—Textbooks for foreign speakers. 2. International English Language Testing System—Study guides. 3. Vocabulary. 4. English language—Spoken English. I. Barron's Educational Series, Inc. II. Title.
    PE1128.L6437 2011
    428.3'4—dc22

                                     2010043858

PRINTED IN THE UNITED STATES OF AMERICA
9 8 7 6 5 4 3 2

CD Track Listing

Unit 10: Inventions—The Transatlantic Cable

Narrator: Listen to a tour guide at a museum.

Tour Guide:
Welcome to the City Museum of Invention. We'll begin our tour with a brief overview of the history of the museum. This museum first opened its doors in 1985, the result of years of effort by the mayor and others in our city. In 1975, the city's mayor first got the idea to start a museum about inventions. After he got several experts interested, he set out to rally the necessary funds. In 1976, several events were held to raise the requisite amount of money to begin construction of a building to house the museum. They had almost raised enough money when there was an unexpected setback. A family that had promised a large percentage of the needed funds inexplicably withdrew their offer. It was toward the end of 1977 that this large gift was lost. Although there was an inquiry, it was never made clear why the funds were withdrawn. Plans for the museum were put aside for five or six years. But a group of interested people renewed the efforts, and by 1982 they had rallied enough monetary support to go ahead with the plans. That year, construction on the building began. In just under three years, the museum was completed, the result of the perseverance of a number of dedicated people. The museum continues to be a popular part of our city's culture. Although everything in the museum follows the theme of inventions, the variety of the exhibits will appeal to visitors of disparate interests. Our most popular exhibit, which is all about cable TV, was first opened in 1998.

Introduction

Barron's Essential Words for the IELTS will help familiarize you with the vocabulary you will find on the reading and listening sections of the IELTS exam (International English Language Testing System). As the number of words you understand when you are reading and listening increases, your speaking and writing vocabulary will improve as well.

VOCABULARY AND THE IELTS

Vocabulary is not tested directly on the IELTS. There are no questions on the IELTS that ask specifically for the meaning of a word. However, comprehension *is* tested. Can you understand what you read? Can you understand what you hear? The more words you know, the more you will understand. The more words you know, the more fluently you will be able to speak and write.

Essential Words for the IELTS will teach you 600 words that you might find on the exam in reading and listening and that you might use in writing and speaking. You will also learn skills that will help you learn new words easily.

- *Essential Words for the IELTS* will teach you how to use context clues. The context provides clues to the meaning of a word. These clues may be in the same sentence or in the same paragraph. You will learn to look for definitions, synonyms, or paraphrases within the text.
- Punctuation is another context clue. A definition or a synonym is often set apart by parentheses, commas, dashes, or a colon. You will learn to recognize these clues.
- Analyzing a word also helps you determine the meaning of a word. Compound words, prefixes, and suffixes are other context clues. You will learn to recognize common prefixes and suffixes and how words are joined together.
- If context clues cannot help you determine the meaning of a word, you can use a dictionary designed for learners of English. You will learn dictionary skills to help you choose the correct definition of a word.
- You will also learn about word families. These are the different parts of speech—noun, verb, adjective, and adverb—that share a similar meaning. The book presents charts with example sentences for each part of speech. The word-family charts include the most common forms as well as multiple forms.

In *Essential Words for the IELTS* you will practice one very effective vocabulary strategy that will improve your comprehension. This effective strategy is to use a word four ways: **Read** the word, **write** the word, **listen** to the word, and **speak** the word. Every activity in each chapter will help you develop this skill.

When you learn a new word, you should practice the same strategy. If you hear a new word, write the new word in a sentence. Read the sentence to yourself. Say the sentence aloud. Every chance you get, review the words you are learning. Say them, write them, read them, and listen to them.

IELTS STUDY CONTRACT

You must make a commitment to study English. Sign a contract with yourself. You should never break a contract—especially a contract with yourself.

- Print your name below on line 1.
- Write the time you will spend each week studying English on lines 4–8. Think about how much time you have to study every day and every week, and make your schedule realistic.
- Sign your name and date the contract on the last line.
- At the end of each week, add up your hours. Did you meet the requirements of your contract?

MY IELTS STUDY CONTRACT

I, _____ , promise to study for the IELTS. I will begin my study with *Barron's Essential Words for the IELTS*, and I will also study English on my own.

I understand that to improve my English I need to spend time on English.

I promise to study English _____ a week. I promise to learn _____ new words every day.

I will spend _____ hours a week listening to English.
I will spend _____ hours a week writing English.
I will spend _____ hours a week speaking English.
I will spend _____ hours a week reading English.

This is a contract with myself. I promise to fulfill the terms of this contract.

_____   _____
Signed   Date

SELF-STUDY ACTIVITIES

Here are some ways you can improve your English vocabulary on your own. Check the ones you plan to try. Add some of your own ideas.

Internet-Based Self-Study Activities:

LISTENING
- ___ Podcasts on the Internet
- ___ News websites: CNN, BBC, NBC, ABC, CBS
- ___ Movies in English
- ___ YouTube
- ___ _____
- ___ _____

SPEAKING
- ___ Use Skype to talk to English speakers (*http://www.skype.com*)
- ___ _____
- ___ _____

WRITING
- ___ Write e-mails to website contacts
- ___ Write a blog
- ___ Leave comments on blogs
- ___ Post messages in a chat room
- ___ Use Facebook and MySpace
- ___ _____
- ___ _____

READING
- ___ Read news and magazine articles online
- ___ Do web research on topics that interest you
- ___ Follow blogs that interest you
- ___ _____
- ___ _____

Other Self-Study Activities

LISTENING
- ___ Listen to CNN and BBC on the radio
- ___ Watch movies and TV in English
- ___ Listen to music in English
- ___ _____
- ___ _____

SPEAKING

___ Describe what you see and do out loud
___ Practice speaking with a conversation buddy

___ _____

___ _____

WRITING

___ Write a daily journal
___ Write a letter to an English speaker
___ Make lists of the things you see every day
___ Write descriptions of your family and friends

___ _____

___ _____

READING

___ Read newspapers and magazines in English
___ Read books in English

___ _____

___ _____

Suggestions for Self-Study Activities

Whether you read an article in a newspaper or on a website, you can use that article in a variety of ways to improve your vocabulary while you practice reading, writing, speaking, and listening in English.

- Read about it.
- Paraphrase and write about it.
- Give a talk or presentation about it.
- Record or make a video of your presentation.
- Listen to or watch what you recorded. Write down your presentation.
- Correct your mistakes.
- Do it all again.

PLAN A TRIP

- Go to *www.concierge.com.*
- Choose a city, choose a hotel, go to that hotel's website and choose a room, and then choose some sites to visit (*reading*).
- Write a report about the city. Tell why you want to go there. Describe the hotel and the room you will reserve. Tell what sites you plan to visit and when. Where will you eat? How will you get around? Now write a letter to someone recommending this place (*writing*).

- Pretend you have to give a lecture on your planned trip (*speaking*). Make a video of yourself talking about this place. Then watch the video and write down what you said (*listening*). Correct any mistakes you made and record the presentation again. Then choose another city and do this again.

SHOP FOR AN ELECTRONIC PRODUCT

- Go to *www.cnet.com.*
- Choose an electronic product and read about it (*reading*).
- Write a report about the product. Tell why you want to buy one. Describe its features. Now write a letter to someone recommending this product (*writing*).
- Pretend you have to give a talk about this product (*speaking*). Make a video of yourself talking about this product. Then watch the video and write down what you said (*listening*). Correct any mistakes you made and record the presentation again. Then choose another product and do this again.

DISCUSS A BOOK OR A CD

- Go to *www.amazon.com.*
- Choose a book or CD or any product. Read the product description and reviews (*reading*).
- Write a report about the product. Tell why you want to buy one or why it is interesting to you. Describe its features. Now write a letter to someone and recommend this product (*writing*).
- Pretend you have to give a talk about this product (*speaking*). Make a video of yourself talking about this product. Then watch the video and write down what you said (*listening*). Correct any mistakes you made and record the presentation again. Then choose another product and do this again.

DISCUSS ANY SUBJECT

- Go to *http://simple.wikipedia.org/wiki/Main_Page*. This website is written in simple English.
- Pick any subject and read the entry (*reading*).
- Write a short essay about the topic (*writing*).
- Give a presentation about it (*speaking*). Record the presentation. Then watch the video and write down what you said (*listening*). Correct any mistakes you made and record the presentation again. Choose another topic and do this again.

FOLLOW THE NEWS

- Go to *http://news.google.com*. Google News has a variety of links.
- Pick one event and read the articles about it (*reading*).
- Listen to an English-language news report on the radio or watch a news program on TV about the same event (*listening*). Take notes as you listen.
- Write a summary of what you read and heard. Then write a short essay about the event (*writing*).
- Pretend you are a news reporter. Use the information from your notes to report the news (*speaking*). Record the presentation. Then watch the video and write down what you said (*listening*). Correct any mistakes you made and record the presentation again. Then choose another event and do this again.

EXPRESS AN OPINION

- Read a letter to the editor in the newspaper (*reading*). You can read sample letters to the editor at *www.publishaletter.com*.
- Write a letter in response in which you say whether or not you agree with the opinion expressed in the first letter. Explain why (*writing*).
- Pretend you have to give a talk explaining your opinion (*speaking*). Record yourself giving the talk. Then watch the video and write down what you said (*listening*). Correct any mistakes you made and record the presentation again. Then read another letter to the editor and do this again.

REVIEW A BOOK OR MOVIE

- Read a book (*reading*). Think about your opinion of the book. What did you like about it? What didn't you like about it? Who would you recommend it to and why?
- Pretend you are a book reviewer for a newspaper. Write a review of the book with your opinion and recommendations (*writing*). You can find examples of book reviews at *www.powells.com/review*.
- Give an oral presentation about the book. Explain what the book is about and what your opinion is (*speaking*). Record yourself giving the presentation. Then watch the video and write down what you said (*listening*). Correct any mistakes you made and record the presentation again. Then read another book and do this again.
- You can do this same activity after watching a movie (*listening*). You can find links to movie reviews to use as models at *www.mrqe.com*.

SUMMARIZE A TV SHOW

- Watch a TV show in English (*listening*). Take notes as you listen.
- After watching, write a summary of the show (*writing*).
- Use your notes to give an oral summary of the show. Explain the characters, setting, and plot (*speaking*). Record yourself speaking. Then watch the video and write down what you said (*listening*). Correct any mistakes you made and record the presentation again. Then watch another TV show and do this again.

HOW TO USE THIS BOOK

The book is divided into ten units, each one focusing on a different theme. There are three topics per unit, and each introduces twenty new vocabulary words in the context of the unit theme. You will practice these vocabulary words by doing exercises that look just like the questions on the IELTS. You can use this book in conjunction with *Barron's IELTS* and *Barron's IELTS Practice Exams* to reinforce the skills practiced in those books and improve your performance on the practice tests.

You can study the units in any order you like. Many of the words introduced in earlier units are repeated in later units. For this reason, you may find it helpful to study the units in order, but it isn't necessary.

NOTE
The book includes many footnotes to show you the British English equivalents of American English words. You will also hear a variety of accents on the audio so that you can become more comfortable with the variations in English. Both British English and American English spelling are acceptable on the exam.

Each unit follows the same format:

Words and Definitions
Each lesson begins with a list of twenty vocabulary words and a separate list of twenty definitions, followed by a reading passage. You will look for the vocabulary words as you read the passage and use the context to help you match each word with its correct definition.

Reading Comprehension
The reading passage is followed by IELTS-style reading comprehension questions that focus on the vocabulary words of the unit. There are a variety of question types throughout the book so you will have an opportunity to practice most of the types of reading comprehension questions that appear on the IELTS.

Word Families
Next you will find word family charts—noun, verb, adjective, and adverb forms of five or six words selected from the unit vocabulary list. You will practice these words in an exercise that asks you to select the correct form of a word to complete each sentence.

Dictionary Skill/Word Skill
This section uses one or two words from the vocabulary list to help you practice using a dictionary or analyzing a word to determine its meaning.

Listening
You will listen to a talk or conversation and answer IELTS-style listening comprehension questions that focus on words from the unit vocabulary list. The different types of talks and conversations and the different question types found in the four listening sections of the IELTS are distributed throughout the book, so you will get practice with listening comprehension from all four sections of the IELTS listening test.

Writing
You will write in response to an IELTS-style writing task that uses words from the unit vocabulary list. This is also an opportunity for you to use some of the vocabulary words in your response. IELTS Task 1– and Task 2–type writing tasks are evenly distributed throughout the book.

Speaking
You will practice speaking in response to two or three IELTS-style speaking questions that use words from the unit vocabulary list. This is also an opportunity for you to use some of the vocabulary words in your response.

Unit 1: The Natural World

ENVIRONMENTAL IMPACTS OF LOGGING

Words

Look for the following words as you read the passage. Match each word with its correct definition.

Words

1. aquatic
2. array
3. defense[1]
4. deforestation
5. environment
6. erosion
7. extend
8. fell
9. habitat
10. impact
11. inhibit
12. intercept
13. logging
14. myriad
15. nutrient
16. pollution
17. stabilize[2]
18. terrestrial
19. vanish
20. vegetation

Definitions

A. n., the natural world
B. v., to reach past, get bigger
C. n., a large number, a collection
D. n., loss of soil from action of water or wind
E. adj., living in the water
F. adj., living on the land
G. v., to cut down
H. n., the natural area where a plant or animal lives
I. n., a strong effect
J. n., protection
K. v., to prevent, slow down
L. n., plants
M. n., the removal of all trees from a large area
N. n., the cutting down of trees for commercial purposes
O. v., to disappear
P. adj., many, numerous
Q. n., damage to air, water, etc.
R. v., to keep from changing, maintain
S. v., to catch
T. n., food

[1]BrE: defence
[2]BrE: stabilise

Reading

Environmental Impacts of Logging

A

From shipping crates to paper bags, the logging industry supplies the raw materials for an array of products. However, this is not without untold harm to the environment. The damage includes habitat loss, pollution, and climate change, with the effects spanning the globe from the rain forests of Central Africa, Southeast Asia, and South America to the northern forests of Canada and Scandinavia. The effects of logging extend beyond just the felling of a swath of trees. Nutrients, water, and shelter for plants, animals, and microorganisms throughout the ecosystem are also lost; many life forms—both terrestrial and aquatic—are becoming endangered as forests vanish.

B

Trees protect the soil beneath them; thus, tree loss can affect soil integrity. For example, the rain forest floor, home to myriad plant life as well as insects, worms, reptiles and amphibians, and small mammals, relies on a dense canopy of branches and leaves to keep it healthy and intact. The canopy prevents surface runoff by intercepting heavy rainfall so that water can drip down slowly onto the porous earth. Tree roots also stabilize the soil and help prevent erosion. In return, a healthy soil encourages root development and microbial activity, which contribute to tree growth and well-being. A major factor in logging-related soil damage comes from road building, with trucks and other heavy equipment compressing the spongy soil, creating furrows where water collects, and disrupting the underground water flow. Eventually, the topsoil wears away, leaving behind an infertile layer of rocks and hard clay.

C

Logging can also damage aquatic habitats. Vegetation along rivers and stream banks helps maintain a steady water flow by blocking the entry of soil and other residue, and tree shade inhibits the growth of algae. Removing trees obliterates these benefits. When eroding soil flows into waterways, the organic matter within it consumes more oxygen, which can lead to oxygen depletion in the water, killing fish and other aquatic wildlife.

D

Trees provide a natural defense against air pollution. They remove carbon dioxide from the atmosphere while they emit oxygen, and their leaves filter pollutants from the air. Cutting down trees keeps pollutants airborne, where they can mix with water vapor[1] and form acid rain. Water quality in nearby streams and rivers also deteriorates as tree loss contributes to increased sedimentation.

E
In a healthy forest ecosystem, trees draw moisture from the soil and release it into the atmosphere while they provide shade to lessen evaporation. Thus, deforestation impacts rainfall patterns, leading to flooding as well as drought and forest fires. Deforestation is responsible for about one-fifth of carbon dioxide emissions worldwide, making it a major contributor to climate change—in particular, global warming. In the Amazon basin alone, deforestation is responsible for millions of tons of carbon dioxide being released into the atmosphere annually. Some logging companies burn large tracts of forest just to facilitate access to one area—a practice[2] that discharges even more carbon dioxide.

F
Forests, especially the tropical rain forests, are a vital natural resource with extensive biodiversity and irreplaceable wildlife habitats. More responsible logging practices would help ensure that they are protected for future generations.

Answer the questions about **Environmental Impacts of Logging**.

Questions 1–4

*The reading passage contains six paragraphs, **A–F**.*
Which paragraphs discuss the following information?
*Write the correct letter, **A–F**.*

_____ 1. The impact of logging on the weather

_____ 2. How trees inhibit soil erosion

_____ 3. How deforestation contributes to air pollution

_____ 4. The impact of erosion on fish

[1]BrE: vapour
[2]BrE: practice *n.*, practise *v.*

Questions 5–8

Complete the summary using words from the list below.

The logging industry **5**.......... trees to get the wood that is used to make many products. This practice has **6**.......... effects on the environment. The natural **7**.......... of many terrestrial and aquatic animals are damaged. Trees protect the environment in many ways. They are an effective **8**.......... against both air pollution and soil erosion.

aquatic	defense	habitats	myriad
arrays	fells	intercepts	vegetation

My Words

Write the words that are new to you. Look them up in the dictionary and write their definitions.

Words   Definitions

_____   _____

_____   _____

_____   _____

_____   _____

_____   _____

_____   _____

_____   _____

_____   _____

Word Families

noun	defense	The shade from trees provides a defense against the drying effects of the sun.
noun	defender	Defenders of the environment work to protect plants and animals from damage caused by logging.
verb	defend	Fish cannot defend themselves from the effects of water pollution.

noun	environment	The environment needs to be protected from the effects of logging.
adjective	environmental	Logging causes a great deal of environmental damage.
adverb	environmentally	It is important to develop more environmentally friendly logging practices

noun	erosion	Soil erosion leads to the pollution of streams and rivers.
verb	erode	When soil erodes, there are no nutrients left to help plants grow.

noun	extent	The extent of environmental damage caused by logging is frightening.
verb	extend	The Amazon rain forest extends from Brazil into neighboring countries.
adjective	extensive	The Amazon rain forest is the most extensive rain forest in the world.
adverb	extensively	Rain forests around the world have been extensively logged.

noun	pollution	Deforestation contributes to the effects of both air and water pollution.
noun	pollutant	Factories add pollutants to the air and water.
verb	pollute	Eroding soil pollutes water.

noun	stability	The stability of the natural environment depends on the interaction of many factors.
verb	stabilize	We need to stabilize the damage caused by logging before it gets worse.
adjective	stable	If the banks of the river continue to erode, they will no longer be stable.

Word Family Practice

Choose the correct word family member from the list below to complete each blank.

Modern industry has caused damage to our natural **1**.......... in many ways. The air and water are filled with **2**.......... . One result of this is acid rain, which has caused **3**.......... damage to vegetation in many areas. When large amounts of vegetation die off, the environment loses **4**.......... . If there are no plants to hold the soil, it starts to **5**.......... . This leads to myriad problems, including water pollution and habitat loss. **6**.......... of wildlife work hard to prevent further damage to natural areas.

1. environment   environmental   environmentally

2. pollution   pollutants   pollutes

3. extent   extend   extensive

4. stability   stabilizes   stable

5. erosion   erode   eroded

6. Defenses   Defenders   Defends

Word Skill

Prefix *de-*
The prefix *de-* can mean "remove."

Read the sentences. Write a definition for each underlined word.

---

1. When we <u>deforest</u> an area, many animals lose their habitat.

   deforest: _____

2. Some people prefer to <u>deseed</u> fruit before eating it.

   deseed: _____

3. I had to <u>deice</u> the windshield before I could drive.

   deice: _____

Listening

 *Listen to the lecture. Choose the correct letter, **A**, **B**, or **C**.*

1. Trees provide a habitat for
   A birds only.
   B a myriad of animals.
   C aquatic animals.

2. _____ are a source of nutrients for birds.
   A Insects
   B Roots
   C Leaves

3. Trees provide aquatic animals with a defense from
   A coolness.
   B rain.
   C heat.

4. _____ inhibit soil erosion.
   A Branches
   B Roots
   C Trunks

Writing

Deforestation caused by human activity is happening in many parts of the world, with serious results for the environment. What do you think can be done to solve this problem?

Support your opinion with reasons and examples from your own knowledge and experience.

> *Write at least 250 words.*

Speaking

> *Talk about the following topics.*

What kinds of natural environments do you enjoy spending time in?

What do you think can be done to help solve the problems of environmental pollution?

BIRD MIGRATION

Words

> Look for the following words as you read the passage. Match each word with its correct definition.

Words

1. aspect
2. breed
3. diurnal
4. endure
5. evolve
6. fascinate
7. feat
8. fuel
9. hemisphere
10. imperative
11. inhabit
12. migration
13. navigation
14. nocturnal
15. observer
16. obscure
17. optimal
18. species
19. stray
20. windswept

Definitions

A. n., type; a basic group in biological classification

B. v., to live under difficult conditions

C. n., a priority; an urgent need

D. n., a part or feature

E. v., to interest greatly

F. n., a person who watches something

G. v., to provide energy

H. v., to live in

I. adj., active during the day

J. n., a difficult act or achievement

K. n., movement from one place to another

L. v., to reproduce

M. adj., active at night

N. adj., unprotected from the wind

O. v., to make difficult to see

P. v., to leave the correct route; become separated from the group

Q. adj., best, most favorable[1]

R. n., finding the way from one place to another

S. n., one half of the Earth; also, one half of a sphere

T. v., to develop gradually

[1]BrE: favourable

Reading

Bird Migration

Migration is the regular movement of animals between their breeding grounds and the areas that they inhabit during the rest of the year. Many types of animals migrate, but bird migration in particular has fascinated observers for centuries. Migration is an excellent example of how nature has responded to the biological imperative for species to evolve and spread out into all possible ecological niches that can provide the conditions necessary for species to breed and raise young.

The most common form of bird migration involves traveling[1] to higher latitudes to breed during the warm season and then returning to lower latitudes during the nonbreeding period. This form of migration allows birds to breed in areas that provide optimal conditions for nesting and feeding their young. Because of the way in which the continents are situated upon Earth, migration of this type takes place primarily into the higher latitudes of the Northern Hemisphere. No land birds are known to migrate into the higher latitudes of the Southern Hemisphere; only species of seabirds migrate to the Southern Hemisphere to breed.

Although most bird migration takes place between the lower and higher latitudes of the Northern Hemisphere, many species are transequatorial, living in the Northern Hemisphere during the breeding season and in the Southern Hemisphere during the remainder of the year. A well-known example of transequatorial migration is the arctic tern. This tern, which breeds in the arctic regions and winters in antarctic waters, travels 24,000 miles a year during migration.

Not all migration is long distance. Some species exhibit altitudinal migration. Their breeding areas are in higher elevations, near or at the peaks of mountains, and they spend the nonbreeding season in neighboring[2] valleys or other nearby low country. This variety of migration is typical of many grouse species, including the ptarmigan, a type of arctic grouse. Many rock ptarmigan never leave the high arctic tundra, spending their breeding season atop windswept arctic peaks and the winter season in nearby valleys, enduring some of the coldest conditions on Earth.

During migration, most birds fly for a limited period each day, probably about six to eight hours, typically flying distances of several hundred miles. Some birds, however, undertake much longer flights when their routes include crossing large bodies of water or other geographic features such as deserts and mountains. For example, many species regularly cross the Gulf of Mexico, a trip that requires a continuous flight of more than 1,000 miles and takes from twenty-four to thirty-six hours or longer. An extreme example of nonstop bird migration is done by the

[1]BrE: travelling
[2]BrE: neighbouring

bar-tailed godwit, which makes a continuous flight of more than 11,000 miles from Alaska to New Zealand each year. At the start of its trip, about 55 percent[3] of its body weight is made up of the fat necessary to fuel this amazing journey.

How birds manage to unerringly travel between distant locations is one aspect that has fascinated observers for centuries. Modern-day researchers have attempted to understand this feat. Most studies have found that migratory birds all have some ability to navigate and an innate drive to travel in a particular direction. Nocturnal migrants, those species that travel at night, seem to take their navigational cues from the stars. When the stars are obscured by clouds, nocturnal migrants may become confused and return to land or stray off course. Diurnal migrants, those migrating during the day, take their cues from the location of the sun. In addition, diurnal migrants have also been shown to use geographic features such as mountain ranges or seacoasts as other cues for navigation. Because the stars and the sun move constantly over the course of twenty-four hours, this suggests that migrating birds also have some sense of time.

Answer the questions about **Bird Migration**.

Questions 1–4

Do the following statements agree with the information in the reading passage?
Write

TRUE	if the statement agrees with the information.
FALSE	if the statement contradicts the information.
NOT GIVEN	if there is no information on this in the passage.

_____ 1. Transequatorial birds cross from one hemisphere to the other when they migrate.

_____ 2. Many migratory birds breed in the Southern Hemisphere.

_____ 3. Migrating birds spend the warm months where conditions for breeding are optimal.

_____ 4. Many birds fail in their migration because they do not have enough body fat to fuel the journey.

[3]BrE: per cent

Questions 5–8

> *Look at the following descriptions of migratory habits.*
> *Match each type of bird with the correct description.*
> *Write the correct letter, **A** or **B**.*
>
> **A** Diurnal species of birds
> **B** Nocturnal species of birds

_____ 5. They navigate by looking at the sun.

_____ 6. They navigate by looking at the stars.

_____ 7. They may stop flying when clouds obscure the sky.

_____ 8. They navigate by looking at landforms.

My Words

> *Write the words that are new to you. Look them up in the dictionary*
> *and write their definitions.*

Words   Definitions

_____   _____

_____   _____

_____   _____

_____   _____

_____   _____

_____   _____

_____   _____

Word Families

noun	evolution	Our research plans have gone through many evolutions and are now quite different from our original plans.
verb	evolve	Scientists believe that birds evolved from dinosaurs.
adjective	evolutionary	Through the evolutionary process, birds have developed adaptations that allow them to survive in different environments.

noun	fascination	His fascination with birds is not hard to understand, because there are several bird-watchers in his family.
verb	fascinate	The study of the lives of birds fascinates many people.
adjective	fascinating	The study of birdsong is a fascinating subject.

noun	migration	Bird migration generally takes place twice a year, in the spring and autumn.
noun	migrant	Migrants stop to rest several times during their journey.
verb	migrate	Some birds migrate thousands of miles to reach their summer breeding grounds.
adjective	migratory	Scientists study the habits of migratory birds.

noun	navigation	Birds use the sun, stars, and landforms for navigation.
noun	navigator	Migratory birds are amazing navigators.
verb	navigate	Birds navigate by looking at the sun and stars.
adjective	navigational	Migratory birds are born with navigational skills; they don't have to learn them.

noun	observation	We can learn a great deal about the lives of birds through simple observation.
noun	observer	If birds become aware of the presence of an observer, they quickly fly away.
verb	observe	Many people observe birds as a hobby.
adjective	observant	You have to be really observant to spot most types of birds.

Unit 1

Word Family Practice

Choose the correct word family member from the list below to complete each blank.

Birds are **1**.......... to many people, and bird watching is a popular hobby. The best time to watch birds is in the early morning, because birds are usually very active at that time of day. The **2**.......... must keep still and quiet in order not to frighten the birds away. If you live in a part of the world where **3**.......... birds spend their breeding season, then you will have the opportunity to see nest-building activity. Over the ages, different species of birds have **4**.......... with different types of nest-building skills. It makes an interesting study to look at the different types of nests built by birds and to watch them as they build their nests. After the breeding season is over and the babies have left the nest, it is time for the birds to head for warmer parts of the world to spend the winter months. Birds **5**.......... to their winter feeding grounds, using the stars or the sun as their guide.

1. fascination	fascinate	fascinating
2. observation	observer	observe
3. migration	migrate	migratory
4. evolution	evolved	evolutionary
5. navigation	navigate	navigational

Unit 1

Dictionary Skill

Parts of Speech
The word *imperative* can be a noun or an adjective.

Read the dictionary definitions below. Then read the sentences and write the letter of the correct definition for each sentence.

im-per-a-tive [im-PER-uh-tiv]
A *adjective.* very important; essential
B *noun.* a priority; an urgent need

_____ 1. It is our *imperative* to protect the natural environment.

_____ 2. It is *imperative* to keep dogs and cats away from the bird breeding area.

Listening

CD 1
Track
3

*Listen to the talk. Look at the map below labeled A–E. Look at the list of places and write the correct letter, **A–E**, next to numbers **1–5**.*

_____ 1. species list

_____ 2. restricted area

_____ 3. observation platform

_____ 4. gift shop

_____ 5. donation box

E   D

C

A   B

↑
Entrance

Writing

The chart[1] below shows information about different species of birds observed in Woodchuck County at different times of the year.

Summarize[2] the information by selecting and reporting the main information and making comparisons.

Write at least 150 words.

Species of Birds Observed
in Woodchuck County by Season
(partial list)

Species	Winter	Summer
bluebirds		X
cardinals	X	X
crows	X	X
juncos	X	
mockingbirds		X
orioles		X
vireos		X
woodpeckers	X	X

Speaking

Talk about the following topics.

Many people enjoy observing birds because they find them fascinating. Why do you think people are fascinated by birds?

Are you fascinated by birds? Why or why not?

What animals are fascinating to you?

[1]BrE: table
[2]BrE: summarise

PLANT LIFE IN THE TAKLIMAKAN DESERT

Words

Look for the following words as you read the passage. Match each word with its correct definition.

Words	Definitions
1. accumulate	A. adj., relating to change from one type to another
2. adapt	B. n., behavior[2] to deal with difficult situations
3. determine	C. v., to gradually increase over time
4. dilute	D. v., to be in a place; exist in
5. diverse	E. v., to reduce to the least possible amount
6. evaporation	F. v., to grow well
7. extreme	G. n., the edge of something
8. fringe	H. adj., varied, of many kinds
9. mechanism	I. v., to change to fit a situation or environment
10. minimize[1]	J. adj., strong; sudden and destructive
11. moisture	K. n., wetness or water
12. occupy	L. adj., tough, able to endure difficult conditions
13. prolific	M. adj., small in numbers or amount
14. resilient	N. adj., very severe or difficult
15. sparse	O. v., to make weaker by mixing with water
16. stressor	P. n., the change from liquid to gas; loss of water to the air
17. swing	Q. n., a sudden or big change
18. thrive	R. v., to decide
19. transitional	S. n., something that causes great difficulties
20. violent	T. adj., producing a lot of something

[1]BrE: minimise
[2]BrE: behaviour

Reading

Plant Life in the Taklimakan Desert

The Taklimakan Desert, second in size only to Africa's Sahara Desert, occupies some 337,600 square kilometers[1] (130,300 square miles) of northwestern China—an area about the size of Finland. Sparse rainfall, daily temperature swings of up to 20°C (68°F), and violent sandstorms make it one of the most extreme environments on Earth.

Eighty-five percent[2] of the Taklimakan Desert consists of shifting sand dunes, some up to 250 meters[3] tall, that are largely free of vegetation. Yet, transitional areas between the open desert and oases on the desert fringe support diverse plant forms that not only have adapted to the harsh conditions but actually thrive there.

Successful desert plants are resilient to scorching summers and frigid winters, drought, and high-salt conditions. The plants' principal defense[4] against these environmental stressors consists of drawing in as much water as possible while minimizing moisture loss. Three Taklimakan plants—*Populus euphratica, Tamarix ramosissima,* and *Alhagi sparsifolia*—represent some of the most diverse, prolific vegetation in the area; although they share many survival strategies, each has developed unique coping mechanisms of its own.

The Euphrates poplar, *Populus euphratica,* the only tall tree in the Taklimakan ecosystem, has an extensive root system that allows it to absorb water far from the standing tree. *P. euphratica* controls evaporation by opening and closing the stomata, or tiny pores, on the leaf surface in response to the amount of moisture being lost through the leaves to the surrounding air. These stomata generally remain open during the day while the plant conducts photosynthesis.

P. euphratica can endure high-salt concentrations in the soil. It takes in unlimited amounts of salt through the roots, up the stem, and into leaves, where it dilutes the normally toxic salt by increasing the number and volume of its cells.

Tamarix ramosissima, a small tree with needlelike leaves commonly known as tamarisk or salt cedar, takes in enormous amounts of water via a far-reaching root system many times the size of the plant above ground. Like *P. euphratica,* tamarisk can naturally determine when to close stomata to inhibit evaporation and regulate photosynthesis.

[1]BrE: kilometres
[2]BrE: per cent
[3]BrE: metres
[4]BrE: defence

Tamarisk has a high tolerance for salty conditions and even produces its own salt, which it accumulates in special glands between the leaves and then releases onto leaf surfaces. Leaves dropping to the ground make the soil more saline, or salty, giving tamarisk a competitive advantage over less salt-tolerant plants.

Alhagi sparsifolia, a spiny shrub, thrives in the Taklimakan Desert even though it uses large amounts of water, especially during the summer months. With only a few wispy roots in the upper soil, it is unaffected by occasional flooding. Most of its roots reach down deep, where they take up water from as far as sixteen meters below ground. Unlike *P. euphratica* and *T. ramosissima,* which open and close stomata according to conditions on the leaf surface, *A. sparsifolia* does so according to hydraulic conductance—that is, the ease with which it takes up groundwater.

Although desert plants have adapted for their own survival, they also help protect their ecosystem by stabilizing sand dunes, preventing erosion, presenting a barrier to sandstorms, and conserving biodiversity.

Answer the questions about **Plant Life in the Taklimakan Desert**.

Questions 1–3

> *Choose the correct letter,* ***A, B, C,*** *or* ***D.***

1. Most of the Taklimakan Desert is covered with
   A tamarisk.
   B spiny plants.
   C sand dunes.
   D diverse plant life.

2. Plants in the Taklimakan Desert
   A grow only in areas above 250 meters high.
   B thrive in extreme conditions.
   C are not very hardy.
   D are mostly tall trees.

3. Environmental stressors in the Taklimakan Desert include
   A sparse sunlight.
   B lack of salt in the soil.
   C extreme temperatures.
   D periods of heavy rainfall.

Questions 4–7

> *Which of the following mechanisms used by plants to survive in the desert environment are mentioned in the passage? Choose **four** answers from the list below.*

A Having strong roots that can hold on during violent sandstorms

B Closing pores to minimize loss of moisture

C Occupying a place in the shade of a larger plant to avoid the scorching desert sun

D Diluting the salt that the plant takes in

E Having large root systems that can reach water far from the plant

F Adding salt to the soil to minimize competition from other plants

G Accumulating water in the leaves of the plant

My Words

> *Write the words that are new to you. Look them up in the dictionary and write their definitions.*

Words   Definitions

_____   _____

_____   _____

_____   _____

_____   _____

_____   _____

_____   _____

_____   _____

_____   _____

Word Families

noun	adaptation	Plants in the Taklimakan Desert have adaptations that allow them to live in the dry, salty conditions.
verb	adapt	One way that plants adapt to the dry desert is by developing deep root systems.
adjective	adaptable	Most plant species are not adaptable to a desert environment.

noun	diversity	There is a great diversity of plant life on the fringe of the Taklimakan Desert.
noun	diversification	Change in climate can result in species diversification.
verb	diversify	As climate changes, plant species in an area may diversify if conditions improve.
adjective	diverse	The diverse ways that plants adapt to desert conditions makes a fascinating study.

noun	extreme	Temperatures in the Taklimakan Desert reach an extreme during hot summer days.
adjective	extreme	Many plants cannot endure the extreme heat of the desert.
adverb	extremely	The weather in a desert is usually extremely dry.

noun	resilience	The resilience of certain plants allows them to thrive in the desert.
adjective	resilient	Desert plants are resilient to heat and dryness.
adverb	resiliently	Desert plants grow resiliently in the heat.

noun	stress	A long period of dryness causes a lot of stress to plants.
noun	stressor	The main stressor in a desert is lack of rain.
verb	stress	Heat and drought both stress plants.
adverb	stressful	Certain plants thrive in the desert despite the stressful conditions.

noun	violence	The violence of sandstorms keeps many plants from thriving in the desert.
adjective	violent	Violent winds tear up many plants or cover them with sand.
adverb	violently	The winds blow violently during a sandstorm.

Word Family Practice

Choose the correct word family member from the list below to complete each blank.

Desert plants have a variety of **1**.......... that allow them to endure the desert environment. Because a desert is **2**.......... dry, plants need to be able to take in as much water as possible when it rains and to store the water for a long time. Special root systems and types of leaves enable them to do this. Another source of **3**.......... in a desert is the high temperature, so desert plants need to have **4**.......... . **5**.......... storms can occur in a desert, and plants with strong roots will be able to endure the storms. Considering the difficult conditions in a desert, the **6**.......... of plants that can be found there is truly amazing.

1. adaptations	adapts	adapted
2. extreme	extremes	extremely
3. stressor	stress	stressful
4. resilience	resilient	resiliently
5. Violence	Violent	Violently
6. diversity	diversify	diverse

Dictionary Skill

Different Meanings
Many words have more than one meaning.

> *Read the definitions below. Then read the sentences and write the letter of the correct definition for each sentence.*
>
> swing [SWING]
> **A** *noun.* a sudden or big change
> **B** *noun.* back-and-forth movement
> **C** *noun.* a hanging seat that moves back and forth

_____ 1. The children played on the *swing* all afternoon.

_____ 2. After a rainstorm in the desert, there is a noticeable *swing* back to life.

_____ 3. The *swing* of the branches in the breeze made a creaking noise.

Listening

> *Listen to the discussion. Complete the notes below.*
> *Write **NO MORE THAN ONE WORD** for each answer.*

Taklimakan Desert Plants

> Many plants live in the **1** .... areas.
> Stressors:
>
> little rain
>
> **2** .... temperatures
>
> rapid **3** ....
>
> Adaptations:
>
> ability to close pores
>
> large root systems to **4** .... water

Writing

The charts below show information about three different deserts around the world.

Summarize[1] the information by selecting and reporting the main information and making comparisons.

Write at least 150 words.

Sahara Desert (Africa)

Size	9,000,000 sq km
Average annual rainfall	7.6 cm (north) 12.7 cm (south)
Average temperatures	30°C (summer) 13°C (winter)
Temperature extremes	58°C = highest recorded

Taklimakan Desert (Asia)

Size	270,000 sq km
Average annual rainfall	3.8 cm (west) 1.0 cm (east)
Average temperatures	25°C (summer) −9°C (winter)
Temperature extremes	−26.1°C = lowest recorded

Great Basin Desert (North America)

Size	305,775 sq km
Average annual rainfall	5.1–51 cm
Average temperatures	30°C (summer) −8°C (winter)
Temperature extremes	57°C = highest recorded

[1]BrE: summarise

Speaking

> *Talk about the following topics.*

Are you interested in visiting extreme environments, such as deserts or high mountains? Why or why not?

Why do you think people like to visit extreme environments?

When you travel, do you adapt easily to new climates?

Unit 2: Leisure Time

PERIPHERAL VISION IN SPORTS

Words

> *Look for the following words as you read the passage. Match each word with its correct definition.*

Unit 2

Words	Definitions
1. anticipate	A. n., area
2. athlete	B. n., a movement
3. blur	C. n., how well a person or machine does something
4. boundary	D. v., to expect, be ready for something to happen
5. complicate	E. v., to notice, become aware of
6. coordinate	F. adv., in a way that is impossible to see or notice
7. demonstrate	G. adj., unclear
8. detect	H. adv., without thinking, automatically
9. distracting	I. n., a person who plays sports[2]
10. focus	J. n., an edge, border
11. indiscernibly	K. adj., at the edge
12. indistinct	L. v., to look over
13. maneuver[1]	M. v., to accept, allow
14. performance	N. v., to organize[3]; make work together
15. peripheral	O. n., something not seen clearly
16. range	P. n., the ability to see; sight
17. scan	Q. v., to cause to be more difficult
18. tolerate	R. v., to center attention on one object; concentrate
19. unconsciously	S. adj., taking attention away from something
20. vision	T. v., to show; model

[1]BrE: manoeuver
[2]BrE: sport
[3]BrE: organise

Reading

Peripheral Vision in Sports

Focus in on something as small as a pin. Notice that everything else that fills your whole area of possible sight is indistinct, lacking in detail. We tolerate this large outlying field of blur, this peripheral view, without taking note. We unconsciously accept it. Sometimes we take charge of how we process all that blur surrounding the tiny center[1] that our vision is focused on. Athletes best demonstrate just how much we can use the entire range of our vision, fanning out to the periphery.

An athlete's performance, necessitating high levels of coordination and reaction time, depends on training visual abilities, not just tuning muscles. Detecting and keeping track of as much motion as possible while performing physical maneuvers is quite a feat. Peripheral visual information is processed quickly. The office worker might notice the tiny distracting insect moving beside the computer, but the fast-moving athlete must detect all kinds of motion from every angle and never lose concentration. Each peripherally viewed movement must be immediately processed as more and varied movements from different sources and directions keep coming rapidly. Good footwork and body positioning will help the athlete gain viewing time in this intense environment, improving the opportunity to anticipate what will happen next.

The athlete's view, full of movement, requires rapid scanning with visual focus changing rapidly among various distances. Tracking fast objects is often complicated by the need for the athlete's body to move in response to other aspects of the activity, and head motion must coordinate with eye movement to assist in balance. A volleyball player, for example, must pay attention to body positioning in relation to the speed and angle of the moving ball as well as to the court boundaries, all the while scanning the movement of the other players. Athletes need as much peripheral range as possible.

The environment contributes to athletes' visual sharpness. Contrasting court backgrounds, adequate lighting, nonconfusing uniform color combinations, and less off-court motion all help the athlete's peripheral concentration. It seems odd that visiting baseball teams are allowed to dress in gray uniforms when bright colors would help the home team keep a better eye on them.

Everything that catches the athlete's attention causes the eyes to pause almost indiscernibly as they gather a quick view of focused detail. As the eyes move in and out of focus, there is a momentary blur between each pause. This is when visual tracking errors can occur. Even the act of blinking, usually at a rate of twenty-five blinks per minute, or one-tenth

[1]BrE: centre

of a second per blink, interferes with the athlete's vision. Normal, natural blinking means the eyes are closed for two and half seconds out of every minute, and more than that if the athlete is anxious. This is added to the rapid blurs that occur as the athlete's eyes move in and out of focus on specific objects. These nonvisual moments can be somewhat compensated for if the athlete thoroughly tunes in to the game. Anticipation, a learned and practiced[2] art, can serve the athlete well in many ways.

Answer the questions about **Peripheral Vision in Sports**.

Questions 1–7

Do the following statements agree with the information in the reading passage?

Write

> **TRUE**   if the statement agrees with the information.
> **FALSE**   if the statement contradicts the information.
> **NOT GIVEN**   if there is no information on this in the passage.

_____ 1. Peripheral vision refers to what we see near the boundaries of our visual range.

_____ 2. Focusing our eyes on one object only will cause that object to look indistinct.

_____ 3. In addition to physical abilities, athletes need to be skilled at detecting movements all around them.

_____ 4. Office workers tend to find that certain kinds of movements are more distracting than others.

_____ 5. A volleyball player does not need to focus on the movements of the other players on the court.

_____ 6. Poor lighting and confusing color combinations on uniforms can have a negative effect on an athlete's performance.

_____ 7. Athletes blink more often when they are feeling anxious.

[2]BrE: practised

My Words

> *Write the words that are new to you. Look them up in the dictionary and write their definitions.*

Words   Definitions

_____   _____

_____   _____

_____   _____

_____   _____

_____   _____

_____   _____

_____   _____

_____   _____

Word Families

noun	complication	Playing a ball game is not as simple as it may look; there are many complications.
verb	complicate	The need to pay attention to many things at once complicates the game for an athlete.
adjective	complicated	A game can become very complicated when there are many players on the field.

noun	coordination	It is important for an athlete to have good physical coordination.
verb	coordinate	An athlete must coordinate physical skill with sharp vision to play a game well.
adjective	coordinated	The coordinated movements of all the team members will help them win the game.

noun	demonstration	The athlete gave a demonstration of the correct way to throw the ball.
verb	demonstrate	Professional athletes demonstrate a high level of skills.
adjective	demonstrative	The way that goal was scored was demonstrative of good teamwork in action.

noun	performance	The team gave an excellent performance at last night's game.
noun	performer	All the performers did a good job.
verb	perform	The entire team performed well during the game.

noun	tolerance	An athlete should have tolerance for hard physical activity.
verb	tolerate	Athletes need to be able to tolerate a high level of action around them.
adjective	tolerant	Good athletes always try to do their best but must still be tolerant of occasional failure.

Unit 2

noun	vision	Good vision is important for playing sports well.
adjective	visual	In sports, visual abilities can be as important as physical abilities.
adverb	visually	The coach used drawings to explain the game visually.

Word Family Practice

Choose the correct word family member from the list below to complete each blank.

In order to **1**.......... well, an athlete must have a number of different abilities. Naturally, she should **2**.......... excellent physical skills. In addition to strength, **3**.......... of all parts of the body while moving around the court or field is very important. The athlete also needs to have good **4**.......... abilities. She needs to be able to see what is happening around her so that she can respond to the other players' maneuvers. She has to be **5**.......... of activity around her without losing her ability to focus on her own part in the game. Finally, she needs to be a fast thinker. **6**.......... can occur in any game, and the athlete needs to be able to respond to them quickly.

1. performance   performer   perform

2. demonstrations   demonstrate   demonstrative

3. coordination   coordinate   coordinated

4. vision   visual   visually

5. tolerance   tolerate   tolerant

6. Complications   Complicate   Complicated

Dictionary Skill

Parts of Speech
Focus can be either a noun or a verb. *Blur* can also be either a noun or a verb.

> *Read the dictionary definitions below. Then read the sentences and write the letter of the correct definition for each sentence.*
>
> QUESTIONS 1–2
>
> fo-cus [FO-kus]
> **A** *noun.* the center of attention
> **B** *verb.* to center attention on one object; concentrate

_____ 1. When playing a game, always *focus* on the ball.

_____ 2. Keep your *focus* on the goal.

> QUESTIONS 3–4
>
> blur [BLUR]
> **A** *noun.* something not seen clearly
> **B** *verb.* make unclear

_____ 3. I couldn't follow the game; it was all a big *blur* to me.

_____ 4. Poor lighting can *blur* the players' vision.

Listening

> *Listen to the discussion. Complete the notes below.*
> *Write **NO MORE THAN ONE WORD** for each answer.*

Vision and Basketball

Basketball players have to **1**........... on the ball. They have to **2**.........
the other players' maneuvers. They **3**............ the whole court to see the
actions of the rest of the players. They don't think about this; they do
it **4**............. .

Writing

Do you believe that professional athletes make good role models for young people?

Support your opinion with reasons and examples from your own knowledge or experience.

Write at least 250 words.

Speaking

Talk about the following topics.

Do you focus better on your studies or work when you are in a quiet environment, or do you prefer to have activity going on around you?

What kinds of things are distracting to you when you study or work?

Do you anticipate any major changes in your work or study situation in the next year?

HISTORY OF THE CIRCUS

Words

Look for the following words as you read the passage. Match each word with its correct definition.

Words

1. ancient
2. band
3. century
4. develop
5. entertainment
6. exhibit
7. exotic
8. found
9. grandeur
10. massive
11. permanently
12. popular
13. reduce
14. remnant
15. renovation
16. spectator
17. survive
18. talent
19. trainer
20. venue

Definitions

A. v., to make something smaller

B. v., to continue, stay alive

C. n., something shown to the public; a display

D. n., a special ability

E. n., a small group

F. n., a person who watches an event

G. n., a period of 100 years

H. n., a small leftover piece

I. v., to grow and change

J. adj., very old, of the distant past

K. n., place where an event is held

L. n., a performance or show

M. n., a person who teaches skills to people or animals

N. n., greatness

O. adj., very big

P. adv., for always

Q. n., repair or rebuilding

R. v., to start or establish an institution

S. adj., liked by many people

T. adj., unusual, from a foreign place

Reading

History of the Circus

The circus is one of the oldest forms of entertainment in history. Although the modern circus has been around for a few centuries, related forms of public entertainment have been in existence for millennia. The animal trainers, clowns, and other circus performers who are familiar to us today can trace their roots to the coliseums, stadiums, and racetracks of the ancient world.

The ancient Romans were the first to enjoy the circus. Around the sixth century B.C., the Circus Maximus was founded in Rome as a venue for public entertainment, mostly chariot races, which were a popular spectator sport. Other events held at the Circus Maximus included gladiator fights and exhibits of exotic animals such as elephants and tigers. These entertainments were less common than chariot races but still very popular. The original Circus Maximus venue was built entirely of wood. By the height of the Roman Empire, it had gone through several renovations and had become a massive marble stadium that could seat more than 200,000 spectators.

Chariot races continued to be held at the Circus Maximus for almost a century after the last remnants of the Roman Empire had vanished. Eventually, the site was permanently retired, and public entertainment was reduced to small bands of traveling[1] performers and animal trainers. It was during the Dark Ages that the circus began to develop into what we know today. The monarchs of Europe had court jesters, whose duty it was to provide amusement for the court. They combined the talents of jugglers, mimes, and clowns. The more common people enjoyed the performances of traveling entertainers, who went from village to village, putting on shows during festivals. These performers made up the medieval circus, which had little in common with the Circus Maximus other than adopting the word *circus* as its name. Leisure time was extremely rare during the Dark Ages, and people had few opportunities to enjoy circus performances. However, the circus survived to make a return to its former grandeur in the eighteenth century.

England was one of the first nations to embrace the modern circus. During the late 1700s, an Englishman named Philip Astley founded the first modern circus. He was a skilled rider who invented stunt riding on horseback. He performed his stunts in a circus ring, another of his ideas, within an indoor stadium. After his act became popular in London, he was asked by Louis XV to perform in France. He later expanded his act to include clowns, acrobats, and parades of trained animals. The last addition to his act was slapstick humor. He had horseback riders

[1]BrE: travelling

pretend to fall off their horses and then go stumbling after them. Shortly after Astley's death, the circus spread to America.

During the early 1800s, the United States took to the circus quickly after learning of its popularity in Europe. Joshua Brown, an American businessman, introduced the circus tent in 1825. The use of portable tents allowed him to take his act all over the country. His traveling circus was a massive success as a business enterprise and loved by audiences everywhere. Most circuses today are variations of Brown's circus.

Answer the questions about **History of the Circus**.

Questions 1–4

Do the following describe the ancient circus, the modern circus, or both? Write the correct letter, **A**, **B**, *or* **C**.

    A Ancient circus
    B Modern circus
    C Both the ancient circus and the modern circus

_____ 1. had animal exhibits

_____ 2. entertained spectators with races

_____ 3. entertainments included falling off horses

_____ 4. took place in a massive venue

Questions 5–7

Choose the correct letter, **A**, **B**, **C**, *or* **D**.

5. The Circus Maximus
    A was not a popular place to visit.
    B developed during the Dark Ages.
    C went through a number of renovations.
    D took place in a portable tent.

6. The court jesters of the Dark Ages usually
   A were skilled animal trainers.
   B had several different talents.
   C performed at village festivals.
   D entertained the common people.

7. In the eighteenth century, the modern circus was founded by
   A a horse rider from England.
   B a Roman businessman.
   C some performers in France.
   D a band of American entertainers.

My Words

Write the words that are new to you. Look them up in the dictionary and write their definitions.

Words   Definitions

_____   _____

_____   _____

_____   _____

_____   _____

_____   _____

_____   _____

_____   _____

_____   _____

Word Families

noun	development	Joshua Brown's introduction of the circus tent was an important contribution to the development of the circus.
noun	developer	Philip Astley is known as the developer of stunt riding.
verb	develop	The circus has developed in different ways over the years.

noun	entertainment	The circus is still a favorite form of entertainment today.
noun	entertainer	The job of a circus entertainer looks like fun, but it is really very difficult.
verb	entertain	People often hire clowns to entertain children at parties.
adjective	entertaining	We spent a very entertaining afternoon at the circus.

noun	permanence	The permanence of the circus as a form of entertainment shows how much people enjoy it.
adjective	permanent	Unlike the traveling bands of performers, court jesters had permanent jobs.
adverb	permanently	Circuses don't stay in one place permanently but travel around from city to city.

Unit 2

noun	popularity	The circus still enjoys great popularity.
verb	popularize[1]	Joshua Brown helped to popularize the circus in America.
adjective	popular	The circus is popular all over the world.
adverb	popularly	The modern circus is popularly known as the Big Top.

noun	survival	The survival of the circus is due to its ability to change with the times.
noun	survivor	The circus as a form of entertainment is a survivor of the hard times of the Dark Ages.
verb	survive	The circus has survived in many forms throughout the centuries.

noun	trainer	A circus animal trainer has to be able to work with exotic animals.
verb	train	Some animals are easier to train than others.
adjective	trained	Many circuses use trained elephants in their show.

[1]BrE: popularise

Word Family Practice

Choose the correct word family member from the list below to complete each blank.

The **1**.......... of the modern circus began in England in the eighteenth century. A skilled horseback rider[1] **2**.......... audiences with stunt riding. He later added other kinds of performances to the show, such as clowns and **3**.......... animals. The show became very **4**.........., and the idea spread to other countries. The circus has **5**.......... the test of time and is still enjoyed by people today. It holds a **6**.......... place in our hearts.

1. development	developer	developed
2. entertainment	entertainer	entertained
3. trainers	trains	trained
4. popularity	popularize	popular
5. survival	survivors	survived
6. permanence	permanent	permanently

[1]BrE: horse rider

Dictionary Skill

Different Meanings
Many words have more than one meaning.

Read the definitions below. Then read the sentences and write the letter of the correct definition for each sentence.

QUESTIONS 1–2

found [FOWND]
A *verb.* to start or establish an institution
B *verb.* past tense and past participle of the verb *find*

_____ 1. After we *found* our seats, we sat down and enjoyed the circus performance.

_____ 2. It takes a lot of money, effort, and daring to *found* an entertainment business.

QUESTIONS 3–4

band [BAND]
A *noun.* a small group
B *noun.* a strip of cloth

_____ 3. People walked around the tent in bands while they waited for the circus performance to begin.

_____ 4. The performers wore brightly colored bands around their waists.

Listening

 *Listen to the talk. Choose the correct answer, **A, B,** or **C.***

1. When was the Springfield Circus founded?
   A 25 years ago
   B 75 years ago
   C 100 years ago

2. What has not changed since the circus was founded?
   A The venue
   B The ticket price
   C The number of performers

3. What kinds of animals begin the show?
   A Exotic
   B Trained
   C Massive

4. What is the most popular part of the show?
   A Animals
   B Clowns
   C Dancers

Unit 2

Writing

In your opinion, why is the circus still a popular form of entertainment in the modern electronic age?

Support your opinion with reasons and examples from your own knowledge or experience.

Write at least 250 words.

Speaking

Talk about the following topics.

What forms of entertainment are popular in your city?

Do you prefer to watch TV and movies or to see live entertainment?

Are you talented in any performing arts? What talents do you have that you would like to develop more?

USES OF LEISURE TIME

Words

> *Look for the following words as you read the passage. Match each word with its correct definition.*

Words
1. acknowledge
2. authority
3. chunk
4. crucial
5. deliberately
6. depression
7. emotion
8. engage
9. industrious
10. intellectual
11. merely
12. obesity
13. obvious
14. overwhelming
15. passive
16. pastime
17. physical
18. rejuvenate
19. reluctant
20. suffer

Definitions
A. adj., not active
B. adv., only
C. n., a strong feeling such as anger or love
D. n., a large piece
E. v., to admit, accept as true
F. adj., very important
G. adj., overpowering; very large
H. v., to refresh, restore
I. adv., intentionally, on purpose
J. n., person with power or special knowledge
K. v., to participate in something
L. n., a free-time activity
M. adj., not wanting to do something; unwilling
N. adj., related to thinking
O. adj., easy to see, clear
P. v., to experience something difficult or painful
Q. adj., related to the body
R. adj., hardworking
S. n., constant sadness
T. n., the condition of being very overweight

Unit 2

Reading

Uses of Leisure Time

A

Although it may seem that people are working more, studies show that we have more leisure time than ever before. Yet researchers are reporting higher levels of both stress and obesity. These reports appear to be a sign that we are not using our leisure time to our best advantage.

B

Health experts agree that the best way to restore body and mind is to spend time in nature pursuing a comfortable level of physical exercise. Spending time in natural surroundings is especially crucial now because, for the first time, a majority of the world's population live in cities. Recent studies show that intellectual function weakens as a result of the energy expended simply sorting out the overwhelming stimuli of city life. Tests demonstrate that people suffer decreases in attention span, memory, and problem-solving ability after taking a short walk on a busy city street or merely seeing pictures of city life. Tests also show that time spent in the city results in a decreased ability to concentrate and to control emotions and impulses. On the other hand, spending time in the country produces the opposite effects.

C

Unfortunately, as society becomes more centered[1] on city life, we have to rejuvenate ourselves in nature deliberately rather than as a matter of course. Yet research shows that we are not spending our leisure time rejuvenating ourselves. Around the world, the most popular way to spend free time is watching television. This, the most passive of pastimes, is how Americans spend more than half their leisure time. Globally, the next most popular is using the Internet, also passive, and it ranks as the most favored[2] among the billions in China. The third is shopping, which may be slightly more active but is still as far from nature as possible. Modern shopping malls remove shoppers from everything natural, leaving them to experience the outdoors only between the paved parking lot[3] and the mall doors.

[1]BrE: centred
[2]BrE: favoured
[3]BrE: car park

D

Children are most negatively affected by city life. Parents are reluctant to let children play freely in the city, fearing for their health and safety, and nature is something many children in the city may never have a chance to experience. Childhood obesity and depression are reaching epidemic levels. Authorities have begun to acknowledge the problem, and innovative programs[4] that give children an opportunity to spend time in nature are being introduced in countries around the world.

E

Vacations[5] are the most obvious chunk of leisure time. The countries with the most vacation time are Italy, with an average of forty-two days a year, and France, with thirty-seven. The industrious Americans have the least: thirteen days. Yet the country most satisfied with their vacations are not the Italians but the British. The British usually divide up their vacation time, taking it in pieces throughout the year rather than all at once. Of all nationalities, the British spend the most time vacationing outdoors in their national-trust parks, where they engage in a comfortable level of physical activity. The British report the greatest satisfaction with their leisure time. Perhaps the rest of the world would do well to follow their lead.

Answer the questions about **Uses of Leisure Time**.

Questions 1–3

*The reading passage contains five paragraphs, **A–E**.*
Which paragraphs discuss the following information?
*Write the correct letter, **A–E**.*

_____ 1. The most popular pastimes in different countries around the world

_____ 2. Why it is crucial to spend time in nature

_____ 3. In which country people spend the largest chunk of vacation time engaged in outdoor activities

[4]BrE: programmes
[5]BrE: Holidays

Questions 4–6

*Choose the correct letter, **A**, **B**, **C**, or **D**.*

4. We can best rejuvenate ourselves by spending time engaged in
    A physical activities.
    B passive activities.
    C activities with children.
    D activities in the city.

5. When children do not spend time in nature, they
    A fear for their health and safety.
    B suffer from obesity and depression.
    C are reluctant to spend time with their parents.
    D have more time to develop their intellectual functioning.

6. The overwhelming character of city life affects our
    A interest in nature.
    B choice of pastimes.
    C relationships with children.
    D emotions and intellectual function.

My Words

Write the words that are new to you. Look them up in the dictionary and write their definitions.

Words   Definitions

_____   _____

_____   _____

_____   _____

_____   _____

_____   _____

_____   _____

_____   _____

Word Families

noun	authority	The authorities decided to keep the park open in the evenings so families could spend more time in nature.
verb	authorize[1]	The school director authorized the teachers to spend a larger chunk of the school day outdoors with their students.
adjective	authoritative	According to an authoritative source, spending time in nature improves our health.
adverb	authoritatively	The expert wrote authoritatively about the topic of exercise and its effects on mental health.

noun	deliberation	After deliberation, he decided to spend some time every day engaged in outdoor activities.
verb	deliberate	The group deliberated for an hour before reaching a decision.
adjective	deliberate	It is obvious that people need to make a deliberate decision to spend more time in nature.
adverb	deliberately	We need to spend time in nature deliberately.

noun	emotion	The stress of city life can make emotions difficult to control.
adjective	emotional	Children who don't spend a lot of time playing outdoors can end up with emotional problems.
adverb	emotionally	People respond emotionally to the overwhelming stimuli of the city.

[1]BrE: authorise

Unit 2

noun	industry	His favorite pastime is building model ships, and he always goes about this activity with great industry.
adjective	industrious	He is always industrious even when engaged in leisure-time activities.
adverb	industriously	He worked on his project industriously.

noun	intellect	The stress of city life has effects on the intellect.
noun	intellectual	I enjoy reading the works of the great intellectuals of the nine-teenth century.
adjective	intellectual	Some people enjoy spending their leisure time engaged in intellectual activities.
adverb	intellectually	Some people look for experiences that engage them intellectually.

noun	reluctance	Reluctance to spend time in nature is a problem for modern children.
adjective	reluctant	People can be reluctant to leave their familiar city surroundings to explore unknown places.
adverb	reluctantly	They reluctantly agreed to spend their vacation at a national park.

Word Family Practice

Choose the correct word family member from the list below to complete each blank.

It is crucial to acknowledge the importance of leisure-time activities. They are not merely a way to use up free time. They are important for our physical and **1**.......... health. We need to choose activities that rest our minds and bodies so that we can feel rejuvenated when we return to work and can do our jobs more **2**.......... . Some people enjoy **3**.......... pastimes; other people choose different sorts of leisure-time activities. The key is to be **4**.......... about choosing a pastime that is active rather than passive. Many people feel **5**.......... to be physically active after a tiring week at work. However, **6**.......... tell us that this is actually the best way to decrease stress and relax.

1. emotions   emotional   emotionally

2. industry   industrious   industriously

3. intellect   intellectual   intellectually

4. deliberation   deliberate   deliberately

5. reluctance   reluctant   reluctantly

6. authorities   authorizes   authoritative

Dictionary Skill

Different Meanings
Many words have more than one meaning.

Read the definitions below. Then read the sentences and write the letter of the correct definition for each sentence.

QUESTIONS 1–2

> en-gage [en-GAYJ]
> **A** *verb.* to participate
> **B** *verb.* to hire

_____ 1. The school *engaged* a special teacher to teach classes about nature.

_____ 2. Every afternoon, the children *engage* in outdoor activities.

QUESTIONS 3–4

> in-dus-try [IN-dus-tree]
> **A** *noun.* hard work
> **B** *noun.* production and sale of goods

_____ 3. Many people in this city work in the clothing *industry*.

_____ 4. *Industry* will help you move up in your profession, but don't forget to spend some time in leisure activities as well.

Listening

Listen to the talk. Complete the notes below.
Write **NO MORE THAN ONE WORD** *for each answer.*

Research on Leisure

People engaged in **1**.......... pastimes don't feel rejuvenated.

Popular Pastimes:
2.......... Activities
• Sports
• Playing with children
• Gardening

3.......... Activities
• Reading
• Playing computer games
• Doing puzzles
• Using the Internet

Activities that exercise both our minds and bodies help us avoid **4**.......... and **5**.......... .

Unit 2

Writing

The numbers below show basic information about uses of leisure time among different age groups.

Summarize[1] the information by selecting and reporting the main information and making comparisons.

Write at least 150 words.

**Pastimes by Age
(minutes per weekend day)**

	Reading	Computer (leisure use)	Sports and exercise
13–19 years old	5	75	60
20–65 years old	30	30	120
66+ years old	60	30	20

Speaking

Talk about the following topics.

What are some of your favorite pastimes? Why do you enjoy them?

Do you prefer physical or intellectual activities for relaxation?

[1]BrE: summarise

Unit 3: Transportation

FIRST HEADLAMPS

Words

Look for the following words as you read the passage. Match each word with its correct definition.

Words
1. cast
2. disaster
3. display
4. drawback
5. efficient
6. equip
7. freight
8. generate
9. illuminator
10. innovation
11. intense
12. knot
13. locomotive
14. mode
15. portable
16. reflector
17. rugged
18. stringent
19. tricky
20. vulnerable

Definitions
A. n., the engine of a train
B. n., a method or type
C. v., to show or exhibit
D. v., to throw light on something
E. adj., easy to carry
F. adj., very strong
G. n., a problem; disadvantage
H. n., cargo carried by a train, truck, or ship
I. adj., weak; without defense[1]
J. n., a terrible event
K. n., a hard bump in wood
L. v., to make or produce
M. adj., difficult
N. n., an object that produces light
O. adj., able to work without waste
P. n., an object that sends light back or makes it stronger
Q. adj., strict, firm
R. v., to provide with something
S. adj., strong; able to stand rough treatment
T. n., a new idea or product

[1]BrE: defence

Unit 3

Reading

First Headlamps

A

Before electricity, light was tricky business. Flames cast limited light, are vulnerable to winds and weather, and can lead to disaster. Making fire portable and dependable was so difficult that lights on moving vehicles were hardly ever considered.

B

The early trains traveled[1] only during the day. The tracks were too dangerous during the dark of night, and passengers wanted to see where they were traveling anyway. In the late 1830s, railroad traffic became heavy enough for freight trains to delay passenger trains. To avoid these delays, railroads started running freight trains at night. Horatio Allen's 1831 innovation, the "Track Illuminator," was suddenly in demand. It was a pile of pine knots burning in an iron grate that sat in a box of sand on a platform car. The car was pushed ahead of the locomotive. The illuminator did not cast much light, but it warned of the approaching train and was the best technology available.

C

In 1841, some trains used an oil[2] lamp backed by a curved reflector, an improvement, but oil lamps blew out easily in the wind, including the wind generated by the movement of the train. At about the same time, Schenectady and Troy Railroad trains displayed a whale oil lamp positioned between a reflector and a lens about twelve inches high; it threw light up to 100 feet ahead of the train. Although this was an improvement, the braking distance the trains required was more than the 100 feet of track that were illuminated. In 1849, a calcium lamp was developed that threw light 1,000 feet and lasted four hours; however, the only railroad company to use it was Camden and Amboy. Limelights, which were used to light theater[3] stages on both sides of the Atlantic, were considered too intense for trains. Eventually, acetylene, which did not extinguish in the wind, replaced oil in headlamps.

D

In 1851, the first electric headlamp was developed. This headlamp had two major drawbacks: It required its own generator, which did not become portable until the 1890s when steam generators became common, and the delicate parts broke easily as a result of the rough rails over which the trains traveled. Russia ran the first train equipped with

[1]BrE: travelled
[2]BrE: kerosene
[3]BrE: theatre

a battery-powered electric headlamp. The French first used steam generators to power electric headlamps on trains. In the United States in 1897, George C. Pyle developed an efficient electric headlamp. By 1916, federal law required trains to have electric headlamps.

E

Automobiles, the exciting new mode of transportation[4] at that time, needed headlamps, too. The requirements for car headlamps were more stringent than those for trains: Because roads were even rougher than rails, cars required more rugged parts, and the steam generators had to be smaller than those in trains. Despite these tougher requirements, the Columbia Electric Car was equipped with electric headlamps in 1898.

F

Electric headlamps made travel at all hours and in almost all weather possible, something we take for granted today.

Answer the questions about **First Headlamps**.

Questions 1–8

*The reading passage contains six paragraphs, **A–F**.*
Which paragraphs discuss the following information?
*Write the correct letter, **A–F**.*

_____ 1. a lamp that used burning wood

_____ 2. lamps rugged enough to use with cars

_____ 3. a lamp that generated its own electricity

_____ 4. the drawbacks of using flames for light

_____ 5. lamps that used reflectors to cast more intense light

_____ 6. the year the first train was equipped with electric headlamps

_____ 7. a reason why acetylene lamps are more efficient than oil lamps

_____ 8. a reason why freight trains traveled at night

[4]BrE: transport

Unit 3

My Words

Write the words that are new to you. Look them up in the dictionary and write their definitions.

Words   Definitions

_____   _____

_____   _____

_____   _____

_____   _____

_____   _____

_____   _____

_____   _____

Word Families

noun	efficiency	Efficiency is an important quality for any new product.
adjective	efficient	Efficient headlamps made safe travel at night possible.
adverb	efficiently	Candles do not light a room very efficiently.

noun	generator	If the power lines are down, you can use a gasoline generator to have electricity in your house.
noun	generation	The generation of electricity can cause air pollution.
verb	generate	There are a variety of ways to generate electricity.

noun	illuminator	An illuminator can provide an area with light.
noun	illumination	The illumination of an electric lamp is stronger than that of a candle.
verb	illuminate	In the past, people used candles to illuminate their houses.

noun	innovation	The innovation of electric headlamps made travel much easier.
noun	innovator	Several innovators worked on the development of electric headlamps.
adjective	innovative	The development of electric headlamps was the work of a number of innovative people.

noun	intensity	A locomotive needs a headlamp with high intensity.
verb	intensify	Using a stronger battery will intensify light.
adjective	intense	The light from candles is not very intense.
adverb	intensely	Some materials burn more intensely than others.

Unit 3

noun	reflector	A reflector on a lamp makes the light more intense.
noun	reflection	You can see your reflection in a mirror.
verb	reflect	A piece of metal can be used to reflect light.
adjective	reflective	If a lamp is coated with reflective material, it will cast a stronger light.

Word Family Practice

Choose the correct word family member from the list below to complete each blank.

Traveling at night was tricky before people had developed headlamps that worked **1**.......... . Early **2**.......... for use on locomotives included lamps that **3**.......... by burning pine knots or whale oil. Some of these lamps used metal as a **4**.......... material to **5**.......... the light. Later, electric headlamps were developed. The problem with these lamps involved finding a portable way to **6**.......... the electricity that they used.

1. efficiency   efficient   efficiently

2. innovators   innovations   innovative

3. illumination   illuminator   illuminated

4. reflector   reflect   reflective

5. intensity   intensify   intensely

6. generation   generators   generate

Dictionary Skill

Different Meanings
Many words have more than one meaning.

Read the definitions below. Then read the sentences and write the letter of the correct definition for each sentence.

QUESTIONS 1–2

dis-play [dis-PLAY]
    A *noun.* a showing, an exhibit
    B *verb.* to show or exhibit

_____ 1. The new, more efficient headlamps for use on trains were on *display*.

_____ 2. Everyone was excited to see cars that *displayed* the new electric headlamps.

QUESTIONS 3–4

knot [NOT]
    A *noun.* a hard bump in wood
    B *verb.* tie something in a certain way

_____ 3. Burning pine *knots* is a way to create light.

_____ 4. If you *knot* your shoelaces well, they won't untie.

Listening

---

*Listen to the lecture. Choose **FOUR** letters, **A–G**.*

Which **FOUR** drawbacks of early train travel does the lecturer mention?

A difficulty traveling at night   **E** cost of tickets

B frequent delays   **F** uncomfortable rides

C safety problems   **G** crowded passenger cars

D dirt

Unit 3

Writing

In your opinion, what has been the most significant transportation innovation of the past 200 years?

Support your opinion with reasons and examples from your own knowledge or experience.

Write at least 250 words.

Speaking

Talk about the following topics.

What modes of transportation are commonly used in your city? Which do you think are the most efficient?

What do you think are some of the advantages of train travel?

What do you think are some drawbacks of train travel?

MAJOR SUBWAYS OF EUROPE

Words

> Look for the following words as you read the passage. Match each word with its correct definition.

Words	Definitions
1. architecture	A. v., to compete with
2. centerpiece[1]	B. n., central office for a military commander
3. clog	
4. decorate	C. n., the act of ruining something
5. destruction	D. n., something that serves as protection
6. disruptive	E. n., an opening to let air, steam, or smoke out
7. expand	F. v., to make bigger
8. headquarters	G. n., a setting in which to present something
9. intrinsic	
10. operation	H. v., to make an object or place beautiful
11. pedestrian	I. n., the style of a building
12. release	J. v., to use
13. rival	K. adj., basic
14. shield	L. n., the working of something, being used
15. showcase	M. adv., below the ground
16. spring up	N. v., to let something out
17. surface	O. n., the outer part or top of something
18. underground	P. adj., stopping the usual course of activity
19. utilize[2]	Q. n., the main or most important feature
20. vent	R. v., to fill so much as to make movement difficult
	S. v., to appear
	T. n., a person traveling[3] on foot

[1]BrE: centrepiece
[2]BrE: utilise
[3]BrE: travelling

Unit 3

Reading

Major Subways of Europe

Public transportation[1] is an intrinsic part of every modern city. Many big cities have an underground rail system as their centerpiece. Three of the biggest and busiest underground rail systems in Europe are in London, Paris, and Moscow. The character of each city imprints its railways.

The first of these subways was London's Underground, which opened in 1863. By that time, horses and pedestrians had so clogged the streets of London that city government ruled that no railroads could enter the city except underground. The method used for laying the first underground tracks is called "cut and cover," meaning the streets were dug up, the track was laid, a tunnel was built, and then everything was buried. Although the method was disruptive, it worked. Steam engines chugged under London, releasing steam through vents along the city streets. In its initial day of operation, the London Underground carried 30,000 passengers.

This cut-and-cover method caused massive disruptions in the city and required the destruction of the structures above the tunnel. A better means of expanding the original Underground was needed, and builders did not have to look far to find it. London was also home to the first underwater tunnel, a pedestrian tunnel that had been built under the Thames River in 1825, made possible by the engineer Marc Brunel. He had devised a way of supporting the tunnel while the workers dug, called the Brunel Shield. Two young engineers improved the Brunel Shield for use in expanding the London Underground. The new Harlow-Greathead Shield carved a circular tube more than seven feet in diameter, which is why the London Underground is called the Tube. By then, the tunnels could be deeper than the original ones because electric train engines had become available. These trains did not have to be close to the surface to release steam. The shield could be used to dig deeper tunnels without destroying the surface structures above them.

Paris started designing an underground rail service to rival London's. The first part of its system was not opened until the World's Fair and Olympics were held in that city in 1900. The Paris Metro is shorter than London's, but it carries more passengers every day, second in Europe only to Moscow. Whereas London's Underground is known for its engineering, Paris's Metro is known for its beauty. The stations and entrances are examples of art nouveau architecture, and they are decorated with mosaics, sculptures, paintings, and innovative doors and walls.

The Moscow Metro opened in 1935. It was based on the design of the London Tube, except much of the track is above ground. When Stalin

[1]BrE: transport

came to power, he used the stations as showcases of Russian art, culture, and engineering. The underground Moscow stations are filled with statuary, painting, and mosaics.

Underground railways are not only for transportation. During World War II, all three underground systems were used as bomb shelters for the populace. The Moscow subway was even used as a military headquarters. Stores and malls have sprung up by stations, something that is especially convenient in cold climates.

All three systems are continuing to expand, providing service to more riders in more distant locales. This is all part of an effort to decrease greenhouse gases emitted from personal vehicles.

Answer the questions about **Major Subways of Europe**.

Questions 1–4

> *Do the following describe the subway system in London, Paris, or Moscow?*
>
> *Write the correct letter,* **A**, **B**, *or* **C**.
>
> **A**   London
> **B**   Paris
> **C**   Moscow

_____ 1. It was used as a military headquarters during World War II.

_____ 2. It has a large percentage of its track above the ground.

_____ 3. It was originally built for the operation of steam trains.

_____ 4. It is famous for its beautiful architecture.

Questions 5–7

> *Choose the correct letter,* **A**, **B**, **C**, *or* **D**.

5. The Paris Metro stations are decorated with
   A   pictures of the Olympics.
   B   different kinds of artwork.
   C   photographs of the World's Fair.
   D   examples of engineering.

Unit 3

6. The London Underground was first built because
   A the underwater pedestrian tunnel had been damaged.
   B a new method for digging tunnels had been developed.
   C the city streets were too clogged for trains on the surface.
   D the city wanted to rival the transportation system in Paris.

7. The introduction of electric train engines allowed for
   A deeper tunnels.
   B more pedestrians.
   C innovative doors and walls.
   D more art showcases in the stations.

My Words

Write the words that are new to you. Look them up in the dictionary and write their definitions.

Words   Definitions

_____   _____

_____   _____

_____   _____

_____   _____

_____   _____

_____   _____

_____   _____

Word Families

noun	architect	The architect is working on a plan for a new train station.
noun	architecture	The architecture of the stations is an important part of subway system design.
adjective	architectural	From an architectural point of view, it's a very interesting building.
adverb	architecturally	Its art nouveau decorative features make the Paris Metro architecturally significant.

noun	decoration	People enjoy looking at the decorations in the station while they wait for the train to arrive.
noun	decorator	The decorator planned the art for the station very carefully.
verb	decorate	Sometimes they decorate the trains for the holidays.
adjective	decorative	That column is there for decorative purposes only; it has no real use.

noun	destruction	The destruction of buildings was part of the process of creating the subway system.
verb	destroy	It was necessary to destroy some buildings to dig the subway tunnels.
adjective	destructive	Digging deeper tunnels makes subway construction less destructive to buildings and roads on the surface.

Unit 3

noun	disruption	Building a subway system can cause a lot of disruptions to traffic on the streets.
verb	disrupt	They try to disrupt traffic as little as possible during subway construction.
adjective	disruptive	The process of building a subway can be disruptive, but the result is well worth it.

noun	expansion	The expansion of the subway system cost a great deal of money.
verb	expand	By the time they were ready to expand the subway system, a new method for digging tunnels had been developed.
adjective	expandable	The subway system was designed to be expandable.

noun	operation	The Paris Metro began operation in 1900.
noun	operator	A subway train operator needs special training for the job.
verb	operate	Modern subway systems use computers to operate the trains.

Word Family Practice

Choose the correct word family member from the list below to complete each blank.

The planning and construction of a subway system requires a great deal of time and effort. In addition to planning the routes, digging the tunnels, and laying the tracks, the stations have to be built. **1**.......... are hired to plan the stations. Often, the station plan includes **2**.......... features such as murals showing local scenes, or a station may be used as a showcase for the work of important local artists. Building a new subway system may require the **3**.......... of buildings on the surface, but attempts are made to cause as little **4**.......... as possible. The **5**.......... of an already-existing subway system can also be quite disruptive. Everyone looks forward to the day when the construction is over and the subway begins to **6**.......... . Often businesses spring up in and around a new subway station, contributing to the life of the neighborhood.

1. Architecture   Architects   Architectural

2. decorates   decorations   decorative

3. destruction   destroy   destructive

4. disruption   disrupts   disruptive

5. expansion   expand   expandable

6. operation   operator   operate

Unit 3

Word Skill

Compound Words
When two or more words join to form a new word, that word is called a compound word. Often, the meaning of the compound word is related to the meanings of the two separate words.

> underground = under + ground
> Meaning: below the surface of the ground

Read the sentences. Write a definition for each underlined word.

1. They built an <u>underwater</u> tunnel for pedestrians below the Thames River.

   underwater: _____

2. Before they could paint the mural in the station, they had to cover the wall with an <u>undercoat</u> of special paint.

   undercoat: _____

3. Instead of a bridge, they built an <u>underpass</u> so that cars could cross the tracks from below.

   underpass: _____

Listening

CD 1
Track
9

Listen to the conversation. Complete the outline below.
*Write **NO MORE THAN ONE WORD** for each answer.*

The London Underground: (1863)

Steam engines were used, so
- it had to be close to the **1**.......... .
- it had **2**.......... so engines could release steam.

Electric engines were introduced, so
- tunnels could be deeper.
- a **3**.......... was used to support the tunnel.
- digging the deeper tunnels did not **4**..........
  streets and buildings.

Writing

The chart[1] below shows information about subway systems in three major European cities.

Summarize[2] the information by selecting and reporting the main information and making comparisons.

Write at least 150 words.

Unit 3

Size of Subway Systems

	Total track length (both underground and on the surface)	Number of stations in operation	Number of daily passengers
London Underground	408 km	275	3 million
Paris Metro	214 km	300	4.5 million
Moscow Metro	300 km	182	6.5 million

[1]BrE: table
[2]BrE: summarise

Speaking

Talk about the following topics.

Are there any subway or train stations or other buildings in your city that have especially beautiful architecture? Describe them.

Are there any public spaces in your city that are used to showcase the work of local or national artists? Do you think it is a good idea to use public spaces in this way? Why or why not?

ELECTRIC CARS AROUND THE GLOBE

Words

> *Look for the following words as you read the passage. Match each word with its correct definition.*

Words

1. accelerate
2. appeal
3. charge
4. classify
5. commuter
6. consume
7. embrace
8. flair
9. fume
10. hamper
11. incentive
12. markedly
13. monetary
14. plodding
15. rural
16. span
17. sprawl
18. standard
19. suburban
20. urban

Definitions

A. v., to accept something enthusiastically

B. n., a person who travels regularly between home and work

C. adj., related to the area just outside a city

D. n., elegant style

E. n., the amount of power a battery can store

F. v., to make things difficult, get in the way

G. adj., related to the city

H. n., reason to do something, reward

I. n., the normal or common thing

J. v., to cross

K. v., to divide into groups by type

L. adv., noticeably

M. adj., related to money

N. v., to gain speed

O. adj., related to the countryside

P. n., harmful gas or smoke in the air

Q. v., to be of interest

R. v., to use

S. n., an area of spreading growth

T. adj., slow

Unit 3

Reading

Electric Cars Around the Globe

Cars have reshaped our world since they first rolled off mass-production lines in the early twentieth century. One- and two-thousand-year-old Roman roads have been replaced by highways. Longer and wider bridges span rivers. The sharp division between urban and rural landscapes has been replaced by suburban sprawl, town and country linked by eight-lane expressways with stop-and-go traffic. Gas[1] stations are everywhere. Countries with oil reserves are enormously rich and powerful. After a century, the romance with internal combustion engines is on the wane. As the price of oil rises, the reserves of irreplaceable oil are consumed, and exhaust fumes hamper life in urban areas, alternatives to gas-powered vehicles are becoming more attractive.

In the early twentieth century in North America, electric cars shared the roads with gas-fueled cars, but after a short time, gas-fueled cars became the standard. Although electric cars were quieter, cleaner, and easier to start, they were not able to travel the required distances, and their plodding speed failed to capture the imagination.

Lately, in Europe and in Asia, where commuting distances are shorter and gas is more expensive than in the United States, electric cars have grown in popularity. Electric recharging stations are appearing in cities. The government of China has offered monetary incentives to car manufacturers for each electric car they manufacture as well as to the people who purchase the electric cars. Taxi drivers in Tokyo have embraced electric vehicles. Major car manufacturers, including Mitsubishi, Nissan, Toyota, and Mercedes Benz, all offer electric cars everywhere but in North America.

In North America, slow, short-ranged electric vehicles with a high initial cost have thus far appealed to a limited audience. An American electric car that appeared briefly in the 1990s had a cruising speed of twenty-five miles per hour and could travel eighty-five miles on a single charge. Since then, battery technology has improved markedly. More recently, a North American company introduced an electric sports car that can travel 300 miles on a single charge and accelerate from 0 to 60 mph in 3.7 seconds, similar to the best sports car. The hope is that North Americans will embrace the new technology when they see an electric car as appealing as a conventional sports car.

Other American auto manufacturers are marketing electric cars as they do in Europe, as commuter cars. The design of many of these cars is innovative: Some are made of light composites and seat only two

[1]BrE: Petrol

people. One is a three-wheeler that is classified as a motorcycle. Another electric car, the Tango, is five inches narrower than a large motorcycle and seats two, one behind the other. Four of these vehicles fit in a single parking space. The vehicle is marketed as a great way to drive between lanes of stopped traffic.

All electric cars will help to reduce exhaust and greenhouse gases; some will do it with greater flair than others.

Answer the questions about **Electric Cars Around the Globe**.

Questions 1–7

Complete the summary using words from the list below.

Cars have had enormous effects on the way our world looks. The landscape is now covered with highways and big bridges. New **1**.......... neighborhoods have developed between the cities and the rural areas. Cars are also causing serious problems. Oil is expensive, and we have already **2**.......... a lot of oil that cannot be replaced. Gas-powered cars also pollute the air with their **3**........... . In the early days, both electric and gas-powered cars were common, but people felt that electric cars did not have the flair that gas-powered cars had. For example, electric cars traveled at a more **4**.......... speed. Gas-powered cars became more popular, and now they are the **5**........... . However, there is a renewed interest in electric cars, and they have been **6**.......... by people in many countries around the world. Manufacturers are developing electric cars to sell to **7**.......... in both Europe and North America, because these cars are a good way to get to work.

accelerated	embraced	incentives	suburban
commuters	fumes	plodding	urban
consumed	hampered	standard	

Unit 3

My Words

Write the words that are new to you. Look them up in the dictionary and write their definitions.

Words   Definitions

_____   _____

_____   _____

_____   _____

_____   _____

_____   _____

_____   _____

_____   _____

Word Families

noun	appeal	The appeal of an electric car is that it doesn't cause pollution.
verb	appeal	A car that uses less gasoline would appeal to commuters.
adjective	appealing	Electric cars are appealing to many people.

noun	class	The new class of electric cars is very different from the electric cars of the early twentieth century.
noun	classification	The classification of a car as a sports car can make it more appealing to certain people.
verb	classify	If you classify your car as a commercial vehicle, you will need to get a special license[1].

noun	commuter	Commuters are worried about the increase of traffic on the highways.
noun	commute	I have an hour-long commute to work every day.
verb	commute	Many people commute from the suburbs to their jobs in the city.

noun	consumer	Consumers of gasoline are paying higher and higher prices.
noun	consumption	As the price of oil increases, consumption may go down.
verb	consume	Electric cars are attractive because they don't consume gasoline.

[1]BrE: licence

noun	mark	The new hybrid vehicles have made their mark with consumers.
verb	mark	The twenty-first century marked a renewed interest in electric cars.
adjective	marked	In the past, before cars became common, the difference between urban and rural areas was more marked.
adverb	markedly	The popularity of electric cars has grown markedly over the past few years.

noun	money	Although cars cost a great deal of money, many people own them.
adjective	monetary	As gasoline becomes more expensive, monetary reasons will cause more people to be interested in buying electric cars.
adverb	monetarily	Electric cars may be out of reach for some people monetarily.

Word Family Practice

Choose the correct word family member from the list below to complete each blank.

Car manufacturers are developing a **1**.......... of electric car especially for **2**.......... . These cars are quite small and may have room for only one or two people. They are not intended for carrying large loads or many passengers. Their main purpose is to get the driver to and from work. Because of their small size, they **3**.......... little energy. They are **4**.......... because they cost much less **5**.......... than larger cars to run. In fact, there is a **6**.......... difference in fuel costs between these new small cars and the larger cars that we are used to seeing.

1. class	classification	classify
2. commuters	commutes	commute
3. consumer	consume	consumption
4. appeal	appeals	appealing
5. monetarily	monetary	money
6. marked	markedly	mark

Unit 3

Dictionary Skill

Different Meanings
Many words have more than one meaning.

Read the definitions below. Then read the sentences and write the letter of the correct definition for each sentence.

QUESTIONS 1–2

ap-peal [a-PEEL]
A *verb.* to be of interest
B *verb.* to ask a court of law to hear a case again

_____ 1. The driver didn't agree that he was guilty of speeding and planned to *appeal* to the court to change the decision.

_____ 2. A car that is inexpensive to buy and easy to maintain would *appeal* to many people.

QUESTIONS 3–4

charge [CHARJ]
A *noun.* the amount of power a battery can store
B *noun.* the price of a service or purchase

_____ 3. The *charge* for car repairs is often quite high.

_____ 4. This car can travel about 100 miles on one battery *charge.*

Listening

 CD 1 Track 10

*Listen to the talk. Look at the map labeled **1–4**.*
Complete the labels.

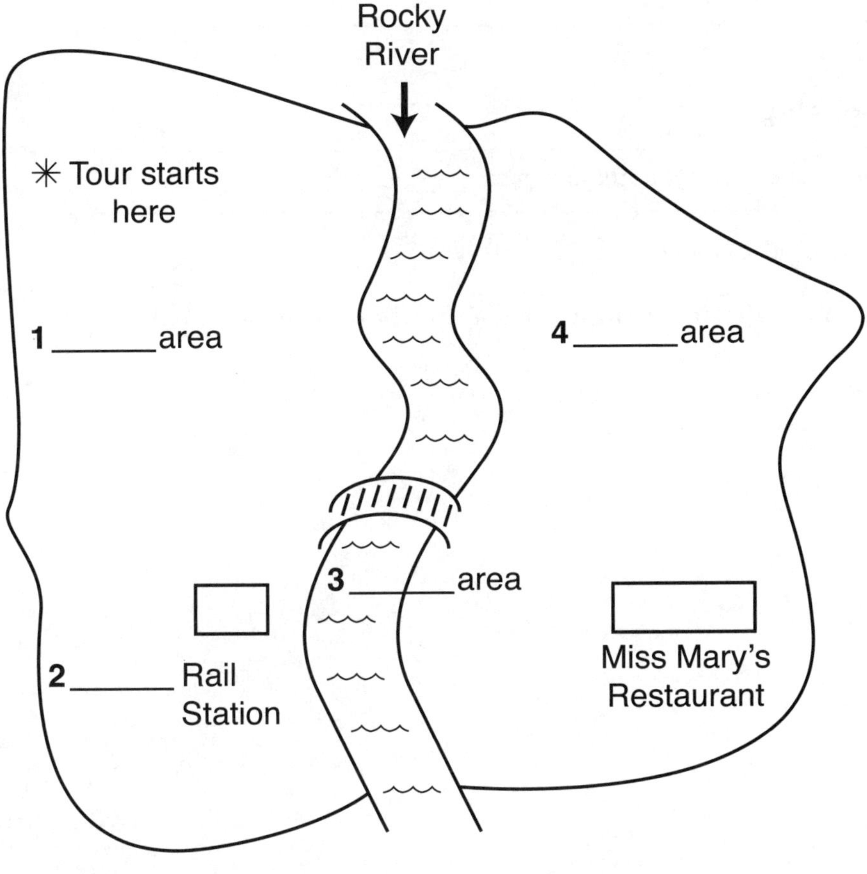

Rocky
River
↓

✳ Tour starts
here

1_____area

4_____area

3_____area

☐

2_____ Rail
Station

☐
Miss Mary's
Restaurant

Unit 3

Writing

In your opinion, what incentives could be offered that would persuade more people to embrace electric cars?

Support your answer with reasons and examples from your own knowledge or experience.

Write at least 250 words.

Speaking

Talk about the following topics.

What kind of car is appealing to you?

Do you prefer to live in a rural, suburban, or urban area?

Unit 4: Culture

ORIGINS OF WRITING

Words

> *Look for the following words as you read the passage. Match each word with its correct definition.*

Words
1. adopt
2. agricultural
3. attribute
4. carve
5. civilization[1]
6. creator
7. deed
8. encompass
9. excavation
10. function
11. inscribe
12. literacy
13. mythology
14. property
15. scholar
16. settle
17. specialized[2]
18. structure
19. tablet
20. token

Definitions
A. v., to include
B. n., the ability to read and write
C. v., to cut and shape hard material
D. n., a thin, flat piece of material to write on
E. n., something that is built, such as a building or bridge
F. n., an area of digging, especially to find objects from past cultures
G. adj., related to farming
H. n., the first maker of something
I. v., to perform well
J. n., human society, its organization[3] and culture
K. v., to mark a surface with words or letters
L. n., an act, especially a good or bad one
M. v., to give credit for or see as the origin of something
N. n., set of traditional stories used to explain the origins of things
O. v., to accept or start to use something new
P. adj., relating to a particular area or type of work
Q. v., to establish a permanent place to live
R. n., an object used to represent something else
S. n., person who has a lot of knowledge about a particular subject
T. n., something that is owned

[1]BrE: civilisation
[2]BrE: specialised
[3]BrE: organisation

Reading

Origins of Writing

Ancient civilizations attributed the origins of writing to the gods. For the ancient Egyptians, their god Thoth was the creator of writing and, in some stories, also the creator of speech. The ancient Sumerians and Assyrians also believed that writing originated with certain gods, as did the ancient Maya. In Chinese mythology, the creation of writing is attributed to an ancient sage and was used for communication with the gods. Clearly, writing was highly valued even by ancient peoples.

Humans began painting pictures on cave walls 25,000 years ago or more, but writing systems did not develop until groups of people began settling in farming communities. Scholars say that writing systems developed independently in at least three different parts of the world: Mesopotamia, China, and Mesoamerica.

The oldest known writing system developed among the ancient Sumerians in Mesopotamia around 3000 B.C. Along with the rise of agricultural societies came the development of property ownership and the need to keep records of it. In early agricultural societies, property consisted largely of land, livestock such as cattle, and grain. Originally, clay tokens of various shapes were used to count these possessions. From this developed a system of impressing the shapes onto clay tablets. One of the earliest clay tablets of this type was found in excavations in Mesopotamia and dates from the time of the Sumerian culture. Scribes then began using reeds instead of tokens to mark the clay, developing a system of wedgelike shapes to represent the tokens. This system of writing using wedge shapes is known as cuneiform. It was later adopted by other cultures and became the basis for other writing systems. Originating in a system that used pictures to represent objects, cuneiform writing eventually developed into systems that used symbols to represent the sounds of language.

The oldest form of Chinese writing dates from around 1500 B.C. It is called oracle bone script because it was carved on animal bones and shells that were used for predicting the future. At a later period, Chinese writing appeared on bronze vases and later still developed into a system that was used to record government affairs. The Chinese writing system was also the original basis for both the Japanese and Korean writing systems.

In Mesoamerica, a region that encompasses parts of Mexico and Central America, it is the ancient Mayans who are famous for the writing they inscribed on temple walls and other religious structures. However, scholars believe that writing in that part of the world may have begun before the rise of the Mayan civilization. The Zapotec culture, centered[1] on Oaxaca, Mexico, was already using writing around 400 B.C., or possibly earlier. The Olmec culture may have developed a writing system even earlier than that. Recent discoveries show that the Mayans may have begun writing around 2,300 years ago. They used a system of symbols that represented words and syllables to record information about the deeds of their rulers as well as information connected to their calendar and astronomy. Their system of writing survived until the time of the Spanish Conquest in the 1500s.

In ancient times, only specialized[2] people such as scholars, priests, or government officials used writing. Today, close to three-quarters of the world's adult population can read and write, and literacy is considered a basic skill necessary to function in the modern world.

Answer the questions about **Origins of Writing**.

Questions 1–7

> Do the following describe the ancient Sumerians, the ancient Chinese, or the ancient Maya?
>
> Write the correct letter, **A**, **B**, or **C**.
>
>   **A** Ancient Sumerians
>
>   **B** Ancient Chinese
>
>   **C** Ancient Maya

_____ 1. inscribed symbols on bones

_____ 2. inscribed symbols on religious structures

_____ 3. inscribed symbols on clay tablets

_____ 4. used tokens to keep records of their property

_____ 5. used writing to record the deeds of their rulers

_____ 6. developed a writing system that was adopted by the Japanese

_____ 7. settled in Mesopotamia

Unit 4

[1]BrE: centred
[2]BrE: specialised

Questions 8–10

Do the following statements agree with the information in the reading passage?

Write

TRUE   *if the statement agrees with the information.*
FALSE   *if the statement contradicts the information.*
NOT GIVEN   *if there is no information on this in the passage.*

_____ 8. The ancient Maya attributed the origin of writing to the gods.

_____ 9. Scholars have discovered similarities between Zapotec and Mayan writing.

_____ 10. Literacy was common in most ancient civilizations.

My Words

Write the words that are new to you. Look them up in the dictionary and write their definitions.

Words   Definitions

_____   _____

_____   _____

_____   _____

_____   _____

_____   _____

_____   _____

_____   _____

Word Families

noun	agriculture	People settled in Mesopotamia because it was a good area for agriculture.
adjective	agricultural	Wheat was one of the first agricultural products.
adverb	agriculturally	Mesopotamia was an agriculturally important part of the world.

noun	creator	The ancient Maya were the creators of temples and other beautiful structures.
noun	creation	The ancient Sumerians used clay and reeds for the creation of property records.
verb	create	The ancient Sumerians created tokens out of clay.
adjective	creative	Ancient peoples developed creative ways to record information.
adverb	creatively	Ancient peoples recorded information creatively, using materials such as clay.

noun	excavation	Early clay tablets and clay tokens have been found in excavations in Mesopotamia.
noun	excavator	Excavators found a clay tablet that dates from the time of the ancient Sumerians.
verb	excavate	When archeologists[1] excavated the area, they found some ancient oracle bones.

Unit 4

[1]BrE: archaeologists

noun	literacy	Literacy was not considered necessary before modern times.
noun	illiteracy	Illiteracy is a problem throughout the modern world.
adjective	literate	Few people were literate in the ancient world.
adjective	illiterate	An illiterate person cannot read or write.

noun	mythology	Mythology was very important in ancient civilizations.
noun	myth	Today we read the myths that were told in ancient times.
adjective	mythological	The Maya included mythological creatures in their writing system.

noun	specialty	That scholar's specialty is ancient Mayan culture.
noun	specialization	With the growth of agriculture, people developed specializations.
verb	specialize	Some scholars specialize in ancient studies.
adjective	specialized	Specialized skills are needed to identify ancient objects found in excavations.

Word Family Practice

Choose the correct word family member from the list below to complete each blank.

1.......... working at ancient sites uncover objects that give us clues about life in the past. Household objects and tools that were used for **2**.......... can tell us a lot about how people lived long ago. Ancient people used a variety of materials to make the objects they used in daily life. Tools that were carved from wood, stone, and bone, and jars that were **3**.......... from clay are some examples of objects that have been found. Some of these objects are quite beautiful, and it is clear that they were made by people with **4**.......... skills. In ancient times, most people were not **5**.......... . However, traditional stories were an important part of ancient civilizations, and people told the **6**.......... of their culture to their children and grandchildren.

1. Excavations   Excavators   Excavates

2. agriculture   agricultural   agriculturally

3. creation   creators   created

4. specialty   specializes   specialized

5. literacy   illiterate   literate

6. mythology   myths   mythological

Unit 4

Dictionary Skill

Parts of Speech
The word *function* can be a verb or a noun.

> Read the definitions below. Then read the sentences and write the letter of the correct definition for each sentence.
>
> func-tion [FUNGK-shun]
> **A** *verb.* to perform well
> **B** *noun.* purpose, role

_____ 1. The skills needed to *function* in modern society are very different from those needed in the ancient world.

_____ 2. Mythology had an important *function* in ancient cultures.

Listening

> Listen to the talk. Look at the map below labeled A–E. Look at the list of places and write the correct letter, **A–E**, next to numbers **1–5**.

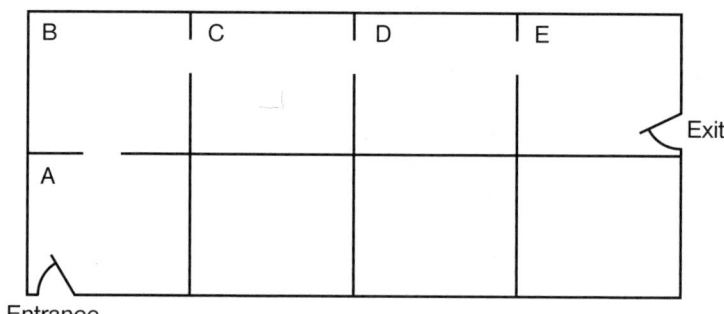

_____ 1. Visiting Scholars' Room

_____ 2. Agricultural Tools Exhibit

_____ 3. Recent Excavations Exhibit

_____ 4. Mythology Exhibit

_____ 5. Gift Shop

Writing

The chart[1] below shows literacy rates in several different countries around the world.

Summarize[2] the information by selecting and reporting the main information and making comparisons.

Write at least 150 words.

Adult Literacy Rates
(age 15 and over)

Country	Total Population	Male	Female
Country A	47.8%	63.5%	32.7%
Country B	50%	70.5%	30%
Country C	90.3%	93.9%	86.9%
Country D	99%	99%	99%
World	82%	87%	77%

Speaking

Talk about the following topics.

Do you believe that it is better to have a teacher who specializes in the subject he or she teaches or a teacher who is highly skilled at teaching? Why?

What skills do you think are necessary to teach today's children to help them function in a society where technology is changing so rapidly?

Unit 4

[1]BrE: table
[2]BrE: summarise

HULA DANCING IN HAWAIIAN CULTURE

Words

> *Look for the following words as you read the passage. Match each word with its correct definition.*

Words	Definitions
1. accompany	A. n., a decorative rope of flowers or leaves
2. altar	B. n., a set of actions used as part of a ceremony
3. benefit	
4. celebration	C. adj., having a lot of energy
5. discourage	D. v., to move back and forth
6. elaborate	E. n., a fixed idea people have, especially one that is wrong
7. energetic	
8. evidence	F. v., to bring to mind
9. evoke	G. adj., related to flowers
10. floral	H. v., to try to stop or prevent something
11. garland	I. adj., having beauty of movement
12. graceful	J. n., a table or similar structure for religious ceremonies
13. image	
14. influence	K. n., a mental picture
15. reign	L. n., a social event to mark a special day or occasion
16. revive	
17. ritual	M. n., the period of time that a king or queen is in power
18. stereotype	
19. sway	N. n., a custom or belief of a group of people
20. tradition	
	O. n., the use, advantage of
	P. adj., having a lot of detail and decoration
	Q. v., to bring back to life
	R. v., to go with, happen at the same time
	S. n., signs, proof something is or is not true
	T. n., an effect, power

Reading

Hula Dancing in Hawaiian Culture

Many people dream of visiting the beautiful Hawaiian Islands. Mention of this Pacific paradise evokes images of women in grass skirts swaying their hips as they perform graceful island dances for the benefit of tourists. Although this image is a common stereotype of Hawaii, it has its roots in a real tradition that continues to play an important role in Hawaiian culture.

Hula dancing has always been part of Hawaiian life. Hawaiian mythology includes various stories that explain the origins of hula, each story attributing its creation to a different god or goddess and its first appearance to a different location. In reality, hula dancing is such an ancient tradition that it is impossible to say when or where it first appeared. It was most likely originally performed in front of an altar in honor of gods and accompanied by great ritual. It is a common belief that the ancient hula was danced only by men, but some scholars point to evidence suggesting that hula was traditionally danced by both men and women.

The English explorer Captain James Cook's visit to the islands in the eighteenth century caused many changes to Hawaiian society as a result of the contact with European culture. Although hula did not completely disappear after contact, it was discouraged. King David Kalakaua is credited with reviving hula dancing during his reign in the late nineteenth century. He was interested in reestablishing lost traditions, and hula was performed at celebrations held in his honor[1].

In the 1960s, a Hawaiian cultural festival was established as part of an effort to attract more tourists to the islands. A major part of this festival consisted of hula competitions, which were organized into categories of *hula kahiko*, or hula danced in the ancient style, and *hula auana*, or modern hula. This festival, called the Merrie Monarch Festival in honor of King David Kalakaua, has become a major annual cultural event. The hula competition is a central part of the festival and has had a significant influence on modern hula dancing.

Hula continues to be danced in both the ancient and modern styles. Traditional hula is an energetic dance performed to the accompaniment of chants and the beating of drums. The dancers wear traditional costumes consisting of garlands of leaves, skirts of tapa (a type of bark), and anklets made of animal bone. Many of the movements of modern hula are based on the ancient hula, but the modern style is slower and more graceful. It is danced to flowing guitar and ukulele music, and the dancers wear elaborate costumes, including the famous Hawaiian floral garlands known as leis.

[1]BrE: honour

Unit 4

Hula has attracted the interest of people outside the islands, and hula schools can be found in many parts of the world. Although people of other nationalities learn to dance some form of hula, it is also danced by Hawaiians who live away from the islands, on the mainland United States, in Europe, and elsewhere. It has become a way for native Hawaiians to maintain their cultural identity even while living away from their island homeland. What was once a religious ritual has become a form of entertainment, not only for tourists, but also for native Hawaiians who seek to maintain connections with their cultural heritage.

Answer the questions about **Hula Dancing in Hawaiian Culture**.

Questions 1–4

Choose the correct letter, **A**, **B**, **C**, *or* **D**.

1. Originally, hula was danced
   A by dancers wearing floral garlands.
   B for the benefit of kings.
   C in competitions.
   D near an altar.

2. Hula dancing was discouraged
   A in certain ancient rituals.
   B after contact with Europeans.
   C in the 1960s.
   D during traditional celebrations.

3. Hula was revived in the nineteenth century by
   A a Hawaiian king.
   B an English explorer.
   C Hawaiians in Europe.
   D the tourist industry.

4. Modern hula dances are accompanied by
   A drums.
   B guitars.
   C chants.
   D violins.

Questions 5–7

Complete the summary using words from the list below.

Hula dancing has been part of Hawaiian culture since ancient times, although the styles of dancing have changed over time. The traditional style of hula dancing, which is still performed, is fast, whereas modern hula is more **5**.......... and flowing. Dancers of modern hula wear costumes that are **6**.........., and dancers of ancient hula wear simpler traditional costumes. People everywhere are interested in hula, including Hawaiians living in other parts of the world. The fact that hula is danced by Hawaiians living away from their homeland is **7**.......... of its importance to Hawaiian culture.

elaborate	evidence	influence
energetic	graceful	reign

My Words

Write the words that are new to you. Look them up in the dictionary and write their definitions.

Words   Definitions

_____   _____

_____   _____

_____   _____

_____   _____

_____   _____

_____   _____

_____   _____

_____   _____

Unit 4

Word Families

noun	accompaniment	The accompaniment of drums and chants helps the hula dancers maintain their energy.
verb	accompany	Guitars often accompany modern hula dances.

noun	benefit	A benefit of hula dancing is that it attracts people to Hawaii.
verb	benefit	Hawaii benefits from the large numbers of tourists who visit the islands.
adjective	beneficial	Tourism is beneficial to the economy of Hawaii.

noun	celebration	Hula dances are often performed at cultural celebrations.
verb	celebrate	People like to celebrate important events by dancing.
adjective	celebratory	Celebratory dances were performed in honor of the king.

noun	energy	It takes a great deal of energy to dance hula.
verb	energize[1]	The beating of the drums energized the crowd.
adjective	energetic	Energetic chants and drumming accompany the hula dancers.
adverb	energetically	The dancers performed energetically all evening.

noun	influence	The influence of other cultures has changed the way hula is danced.
verb	influence	Ancient hula influenced the modern style of hula dancing.
adjective	influential	King David Kalakaua was influential in the return to old traditions.

noun	tradition	Hula dancing is an ancient tradition.
adjective	traditional	Hula is the traditional dance of Hawaii.
adverb	traditionally	Hula was traditionally performed in honor of the gods.

Unit 4

[1]BrE: energise

Word Family Practice

Choose the correct word family member from the list below to complete each blank.

Hula is a **1**.......... dance from Hawaii. Originally, it was performed as part of religious rituals. It was danced **2**.......... to the **3**.......... of drums and chants. Over time it has been **4**.......... in different ways, and styles have changed. Modern hula is a more graceful dance performed to guitar and ukulele music. It is performed for tourists and also as part of **5**.......... . The wide interest in hula dancing is **6**.......... for Hawaii, because it helps attract tourists to the islands.

1. tradition   traditional   traditionally

2. energy   energetic   energetically

3. accompaniment   accompany   accompanies

4. influences   influenced   influential

5. celebrations   celebrates   celebratory

6. benefits   benefited   beneficial

Dictionary Skill

Different Meanings
Many words have more than one meaning.

> *Read the definitions below. Then read the sentences and write the*
> *letter of the correct definition for each sentence.*
>
> im-age [IM-mij]
> **A** *noun.* a mental picture
> **B** *noun.* impression, appearance

_____ 1. The word *Hawaii* carries *images* of sunny beaches, volcanoes, and hula dancing.

_____ 2. King David Kalakaua was known as the Merrie Monarch because of his *image* as a happy party host.

Listening

CD 1 Track 12

> *Listen to the conversation. Choose* **FOUR** *letters,* **A–G.**

Which **FOUR** of the following will be included in the hula demonstration?

A floral decorations

B elaborate costumes

C garlands of leaves

D an altar

E energetic dances

F graceful movements

G traditional music

Unit 4

Writing

Most countries have traditional celebrations that occur annually.
In your opinion, what benefits do these celebrations have for society?

Support your opinion with reasons and examples from your own knowledge or experience.

> *Write at least 250 words.*

Speaking

> *Talk about the following topics.*

What are some important traditional celebrations in your country?

What are some rituals connected with traditional celebrations in your country?

THE ART OF MIME

Words

> Look for the following words as you read the passage. Match each word with its correct definition.

Words
1. abstract
2. atmosphere
3. conflict
4. considerably
5. culminate
6. effectively
7. emerge
8. exaggerated
9. frailty
10. gesture
11. humorous[1]
12. illusion
13. literal
14. merge
15. portray
16. prominent
17. prop
18. reminiscent
19. renowned
20. sharpen

Definitions
A. adj., funny, entertaining
B. v., to represent, act out
C. adj., not concrete, related to ideas or feelings
D. adj., similar to, reminding of something
E. n., appearance of being real, false impression
F. adv., well, successfully
G. v., to appear, develop
H. n., weakness and lack of strength
I. adv., a great deal, noticeably
J. n., a movement to express a feeling or idea
K. n., the feeling of a place
L. adj., important, major
M. n., difficulty, opposition
N. v., to result in, end with
O. v., to improve, perfect
P. adj., following the exact meaning
Q. adj., famous
R. v., to combine
S. adj., made to seem more or bigger
T. n., an object used by actors

[1]BrE: humourous

Unit 4

Reading

The Art of Mime

Miming dates back to the theaters[1] of ancient Greece and Rome. Mimes use movements, gestures, and facial expressions to portray a character or an emotion or to tell a story—all without words. Over the centuries, the art of miming grew to include acrobatics, props, and costumes, culminating in the fine-tuned art form that people recognize[2] today.

Miming can be abstract, literal, or a combination of the two. Abstract miming usually has no plot or central character but simply expresses a feeling such as sorrow or desire. Literal miming, on the other hand, tells a story and is often comedic, using body gestures and facial expressions to present a main character facing some type of conflict in a humorous way, for example, acting out a tug-of-war without the aid of rope or other props.

The twentieth-century style of miming reflects outside influences of the period, most notably silent films, in which actors relied on their ability to communicate thoughts and stories through facial expressions and exaggerated gestures. Two superstars of the silent movie era, Buster Keaton and Charlie Chaplin, sharpened their miming skills in the theater before using them in movies. Both were so successful that they have continued to influence mimes and other live performers long after their deaths. People still consider Chaplin a master of the miming technique, in particular, his tragicomic "little tramp" character, who so effectively portrays human frailty through physical comedy, also known as slapstick.

Another twentieth-century influence on modern miming involves a renowned French mime and acting teacher named Etienne Decroux, who developed what was known as corporeal mime. This art form focused on the body, showing thought through movement, and became the prominent form of the modern mime era. In the 1930s, Decroux founded a mime school in Paris based on corporeal mime. One of his students, a young Frenchman named Marcel Marceau, emerged as what many consider the master of modern mime.

Marceau added his personal touch to the art of miming and presented it to the world for half a century on television and in theaters. Among his well-known illusions are portrayals of a man walking against the wind and a man trapped inside a shrinking box. Marceau also created his own special character, Bip the clown. White-faced and dressed in a striped shirt and floppy top hat with a red flower, Bip is reminiscent of both Chaplin's little tramp and Pierrot, the traditional downtrodden mime character from centuries earlier.

[1]BrE: theatres
[2]BrE: recognise

Miming is still taught in dance, drama, and acting schools worldwide, although it has changed considerably since the ancient Greek plays and even since the solo performances of Marceau. Group miming is now in fashion, and sounds, lighting, and other special effects are included to help create the desired atmosphere. Current examples include the U.S. dance troupe Pilobolus, which merges modern dance, acrobatics, gymnastics, and mime to create elaborate geometric shapes with their bodies, and the Canadian Cirque du Soleil, which uses lighting, spectacular costumes, and special effects to produce striking illusions.

Answer the questions about **The Art of Mime**.

Questions 1–8

> *Complete the summary using words from the list below.*

Mime is a type of theater performance that uses **1**.......... and expressions to tell a story or show a character. There are two types of mime. The first is **2**.......... mime, which tells a story and is often **3**........... . It makes people laugh. The second is **4**.......... mime, which portrays feelings. Two influential actors **5**.......... during the silent film era. They were Charlie Chaplin and Buster Keaton, whose years of experience in the theater **6**.......... in miming skills that they were able to use effectively in silent films. Their techniques influenced mimes for many years. The French mime Etienne Decroux developed the form known as corporeal mime. One of his students, Marcel Marceau, became a prominent modern mime. Marceau's **7**.......... illusions include a man walking against the wind and a man trapped in a box. Now mimes often perform in groups. They have **8**.......... a variety of skills, such as dance, acrobatics, and gymnastics, as well as mime, in their performances.

abstract	gestures	merged	sharpened
conflicts	humorous	props	
culminated	illusion	reminiscent	
emerged	literal	renowned	

My Words

Write the words that are new to you. Look them up in the dictionary and write their definitions.

Words   Definitions

_____   _____

_____   _____

_____   _____

_____   _____

_____   _____

_____   _____

_____   _____

_____   _____

Word Families

adjective	considerable	It takes considerable skill to perform mime.
adverb	considerably	The mime's audiences grew considerably as word of his skill spread.

noun	effect	His skilled performance was the effect of years of experience.
verb	effect	He worked hard to effect change.
adjective	effective	A really effective mime perform-ance makes the audience believe in the illusion.
adverb	effectively	A skilled mime can effectively perform a variety of illusions.

noun	exaggeration	A mime uses exaggeration to create illusions.
verb	exaggerate	A mime may exaggerate certain gestures.
adjective	exaggerated	The exaggerated gestures of a mime are used for humorous effect.

Unit 4

noun	frailty	Mimes can make us laugh at our own frailty.
noun	frailness	The mime portrayed the frailness of old age.
adjective	frail	Humans are frail, and mimes can make us laugh at this.
adverb	frailly	The mime moved frailly around the stage as if he were 100 years old.

noun	portrayal	Charlie Chaplin is renowned for his portrayal of the little tramp character.
noun	portrayer	Mimes are often portrayers of human frailty.
verb	portray	Mimes portray common situations in humorous ways.
adjective	portrayable	Almost any everyday situation is portrayable through mime.

noun	reminiscence	Reminiscences of the early days of film would include stories of stars such as Charlie Chaplin and Buster Keaton.
verb	reminisce	People like to reminisce about the great performers of the past.
adjective	reminiscent	Marcel Marceau's clown character was reminiscent of characters performed by earlier mimes.

Word Family Practice

Choose the correct word family member from the list below to complete each blank.

Everyone enjoys watching mimes perform. A really good mime makes the job look easy, but in reality it is impossible to **1**.......... the skill required to perform mime **2**.......... . It takes a **3**.......... amount of time to develop techniques and learn to perform them well. Mimes need to be able to **4**.......... characters who will interest their audience, as well as perform a variety of illusions. The best mimes can show us our **5**.......... while making us laugh at ourselves at the same time. Although mime has changed over the years, people still **6**.......... about some of the popular mimes of the past, who have inspired today's performers.

1. exaggeration exaggerate exaggerated

2. effect   effective   effectively

3. considerable considerably

4. portrayal   portrayer   portray

5. frailties   frail

6. reminiscence reminisce   reminiscent

Unit 4

Dictionary Skill

Different Meanings
Many words have more than one meaning.

Read the definitions below. Then read the sentences and write the letter of the correct definition for each sentence.

QUESTIONS 1–2

at-mos-phere [AT-mu-sfeer]
A *noun.* the feeling of a place
B *noun.* the air, or mixture of gases, surrounding Earth and other planets

---

_____ 1. The *atmosphere* helps hold warmth from the sun.

_____ 2. The bright lighting in the theater created a happy *atmosphere.*

QUESTIONS 3–4

ef-fect [i-FEKT]
A *noun.* result
B *noun.* special sound or lighting in a theater or movie

_____ 3. The *effect* of watching Charlie Chaplin's little tramp character is a mixture of sadness and laughter.

_____ 4. Modern mime performances often include special *effects* as part of the illusions they create.

Listening

CD 1
Track
13

Listen to the talk. Complete the notes below.
*Write **NO MORE THAN ONE WORD** for each answer.*

Mime

Performed without **1** ....

2 .... of everyday activities
  • climbing stairs
  • opening a window

Use **3** .... to show presence of objects

Act out stories
  • **4** .... different characters
  • Show the characters in **5** ....

Unit 4

Writing

The chart[1] below shows information about ticket sales for performances at the National Theater over a six-month period.

Summarize[2] the information by selecting and reporting the main information and making comparisons.

> Write at least 150 words.

National Theater
Ticket Sales: January–June

Performers	Performance title	Number of tickets sold
National Mime Troupe	"Humorous Situations"	5,000
City Opera	Carmen	2,500
National Symphony Orchestra	"Works of Beethoven"	3,000
City Ballet	Swan Lake	4,750
Rock Stars Rock Band	"Rock Stars Live!"	4,750

Speaking

> Talk about the following topics:

When you see a live performance, do you prefer humorous types of performances or more serious types? Why?

Who are some of the more renowned performers in your country?

Do you enjoy movies that portray real people and events, or do you prefer movies with made-up stories?

[1]BrE: table
[2]BrE: summarise

Unit 5: Health

NURSE MIGRATION

Words

> *Look for the following words as you read the passage. Match each word with its correct definition.*

Words
1. abroad
2. administer
3. bulk
4. complex
5. cripple
6. decade
7. decline
8. epidemic
9. estimate
10. lure
11. primary
12. qualified
13. rampant
14. retain
15. rudimentary
16. shortage
17. standpoint
18. stem
19. supply
20. vacancy

Definitions
A. v., to keep
B. adj., not simple
C. v., to gradually go lower, become smaller
D. adj., main, most important
E. v., to attract
F. n., a position or job that needs to be filled
G. n., point of view
H. n., the total amount available
I. n., period of ten years
J. v., to guess based on information
K. v., to give medicine or medical treatment
L. v., to cause serious damage; weaken
M. adj., skilled, able to do a job
N. adv., in a foreign country
O. v., to come from, originate
P. n., the largest part
Q. adj., spreading out of control
R. adj., basic, not well developed
S. n., rapid spread of a disease
T. n., a lack of something

Reading

Nurse Migration

There are more nurses today than at any time in history, yet a global nursing shortage threatens to cripple health care systems worldwide. Because the underlying causes are complex and vary in different regions, a simple, short-term fix will not remedy the situation.

In developing nations—particularly in sub-Saharan Africa, South Asia, and Latin America—a major reason for the shortage is nurse migration to developed countries in Europe and North America as well as Australia to help fill vacancies there.

Nurse migration is hardly a recent phenomenon. The Philippines have for years trained many more nurses than the country needs, with thousands working abroad and sending money to relatives back home (nearing $1 billion annually). From that standpoint, migration of nurses from poorer to wealthier countries would appear to benefit all involved. But there is another side to the story. Today, even the Philippines feels the effects of the nursing shortage, with nurses continuing to migrate abroad while positions at home go unfilled.

Lured by the higher salaries and better quality of life available in wealthier countries, nurses from developing countries frequently leave behind already overburdened health care systems, where nurses are often the primary caregivers because doctors, too, are in short supply. Conditions then deteriorate further as the nurse-to-population ratio declines, a number that is estimated to be ten times higher in European than in African countries. Some Latin American countries are experiencing such a shortage of nurses that doctors actually outnumber them, leaving the bulk of health care up to assistant nurses, who have only rudimentary training.

Routine immunizations and prenatal care fall victim to the nursing shortage in developing countries, and in many cases the results can be life threatening. In African countries where the HIV/AIDS epidemic is rampant, some patients go untreated not because lifesaving drugs are unavailable but because there are not enough nurses to administer them.

In developed countries in Europe and North America, the nursing shortage largely stems from an aging population, who require more health care services, coupled with a dwindling supply of nurses, many of whom are likewise nearing retirement age, with fewer young people preparing to replace them.

A common thread among nurse-importing countries—underinvestment in nursing education dating back two or more decades—has prevented them from creating a stable workforce to meet current and future needs. The United Kingdom, for example, still feels the effects of a cut-back in nurse training some twenty years ago. In the United States, nursing schools turn down thousands of qualified applicants every year because of their own shortages of nursing faculty. Developed countries need to invest in nursing education and focus on retaining and reward-ing nurses appropriately, both financially and through high-quality working conditions.

Widespread nurse migration helps neither the host country nor the country of origin in the long run, does nothing to remedy the underlying cause of the shortage, and results in millions of people being deprived of the health care they need.

Answer the questions about **Nurse Migration**.

Questions 1–6

> *Complete the summary using the list of words below.*

The **1**........... of nurses in developing nations is largely caused by nurses leaving their countries to work **2**............ . It is difficult for poorer nations to retain their nurses because better salaries and living condi-tions **3**........... many nurses to work in wealthier countries. When nurses migrate to other countries, there are fewer **4**........... health care givers left in their own countries. The lack of trained doctors as well as nurses means that health care is often **5**........... by workers who have only **6**........... skills.

abroad	complex	qualified
administered	cripple	rudimentary
bulk	lure	shortage

Questions 7–9

> *Do the following statements agree with the information in the reading passage?*
> *Write*
>
> **TRUE**   *if the statement agrees with the information.*
> **FALSE**   *if the statement contradicts the information.*
> **NOT GIVEN**   *if there is no information on this in the passage.*

_____ 7. A primary reason for the nursing shortage in developed countries is the health care needs of the aging population.

_____ 8. There is not a large enough supply of qualified applicants for nursing schools in the United States.

_____ 9. In the United Kingdom, a high percentage of nurses have retired during the past two decades.

My Words

> *Write the words that are new to you. Look them up in the dictionary and write their definitions.*

Words   Definitions

_____   _____

_____   _____

_____   _____

_____   _____

_____   _____

_____   _____

_____   _____

_____   _____

Word Families

noun	complexity	The complexity of the nursing shortage problem makes it difficult to solve.
adjective	complex	The reasons for the worldwide nursing shortage are complex.
adverb	complexly	Some modern health care delivery systems have been complexly developed.

noun	qualification	A nurse who has the right qualifications will have no trouble finding a job.
verb	qualify	At nursing school, a student learns the skills to qualify for a career in nursing.
adjective	qualified	Qualified nurses are needed everywhere.

noun	rampancy	The epidemic spread with a rampancy that was frightening.
adjective	rampant	The rampant spread of the epidemic made it difficult to control.
adverb	rampantly	The disease spread rampantly throughout the region.

Unit 5

noun	shortage	The nursing shortage is affecting countries around the world.
verb	shorten	Lack of proper medical care can shorten a patient's life.
adjective	short	Both nurses and doctors are in short supply in many places.
adverb	shortly	The nurse said, "The doctor will be with you shortly."

noun	vacancy	When a nurse leaves a job, it is not always easy to fill the vacancy.
verb	vacate	Many nurses vacate their jobs in their native countries in favor of better positions elsewhere.
adjective	vacant	A vacant position at a hospital will be filled quickly if the salary and benefits are attractive.
adverb	vacantly	The patient stared vacantly as the nurse tended to him.

Word Family Practice

Choose the correct word family member from the list below to complete each blank.

Nurses are in **1**.......... supply in many parts of the world. There are many reasons for this lack of nurses; the issue is filled with **2**.......... . A solution needs to be found soon, because the problem has become **3**.......... . When nurses **4**.......... their positions at hospitals and health care centers, it is not easy to find other nurses to replace them. The ability to administer health care where it is needed is crippled when there are not enough **5**.......... nurses.

1. shortage	shorten	short
2. complexities	complex	complexly
3. rampancy	rampant	rampantly
4. vacancies	vacate	vacant
5. qualifications	qualifies	qualified

Unit 5

Word Skill

Compound Words
When two or more words join to form a new word, that word is called a compound word. Sometimes, the meaning of the compound word is related to the meanings of the two separate words.

> standpoint = stand + point
> Meaning: the place where you stand, the position from
>   which you see and understand things.

Read the sentences. Write a definition for each underlined word.

---

1. Work at the health care center came to a <u>standstill</u> because there was not enough money to pay the staff.

    standstill: _____

2. The new nurse has been a real <u>standout</u> with excellent reviews from doctors and patients alike.

    standout: _____

Listening

 Listen to the talk. Complete the sentences below.
*Write **ONE NUMBER ONLY** for each answer.*

1. In the United States, the bulk of nursing school programs take .... years.

2. In the United Kingdom, ... percent of nurses have degrees.

3. There has been a decline of .... percent or more of people applying to nursing schools in the United States.

4. By 2015, there may be as many as .... vacancies for nurses in the United States.

Writing

The chart[1] below shows information about wages for health care professionals in four different countries.

Summarize[2] the information by selecting and reporting the main information and making comparisons.

Write at least 150 words.

Average Monthly Salaries
for Qualified Health Care Professionals

	Nurses	Doctors
Country A *	$35	$64
Country B *	$350	$700
Country C **	$2,900	$5,500
Country D **	$3,420	$10,200

*Source countries: supply health care professionals to other countries
**Destination countries: receive health care professionals from abroad

Speaking

Talk about the following topics:

What profession do you work in or plan to work in? What were your primary reasons for choosing this profession?

What are your professional goals for the next decade?

What kinds of opportunities does your profession offer for working abroad?

[1]BrE: table
[2]BrE: summarise

Unit 5

AEROBIC EXERCISE AND BRAIN HEALTH

Words

> Look for the following words as you read the passage. Match each
> word with its correct definition.

Words
1. aerobic
2. capacity
3. cognition
4. concentration
5. counteract
6. dementia
7. deterioration
8. diagnose
9. disorder
10. gravity
11. impaired
12. indicate
13. link
14. mood
15. previously
16. regulate
17. rodent
18. spatial
19. stave off
20. stimulate

Definitions
A. n., the use of mental processes
B. n., the situation of becoming worse
C. adj., of or relating to space
D. v., to cause a response
E. n., a feeling, a state of mind
F. v., to identify an illness
G. n., a large amount of something in the same place
H. v., to show
I. adj., relating to energetic exercise
J. n., seriousness
K. adj., damaged or weakened
L. n., a disease or illness
M. v., to work against
N. n., the group of small animals that includes mice and rats
O. v., to prevent
P. n., total amount available
Q. adv., before
R. n., connection
S. v., to control
T. n., the loss of intellectual functioning of the brain

Reading

Aerobic Exercise and Brain Health

The disease-fighting, weight-controlling benefits of physical exercise, especially aerobic exercise, have long been known. Now, researchers have discovered another advantage: Physical exercise has a powerful effect on brain health, and the benefits go beyond the release of endorphins, the chemical in the brain that improves mood. Exercise affects the brain's plasticity—that is, its ability to reorganize[1] itself—and can reduce the age-associated loss of brain tissue that decreases cognition in the elderly and in those who have disorders such as Alzheimer's disease.

Recent studies have found that exercise activates a number of factors in the brain, including a protein known as *brain-derived neurotrophic factor* (BDNF), that stimulate the growth and development of brain cells. BDNF regulates the production of synapses, the connections between neurons that are essential for transmitting signals from one nerve cell to the next, and may also be involved in producing new nerve cells. Using rodent models, researchers found increased concentrations of BDNF in the hippocampus, an area of the brain involved in learning and memory and associated with dementia, after only one week of regular exercise. A study in older humans found a correlation between aerobic fitness, the size of the hippocampus, and performance on spatial memory tests. Other human studies noted that aerobic exercise increased the volume of gray[2] matter in some parts of the brain.

Regular exercise can help stave off some effects of normal aging and delay or diminish the gravity of conditions such as Alzheimer's disease, depression, and multiple sclerosis. Even over a relatively short time, exercise can repair some of the loss in brain capacity associated with aging. The greatest effects have been found in processes such as decision-making. Aerobic exercise can also improve short-term memory in the elderly. Exercise has been found to lower the risk of Alzheimer's disease in mice by decreasing the buildup of a protein known as beta-amyloid, which forms the brain plaques that precede Alzheimer's. The mice also outperformed nonexercising mice in a memory test. In a study of multiple sclerosis patients, those who exercised regularly fared better than those who exercised less. The exercise group scored better on tests of cognitive function, and their brain scans showed less deterioration and more gray matter.

In addition to increasing brainpower, exercise can help relieve depression. Although it is well known that endorphins help relieve stress and

[1]BrE: reorganise
[2]BrE: grey

Unit 5

reduce anxiety and depression, BDNF plays a role as well. Human studies have shown that people who have received a diagnosis of major depression typically have lower concentrations of BDNF in their blood. Animal studies indicate that corticosteroids, which the body produces in response to stress, decrease the availability of BDNF in the hippocampus. Exercise can counteract this effect. Exercise also lessens depression by increasing blood flow to the brain.

The link between aerobic exercise and improved brain function in the elderly and in people with impaired cognition could lead to new ways to prevent and treat brain disorders. Meanwhile, people may have more control over their own brain health than was previously believed.

Answer the questions about **Aerobic Exercise and Brain Health**.

Questions 1–8

Complete the sentences below.
Choose **NO MORE THAN ONE WORD** from the text for each answer.

1. Exercise helps people feel good mentally because it releases endorphins, which put people in a better ....

2. BDNF improves the connections between nerve cells in the brain because it .... how those connections, or synapses, are made.

3. Studies on rodents showed that there were larger .... of BDNF in the brain after just one week of exercise.

4. Exercise may lessen the .... of Alzheimer's disease and other disorders that affect the brain.

5. As people age, they may not function as well because they lose some brain ...., but exercise can repair some of this lost ability.

6. A study with multiple sclerosis patients showed that those who exercised more had less .... of the brain.

7. Usually, smaller amounts of BDNF are found in the blood of people .... with depression.

8. Exercise may lessen the effects of stress because it can .... the effects of corticosteroids, which are produced by stress.

My Words

> *Write the words that are new to you. Look them up in the dictionary and write their definitions.*

Words   Definitions

_____   _____

_____   _____

_____   _____

_____   _____

_____   _____

_____   _____

_____   _____

Word Families

noun	diagnosis	The doctor asks the patient a series of questions to make a diagnosis.
noun	diagnostician	The doctor is an outstanding diagnostician.
verb	diagnose	It is not always easy to diagnose a disease.
adjective	diagnostic	Doctors use different diagnostic tests to identify diseases.

Unit 5

noun	gravity	Because of the gravity of her condition, the patient was kept in the hospital.
adjective	grave	The patient arrived at the hospital in grave condition.
adverb	gravely	The patient was gravely ill.

noun	indication	Forgetfulness may be an indication of Alzheimer's disease, or it may just be a normal part of aging.
noun	indicator	There are several key indicators that doctors look for in their diagnoses.
verb	indicate	Studies indicate that exercise helps increase brainpower.
adjective	indicative	Memory loss may be indicative of a more serious condition.

noun	impairment	Multiple sclerosis patients suffer many physical impairments.
verb	impair	Aging can impair short-term memory.
adjective	impaired	Impaired memory can be improved by regular exercise.

noun	mood	People are often in a good mood after exercising.
noun	moodiness	A person who suffers from moodiness may be helped by regular exercise.
adjective	moody	If you are feeling moody, get some exercise.
adverb	moodily	The patient replied moodily when asked if he was feeling much pain.

Word Family Practice

Choose the correct word family member from the list below to complete each blank.

If you are suffering from a bad **1**.......... that won't go away, it is important to see a doctor. Mild depression may be a temporary response to the normal stresses of life, but ongoing depression could **2**.......... a more serious condition. The doctor will ask you a series of questions and may recommend some tests to come up with a **3**.......... . If your condition is **4**.........., the doctor may give you medication. If, on the other hand, you are not suffering any serious disorder or **5**.........., the doctor may recommend something as simple as regular exercise.

1. mood	moodiness	moody
2. indication	indicate	indicative
3. diagnosis	diagnose	diagnostic
4. gravity	grave	gravely
5. impairment	impair	impaired

Dictionary Skill

Different Meanings
Many words have more than one meaning.

Read the definitions below. Then read the sentences and write the letter of the correct definition for each sentence.

QUESTIONS 1–2

      gra-vi-ty [GRA-vuh-tee]
      A *noun.* seriousness
      B *noun.* the force that holds objects on the Earth

_____ 1. *Gravity* makes it easier to walk downhill than uphill.

_____ 2. Because of the *gravity* of his injury, the doctor told him not to exercise for several months.

QUESTIONS 3–4

      dis-or-der [dis-OR-der]
      A *noun.* a disease or illness
      B *noun.* confusion; lack of order

_____ 3. The doctor's office was in such *disorder* that she couldn't find the test results.

_____ 4. Depression is a serious *disorder,* but there are ways to treat it.

Listening

Listen to the conversation. Complete the form below.
*Write **NO MORE THAN ONE WORD** for each answer.*

Hospital Fitness Center[1]

New Patient Information

Patient Name: *Amanda* **1**..........

Interests: **2** .... *exercise classes*

Level: *beginner, but previously took* **3**.......... *classes*

Referral? *Yes, recommended by doctor in order to*

improve **4**.......... *and stave off* **5** .... *gain.*

[1]BrE: Centre

Writing

The charts[1] below show changes in mental capacity in patients who have been given a diagnosis of mild cognitive impairment, a condition that can develop into Alzheimer's disease or other types of dementia.

Summarize[2] the information by selecting and reporting the main information and making comparisons.

Write at least 150 words.

Group A (followed a program of 1 hour of aerobic exercise daily for 6 months)

Memory	Thinking Speed	Word Fluency
=	+	+

Group B (followed a program of 1 hour of nonaerobic [stretching and balancing] exercise daily for 6 months)

Memory	Thinking Speed	Word Fluency
−	−	−

Key:
− .... deteriorated
= .... no change
+ .... improved

[1]BrE: tables
[2]BrE: Summarise

Speaking

Talk about the following topics.

Do you find that exercise improves your mood? What other things do you do to feel better when you are in a bad mood?

Now that researchers have found links between exercise and improved brain capacity, do you think exercising will become more popular? Why or why not?

Because exercising has so many health benefits, do you think more should be done to stimulate people to exercise more?

Unit 5

HOW DRUGS ARE STUDIED

Words

Look for the following words as you read the passage. Match each word with its correct definition.

Words
1. absorb
2. alleviate
3. ascertain
4. chronic
5. combat
6. culture
7. deem
8. desirable
9. enhance
10. fraction
11. interval
12. investigation
13. manufacture
14. monitor
15. outcome
16. recur
17. substance
18. target
19. theoretical
20. toxic

Definitions
A. v., to improve
B. n., a small part
C. v., to produce
D. v., to lessen, ease
E. v., to take in
F. n., result
G. adj., poisonous
H. v., to believe; judge
I. v., to watch; observe
J. v., to focus on
K. v., to happen or occur again
L. adj., long-lasting
M. n., a study
N. adj., abstract; based on theory
O. v., to determine; find out
P. n., the growing of organic materials in a laboratory setting
Q. n., the period between two times or events
R. n., material
S. v., to fight against
T. adj., wanted; worth having

Reading

How Drugs Are Studied

A

It takes years, and sometimes decades, for a drug to move from the theoretical stage to the pharmacy shelf. Of the thousands of drugs under investigation at any one time, only a small fraction will produce the desired result without unacceptable side effects.

B

First, scientists target a step in the disease process where they believe a drug can have an effect. Then they manufacture compounds or take them from organisms such as viruses and fungi and test them in laboratory cultures. Once scientists isolate a chemical that produces a desirable effect, they analyze[1] its structure and alter it as necessary to enhance the outcome.

C

The next step involves testing the drug in animals. Scientists look at how much drug is absorbed into the bloodstream, how it distributes to different organs, how quickly it is excreted or leaves the body, and whether it has any toxic effects or by-products. Researchers usually test at least two animal species because the same drug may affect species differently.

D

If a chemical passes laboratory and animal testing and is deemed appropriate to analyze in human volunteers, it is ready for clinical trials. Researchers follow a protocol that describes who may participate in the study, tests and procedures to follow, the length of the study, and outcomes to be measured. Drug trials may focus on treating a disease, preventing a disease from occurring or recurring, or enhancing the quality of life for people living with incurable, chronic conditions.

E

There are four phases of clinical trials; the first three phases study whether the drug is effective and can be safely administered to patients, and the fourth phase evaluates long-term safety and use once a drug is on the market.

F

Phase I clinical trials test a drug in small groups of healthy volunteers (fewer than 100) to ascertain its safety and the appropriate dose range. These studies last for six months to one year.

[1]BrE: analyse

Unit 5

G

Phase II clinical trials test several hundred volunteers to determine how effectively the drug combats the disease being studied. These trials continue to evaluate safety, side effects, and optimal dose. Phase II studies also last for six months to one year.

H

Phase III trials test thousands of volunteers for several years, with researchers closely monitoring study participants at regular intervals. These studies typically compare the drug under investigation with a control: either a drug known to cure or alleviate a specific disease or, if one does not exist, a substance that has no medicinal effects, known as a placebo. Phase III trials are typically blind studies (participants do not know which drug they are receiving) or double-blind studies (neither participants nor researchers know which drug an individual is receiving until the trial is completed).

I

Once a drug passes the first three phases and is found to be safe and effective, drug companies may apply for the right to market the product. After a drug is approved and on the market, Phase IV trials may investigate longer-term effects, effects in different groups of patients such as the elderly, or use of the medication for a different condition such as using a cancer drug to treat AIDS.

Answer the questions about **How Drugs Are Studied**.

Questions 1–4

---

*The reading passage contains nine paragraphs, **A–I**.*
Which paragraph discusses the following information?
*Write the correct letter, **A–I**.*

_____ 1. Drug tests that involve growing biological material in a laboratory

_____ 2. Investigations of the effects of drugs on animals

_____ 3. Studies to determine how safe a drug is and how much a patient should take

_____ 4. Studies to monitor how well a drug fights a disease

Questions 5–7

*Choose the correct letter, **A**, **B**, **C**, or **D**.*

5. Drug tests on animals look at
   A how the drug is absorbed by the body.
   B how effective the drug is for chronic conditions.
   C how well the drug prevents a disease from recurring.
   D how quickly the drug alleviates the disease.

6. During Phase II clinical trials, study participants are monitored for
   A chronic conditions.
   B toxic doses.
   C speed of cure.
   D possible side effects.

7. After a drug is deemed safe and effective, a drug company may do further tests to ascertain
   A the best way to market it.
   B possible effects over time.
   C how it compares with other drugs.
   D the best group of people to use it.

My Words

Write the words that are new to you. Look them up in the dictionary and write their definitions.

Words   Definitions

_____   _____

_____   _____

_____   _____

_____   _____

_____   _____

_____   _____

_____   _____

_____   _____

Unit 5

Word Families

noun	absorption	As part of their research, scientists look at the absorption of a drug into the bloodstream.
verb	absorb	The body absorbs some drugs very quickly.
adjective	absorbent	Cotton makes a good cleaning material because it is so absorbent.

noun	desire	The desire to help others attracts many people to medical professions.
verb	desire	Patients desire drugs that will treat their conditions effectively.
adjective	desirable	The most desirable type of drug is one that is effective and has no side effects.
adverb	desirably	The drug in the investigation had desirably few side effects.

noun	investigation	The investigation of a potential new drug costs a great deal of money and takes a long time.
noun	investigator	The investigator submitted a report about the crime.
verb	investigate	Researchers may investigate several possible uses of a new drug.
adjective	investigative	An investigative report showed the drug to be ineffective in fighting the disease.

noun	theory	The scientists set up the study to test the theory.
verb	theorize	Scientists theorize that a substance will have a certain medical effect, and then they set up a research study.
adjective	theoretical	Ideas are theoretical before they are tested.
adverb	theoretically	It was a good idea theoretically, so they decided to test it.

noun	toxin	Some substances can release toxins into the blood.
noun	toxicity	Potential drug toxicity is a part of every study.
adjective	toxic	Part of drug research involves testing for toxic effects.
adverb	toxically	If one drug reacts toxically with another, you cannot take them together.

Unit 5

Word Family Practice

> *Choose the correct word family member from the list below to complete each blank.*

A good deal of time, effort, and money is required to thoroughly **1**..........
a new drug before it can be put on the market. Scientists develop a
2.......... about the ability of a certain substance to combat a specific
disease or medical condition. Then they have to test their idea. After
manufacturing the drug in the laboratory, they test it first on animals
and then on people. They monitor the **3**.......... of the drug by the body,
and they look for any **4**.......... that may be produced as the drug moves
through the body. Then they test the drug's ability to combat the
disease. If they get the outcome that they **5**.......... and the drug cures
the disease or alleviates the condition, then it's time to work on marketing the product.

1. investigation   investigator   investigate

2. theory   theorize   theoretical

3. absorption   absorb   absorbent

4. toxins   toxic   toxically

5. desires   desire   desirably

Dictionary Skill

Different Meanings
Many words have more than one meaning.

> *Read the definitions below. Then read the sentences and write the letter of the correct definition for each sentence.*
>
> cul-ture [KUL-cher]
> **A** *noun.* the growing of organic materials in a laboratory setting
> **B** *noun.* a shared system of beliefs, customs, and language
> **C** *noun.* the arts

_____ 1. It is always interesting to learn about the *culture* of another country.

_____ 2. A clinic might use a *culture* from the patient to diagnose a disease.

_____ 3. Because of their museums, theaters, and libraries, cities have a lot more to offer in terms of *culture* than small towns do.

Listening

CD 1 Track 16

> *Listen to the conversation. Complete the notes below.*
> *Write **NO MORE THAN ONE WORD** for each answer.*

Laboratory Research Project

> Steps to follow:
>
> • Grow **1** .... in the laboratory.
>
> • Introduce different substances.
>
> • **2**............ at regular intervals.
>
> • **3**............. if there are changes.
>
> • Describe the **4**............ in the final report.

Unit 5

Writing

Modern medical science has made it possible to combat many diseases. This is one reason that people are living longer lives now than they did in the past. Discuss the effects this might have on society.

Support your answer with reasons and examples from your own knowledge or experience.

> *Write at least 250 words.*

Speaking

> *Talk about the following topics.*

A lot of money is spent on investigating drugs. Do you think it is desirable to spend so much money on developing new drugs, or should more money be spent on other areas of health care?

What do you think are some of the most important health issues to target?

What do you think is the best way to combat common but potentially dangerous diseases such as influenza?

Unit 6: Tourism

HIKING THE INCA TRAIL

Words

Look for the following words as you read the passage. Match each word with its correct definition.

Words

1. accessible
2. adventurous
3. archeologist[1]
4. ceremonial
5. construct
6. draw
7. imagination
8. institute
9. luxury
10. marvel
11. mystery
12. native
13. network
14. pertain
15. precisely
16. preserve
17. restriction
18. site
19. spectacular
20. upside

Definitions

A. n., a wonderful thing

B. n., something expensive and desirable but unnecessary

C. v., to attract, pull

D. adj., reachable, easy to get

E. adj. related to traditional or formal practices

F. n., advantage, good part

G. n., official limit on something

H. v., to build

I. v., to start, put in place

J. n., place

K. adj. original to a place

L. adj., daring, willing to try new or dangerous activities

M. adv., exactly

N. v., to protect, save

O. n., the ability to think creatively, form pictures in the mind

P. v., to be related to something

Q. n., a system of various parts that work together

R. adj., wonderful to see

S. n., a person who studies ancient cultures

T. n., something strange, unknown, or difficult to understand

[1]BrE: archaeologist

Reading

Hiking the Inca Trail

Sitting high in the Andes Mountains in Peru, the ancient ruins of Machu Picchu have captured the imaginations of travelers[1] ever since they were rediscovered by archeologist Hiram Bingham in 1911. The name Machu Picchu means "old peak" in the native Incan language, and the site had probably been considered a sacred place since long before the ancient Incas arrived there. The Incas built a ceremonial city on the site that included palaces, temples, storage rooms, baths, and houses, all constructed from heavy blocks of granite fitted precisely together. Although little is known about the activities that took place in the ancient city, it appears that one of its functions was as an astronomical observatory. The so-called Intihuatana stone, located at the site, was used to mark the autumn and spring equinoxes as well as other astronomical events.

The spectacular natural setting, the wonders of architectural and engineering skills embodied in the well-preserved buildings, and the mysteries of the ancient culture draw thousands of tourists from around the world every year. The nearest city is Cuzco, about thirty miles away. From there, tourists can take trains and buses to the ruins. A popular route for the more adventurous is to hike along the Inca Trail. The ancient Inca created a network of trails throughout the mountains, some of which are still in existence. The Inca Trail to Machu Picchu, used by hikers today, was likely considered a sacred route in its time, used by travelers making pilgrimages to that ceremonial site.

Although the Inca Trail leads to the wonders of Machu Picchu, it offers many marvels of its own. Hikers are treated to magnificent views of glacier-covered peaks above and tropical valleys below in their journey over high mountain passes. Many species of orchids can be seen, as well as all kinds of birds, from tiny hummingbirds to the splendid Andean condor. The Inca Trail also passes by ruins of other ceremonial sites on the way to the grand destination of Machu Picchu.

Tourists have been hiking the Inca Trail since the early part of the twentieth century, and for much of that time there were no regulations. Hikers could travel when they pleased and camp wherever they chose. However, the trip has become so popular that in 2005, the Peruvian government instituted a set of restrictions on the use of the trail. To protect the natural environment and preserve the ruins, no more than 500 people a day are allowed to enter the trail. Because each group that sets out includes guides and porters, the number of tourists entering the trail

---

[1]BrE: travellers

each day is probably closer to 200. In addition, both tour companies and individual guides must be licensed. There are also legal requirements that pertain to the minimum wage that porters must be paid as well as the maximum weight load they can be required to carry. Fees for trail use help pay for upkeep of the trail and the ruins. All these regulations and fees combine for a more expensive trip, and this has made it a luxury accessible to fewer people. The upside is that the environment and the workers are protected.

Answer the questions about **Hiking the Inca Trail**.

Questions 1–9

> Complete the summary below.
> Choose **NO MORE THAN ONE WORD** from the text for each answer.

Machu Picchu is an ancient **1**.......... city in the Andes Mountains of Peru. It was rediscovered by an **2**.......... in 1911. It is not precisely clear how the ancient Inca used the site, but experts believe that at least some of its **3**.......... pertained to astronomy. The wonders of Machu Picchu **4**.......... visitors from all around the world. Many visitors like to reach the site by hiking the Inca Trail, part of a **5**.......... of trails originally made by the ancient Inca. This is a trip for **6**.......... people. Along the way, hikers can enjoy many **7**.......... such as spectacular views and interesting flowers and birds. Because such large numbers of people use the Inca Trail, the Peruvian government has had to take steps to **8**.......... the ruins and the environment. It has instituted a number of restrictions as well as fees. Because of this, hiking the trail has become an expensive **9**.......... that many people cannot afford.

My Words

Write the words that are new to you. Look them up in the dictionary and write their definitions.

Words   Definitions

Word Families

noun	access	The Inca Trail provides one way to gain access to Machu Picchu.
noun	accessibility	The train from Cuzco increases accessibility to Machu Picchu.
verb	access	Fewer people can access the site because the trip has become so expensive.
adjective	accessible	Machu Picchu is accessible by plane, train, or hiking.
adjective	inaccessible	Machu Picchu is inaccessible except by plane, train, or hiking.

noun	adventure	Our trip to Machu Picchu was a great adventure.
noun	adventurer	We felt like modern-day adventurers.
verb	adventure	We adventured into places where few people visit.
adjective	adventurous	Adventurous people enjoy hiking in the Andes Mountains.
adverb	adventurously	We hiked adventurously over tall peaks and steep cliffs.

noun	archeologist	An archeologist is interested in ancient cultures.
noun	archeology	The field of archeology has taught us a great deal about the ancient world.
adjective	archeological	Machu Picchu is one of the most visited archeological sites in the world.

noun	luxury	Hiring porters to carry your equipment on a hiking trip is quite a luxury.
verb	luxuriate	After returning from a week of hiking in the mountains, we luxuriated in the comfort of our beds.
adjective	luxurious	A simple bed felt luxurious after a weeklong hiking trip.
adverb	luxuriously	We dined luxuriously on champagne and chocolate.

noun	restriction	Restrictions are necessary to preserve the environment.
verb	restrict	The government restricts large numbers of people from entering the area.
adjective	restrictive	The rules may seem restrictive, but they are meant to protect the area.

noun	precision	The blocks were fitted together with great precision.
adjective	precise	Archeologists have many theories but few precise ideas about the ceremonial functions of Machu Picchu.
adverb	precisely	We arrived at the site at precisely five o'clock.

Word Family Practice

> *Choose the correct word family member from the list below to complete each blank.*

Hiking the Inca trail is a popular way to **1**.......... Machu Picchu. However, the Peruvian government has **2**.......... use of the trail, so not everyone is able to make the trip. The upside is that hiking is not the only way to get there, and because it is not a particularly **3**.......... way to travel, other methods might be preferable. You can get to the **4**.......... site by train and bus, and they will get you there much faster than hiking. When you arrive in Cuzco, you can check the schedules. You may not be able to leave at **5**.......... the time you wish, but you should be able to work out a schedule that is convenient. Whatever method you choose to get there, a trip to Machu Picchu is always a great **6**........... .

1. access   accesses   accessible

2. restrictions   restricted   restrictive

3. luxury   luxurious   luxuriously

4. archeology   archeologist   archeological

5. precision   precise   precisely

6. adventure   adventured   adventurous

Dictionary Skill

Different Meanings
Many words have more than one meaning.

Read the definitions below. Then read the sentences and write the letter of the correct definition for each sentence.

QUESTIONS 1–2

in-sti-tute [IN-sti-toot]
A *verb.* to start, put in place
B *noun.* a type of organization

_____ 1. The government founded an *institute* of archeology to promote the study of ancient cultures.

_____ 2. The school plans to *institute* a summer program for students who are interested in archeology.

QUESTIONS 3–4

draw [DRAW]
A *verb.* to attract, pull
B *verb.* to make a picture using pencils or crayons

_____ 3. People like to *draw* the beautiful mountain scenery around Machu Picchu.

_____ 4. The interesting birds and flowers *draw* many people to the mountains around Machu Picchu.

Listening

Listen to the talk.
Complete the information about the archeological site.
*Write **NO MORE THAN ONE WORD** for each answer.*

Unit 6

Information for Visitors

Restrictions:
Stay on the **1**.......... of paths.
2.......... the buildings between 10:00 A.M. and 4:00 P.M. only.
Enter the **3**.......... area only with a guide.

Entry Fees:
Adults: $15
Children: $10

4.......... crafts are available for sale in the gift shop.

Writing

Large numbers of visitors endanger sensitive archeological sites such as Machu Picchu. In your opinion, is it more important to try to preserve such sites or to allow public access to them?

Support your opinion with reasons and examples from your own knowledge or experience.

Write at least 250 words.

Speaking

Talk about the following topics.

What kinds of adventures are attractive to you?

What kinds of luxuries do you enjoy?

Is it important to you to have luxuries?

WHAT IS ECOTOURISM?

Words

> Look for the following words as you read the passage. Match each word with its correct definition.

Words
1. accommodations[1]
2. avoid
3. barrier
4. category
5. concept
6. culprit
7. delicate
8. destination
9. dump
10. injure
11. pleasure
12. practice[2]
13. principle
14. publicity
15. recycling
16. remote
17. strive
18. volunteer
19. wary
20. wilderness

Definitions
A. v., to work for no pay; freely offer to do something
B. v., to get rid of garbage and trash[3]
C. adj., not completely trusting
D. n., guilty party, origin of a problem
E. adj., easily hurt or broken
F. n., natural region away from towns and cities
G. n., the place somebody or something is going to
H. v., to hurt
I. n., enjoyment
J. v., to work very hard to do something
K. n., rule, basic idea behind a system
L. n., a place to stay such as a hotel
M. n., something that blocks or separates
N. n., activity that makes something known to the public
O. n., idea
P. n., collection and treatment of trash for reuse
Q. v., to prevent from happening; stay away from
R. adj., far away
S. n., a custom, method
T. n., a group of things that have something in common

[1]BrE: accomodation
[2]BrE: practice n., practise v.
[3]BrE: rubbish

Reading

What Is Ecotourism?

The concept of ecotourism has been gaining publicity over the past couple of decades. It arose out of the "green movement"—a growing interest in developing practices in all aspects of daily life that preserve rather than injure the natural environment. Ecotourists strive to have minimal impact on the places they visit, in terms of both the local ecology and the local culture. Some followers take the concept even further and define ecotourism as travel that aims not only to avoid harming the environment, but also to make a positive contribution to the local ecology and culture.

The types of vacations[1] that fit into the category of ecotourism vary widely. Ecotourism might involve travel to a natural destination such as a national park or a nature preserve to learn about the natural environment and, in some cases, to volunteer on environmental protection projects. It could be a few weeks spent with local artisans learning how to do a traditional craft. Trips that involve hiking or rafting through wilderness areas with no regard for the natural habitats one passes through would not be included in the definition of ecotourism. Neither, of course, would be trips with a focus on hunting.

Ecotourists seek out accommodations that follow environmentally friendly practices such as using renewable resources and recycling. Ecotourists look for hotels and tour companies that hire mainly local staff, keeping tourist dollars within the local economy. Ecotourists might choose to join a bicycling or walking tour rather than a bus tour that adds to air pollution and allows tourists to see the local area only through a barrier of glass windows.

Ecotourists often shun cruise ships, because these are among the biggest culprits in the tourism industry in terms of environmental pollution. Massive cruise ships release large quantities of harmful emissions into the air as well as pollute the waters they sail through with fuel from their engines. The huge numbers of passengers on these ships generate many tons of garbage and wastewater, which is often dumped into the sea. Cruise ships also cause damage to coral reefs and other delicate ecosystems that they travel near. Perhaps in part because of the growing interest in ecotourism, some cruise companies are now making an effort to be more environmentally friendly. These efforts include recycling wastes and using fuel more efficiently. Vacationers who are interested in ecotourism and still get pleasure from cruises can travel with cruise companies that follow these practices.

[1]BrE: holidays

Because of the growing interest in ecotourism, many companies advertise themselves as ecotourism companies, especially those that offer trips to remote, natural areas, the type of destination that eco-tourists favor[2]. Travelers need to be wary and do their research carefully. Not all of these companies follow the principles of ecotourism. Some are simply trying to take advantage of the current interest in this type of travel. The positive side of this, however, is that it may actually be an indication that the movement is gaining in popularity.

Answer the questions about **What Is Ecotourism?**

Questions 1–7

Do the following statements agree with the information in the reading passage?
Write

          TRUE   if the statement agrees with the information.
        FALSE   if the statement contradicts the information.
NOT GIVEN   if there is no information on this in the passage.

_____ 1. Ecotourism refers only to trips made to remote wilderness destinations.

_____ 2. Ecotourists are interested in preserving delicate natural areas.

_____ 3. Ecotourists prefer less expensive accommodations.

_____ 4. Ecotourists strive to support the local economy where they travel.

_____ 5. Many large cruise ships injure the environment by dumping garbage into the sea.

_____ 6. Hunting trips can be included in the category of ecotourism.

_____ 7. An ecotourism trip might include volunteering to work on local projects.

_____ 8. Some cruise companies are changing their practices to become more environmentally friendly.

_____ 9. Cruise ships do not recycle paper and plastic because it is too expensive.

[2]BrE: favour

My Words

Write the words that are new to you. Look them up in the dictionary and write their definitions.

Words   Definitions

_____   _____

_____   _____

_____   _____

_____   _____

_____   _____

_____   _____

_____   _____

_____   _____

Unit 6

Word Families

noun	accommodations	The accommodations on our trip were very comfortable.
verb	accommodate	It's a small hotel that can accommodate only about fifty guests.
adjective	accommodating	We found our hosts very accommodating.

noun	avoidance	Avoidance of environmental damage is an important part of ecotourism.
verb	avoid	We can avoid damaging the environment if we are careful to follow certain practices.
adjective	avoidable	Following certain practices makes damage to the environment avoidable.

noun	concept	Ecotourism is a concept that is growing in popularity.
verb	conceive	It is not hard to conceive of ways to protect the environment.
adjective	conceptual	Ecotourism has gone beyond the conceptual stage to become something that many people have put into practice.
adverb	conceptually	Ecotourism differs conceptually from regular tourism.

noun	injury	Large cruise ships cause several types of injury to the environment.
verb	injure	Ecotourists try not to injure the environment.
adjective	injurious	Some practices, such as anchoring large cruise ships close to coral reefs, are injurious to the environment.

noun	publicity	The more publicity ecotourism gets, the more people will become interested in this type of travel.
verb	publicize[1]	Many companies publicize them-selves as ecotourism companies, but not all of them follow ecotourism principles.
adjective	public	Tour companies make their serv-ices public through advertisements on the Internet and in magazines.
adverb	publicly	The need to protect the environment is being discussed publicly.

noun	wild	Many tourists enjoy photographing animals in the wild.
noun	wilderness	Many people enjoy spending time in the wilderness.
adjective	wild	Some tours are organized to destinations where wild animals can be observed.
adverb	wildly	Places such as Machu Picchu and the Galapagos Islands have become wildly popular ecotourism destinations.

[1]BrE: publicise

Word Family Practice

Choose the correct word family member from the list below to complete each blank.

Ecotourism companies operate on the principle that **1**.......... of harm to the environment is not only possible but an important part of pleasure trips. The basic **2**.......... of ecotourism is to respect the places you visit, in terms of both the culture and the natural environment. Ecotourism companies offer a wide range of tours. Some include stays in luxury hotels, whereas others take travelers to remote destinations where only the simplest **3**.......... are available. On some trips, travelers learn about the **4**.......... plants and animals that live in the area. On others, they learn about the local traditions. On all trips, travelers are careful not to cause any type of **5**.......... to the environment. Where environmental harm is concerned, they don't want to be among the culprits. If you are interested in ecotourism, it's easy to find out about trips being offered. Ecotourism companies **6**.......... their trips in travel magazines and on travel websites.

1. avoidance   avoid   avoidable

2. concept   conceive   conceptual

3. accommodations   accommodate   accommodates

4. wilderness   wildly   wild

5. injury   injure   injurious

6. publicity   publicize   public

Dictionary Skill

Parts of Speech
Volunteer can be a noun, a verb, or an adjective.

Read the dictionary definitions below. Then read the sentences and write the letter of the correct definition for each sentence.

vol-un-teer [vol-un-TEER]
A *noun.* a person who offers to do work for no pay; a person who freely offers a service
B *verb.* to work for no pay; freely offer to do something
C *adjective.* done by volunteers

_____ 1. Many environmental protection projects depend on *volunteer* work.

_____ 2. A *volunteer* not only provides a service but also has the opportunity to gain valuable experience.

_____ 3. Many people *volunteer* to spend their vacation time helping out on environmental protection projects.

Listening

CD 1 Track 18

Listen to the conversation. Complete the form below.
*Write **NO MORE THAN ONE WORD** for each answer.*

Excellent Eco Tours

Customer Name: *Bob Henderson*

Trip: **1**........ *Adventure*

Dates **2**.......... *12–25*

Type of **3**.......... : *campground*

How did customer hear about us?

Saw **4**........ *in a travel magazine*

Writing

The charts[1] below show information about environmentally friendly practices followed by three different cruise ship companies in two different years.

Summarize[2] the information by selecting and reporting the main information and making comparisons.

Write at least 250 words.

Year: 2000

	Recycles at least 75% of waste	Has system to reduce air pollution	Avoids dumping waste water into the sea	Avoids destinations with delicate underwater ecosystems
Sun Cruises	yes	no	yes	no
Sea Adventure	no	no	no	no
Water World Tours	yes	yes	yes	no

Year: 2010

	Recycles at least 75% of waste	Has system to reduce air pollution	Avoids dumping waste water into the sea	Avoids destinations with delicate underwater ecosystems
Sun Cruises	yes	yes	yes	yes
Sea Adventure	yes	no	yes	no
Water World Tours	yes	yes	yes	yes

[1]BrE: tables
[2]BrE: Summarise

Speaking

> *Talk about the following topics.*

When you travel, do you enjoy going to wilderness destinations, or do you prefer visiting cities or some other kind of place?

What kinds of places do you avoid visiting when you travel?

What kinds of accommodations do you like? Is luxury important to you when choosing accommodations?

Unit 6

LEARNING VACATIONS

Words

Look for the following words as you read the passage. Match each word with its correct definition.

Words
1. acquire
2. breeze
3. broad
4. budget
5. colorful[1]
6. content
7. costly
8. cuisine
9. economical
10. endeavor[2]
11. enroll
12. hone
13. ingredient
14. ongoing
15. residential
16. resort
17. sponsor
18. supervision
19. survey
20. taste

Definitions
A. n., a vacation place
B. n., style of cooking
C. n., direction, assistance
D. adj., interesting and unusual
E. n., preference
F. v., to learn something or get something
G. n., subject matter
H. adj., with living accommodations, related to housing
I. n., light wind
J. adj., inexpensive
K. adj., wide or large
L. n., activity with a specific purpose, effort
M. v., to sign up for a class
N. n., a study of opinions in a sample of the population
O. n., a plan for spending money
P. n., an item in a recipe
Q. adj., continuing
R. adj., expensive
S. v., to organize and be responsible for
T. v., to sharpen, improve

[1]BrE: colourful
[2]BrE: endeavour

Reading

Learning Vacations

A couple spends a week in Thailand learning to cook in the local style. A group flies to Turkey to join an ongoing archeological[1] dig for the summer. A history professor leads a tour of historical sites of Europe.

The participants in these trips are all enjoying a different kind of travel: learning vacations[2]. Rather than spending their vacations relaxing on a beach or taking a bus[3] tour of ten cities in eight days, they have opted to enjoy their time off by learning something new. From attending summer camps for adults to studying botany in the rain forest, people everywhere are experiencing the value of a vacation with a purpose. According to surveys, close to one-third of travelers[4] each year choose learning programs over other types of vacations, and their numbers are growing.

In the past, these types of vacations were generally considered to be for young people still in school. A student of French might spend the summer studying that language in Paris. A marine biology major could learn to scuba dive and spend a few months at sea assisting researchers. Now, it has become common for adults, too, to spend their vacation time in educational endeavors, and various types of travel programs[5] have grown up around this interest.

Art schools and writing programs sponsor trips to interesting parts of the world. Trip participants hone their creative skills under the supervision of professional artists and writers while at the same time enjoying, for example, the warm breezes of the Caribbean islands or the colorful villages of Spain. Cooking is a popular hobby, and tour companies have developed trips that focus on the cuisine of different regions of the world. Travelers may learn all about how traditional meals are prepared and what ingredients are used. Or, for those who want to improve their abilities in the kitchen, they may actually receive hands-on lessons, acquiring new skills that they can take home with them. Travelers to Britain can enroll in courses at any of the twenty-plus adult residential colleges around the country. The courses at these schools generally last just a few days and range in content from activities such as photography and dancing to more serious subjects such as history, philosophy, and literature.

[1]BrE: archaeological
[2]BrE: holidays
[3]Bre: coach
[4]BrE: travellers
[5]BrE: programmes

These are just a few examples of the many types of learning vacations that people enjoy every year. In addition to gaining knowledge and skills, another advantage of these types of vacations is that they can be more economical than traditional vacations. Camping out near an archeological site or sleeping in a college dormitory or youth hostel certainly costs less than staying at a luxury hotel or vacation resort. And the fact that many of these trips can be organized[6] by the travelers themselves without the services of a tour company or travel agency makes them even more economical. Of course, it all depends on the type of trip one chooses, and some companies offer learning vacations to exotic locales with expert professionals that are quite costly. With the broad range of possibilities available, there are options to suit all tastes and budgets.

Answer the questions about **Learning Vacations**.

Questions 1–3

*Which of the following types of learning vacations are mentioned in the passage? Choose **three** answers from the list below.*

A Honing cooking skills

B Working on artistic endeavors

C Enrolling in an archeology course

D Studying the Spanish language

E Taking classes at a residential college

F Acquiring knowledge about Thailand's history

[6]BrE: organised

Questions 4–7

> Do the following statements agree with the information in the reading passage?
>
> Write
>
> | | |
> |---|---|
> | **TRUE** | if the statement agrees with the information. |
> | **FALSE** | if the statement contradicts the information. |
> | **NOT GIVEN** | if there is no information on this in the passage. |

_____ 4. Most participants in learning vacations are young people.

_____ 5. Surveys show that around 30 percent of travelers take learning vacations.

_____ 6. It is common for colleges to sponsor learning vacations.

_____ 7. Learning vacations are generally less costly than resort vacations.

My Words

> Write the words that are new to you. Look them up in the dictionary and write their definitions.

Words   Definitions

_____   _____

_____   _____

_____   _____

_____   _____

_____   _____

_____   _____

_____   _____

Word Families

noun	acquisition	The acquisition of new skills is just one of the goals of learning vacations.
verb	acquire	It is fun to acquire new skills while on vacation.

noun	cost	The cost of a learning vacation can be lower than other types of vacations.
verb	cost	A learning vacation could cost less than another type of vacation.
adjective	costly	Learning vacations can be costly, but usually they are not.

noun	economy	A family that doesn't have a lot of money to spend must pay attention to economy when planning a vacation.
verb	economize[1]	People can economize by avoiding resort vacations.
adjective	economical	Taking a learning vacation can be an economical way to travel.
adverb	economically	By planning economically, you can save money and still have a great vacation.

[1]BrE: economise

noun	enrollment	If enrollment is low, they will cancel the class.
noun	enrollee	Enrollees had to pay a deposit for the class.
verb	enroll	One way to take a learning vacation is to enroll in a class.

noun	resident	The local residents are always helpful to visitors.
noun	residence	The student residence is simple but comfortable.
verb	reside	This place is convenient for a learning vacation because you can reside right at the college.
noun	residential	Residential colleges are popular places for learning vacations.

noun	supervision	You will always have the supervision of an experienced art teacher during the painting trip.
noun	supervisor	A professional artist will act as supervisor of the trip.
verb	supervise	Experienced art teachers will supervise your work.
adjective	supervisory	The professor will be in a supervisory role on the trip.

Word Family Practice

Choose the correct word family member from the list below to complete each blank.

Many people are interested in the concept of a learning vacation because it is a fun way to **1**.......... skills while traveling. Learning vacations don't necessarily **2**.......... a great deal, so they are a good option for people on a budget. If you would like to travel to colorful parts of the world, taste exotic cuisine, and learn something new at the same time, then a learning vacation might be a good choice for you. If you want to **3**.......... , you can plan your vacation on your own. **4**.......... in a short course on a topic of special interest is a common way to spend a learning vacation and an easy one to arrange. If the school that offers the course also has a **5**.......... for students, that will make your plans even easier. You don't need the **6**.......... of a professional to organize your vacation. A little research online might provide you with all the information you need.

1. acquisition   acquire   acquires

2. cost   costs   costly

3. economy   economize   economical

4. Enrollment   Enroll   Enrolled

5. residence   reside   residential

6. supervisor   supervision   supervise

Unit 6

Dictionary Skill

Changing Stress
The meanings of some words change when different syllables are stressed. These words are spelled the same but are pronounced with different stress. Most are also different parts of speech.

> *Read the definitions below. Then read the sentences and write the letter of the correct definition for each sentence.*
>
> con-tent [KON-tent]
> **A** *noun.* subject matter
>
> con-tent [kon-TENT]
> **B** *adjective.* happy

_____ 1. The *content* of the article was quite interesting—it was all about learning vacations.

_____ 2. We were *content* to spend our vacation painting and enjoying the scenery.

Listening

CD 1
Track
19

> *Listen to the conversation. Complete the chart¹ below.*
> *Write **NO MORE THAN ONE WORD** for each answer.*

	Accommodations	**3**..........	**4**.......... ends
Painting trip	Beach **1**..........	Springfield University	June 15
Cooking trip	**2**.......... college	National Cooking Institute	July 1

¹BrE: table

Writing

The chart[1] below shows information about enrollment in courses at an adult residential college.

Summarize[2] the information by selecting and reporting the main information and making comparisons.

Write at least 250 words.

Barkford Adult Residential College

Enrollment by subject area (percentage of total students enrolled) Summer 2010	
Cuisine	35%
Photography	20%
Painting and Drawing	25%
History	10%
Philosophy	5%
Science	5%

Speaking

Talk about the following topics.

What are some dishes that are typical of the cuisine of your country or region?

What are some common ingredients in your country or region's cuisine?

How has the cuisine of your country changed over the past century? How do you think it will be different in the future?

[1]BrE: table
[2]BrE: summarise

Unit 7: Business

WHAT MAKES A SMALL BUSINESS SUCCESSFUL?

Words

> Look for the following words as you read the passage. Match each word with its correct definition.

Words		Definitions	
1.	afloat	A.	adj., first, beginning
2.	characteristic	B.	n., money earned after paying costs
3.	compete	C.	n., a piece of advice
4.	edge	D.	v., to do as well as or better than others
5.	financial	E.	n., an advantage
6.	inevitably	F.	n., reason for doing something
7.	initial	G.	adj., related to money
8.	motivation	H.	adj., special, different from all others
9.	niche	I.	adj., having enough money to pay what you owe
10.	particular	J.	adj., very important, necessary for success
11.	personalized[1]	K.	adj., specific
12.	potential	L.	adj., possible
13.	product	M.	n., a position or place that is very suitable
14.	profit	N.	n., the general opinion about something or somebody
15.	project	O.	adj., made or done especially for a certain person
16.	reputation	P.	adj., healthy, without financial risk
17.	sound	Q.	n., something that is made
18.	tip	R.	adv., certainly, to be expected
19.	unique	S.	n., a feature, quality
20.	vital	T.	v., to estimate, calculate a future amount

[1]BrE: personalised

Reading

What Makes a Small Business Successful?

The U.S. Small Business Administration (SBA) defines small businesses as those employing fewer than 500 employees, and many are much smaller than that. In the United States, about a third of small businesses employ fewer than twenty employees. Many thousands of new small businesses are started every year, but few survive. In fact, according to the SBA, one in three fails during the first two years, and only one in two survives beyond five years.

People start small businesses for a variety of reasons, but whatever the particular motivation, certain characteristics make a small business more likely to succeed. Business advisers point to the importance of finding a niche. It is difficult for a small business to compete with the array of products or services a large business can offer. Instead, the small business that has defined what is unique about the product or service it provides has a greater chance of success. A small business can offer customers personalized service and specialized products or knowledge that can be more difficult to find in a large chain store, for example.

Related to the concept of finding a niche is the importance of maintaining a competitive edge. To be successful, a business has to look at what its competitors, whether large or small, are doing and find a way to stay ahead of the game. In addition to offering a specialized product or service, a business that has more efficient production or distribution systems, a better location, or a reputation for excellence in customer service can do well in a competitive market.

Research and planning are vital steps in setting up a small business. It is essential to determine who the potential customers are and the best way to reach them. It is also necessary to develop a sound business plan that, among other things, shows how the business will make a profit and projects the cash flow that will help the business stay afloat.

Naturally, a successful small business starts out with proper financial support. In addition to the costs of starting the business, there are also the costs of running it until it starts turning a profit. Typically, a small business takes one to two years to become profitable. During that time, there are still expenses that have to be met. Rent has to be paid, employees have to be paid their wages, and supplies have to be bought. If plans have not been made for supporting the costs of the business until it brings in a profit, inevitably it will fail.

One important tip is to start small. This allows owners the opportunity to learn little by little without making huge costly mistakes. Working alone in one's basement during the initial phases of the business, for example, costs a great deal less than renting a space and hiring staff. If the business generates less income than expected or if the market needs to be redefined, the financial losses will be much less if expenses have been kept to a minimum.

About half of private-sector employees in the United States work for small businesses. This number is even greater in other parts of the world. Successful small businesses make important contributions to the economy everywhere.

Answer the questions about **What Makes a Small Business Successful?**

Questions 1–3

> *Choose the correct letter,* ***A***, ***B***, ***C***, *or* ***D***.

1. How many small businesses fail during their initial two years in business?
   A One-half
   B One-third
   C One-fourth
   D One-fifth

2. What kind of edge can a small business have over a large business?
   A Better business advisers
   B A wider array of products
   C Greater motivation to succeed
   D More personalized service

3. How long does it usually take a small business to start earning a profit?
   A Less than one year
   B Between one and two years
   C More than two years
   D At least five years

Questions 4–7

> Complete the summary below.
> Choose **NO MORE THAN ONE WORD** from the text for each answer.

Vital Steps to Starting a Small Business

- Define what makes your product or service **4** .... or different from others in your sector.
- Identify your **5** .... customers.
- Write up a **6** .... business plan.
- Make sure you have the **7** .... support to keep the business running until you earn a profit.

My Words

> Write the words that are new to you. Look them up in the dictionary and write their definitions.

Words   Definitions

_____   _____

_____   _____

_____   _____

_____   _____

_____   _____

_____   _____

_____   _____

Word Families

noun	competition	There is a lot of competition for the attention of customers.
noun	competitor	Business owners need to pay attention to what competitors are doing.
verb	compete	A small business can compete with large businesses by providing a specialized service.
adjective	competitive	A small business must stay competitive to succeed.
adverb	competitively	Some small businesses are competitively positioned to grab a market.

noun	inevitability	The owner worried whether failure was an inevitability.
adjective	inevitable	The failure of a small business is not inevitable if all the important pieces are in place.
adverb	inevitably	If a businessman sells an inferior product, it will inevitably affect his reputation.

noun	initiation	There is a lot of hard work and planning behind the initiation of a new business.
noun	initiator	No one knew who the initiator was, but it changed the way companies did business.
verb	initiate	In addition to good planning, financial support is necessary to initiate a business.
adjective	initial	Many small businesses fail during the initial stages.
adverb	initially	It is a good idea to keep your business small initially.

Unit 7

noun	motivation	A strong motivation to succeed keeps many small businesses afloat.
noun	motivator	The possibility of earning a lot of money was the key motivator.
verb	motivate	Many different situations motivate people to start businesses.
adjective	motivated	The motivated business owner will find a way to make his business succeed.
adjective	motivating	We looked for different motivating factors.

noun	production	The production of handmade items is very time consuming.
noun	product	The success of a small business depends in part on how much customers want the product it sells.
noun	producer	That company is a major producer of electronic equipment.
verb	produce	Some small businesses also produce the items that they sell.
adjective	productive	The business owner wants the employees to be productive.
adverb	productively	He hoped to be productively employed in his field.

noun	profit	It usually takes several years for a small business to earn a profit.
verb	profit	It is a good idea to look at what other similar businesses have done so that you can profit from their experience.
adjective	profitable	If your business is not profitable, you will have to figure out what changes can be made.
adverb	profitably	Some businesses never manage to function profitably.

Word Family Practice

Choose the correct word family member from the list below to complete each blank.

Many small businesses fail. You don't want yours to be one of them. How can you make sure your business succeeds? The answer lies in careful thought and planning. Before you **1**.......... your business, think about your reasons for doing so. What is your **2**..........? Being clear about this will help you keep going even when things get difficult. Then, do your research. What similar businesses are in your area? Will you be able to **3**.......... with them? How? Take the time to develop a sound plan. What will your business be about? Will you **4**.......... a unique item or provide a personalized service? Whatever you do, make sure it is different in some way from what other businesses are offering. As you make your plan, remember that it normally takes several years before a business becomes **5**.......... . Make sure you have enough money to keep going until then. If you follow all these tips, it is not **6**.......... that your business will fail.

1. initiation	initiate	initial
2. motivation	motivate	motivated
3. competitor	compete	competitive
4. product	produce	productive
5. profit	profitably	profitable
6. inevitable	inevitably	inevitability

Dictionary Skill

Changing Stress
The meanings of some words change when different syllables are stressed. These words are spelled the same but are pronounced with different stress. Most are also different parts of speech.

> *Read the definitions below. Then read the sentences and write the letter of the correct definition for each sentence.*
>
> pro-ject [pro-JEKT]
> **A** *verb.* to estimate, calculate a future amount
>
> pro-ject [PRO-jekt]
> **B** *noun.* a task, a defined program of work

_____ 1. Our first *project* is to study the market and identify our potential customers.

_____ 2. We *project* that we will start earning a profit by the end of next year.

Listening

> *Listen to the conversation. Choose* **FOUR** *letters,* **A–G.**

Which **FOUR** of the following characteristics of a successful small business describe the Sunshine Bakery?

A It does not have nearby competitors.

B It offers a unique product.

C It has a good reputation.

D The idea for it was based on research of potential customers.

E It was started with a sound business plan.

F It became profitable in the first year.

G It was started with the necessary financial support.

Writing

In many places, large chain stores are taking over the marketplace, making it impossible for small businesses to compete with them. What are the advantages and disadvantages of this situation?

Support your opinion with reasons and examples from your own knowledge or experience.

Write at least 250 words.

Speaking

Talk about the following topics:

Think of a store where you enjoy shopping. What characteristics draw you to it?

People spend money on different kinds of things. What kinds of products do you feel are worth spending a lot of money on?

What tips do you have for someone who is planning to buy an expensive product?

BRAND LOYALTY

Words

> *Look for the following words as you read the passage. Match each word with its correct definition.*

Words
1. bond
2. brand
3. burgeoning
4. conglomerate
5. consistently
6. convince
7. endorsement
8. fleeting
9. ignore
10. loyalty
11. outperform
12. passion
13. phenomenon
14. prevail
15. promote
16. reverse
17. selective
18. staple
19. status
20. thirst

Definitions
A. adj., intentionally choosing some things and not others
B. v., to get somebody to do or believe something
C. n., public support for something
D. v., to be common among certain groups
E. n., large company that owns smaller companies
F. v., to not pay attention to
G. n., faithfulness, belief in something
H. n., connection
I. v., to perform better than
J. n., very strong feeling or interest in
K. n., company name for a product
L. n., a strong enthusiasm for something
M. n., social position
N. adj., brief, ending quickly
O. v., to advertise
P. adv., regularly, always
Q. v., to turn around, change to its opposite
R. adj., growing
S. n., something unusual that happens, a fact
T. n., a basic household item

Reading

Brand Loyalty

From the neighborhood[1] barber to the international conglomerate, most businesses have a common goal: repeat customers. Developing a committed clientele can be more valuable than attracting new customers, whose loyalty to a company's products may be fleeting.

Brand loyalty is a psychological bond that, once established, is difficult to reverse—and it is more complicated than simply buying the same product time and again. True brand loyalty differs from what some marketing researchers refer to as spurious loyalty—a passive type of buying motivated by habit, convenience, price, and availability but not the result of any true loyalty or passion for the actual merchandise. Convincing consumers with spurious loyalty to try another brand can be quite easy.

Products that create true consumer loyalty tend to be nonessential day-to-day items such as tobacco, beverages, candy, and beauty products, as well as luxury purchases such as designer clothes and cars. Household staples such as milk, eggs, sugar, and paper products create little brand loyalty, with most consumers just as likely to purchase private labels or store brands or whatever is on sale.

A product must have acceptable quality to establish true brand loyalty, but even top quality is not enough on its own to forge a strong connection with a consumer. Customers relate to products for emotional and symbolic reasons. People identify with the image associated with a brand, for example, as a result of a celebrity endorsement or because of the social values of the company. In addition, people consistently purchase pricey items because of the perceived status those items confer.

Brand-loyal consumers are unlikely to defect to the competition because loyal consumers develop a preference for a product, ignore negative associations, and believe it outperforms others, even when there is little difference among brands. For example, beverage drinkers in blind taste tests regularly fail to select their favored brand—even though they mention taste as the primary reason for their loyalty.

Brand loyalty is a worldwide phenomenon, but it is a luxury that prevails where people have more money to spend. In China's burgeoning economy, sales are soaring for certain top-of-the-line luxury cars after concerted efforts were made to promote them. At the same time, European fashion companies are taking advantage of Chinese consumers' thirst for designer labels, selling goods worth billions of U.S. dollars a year.

Consumers become less selective about brands in economic downturns. During the recession of the early-twenty-first century, more con-

[1]BrE: neighbourhood

sumers in Europe and North America turned to brands that cost less instead of the ones they preferred, and more retailers packaged goods under their own private labels. Although private labels are also influencing shoppers in South Africa and Japan, they have had little effect in Hong Kong, where people have more disposable income and therefore remain loyal to the higher-priced brands.

Brand loyalty is less prevalent in poorer countries where consumers have fewer choices and price is usually the priority.

Answer the questions about **Brand Loyalty**.

Questions 1–8

> Do the following statements agree with the information in the reading passage?
>
> Write
>
>   **TRUE**   if the statement agrees with the information.
>   **FALSE**   if the statement contradicts the information.
> **NOT GIVEN**   if there is no information on this in the passage.

_____ 1. International conglomerates are more successful at creating brand loyalty than small businesses are.

_____ 2. New customers may have only a fleeting interest in a particular brand.

_____ 3. Brand loyalty occurs more often with household staples than with luxury items.

_____ 4. Brand loyalty includes the belief that one brand outperforms other brands.

_____ 5. Endorsement of a product by a famous person can help create brand loyalty.

_____ 6. Companies can convince consumers to change their brand loyalty by lowering prices.

_____ 7. The phenomenon of brand loyalty is seen in countries around the world.

_____ 8. Consumers are drawn to certain brands because they believe these brands give them status.

My Words

*Write the words that are new to you. Look them up in the dictionary
and write their definitions.*

Words   Definitions

_____   _____

_____   _____

_____   _____

_____   _____

_____   _____

_____   _____

_____   _____

_____   _____

Unit 7

Word Families

noun	consistency	Brand loyalty is about the consistency with which consumers buy a certain brand.
adjective	consistent	Not all consumers are consistent when it comes to buying certain brands.
adverb	consistently	A company wants consumers to consistently buy its brands.

noun	loyalty	A company wants the loyalty of its customers.
adjective	loyal	A customer who feels loyal to a certain brand will always buy that brand even when the price rises.
adverb	loyally	Customers may loyally buy all the brands of a particular company.

noun	passion	Customers may have a passion for a particular brand.
adjective	passionate	A person who feels passionate about a brand tends to ignore any problems the product may have.
adverb	passionately	Loyal customers passionately defend their favorite brands.

noun	prevalence	The prevalence of certain brands is a result of the effort companies put into promoting them.
verb	prevail	Brand loyalty usually prevails over price.
adjective	prevalent	Brand loyalty is more prevalent in places where people have more money to spend.

noun	selection	Larger stores can offer a wide selection of brands.
verb	select	People may select a brand that they believe gives them status.
adjective	selective	Some people are very selective about the brands they buy.
adverb	selectively	Some people shop selectively, whereas others just buy whatever they see on the shelf.

noun	thirst	As long as there is a thirst for luxury items, companies will keep producing them.
verb	thirst	Some consumers thirst for the newest of everything.
adjective	thirsty	In a burgeoning economy, consumers are thirsty for products that were not available to them in the past.
adverb	thirstily	People shop thirstily for new products that appear on the market.

Unit 7

Word Family Practice

Choose the correct word family member from the list below to complete each blank.

In promoting their brands, companies try to create a **1**.......... for their products so that large numbers of people will want to buy them. Consumers who make purchases **2**.......... will choose the brands that they feel are the best ones. Therefore, companies try to create an image for their brands that is attractive to consumers. They want their brands to appear exciting. If consumers feel **3**.......... about certain brands, then they are likely to be **4**.......... in buying them. When a company introduces new products to the market, **5**.......... customers will buy them because they already feel good about the company's brands and trust them. Companies that are successful in creating brand loyalty **6**.......... in the market.

1. thirst	thirsty	thirstily
2. select	selective	selectively
3. passion	passionate	passionately
4. consistency	consistent	consistently
5. loyalty	loyal	loyally
6. prevalence	prevail	prevalent

Word Skill

Prefix *out-*
The prefix *out-* can mean *better* or *greater.*

> *Read the sentences. Write a definition for each underlined word.*

1. The company introduced a new car that <u>outperforms</u> other similar cars.

    outperform: _____

2. This company is very good at promoting its brands, and its products always <u>outsell</u> the competitors.

    outsell: _____

3. This company's products are very popular, and its loyal customers <u>outnumber</u> those of other companies.

    outnumber: _____

Listening

> *Listen to the talk. Complete the notes below.*
> *Write **NO MORE THAN ONE WORD** for each answer.*

Creating Brand Loyalty

> Make your brand seem special.
>
> Customers want to feel that your brand gives them **1**............ .
>
> Get **2**.......... from famous people.
>
> Give the idea that the brand is bought by **3**.......... people.
>
> Make customers feel **4**.......... about your brand.

Writing

The charts below show information about consumer decisions regarding mobile phone purchases in two different countries.

Summarize[1] the information by selecting and reporting the main information and making comparisons.

Write at least 150 words.

Most Important Factors in Choosing a Mobile Phone

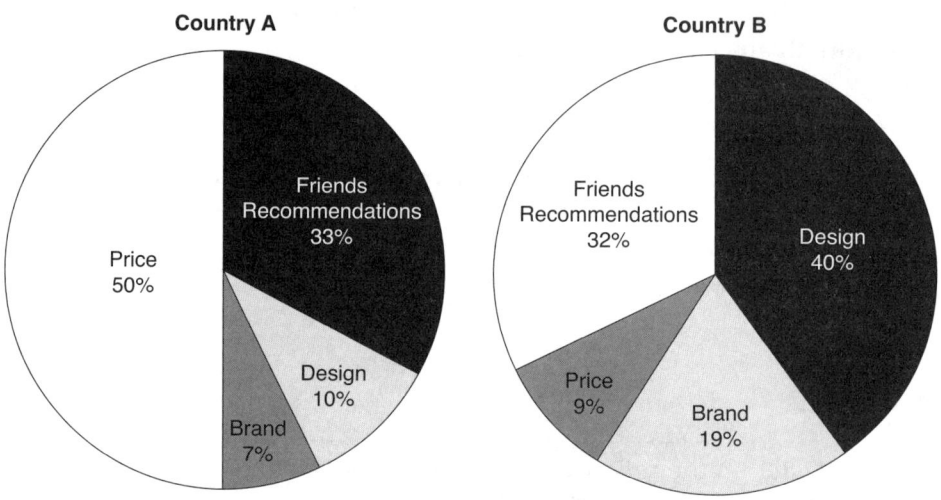

Speaking

Talk about the following topics.

Are you loyal to any particular brands? Why or why not?

Why do you think celebrity endorsements convince people to buy certain brands?

[1]BrE: summarise

GLOBAL OUTSOURCING

Words

> *Look for the following words as you read the passage. Match each word with its correct definition.*

Words

1. boon
2. branch
3. catch up
4. coincide
5. confront
6. controversy
7. decisive
8. enticing
9. epicenter[1]
10. firm
11. looming
12. opponent
13. point
14. preponderance
15. proponent
16. remainder
17. routinely
18. shift
19. turnover
20. wealthy

Definitions

A. v., to call attention to
B. n., central or most important place
C. v., to reach someone or something that is ahead
D. adj., rich
E. adj., attractive
F. n., supporter
G. v., to happen at the same time
H. n., period of work time
I. adv., on a regular basis
J. n., someone who disagrees and speaks out
K. n., local office of a larger company
L. n., the rate at which employees leave and are replaced
M. n., a lot of disagreement affecting many people
N. v., to face a difficulty
O. adj., important, affecting a decision
P. adj., nearing, usually said of a threat or difficulty
Q. n., a company, business organization[2]
R. n., a benefit; advantage
S. n., the largest amount
T. n., the rest, what is left

[1]BrE: epicentre
[2]BrE: organisation

Reading

Global Outsourcing

Outsourcing, subcontracting work to another company, has always been a part of doing business. Firms hire other firms to do work they cannot do themselves or can have done more cheaply elsewhere. With today's global economy, the practice is now so prevalent that even companies in the business of outsourcing are outsourcing work to others.

Wealthy nations routinely send all types of work to countries where labor costs are cheaper, but currently the most frequently outsourced jobs are in information technology (IT), software, and customer service. Japan, Western European countries, and the United States outsource the most work, and India and China take in the most.

Language skills are a decisive factor in where work is sent, with India and the Philippines serving English-speaking clients, Argentina working with Spain, Mexico serving Spanish speakers in the United States, and China handling Asian languages such as Mandarin, Cantonese, and Korean. As a preponderance of corporations conduct business in English, the bulk of outsourcing jobs in recent decades have gone to India, where its status as a former British colony resulted in millions of people speaking English as their first language. About half of India's outsourcing work comes from the United States, with about a quarter from European countries and the remainder from countries such as Japan and Australia.

Some of the largest outsourcing firms in the world have headquarters in India. However, confronted with increasing demand, a looming shortage of skilled workers, and rising wages at home as the Indian economy grows, some of those outsourcing companies are now turning to other countries to help meet their own staffing needs. They outsource largely to China but also to dozens of other countries, including the Philippines, Mexico, Brazil, Saudi Arabia, and, in some cases, the country where the work originated. For example, a U.S.-based software company might outsource IT support to a company based in India, which then subcontracts part of the work to a company in the United States.

Much of the IT support market is now moving to China, where a vast supply of highly trained people are willing to work for lower wages than people in India. With newer Chinese companies not yet well established in the outsourcing business, Indian firms are opening branches there, where their knowledge of English and well-developed managerial skills give them an advantage, at least for now, in dealing with international clients.

Outsourcing has long been a source of controversy, with opponents pointing to the loss of jobs and damage to the economy in the home country and proponents viewing the savings in labor costs as a boon to business. The receiving countries generally consider the well-paying jobs a benefit to their economy, but employees are not always happy with the work. Staff turnover can be high when employees have to work long night shifts to coincide with the business day in the outsourcing country.

India remains the outsourcing epicenter for now, with China slowly catching up, but the situation will continue to change. Once wages rise high enough in India and China, foreign workers somewhere else will be as enticing to outsourcing countries as India and China now are to Europe, Japan, and the United States.

Answer the questions about **Global Outsourcing**.

Questions 1–7

Complete the summary using words from the list below.

Outsourcing is very common in today's global economy. A preponderance of companies in **1**.......... nations send work to countries where wages are lower. These countries are **2**.......... to large companies because labor costs are cheap. Because English is the language used by a large number of international corporations, a large percentage of outsourcing work has gone to India, and the **3**.......... has been sent to other countries. Now wages are rising in India, and more outsourcing work is being sent to other countries. Proponents of outsourcing point out that, as well as being beneficial to the outsourcing companies, it is also a major **4**.......... to the economies of receiving countries. Outsourcing companies **5**.......... some disadvantages, however. For example, there is sometimes a high **6**.......... of employees, who aren't always happy with nighttime work schedules. Labor costs are rising in India and China. When costs in these countries start to **7**.......... with costs in wealthier countries, companies will start sending their work to other places.

boon	confront	firm	turnover
branch	enticing	looming	wealthy
catch up	epicenter	remainder	

My Words

Write the words that are new to you. Look them up in the dictionary and write their definitions.

Words   Definitions

_____   _____

_____   _____

_____   _____

_____   _____

_____   _____

_____   _____

_____   _____

_____   _____

Word Families

noun	controversy	There has been a good deal of controversy around the issue of outsourcing labor.
adjective	controversial	Outsourcing labor is a controversial issue.
adverb	controversially	Many major firms are controversially sending more and more work to countries where labor is cheap.

noun	decision	Many large firms have made the decision to outsource labor to other countries.
verb	decide	Some firms decide not to outsource labor to other countries and hire local workers instead.
adjective	decisive	The cost of labor is a decisive factor for outsourcing work.
adverb	decisively	The company responded decisively by sending the work overseas.

noun	enticement	Low wages are often an enticement for companies looking to cut costs.
verb	entice	Low labor costs entice outsourcing companies to open branches in certain parts of the world.
adjective	enticing	Outsourcing companies find low labor costs enticing.

noun	opponent	Opponents of the practice of outsourcing labor say that it is bad for the economy of the home country.
noun	opposition	There has been a certain amount of opposition to the practice of outsourcing labor.
verb	oppose	Many people who have lost their jobs oppose outsourcing labor to other countries.
adjective	opposing	People hold opposing views on the issue of outsourcing.

noun	preponderance	A preponderance of outsourcing work comes from the United States, Europe, and Japan.
adjective	preponderant	Jobs from international companies play a preponderant role in the economies of a number of countries.
adverb	preponderantly	The work shifts at these companies are preponderantly long.

noun	routine	The job is not difficult as all employees follow the same routine.
adjective	routine	The work is routine and not very interesting.
adverb	routinely	Employees routinely work night shifts.

Word Family Practice

> *Choose the correct word family member from the list below to complete each blank.*

Many customer service companies outsource their work to other countries. The **1**.......... to do this is generally based on labor costs, because wages are lower in certain parts of the world. There are many people who **2**.......... this practice because it leads to loss of employment for workers in the company's home country. This is one reason why the outsourcing of labor has become **3**.......... . For the receiving countries, on the other hand, global outsourcing offers economic opportunities. Inconvenient night shifts are **4**.......... in customer service jobs and the work can be boring and **5**.......... , but the **6**.......... is regular employment at a relatively decent wage.

1.	decision	decide	decisive
2.	opponent	opposition	oppose
3.	controversy	controversial	controversially
4.	preponderance	preponderant	preponderantly
5.	routines	routine	routinely
6.	enticement	entice	enticing

Dictionary Skill

Different Meanings
Many words have more than one meaning.

Read the definitions below. Then read the sentences and write the letter of the correct definition for each sentence.

QUESTIONS 1–2

firm [FURM]
A *noun.* a company, business organization
B *adjective.* hard; steady; unchanging

_____ 1. The prices on our products are *firm,* and we are not willing to change them.

_____ 2. The directors of the *firm* are thinking about outsourcing some of the work to another company.

QUESTIONS 3–4

shift [SHIFT]
A *noun.* period of work time
B *verb.* move; change

_____ 3. They decided to *shift* some of the work to another branch of the company.

_____ 4. The *shifts* at this company are generally eight hours long.

Listening

CD 1
Track
22

Listen to the talk. Complete the timeline below.
*Write **NO MORE THAN TWO WORDS AND/OR A NUMBER***
for each answer.

1......	The firm built the first factory.
1910	Owners decided to have a **2**......
3......	First branch factory built
1940	Original factory replaced
1998	The most **4**...... year for the company: no outsourcing of labor
Present:	Apex is a major employer in the region, with low **5**......

Writing

There has been some controversy about the practice of companies in wealthy countries outsourcing labor to countries where wages are lower. What do you feel are the advantages and disadvantages of this practice?

Support your opinion with reasons and examples from your own knowledge or experience.

Write at least 250 words.

Speaking

> *Talk about the following topics.*

Tell about a decisive moment in your life.

What are some difficulties you confront in your daily life as a professional (or student)?

Unit 8: Society

SOCIAL NETWORKING

Words

> *Look for the following words as you read the passage. Match each word with its correct definition.*

Words

1. acquaintance
2. adolescent
3. apparently
4. carry out
5. community
6. consequence
7. contact
8. eradicate
9. exchange
10. explode
11. immense
12. impose
13. interact
14. post
15. pursue
16. statistics
17. susceptible
18. trend
19. undergo
20. unfold

Definitions

A. v., to remove completely

B. adv., seemingly

C. n., information in the form of numbers; data

D. n., a friend you do not know well

E. adj., easily affected

F. n., result

G. n., communication, connection

H. n., person between the ages of thirteen and nineteen

I. n., movement in a certain direction, popular fashion

J. adj., very big; huge

K. v., to trade something

L. v., to experience, suffer

M. n., a social group

N. v., to display information in a public place

O. v., to grow suddenly and rapidly

P. v., to do, perform

Q. v., to develop; open up

R. v., to force

S. v., to communicate with

T. v., to hunt for; seek

Reading

Social Networking

A

During the first decade of the twenty-first century, the phenomenon of social networking on the Internet exploded across the globe. Online social networking sites are websites that allow people to post personal information about themselves and to connect with people who have similar interests. It is a way of forming community, but a community that exists online rather than in physical space. Facebook, MySpace, LinkedIn, and Twitter are examples of some of the most commonly used social networking sites.

B

Recent statistics show that 75 percent[1] of Internet users around the world use social networking sites to some extent and that 22 percent of all time spent online is spent on these sites. Of all the countries in the world, Italy is apparently the place where social networking is most popular. Italians spend an average of six and a half hours per month per person on social networking sites, followed by Australians, with an average time of just over six hours a month. In comparison, the Japanese are much less interested in social networking, spending an average of just two and a half hours per person per month on these sites. The global average is close to five and a half hours per month. The social networking trend has increased among people of all ages.

C

The phenomenon of social networking sites may present unanticipated consequences for people's lives in the future. The immense popularity of these sites is evidence that they contribute to users' lives in positive ways, but there are drawbacks as well. Social networking sites allow people to broaden their social reach both personally and professionally. These sites allow users to stay in contact with friends and relatives and reconnect with old friends from the past. The sites also provide opportunities for people to connect with strangers in far-distant places who share similar interests or to seek support when undergoing difficulties such as a grave illness. In the business world, people use social networking sites to carry out business, pursue employment opportunities, or seek new business clients. Students of all ages discuss homework assignments and future educational and career plans. Social networking sites eradicate the limits imposed by the physical world and make it possible to communicate and exchange information with people everywhere.

[1]BrE: per cent

D

On the other hand, concerns are growing about online social networking. As people spend more time interacting with each other online, they spend less time in face-to-face communication. Social networking can actually lead to separation as families and neighbors[2] spend less time together while they are busy using the Internet. There are also potential risks. Social networking involves making personal information available online, which means that, unless the user is careful, anyone can have access to that information. Adolescents may be particularly susceptible to this danger. It is also impossible to know anyone's true identity online. Acquaintances found on the Internet may not be who people think they are. The effects that social networking will have on our social relationships and sense of safety remain to be seen as the future unfolds.

Answer the questions about **Social Networking**.

Questions 1–4

> *The reading passage contains six paragraphs,* ***A–D***.
> *Which paragraphs discuss the following information?*
> *Write the correct letter,* ***A–D***.

_____ 1. The different reasons people pursue contacts on social networking sites

_____ 2. Possible negative consequences of social networking

_____ 3. The amount of time people spend interacting on social networking sites

_____ 4. When the social networking trend became big

[2]BrE: neighbours

Questions 5–9

Complete the summary using words from the list below.

Recently, the popularity of social networking sites has **5**........... . There are **6**........... advantages to these sites. People use these sites to post information about themselves, seek new **7**..........., and **8**.......... professional opportunities. There are also drawbacks. Social networking online may mean that people **9**.......... less with the people around them. It also gives strangers access to personal information.

acquaintances	immense	statistics
exchanged	interact	susceptible
exploded	pursue	undergo

My Words

Write the words that are new to you. Look them up in the dictionary and write their definitions.

Words   Definitions

_____   _____

_____   _____

_____   _____

_____   _____

_____   _____

_____   _____

_____   _____

Word Families

noun	adolescence	As children enter adolescence, they start spending more time on the Internet, pursuing both educational and social activities.
noun	adolescent	These days, adolescents are used to making new acquaintances on the Internet.
adjective	adolescent	Parents need to be aware of how their adolescent children spend time on the Internet.

noun	eradication	Internet communication could lead to the eradication of face-to-face communication in many aspects of our lives.
verb	eradicate	The Internet eradicates the need for face-to-face communication.
adjective	eradicable	Internet communication has made the limits of the physical world eradicable.

noun	explosion	Countries around the world are experiencing the explosion of online social networking.
verb	explode	Interest in online social networking has exploded everywhere.
adjective	explosive	The explosive growth of online social networking has rapidly changed the way we communicate.

Unit 8

noun	immensity	The immensity of the effects that online social networking will have on our lives remains to be seen.
adjective	immense	Online social networking will have immense effects on the way we communicate.
adverb	immensely	Adolescents are immensely interested in online social networking.

noun	interaction	Online interaction is very different from face-to-face interaction.
verb	interact	The Internet makes it possible to interact with people in faraway places.
adjective	interactive	Some computer games are highly interactive.
adverb	interactively	Some sites allow users to communicate interactively.

noun	statistics	We can learn a lot from statistics, but we need to be careful about how we interpret them.
noun	statistician	Statisticians tell us that online social networking communities have grown explosively.
adjective	statistical	Statistical information is important, but it doesn't give us a complete picture.
adverb	statistically	The differences in the data were not statistically significant.

Word Family Practice

Choose the correct word family member from the list below to complete each blank.

These days, many people are spending more time in online **1**.......... than they do in face-to-face communication with the people around them. The **2**.......... of interest in online social networking is especially prevalent among the **3**.......... age group. **4**.......... who study this trend report that a significant number of teenagers spend a large percentage of their free time online and that much of this time is spent on social networking sites. The Internet has apparently **5**.......... limits to communication. It is too soon to tell how **6**.......... this will affect teenagers' lives as they grow up. For now, experts recommend that parents impose restrictions on the amount of time their children spend on the Internet.

1. interactions	interacts	interactive
2. explosion	exploded	explosive
3. adolescence	adolescent	adolescents
4. Statistics	Statisticians	Statistical
5. eradication	eradicated	eradicable
6. immensity	immense	immensely

Unit 8

Word Skill

Phrasal Verbs with carry
Phrasal verbs are made up of two parts: a verb and one or two particles. The meaning of the phrasal verb is usually not related to the meanings of the individual parts.

Phrasal Verb		**Meaning**
carry	*out*	do or perform
verb	particle	
carry	*through*	complete successfully
verb	particle	
carry	*on*	continue
verb	particle	

> *Choose the correct phrasal verb from the list above to complete each sentence.*

1. We thought our friendship would end after we graduated from school, but we have been able to _____ being friends through the Internet.

2. Some people _____ all their business completely online.

3. They will _____ with their plans to start a community center[1] for adolescents.

Listening

 Listen to the conversation. Complete the notes below.
*Write **NO MORE THAN ONE WORD** for each answer.*

Online Social Networking

Advantages
1.......... with people all over the world
2......... personal and professional opportunities

Disadvantages
loss of local **3**..........
don't know true identity of online **4**..........

[1]BrE: centre

Writing

The statistics below show basic information about users of three different online social networking sites.

Summarize[1] the information by selecting and reporting the main information and making comparisons.

Write at least 150 words.

Use of different social network sites by age group. Percentages are of total membership.

	Adolescents (13–17)	Younger adults (18–25)	Older adults (25+)
Site A	20%	47%	33%
Site B	7%	27%	66%
Site C	55%	35%	10%

Speaking

Talk about the following topics.

What kinds of information do you generally exchange with your friends online?

Do you feel that parents should impose any kinds of limits on their adolescent children's use of the Internet? Why or why not?

Do you believe that the online social networking trend will continue in the future?

[1]BrE: summarise

Unit 8

WHY ARE WOMEN LEAVING SCIENCE CAREERS?

Words

> *Look for the following words as you read the passage. Match each word with its correct definition.*

Words	Definitions
1. absence	A. n., a person who gives help and advice
2. academic	B. n., demands; responsibilities
3. approximately	C. adj., similar in size or amount
4. bear	D. v., to give, commit
5. commensurate	E. adj., very serious or extreme; very bad
6. devote	F. n., not being present, time away
7. dire	G. v., to move forward
8. discrepancy	H. n., difference between two things that should be the same
9. equality	
10. frustration	I. adv., close but not exactly
11. funding	J. v., to continue
12. guidance	K. n., being the same, having the same rights and opportunities
13. inordinate	
14. invaluable	L. v., to confirm, make a person feel valued
15. mentor	
16. persist	M. n., lack of satisfaction, inability to reach goals
17. pressure	
18. progress	N. adj., related to school, especially university
19. struggle	
20. validate	O. n., financial support
	P. v., to fight
	Q. adj., more than is reasonable
	R. adj., very valuable; extremely useful
	S. v., to carry, have responsibility for
	T. n., advice, assistance

Reading

Why Are Women Leaving Science Careers?

Generations of women struggled for the right to pursue careers in science and technology, yet today nearly half the women scientists in Europe and the Americas leave their careers. The difference in numbers between men and women who advance and persist in their fields cannot be attributed to race, ethnic, or social group. The dire consequences of this loss may become more acute as the number of women entering science careers increases. Since the 1990s, more women than men have enrolled in college, earned higher grades, and majored in science or technology fields. If the trend continues and more than half these women leave their careers by their mid-forties, approximately one-third of all scientists will leave their careers in the next twenty years. So why are women leaving the science careers they worked so hard to attain? Studies by academic and professional associations show the causes for the loss of this valuable resource are threefold: time, family responsibilities, and lack of role models.

High-level jobs in science, in both the corporate and the academic world, require inordinate amounts of time. With increased use of the Internet, cell phones, and other electronic forms of communication, scientists are not only required to be in the lab or office ten to twelve hours a day, but expected to be available the rest of the time, too. Professional time demands are the same for both men and women, but many more women opt out than men because of significant issues that men do not face.

Although women are nearing equality in the professional world, the pressures of caring for family still rests largely with women. According to studies, professional women with children still bear the majority of the responsibilities at home. They spend more time with the children and on taking care of the home than men. Biology dictates that women require extended leaves of absence when they are pregnant and give birth, yet to advance in their careers, women cannot afford to take time off until their late thirties, when the optimal time for having healthy babies is ending. Women can devote the necessary attention to neither career nor home life, often creating intense frustration.

Discrepancies in opportunities and salaries still exist between the sexes. Because there are fewer female role models in the upper levels of science and technology fields, women have fewer mentors, who provide invaluable support. Without mentors, women in the sciences go without the support, guidance, and networking needed to lead them through the complications of corporate culture, to validate their ideas and secure funding for research, and to access those who can help them progress in their careers. Mentors also help scientists develop business expertise:

Unit 8

Mentored scientists hold more patents, an important source of wealth. Women hold only 14 percent[1] of new patents awarded. Without mentors, women have to work harder to reach the same goals as men, and all the while, many women are still paid less than men for commensurate work.

To keep women scientists in the workforce, some companies are instituting mentoring programs, on-site child care, flex-time, and other innovative accommodations. Unfortunately, many companies are content to outsource or to bring in men from other countries to fill positions that valuable but frustrated women scientists leave behind.

Answer the questions about **Why Are Women Leaving Science Careers?**

Questions 1–3

> *Choose an ending from the list to complete each sentence. There are more endings than sentences, so you will not use them all.*
>
> **A** funding offered by the government.
>
> **B** discrepancies in opportunities for men and women.
>
> **C** pregnancy and childbirth.
>
> **D** the type of guidance they receive in school.
>
> **E** the need to divide their time between career and home life.

_____ 1. Women may request permission for long periods of absence from work because of

_____ 2. Women in science careers experience frustration because of

_____ 3. Women often don't progress as far as men in science careers because of

[1]BrE: per cent

Questions 4–7

Do the following statements agree with the information in the reading passage?

Write

> **TRUE**   *if the statement agrees with the information.*
> **FALSE**   *if the statement contradicts the information.*
> **NOT GIVEN**   *if there is no information on this in the passage.*

_____4. Women scientists are hired for academic jobs more often than for research jobs.

_____5. Both men and women in science careers are expected to devote inordinate amounts of time to their jobs.

_____6. Women in science careers tend to get less support from mentors than men do.

_____7. Salaries for women in science careers are commensurate with men's salaries.

My Words

Write the words that are new to you. Look them up in the dictionary and write their definitions.

Words   Definitions

_____ _____

_____ _____

_____ _____

_____ _____

_____ _____

_____ _____

_____ _____

_____ _____

Word Families

noun	approximation	Researchers don't know the exact numbers of women leaving science careers; these statistics are only an approximation.
verb	approximate	Studies often approximate numbers.
adjective	approximate	The studies tell us the approximate numbers of women leaving science careers.
adverb	approximately	Scientists are required to spend approximately sixty hours a week at their jobs.

noun	equal	Women have struggled for decades to be treated as equals.
noun	equality	Women have struggled for decades for equality in the workplace.
verb	equal	Fifty percent equals one-half.
verb	equalize[1]	Numbers of men and women in the sciences have equalized over time.
adjective	equal	Men and women do not always receive equal pay for equal work.
adverb	equally	Men and women are not always treated equally in the workplace.

[1]BrE: equalise

noun	frustration	The difficulties of balancing career and family responsibilities is a cause of frustration for many women.
verb	frustrate	The lack of equality in the work-place frustrates many women.
adjective	frustrated	Many women are frustrated by the combined pressures of family and career.
adjective	frustrating	The lack of mentors for women in science careers is frustrating.

noun	guidance	Mentors provide guidance to their less experienced colleagues.
noun	guide	It is helpful to have someone who can act as a guide when starting out in your career.
verb	guide	People new to the field need a more experienced person to guide them through the complications of corporate culture.

Unit 8

noun	persistence	Persistence is an important part of success in any profession.
verb	persist	Some women persist in their careers despite the responsibilities they bear at home.
adjective	persistent	A persistent person will progress in her career.
adverb	persistently	Women have struggled persistently to achieve equality in the workplace.

noun	validity	People doubted the validity of the research.
noun	validation	Validation is important for any professional.
verb	validate	It is important to have someone to validate your ideas.
adjective	valid	Scientists need to be certain that their research is valid.

Word Family Practice

Choose the correct word family member from the list below to complete each blank.

The lack of **1**.......... for women in the workplace is a dire problem that has **2**.......... over the years. Many well-educated women feel **3**.......... by the lack of opportunities to progress in their fields as far as men do. Women in male-dominated fields such as science and technology do not have role models to **4**.......... them. They cannot feel sure that they will get **5**.......... for their ideas. Although it is uncertain exactly what percentage of women scientists leave their careers every year, an **6**.......... figure is 50 percent.

1. equality	equal	equally
2. persistence	persisted	persistently
3. frustration	frustrate	frustrated
4. guidance	guides	guide
5. validation	validated	valid
6. approximation	approximate	approximately

Dictionary Skill

Parts of Speech
Progress can be a noun or a verb. The stress changes with the part
of speech.

---

*Read the definitions below. Then read the sentences and write the
letter of the correct definition for each sentence.*

> pro-gress [pro-GRESS]
> **A** *verb.* to move forward
> pro-gress [PRO-gress]
> **B** *noun.* movement forward; advancement

_____ 1. Scientists need to spend long hours at work to *progress* in
their field.

_____ 2. After many months of research, the scientists finally felt
that they had made some *progress* in their work.

Listening

*Listen to the talk. Choose the correct letter, **A**, **B**, or **C**.*

1. The Robertson Research Lab is devoted to _____ research.
   A governmental
   B academic
   C scientific

2. It took _____ to get the funding to build the lab.
   A exactly ten years
   B more or less than ten years
   C much more than ten years

3. _____ bears the responsibility for running the lab.
   A The university
   B The government
   C The Robertson family

4. Lab researchers provide science students with
   A funding.
   B guidance.
   C validation.

Writing

Modern professional women confront a difficulty that men don't generally face: the struggle to balance the pressures of work and home. In your opinion, how can this difficulty best be solved?

Give reasons for your answer and include examples from your own knowledge or experience.

Write at least 250 words.

Speaking

Talk about the following topics.

What career advice have you received that you feel is invaluable?

What are some of the common pressures of your profession?

WHEELCHAIR-ACCESSIBILITY ISSUES

Words

> *Look for the following words as you read the passage. Match each word with its correct definition.*

Words
1. abound
2. account for
3. capable
4. compact
5. corridor
6. curb[1]
7. disability
8. exterior
9. incapacitated
10. interior
11. necessitate
12. poverty
13. ramp
14. recreation
15. slippery
16. slope
17. switch
18. terrain
19. unwieldy
20. update

Definitions
A. n., the condition of being poor
B. n., a smooth surface that allows access between levels
C. n., leisure activities
D. v., to make necessary
E. n., the outside of something
F. adj., small
G. v., to exist in large numbers
H. adj., causing things to slide or slip, difficult to hold or stand on
I. n., the raised edge of the street
J. n., a surface at an angle, with the top higher than the bottom
K. n., a button used to turn on lights or machines
L. adj., able to do something
M. n., the surface of land
N. n., the inside of something
O. adj., difficult to manage
P. n., a condition that makes it difficult to do things other people do
Q. v., to modernize[2], improve
R. adj., unable to do things normally
S. n., hallway
T. v., to be responsible for, be the cause of

Unit 8

[1]BrE: kerb
[2]BrE: modernise

Reading

Wheelchair-Accessibility Issues

As many as 650 million people worldwide live with some form of physical disability, and about 100 million of the disabled need a wheelchair at least part of the time. Industrialized[1], higher-income nations in Asia, Europe, and North America are seeing an older population grow more incapacitated as they age, whereas in lower-income countries of Africa, Asia, and Latin America, poverty, conflict, injuries, and accidents account for most disabilities, many of them in children.

Wheelchairs provide a more independent lifestyle, but they come with their own set of problems: They are wide, unwieldy, and difficult to maneuver[2] in tight spaces, on slippery surfaces, and on steep slopes—not to mention impassable stair steps. Accessibility issues abound at home, work, and school; in recreation activities; and in transportation[3].

One of the most difficult places to use a wheelchair is the home. The average doorway width of about 76 centimeters[4] (30 inches) falls some 5 to 15 centimeters (2 to 6 inches) short of the space necessary to accommodate a wheelchair. To be accessible to a person in a wheelchair, bathrooms require grab bars in showers and tubs[5], built-in shower seats, lower sinks and mirrors, and higher toilet seats. Kitchens need lower counters and shelves as well as accessible switches for lights, garbage disposals, and exhaust fans. Also, because most homes have at least a few steps, a wheelchair ramp is a must.

Many countries have laws requiring public buildings—workplaces, stores, restaurants, and entertainment and sports[6] facilities—to be wheelchair accessible. To accommodate wheelchairs, building exteriors need wide sidewalks[7] with curb cuts and ramps. Automatic doors, including those on elevators[8], must be broad and remain open long enough for a person in a wheelchair to come and go with ease. In a building interior, corridors must be wide enough for a person in a wheelchair and another person on foot to pass side by side, and carpeting should be firm enough for wheelchairs to roll over easily. Restrooms[9] must be wheelchair accessible, too. Although many countries have made these improvements, many more have yet to follow their example.

[1]BrE: Industrialised
[2]BrE: manouever
[3]BrE: transport
[4]BrE: centimetres
[5]BrE: baths
[6]BrE: sport
[7]BrE: pavements
[8]BrE: lifts
[9]BrE: Toilets

With appropriate technology, some wheelchair users can drive cars, although getting in and out of a vehicle while in a wheelchair usually necessitates a portable ramp. Many cities have subway and bus systems that accommodate wheelchairs, and the list is growing. For example, Beijing updated its subway system for the 2008 Olympics, providing disabled riders there access to it for the first time.

In most developing countries, a major concern is not so much wheelchair accessibility as access to a wheelchair. Growing public awareness is contributing to less expensive types of wheelchairs being designed for specific environments—for example, chairs capable of maneuvering across dirt roads and rugged terrain but lightweight and compact so they can fold up to fit in crowded spaces, such as the aisle of a bus. These wheelchairs also must be affordable and constructed of locally available materials for easy repair.

The number of people needing a wheelchair is expected to increase by 22 percent[10] over the next decade, with most of the increase coming in developing countries, where fewer than 1 percent of those in need now have access to one.

Answer the questions about **Wheelchair-Accessibility Issues**.

Questions 1–3

Choose the correct letter, *A*, *B*, *C*, *or* *D*.

1. In industrialized nations, disabilities are found more often among
   A older people.
   B children.
   C students.
   D injured people.

2. To be accessible to wheelchairs, buildings need
   A more compact curbs.
   B wider doors and corridors.
   C elevators on the exterior.
   D carpets in the interior.

3. Compact wheelchairs are
   A more unwieldy.
   B easier to use on a bus.
   C less affordable.
   D much wider.

[10]BrE: per cent

Questions 4–7

Complete the summary using words from the list below.

For people in wheelchairs, accessibility is an issue in most areas of their lives, whether they are at home or at school, working, or enjoying **4**………. during their free time. In homes, things need to be arranged so that they can be reached by a person in a wheelchair. Counters, shelves, and **5**………. need to be placed lower than usual, and **6**………. must be built in place of the usual front steps. Public buildings also need to be arranged to allow access to people in wheelchairs. Transportation is also an issue. Many cities have **7**………. their buses and subways so that it is easier now than it was in the past for people in wheelchairs to get around.

necessitated	ramps	slopes	terrain
poverty	recreation	switches	updated

My Words

Write the words that are new to you. Look them up in the dictionary and write their definitions.

Words   Definitions

_____   _____

_____   _____

_____   _____

_____   _____

_____   _____

_____   _____

_____   _____

Word Families

noun	capability	If a wheelchair has certain capabilities, it is easier to take on a crowded bus or subway.
adjective	capable	Some wheelchairs are capable of being folded.
adverb	capably	People can get around quite capably with a wheelchair.

noun	disability	A disability does not have to prevent a person from living a complete life.
noun	disabled	The disabled require many adjustments to a house.
verb	disable	An accident can disable a person for life.
adjective	disabled	Wheelchairs have helped many disabled people get around.

noun	incapacity	His growing incapacity did not stop him from enjoying life.
noun	incapacitation	Incapacitation caused by aging is one reason that people use wheelchairs.
verb	incapacitate	Age, injury, and illness are all things that can incapacitate people.
adjective	incapacitated	People can become incapacitated with age.

noun	necessity	He uses a wheelchair out of necessity.
verb	necessitate	Wheelchairs necessitate ramps and wide corridors.
adjective	necessary	Ramps are necessary to accommodate wheelchairs.
adverb	necessarily	Corridors in hospitals are necessarily wide to accommodate wheelchairs.

noun	slip	Slips and falls are a major cause of injury in the elderly.
noun	slipperiness	The slipperiness of the roads after an ice storm accounts for many accidents.
verb	slip	A wheelchair can slip on a wet or icy surface.
adjective	slippery	Ice can make a sidewalk too slippery for a wheelchair.

Word Family Practice

> *Choose the correct word family member from the list below to complete each blank.*

Physical **1**.......... does not **2**.......... mean that one has to live a limited life. Wheelchairs, for example, help millions of **3**.......... people get around and live independent lives. Wheelchairs are **4**.......... of going just about everywhere. As with any form of transportation, the user has to be careful to avoid accidents. For example, after a snowstorm or rain-storm, the **5**.......... of sidewalks may make it difficult to maneuver a wheelchair safely.

1. incapacitation	incapacitate	incapacitated
2. necessitate	necessary	necessarily
3. disability	disable	disabled
4. capability	capable	capably
5. slipperiness	slip	slippery

Unit 8

Dictionary Skill

Parts of Speech
Exterior can be a noun or an adjective. *Interior* can also be a noun or an adjective.

Read the definitions below. Then read the sentences and write the letter of the correct definition for each sentence.

QUESTIONS 1–2

ex-te-ri-or [ex-TEE-ree-or]
A *noun.* the outside of something
B *adjective.* on or of the outside

_____ 1. The *exterior* doors need to be wide enough to allow wheelchairs to enter the building.

_____ 2. We need to make sure that the building's *exterior* can accommodate wheelchairs.

QUESTIONS 3–4

in-te-ri-or [in-TEE-ree-or]
A *noun.* the inside of something
B *adjective.* on or of the inside

_____ 3. The *interior* has been altered to accommodate wheelchairs.

_____ 4. The *interior* rooms need wider doors.

Listening

CD 1
Track
25

*Listen to the conversation. Choose **FOUR** letters, **A–F**.*

Which **FOUR** accommodations for wheelchairs are already in place in the building?

A wide corridors

B wide doors

C ramp

D curb cuts

E elevator

F low switches

Writing

The graphs below show basic information about employment among people with and without disabilities in a certain country.

Summarize[1] the information by selecting and reporting the main information and making comparisons.

> *Write at least 250 words.*

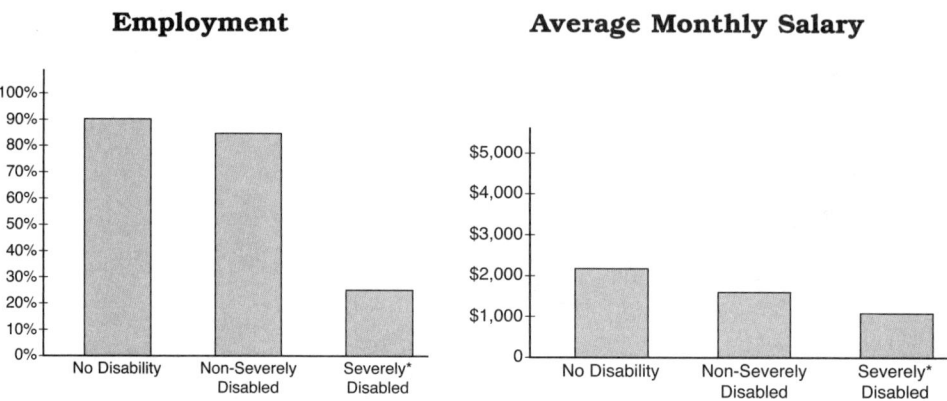

Employment   **Average Monthly Salary**

*Severely Disabled is defined as needing a wheelchair, crutches, or a cane and requiring assistance with personal activities.

Speaking

> *Talk about the following topics.*

Are there laws in your country that require public buildings to be accessible to disabled people? Do you think such laws are a good idea?

Think about the building where you work or study. Is it accessible to people in wheelchairs? In what ways could accessibility be improved?

[1]BrE: summarise

Unit 9: Education

LEARNING STYLES

Words

> Look for the following words as you read the passage. Match each word with its correct definition.

Words

1. approach
2. auditory
3. blend
4. circumstance
5. confidence
6. conventional
7. diagram
8. dominant
9. encouragement
10. expose
11. facial
12. fidget
13. hinder
14. incorporate
15. kinesthetic[1]
16. manipulate
17. obstruction
18. recite
19. solitary
20. verbal

Definitions

A. v., to move constantly in a nervous manner

B. n., method

C. adj., related to words

D. adj., related to the face

E. v., to say or repeat out loud

F. n., a simple drawing to explain how something works

G. adj., normal, traditional

H. n., praise, support to keep going

I. adj., more important, stronger

J. n., situation

K. adj., related to hearing

L. adj., related to body motion

M. n., something that blocks or stands in the way

N. v., to add in, bring together

O. v., to give an opportunity to experience or learn new things

P. n., a mixture, combination

Q. adj., done alone; independent

R. v., to prevent, get in the way

S. v., to move things around with the hands

T. n., belief in one's abilities

[1]BrE: kinaesthetic

Reading

Learning Styles

There are three basic types of classroom learning styles: visual, auditory, and kinesthetic. These learning styles describe the most common ways that people learn. Individuals tend to instinctively prefer one style over the others; thus each person has a learning style that is dominant even though he or she may also rely somewhat on the other approaches at different times and in different circumstances.

Visual learners prefer to sit somewhere in the classroom where no obstructions hinder their view of the lesson. They rely on the teacher's facial expressions and body language to aid their learning. They learn best from a blend of visual displays and presentations such as colorful[1] videos, diagrams, and flip-charts. Often, these learners think in pictures and may even close their eyes to visualize[2] or remember something. When they are bored, they look around for something to watch. Many visual learners lack confidence in their auditory memory skills and so may take detailed notes during classroom discussions and lectures.

Auditory learners sit where they can hear well. They enjoy listening and talking, so discussions and verbal lectures stimulate them. Listening to what others have to say and then talking the subject through helps them process new information. These learners may be heard reading to themselves out loud because they can absorb written information better in this way. Sounding out spelling words, reciting mathematical theories, or talking their way across a map are examples of the types of activities that improve their understanding.

Kinesthetic learners may find it difficult to sit still in a conventional classroom. They need to be physically active and take frequent breaks. When they are bored, they fidget in their seats. They prefer to sit someplace where there is room to move about. They benefit from manipulating materials and learn best when classroom subjects such as math, science, and reading are processed through hands-on experiences. Incorporating arts-and-crafts activities, building projects, and sports into lessons helps kinesthetic learners process new information. Physical expressions of encouragement, such as a pat on the back, are often appreciated.

In addition to these traditional ways of describing learning styles, educators have identified other ways some students prefer to learn. Verbal learners, for example, enjoy using words, both written and spoken. Logical learners are strong in the areas of logic and reasoning. Social

[1]BrE: colourful
[2]BrE: visualise

learners do best when working in groups, whereas solitary learners prefer to work alone. Research shows that each of these learning styles, as well as the visual, auditory, and kinesthetic styles, uses different parts of the brain. Students may prefer to focus on just one style, but practicing[3] other styles involves more of the brain's potential and therefore helps students remember more of what they learn.

Teachers who present their lessons using varied techniques that stimulate all learning styles expose students to both their dominant and less preferred methods of learning, aiding them to more fully reach their potential as learners.

Answer the questions about **Learning Styles**.

Questions 1–6

> *Look at the following descriptions of different styles of learners.*
> *Match each type of learner with the correct description.*
> *Write the correct letter,* **A**, **B**, *or* **C**, *next to numbers 1–6.*
>
> **A** Visual learners
>
> **B** Auditory learners
>
> **C** Kinesthetic learners

_____ 1. They are stimulated by lessons that incorporate discussions and verbal lectures.

_____ 2. Facial expressions are important to them.

_____ 3. They learn best in circumstances where they can manipulate objects.

_____ 4. Taking notes is one approach they use for processing information.

_____ 5. They often fidget in a conventional classroom setting.

_____ 6. Reciting information helps them absorb it better.

Unit 9

[3]BrE: practising

Questions 7–9

Choose the correct letter, **A**, **B**, **C**, *or* **D**.

7. Verbal learners are
    A better at writing than speaking.
    B good with words.
    C solitary people.
    D skilled at reasoning.

8. Social learners need
    A other people around them.
    B very little encouragement.
    C both spoken and written instructions.
    D information presented through diagrams.

9. When teachers expose students to all learning styles, the students
    A change their dominant style.
    B lose their confidence.
    C get confused.
    D learn more.

My Words

Write the words that are new to you. Look them up in the dictionary and write their definitions.

Words   Definitions

_____   _____

_____   _____

_____   _____

_____   _____

_____   _____

_____   _____

_____   _____

_____   _____

Word Families

noun	confidence	Developing confidence in one's abilities is an important part of learning.
adjective	confident	Students who feel confident do better in school.
adverb	confidently	Students learn confidently when they are allowed to use learning styles that they feel comfortable with.

noun	convention	Classroom conventions sometimes need to be adapted to fit the learning styles of all the students.
adjective	conventional	Conventional teaching methods are changing as educators understand the need to address all styles of learning.
adverb	conventionally	A conventionally taught lesson may not incorporate approaches suited to all the students' learning styles.

noun	dominance	The dominance of one learning style over others does not mean that the learner relies on that one style alone.
verb	dominate	In each individual, one learning style tends to dominate over the others.
adjective	dominant	Students can learn to use other styles in addition to the one that is dominant.

Unit 9

noun	exposure	Students benefit a great deal from exposure to different styles of learning.
verb	expose	It is a good idea for teachers to expose students to a variety of learning experiences.

noun	face	Visual learners like to be able to see the teacher's face during a lesson.
verb	face	Visual learners like to face the teacher during a lesson.
adjective	facial	Facial expressions are an important part of communication.
adverb	facially	People may express their feelings facially even if they don't say a word.

noun	solitude	Some students prefer to work in solitude.
adjective	solitary	Solitary learners would rather work alone than in a group.
adverb	solitarily	Some students do better when they can work solitarily.

Word Family Practice

Choose the correct word family member from the list below to complete each blank.

1.......... approaches to learning have students sitting at their desks listening to the teacher or working in their textbooks. These days, however, teachers have changed their methods, and modern classrooms no longer look like this, at least not all the time. Teachers now incorporate activities into their lessons that address the learning needs of all the students. Although students each have a particular learning style that **2**.........., it is important to give them the opportunity to practice other learning styles as well. **3**.......... to a variety of activities encourages students to use different parts of their brains, thus increasing their learning potential. Students who have a tendency to work in **4**.........., for example, will benefit from working in small groups some of the time. Students who get used to different ways of working in the classroom will become more **5**.......... learners. The results will be seen in the quality of the work they do, and on their proud and happy **6**.......... as well.

1. Conventions	Conventional	Conventionally
2. dominance	dominates	dominant
3. Exposure	Exposes	Exposed
4. solitude	solitary	solitarily
5. confidence	confident	confidently
6. faces	facial	facially

Dictionary Skill

Parts of Speech
Blend can be a noun or a verb.

Read the definitions below. Then read the sentences and write the letter of the correct definition for each sentence.

blend [BLEND]
A *noun.* a mixture, combination
B *verb.* to mix, combine

_____ 1. There is a *blend* of leaning styles in every classroom.

_____ 2. When forming learning groups in the classroom, it is a good idea to *blend* students with different learning styles.

Listening

 Listen to the lecture. Complete the notes below.
*Write **NO MORE THAN ONE WORD** for each answer.*

Needs of Different Students

Visual Learners:
    They need to see the teacher's face.
    They need lessons with **1**.......... and pictures.

Auditory Learners:
    They need to hear words.
    They need to read aloud and **2**.......... rules.

Kinesthetic Learners
    They need to do things.
    They need to move around and **3**.......... items.

All students need **4**.......... .

Writing

Confidence in oneself is an important part of learning. What factors in a classroom can contribute to a student's feeling of confidence?

Give reasons for your answer and include examples from your own knowledge or experience.

Write at least 250 words.

Speaking

Talk about the following topics.

Think about the three learning styles—visual, auditory, and kinesthetic. Which do you think is your dominant style? Why?

Would you describe yourself as a solitary learner or a social learner?

What things hinder your learning?

Unit 9

THE HOMESCHOOL OPTION

Words

> *Look for the following words as you read the passage. Match each word with its correct definition.*

Words
1. address
2. adequately
3. alternative
4. compulsory
5. concerned
6. dissatisfied
7. exceptional
8. instruction
9. latter
10. majority
11. mandate
12. novel
13. obligatory
14. periodic
15. philosophy
16. prior
17. relatively
18. tutor
19. vast
20. widespread

Definitions
A. n., teaching
B. adj., special, above average
C. adj., near the end
D. n., a private teacher
E. n., a choice
F. adj., required
G. n., the larger part, most
H. adj., before, previous
I. adj., required
J. adj., worried
K. n., set of beliefs and values
L. adj., not pleased
M. adj., common
N. adv., well enough
O. adj., very big
P. adv., in comparison to something else
Q. adj., new and unusual
R. v., to deal with a problem or issue
S. adj., repeated regularly
T. v., to order officially; require

Reading

The Homeschool Option

Educating children at home as an alternative to formal education is an option chosen by families in many parts of the world. The homeschooling movement is popular in the United States, where close to one million children are educated at home. In Canada, 1 percent[1] of school-age children are homeschooled, and the idea also enjoys growing popularity in Australia, where 20,000 families homeschool their children. The movement is not limited to these countries. Homeschooling families can be found all over the world, from Japan to Taiwan to Argentina to South Africa.

Homeschooling is not a novel idea. In fact, the idea of sending children to spend most of their day away from home at a formal school is a relatively new custom. In the United States, for example, it was not until the latter part of the nineteenth century that state governments began making school attendance compulsory. Before that, the concept of a formal education was not so widespread. Children learned the skills they would need for adult life at home from tutors or their parents, through formal instruction or by working side by side with the adults of the family.

In the modern developed world, where the vast majority of children attend school, families choose homeschooling for a variety of reasons. For people who live in remote areas, such as the Australian outback or the Alaskan wilderness, homeschooling may be their only option. Children who have exceptional talents in the arts or other areas may be homeschooled so that they have more time to devote to their special interests. Much of the homeschooling movement is made up of families who, for various reasons, are dissatisfied with the schools available to them. They may have a differing educational philosophy, they may be concerned about the safety of the school environment, or they may feel that the local schools cannot adequately address their children's educational needs.

The legal environment surrounding homeschooling varies. In some places, a government-approved course of study is mandated, whereas in others, homeschoolers may be required only to follow general guidelines, or even none at all. Sometimes periodic progress reports, tests, or professional evaluations are obligatory. There are different approaches to homeschooling that individual families can take. Some follow a particular educational philosophy, such as the Montessori method or Waldorf education. Others use a mixed approach, borrowing from a variety of methods and materials. A large selection of prepared educational prod-

[1]BrE: per cent

ucts is available to specifically address the needs of homeschooling families, and correspondence courses can also be purchased. In addition, homeschooling magazines and websites give families the opportunity to read about others' experiences and get ideas for different kinds of educational activities to try. As the homeschooling movement grows around the world, so, too, do the opportunities for homeschooling families to share experiences and ideas at conferences and on the Internet. Although most families continue to choose a traditional classroom education for their children, homeschooling as an alternative educational option is becoming more popular.

Answer the questions about **The Homeschool Option**.

Questions 1–3

> *Which of the following reasons that families choose homeschooling are mentioned in the passage?*
> *Choose* **three** *answers from the list below.*

A The large size of local schools

B The exceptional talents of their children

C The lack of variety of instruction in the majority of schools

D Disagreement with the educational philosophy of local schools

E Belief that local schools cannot adequately meet their children's needs

F Opposition to the periodic testing of their children

Questions 4–8

> *Do the following statements agree with the information in the reading passage?*
> *Write*
>
>   **TRUE**   *if the statement agrees with the information.*
>   **FALSE**   *if the statement contradicts the information.*
> **NOT GIVEN**   *if there is no information on this in the passage.*

_____ 4. School attendance was mandated in the United States near the beginning of the nineteenth century.

_____ 5. Before modern times, the majority of children did not attend school.

_____ 6. Many nineteenth-century tutors were not adequately trained for the job.

_____ 7. The majority of homeschooling families follow a similar educational philosophy.

_____ 8. Although there is growing interest in homeschooling, relatively few families practice[1] it.

My Words

Write the words that are new to you. Look them up in the dictionary and write their definitions.

Words   Definitions

_____   _____

_____   _____

_____   _____

_____   _____

_____   _____

_____   _____

_____   _____

_____   _____

Unit 9

[1]BrE: practise

Word Families

noun	alternative	Some families choose private school as an alternative to public school.
noun	alternate	Because our first choice for the class trip was too expensive, we went with our alternate instead.
adjective	alternative	Some homeschooling families follow an educational program similar to that found in formal schools, whereas others choose alternative methods.
adjective	alternate	We made alternate arrangements for the class trip.
adverb	alternatively	Parents can choose to teach their children themselves; alternatively, they can join homeschooling groups and share teaching responsibilities with other families.

noun	concern	The safety of the school environment is a concern for many modern parents.
verb	concern	The quality of public schools concerns a growing number of families.
adjective	concerned	Parents feel concerned when their children don't do well in school.

noun	instruction	Parents want their children to get the best instruction.
noun	instructor	Some people feel that parents are the best instructors for their children.
verb	instruct	Some homeschooling parents instruct their children for a set number of hours every day, whereas others follow a less structured schedule.
adjective	instructive	Homeschooling parents try to provide their children with a variety of instructive experiences.
adjective	instructional	Homeschooling parents try to provide their children with good instructional materials.
adverb	instructionally	Materials used for homeschooling must be instructionally sound.

noun	obligation	Parents have the obligation to protect their children and provide for their needs.
verb	obligate	A teacher might obligate his students to spend several hours a day doing homework.
adjective	obligatory	School is obligatory for young children in most parts of the world.

noun	period	Children should be given several rest periods during the school day.
adjective	periodic	In some places, homeschooling families are required to receive periodic visits from professional educators.
adverb	periodically	Teachers give their students tests periodically.

Unit 9

Word Family Practice

> *Choose the correct word family member from the list below to complete each blank.*

Many families are interested in **1**.......... forms of education. Some send their children to private schools that follow certain educational methods, and others choose to **2**.......... their children themselves at home. Providing children with a thorough education in all subject areas can be a **3**.......... for homeschooling families. However, there are many places they can turn to for support. There are several homeschooling organizations[1] that can give them guidance with this. Communicating with other homeschooling families **4**.......... to exchange ideas and discuss problems is an important source of support for many homeschoolers. Whether they choose formal schooling or homeschooling, parents have the **5**.......... to make sure that their children get a good education.

1. alternative	alternatives	alternatively
2. instructor	instruct	instruction
3. concern	concerns	concerned
4. period	periodic	periodically
5. obligation	obligate	obligatory

[1]BrE: organisations

Word Skill

Prefix *dis–*
The prefix *dis–* makes the meaning of the word negative.

> *Read the sentences. Write a definition for each underlined word.*

1. Many families are <u>satisfied</u> with the results they get from homeschooling and would never send their children back to a traditional school.

   satisfied: _____

2. Parents who are <u>dissatisfied</u> with traditional education look for alternative schools for their children.

   dissatisfied: _____

Listening

CD 1
Track
27

> *Listen to the talk. Choose **FOUR** letters, **A–G**.*

Which **FOUR** of the following are compulsory for parents who homeschool their children in the speaker's city?

A Informing the city of their plans to homeschool

B Hiring professional tutors

C Having prior experience teaching

D Addressing all subjects taught in the local school

E Using books provided by the city

F Giving periodic tests

G Submitting a yearly report

Unit 9

Writing

Interest in homeschooling is becoming more widespread around the world. In your opinion, should school be compulsory for all children, or should families be allowed the right to choose to educate their children at home?

Support your opinion with reasons and examples from your own knowledge and experience.

Write at least 250 words.

Speaking

Talk about the following topics.

For what ages should education be compulsory, in your opinion?

Which subjects do you think should be obligatory in high schools?

What concerns do you have about education in your country?

EDUCATING THE GIFTED

Words

Look for the following words as you read the passage. Match each word with its correct definition.

Words	Definitions
Words	**Definitions**
1. assess	A. adj., improved, describing something of higher quality
2. constructive	
3. curriculum	B. v., to identify
4 dedicate	C. n., understanding
5. discipline	D. n., the set of subjects taught at a school
6. enriched	E. v., to measure
7. extraordinary	F. adj., having special talents or abilities
8. gifted	G. adj., advanced, complex
9. inquisitiveness	H. n., maintaining correct behavior[2]
10. interpretation	I. v., to become
11. moderately	J. adj., describing education programs to address some area of difficulty
12. peer	
13. profoundly	K. adv., greatly, extremely
14. recognize[1]	L. n., a person at an equal level with another
15. remedial	
16. simultaneous	M. v., to give, devote
17. sophisticated	N. n., desire for knowledge
18. transfer	O. n., not wanting to participate
19. turn into	P. adj., happening at the same time
20. withdrawal	Q. v., to move from one place to another
	R. adv., slightly
	S. adj., positive, beneficial
	T. adj., special, exceptional

[1]BrE: recognise
[2]BrE: behaviour

Reading

Educating the Gifted

What is a gifted child? There are different ways to define this term. It may refer to special talents in the arts or to a high level of academic abilities. A child may be gifted in one specific area, such as music, or have talents in many areas. According to the U.S. National Association for Gifted Children, a gifted child shows an "exceptional level of performance" in one or more areas. In general usage, giftedness includes high levels of cognitive ability, motivation, inquisitiveness, creativity, and leadership. Gifted children represent approximately 3 to 5 percent[1] of the school-aged population.

Although giftedness cannot be assessed by an intelligence test alone, these tests are often used to indicate giftedness. By and large, giftedness begins at an IQ of 115, or about one in six children. Highly gifted children have IQs over 145, or about one in a thousand children. Profoundly gifted children have IQs over 180, or about one in a million children. Because very few education programs include any courses on teaching the gifted, teachers are often not able to recognize the profoundly gifted. Teachers are more likely to recognize moderately gifted children because they are ahead of the other children but not so far ahead as to be unrecognizable. For instance, children who can read older children's books in first and second grade are often transferred into gifted classes, but children who are reading adult books are told to stop reading them. Those profoundly gifted students who are not recognized often turn into discipline problems when they are not offered constructive ways to focus their extraordinary creativity.

The practice of creating a separate, enriched curriculum for gifted students began in the early twentieth century. At that time, social scientists noted that gifted children often speak, read, and move at an earlier age than their peers. At a younger age they are able to work at a higher conceptual level, develop more sophisticated methods to solve problems, and show more creativity in their methods and interpretation of assignments. After the first schools for the gifted were established, these students were followed for many years to see if enriched education made a difference. It did. Gifted students who were grouped together and taught a special curriculum earned fifty times more doctoral degrees than gifted students who were not given an enriched curriculum. When gifted programs[2] have been cut, the parents of the participants have reported decreased inquisitiveness, motivation, and energy levels in their children, and a simultaneous withdrawal from the class-

[1]BrE: per cent
[2]BrE: programmes

room experience. Identified gifted students who attend schools without any program for the gifted show a steady decrease in motivation and test scores between first and sixth grade.

There are still very few opportunities for educating the gifted in the lowest socioeconomic levels. The schools that service the poorest areas often dedicate their efforts toward remedial teaching rather than accelerated curriculum, and students with extraordinary talents are often not recognized. About 25 percent of the world's gifted population are too poor to be noticed.

Answer the questions about **Educating the Gifted**.

Questions 1–9

> *Complete the summary using words from the list below.*

Gifted children are children with **1**.......... talents. Their talents may be artistic or academic. There are different levels of giftedness. The most gifted children are called **2**.......... gifted, but very few children are so gifted. It is more common to see **3**.......... gifted children, and it is easier for teachers to **4**.......... them. These are the children who are ahead of their **5**.......... but not too far ahead. These children are more likely to be **6**.......... from regular classes to classes where a special **7**.......... for the gifted is taught. When schools **8**.......... programs to gifted education, the participants do well in school. When these programs are cut, the children appear to lose interest in school learning and their levels of **9**.......... decline.

assessed	discipline	moderately	remedial
constructive	extraordinary	peers	transferred
curriculum	inquisitiveness	profoundly	
dedicate	interpretation	recognize	

My Words

> *Write the words that are new to you. Look them up in the dictionary and write their definitions.*

Words   Definitions

_____   _____

_____   _____

_____   _____

_____   _____

_____   _____

_____   _____

_____   _____

_____   _____

Word Families

noun	assessment	It is not always easy to find the proper assessment for gifted children.
noun	assessor	The school used one of the teachers as an assessor for the program.
verb	assess	Different methods are used to assess gifted children.

noun	enrichment	A school system's approach to educating gifted children usually includes enrichment of the regular curriculum.
verb	enrich	Providing special programs for gifted children enriches their school experience.
adjective	enriched	Parents hope that programs for the gifted will provide their children with an enriched school experience.
adjective	enriching	Participants found the whole experience quite enriching.

noun	recognition	Gifted children don't always get recognition for their extraordinary talents.
verb	recognize	Teachers need to be trained to recognize gifted children in their classrooms.
adjective	recognizable	Children with recognizable talents may be transferred to a gifted education program.
adjective	unrecognizable	Profoundly gifted children are so different from their peers that their talents may be unrecognizable.

Unit 9

255

| **adjective** | simultaneous | We usually see a simultaneous improvement in test scores when a gifted child enters a program with an enriched curriculum. |
| **adverb** | simultaneously | When gifted children are transferred to special programs, their scores rise simultaneously. |

| **noun** | sophistication | Gifted children can solve problems with great sophistication. |
| **adjective** | sophisticated | Gifted children take sophisticated approaches to problem solving. |

noun	withdrawal	Withdrawal from classroom activities is a sign that a child needs special attention.
verb	withdraw	The gifted child who was bored in his regular classroom soon withdrew from all classroom activities.
adjective	withdrawn	A gifted child who is kept in a regular classroom may either become withdrawn or turn into a discipline problem.

Word Family Practice

Choose the correct word family member from the list below to complete each blank.

Education of the gifted starts with **1**.......... . Gifted children may show certain characteristics. For example, they may solve problems more quickly and with greater **2**.......... than their peers do. Once a teacher identifies a potentially gifted student, then **3**.......... are used to determine the giftedness of the child. Identified gifted children are placed in special classes for educational **4**.......... . It has been observed that gifted students' level of interest in school usually increases **5**........... Gifted children who are not identified and not placed in special programs may lose interest in school and **6**.......... from classroom participation.

1. recognition   recognizes   recognizable

2. sophistication   sophisticated

3. assessments   assesses   assessing

4. enrichment   enrich   enriched

5. simultaneous   simultaneously

6. withdrawal   withdraw   withdrawn

Unit 9

Word Skill

Phrasal Verbs with turn.
Phrasal verbs are made up of two parts: a verb and one or two particles. The meaning of the phrasal verb is usually not related to the meanings of the individual parts.

Phrasal Verb		Meaning
turn	*into*	become
verb	particle	
turn	*up*	appear, arrive
verb	particle	
turn	*out*	result
verb	particle	

> *Choose the correct phrasal verb from the list above to complete each sentence.*

1. We expect at least 100 people to _____ at the school meeting about gifted education.

2. Our school's gifted education program serves only a few children now, but we hope it will _____ a large program some day.

3. The children enjoyed the trip to the museum with their teachers, so the day _____ well.

Listening

CD 1
Track
28

Listen to the discussion. Complete the notes below.
*Write **NO MORE THAN ONE WORD** for each answer.*

How to **1**.......... gifted children
- They read books for older children or adults.
- They have **2**.......... approaches to problem solving.
- They may need help with **3**.......... .

How to support:
- Give them **4**.......... activities.
- Provide a special **5**.......... .

Writing

The charts[1] below show information about the percentage of first-year students enrolled in remedial education courses at two different universities.

Summarize[2] the information by selecting and reporting the main information and making comparisons.

Write at least 150 words.

Percent of First-Year Class
Enrolled in Remedial Education Courses

University A

Reading, Writing, or Math	Reading	Writing	Math
45%	22%	26%	35%

University B

Reading, Writing, or Math	Reading	Writing	Math
15%	12%	10%	5%

[1]BrE: tables
[2]BrE: summarise

Speaking

> *Talk about the following topics.*

If you could choose to have any extraordinary talent, what would you choose?

What programs for gifted children are there in your country?

How do you think education for gifted children will be different in the future?

Unit 10:
Technology/Inventions

THE DEVELOPMENT OF THE LIGHTBULB

Words

> *Look for the following words as you read the passage. Match each word with its correct definition.*

Words
1. back
2. clamp
3. critical
4. current
5. derive
6. device
7. entrepreneur
8. file
9. infringement
10. inspiration
11. invalid
12. inventor
13. investor
14. patent
15. ransack
16. refinement
17. ruling
18. specifically
19. suitable
20. unveil

Definitions

A. n., an action that breaks a rule or law

B. n., a flow of electricity, water, or air

C. v., to hold tightly

D. adj., appropriate, acceptable for something

E. v., to search thoroughly, often violently or carelessly

F. n., a legal decision

G. v., to support, esp. financially

H. n., somebody who starts a business

I. v., to officially record something

J. n., a person who creates new things

K. n., a person who puts money into a business

L. adv., exactly; for a particular reason

M. n., a right to an invention granted by the government

N. n., a machine or tool

O. adj., very important

P. v., to make public; uncover

Q. n., improvement

R. v., to get something from something else, originate

S. n., a sudden good idea; a role model for creativity

T. adj., not legal or correct

Reading

The Development of the Lightbulb

Thomas Edison is generally credited with the invention of the light-bulb. In fact, he was just one inventor among many involved in the process of moving the concept of incandescent light from inspiration to marketable reality. What he actually invented in 1879 was a carbon filament that lasted for forty hours. In 1880, he improved his idea, producing a filament derived from bamboo that burned for 1,200 hours.

The first person to successfully produce light with electricity was Humphry Davy, who connected a carbon filament to a battery in 1809. Other inventors worked on refinements of this idea. In 1835, James Lindsay unveiled an electric lamp, which cast enough light to read a book one and a half feet away. In 1854, Henrich Globel created the first actual lightbulb—a glass bulb containing a filament that glowed when electrical current passed through it. However, it burned out too quickly to have any commercial value. Then, Hermann Sprengel developed the Sprengel Pump, a device that used mercury to create a vacuum. Reducing the oxygen in the bulb allowed the filament to glow longer before burning out.

In 1874, Henry Woodward and Matthew Evans filed a patent for a light specifically described as "a shaped piece of carbon held between two electrodes enclosed in a glass vessel." Woodward and Evans attempted to raise the necessary money to improve and market their invention; however, as entrepreneurs, they had little success finding anyone to back them financially. Eventually they sold the rights to their patents to Thomas Edison.

Edison had already been working on the same idea, but for him money was not a critical issue. He was no longer a solitary inventor working in his basement, but the head of a laboratory with the support of investors. He worked to refine the Woodward and Evans light because its filament burned out too quickly. Edison set about testing every material possible for use as a filament. "Before I got through," Edison recalled, "I tested no fewer than 6,000 vegetable growths, and ransacked the world for the most suitable filament material." He even considered using tungsten, which is the material currently used. Eventually, Edison tried a carbonized cotton thread filament clamped to platinum wires. When tested, it lasted forty hours. In 1880, he received a patent for this invention. By the end of the year, Edison had perfected a sixteen-watt bulb that lasted for 1,500 hours.

At the same time, Sir Joseph Swan was working on similar ideas in England. In 1860, he obtained a patent for a carbon filament incandescent lamp, and in 1878, another for an improved version of his lightbulb.

He presented it in a public lecture in 1879. In 1882, Swan sued Edison for patent infringement. As part of the settlement, Edison had to take Swan as a partner in his British electric works. Also, in 1877 and 1878, William Edward Sawyer and Albon Man were granted patents for electric lamps. Based on these patents, the U.S. Patent Office ruled in 1883 that Edison's patents were invalid. Edison fought to appeal that ruling, and in 1889, the court determined that his patents were indeed valid.

Edison is famous for having said, "Genius is one percent inspiration and ninety-nine percent perspiration." It is an understandable statement coming from someone whose laboratory tested more than 6,000 filament possibilities. Nevertheless, one might also consider the adage "History is written by the winners." Edison may not have been the actual inventor of the lightbulb, but he was the man who had the genius, the business sense, and the financial backing to invent the first one that was commercially viable.

Answer the questions about **The Development of the Lightbulb**.

Questions 1–5

> *Complete the summary using the list of words below.*

In the 1800s, many **1**............. experimented with using electrical **2**.......... to produce light. James Lindsay **3**............ his version of an electric light in 1835. It was bright enough for reading a book. Henrich Globel developed the first lightbulb in 1854. His **4**............ , unfortunately, did not have commercial value. It needed **5**............ because it burned out very quickly.

backers	current	filed	refinement
clamped	device	inventors	unveiled

Questions 6–9

Choose an ending from the list to complete each sentence. There are more endings than sentences, so you will not use them all.

A a cotton thread filament that he clamped to wires.

B a filament derived from bamboo.

C a tungsten filament like those used today.

D a long-lasting lightbulb filament.

E a filament that burned out very quickly.

F the most suitable material for a lightbulb filament.

_____ 6. Edison did not invent the lightbulb in 1879; he invented

_____ 7. Edison ransacked the world searching for

_____ 8. Edison's first lightbulb consisted of

_____ 9. Edison later refined his idea with the development of

My Words

Write the words that are new to you. Look them up in the dictionary and write their definitions.

Words   Definitions

_____   _____

_____   _____

_____   _____

_____   _____

_____   _____

_____   _____

_____   _____

_____   _____

Unit 10

Word Families

noun	inventor	Thomas Edison is probably the most well-known American inventor.
noun	invention	The computer is an invention that has completely changed our way of life.
verb	invent	People invent new things every day.

noun	investor	Every investor hopes to get a good return on his or her money.
noun	investment	Keeping all your money in the bank is not a good investment.
verb	invest	If you invest wisely, you can make a good deal of money.

noun	inspiration	Edison's achievements have been an inspiration to many people.
verb	inspire	The president's speech inspired people to action.
adjective	inspiring	It is inspiring to look at the work of great artists.
adverb	inspired	I felt inspired after my visit to the museum.

noun	refinement	Any piece of work can always use refinement.
verb	refine	Edison worked very hard to refine his inventions.
adjective	refined	In 1880, Edison developed a lightbulb that was a refined version of his earlier lightbulb.

noun	specification	The customer changed the specifications for the new lightbulbs.
verb	specify	The customer ordered some lightbulbs, but he didn't specify which kind he wanted.
adjective	specific	The professor gave specific directions about how she wanted the assignment to be done.
adverb	specifically	Edison made an important contribution to the development of the lightbulb, specifically, a long-lasting filament.

noun	suitability	There were doubts about the suitability of the new location.
verb	suit	She is a solitary person, so it suits her to work alone.
adjective	suitable	It's important to wear suitable clothes to a job interview so that you give the right impression.
adverb	suitably	They decided to rent the office because it was suitably located.

Unit 10

Word Family Practice

> *Choose the correct word family member from the list below to complete each blank.*

It takes a creative person to come up with ideas for new products. However, **1**.......... is not enough. It takes more than good ideas to develop an **2**.......... into a product that is practical and useful and can be successfully marketed. It takes hard work and determination. Teams must test new products and then **3**.......... the design, again and again, until there are no improvements to be made. Once the design is perfected, the new product is ready for mass production. This takes money. It takes finding people who believe in the product enough to **4**.......... money in it. **5**.......... people should be found, that is, people who not only can provide the financing, but are interested in the product and in the business. In addition, market research needs to be done to target the **6**.......... groups of people who might be interested in buying the product. Marketing to certain types of people rather than to a general audience can be a very successful approach.

1. inspiration   inspire   inspiring

2. inventor   invention   invent

3. refinement   refine   refined

4. investor   investment invest

5. Suit   Suitable   Suitably

6. specify   specific   specifically

Dictionary Skill

Different Meanings
Many words have more than one meaning.

Read the definitions below. Then read the sentences and write the letter of the correct definition for each sentence.

> cur-rent [KUR-uhnt]
> **A** *noun.* a flow of electricity, water, or air
> **B** *adjective.* of the present time

_____ 1. Don't touch a wire that has an electric *current* running through it.

_____ 2. We are able to do many things now that were difficult just a few years ago because of the *current* state of technology.

Listening

Listen to the talk. Complete the notes below.
*Write **NO MORE THAN THREE WORDS** for each answer.*

Getting Ready to Market Your Invention

First, do a **1**............ .

Next, file **2**............ .

At the same time, you will have to **3**............ .

Look for financial **4**............ .

Unit 10

Writing

In your opinion, what has been the most important invention of the past 100 years?

Support your opinion with reasons and examples from your own knowledge or experience.

Write at least 250 words.

Speaking

Talk about the following topics.

Who was an inspiration to you when you were growing up?

Who is an inspiration to you now?

Do you find any type of music or art inspiring? How does it inspire you?

THE INVENTION OF VARIABLE-PITCH PROPELLERS

Words

Look for the following words as you read the passage. Match each word with its correct definition.

Words
1. aviation
2. blade
3. coarse
4. confer
5. cruise
6. curiosity
7. design
8. enthusiast
9. handle
10. inflexibility
11. isolation
12. pitch
13. prolonged
14. propeller
15. reliably
16. revolutionize[1]
17. rotation
18. sustained
19. turbulence
20. variable

Definitions
A. n., a person who is very interested in something
B. n., a device that causes an airplane or boat to move
C. v., to travel at a steady speed
D. n., the development, design, and use of aircraft
E. n., interest; need to know
F. adj., rough; not smooth
G. n., a plan for making something
H. v., to manage; work well with
I. n., strong, sudden movements in air
J. adj., able to change
K. n., inability to change
L. v., to discuss, consult with somebody
M. n., the condition of being alone or separated from others
N. adj., continuing for a long time, often in a negative sense
O. n., a thin, flat part of a machine
P. n., turning motion
Q. v., to change completely
R. adv., dependably
S. adj., having the ability to continue for a long time
T. n., the angle or slope of something

[1]BrE: revolutionise

Reading

The Invention of Variable-Pitch Propellers

Until the late 1920s, airplane propellers were made of a single piece of wood attached at the center[1] to the driveshaft of the engine. The tilt of the propeller, that is, how flatly it faced the wind, was fixed, which meant planes flew as if they had only one gear. If the plane had a fine propeller, it traveled the entire time as if in first gear, working well on takeoff and landing but working inefficiently during sustained flight. If the plane had a thick, coarse propeller, it traveled the entire time as if in high gear, working efficiently during sustained flight, but making takeoffs and landings dangerous and prolonged. This inflexibility meant that commercial uses of such aircraft were limited because the planes could not carry heavy loads either safely or efficiently.

In 1922, Wallace Rupert Turnbull patented his latest invention, the Variable-Pitch propeller. His propeller in effect gave airplanes gears. The propeller's blades were separate from each other, attached at the driveshaft in the center, and could be moved independently or together to chop the air at different angles. The propellers could be tilted at takeoff and landing to act as if in first gear, chopping less air with each rotation, and could be tilted when cruising to act as if in high gear, chopping more air with each rotation. With this Variable-Pitch propeller, planes could now take off and land more safely and reliably, carry varying weights, and handle greater variations in wind speed and turbulence.

Turnbull was born in New Brunswick in eastern Canada in 1876. He studied mechanical engineering at Cornell, then continued his postgraduate studies in Europe, and returned to work at the Edison labs in New Jersey. In 1902, just one year before the Wright brothers made their historic flight, Turnbull went back home, set up his own lab in a barn, and started running his own aviation experiments.

To begin, Turnbull needed a wind tunnel. He built a wind tunnel, the first in the world, out of packing materials. In it, he tested different designs for propellers and wings; his research is the basis for many of the successful designs still in use today. Alone in his barn, Turnbull designed and tested his Variable-Pitch propeller. It was tested successfully in flight in Borden, Ontario, on June 6, 1927.

Turnbull spent his life experimenting and designing for the new science of aviation in his barn in Rothesay. He sometimes conferred with fellow aviation enthusiast Alexander Graham Bell in Nova Scotia, but for the most part, he worked in isolation. Unlike most engineers, he chose not to work in a university laboratory or in a lab such as Edison's, where

[1]BrE: centre

he would have been supported by like-minded engineers and physicists. Instead, he spent his adult life in a barn he equipped himself. Depending only on his intelligence, curiosity, and work ethic, he revolutionized flight. He is honored[2] in Canada as a pioneer in aviation and a genius in the study of aerodynamics.

Answer the questions about **The Invention of Variable-Pitch Propellers**.

Questions 1–5

> *Do the following statements agree with the information in the reading passage?*
>
> *Write*
>
> > **TRUE**   *if the statement agrees with the information.*
> > **FALSE**   *if the statement contradicts the information.*
> > **NOT GIVEN**   *if there is no information on this in the passage.*

_____ 1. A coarse propeller worked better during sustained flight than during landing.

_____ 2. Variable-Pitch propellers caused problems because of their inflexibility.

_____ 3. The blades of a Variable-Pitch propeller could be moved to different angles.

_____ 4. A plane with a Variable-Pitch propeller was easier to handle in turbulence.

_____ 5. Variable-Pitch propellers were expensive to manufacture.

Unit 10

[2]BrE: honoured

Questions 6–7

Choose the correct letter, **A***,* **B***,* **C***, or* **D***.*

6. Wallace Rupert Turnbull designed his Variable-Pitch propeller
   A at Cornell University.
   B in Canada.
   C at the home of Alexander Graham Bell.
   D in Edison's lab.

7. Turnbull preferred to work
   A with other inventors.
   B in a university lab.
   C with like-minded engineers.
   D in isolation.

My Words

Write the words that are new to you. Look them up in the dictionary and write their definitions.

Words   Definitions

_____   _____

_____   _____

_____   _____

_____   _____

_____   _____

_____   _____

_____   _____

_____   _____

Word Families

noun	enthusiast	Aviation enthusiasts are very interested in flying.
noun	enthusiasm	Turnbull's enthusiasm for aviation kept him searching for a better propeller design.
adjective	enthusiastic	Turnbull was enthusiastic about aviation.
adverb	enthusiastically	The inventor worked enthusiastically to turn his idea into reality.

noun	inflexibility	The inflexibility of early propellers made planes difficult to fly.
adjective	inflexible	The successful inventor cannot be inflexible.
adverb	inflexibly	An inventor should not work inflexibly.

noun	isolation	Inventors often prefer to work in isolation.
verb	isolate	An inventor may need to isolate herself to do her best work.
adjective	isolated	Turnbull set up his lab in an isolated location.

Unit 10

noun	reliance	His reliance on others' work caused some to question his research.
verb	rely	Early pilots could not rely on their planes to carry heavy loads.
adjective	reliable	The Variable-Pitch propeller made planes more reliable.
adverb	reliably	A plane with a Variable-Pitch propeller flew more reliably than earlier planes.

noun	revolution	The invention of the Variable-Pitch propeller led to a revolution in flight.
verb	revolutionize	New inventions revolutionize the way we do things.
adjective	revolutionary	Turnbull's propeller was a revolutionary invention.

noun	variable	Researchers look at different variables in their studies.
verb	vary	Planes carry different kinds of loads, and the size of the load will vary.
adjective	variable	It might be more difficult to fly if the winds are variable.
adverb	variably	Planes carry variably heavy loads.

Word Family Practice

Choose the correct word family member from the list below to complete each blank.

Like most inventors, Wallace Rupert Turnbull was filled with curiosity about many things. He became **1**.......... about designing a propeller that would fly more efficiently, during takeoff and landing as well as while cruising. Propellers on early planes were **2**.......... , that is, the angle could not be changed, so they did not fly efficiently under certain conditions. Because of this, pilots could not always **3**.......... on their planes to perform well. Turnbull worked in an **4**.......... barn in New Brunswick to develop a new kind of propeller. He could **5**.......... the angle, or pitch, of this propeller, which made it efficient under different conditions. Turnbull's invention led to a **6**.......... in flight.

1. enthusiast	enthusiastic	enthusiastically
2. inflexibility	inflexible	inflexibly
3. rely	reliable	reliably
4. isolation	isolate	isolated
5. vary	variable	variably
6. revolution	revolutionize	revolutionary

Word Skill

Prefix *in–*
The prefix *in–* can make the meaning of a word negative.

> *Read the sentences. Write a definition for each underlined word.*

1. Inventing involves trying out different ways of doing things, so it is important for an inventor to be <u>flexible</u>.

    flexible: _____

2. Because the position of the propeller on early airplanes was <u>inflexible</u>, it was always set at the same angle.

    inflexible: _____

Listening

 *Listen to the conversation. Choose **FOUR** letters, **A–G**.*

Which **FOUR** facts about the flight demonstration will the students include in their report?

A the name of the plane's designer

B the names of the passengers

C the number of passengers

D the size of the propeller

E the speed of rotation

F the length of the flight

G the weather conditions

Writing

The charts[1] below show basic information about different models of light sport aircraft and very light jets for aviation enthusiasts.

Summarize[2] the information by selecting and reporting the main information and making comparisons.

Write at least 150 words.

Light Sport Aircraft

Manufacturer	Cruise Speed	Passenger Capacity	Price
Airways	75 mph	0	$39,000
Tiger, Inc.	115 mph	1	$134,000
McGregor	130 mph	1	$194,000

Very Light Jets

Manufacturer	Cruise Speed	Passenger Capacity	Price
Airways	300 mph	2	$900,000
Tiger, Inc.	350 mph	4	$2,250,000
McGregor	425 mph	6	$3,650,000

Speaking

Talk about the following topics.

Do you prefer to work with a group or in isolation? Why?

When you run into a problem with work, do you confer with others or do you prefer to find your own solution?

What makes you feel enthusiastic about your work?

[1]BrE: tables
[2]BrE: summarise

Unit 10

THE TRANSATLANTIC CABLE

Words

> *Look for the following words as you read the passage. Match each word with its correct definition.*

Words

1. cable
2. catastrophic
3. compensate
4. disparate
5. flaw
6. indispensable
7. inexplicably
8. inquiry
9. insulation
10. perseverance
11. rally
12. requisite
13. set out
14. snap
15. tow
16. transmit
17. triumph
18. utterly
19. vilified
20. voltage

Definitions

A. n., material used to prevent passage of electricity, heat, or sound

B. n., a mistake or weakness, especially in design

C. n., continuation with a task despite difficulties

D. v., to make up for; balance out

E. adj., extremely bad

F. n., an official investigation

G. v., to succeed; win

H. v., to gather support

I. adj., different

J. n., a need; requirement

K. v., to send

L. v., to start an activity

M. adv., totally

N. n., measure of electric power

O. v., to pull behind

P. adj., completely necessary

Q. adv., without explanation

R. adj., having one's reputation ruined; being spoken about in a bad way

S. n., wire used for sending electric signals

T. v., to break suddenly

Reading

The Transatlantic Cable

Laying the transatlantic cable was the culmination of the unflagging perseverance of one man leading like-minded men, of disparate technical and scientific advances, and of the need for faster communication. The first attempts at laying the cable in the 1850s, each of which cost an enormous amount of money, failed utterly. Yet as technology and science improved, and the need for faster communication increased, perseverance finally paid off.

The man who rallied support and raised money for the transatlantic cable venture was Cyrus Field, a New York businessman, who started the New York, Newfoundland, and London Telegraph Company in 1854. For the next twelve years, Field raised money and expectations in North America and England for repeated attempts at laying a cable, despite catastrophic cable breaks and a formal inquiry when the first cable stopped working within days.

The scientific and technological advances began with electricity, the study of which was attracting the greatest minds of the age. Samuel Morse invented a code that made it possible to send information over electric wires, and he made the first successful transmission in 1842. The next year, d'Alameida, a Portuguese engineer, announced the use of gutta-percha, a rubberlike sap from the gutta tree, as an insulation for wires. Thus, two of the requisites for an underwater cable were met. In the next several years, telegraph cables were laid in Atlantic Canada, across the English Channel and around Europe, and across the United States.

In 1857, the company Field founded set out to lay the cable that had taken months and almost a million dollars to make. The cable was made of 340,000 miles of copper and iron wire and three tons of gutta-percha insulation, too much for one ship to carry. The cable was divided between two ships, each towed by another, all four provided by the British and American navies. After only 255 miles of cable had been laid, the cable stopped transmitting and then snapped, sinking to the depths of the ocean. The second attempt was made in 1858, beginning at the midpoint of the Atlantic, from which each ship lay cable as she sailed to her home shores. Again, the cable inexplicably stopped working. They tried again a month later, beginning again from the middle and sailing in opposite directions. This time, success! Queen Victoria sent a message to President Buchanan, and both countries celebrated. Within hours, however, the signal began failing. To compensate for the fading

Unit 10

transmissions, Whitehouse, the American engineer, transmitted messages at higher voltages, eventually burning out the cable. Once a hero, Field was now vilified.

Work on the transatlantic cable was halted because of the American Civil War. During the war, the telegraph became indispensable, and enthusiasm for a transatlantic cable mounted. In Scotland, William Thomson, who would later be knighted Lord Kelvin for his work, corrected the design flaws in Whitehouse's cable. Kelvin also designed a mirror-galvanometer that could detect weak currents, thus allowing lower voltages and weaker currents to transmit information. In 1866, the world's largest steamship laid Kelvin's new cable, an unqualified success. Field's perseverance had triumphed in the end.

Answer the questions about **The Transatlantic Cable**.

Questions 1–4

*Look at the following inventors and the list of descriptions below. Match each inventor with the correct description, **A–F**.*

A burned out the first transatlantic cable by using high voltages

B was the first to be utterly successful in getting the transatlantic cable laid

C invented a type of insulation from the sap of a tree

D sent a telegraph message to President Buchanan

E was the first to attempt to have a transatlantic cable laid

F developed a code for transmitting messages by electric cable

_____ 1. Morse

_____ 2. d'Alameida

_____ 3. Field

_____ 4. Kelvin

Questions 5–9

Complete the summary using words from the list below.

In the 1850s, several unsuccessful attempts were made to lay a telegraph cable across the Atlantic Ocean. For the first attempt, a cable was manufactured of copper and iron wire with gutta-percha **5**.......... . It was so heavy that the ships that carried it had to be **6**.......... by other ships. This cable failed because it **7**.......... and sank beneath the sea. The second attempt also failed. The third attempt appeared to be successful, and a message was **8**.......... from England to the United States. However, the telegraph company did not **9**.......... this time either. This attempt also turned out to be a failure when the cable stopped working, and the reputations of the project leaders were vilified.

compensated	rallied	towed	triumph
insulation	snapped	transmitted	voltage

Unit 10

My Words

> *Write the words that are new to you. Look them up in the dictionary and write their definitions.*

Words	Definitions
_____	_____
_____	_____
_____	_____
_____	_____
_____	_____
_____	_____
_____	_____

Word Families

noun	catastrophe	The initial attempts to lay a transatlantic cable ended in catastrophe for Field.
adjective	catastrophic	The failure of the initial attempts to lay the transatlantic cable resulted in a catastrophic loss of money.
adverb	catastrophically	Field failed catastrophically in his attempts to lay a transatlantic cable.

noun	compensation	There is no compensation for hard work and perseverance.
verb	compensate	Hard work can sometimes compensate for bad luck.
adjective	compensative	When the signals began to fade, they took compensative measures to keep the cable working.

noun	insulation	Rubber makes good insulation for an electric wire.
noun	insulator	Rubber is a good insulator.
verb	insulate	It was important to find a practical way to insulate the cable.
adjective	insulated	The transatlantic cable was insulated with gutta-percha.

noun	perseverance	Because of Field's perseverance, a telegraph cable was eventually laid under the Atlantic Ocean.
verb	persevere	An inventor must persevere to turn his ideas into reality.
adjective	perseverant	A perseverant person can find a way to achieve her dreams.

noun	triumph	The laying of the cable in 1866 was a triumph for Kelvin.
verb	triumph	Many people worked hard to make the idea of a transatlantic cable into a reality, and they finally triumphed.
adjective	triumphant	It was a triumphant day when the English queen sent a telegraph message to the American president.
adverb	triumphantly	They triumphantly announced the completion of the project.

Unit 10

Word Family Practice

Choose the correct word family member from the list below to complete each blank.

Invention is all about hard work. An inventor may have a brilliant idea, but he has to test it many times. The process may be filled with **1**.......... . It is the **2**.......... inventor who will eventually be **3**.......... . For example, there were many failed attempts before the transatlantic telegraph cable was successfully manufactured and laid. After a material was found that could suitably **4**.......... the cable, they thought the major difficulties had been solved. However, they met with many more difficulties when they actually tried to put the cable in place. They tried to **5**.......... for the flaws in their method but were unsuccessful. It wasn't until almost ten years later that another group of people succeeded in laying the cable.

1. catastrophes   catastrophic   catastrophically

2. perseverance   persevere   perseverant

3. triumph   triumphs   triumphant

4. insulation   insulate   insulated

5. compensation   compensate   compensative

Word Skill

Phrasal Verbs with set.
Phrasal verbs are made up of two parts: a verb and one or two particles. The meaning of the phrasal verb is usually not related to the meanings of the individual parts.

Phrasal Verb		**Meaning**
set verb	*out* particle	begin a project
set verb	*back* particle	delay
set verb	*up* particle	arrange

> *Choose the correct phrasal verb from the list above to complete each sentence.*

1. The two inventors _____ to design a new kind of cable.

2. They _____ a meeting to talk about their project.

3. The meeting was _____ several days because of bad weather.

Listening

CD 1
Track
31

Listen to the talk. Complete the timeline below.
*Write **NO MORE THAN TWO WORDS AND/OR A NUMBER***
for each answer.

1..... The mayor got the idea for a museum.

1976 The mayor **2**....... to get the requisite money.

1977 A large gift of money was lost.

3..... Construction of the museum began.

4..... museum opened

1998 opening of exhibit on **5**.....

Writing

In your opinion, which is more important for success, perseverance or good luck?

Support your opinion with reasons and examples from your own knowledge or experience.

Write at least 250 words.

Speaking

Talk about the following topics.

What profession do you work in or do you plan to work in? What are the usual requisites for entering this profession?

In your opinion, what personal qualities are indispensable for success in your profession?

APPENDIX

Answer Key

UNIT 1: NATURAL WORLD

Environmental Impacts of Logging

WORDS

1. E	6. D	11. K	16. Q
2. C	7. B	12. S	17. R
3. J	8. G	13. N	18. F
4. M	9. H	14. P	19. O
5. A	10. I	15. T	20. L

READING

1. E	3. D	5. fells	7. habitats
2. B	4. C	6. myriad	8. defense

WORD FAMILIES

1. environment	3. extensive	5. erode
2. pollutants	4. stability	6. Defenders

WORD SKILL

1. remove the forest
2. remove the seeds
3. remove the ice

LISTENING

1. B	2. A	3. C	4. B

WRITING

(sample response)

    Deforestation is a serious problem, and finding a solution to it will not be simple. It involves a lot of different countries and many political and economic factors. However, as individuals we can each make our contribution to the solution. It involves being more responsible about our use of products that come from logging.

Logging companies fell trees so that we can have wood to make a lot of useful products: houses, bags and boxes, writing paper, furniture. We all use these things in our daily lives and would not want to give them up. We can, however, be less wasteful in the way we use these things. Paper products, in particular, offer many opportunities for reusing, recycling, and reducing our use of them.

Many paper products can be reused. We tend to go shopping, carry our purchases home in a paper bag, and then throw the bag away. That means the bag is used only once, when it really has enough life in it to be used several times. We can take the bag with us on our next shopping trip or find other uses for it around the house. This is just one example of a paper product that can be reused.

Recycling is another important part of being less wasteful. Most kinds of household and office paper can be recycled, and these days most cities have recycling centers. Recycling paper is so easy that there is really no excuse not to do it.

Reducing our use of paper might be the most effective action of all. Electronic technology makes a lot of uses of paper unnecessary. We can create documents and read news articles on a computer without using paper. There are many other things we can do in our daily lives, such as using cloth napkins and towels instead of paper ones, to reduce our use of paper.

These actions may seem small compared with the terrible impacts of deforestation. However, they are things that we can each do and that, when added up, really can make a difference.

SPEAKING

(sample response)

I don't get a lot of time to spend in nature, but when I do, I like being in the mountains. When you're in the mountains, you're really far away from everything, from cities, I mean, and civilization. You can really feel like you're in nature. Also, mountains are different from other environments. They're higher up, so you see different kinds of vegetation, and if you go up high enough, there aren't even any trees, just plants low down to the ground. I really enjoy hiking. That's the main reason I like mountains. I like to hike to the top of a mountain, breathe the fresh, cool air, and enjoy the view.

There are a lot of different causes of environmental pollution, so there are a lot of different solutions. One of my favorites is transportation. Cars really pollute the air a lot. They really have an impact on the environment. Think about how it would be if no one drove cars. The air would be really clean! Of course, that won't happen. However, people would drive less if better public transportation was available. If we had good bus and train and subway systems, we would need fewer cars. I think that would be a really important part of any solution.

Bird Migration

WORDS

1. D	6. E	11. H	16. O
2. L	7. J	12. K	17. Q
3. I	8. G	13. R	18. A
4. B	9. S	14. M	19. P
5. T	10. C	15. F	20. N

READING

1. True	4. Not Given	7. B
2. False	5. A	8. A
3. True	6. B	

WORD FAMILIES

1. fascinating	3. migratory	5. navigate
2. observer	4. evolved	

DICTIONARY SKILL

1. B	2. A

LISTENING

1. B	3. E	5. C
2. A	4. D	

WRITING

(sample response)

The chart shows a list of some of the species of birds that can be seen in Woodchuck County in two different seasons: winter and summer. Information is given about eight different species of birds. Three of the species listed—cardinals, crows, and woodpeckers—are observed in both summer and winter. That means that they are probably not migratory birds but live in the region all year. They can tolerate the winter weather in that area. Four of the species listed—bluebirds, mockingbirds, orioles, and vireos—are observed only in the summer. They must be migratory birds that travel to Woodchuck County for their breeding season and spend the winter in another place where the weather is warmer. One species of bird—juncos—is seen in Woodchuck County in the winter but not in the summer. Perhaps it migrates farther north in the summer for its breeding season.

SPEAKING

(sample response)

I think people are fascinated by birds because they seem so free. They can fly, so it seems like they can go anywhere. People can't fly and are stuck on the ground. So birds are very different from us in that way. Some birds are also very beautiful. Some are very colorful. Swans are very graceful. So I think people are also fascinated by birds because of their beauty.

I'm not particularly fascinated by birds. I live in the city, so I don't see any interesting birds around me in my everyday life. I just see those brown and gray city birds. They aren't pretty, and they're a bit dirty, so I don't like them. If I lived somewhere where there were more interesting birds, probably I would be interested in them.

I'm not fascinated by animals in general, but I am a little bit interested in pet cats. I think they have very nice lives. They nap all day on a soft chair or in the sun, and then in the evening they get fed. They just nap and eat. They can chase mice if they feel like it. They can do whatever they like. What a life!

Plant Life in the Taklimakan Desert

WORDS

1. C	6. P	11. K	16. S
2. I	7. N	12. D	17. Q
3. R	8. G	13. T	18. F
4. O	9. B	14. L	19. A
5. H	10. E	15. M	20. J

READING

1. C	3. C	5. D	7. F
2. B	4. B	6. E	

WORD FAMILIES

1. adaptations	3. stress	5. Violent
2. extremely	4. resilience	6. diversity

DICTIONARY SKILL

1. C	2. A	3. B

LISTENING

1. transitional
2. extreme
3. evaporation
4. accumulate

WRITING

(sample response)

The charts show information about the size, rainfall, and temperatures of three deserts on three different continents. At 9,000,000 square kilometers in area, the Sahara Desert in Africa is much larger than the other two deserts shown. The Taklimakan, at 270,000 square kilometers, and the Great Basin, at 305,775 square kilometers, are similar to each other in size. The Taklimakan has the sparsest rainfall, with an average of 1 to 3.8 centimeters per year. The three deserts have similar summer temperatures: 30°C in the Sahara and Great Basin deserts and 25°C in the Taklimakan Desert. However, winters in the Sahara, with an average temperature of 13°C, are much warmer than in the other two deserts, where the average winter temperatures are –8°C and –9°C. The highest temperatures recorded in the Sahara and Great Basin are almost the same: 57°C and 58°C. The other extreme, the lowest recorded temperature, is not shown for those two deserts, but it is shown for the Taklimakan: –26.1°C.

SPEAKING

(sample response)

I don't think I would like to go to the top of a high mountain because I don't like to be cold. And I think climbing high mountains like Mount Everest is dangerous. It might be interesting to visit a desert because I would like to see the different kinds of plants that grow there. I think they would be very unusual and interesting to look at. But I don't like to be too hot, either, so I wouldn't want to stay in the desert for a long time. I don't really like extreme environments. I prefer to be comfortable.

I think people like extreme environments for two reasons. One is adventure. Some people like doing unusual or dangerous things. They want to see if they can climb to the top of high mountains or endure extreme hot or cold. They want to prove how strong they are and how much they can endure. The other reason is interest. Some people are interested in studying unusual plants or animals or rocks, different kinds of things, so they have to go to unusual places to find these things.

I can adapt easily to new climates as long as they aren't extreme! In the wintertime it's very cold in my city. If I have the opportunity, I like to take a vacation at that time and go to a warm place with a nice beach. I certainly can adapt easily to a warm beach climate, especially when I think about the cold weather I have left behind at home! However, I don't like to go anywhere that's too hot, or too cold either. I can't adapt to that.

UNIT 2: LEISURE TIME

Peripheral Vision in Sports

WORDS

1. D	6. N	11. F	16. A
2. I	7. T	12. G	17. L
3. O	8. E	13. B	18. M
4. J	9. S	14. C	19. H
5. Q	10. R	15. K	20. P

READING

1. True
2. False
3. True
4. Not Given
5. False
6. True
7. True

WORD FAMILIES

1. perform
2. demonstrate
3. coordination
4. visual
5. tolerant
6. Complications

WORD SKILL

1. B
2. A
3. A
4. B

LISTENING

1. focus
2. anticipate
3. scan
4. unconsciously

WRITING

(sample response)

People everywhere like watching sports. Many top athletes are admired throughout their countries, and some even have fans all around the world. These athletes are good role models for young people in many ways, although in some ways they can also be a bad example.

Top athletes get the attention of young people. Most children and teenagers like to follow professional sports. Professional athletes become heroes to them, and children want to be like their heroes. This means they will want to play sports, which is good for their health. Playing sports also teaches important lessons such as teamwork and learning how to lose (and win) gracefully. Professional athletes also demonstrate the importance of working hard for your goals, of practicing regularly to become good at something. This is a good example for children to follow.

However, professional athletes are not always good role models. For one thing, the most famous athletes get paid very high salaries, much higher than most normal people can expect to earn. They also get a lot of attention, not only when they play their sports, but in other parts of their lives as well. This can lead children to believe that money and fame are an important part of sports. Children might focus more on these aspects than on the fun of the game or on the challenge of learning how to play well. Then there are those athletes who behave badly. For example, some take drugs to improve their performance in their game. This kind of behavior sends the wrong message to children.

Professional athletes can be very good role models for children, as long as they focus on the positive aspects of playing sports.

SPEAKING

(sample response)

I know that some people find noise distracting, but I actually prefer to study in a noisy environment. I don't know why. When things are quiet, somehow I seem to notice that. It distracts me in a way. But when there is some noise around me—I don't mean loud noise like a rock concert or anything like that, but when I hear people talking in the next room, or people walking down the hall, just people going about their normal activities around me—I feel comfortable. I guess then I know I'm not alone. That feeling of having people around me actually helps me focus on my studies.

Like I said, being in a noisy environment isn't distracting to me, but sudden loud noises, such as the telephone ringing or a car horn honking, really bother me. Then it takes me a few minutes to get my focus back and go on studying. Also, as I mentioned before, quiet can be distracting to me. If there are no noises around me, no people talking or no cars rushing by, I notice the lack of noise. I just don't like it. That's why I don't really like to study at the library. It's too quiet!

I anticipate a big, big change in my study situation. For one thing, I will graduate in a few months. That's a major change. Then, I'm hoping to be able to go to graduate school. I'm working on the applications now, so it will be a while before I find out whether I'm accepted at any of the schools. All the schools I'm applying to are in other countries, so maybe a year from now I'll be living in a foreign country. That would be a huge change. If I don't get accepted at any of the schools, then I'll have to find a job and work for a while and apply to graduate school again. Whatever happens, by next year my life will be very different from what it is now.

History of the Circus

WORDS

1. J	6. C	11. P	16. F
2. E	7. T	12. S	17. B
3. G	8. R	13. A	18. D
4. I	9. N	14. H	19. M
5. L	10. O	15. Q	20. K

READING

1. C	3. B	5. C	7. A
2. A	4. A	6. B	

WORD FAMILIES

1. development	3. trained	5. survived
2. entertained	4. popular	6. permanent

DICTIONARY SKILL

1. B	2. A	3. A	4. B

LISTENING

1. C	2. A	3. A	4. B

WRITING

(sample response)

These days, technology has made it possible for us to be entertained without even leaving our homes. TV, DVDs, and computers can provide us with endless hours of entertainment. It may seem strange that people still like to go out to see live performances such as a circus. The circus, however, can provide things that electronic entertainment cannot.

I think the most attractive aspect of the circus is that, compared with the electronics we are used to, it seems exotic. Seeing a circus is very different from the things we are used to seeing and experiencing in our daily lives. We do not normally get to see live animals, especially trained ones that perform, or real people who dress in funny clothes and do difficult tricks. In ancient times, circus audiences may have been awed to see things they had never even heard of. In modern times, we have heard of these things and have probably even seen them on TV, but we rarely get to see these interesting things in real life.

Going to the circus is a special experience because it is different from the things we normally do. We get to leave the house and go to a special stadium or circus tent. We get to hear all the sounds and smell all the smells and eat all the special circus junk food that is sold before the performance. It takes us out of our daily experience and transports us for a short while to a different world in a way that electronic games or TV shows cannot. It is something that is not available to us every day, and that makes it even more special.

Even though we live in a world filled with modern technology, the circus can still offer us a special and exciting experience.

SPEAKING

(sample response)

In my city, there are a lot of different forms of entertainment. There are movies, theaters, concerts, and nightclubs. It's a big city, so you can find almost anything to do that you want. I suppose a special form of entertainment we have is the summer theater festival. During the summer, there are live theater performances in the park. Some of the shows are free, and others you have to buy tickets for. When festival time comes around, almost everybody goes to at least one of the performances. That's one kind of entertainment we have that's very popular, and everyone talks about it. During the winter holidays, we also have a series of concerts that a lot of people enjoy. Other than those special events, people in my city mostly just enjoy the usual kinds of entertainment that people everywhere like.

I definitely prefer to see live entertainment. I really enjoy going to concerts, and nothing beats seeing a live concert performance. It really makes a difference to be in the same room with the musicians and to be able to watch them as they perform. It's a totally different experience from listening to recorded music. For music, seeing a live performance is really important. For other kinds of entertainment, it doesn't matter to me as much. Going to a play in a theater or watching a movie on TV is all the same to me.

I like to play the guitar, but I don't think I can say that I'm very talented at it. I wish I were, but I enjoy it anyway because I love music. I don't have any other performing arts talents. I have some artistic talents, though. I like to paint and draw, and I'm trying to develop those talents more. I take art classes occasionally. That's about all the talents I have.

Uses of Leisure Time

WORDS

1. E	6. S	11. B	16. L
2. J	7. C	12. T	17. Q
3. D	8. K	13. O	18. H
4. F	9. R	14. G	19. M
5. I	10. N	15. A	20. P

READING

1. C	3. E	5. B
2. B	4. A	6. D

WORD FAMILIES

1. emotional	3. intellectual	5. reluctant
2. industriously	4. deliberate	6. authorities

DICTIONARY SKILL

1. B	3. B
2. A	4. A

LISTEN

1. passive	4. obesity (*or*	5. depression (*or*
2. physical	depression)	obesity)
3. intellectual		

WRITING

(sample response)

The chart shows how much time people of different ages spend engaged in various pastimes. It shows two intellectual activities—reading and computer use. There is also a column for physical activities—sports and exercise. The information is about how people spend their leisure time on weekends. According to the chart, teenagers spend the least amount of time reading, much less than adults do. They spend just five minutes a day reading, whereas adults aged twenty to sixty-five years old spend thirty minutes a day and adults aged sixty-six and older spend an hour a day in this pastime. Teenagers spend more time on the computer than people in the other two age groups—seventy-five minutes a day. The age group that spends the most time engaged in physical activities is adults aged twenty to sixty-five, and the age group that spends the most time reading is adults sixty-six and older. Adults aged sixty-six and older are the ones who spend the least amount of time engaged in physical activities—just twenty minutes a day.

SPEAKING

(sample response)

One of my favorite pastimes is going to the movies. I really enjoy movies of all kinds. I like drama and comedy and action movies. I like going to the movies with my friends and then talking about the movie afterward. We often go to a restaurant or a café and talk about the movie: whether or not we liked it and why, what we thought about the actors, how it compares with other movies, things like that. It's really interesting. So I think I could say that's my favorite pastime. I also like to read, I enjoy watching sports, and sometimes I play a little tennis.

I enjoy both physical and intellectual activities, but I guess I prefer intellectual activities a little more. As I said, I love discussing movies. I also like talking about books I read or articles I read in the newspaper. It's great to spend an evening at a café with my friends talking about these kinds of things. But physical activities are important, too. Maybe I don't do them every day, but I like to get some exercise a few times a week. I like to play tennis or sometimes just take a walk.

UNIT 3: TRANSPORTATION

First Headlamps

WORDS

1. D	6. R	11. F	16. P
2. J	7. H	12. K	17. S
3. C	8. L	13. A	18. Q
4. G	9. N	14. B	19. M
5. O	10. T	15. E	20. I

READING

1. B	3. D	5. C	7. C
2. E	4. A	6. D	8. B

WORD FAMILIES

1. efficiently	3. illuminated	5. intensify
2. innovations	4. reflective	6. generate

DICTIONARY SKILL

1. A	2. B	3. A	4. B

LISTENING

1. A   2. B   3. D   4. F

WRITING

(sample response)

Trains, planes, and automobiles have all become common modes of travel within the past 200 years, and they have all had significant effects on the way we live. If I had to choose which one of these three was the most significant, I would choose automobiles. Automobiles affect the way we live and work, and they affect the way the world around us looks.

Automobiles have given us easy access to many things in our daily lives, so we have more choices about a lot of different things. We can shop at a variety of stores, for example, because we can get to them by car. We do not have to shop only at the stores that are nearby. We have more choices about which doctors we want to have treat us or which lawyer we want to hire or which hairstylist we want to use because automobiles have increased the distances that we can easily travel. We have more choices about places to study or work because we can get to more places by car.

Automobiles have also affected the way the world around us looks. Because so many people depend on automobiles, there are paved roads and parking lots everywhere. This was not true in the days before automobiles. Houses, shopping malls, and apartment buildings are all built with garages attached to accommodate cars. Gas stations are everywhere. The world today looks very different than it did 100 years ago, and much of this is because of the automobile.

Automobiles have made a lot of changes in the way people go about their daily lives. This is why I think the automobile is the most significant transportation innovation of recent times.

SPEAKING

(sample response)

In my city, people generally use buses, bicycles, and cars to get around. In my opinion, bicycles are the most efficient mode of transportation. I say this because there's a lot of traffic on our streets, especially during rush hour. Sometimes the cars and buses don't seem to move at all because there are so many of them. We have terrible traffic jams. For me, however, this isn't a problem because I almost always use my bike to get around. When all the cars and buses are sitting there waiting to move, I speed right by them on my bike. I never get stuck in traffic jams. I get everywhere quickly and efficiently on my bike. I really love it. The only time I don't like riding my bike is when it rains.

I think trains are great for long-distance travel. They're a lot more comfortable than buses because they have more space. You can get up and walk around on a train, but you can't do that on a bus. Trains are more relaxing than cars because you don't have to do the driving yourself and you don't have to deal with traffic jams or worry about getting lost. Trains usually have comfortable seats. They have large windows so you can enjoy the scenery. I love traveling by train.

In my opinion there are very few drawbacks to train travel. Sometimes the tickets are expensive, but that depends on where you're going . Sometimes the schedule isn't completely convenient, but I don't mind changing my plans a little to fit a train schedule. A lot of people don't like trains because they don't give you the same independence that traveling by car does, but I don't mind that.

Major Subways of Europe

WORDS

1. I	6. P	11. T	16. S
2. Q	7. F	12. N	17. O
3. R	8. B	13. A	18. M
4. H	9. K	14. D	19. J
5. C	10. L	15. G	20. E

READING

1. C	3. A	5. B	7. A
2. C	4. B	6. C	

WORD FAMILIES

1. Architects	3. destruction	5. expansion
2. decorative	4. disruption	6. operate

WORD SKILL

1. below the surface of the water
2. a coat of paint below the surface coat of paint
3. a road that passes below another road or structure

LISTENING

1. surface	3. shield
2. vents	4. destroy

WRITING

(sample response)

The chart shows the size of three different subway systems using different measures: track length, number of stations, and number of passengers. Each one of the subway systems shown could be said to be the largest one, depending on which measure you use. The London Underground has the most track, the Paris Metro has the most stations, and the Moscow Metro carries the most passengers. The London Underground has almost twice as much track as the Paris Metro but twenty-five fewer stations, so the stations on the Paris Metro must be much closer together. In fact, of the three systems shown, Paris has the most stations but the least total track length. The Moscow Metro carries twice as many passengers as the London Underground, although it is only about three-quarters the size of the London system. Its trains might be very crowded. Although the Moscow Metro carries the most passengers of the three systems, it has the fewest stations.

SPEAKING

(sample response)

The subway stations in my city do not have interesting architecture, in my opinion. They are very modern, and I don't like that style. It just isn't warm and inviting. It isn't comfortable. It's all straight lines and no pretty decorations. Our train station, on the other hand, has very beautiful architecture. It's an old building and was built in the classical Greek style, which I like very much. It has columns and statues of mythological figures. It's a very interesting building to look at.

Our city library usually has exhibits of paintings and other kinds of art by local artists. It's interesting because they change the exhibits several times a year, so there's often something new to see. I think this is a great way to use space in the library, because a lot of people go there. They get to see what artists in our community are doing. I think there's also work by local artists in our city hall, but the problem with that is that most people don't go there very often. They don't have a reason to go there, so that art doesn't get seen by as many people. The library is a better place. Subway stations would be a good place, too, because most people use the subway. However, in my city, there isn't any artwork in the subway stations, unfortunately.

Electric Cars Around the Globe

WORDS

1. N	6. R	11. H	16. J
2. Q	7. A	12. L	17. S
3. E	8. D	13. M	18. I
4. K	9. P	14. T	19. C
5. B	10. F	15. O	20. G

READING

1. suburban
2. consumed
3. fumes
4. plodding
5. standard
6. embraced
7. commuters

WORD FAMILIES

1. class
2. commuters
3. consume
4. appealing
5. money
6. marked

DICTIONARY SKILL

1. B
2. A
3. B
4. A

LISTENING

1. Urban
2. Commuter
3. Bridge
4. Suburban

WRITING

(sample response)

If more people drove electric cars, that would help solve some of the problems created by gasoline-powered cars. I believe that money, convenience, and education are the three major factors that would persuade more people to drive electric cars.

Money is a powerful incentive. If electric cars are cheaper to buy than gasoline-powered cars, then people will become interested in them. If electricity is cheaper to use than gasoline, then people will want to own electric cars. Clearly, gasoline is becoming more expensive every day. If car manufacturers can produce electric cars cheaply, then the monetary incentives will be in place and more and more people will start buying electric cars.

Convenience is almost as important as money. Electric cars need to be easy to use for them to be appealing. If putting a charge in a car battery is as easy or easier than filling up the tank with gasoline, then people will find electric cars attractive. If electric cars are small and easier to park than larger gasoline-powered cars, that would be another attraction. If people see electric cars as easy to own and easy to use, they will be more interested in buying them.

The third factor is education. People will become more interested in driving electric cars when they understand the problems with gasoline-powered cars. Educating the public about issues of pollution and decreasing oil reserves may persuade more people to consider electric cars.

If people believe that electric cars are cheap and easy to use and if they understand the reasons why we need to move away from gasoline, they will be more likely to embrace them.

SPEAKING

(sample response)

I'm not very interested in cars. I just want something that will take me places. I don't care if a car has flair. I don't care if it can go really fast or what color it is or anything. I just want a car that is easy to take care of and that doesn't need repairs all the time. I know some people are very interested in cars and know all about the different models and the different things that different cars can do, but that's not me. I just need transportation.

I prefer to live in an urban area. I grew up in the city, and I still live there. I can't imagine living anywhere else. A city has everything. It has all kinds of stores so you can buy anything you need. It has movies and theaters and museums and restaurants. All my friends live in the city, and most of my relatives do, too, so I feel like I have everybody nearby. I don't like rural areas. They are so quiet, it makes me feel afraid. And there's nothing to do. There are no stores or museums or anything. And the suburbs just seem so boring. I don't know why anybody would live anywhere that wasn't a city.

UNIT 4: CULTURE

Origins of Writing

WORDS

1. O	6. H	11. K	16. Q
2. G	7. L	12. B	17. P
3. M	8. A	13. N	18. E
4. C	9. F	14. T	19. D
5. J	10. I	15. S	20. R

READING

1. B	4. A	7. A	10. False
2. C	5. C	8. True	
3. A	6. B	9. Not Given	

WORD FAMILIES

1. Excavators
2. agriculture
3. created
4. specialized
5. literate
6. myths

DICTIONARY SKILL

1. A
2. B

LISTENING

1. D
2. A
3. C
4. B
5. E

WRITING

(sample response)

The chart shows literacy rates for the adult population in four different countries, as well as literacy rates for the entire world. It also shows the differences in male and female literacy rates. Two countries have literacy rates higher than the world rate of 82 percent. Country D has almost 100 percent literacy, and the rate is the same for both the male and female populations. Country C has a literacy rate just over 90 percent, but there is a significant difference between the male and female rates. In fact, in all the countries except for Country D, there is a difference between the male and female literacy rates. This reflects the world literacy rates, which show a 10 percent difference between male and female rates. In Countries A and B, the difference between male and female literacy is very large. In Country A there is a 30 percent difference, and in Country B there is a 40 percent difference. Around the world, there are more literate men than literate women.

SPEAKING

(sample response)

Of course it would be best to have a teacher who specializes in the subject being taught and is also very skilled at teaching, but if I had to make a choice, I think I would choose the one who is skilled at teaching. Of course, I assume this teacher would have a certain amount of knowledge about the subject. I think the best teachers are the ones who make their students want to learn and can show them how to learn. If you know how to learn, you can find any information you need. And if you want to learn, you will look for that information. So a teacher might not know every last piece of information about something, but a good teacher can help the students figure out how to find that information. I have had teachers who knew a lot about their subjects but who were so boring that I learned very little from them. To me it didn't matter what they knew. They still didn't help me learn about it.

Clearly, the most basic skills children need to learn to function in modern society are computer skills. Computers in today's world are like books have been, or were. Nowadays, computer literacy is as important as reading and writing. Children have to learn how to use different kinds of software and how to find information on the Internet and things like that. But I also think there is a skill even more basic than that that we need to function in modern society. That skill is the ability to change rapidly. Technology changes rapidly, and we have to keep up with it. Today, we use computers in a certain way, but a few years from now everything might be different and we'll have to adopt new methods of work and communication. What we teach children in school today might not be completely useful by the time they graduate. Learning the skill of changing is as important as anything else.

Hula Dancing in Hawaiian Culture

WORDS

1. R	6. P	11. A	16. Q
2. J	7. C	12. I	17. B
3. O	8. S	13. K	18. E
4. L	9. F	14. T	19. D
5. H	10. G	15. M	20. N

READING

1. D	3. A	5. graceful	7. evidence
2. B	4. B	6. elaborate	

WORD FAMILIES

1. traditional	3. accompaniment	5. celebrations
2. energetically	4. influenced	6. beneficial

DICTIONARY SKILL

1. A	2. B

LISTENING

1. A   2. D   3. E   4. G

WRITING

(sample response)

Celebrations are very important for any society. They bring families together, give people a sense of identity, and provide a break from the usual routines of life.

An important benefit of traditional celebrations is that they give family members opportunities to spend time together. This is especially important in the modern world, where families are becoming more separated. Family members often do not live in the same city, or even the same country, like they did in the past. When there is an important celebration, family members usually want to spend it together. Often they have special family traditions such as preparing special food together or gathering at a certain place. Families look forward to the special days in the year when they can do these things together.

Traditional celebrations give people a sense of identity. Celebrations that are traditional in a certain place or for a certain culture help people feel more connected to their place or their culture. They help people feel like they are part of something that is meaningful.

Celebrations give people a break from their normal routines. Whether it is something that takes place every year or a one-time special event, a celebration is a chance to relax and have fun with friends and relatives. It is something that adds a little bit of excitement to life. Annual celebrations are especially important because they give people something to look forward to throughout the year.

Humans have been enjoying celebrations since ancient times. Celebrations are important to individuals, families, and society as a whole.

SPEAKING

(sample response)

At the beginning of the year, New Year's Day celebrations are important. Everybody enjoys this celebration because we stay up and have a party until very late. We want to be awake at midnight when the new year begins, and the party usually continues past that hour. Another very important day in my country is Independence Day. Everybody in the whole country is excited when that day is approaching. It's a day with a lot of meaning for us. We have many other traditional celebrations throughout the year. We really like to celebrate in my country!

In my country, Mexico, we celebrate the Day of the Dead at the beginning of November. It's the day when we remember our loved ones who have died. The traditional ritual is to make an altar in the house. We put

*special food on the altar and things that remind us of our dead loved
ones. We decorate it with yellow flowers and other traditional decorations. Some people make very beautiful altars. It's a very old tradition.*

The Art of Mime

WORDS

1. C	6. F	11. A	16. L
2. K	7. G	12. E	17. T
3. M	8. S	13. P	18. D
4. I	9. H	14. R	19. Q
5. N	10. J	15. B	20. O

READING

1. gestures	4. abstract	7. renowned
2. literal	5. emerged	8. merged
3. humorous	6. culminated	

WORD FAMILIES

1. exaggerate	3. considerable	5. frailties
2. effectively	4. portray	6. reminisce

DICTIONARY SKILL

1. B	3. A
2. A	4. B

LISTENING

1. props	3. gestures	5. conflict
2. illusions	4. portray	

WRITING

(sample response)

   The chart shows ticket sales at the National Theater for the six-month
period from January through June. The most popular group of performers during that time was the National Mime Troupe. Five thousand tickets were sold for their performance titled "Humorous Situations." Only
half as many tickets were sold for the performance of *Carmen*, put on by
the City Opera. That was the least popular of all the performances listed
on the chart. The second least popular performance was "Works of
Beethoven" by the National Symphony Orchestra, with 3,000 tickets
sold. The "Rock Stars Live!" concert and the *Swan Lake* ballet were both

almost as popular as the "Humorous Situations" mime performance. There were 4,750 tickets sold for each of those performances. Opera and classical music do not appear to be very popular forms of entertainment at the National Theater. People appear to prefer less serious forms of entertainment such as humorous mime and rock music.

SPEAKING

(sample response)

I usually prefer to see humorous performances. I like to see funny things and hear jokes. If I spend the money and time to go to the theater to see a live performance, then I want to have a good time. I want to laugh. I want to relax and forget about my worries. I actually enjoy serious performances, too. The most important thing, really, is to have the chance to watch skilled performers. But I choose to see humorous performances more often than serious ones.

My country is small. We have some renowned actors and musicians whom we really love, but they're known only to people in our country. They aren't famous in other places. We also enjoy performers from other countries. We like the famous Hollywood actors and musicians from different places. We like all the international stars, just like people everywhere.

I like both kinds of movies. I like real stories and made-up ones, but I particularly enjoy movies that portray real events and people from history. I enjoy seeing what life was like during a different period in history. I like to see what the houses looked like, the clothes, the towns and cities, all the details of daily life. I especially enjoy movies that show those details and show them correctly, that make the effort to really show what life was like. Historical events are interesting to learn about, but to me learning about the details of daily life in the past is even more interesting.

UNIT 5: HEALTH

Nurse Migration

WORDS

1. N	6. I	11. D	16. T
2. K	7. C	12. M	17. G
3. P	8. S	13. Q	18. O
4. B	9. J	14. A	19. H
5. L	10. E	15. R	20. F

READING

1. shortage
2. abroad
3. lure

4. qualified
5. administered
6. rudimentary

7. True
8. False
9. Not Given

WORD FAMILIES

1. short
2. complexities

3. rampant
4. vacate

5. qualified

WORD SKILL

1. a situation where something stops or stands still
2. a person or thing that is much better than all others

LISTENING

1. 4
2. 25

3. 5
4. 114,000

WRITING

(sample response)

The salaries paid to nurses and doctors vary widely, according to the information in the chart. The two countries with the lowest salaries, Country A and Country B, are source countries. They provide a supply of health care workers to the destination countries. The salaries paid to doctors and nurses in these source countries are much lower than the salaries paid in Country C and Country D, which are destination countries. The salaries in Country A are much lower even than the salaries in Country B. In Country B, nurses earn ten times as much as in Country A. The difference in doctors' salaries is even greater.

The difference in salaries between the source countries and the destination countries is greater still. Nurses in Country D, for example, earn almost ten times as much as nurses in Country B. Doctors in Country D earn almost fifteen times as much as doctors in Country B. It is easy to see why source countries have a hard time retaining health care professionals. From the standpoint of the doctors and nurses, working abroad is a much better deal.

SPEAKING

(sample response)

I am a journalist. I chose this profession for several reasons. First, I like to write and always have, ever since I was a small child. I'm also interested in politics and current events. I like to keep up with what's happen-

ing and analyze different political situations, and I love telling people my opinion about things. As a journalist, I get to do all these things that I really love: write, follow the news, and tell people my opinion. It's great!

Because I am just starting out in my profession, I hope things will change a lot for me over the next decade. Right now I have a job as a reporter for a small newspaper in my city. I hope that in ten years I will be working for a much larger newspaper. I also hope by then to be working as a foreign correspondent, reporting the news from abroad. That's really my biggest goal. I think I can make it in ten years.

My profession offers a lot of opportunities for working abroad. A lot of people are lured to journalism because they are interested in traveling to other countries. As I mentioned, that's a primary goal for me, too. Some journalists live abroad and report the news regularly back to the newspaper in their own country. Other journalists don't live abroad but travel regularly, depending on where the news is happening. There is always important news happening all over the world, so journalists get to travel a lot if that's what they want to do.

Aerobic Exercise and Brain Health

WORDS

1. I	6. T	11. K	16. S
2. P	7. B	12. H	17. N
3. A	8. F	13. R	18. C
4. G	9. L	14. E	19. O
5. M	10. J	15. Q	20. D

READING

1. mood
2. regulates
3. concentrations
4. gravity
5. capacity
6. deterioration
7. diagnosed
8. counteract

WORD FAMILIES

1. mood
2. indicate
3. diagnosis
4. grave
5. impairment

DICTIONARY SKILL

1. B
2. A
3. B
4. A

LISTENING

1. Clark	3. yoga	5. weight
2. aerobic	4. mood	

WRITING

(sample response)

The chart shows information about two groups of patients who were suffering from mild cognitive impairment. Each group followed a program of one hour of daily exercise for six months, but they did different kinds of exercise. Group A did aerobic exercise, and Group B did non-aerobic exercise. The charts show changes in mental capacity in each group after six months of exercise. Group A showed improvement in two areas: thinking speed and word fluency. Capacity in memory did not change. Group B had a much worse experience, because there was deterioration in all three areas. This information shows that aerobic exercise can have positive effects on mental capacity for patients suffering from cognitive impairment. Although it did not help patients improve their memory, it appeared to at least stave off deterioration in this area. Non-aerobic exercise had no positive effects, and the patients' mental capacity continued to deteriorate during the study.

SPEAKING

(sample response)

I think that exercise improves my mood. I play soccer often with my friends, and I always feel really good afterward. Of course, there are other factors. It's great to spend the time with my friends, and if we win a game, that makes me feel really good. But I think the exercise affects my mood, too. Even if I go for a run by myself, it puts me in a better mood. Other things that help improve my mood are listening to music, if it's happy music, of course, or energetic music. Sad music would only make me feel worse. Watching funny movies usually helps me feel better, too.

I'm not sure if improving brain capacity will make exercising more popular. Exercise won't make you smarter, at least I don't think it will; it just slows the deterioration of the brain as you get older. That's probably important for older people, but younger people are more interested in other things. Some people like to exercise, but a lot of people don't, or they don't have time for it. I don't think this research will change that. I think people will just keep doing whatever they did previously. Some will exercise and others won't, depending on whether or not they enjoy it.

Personally, I think exercising is important and I try to get regular exercise. However, I also think it's up to each individual to choose whether or not to exercise. All the information is there. Everybody knows the benefits of exercise or can easily find them out. If some people choose not to exercise, they're the ones who have to live with the results of that. They might have poor health or be more depressed or something like that, but it's their choice. I think information should always be made available, but after that, each person has to decide what he or she will do with that information.

How Drugs Are Studied

WORDS

1. E	6. P	11. Q	16. K
2. D	7. H	12. M	17 R
3. O	8. T	13. C	18. J
4. L	9. A	14. I	19. N
5. S	10. B	15. F	20. G

READING

1. B	3. F	5. A	7. B
2. C	4. G	6. D	

WORD FAMILIES

1. investigate	3. absorption	5. desire
2. theory	4. toxins	

DICTIONARY SKILL

1. B	2. A	3. C

LISTENING

1. culture	2. Monitor	3. Ascertain	4. outcome

WRITING

(sample response)

Modern medicine has made it possible for people to live longer lives. Drugs have been developed to cure many common diseases and allieviate many chronic conditions. This has obvious benefits for individuals, but the benefits for society are a bit less certain.

Because of modern medicine, people nowadays not only live longer but live healthier lives, too. Fewer people die young of communicable diseases because there are drugs to cure or prevent such diseases. The lives of many older people are enhanced by medicine that prevents or controls many of the conditions that can cause illness in the elderly.

Modern medicine has enabled many people to have many more years to enjoy their lives. Most individuals would agree that this is a desirable outcome.

On the other hand, more people living longer means that a larger fraction of society is made up of older people. If many of these people are past retirement age, that means they are no longer making an economic contribution to society. However, they still require support for themselves. Many people living longer also means that the population is larger. The longer people live, the more resources they use, and society must find a way to provide for their needs.

Modern medical science aims to help people live longer lives and healthier lives, too. This is a good thing in many ways, but it is a situation that also has many complications.

SPEAKING

(sample response)

I think it is important to spend money on investigating new drugs, of course. After all, drugs can cure many diseases and allieviate many conditions. But we also need to think about prevention. It would be a good idea to spend more money on educating the public about things that can be harmful to the health, such as smoking, or drinking too much, or eating junk food. There is education about those things, but people still smoke and drink and do other things that are unhealthy. People need to really understand the effects of bad habits. Too many people have chronic diseases because they drink too much or eat the wrong kind of food. I really think education is an important part of health care.

I think when people live healthy lifestyles, they get sick less frequently. I think targeting dietary and exercise habits is really important. Lack of exercise and a poor diet can have different kinds of negative outcomes. For example, they can lead to obesity, being overweight, which can cause heart disease. Poor diet can also lead to diabetes, which is a serious health problem. I think encouraging people to eat well and exercise frequently are important areas to focus on.

Doctors can give injections that prevent influenza, so everyone should get these injections. That's the easiest way to combat this disease, and many other diseases, too. There are injections to prevent many of the most common diseases. People also need to be educated about good habits to prevent spreading disease, such as washing their hands, or staying home if they are sick. There are some common diseases, such as the common cold, that can't be cured or prevented with an injection. Scientists need to keep investigating these diseases until they discover a way to cure them.

UNIT 6: TOURISM

Hiking the Inca Trail

WORDS

1. D	6. C	11. T	16. N
2. L	7. O	12. K	17. G
3. S	8. I	13. Q	18. J
4. E	9. B	14. P	19. R
5. H	10. A	15. M	20. F

READING

1. ceremonial	4. draw	7. marvels
2. archeologist	5. network	8. preserve
3. functions	6. adventurous	9. luxury

WORD FAMILIES

1. access	3. luxurious	5. precisely
2. restricted	4. archeological	6. adventure

DICTIONARY SKILL

1. B	2. A	3. B	4. A

LISTENING

1. network	2. Access	3. ceremonial	4. Native

WRITING

(sample response)

The preservation of archeological sites is extremely important. The reason is quite simple: Once they are gone, they are gone forever. Those who hope to preserve such sites need to provide education so that the public understands their importance.

Archeological sites contain buildings and objects that have been around for a long time, for thousands of years in some cases. They provide us with a connection to past civilizations, to the people who came before us. They contain valuable information about our ancestors and where we came from. If we lose this information, we lose the possibility of learning many things about our history. It is terrible to think that something that has lasted for thousands of years can be destroyed in a relatively short period of time by the idle curiosity of modern tourists.

Often people are interested in visiting these sites because it is a popular thing to do. They are not drawn to a place out of respect or appreciation for what it represents. They go because everyone else goes or because they want an interesting adventure. Therefore, education is very important. People need to understand the meaning and value of these ancient sites and the impact that tourism has on them. This is an important part of preserving these sites. Then, if access to the sites is restricted, perhaps people will understand the reasons why and will not protest it so much. Whether or not the general public agrees, however, everything possible must be done to preserve archeological sites.

SPEAKING

(sample response)

I'm not really interested in outdoor adventures like hiking or rafting. I don't like physical danger. For me a really interesting adventure is to visit a new city where I've never been before. I like trying to find my way around a new place. I enjoy trying to figure out the people and what life is like in that city and where the interesting places are to go. It's not a dangerous kind of adventure at all, but it's interesting, and it's even more interesting and exciting when you're visiting a city in a foreign country.

When I travel, I like to stay in really comfortable hotels. I like the hotels that have really comfortable rooms with high-quality sheets and blankets on the bed. I like hotels that have really good personal service, and most of all I like hotels with good food. It's a special luxury to order breakfast from room service. I don't mind paying more for a luxury hotel. Staying in a hotel like that is half the fun of traveling.

It's not really important to me to have luxuries in my daily life. Most of the time I'm very practical. I just live a normal life with normal things, and that's okay with me. But I do like to have luxuries on special occasions, like staying in a luxury hotel when I'm traveling, or going to an expensive restaurant on my birthday. When you save luxuries for special occasions, then they're more appreciated. When you have them every day, like driving around in an expensive car, for example, then they don't seem so special any more. You don't even notice them, and they stop feeling luxurious.

What Is Ecotourism?

WORDS

1. L	6. D	11. I	16. R
2. Q	7. E	12. S	17. J
3. M	8. G	13. K	18. A
4. T	9. B	14. N	19. C
5. O	10. H	15. P	20. F

READING

1. False	4. True	7. True
2. True	5. True	8. True
3. Not Given	6. False	9. Not Given

WORD FAMILIES

1. avoidance	4. wild
2. concept	5. injury
3. accommodations	6. publicize

DICTIONARY SKILL

1. C   2. A   3. B

LISTENING

1. Wilderness	3. accommodations
2. January	4. publicity

WRITING

(sample response)

The charts show whether or not three different cruise companies follow certain environmentally friendly practices, and they compare this information in two different years: 2000 and 2010. In 2000, two of the companies were already recycling most of their waste and avoiding dumping wastewater into the sea. These companies were Sun Cruises and Water World Tours. The Sea Adventure company did not follow these practices. None of the three companies had systems to reduce air pollution in 2000, and none of them avoided traveling to places with delicate underwater ecosystems. By 2010, all three companies had made changes to become more environmentally friendly. In fact, in that year, two of the companies, Sun Cruises and Water World Tours, were following all the practices shown on the chart. Sea Adventure was recycling waste and avoiding dumping wastewater into the sea, but they still did not have a system to reduce air pollution and still traveled to destinations with delicate underwater ecosystems. Sun Cruises and Water World Tours are probably more attractive to people who are interested in ecotourism than Sea Adventure is.

SPEAKING

(sample response)

I always choose to spend my vacations somewhere in the wilderness. I live in a big city, and I'm surrounded by crowds and noise all the time, so when I'm on vacation, I want to be in a really quiet place. I try to find as remote a place as possible. I like hiking and camping in the mountains. Once I went on a rafting trip on a river. Really, I'm happy spending my vacation anywhere out in the woods.

When I travel, I avoid any place with crowds. That doesn't mean just cities. Some national parks can get very crowded, too, and then you don't feel like you're in the wilderness. I try to avoid taking my vacation in the summer because that's when everyone else travels and every place is crowded. I like to travel in the fall. It's a beautiful time of year, and it's much easier to avoid crowds then.

Luxury accommodations aren't important to me. In fact, they make me feel a little uncomfortable because I'm not used to them. I like everything plain and simple and especially inexpensive. My favorite place to stay when I'm traveling is in my tent. For one thing, it's inexpensive. For another, it allows me to be in the middle of nature. I go to sleep at night to the sound of the wind blowing through the trees above me. I wake up in the morning surrounded by birdsong. What could be better than that?

Learning Vacations

WORDS

1. F	6. G	11. M	16. A
2. I	7. R	12. T	17. S
3. K	8. B	13. P	18. C
4. O	9. J	14. Q	19. N
5. D	10. L	15. H	20. E

READING

1. A	4. False	7. True
2. B	5. True	
3. E	6. Not Given	

WORD FAMILIES

1. acquire	3. economize	5. residence
2. cost	4. Enrollment	6. supervision

DICTIONARY SKILL

1. A   2. B

LISTENING

1. resort	3. Sponsor
2. Residential	4. Enrollment

WRITING

(sample response)

The chart shows the percentage of the total number of students who enrolled in different types of courses during the summer of 2010. The most popular type of course was cuisine. Thirty-five percent of students enrolled in cuisine courses. Science and philosophy had the lowest enrollment, at 5 percent each. In general, the creative types of courses had higher enrollments. Cuisine, photography, and painting and drawing are all courses where students learn how to do creative things. Taken all together, these courses made up 80 percent of the total enrollment. The courses with more serious content, on the other hand, were much less popular. History, philosophy, and science are all academic types of courses, the kinds of things one might study in a college degree program. Only 20 percent of students signed up for these courses. Perhaps during the summer people prefer to spend their time taking a more relaxing type of course.

SPEAKING

(sample response)

I'm from the coast, so the cuisine of my city is all about seafood. We have a lot of different fish dishes. We are famous for a special kind of seafood stew that we make. We enjoy this dish on all our national holidays. There are also some different kinds of baked fish dishes that are famous in my city. We have a variety of seafood dishes, and tourists always eat them when they come to our city.

Different kinds of fish, of course, are the most common ingredients in our cuisine. Almost all our traditional fish dishes contain garlic, so that's another common ingredient. Also, we eat almost everything with rice. Besides that, because it's a tropical area, we have a lot of tropical fruits that we use in our cooking—mangoes, coconuts, things like that. They're common ingredients in stews and soups as well as in desserts.

We still enjoy the traditional fish dishes that our city has always been famous for, but we use more modern cooking methods now. Instead of cooking over a fire, people usually cook on a gas stove or in a microwave oven. People now have more access to ingredients from other places, for example, different kinds of spices that are common in other countries—people in my country are used to them now, too. They aren't traditional flavors for us, but they're becoming more common in our cooking. I think in the past, people ate the traditional dishes more often, maybe even every day. Now we're so busy, we don't have time to cook as often, so we eat those traditional dishes less often, maybe once a week or even once a month. In the future, I think this will be even more true. People will eat more fast food and more frozen food from the grocery store. They'll have less and less time to cook the traditional dishes, and maybe they'll even forget how to cook them. I hope not, but it could happen.

UNIT 7: BUSINESS

What Makes a Small Business Successful?

WORDS

1. I	6. R	11. O	16. N
2. S	7. A	12. L	17. P
3. D	8. F	13. Q	18. C
4. E	9. M	14. B	19. H
5. G	10. K	15. T	20. J

READING

1. B	3. B	5. potential	7. financial
2. D	4. unique	6. sound	

WORD FAMILIES

1. initiate	3. compete	5. profitable
2. motivation	4. produce	6. inevitable

DICTIONARY SKILL

1. B	2. A

LISTENING

1. A	2. C	3. E	4. G

WRITING

(sample response)

Many people enjoy shopping in large chain stores, whereas many others have a great dislike for them. Large chain stores offer a number of advantages to shoppers. However, they also have several drawbacks.

One of the advantages of large chain stores is that they generally offer a wider selection of products than smaller, locally owned businesses do. Because a chain store is owned by a large company, it has access to many more sources of products than its smaller competitors do. This allows it to offer a greater variety of products on the store shelves. Chain stores can also sell products in their stores at lower prices. One reason is that, being part of a large company, it is easier for them to seek out the manufacturers that charge less. Another reason is that they get discounts for buying in very large quantities.

Chain stores also have disadvantages. They cannot offer the personalized services that small stores can. People who run small stores are very familiar with the products they sell. They can make knowledgeable recommendations to their customers, they can answer questions about the products, and they can special-order items. Employees in chain stores, on the other hand, usually know very little about the items they sell. They often cannot help customers beyond telling them in which part of the store something is located.

Chain stores make things more convenient for shoppers, but they also have the effect of making things less personal. A place that has a balanced mix of large and small stores, if it exists, would offer shoppers the best of both worlds.

SPEAKING

(sample response)

A store where I enjoy shopping is a large bookstore near my house. One characteristic that draws me to it is that it is a welcoming place. Anyone can go there and spend as long as he or she wants. No one bothers you if you sit down with a book and spend a long time reading it. You might buy it or you might not. No one bothers you about it. It's a place where you can feel comfortable just relaxing. Another thing I like is that it has all kinds of books as well as magazines and CDs. Whatever mood I'm in, I'm sure to find something I feel like looking at or buying. The best thing of all is the coffee shop. They sell great coffee and pastries. It's a nice place to spend a Sunday afternoon, reading and sipping coffee, no pressure, just relaxation.

I think it's important to spend money on clothes. I mean professional clothes. The clothes you wear are an important part of your professional image. Your clothes aren't, of course, as important as your professional skills and experience, but they really add to it. I mean, if you look like a professional, people will believe you are one. They will pay more attention to what you can do than if you dress like a slob. I always spend a lot of money on business suits. I buy suits with a good cut and high-quality material. It's really worth the money.

If you're going to spend a lot of money on something, you have to be sure you know what you're buying. It doesn't matter if it's clothes or a car or a house. You want to make sure you're getting what you want. So, you have to do research. Find out what the clothes are made of or which car goes the fastest or if the house is in good condition. Think about why it's worth it to you to spend money on this product, and then make sure that the one you buy has these characteristics. One thing I do before I spend a lot of money on something is find a friend or relative who knows about the thing I want to buy. Before I bought a car, for example, I talked to my uncle because he owns a car similar to the one I wanted. I asked him about his experience with it and how he bought it. That helped me a lot when I finally bought my car. Doing research and asking advice from experienced people are, I think, the most important tips.

Brand Loyalty

WORDS

1. H	6. B	11. I	16. Q
2. K	7. C	12. J	17. A
3. R	8. N	13. S	18. T
4. E	9. F	14. D	19. M
5. P	10. G	15. O	20. L

READING

1. Not Given	4. True	7. True
2. True	5. True	8. True
3. False	6. Not Given	

WORD FAMILIES

1. thirst	3. passionate	5. loyal
2. selectively	4. consistent	6. prevail

WORD SKILL

1. perform better
2. sell better
3. are greater in number

LISTENING

1. status	3. selective
2. endorsements	4. passionate

WRITING

(sample response)

The charts show reasons for consumers' decisions when choosing a mobile phone. The information is given for two different countries. In Country A, price is the top reason, with 50 percent of consumers mentioning it as the most important factor in buying a phone. Brand is the least popular reason, with only 7 percent of consumers mentioning it as the most important factor. Brand loyalty is also low in Country B, although a bit higher than in Country A. In Country B, 19 percent of consumers mention brand as the most important factor in choosing a mobile phone. The top reason in Country B is design, which is the most important factor for 40 percent of consumers. Price, the top reason in Country A, is the least important reason in Country B. Only 9 percent of consumers in that country mentioned price as the most important factor in choosing a mobile phone.

SPEAKING

(sample response)

I like to run. I run almost every day for exercise, so the shoes I wear for running are really important. If my running shoes don't fit me right, I could have a lot of problems. It's not just about comfort, but I could have a lot of physical problems if I don't wear the right shoes, because I run every day. That's why I'm loyal to a certain brand of running shoes. I've found a company that makes shoes that fit me just right. I really like them. I always buy that brand of shoes because I know they're exactly what I want. I think that's the only case where I have brand loyalty. Other things aren't as important to me. I might choose something because the price is right or I like the way it looks or something like that, but not usually because of the brand. I'm really selective only about running shoes.

Celebrity endorsements are used a lot in promoting products, so they must persuade a lot of people to buy certain brands. Some people pay a lot of attention to celebrities; they really admire them and want everything their favorite celebrities have. Some people think that a celebrity endorsement means that the product is better or more popular. But it doesn't convince me. It makes no difference to me what a movie star or athlete buys. Anyhow, I don't think celebrities really buy those things. They make an endorsement, but that doesn't mean they really use the product.

Global Outsourcing

WORDS

1. R	6. M	11. P	16. T
2. K	7. O	12. J	17. I
3. C	8. E	13. A	18. H
4. G	9. B	14. S	19. L
5. N	10. Q	15. F	20. D

READING

1. wealthy	4. boon	7. catch up
2. enticing	5. confront	
3. remainder	6. turnover	

WORD FAMILIES

1. decision
2. oppose
3. controversial
4. preponderantly
5. routine
6. enticement

DICTIONARY SKILL

1. B
2. A
3. B
4. A

LISTENING

1. 1900
2. night shift
3. 1915
4. decisive
5. employee turnover

WRITING

(sample response)

Outsourcing of labor to other countries has become a common practice. The advantages and disadvantages of this practice depend on your point of view. The effects on a customer or worker in the company's home country are different from the effects on the people in other countries that do the outsourced labor.

There are both advantages and disadvantages for people in the company's home country. For the company's customers, there may be the advantage of lower prices. If the company saves money on labor, then it can offer lower prices to its customers. On the other hand, there are some disadvantages when a company outsources customer services to a foreign country. There can be difficulties with communication when the customer service provider does not understand the customer's language or culture very well. In addition to disadvantages for customers, there is the serious disadvantage for workers, who become unemployed when their jobs are sent to workers abroad.

For workers doing the outsourced labor, the significant advantage, of course, is that outsourced labor provides them with opportunities for employment. But there are some disadvantages to this sort of work. Especially for customer service work, employees might have to work night shifts to provide service to customers in a different time zone. In addition, difficulties with understanding a foreign language and culture affect the workers as well as the customers.

The reason that companies outsource labor is that they gain a big advantage—lower costs. The needs of customers and employees are probably not considered. However, customers and employees both feel the effects of this practice.

SPEAKING

(sample response)

    A decisive moment in my life is when I chose my career. This really was the most difficult decision of my life. My father always wanted me to be a doctor. Ever since I was a child, I knew that this was his plan for me. I always accepted it because it was what my father wanted. However, in high school I realized that I didn't want to be a doctor. There was nothing about it that interested me. I decided that I wanted to study architecture and learn how to design buildings. I was afraid to tell my father this because I knew he really wanted me to be a doctor. But I really wanted to study architecture, and I actually applied to be an architecture student. When I was accepted into the program, I knew I had to tell my father. So, I finally dared to tell him. He wasn't very happy about it, but he accepted my decision because he saw how much I wanted to do it. It was a difficult thing for me to do, to ruin my father's dream, but I knew I had to follow my own dream. Now I'm glad I did, and I think my father is, too.

    There are a number of little difficulties I confront every day in my life as a university student. The first one is getting to my morning classes on time, because I like to sleep late. Some days I have class at 8:00 in the morning. I really don't like that. Another difficulty is trying to get all my assignments done. I always have so much studying to do—reading articles and writing research papers and preparing presentations. They give us a lot of work to do, and it isn't always easy to find time to do it all. That's the biggest difficulty, I think. I don't have much difficulty with the content of my classes. I think they're really interesting. And I get along with most of my classmates and my professors. Mostly I enjoy university life—just the workload is sometimes too much.

UNIT 8: SOCIETY

Social Networking

WORDS

1. D	6. F	11. J	16. C
2. H	7. G	12. R	17. E
3. B	8. A	13. S	18. I
4. P	9. K	14. N	19. L
5. M	10. O	15. T	20. Q

READING

1. C	4. A	7. acquaintances
2. D	5. exploded	8. pursue
3. B	6. immense	9. interact

WORD FAMILIES

1. interactions
2. explosion
3. adolescent
4. Statisticians
5. eradicated
6. immensely

WORD SKILL

1. carry on
2. carry out
3. carry through

LISTENING

1. contact
2. pursue
3. community
4. acquaintances

WRITING

(sample response)

The chart shows the percentage of each site's total membership in three different age groups: adolescent, younger adult, and older adult. The statistics show that each site attracts more members of a particular age group. Site A is apparently more popular with younger adults than with adolescents or older adults. Close to half of the members of that site fall into the younger adult age group. Site B is much more popular with older adults than with people of other ages, since two-thirds of its members belong to that age group. At the same time, the site has very few adolescent members—only 7 percent of its total membership. Site C seems to be the site that draws the most adolescent members. More than half of its members are adolescents. A little more than one-third are younger adults. However, very few are older adults—only 10 percent of its total membership.

SPEAKING

(sample response)

The kind of information I exchange with my friends online is usually just everyday information. I tell them what I did today or what my plans for the weekend are. If I go someplace interesting or do something fun, then I take photos and post them online. My friends and I post a lot of photos online. It's fun to see what everyone has been doing. Sometimes if I need some special kind of information, like I want to buy something expensive or if I'm looking for a job, then I post that online and ask my friends for help or advice.

I think it's really important for parents to pay attention to what their kids do online. Adolescents, especially, like to use the Internet a lot. It's the main way they communicate with their friends, but there are a lot of dangers for them online and they're too young to understand that. Parents should know what their kids do online, what sites they like to visit, what acquaintances they make. Maybe they should impose limits about how much time their kids spend online. Knowing how to use the Internet is important, but it's also important to spend time doing other things.

I'm sure the trend will continue, but I can't say exactly how it will unfold. Things change so rapidly. But I believe that online social networking has already become a really important form of communication. Perhaps in the near future it will become the way that most of us find jobs. Maybe it will be the way that we find our husbands and wives. There are a lot of possibilities.

Why Are Women Leaving Science Careers?

WORDS

1. F	6. D	11. O	16. J
2. N	7. E	12. T	17. B
3. I	8. H	13. Q	18. G
4. S	9. K	14. R	19. P
5. C	10. M	15. A	20. L

READING

1. C	4. Not Given	7. False
2. E	5. True	
3. B	6. True	

WORD FAMILIES

1. equality	3. frustrated	5. validation
2. persisted	4. guide	6. approximate

DICTIONARY SKILL

1. A   2. B

LISTENING

1. C	3. A
2. B	4. B

WRITING

(sample response)

Women are an invaluable part of the workforce. We need the contributions that they make. Women should be allowed to devote some of their time and attention to their families without losing opportunities or status at work. The best way to do this, in my opinion, is for governments to pass laws requiring companies to support the needs of women.

Although attitudes have changed a little in some places, modern women continue to bear more responsibilities at home than men do. That is a fact of life in most parts of the world. I think the best thing we can do is acknowledge this situation and provide women with the support they need to meet these responsibilities. That is the only fair way because women's home responsibilities are as important to society as their professional jobs are.

Companies could be required by law to support women's needs. For example, they could be required to allow women time off when they have babies. They could be required to provide child care at the company so women could be close to their babies but still do their work. They could be required to allow mothers (and fathers, too) flexible schedules so that they can meet their children's needs: visit their schools, take them to doctor's appointments, and things like that.

Passing laws that require companies to support women's needs would show that society values women's contributions, both at home and at work. Because everybody benefits from women's work, it seems the fairest thing to do.

SPEAKING

(sample response)

The most important career advice I have received was given to me when I was quite young. I was still in high school. I will always remember it. I was thinking about the university and trying to decide what I would want to study. My uncle told me to choose a career that was interesting to me and not to worry about what other people might say. He said a lot of people might try to influence me to choose certain careers for a lot of different reasons but to always remember that it would be my career. I would have to devote the years to studying for it, and then I would devote the rest of my life to working in it. I should choose something that I wanted to do, that I thought I would like, and I shouldn't choose something based on other people's reasons. That advice seems simple, but it's very important, and I can say it's helped me because I really enjoy my job now.

I'm a lawyer and there are a lot of pressures in this profession. Time is a big pressure. We have a lot of deadlines, and we always have to get a lot of work done in a short time. Another pressure is staying current. Laws and regulations change all the time, and we have to know about the changes, so we have to pay attention. I think those are the two biggest pressures, time and paying attention to changing laws. Then there are the daily pressures of any job, finding new clients, getting along with everyone at the office, things like that.

Wheelchair-Accessibility Issues

WORDS

1. G	6. I	11. D	16. J
2. T	7. P	12. A	17. K
3. L	8. E	13. B	18. M
4. F	9. R	14. C	19. O
5. S	10. N	15. H	20. Q

READING

1. A	4. recreation	7. updated
2. B	5. switches	
3. B	6. ramps	

WORD FAMILIES

1. incapacitation	3. disabled	5. slipperiness
2. necessarily	4. capable	

DICTIONARY SKILL

1. B	2. A	3. A	4. B

LISTENING

1. A	2. C	3. E	4. F

WRITING

(sample response)

Ninety percent of the people without disabilities in this country are employed. At 85 percent, the employment rate among non-severely disabled people is not a great deal lower. However, severely disabled people have a very low employment rate. Only 25 percent of severely disabled people are employed. But even when disabled people are employed, they are still not as comfortable as people who don't have disabilities. The average monthly salary of people without disabilities is $2,200, and for the non-severely disabled it is $600 lower. Severely disabled people are in an even less comfortable situation, with an average monthly wage of just $1,100. That means that they earn half the amount that people without disabilities earn. These statistics show that employment for people with disabilities is not a simple issue. It is not only about getting a job, but also about how high a salary a disabled person can earn.

SPEAKING

(sample response)

There are laws in my country that require public buildings to be accessible to disabled people—not only people in wheelchairs, but also people with other kinds of disabilities. For example, the floor numbers in elevators have to be in Braille so blind people can read them. I think these laws are a good idea because they give disabled people independence. That's really important. Think about if you were in a wheelchair. It would really change your life if you couldn't enter buildings or take the bus because you were in a wheelchair. But if buildings and buses and subways are accessible, you could go on living almost the same life you do now without a wheelchair. There is a drawback though. Changing buildings to make them accessible costs a lot of money. That's really a problem in places where there's a lot of poverty. Accessibility is really important, but it might not always be possible because of the costs.

I work in an office building, and it is accessible to people in wheelchairs. There are elevators, and they are all wide enough for wheelchairs. The buttons on the elevator are low so people in wheelchairs can reach them. On each floor there is a handicapped restroom that can accommodate wheelchairs. There is no need for ramps because the entrance is at the same level as the sidewalk, so there aren't stairs or steps to enter the building. I think the building is really easy for a person in a wheelchair to use, so I can't think of any improvements that are needed.

UNIT 9: EDUCATION

Learning Styles

WORDS

1. B	6. G	11. D	16. S
2. K	7. F	12. A	17. M
3. P	8. I	13. R	18. E
4. J	9. H	14. N	19. Q
5. T	10. O	15. L	20. C

READING

1. B	4. A	7. B
2. A	5. C	8. A
3. C	6. B	9. D

WORD FAMILIES

1. Conventional
2. dominates
3. Exposure
4. solitude
5. confident
6. faces

DICTIONARY SKILL

1. A
2. B

LISTENING

1. diagrams
2. recite
3. manipulate
4. encouragement

WRITING

(sample response)

Confidence is an important element in the learning process. In order to learn, students need to believe that they can learn. When students are given opportunities for success, encouragement from their teachers, and exposure to a variety of experiences, they can develop a strong feeling of confidence.

When students have opportunities to complete tasks successfully, this shows them that they really can learn. If you give a small child a book with lots of pages crowded with words, naturally she will feel it impossible to ever learn to read. However, if you give that child one page with a few simple words on it, she can learn to read the page quite easily. The child understands that learning to read is not only possible, but probably not all that difficult, either. The child gains confidence in her abilities.

Encouragement is also important. The teacher can show the child how to break a difficult task into small parts and praise the child's small successes. The teacher can give the child support to keep going until a difficult task is completed. If the teacher believes in the child's abilities to complete learning tasks and lets the child know this, the child will believe in herself, too.

Having a variety of types of learning experiences also contributes to a child's feeling of confidence. If a child has opportunities to work alone as well as in groups, then she knows she can work in different situations. If she learns to write about what she learns as well as talk about it, then she knows there are different ways that she can communicate information. Knowing that she can learn in different ways and in different circumstances helps her feel confident about her abilities to learn.

Confidence is an important part of learning. Building students' confidence should be part of all classroom activities.

SPEAKING

(sample response)

I think I would have to say that I'm an auditory learner because I like to talk so much. I was always getting into trouble in school because I couldn't keep my mouth closed, especially when the teacher was talking! But now that I think about it, I think that must have been because I am an auditory learner. I need to talk about what I learn. In school, I always liked it best when we had small-group discussions. I enjoyed listening to what others had to say and talking about my ideas with them. I always preferred classroom discussions to reading. It was hard for me to understand something I had read until we talked about it in class.

I'm definitely a social learner because I need to talk about the things I'm learning. I see some students spend a lot of time in the library, reading and taking notes. That's always been difficult for me. When I was in high school, if I had to go to the library to study, I always asked some friends to go with me. I didn't like studying alone. Even if my friends weren't working on the same assignments, I liked being around them when I studied. That must mean I'm a social learner.

Being alone hinders my learning, definitely. I'd rather have company when I study. When I was in high school, sometimes in class we would have to sit quietly and read the assignment. That was usually a waste of time for me. I just couldn't learn that way, in silence. On the other hand, when I'm with people who talk too much, that also hinders me. If I don't get a chance to talk, too, and have people listen to my ideas, that's not helpful to me.

The Homeschool Option

WORDS

1. R	6. L	11. T	16. H
2. N	7. B	12. Q	17. P
3. E	8. A	13. I (or F)	18. D
4. F (or I)	9. C	14. S	19. O
5. J	10. G	15. K	20. M

READING

1. B	3. E	5. True	7. False
2. D	4. False	6. Not Given	8. True

WORD FAMILIES

1. alternative	3. concern	5. obligation
2. instruct	4. periodically	

WORD SKILL

1. pleased   2. not pleased

LISTENING

1. A   2. D   3. F   4. G

WRITING

(sample response)

I strongly believe that school should be compulsory for all children, with very few exceptions. Most parents do not have the professional teaching skills and range of knowledge that their children are exposed to at school. Only children who have special circumstances that prevent them from attending school should be taught at home, in my opinion.

Parents teach their children many things. They teach them skills they need in daily life, such as how to keep their rooms clean or how to tie their shoes. They teach them moral values such as honesty and kindness. These are very important lessons, but they are very different from the academic lessons children learn at school. Most parents, unless they are professional teachers themselves, do not have professional teaching skills. They have not been trained to teach academic skills such as reading, writing, and arithmetic. The best place for children to learn these things is at school under the guidance of professional educators.

Children are exposed to a much wider range of knowledge at school than they ever could be at home, no matter how well educated their parents are. At home, children have their parents and possibly also their grandparents. This is a limited number of adults. At school, on the other hand, children study with a variety of teachers. Each of these teachers has specialized knowledge about his or her subject area. This gives schoolchildren the opportunity to learn about many more things than their parents could teach them at home.

Some children cannot attend school for special reasons. Some live too far away from school. Some are professional actors and have to work during the school day. Some have physical disabilities or health problems that make it difficult for them to move around. In cases such as these, learning at home is the only choice. However, these are exceptional cases.

No matter how well educated parents are or how much they love their children, they cannot provide the same level of education that a school can. That is why I believe that school should be compulsory for all children.

SPEAKING

(sample response)

I think education should be compulsory for ages six through eighteen, that is, for first through twelfth grades. Some people think that compulsory education should start in kindergarten, but I don't think that's necessary. In kindergarten the kids just play and learn things like colors and numbers and look at storybooks. These are all things they can do at home, and five years old is too young, I think, to be away from home all day. Six is a good age to start school. In some countries you have to do only six or eight years of school, but I think it's really important to finish high school. The modern world gets more and more complicated every day, and I think everyone needs the things they learn in high school, even if they don't plan to go to the university afterward.

In most high schools, students have to learn some math, such as algebra and geometry. They have to take the basic science courses: biology, chemistry, and physics. They have to study the history and literature of their own country. I think all these things are important. Usually high school students have to learn a foreign language, and I think that's very important, too. These are all things that an educated person should know. It's basic knowledge. Maybe the only thing I would add would be international politics. The world is getting smaller every day, isn't it? We all should understand something about how other countries operate.

A problem with the schools in my country, especially in the primary schools, is the size of the classes. It isn't unusual to see a classroom with forty or even fifty children in it. Imagine if that's a first grade classroom with forty or fifty six-year-old children. It's impossible for the teacher to give so many children the attention they need. It's a really difficult situation, and the quality of education for little children really suffers from it. I guess it's a problem with money. To make smaller classes they would have to build more classrooms and hire more teachers. I guess the real concern is that the government is not spending enough money on education.

Educating the Gifted

WORDS

1. E	6. A	11. R	16. P
2. S	7. T	12. L	17. G
3. D	8. F	13. K	18. Q
4. M	9. N	14. B	19. I
5. H	10. C	15. J	20. O

READING

1. extraordinary
2. profoundly
3. moderately
4. recognize
5. peers
6. transferred
7. curriculum
8. dedicate
9. inquisitiveness

WORD FAMILIES

1. recognition
2. sophistication
3. assessments
4. enrichment
5. simultaneously
6. withdraw

WORD SKILL

1. turn up
2. turn into
3. turned out

LISTENING

1. recognize
2. sophisticated
3. discipline
4. constructive
5. curriculum

WRITING

(sample response)

The charts show information about enrollment in remedial education at two different universities. The statistics are percentages of first-year students. There are significantly more students enrolled in remedial education at University A than at University B. Close to half (45 percent) of the first-year students at University A take remedial education courses. A little more than a third (35 percent) of first-year students at that school are enrolled in remedial math courses, and close to one-quarter are enrolled in other remedial courses: 22 percent in remedial reading courses and 26 percent in remedial writing courses. At University B, only 15 percent of first-year students are enrolled in remedial education courses. The smallest number, 5 percent, take remedial math courses, and 10 percent are enrolled in remedial writing and 12 percent in remedial reading. Clearly, there are many more students with math difficulties at University A than at University B. University B may have stricter requirements for math when they admit new students.

SPEAKING

(sample response)

If I could choose to have any extraordinary talent, I think I would choose to be a painter. I really enjoy looking at art. I enjoy the work of many famous painters. I love going to museums and studying the paintings. I have tried painting a little myself, but I'm not very good at it. If I could paint even half as well as Picasso, I would be very happy. However, I don't think that's very likely to happen. I'm not gifted in the arts.

I don't know too much about gifted education in my country. I think in some schools they have special programs for gifted children where they spend an hour or two in a class with other gifted children, and then spend the rest of the day in a regular classroom. I don't know of any full-time gifted education programs. Maybe some private schools have them—I'm not sure. When children have special artistic or musical talents, usually their parents hire private teachers to teach them after school.

I think education for everyone will be very different in the future. I think all education will be through the Internet, and that way education can be individualized. That means that any child with exceptional abilities will have a specialized program that fits those abilities. At the same time, children who have difficulties in certain areas will have special instruction to help with those difficulties. The Internet will make this possible because then children won't have to study just with the children who live in their neighborhood or just with the teachers in their local school. They'll be able to find the children and the teachers who match their abilities and needs and study with them. This will be good for everybody, whether or not they have exceptional abilities.

UNIT 10: TECHNOLOGY/INVENTIONS

The Development of the Lightbulb

WORDS

1. G	6. N	11. T	16. Q
2. C	7. H	12. J	17. F
3. O	8. I	13. K	18. L
4. B	9. A	14. M	19. D
5. R	10. S	15. E	20. P

READING

1. inventors	4. device	7. F
2. current	5. refinement	8. A
3. unveiled	6. D	9. B

WORD FAMILIES

1. inspiration	3. refine	5. Suitable
2. invention	4. invest	6. specific

DICTIONARY SKILL

1. A   2. B

LISTENING

1. patent search
2. an application
3. pay a fee
4. backers

WRITING

(sample response)

There have been many important inventions in the past 100 years, and they have changed our lives in dramatic ways. One of the more important of these inventions, in my opinion, is the cell phone. It is a device that has made both our work and our personal lives more convenient.

Because of cell phones, people are no longer tied to their offices. If someone has a business meeting in another part of town, she does not have to miss important phone calls because she is away from the office. Also, since it is possible to send and receive e-mail with many cell phones, it is very easy to take advantage of travel time to catch up on sending and responding to business e-mails. Cell phones are also very useful for people who travel a lot on business. Specifically, they make communication with the home office extremely convenient, and they make it easy for the traveler to continue attending to normal business responsibilities even when on the road. For reasons like these, cell phones have changed the way most companies do business.

Cell phones have also had a big impact on our personal lives. For one thing, they make it easier for families to stay in touch with each other throughout the day. Parents do not have to worry about their children because they can always reach them by cell phone. Children feel secure because they know that their parents are just a phone call away. Cell phones also make it very convenient for people to make or change plans with their friends and relatives. Cell phones have changed the way we interact with each other and the way we go about our daily lives.

Cell phones are always changing and becoming capable of more and more things. As cell phones continue to evolve, their impact on our daily lives will become even greater.

SPEAKING

(sample response)

When I was growing up, my cousin was an inspiration to me. He is a good deal older than I am, maybe ten or twelve years older. When I was a child, he seemed like a grown-up to me. He was always doing interesting things, and I wanted to do what I saw him doing. He was on his school's soccer team, so I wanted to play soccer, too. His favorite subject

*in high school was biology, so I was interested in biology, too. By follow-
ing his example, I learned to apply myself in sports and in school. He
really was a good role model for me.*

*The person who is an inspiration to me now is the president of the com-
pany where I work, Mr. Gomez. It's a small company, but a very successful one. Mr. Gomez started it from nothing. He had an idea, a dream, and
he made it into a reality. He did it with hard work and brains. I'm learning all I can while I work for this company, because one day I want to
start a company of my own just like Mr. Gomez did.*

*I find classical music very inspiring—certain types of it, fast-paced
music. When I'm working, I always play classical music because it helps
me concentrate, and if the music is fast paced or energetic, it gives me
energy to keep working.*

The Invention of Variable-Pitch Propellers

WORDS

1. D	6. E	11. M	16. Q
2. O	7. G	12. T	17. P
3. F	8. A	13. N	18. S
4. L	9. H	14. B	19. I
5. C	10. K	15. R	20. J

READING

1. True	4. True	7. D
2. False	5. Not Given	
3. True	6. B	

WORD FAMILIES

1. enthusiastic	3. rely	5. vary
2. inflexible	4. isolated	6. revolution

WORD SKILL

1. able to change   2. not able to change

LISTENING

1. A	2. C	3. F	4. G

WRITING

(sample response)

By looking at these charts we can see that very light jets are larger and faster than light sport aircraft. Light sport aircraft can carry at the most one passenger, and one of the models shown does not have the capacity to carry any passengers at all. The very light jets, on the other hand, can carry two to six passengers. Very light jets are much faster than light sport aircraft, with cruise speeds between 300 and 425 miles per hour. The fastest light sport aircraft, on the other hand, has a cruise speed of just 130 miles per hour. With their higher passenger capacity and greater speeds, very light jets are naturally a great deal more expensive than light sport aircraft. Prices range from just under $1 million to well over $3 million. Prices for light sport aircraft are much lower, ranging from $39,000 to $194,000 for the models shown.

SPEAKING

(sample response)

I definitely prefer to work in isolation. I think it's much more efficient. When I work alone, I don't have to wait for other people to do their part. I don't have to change my work habits or methods to fit in with other people. I can work the way I work best and at my own pace. I get a lot more done when I work on my own, and I enjoy it a lot more, too.

It depends on the problem. Sometime I have to confer with others. Sometimes I know that a certain other person will have the information I need or has had experience with a similar type of problem. In that case, I confer with that person. But most of the time I try to solve problems on my own. It's like a puzzle. If I can come up with a good solution on my own, I feel proud of myself. Mostly, I prefer working alone, and I prefer solving problems on my own, too.

I like my work because it's all about numbers. I'm an accountant, and I chose this field because I love numbers. I could spend all day working with numbers. It may sound strange, but I really am enthusiastic about numbers. I'm happiest when I'm in my office by myself working on accounts.

The Transatlantic Cable

WORDS

1. S	6. P	11. H	16. K
2. E	7. Q	12. J	17. G
3. D	8. F	13. L	18. M
4. I	9. A	14. T	19. R
5. B	10. C	15. O	20. N

READING

1. F	4. B	7. snapped
2. C	5. insulation	8. transmitted
3. E	6. towed	9. triumph

WORD FAMILIES

1. catastrophes	3. triumphant	5. compensate
2. perseverant	4. insulate	

WORD SKILL

1. set out	2. set up	3. set back

LISTENING

1. 1975	3. 1982	5. cable TV
2. set out	4. 1985	

WRITING

(sample response)

Both perseverance and good luck are helpful ingredients for success. People may work hard to reach their goals, but finding some luck along the way is also nice. However, I believe that perseverance is much more likely to help someone reach success than plain old luck. You may sit around waiting fruitlessly for luck to come your way, but perseverance is something you can always control. In addition, you can create your own luck through perseverance.

From one point of view, luck is something we do not have any control over. Your friend may win the lottery, but you do not. That is not something that happens because your friend is somehow more deserving. It just happens. If you believe that reaching your goals similarly depends on luck, then you probably will not get anywhere at all. You might waste your time just sitting around all day waiting for opportunity to fall into your lap. It will not. It would be better to go out and do something yourself every day that will bring you closer to your goals.

From another point of view, luck is not really luck but the result of our own perseverance. Sometimes people say that getting that special opportunity you have been hoping for is just a matter of being in the right place at the right time—a lucky chance. But how did you get to be in that place at that time? It is probably because you have been working hard toward your goals. If you want to get a certain kind of job, for example, you answer job ads, talk to other people in your field, and do other things to find out where the job openings are. Pursuing these activities makes it more likely that you will come across people who are hiring. You may have to persevere, but eventually you will meet the person who has the job for you. The day you meet this person it might look like luck, but it really comes about because of your own effort.

Luck is nice when it comes our way, but I think that perseverance is the thing that will help us reach our goals.

SPEAKING

(sample response)

I'm in training to become a nurse. I think this is a really interesting profession because it has so many possibilities. To become a nurse you have to have specialized training, but there are different levels of nursing, so your training depends on what level you're interested in. At a minimum you need a certificate that means you've been trained in basic nursing skills like giving medicines and assisting patients. Some nurses have bachelor's degrees and some have master's or doctoral degrees. To get a nursing degree, you study a variety of subjects such as science, public health, administration, and more. You have to know about all these things. You definitely need a certificate or a diploma to become a nurse, but the exact kind you need depends on your goals and interests.

Nurses have to be good at a lot of things; the skills required for this profession are disparate. To be a good nurse you have to have a range of interests and be good at learning new things. You should be good at science and technology. At the same time, you need good "people skills." This is really important because the job of nursing is to help sick people. You have to be able to work well with them, to be kind and compassionate, to transmit a certain type of message through your interactions with your patients: "I care and I'm here to help you." If you don't have that attitude when you set out to care for your patients, you won't be completely successful. Good medical skills can't compensate for a lack of compassion or kindness.

Audioscripts

Unit 1: Natural World—Environmental Impacts of Logging

Narrator: Listen to a lecture about trees.

Lecturer:
When you look at a tree, you may notice only the branches and leaves. A closer look shows that there's actually a great deal more going on. Trees provide homes to a large variety of terrestrial animals, from tiny insects to large birds such as owls. Insects live beneath the bark, providing a source of food for many types of birds. Squirrels and birds nest on the branches or in the trunk. Small animals defend themselves by hiding among the leaves. The benefits of trees also extend to aquatic animals. The shade from trees keeps water cool, protecting aquatic animals from the heat of the summer sun. The roots hold on to the soil, which keeps it from being eroded by the rain. This is a protection for aquatic habitats, as it prevents soil from running into the rivers and polluting them. Clearly trees are very important. If forests vanish because of logging or other activities, the impacts on the environment will be great.

Unit 1: Natural World—Bird Migration

Narrator: Listen to a tour guide at a bird sanctuary.

Tour Guide:
Welcome to the National Bird Sanctuary. The bird sanctuary provides us with the opportunity to study many aspects of the lives of the migratory birds that pass through here every year. This is a breeding area for many different species, and we'll likely see a number of them on our walk today. On our right, just past the entrance, you'll see a list of all the species that have been observed here. You'll notice several nocturnal species as well as diurnal. They spend the warm months here but leave in the autumn, as they can't endure our cold winters. Okay, take a look at your maps. We're beginning here at the entrance. As we walk through the sanctuary, it's imperative that you not stray off the trail and that you be particularly careful to stay out of the restricted area,

all along the trail to the left here. The restricted area protects breeding birds from disturbance. All right, then. That trail over to the right leads to the gift shop, but before we head there, let's continue to the end of this trail on the left, to the observation platform. *[pause]* Here we are. We can look out over the wetlands from here and observe the waterbirds. I'll leave you here to observe as long as you like, and I'll meet you afterward at the gift shop. It's at the end of that trail I pointed out to you earlier. Before I leave you, I'd like to remind you that this bird sanctuary was built entirely by volunteer labor and donations. You can imagine what a feat that was and what it takes to maintain it. Please consider giving a donation before you leave. You'll find a box for that purpose along the trail right before you arrive at the gift shop.

Unit 1: Natural World—Plant Life in the Taklimakan

Narrator: Listen to a class discussion about plants in the Taklimakan Desert.

Professor: We've looked at plant life in various deserts around the world. Let's talk today about plants in the Taklimakan Desert.

Student 1: What I understood from the reading is that there aren't a lot of plants throughout the Taklimakan Desert but that many plants live in the transitional area on the desert fringe.

Professor: That's exactly correct. Conditions in the desert are extremely harsh, but around the edges, plants have been able to adapt and thrive, and some species are actually quite prolific. Of course, the environment there is still extreme, and the plants have some interesting adaptations.

Student 2: There are still a lot of stressors on the desert fringe. The rain there is sparse, right?

Professor: That's true. The desert fringe is very dry and is subject to extreme temperature swings, and these conditions can cause plants a lot of stress.

Student 1: Another stressor is, because of the dry air, there's rapid evaporation, so it's difficult for the plants to hold on to the water they take in.

Student 2: I read that some plants are actually able to determine when they've lost enough moisture and have the ability to close their pores so they don't lose more.

Professor: Yes, that's one of the interesting desert plant adaptations. Another way plants thrive in the desert is by having large root systems so that they can accumulate water taken from deep in the ground.

Unit 2: Leisure Time—Peripheral Vision in Sports

CD 1
Track
5

Narrator: Listen to a class discussion about vision and basketball.

Professor: We've been discussing the way the eye works and the importance of vision. Let's apply some of this and talk today about how vision affects an athlete's performance. Okay, so when a basketball player, let's say, is out there on the court, what does he need to pay attention to?

Student 1: The player needs to focus on the ball. He needs to always know where the ball is.

Professor: Correct. That's important. But that's not all. The player also has to be aware of what the other players are doing. He has to anticipate their maneuvers so he can be ready to respond. This is where peripheral vision is important. The player may be looking directly at the ball, but he also has to be aware of what's going on near the boundaries of his visual range. He has to be aware of the actions around him.

Student 2: Players look at the ball, but they also scan the whole court, right?

Professor: That's right. They need to go back and forth between focusing on one point and scanning the entire game, so they can know what the rest of the players are doing. Of course, they don't stop to think about it. There isn't time. Good athletes do this unconsciously.

Student 1: They do it so fast, it's indiscernible to us when we're watching the game.

Professor: But they don't respond indiscernibly. When you see a player move in to shoot a basket, he's there because he was able to coordinate all the information he took in about the action of the game so he could make his move.

Unit 2: Leisure Time—History of the Circus

Narrator: Listen to a tour guide at a circus.

Tour Guide:
Good afternoon and welcome to the tour of the Springfield Circus. Today you'll get to see the circus rings up close, visit the places where the performers work and rest, and even meet an animal trainer and some animals. Let's start our tour with a brief history of the Springfield Circus. It was founded a century ago right here in Springfield and has been going ever since. The original owner sold it after twenty-five years, and it's been under ownership of the same company for the past seventy-five years. Although the owners have changed, the place has not. The Springfield Circus has always put on its performances in this venue. Unlike other circuses, it has never traveled around with tents but has always held its performances in this permanent spot. When the Springfield Circus was first founded, it put on large entertainments filled with grandeur for massive audiences. Since then, the show has been reduced in size somewhat with fewer performers and acts. The show always begins with its famous parade of exotic animals. This is followed by dancers on horseback, and then the clowns enter the ring. We may get a chance to meet some of them today. They're always the most popular part of the show. Okay, let's go out to the rings now, so we can see where the performers work. Hold on to your tickets, as you will need them to be admitted to the show after the tour.

Unit 2: Leisure Time—Uses of Leisure Time

Narrator: Listen to a talk about leisure time.

Lecturer:
There has been a good deal of research on how we use our leisure time. Study after study has shown the importance of using leisure time well. According to research, people who spend their leisure time engaged in passive pastimes such as watching TV actually end up feeling less rejuvenated than people who choose more active leisure-time activities. People who report feeling the most satisfaction with how they spend their leisure time engage in a range of activities for relaxation, both physical and intellectual. Among the most popular pastimes reported by adults, physical activities include a variety of sports, playing with their children, and gardening. Intellectual activities include reading, playing computer games, doing puzzles, and using the Internet. People who engage in a variety of active pastimes tend to be

healthier, both physically and emotionally. It is obvious that we need to engage in leisure activities that exercise both our minds and bodies to avoid suffering problems such as obesity and depression.

Unit 3: Transportation—First Headlamps

Narrator: Listen to a talk about early train travel.

Lecturer:
Train travel became increasingly common in the mid- to late-nineteenth century, despite the difficulties involved with this mode of travel. In many ways, trains were more efficient than other available means of transportation, but there were still drawbacks. Travel at night was tricky, for example, because trains lacked effective methods of illumination. Rides on early trains were often rough because of the way the train tracks were laid, although this improved over time and riding the train became more comfortable. As train travel became more popular, the tracks became more crowded, and this was one reason why trains were frequently vulnerable to delays. Train travel could also be dirty because the smoke from the locomotive could not be kept away from the rest of the train. In the early years of train travel there were few disasters, so passengers generally felt safe. Trains were the major means of long-distance travel for a long time and had major effects on society and the economy. Clearly, the initial cost of building the railroads was well worth it, despite the drawbacks involved.

Unit 3: Transportation—Major Subways of Europe

Narrator: Listen to two students discussing subways.

Student 1: We need to organize the information for our report on the history of subways. We agreed that our topic would be the London Underground.

Student 2: Yes, it's such an intrinsic part of London. It's famous worldwide. It really is the centerpiece of the city.

Student 1: And it's been around for a long time. We should mention that it first began operation in 1863. I think it's important to point out that at that time they used steam engines to pull the trains.

Student 2: Yes. That's really important information because steam engines were intrinsic to the way the system was built. The tracks couldn't be very deep because the engines had to release steam.

Student 1: Right. The tunnels had to be close to the surface of the ground, and there were vents to release the steam to the streets.

Student 2: So we should explain all that and then talk about how the system changed when electric trains were introduced.

Student 1: That made a big difference because the tunnels could be deeper since they didn't have to worry about releasing steam.

Student 2: And they had developed methods that made it possible to dig deeper tunnels because they used a sort of shield to support the tunnel while the workers were digging.

Student 1: Right. The Harlow-Greathead Shield.

Student 2: People were happy with the deeper tunnels because it wasn't necessary to destroy streets and buildings to dig them.

Unit 3: Transportation—Electric Cars Around the Globe

Narrator: Listen to a tour guide introduce a city tour.

Tour Guide:
Welcome to City Bus Tours. Our tour today will take us not only through the city but also to some of the nearby suburbs as we explore the historical development of the area. Before we begin, let's take a look at this map, which shows the places we'll be visiting today. We'll start here, on the west side of the river, which is all urban area. We'll pass by the commuter rail station here, right by the river and near the bridge. This is a brand new station since the train system was completed just last year. Commuter traffic was becoming a huge problem in our area, and there's been a marked improvement in the traffic situation since the trains started running. After we look at the station, we'll cross this bridge, which spans the Rocky River. The bridge was built 100 years ago. At that time, we had the city on this side, but it was all rural area on the other side of the bridge. The building of the bridge accelerated development on the east side of the river, and now it's a growing suburban area with a lot of sprawl. On that side of the river, we'll take a look at some historic houses that still exist there, and then stop for lunch at Miss Mary's Restaurant.

Unit 4: Culture—Origins of Writing

Narrator: Listen to a tour guide at a museum.

Tour Guide:
Welcome to the university's Museum of Ancient Studies. As you may be aware, this museum was created by professors and students as a place to exhibit objects and information about ancient civilizations that they've uncovered in their research. Visiting scholars to the university have also contributed a great deal to the museum, and there's a room created especially for items they've donated. However, that's in Room D, near the end of our tour, so we'll talk more about that later. We'll begin here near the entrance, in Room A. This room is all about agricultural tools. It encompasses tools from several different cultures, and it's interesting to note the similarities and differences among them. You'll also find a few examples of agricultural-related objects in Room C, where we have an exhibit of items found in more recent excavations, but most of them are here in this room. Let's move ahead now to Room B. This is my favorite part of the museum. The exhibit you see in here explains the mythology of several ancient civilizations. Some of the old myths are lovely, fascinating. If you're interested in mythology, our gift shop has a number of books for sale on the subject. Okay, let's move now to our right, to Room C. Here's the Recent Excavations Exhibit I mentioned earlier. There are a variety of things in here that've been recently uncovered by scholars connected with the university: tools, cooking implements, clay tablets and tokens, and more. Just ahead is the Visiting Scholars' Room, and past that's the gift shop, in Room E. There, in addition to the books I mentioned, you can buy copies of many of the items on exhibit in the museum, so don't forget to spend some time there before you exit. Now, I'd be happy to answer any questions you may have.

Unit 4: Culture—Hula Dancing in Hawaiian Culture

Narrator: Listen to two students planning a hula demonstration.

Student 1: We have to get ready for our hula demonstration for our class. We need to show what we've learned about Hawaiian culture.

Student 2: Let's start with the decorations. I don't think they should be too elaborate, but we want to evoke a feeling of being in Hawaii.

Student 1: I think floral decorations would work. We can make garlands and leis out of paper flowers. They would be easy to make, and still give the right feeling.

Student 2: That's a good idea. What about our costumes? We need to be careful to avoid stereotypes like grass skirts.

Student 1: Since we're going to demonstrate the ancient style of hula, we don't need elaborate costumes. We can make simple costumes that look like tapa bark.

Student 2: Okay, I guess that wouldn't be hard to do. What about garlands of leaves? Aren't they part of the traditional costume?

Student 1: Yeah, they are, but I think the tapa skirts are enough. Otherwise we'll spend all our time making decorations and costumes.

Student 2: I suppose so. No garlands then. But we do need an altar. That's really important because that's part of what we learned about the place of hula dancing in Hawaiian culture.

Student 1: Of course. We'll have to spend some time on creating an altar. But we can't forget to actually practice the dances that we're going to demonstrate.

Student 2: Did we decide to use the graceful movements with all the swaying?

Student 1: No, we're demonstrating the ancient style. Remember? We're doing the energetic dances.

Student 2: Right, of course. With the traditional music, the drums and chants. Okay, let's start practicing.

Unit 4: Culture—The Art of Mime

Narrator: Listen to a talk about mime.

Speaker:
Mime is a type of performance carried out without the use of props or language. The mime's skill is the ability to make the audience believe that objects are present when in reality they're not.

Mimes create illusions of everyday activities. For example, a mime may act out climbing the stairs or opening a window, and do it so skillfully that it almost appears that the stairs or window are really there. Mimes use gestures to show the presence of objects. For example, a mime may use his hands to outline the shape of a box, then climb inside the imaginary box. In addition to interacting with imaginary objects, mimes may act out stories in which they portray different characters. The stories usually show the characters involved in some sort of conflict, but it's all done in a humorous way meant to make the audience laugh.

Unit 5: Health—Nurse Migration

Narrator: Listen to a talk about training for nurses.

Speaker:
Qualified nurses must have several years of specialized training following high school. In the United States, for example, the bulk of nursing schools offer four-year programs. A nurse who graduates from such a program and then passes a licensing test is qualified for a variety of professional-level jobs. Many nurses choose to go on to graduate school and get higher-level degrees. In the United Kingdom, about 25 percent of nurses have graduated from degree programs. The rest generally have studied in two-year programs. This situation will change soon, however, and in the future all nurses in the U.K. will be required to have a degree in order to qualify for professional nursing jobs. Despite the need for nurses everywhere, there is still a decline in applicants for nursing programs. Many nursing schools in the United States have reported a decline of applicants of 5 percent or more over the past decade. This situation stems from a variety of causes. An important one is that more women are interested in professions, such as doctor or lawyer, which in the past were considered to be men's professions. It's been estimated that there will be 114,000 vacant nursing jobs in the United States by the year 2015.

Unit 5: Health—Aerobic Exercise and Brain Health

Narrator: Listen to a woman talking to a trainer at a fitness center.

Patient: Hello? Is this the hospital fitness center?

Trainer: Yes. I'm Tim Smith, a trainer here. How may I help you?

Patient: I'm interested in taking classes.

Trainer: Just let me take down your information. May I have your name?

Patient: Yes, it's Amanda Clark. That's Clark, C-l-a-r-k.

Trainer: R-k. Right. And what kind of classes were you interested in?

Patient: I need to get some exercise. Do you have aerobics exercise classes?

Trainer: Yes, we do. We have several levels of exercise classes. Are you a beginner?

Patient: Yes, I am, for aerobics classes, but I've taken other classes previously. I took yoga classes last year.

Trainer: So you've taken yoga classes. Very good. And why are you interested in exercise classes with us now? Do you have a referral?

Patient: Yes, I do. My doctor told me to call you. I've been feeling depressed, and she said it would improve my mood.

Trainer: I think we'll be able to help you with that problem. Medical research shows a clear link between exercise and mood.

Patient: Also I've been getting a little heavy, and the doctor thought that regular exercise would help me stave off any big weight gain.

Trainer: It certainly will. Exercise has many benefits. We also work a lot with the elderly here, who may be suffering from dementia or decrease of cognition. But you, of course, are much too young for that! However, we can help you with the issues your doctor wants you to work on.

Unit 5: Health—How Drugs Are Studied

Narrator: Listen to two students discussing their research assignment.

Student 1: Our lab assignment is due soon. We need to go over the steps to follow for our experiment.

Student 2: The professor gave us an outline. We're investigating the effects of certain substances on a certain type of bacteria, right? So the first thing we have to do is grow our culture in the lab.

Student 1: Right. Okay. Then we'll have to introduce the different substances to the culture.

Student 2: Yeah, and then carefully monitor it at regular intervals. I think every twelve hours would be about right. We should take turns doing that.

Student 1: Good idea. Let's leave a notebook in the lab so we can each record what we see. We'll have to ascertain whether there are any changes.

Student 2: Yes. It's fairly straightforward, isn't it? At the end we'll get together to write up the report. We'll have to describe the outcome.

Student 1: Okay. I'm ready to get started.

Unit 6: Tourism—Hiking the Inca Trail

Narrator: Listen to a tour guide at an archeological site.

Tour Guide:
Good morning and welcome. I'm sure you'll enjoy your visit to this archeological site. One of the greatest mysteries of this site is the question of how it was built. How were the ancient people able to construct such spectacular buildings out of such heavy stones without the help of modern technology? We'll explore this and other mysteries pertaining to their culture during our tour today. Before we begin, let me go over a few restrictions. In order to preserve the site, we ask you to walk only on the network of paths, which is clearly marked. After the tour, you may walk around the site as you please, but remember that you can access the buildings only between ten o'clock and four o'clock. The grounds stay open until six. You can access any building you wish on your own except for the ceremonial area. That building is open only to groups with guides, and we'll be visiting it on our tour today. If you haven't bought your tickets yet, please do so now. They're available over here at the counter, fifteen dollars for adults and ten dollars for children. After the tour is over, you might want to visit out gift shop, where we have an array of native crafts for sale.

Unit 6: Tourism—What Is Ecotourism?

Narrator: Listen to a customer talking to a tour company agent.

Agent: Good afternoon. Excellent Eco Tours.

Customer: Hello. Yes. I have a vacation coming up, and I haven't taken a pleasure trip in a long time. I'm interested in ecotourism. Can you tell me about any trips you have coming up soon? My vacation is in January.

Agent: I'd be happy to help you. Let me just take down your information. What's your name, please?

Customer: Bob Henderson.

Agent: What kind of tour are you interested in? Our most popular tours are the Wilderness Adventure Tour and the Local Culture Tour.

Customer: Tell me more about the first one.

Agent: That's a nature tour. We take you to a remote area of the rain forest where you learn all about the local plants and animals.

Customer: It sounds interesting, but I'm a little wary of tours that feature wild animals.

Agent: Don't worry. You'll be in the hands of experts, and everything will be perfectly safe. Also, there will always be a barrier between you and the animals.

Customer: It sounds like an interesting trip.

Agent: It is. Shall I sign you up for the Wilderness Adventure Tour then?

Customer: Yes. What are the dates?

Agent: January twelfth through the twenty-fifth.

Customer: That sounds perfect. I have a question about the accommodations. What are they like?

Agent: There are two types. You have a choice between a fairly basic hotel or camping at the campground.

Customer: Oh, I'd definitely prefer the campground.

Agent: Great. I'll put you down for that. Now do you mind if I ask you something? How did you hear about our company? Did you see our publicity somewhere?

Customer: Yes, I saw it in a travel magazine.

Unit 6: Tourism—Learning Vacations

CD 1
Track
19

Narrator: Listen to a customer talking to a tour company agent.

Agent: Good afternoon. Learning Vacations Limited. May I help you?

Customer: I'm interested in taking a learning vacation. I understand you organize vacations with painting classes.

Agent: We do. We offer learning trips for a broad range of tastes and interests, and painting trips are among the most popular. Do you have a particular destination in mind?

Customer: Not really. I'd just like to go someplace pretty with colorful scenery for painting and maybe some nice ocean breezes.

Agent: Then you would probably be interested in our painting trip this summer. You spend two weeks at a beach resort in Mexico and attend painting classes under the supervision of university art professors.

Customer: University professors? That's impressive.

Agent: Yes. The trip is sponsored by the art department at Springfield University. It's part of their summer school.

Customer: That sounds great. My other interest is international cuisine. Do you have any cooking trips?

Agent: We certainly do. However, I don't know whether you'd be interested because almost all our cooking trips take place in a city, not by the ocean. Our clients get to enroll in ongoing cooking classes at the National Cooking Institute, which sponsors the trips.

Customer: So I would really learn to cook, not just watch someone else cook?

Agent: Yes. You learn how to choose ingredients, how to prepare them, everything.

Customer: What are the accommodations like? Would I stay at a hotel?

Agent: No. For the cooking trip, participants stay at a residential college that's close to the National Cooking Institute.

Customer: I think either one of those trips would suit my taste.

Agent: You need to decide soon. You'll have to enroll in the class of your choice, and then we make the travel arrangements for you.

Customer: When would I have to decide?

Agent: Enrollment for the painting classes ends on June 15 and for the cooking classes on July 1.

Customer: Thanks. I'll let you know soon.

Unit 7: Business—What Makes a Small Business Successful?

Narrator: Listen to two students discussing a small business.

Student 1: Okay, so our assignment for our business class is to explain the reasons for the success of a particular small business. We agreed to use the Sunshine Bakery for our model, right?

Student 2: Yes. It's a good example of several of the characteristics that are typical of successful small businesses. For one thing, it has its own particular niche.

Student 1: Uh huh, because there are no other bakeries in the neighborhood.

Student 2: Right. So even though its product isn't unique—it just sells normal baked goods—there aren't any competitors in the area.

Student 1: Yes, I think that's a vital part of its success. And its product is really good, so it already has a great reputation. Everybody knows about the delicious bread you can get there.

Student 2: So it has lots of customers. I don't remember reading anything about market research that the owners did before opening the business, but I guess it doesn't matter because there are lots of customers now.

Student 1: But the owners did start with a sound business plan. I mean, they projected all their expenses and how long it would take to start earning a profit and all that.

Student 2: Right, and the business became profitable in about two years. I think that's pretty good. And since they had enough financial support to start off with, they were able to keep the business afloat until then.

Student 1: Okay, so let's start writing up these ideas for our report.

Unit 7: Business—Brand Loyalty

Narrator: Listen to a lecture in a marketing class.

Lecturer:
We'll talk today about promoting new products. Your main goal in promoting your products is to create brand loyalty, a bond between you and your customers. That way, your customers will keep coming back to you. How do you do this? The main point is to make your customers feel that your brand is somehow special so that they'll feel special when they buy it. They want to feel that using products with your brand gives them status. A common method is to get endorsements from famous people. Customers will think, "If I use the same brand as that movie star or athlete or television actor, then I'll be as special as that person." This also gives the idea that your brand is bought by selective people, which makes customers feel very good about buying it themselves. If you can make customers feel passionate about your brand, then they'll always buy it, whether your products are common household staples or expensive luxury items. This is what you want, a brand loyalty that's hard to reverse.

Unit 7: Business—Global Outsourcing

Narrator: Listen to a tour guide at a factory.

Tour Guide:
Welcome to the Apex factory tour. Let's begin with a little history of the factory. The Apex Manufacturing Firm has been in existence since 1900, when the company built the first factory right here on this site. It was quite a boon to the local economy since it was the first factory in this region. In fact, Apex was at the epicenter of manufacturing in this region for many, many years. Business was so good that in 1910, the firm's owners decided to add a night shift in order to keep the factory operating twenty-four hours a day. As you can imagine, the firm's owners became quite wealthy. The first branch factory was built in 1915. In 1940, the original old factory was completely torn down and

replaced with a new larger one on the same site. That's the building we're standing in now. Over the years, there have been a number of changes, of course. Then came 1998, which was perhaps the most decisive year for the company. The decision had to be made about outsourcing some of the labor, as many other companies were doing and are doing. The firm's owners ultimately decided not to do so. That decision means that at the present time, Apex remains a major employer in this region. There's a high level of satisfaction among our staff, as shown by the fact that our employee turnover is quite low.

Unit 8: Society—Social Networking

Narrator: Listen to a class discussion about social networking.

Professor: Let's talk today about the online social networking trend. There's been an explosion of interest in this form of communication. What effects do you think this will have on our lives as the trend unfolds?

Student 1: It's clear that the advantages are immense. Think about it. These online social networking sites make it possible to have contact with people all over the world.

Student 2: I agree. You can pursue all kinds of opportunities, both personal and professional, through social networking. You can make friends, you can find jobs, you can exchange all kinds of information with people everywhere. It really expands your world.

Professor: These are important advantages, but do you also see any disadvantages to this phenomenon? What might be some of the negative consequences?

Student 1: I see that in one way it expands your world, but in another way it hurts it. I mean, you might spend so much time with your online friends that you don't pay attention to your local friends and family. It can mean the loss of your local community.

Student 2: There are also dangers with your online community. You can make many acquaintances online, but you don't necessarily know a lot about them. You might not know their true identity.

Unit 8: Society—Why Are Women Leaving Science Careers?

Narrator: Listen to a tour guide at a research lab.

Tour Guide:
Welcome to the Robertson Research Lab. On our tour today you'll see where researchers work, and you'll learn what scientific research is all about. Today, the Robertson Research Lab is one of the most important labs devoted to scientific research in the country, but it took a long struggle for the lab to gain the status that it enjoys today in the scientific and academic communities. It required an inordinate effort to get the support necessary to build the lab. In fact, it took approximately ten years to collect enough funding to start construction. That would not have been possible without the invaluable help of a number of individuals whose names are listed here on this wall. Although much of the funding came from government resources, and, of course, some of it also came from the Robertson family, the lab is located here at the university and it's the university that bears the responsibility for maintaining and running the lab. In fact, one purpose of the lab is to give university students experience with research. Professional research scientists at the lab provide guidance to science students as they design and carry out their own research studies.

Unit 8: Society—Wheelchair-Accessibility Issues

Narrator: Listen to two students discussing wheelchair accessibility.

Student 1: We have to plan our report on wheelchair accessibility in this building. The professor wanted us to see what accommodations are already in place and what changes need to be made.

Student 2: Right. So the first thing we need to do is walk around the building and see what's here.

Student 1: We've already done some of that. I have, anyway. I measured the corridors, and they're wide enough to accommodate wheelchairs.

Student 2: That's good to know because I measured some doors, both exterior and interior, and none of them has the necessary width.

Student 1: Then that's the first recommendation we'll have to make: wider doors.

Student 2: I think the building's exterior is fine. There's a ramp at the front entrance so wheelchairs can get inside the building easily.

Student 1: That's true, but didn't you notice that there aren't any curb cuts? The curb is too high for a wheelchair to get over. So, there's a parking place for disabled people in front of the building, but they still can't get a wheelchair over the curb and onto the sidewalk.

Student 2: Yeah, I guess that really would be a problem. So we'll have to recommend curb cuts.

Student 1: The building already has an elevator, so wheelchairs can get to all the floors.

Student 2: Right, so elevators aren't a problem. What about the light switches? Are they low enough on the walls?

Student 1: Yes, I tested some of them by sitting in a chair. They're low enough to reach.

Unit 9: Education—Learning Styles

Narrator: Listen to a lecture about learning styles.

Lecturer:
As teachers, when you plan your lessons, you'll need to keep in mind the different learning styles of your students. Remember that visual learners need to see things. Allow them to sit where they can easily see your face as you give the lesson. Remove any obstructions that might prevent this. Include visual items such as diagrams and pictures in your lesson to address the needs of these students. Auditory learners need to hear things. When they read, they may want to hear the words as well as see them, so allow them to read aloud and to recite information they're studying. Don't hinder their learning by requiring them to keep quiet during study time. Kinesthetic learners need to do things. To help these students, include activities that give them opportunities to move around and to manipulate items. While students may have different learning styles, they all have one thing in common: the need for frequent encouragement.

Unit 9: Education—The Homeschool Option

Narrator: Listen to a parent explain homeschooling requirements in her city.

Speaker:
Welcome to the City Homeschooling Association. Most of you are interested in homeschooling your children, and I know you have many concerns and questions about how to begin. I'll start by explaining to you the legal requirements for homeschoolers in our city, then in the latter part of the program, you'll have a chance to ask questions. There are certain things that are compulsory for homeschoolers in our city. First, to start, you'll need to inform the city that you plan to homeschool your children. Many people think that they'll have to hire professional tutors for their children, but that isn't required. Nor do you need to have prior teaching experience yourself. You do, however, have to follow an educational program mandated by the city, which addresses all the same subjects that are taught in the local schools. The city can provide you with textbooks, but, even though the vast majority of families choose to use these books, they aren't required. You can use any books you want as long as you follow the city's program. Periodic tests, usually twice a year, are required by the city. You can give them to your children in your home and send them to the Board of Education for scoring. It's easy to do and doesn't cost any money. At the end of the school year, you have to submit a report to the city, which is also simple to do. It's a short report, and the city provides you with easy-to-follow guidelines. Homeschooling is no longer considered a novel idea but is becoming more widespread. There are a lot of experienced families around who can help you get started.

Unit 9: Education—Educating the Gifted

Narrator: Listen to a class discussion about gifted children.

Professor: I asked you to read an article about recognizing gifted students in the classroom. So, tell me. How can a teacher recognize gifted children?

Student 1: One thing gifted children do is read. They usually read books for older children, or sometimes books for adults.

Professor: Yes, that's an important sign. Profoundly gifted children, especially, may be seen reading adult books at a very early age. What else?

Student 2: When it comes to problem solving, gifted children use sophisticated approaches, unlike their peers.

Student 1: Not all the signs of giftedness are positive. Gifted children might be bored in the classroom and behave badly. They often need help with discipline.

Professor: That's exactly right, and one reason why it's so important to recognize these children and place them in the proper environment and give them the support they need.

Student 2: One way to support them is to give them constructive activities that are interesting to them. If they don't have activities that satisfy their inquisitiveness and creativity, that's when discipline can become a problem.

Student 1: And, of course, we need to provide a special curriculum for these children. They need more than just some interesting activities. They need a whole course of study that matches their abilities.

Unit 10: Inventions—The Development of the Lightbulb

Narrator: Listen to a talk about producing and marketing inventions.

Lecturer:
When you have an invention that you think you can sell, you have to protect it. You must get a patent so that there will be no infringement on your rights to produce and sell the device you've invented. The first thing you must do is find out if anyone else has a patent on a similar type of invention. This is called a patent search. Often, people hire specialized lawyers to do this for them. Once you've ascertained that there are no patents on inventions similar to yours, then you can get an application and file it with the Patent Office. Generally you'll have to pay a fee when you send in the application. Next, you can start looking for investors. This is critical. Inventors tend to be solitary people and don't give much thought to finding financial backers to help them. However, if you want to successfully market your invention, you'll need people to provide money to start production and begin marketing. You'll need to think like an entrepreneur. Inspiration is not enough. Hard work and money are important ingredients for success.

Unit 10: Inventions—The Invention of Variable-Pitch Propellers

Narrator: Listen to two students discussing a flight demonstration.

Student 1: That was a fascinating flight we saw. Now we have to write up the report for the school newspaper.

Student 2: Okay. Well, we should start with the name of the designer of the plane.

Student 1: Right. I'll just write that down. The designer was Steve Wilson, and the pilot's name was Joe Applewood. What about the names of the passengers? Did you get those?

Student 2: No, but there were two of them, we can just put that. We don't need their names.

Student 1: We should say something about the design of the plane, like the size of the propeller. How big was it?

Student 2: I'm not sure. It was big, but I couldn't say the exact size.

Student 1: Well, we should say something about it. What about the speed of rotation? How fast did that propeller move?

Student 2: I don't know. If we'd had a chance to confer with the pilot, we could've found out. But he left too quickly.

Student 1: Okay, so we can't include that information. We'll have to write more about the flight. It was a really prolonged flight.

Student 2: Yeah, he was cruising up there for at least thirty minutes, a lot longer than I expected. So write that down. And what a flexible machine. It handled the turns really well.

Student 1: Yeah, especially considering the weather conditions. It was so windy and cloudy, there must have been some turbulence.

Student 2: There probably was. We'll put that in the report, too.

BARRON'S

IELTS

INTERNATIONAL ENGLISH LANGUAGE TESTING SYSTEM

Second Edition

Dr. Lin Lougheed

BARRON'S

Acknowledgments

Directions in the Model Tests used with permission of the IELTS partners. Charts on pages 3 and 7 are reprinted from the IELTS Handbook with permission of the IELTS partners.

The author gratefully acknowledges the comments and suggestions of ELT teachers and IELTS administrators around the world. The suggestions of Mary Hernandez of ELS Language Center, Santa Monica, California, have been especially helpful. The author would also like to thank Elisabeth Gillstrom of ELS Language Centers, Grand Rapids, Michigan, for her assistance and Angela Castro of Newburyport, Massachusetts for her insights into tone and register.

The author wishes to thank the following organizations, institutions, bloggers, and clearinghouse for their kind permission to use their source material. If we neglected to list your name, please contact us so we can correct that omission.

(p. 250) Adult Intelligence, by Phillip Ackerman, ED410228, ERIC Clearinghouse on Assessment and Evaluation, Washington, DC, 1996.

(p. 195) Less Television, Less Violence, TV-Free America, *www.tvturnoff.org/lessviolence.htm*.

(p. 199) Issues **Affecting the Southern Resident Orcas** from Declining Fish Populations, The Whale Museum (*www.whalemuseum.org*).

All inquiries should be addressed to:
Barron's Educational Series, Inc.
250 Wireless Boulevard
Hauppauge, New York 11788
www.barronseduc.com

Library of Congress Catalog Card No.: 2009043189

ISBN-13: 978-0-7641-9662-1 (Book with audio CDs)
ISBN-10: 0-7641-9662-6 (Book with audio CDs)

Library of Congress Cataloging-in-Publication Data
Lougheed, Lin, 1946–
  Barron's IELTS : International Language Testing System / Lin Lougheed.—2nd ed.
        p. cm.
  Includes bibliographical references and index.
  ISBN-13: 978-0-7641-4299-4
  ISBN-10: 0-7641-4299-2
  ISBN-13: 978-0-7641-9662-1
  ISBN-10: 0-7641-9662-6
  1. International English Language Testing System—Study guides.   2. English language—Textbooks for foreign speakers.   3. English language—Examinations—Study guides.   I. Barron's Educational Series, Inc.   II. Title.   III. Title: IELTS : International English Language Testing System.   IV. Title: International English Language Testing System.
  PE1128.L6436 2010
  428.1076—dc22

                                                                          2009043189

10%
POST-CONSUMER
WASTE
Paper contains a minimum
of 10% post-consumer
waste (PCW). Paper used
in this book was derived
from certified, sustainable
forestlands.

CONTENTS

SPEAKING SKILLS 149

IELTS MODEL TESTS

ANSWER KEYS FOR THE MODULE ACTIVITIES

EXPLANATORY ANSWERS FOR THE IELTS MODEL TESTS

APPENDIX

INTRODUCTION

Over one million people take IELTS each year. There are more than 500 test centers that administer IELTS in over 100 countries around the world. Today it is one of the most accepted international exams for academic qualification. You can learn more about IELTS by visiting the official website at **www.ielts.org**.

Purpose

IELTS is available for people who need to demonstrate their English language proficiency for specific purposes. There are two formats of IELTS to choose from depending on your needs. You should take the Academic Training modules if you are planning to apply to an international university where English is the spoken language. The Academic Training modules are also used as a measure of professional language proficiency for educators, nurses, veterinarians, and other professionals. The General Training modules are more suitable if you want to work, live, or study at a secondary institution in an English-speaking country.

Test-takers

International students represent the highest percentage of candidates who take IELTS. An IELTS score is a recognized measurement of English proficiency at over 1200 educational facilities around the world. Government departments and businesses around the globe also require an IELTS or equivalent score for employment or immigration. Medical professionals who want to work overseas in the UK may take the IELTS test.

Skills Tested

IELTS consists of four sections testing the full range of English language skills—Reading, Writing, Listening, and Speaking. The Listening and Speaking sections are the same for both the Academic and General Training modules. The Reading and Writing sections are different in the Academic and General Training modules.

Language Tested

IELTS is an international test. The English used in the test and heard on the audio can be British, American, Australian, or New Zealand English. The language tested will be comprehensible to any learner of English. Even though IELTS is created in Britain, test-takers who studied another form of English will not be penalized (or *penalised*).

In this book, we have pointed out the common differences between American English and the English used in other parts of the world. We have provided footnotes to show differences in spelling and differences in usage. Whatever spelling you use when writing your test answers, the examiners will accept your spelling as long as you are consistent throughout.

International users of English are aware of differences in usage and spelling. Most international users understand that *colour* is written *color* in American English and that *organize* is written *organise* in British English. Because of films, international magazines, travel, and the Internet, we know that *apartment* and *flat* and *gas* and *petrol*, *city center* and *downtown* are synonyms. We know that an American form is *filled out* and in Britain is *filled in*. In Britain, a family could take a *holiday* at the *sea*. In America, people head toward land: in Florida, *vacationers* go to the *beach* for a *vacation*; in New Jersey, they go to the *shore*. We may use one synonym, but we understand the other without problem.

We know that the cultural institutions of English speaking countries are organized (*organised*) differently. American and Australian students study for a *semester* or a *term*; British students study for a *term*. In Canada and Britain, students get *marks*; in America, they get *grades*. A British *public* school is a *private* school in America. In America, a building begins on the *first* floor. In Britain, one starts at the *ground* floor. We can understand these differences from the context. Their meanings will not be misunderstood.

The common usage differences in this book are:

American	British
math	maths
college major	subject
city hall	town hall
pharmacy	chemist
parking garage/lot	car park
movies/film	film
movie theater	cinema
sidewalk	pavement
cell phone	mobile phone
graduated from college	left college
school/college/university	college/university
checkroom	cloakroom
check	cheque
downtown	city centre

The common spelling differences in this book are:

Suffixes		Doubling of consonants	
-yze	-yse	traveling	travelling
-ize	-ise	label	labelled
-or	-our		
-am	-amme		
-ck	-que		
-er	-re		
Prefixes		**Use of dipthong** *ae*	
co	co-	anesthesia	anaesthesia
re	re-		

Format

The whole IELTS takes 2 hours and 45 minutes. The Listening, Reading, and Writing modules are taken in one sitting. The Speaking module may be taken within 7 days before or after the other modules. It is usually taken the same afternoon or within 2 or 3 days. You will have to arrange for the Speaking module at your test center.

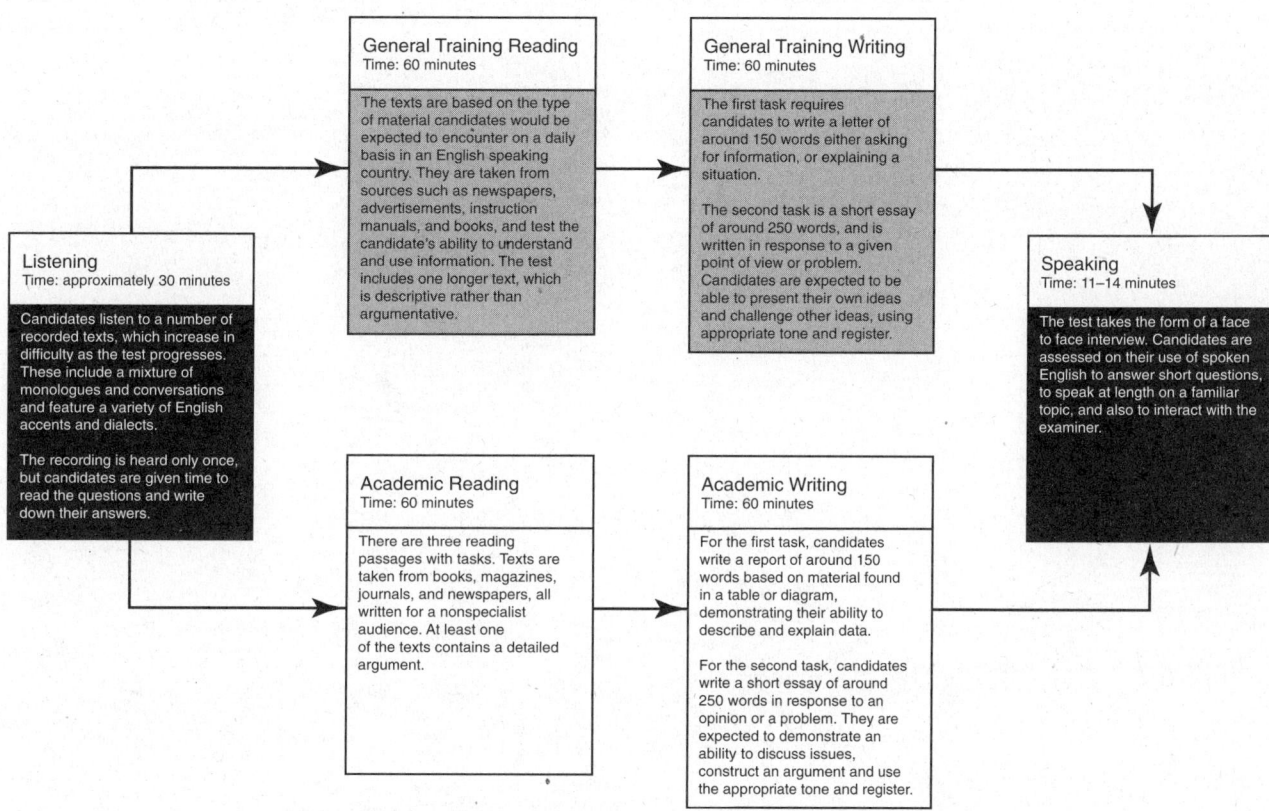

Listening
Time: approximately 30 minutes

Candidates listen to a number of recorded texts, which increase in difficulty as the test progresses. These include a mixture of monologues and conversations and feature a variety of English accents and dialects.

The recording is heard only once, but candidates are given time to read the questions and write down their answers.

General Training Reading
Time: 60 minutes

The texts are based on the type of material candidates would be expected to encounter on a daily basis in an English speaking country. They are taken from sources such as newspapers, advertisements, instruction manuals, and books, and test the candidate's ability to understand and use information. The test includes one longer text, which is descriptive rather than argumentative.

General Training Writing
Time: 60 minutes

The first task requires candidates to write a letter of around 150 words either asking for information, or explaining a situation.

The second task is a short essay of around 250 words, and is written in response to a given point of view or problem. Candidates are expected to be able to present their own ideas and challenge other ideas, using appropriate tone and register.

Speaking
Time: 11–14 minutes

The test takes the form of a face to face interview. Candidates are assessed on their use of spoken English to answer short questions, to speak at length on a familiar topic, and also to interact with the examiner.

Academic Reading
Time: 60 minutes

There are three reading passages with tasks. Texts are taken from books, magazines, journals, and newspapers, all written for a nonspecialist audience. At least one of the texts contains a detailed argument.

Academic Writing
Time: 60 minutes

For the first task, candidates write a report of around 150 words based on material found in a table or diagram, demonstrating their ability to describe and explain data.

For the second task, candidates write a short essay of around 250 words in response to an opinion or a problem. They are expected to demonstrate an ability to discuss issues, construct an argument and use the appropriate tone and register.

*Reprinted from the IELTS Handbook with permission of the IELTS partners.

QUESTIONS AND ANSWERS ABOUT IELTS

Should I take the Academic or General Training exam?

If you are planning on taking an undergraduate or postgraduate course at an English college or university, you should take the Academic Training exam. Your entrance to an institution will be based on this exam. If you are taking the IELTS for professional purposes, you should also take the Academic Training exam. The General Training exam tests the English language communication skills or general communication skills that are needed for those who want to live and work in English-speaking countries. Although the Reading and Writing modules of the Academic exam measure the candidate's ability to function in a higher educational institution, a range of educational and social contexts are used in the Listening and Speaking sections of both tests. It is important that you choose the correct test on your application form. The institution or agency that will be receiving your scores will tell you which exam to take.

Where can I take IELTS?

More than 500 test centers around the world administer IELTS. All test centers are run by the British Council, IELTS Australia, or Cambridge University. Some testing centers also offer off-site testing for large groups by prior arrangement with IELTS. Contact your local examination center or visit **www.ielts.org** to find out where the nearest IELTS test center is located.

Where can I find information about registering for the test?

You can contact your nearest examination center or visit the official IELTS website (**www.ielts.org**) for more information about application procedures and the location of a test center near you.

How much does it cost to take IELTS?

Test fees are set centrally by the British Council and its partners. The fees are generally set for a year at a time. You can find out the cost to take IELTS in your currency by calling your test center. If for some reason you cannot take the test, contact your test center as soon as possible. A partial refund may be available.

Is this a paper-and-pencil test or is there a computer-based version?

As of May 2005, a computer-based IELTS (CB IELTS) became available at select test centers around the world. These tests are usually administered on alternative dates to the paper test. If you are taking the CB IELTS, you will take the Listening and Reading modules on the computer. If you are worried about your typing abilities, you have the option of doing the Writing section on paper. The Speaking section will still be administered face-to-face. CD-ROM versions of the CB IELTS are available for practice. See **www.ielts.org** for a list of test centers that offer the computer-based version.

How is IELTS different from the TOEIC or TOEFL?

- IELTS does not rely as heavily on multiple-choice questions.
- Different accents are used in IELTS including British, New Zealand, Australian, and American.
- Two different formats are offered (Academic and General Training), depending on the purposes of the test-taker.
- IELTS is offered more regularly than TOEIC and TOEFL at most test centers.

What can I take into the testing room?

On your desk you will be allowed only pencils and erasers (rubbers). (On the paper-based test, the answer sheet for the Listening and Reading modules must be written in pencil as parts will be scanned by a computer.) You cannot use correction fluid. You also may not borrow or lend writing utensils during the test. There will be a designated area for you to put your other personal belongings. You will not be allowed to have any electronic devices such as pagers and cell (mobile) phones in the testing room.

What identification is required?

You will need to have two forms of identification (such as a valid photo ID card, passport, driver's license, student ID, or national ID) with you when you register, as well as on test day. When you take the Speaking module, you will have to present your photo ID again. In the United States, only your passport is required.

How many times will I hear the recording in the Listening module?

Each Listening section is played only once. You must take notes in the Listening question booklet as you listen. After the 30-minute section, you will be given 10 minutes to transfer your notes to your answer sheet. In Sections 1, 2, and 3, there are pauses so you can review the questions. There are 30 seconds to check answers after each section. The examiner will not see your notes.

What types of things will I have to talk about in the Speaking section?

You will not be asked to talk about anything that you need background information for. All of the questions deal with common experiences that do not require special knowledge. It is not a good idea to try to memorize answers to questions that you think will be asked because you may not address the question exactly as the examiner asks. You may ask the examiner to repeat a question or clarify a word you are unsure of.

Will I have any time to prepare my Speaking answers?

Part 2 is the only section in which you will be given time to prepare. You will have one minute to organize your thoughts and take notes for your speech. You are allowed to refer to these notes when you speak, but you should look at the examiner as much as possible.

What criteria are my Speaking answers based on?

Your ability to communicate in English is measured in two ways:

1. Fluency and coherence: content, delivery, organization
2. Language use: vocabulary, pronunciation, grammar

How can I find out my results?

Your test results will be sent to your home address or your educational institute within 2 weeks of taking the test. Your overall band score will be given on the Test Report Form, as will a breakdown of your scores in the four separate sections. On the IELTS registration form, you can designate up to five institutions, agencies, or individuals to receive your Test Report Form. There will be a charge for additional reports.

What is a band?

You cannot pass or fail IELTS. The test is scored on a band scale. A band is a level of ability. In each section, you can score anywhere from a band of 0 (nonuser) to a band of 9 (expert user). In the Listening and Reading modules, a mark is given for each correct answer. This number is then converted into a band, with a conversion table. Overall scores are an average of all four sections and can be given in whole or half bands.

How can I interpret my band scores?

A general description of the competency level for each of the nine bands is reprinted from the IELTS website with permission. Scores are reported in whole or half bands. The overall band requirement for each institution or government body may be different. A band of 6.5 or 7 is a common requirement for university admission.

9	Expert user	Has fully operational command of the language: appropriate, accurate, and fluent with complete understanding.
8	Very good user	Has fully operational command of the language with only occasional unsystematic inaccuracies and inappropriacies. Misunderstandings may occur in unfamiliar situations. Handles complex detailed argumentation well.
7	Good user	Has operational command of the language, though with occasional inaccuracies, inappropriacies, and misunderstandings in some situations. Generally handles complex language well and understands desired reasoning.
6	Competent user	Has generally effective command of the language despite some inaccuracies, inappropriacies, and misunderstandings. Can use and understand fairly complex language, particularly in familiar situations.
5	Modest user	Has partial command of the language, coping with overall meaning in most situations, though likely to make many mistakes. Should be able to handle basic communication in own field.
4	Limited user	Basic competence is limited to familiar situations. Has frequent problems in understanding and expression. Is not able to use complex language.
3	Extremely limited user	Conveys and understands only general meaning in very familiar situations. Frequent breakdowns in communication occur.
2	Intermittent user	No real communication is possible except for the most basic information using isolated words or short formulae in familiar situations and to meet immediate needs. Has great difficulty understanding spoken and written English.
1	Nonuser	Essentially has no ability to use the language beyond possibly a few isolated words.
0	Did not attempt the test	No assessable information provided.

* Reprinted from the IELTS Handbook with permission of the IELTS partners.

How long is my score valid?

An IELTS score is generally recognized for two years. Some institutions may accept your score after 2 years if you can provide proof that you have maintained your English language proficiency. If you are applying for admission to a post-secondary institution, your last test score will be used.

When can I retake the test?

You may repeat the test whenever and as often as you wish. However, some studies suggest that 3 months may be the minimum amount of time that average learners need to improve their band score. During these 3 months, candidates must continue their efforts to improve their English through class study or self-study.

How can I improve my score on each of the test sections?

Most importantly you must read, write, speak, and listen to English on a regular basis. *Barron's IELTS* will help you achieve your goal.

PREPARING FOR IELTS

- **A Study Contract**
- **Using This Book**
- **Tips for Success**
  - Listening Tips
  - Reading Tips
  - Writing Tips
  - Speaking Tips
  - Exam Day Tips

A Study Contract

You must make a commitment to study English. Make a contract with yourself. A contract is a document that establishes procedures. You should not break a contract—especially a contract with yourself.

- Print your name below on line 1.
- Write the total amount of time, the time you will spend each week studying English and the time for each skill area. Think about how much time you have to study every day and every week and make your schedule realistic.
- Sign your name and date the contract on the last lines.
- At the end of each week, add up your hours. Did you meet the requirements of your contract?

IELTS STUDY CONTRACT

I, _____, promise to study for the IELTS. I will begin my study with *Barron's IELTS*, and I will also study English on my own.

I understand that to improve my English I need to spend time on English.

I promise to study English _____ a week.

I will spend _____ hours a week listening to English.
I will spend _____ hours a week writing English.
I will spend _____ hours a week speaking English.
I will spend _____ hours a week reading English.

This is a contract with myself. I promise to fulfill the terms of this contract.

_____   _____
Signed   Date

Self-Study

Here are some ways you can study English on your own. Check the ones you plan to try. Add some of your own ideas.

Internet-Based Self-Study Activities:

Listening

____ Podcasts on the Internet
____ News websites: CNN, BBC, NBC, ABC, CBS
____ Movies in English
____ You Tube
____ _____
____ _____

Speaking

____ Use Skype to talk to English speakers

____ _____

____ _____

Writing

____ Write e-mails to website contacts
____ Write a blog
____ Leave comments on blogs
____ Post messages in a chat room
____ Use Facebook and MySpace

____ _____

____ _____

Reading

____ Read news and magazine articles online
____ Do web research on topics that interest you
____ Follow blogs that interest you

____ _____

____ _____

Other Self-Study Activities:

Listening

____ Listen to CNN and BBC on the radio
____ Watch movies and TV in English
____ Listen to music in English

____ _____

____ _____

Speaking

____ Describe what you see and do out loud
____ Practice speaking with a conversation buddy

____ _____

____ _____

Writing

____ Write a daily journal
____ Write a letter to an English speaker
____ Make lists of the things you see every day
____ Write descriptions of your family and friends

____ _____

____ _____

Reading

_____ Read newspapers and magazines in English
_____ Read books in English
_____ Read academic articles in English
_____ Read informational brochures and pamphlets in English

_____ _____

_____ _____

Examples of Self-Study Activities

Whether you read an article in a newspaper or on a website, you can use that article in a variety of ways to practice reading, writing, speaking, and listening in English.

- Read the article.
- Paraphrase and write about it.
- Give a talk or presentation about it.
- Record or make a video of your presentation.
- Listen to or watch what you recorded. Write down your presentation.
- Correct your mistakes.
- Do it all again.

Plan a Trip

Go to **www.concierge.com**
Choose a city, choose a hotel, go to that hotel's website and choose a room, then choose some sites to visit. (*reading*) Write a report about the city (*writing*). Tell why you want to go there. Describe the hotel and the type of room you will reserve. Tell what sites you plan to visit and when. Where will you eat? How will you get around?

Now write a letter to someone recommending this place. (*writing*) Pretend you have to give a lecture on your planned trip. (*speaking*) Make a video of yourself talking about this place. Then watch the video and write down what you said. (*listening*) Correct any mistakes you made and record the presentation again. Then choose another city and do this again.

Shop for an Electronic Product

Go to **www.cnet.com**
Choose an electronic product and read about it. (*reading*) Write a report about the product. (*writing*) Tell why you want to buy one. Describe its features.

Now write a letter to someone recommending this product. (*writing*) Pretend you have to give a talk about this product. (*speaking*) Make a video of yourself talking about this product. Then watch the video and write down what you said. (*listening*) Correct any mistakes you made and record the presentation again. Then choose another product and do this again.

Discuss a Book, a CD, a Product

Go to **www.amazon.com**
Choose a book or CD or any product. Read the item's description and reviews. (*reading*) Write a report about the item. Tell why you want to buy one or why it is interesting to you. Describe its features.

Now write a letter to someone recommending this product. (*writing*) Pretend you have to give a talk about this product. (*speaking*) Make a video of yourself talking about this product. Then watch the video and write down what you said. (*listening*) Correct any mistakes you made and record the presentation again. Then choose another item and do this again.

Discuss any Subject

Go to **http://simple.wikipedia.org/wiki/Main_Page**
This website is written in simple English. Pick any subject and read the entry. (*reading*)
Write a short essay about the topic. (*writing*) Give a presentation about it. (*speaking*) Make a video of yourself giving the presentation. Then watch the video and write down what you said. (*listening*) Correct any mistakes you made and record the presentation again. Choose another topic and do this again.

Discuss any Event

Go to **http://news.google.com**
Google News has a variety of links. Pick one event and read the articles about it. (*reading*)
Write a short essay about the event. (*writing*) Give a presentation about it. (*speaking*) Make a video of yourself giving the presentation. Then watch the video and write down what you said. (*listening*) Correct any mistakes you made and record the presentation again. Then choose another event and do this again.

Report the News

Listen to an English language news report on the radio or watch a news program on TV. (*listening*)Take notes as you listen. Write a summary of what you heard. (*writing*)
Pretend you are a news reporter. Use the information from your notes to report the news. (*speaking*) Make a video of yourself giving the presentation. Then watch the video and write down what you said. (*listening*) Correct any mistakes you made and record the presentation again. Then listen to another news program and do this again.

Express an Opinion

Read a letter to the editor in the newspaper. (*reading*) Write a letter in response in which you say whether or not you agree with the opinion expressed in the first letter. Explain why. (*writing*)
Pretend you have to give a talk explaining your opinion. (*speaking*) Make a video of yourself giving yourself giving the talk. Then watch the video and write down what you said. (*listening*) Correct any mistakes you made and record the presentation again. Then read another letter to the editor and do this again.

Review a Book or Movie

Read a book (*reading*) or watch a movie (*listening*). Think about your opinion of the book or movie. What did you like about it? What didn't you like about it? Who would you recommend it to and why? Pretend you are a book or movie reviewer for a newspaper or a website. Write a review of the book or movie with your opinion and recommendations. (*writing*)
Give an oral presentation about the book or movie. Explain what it is about and what your opinion of it is. (*speaking*) Make a video of yourself giving the presentation. Then watch the video and write down what you said. (*listening*) Correct any mistakes you made and record the presentation again. Then read another book or watch another movie and do this again.

Summarize a TV Show

Watch a TV show in English. (*listening*) Take notes as you listen. After watching, write a summary of the show. (*writing*)

Use your notes to give an oral summary of the show. Explain the characters, setting, and plot. (*speaking*) Make a video of yourself speaking. Then watch the video and write down what you said. (*listening*) Correct any mistakes you made and record the presentation again. Then watch another TV show and do this again.

Using This Book

You can study the material in this book in many ways. You can study it in a class; you can study it by yourself starting with the first page and going all the way to the end; or you can study only those parts where you know you need extra help.

Here are some suggestions for getting the most out of *Barron's IELTS*.

- Look over the Table of Contents so you have an idea of what is in the book.
- Take a Model Test so you understand where you need more help.
- Become familiar with the directions for IELTS. Get to know what the task is. This will help you move quickly through the test.
- Study efficiently. If you don't have much time, only study where you need extra help.
- Use the strategies. These strategies will help you score well on IELTS.
- Use the explanatory answers. These answers will explain why an answer choice is wrong. For many of the items, the answers will only be approximate. Your answer need not match the one provided as a sample.
- Study a little every day. Don't fall behind. Keep at it.

Tips for Success

Listening Tips

- Make sure that you know what the question is asking.
- Practice listening for a full half-hour. Concentrate. Do not let your mind wander. Can you repeat main ideas and details from what you heard? Can you summarize what you heard?
- Use the time before each Listening section to underline key words in the question, such as *who*, *where*, *when,* and *what*.
- Mark your answers carefully. If you are asked to give a letter (A), don't put the phrase.
- Look out for speakers who correct themselves. Their second statement is the one that is usually asked for.
- Be careful not to make simple spelling mistakes. These will be penalized.
- Incomplete or shortened answers (i.e., times and dates) will be marked as incorrect.
- A variety of accents are used including British, Australian, and American. Practice listening to different native English speakers.
- Remember that answers that exceed word limits (even use of *a* or *the*) will be marked as incorrect.

Reading Tips

- Time management is key. Remember that you won't be given ten extra minutes of transfer time at the end of the Reading module as you are in the Listening module. Also, be prepared for the passages to get progressively more difficult and demand more of your time.

- You will have an hour to work on three reading passages, so you should plan to spend about 20 minutes on each one.
- Skimming and scanning are important comprehension skills. You must learn and practice these skills.
- Learn to analyze titles and headings and to predict paragraph subject matter from subtitles and topic sentences.
- Always read twice the section that is relevant to the question.
- Underline important parts as you read. Do this when you are practicing and when you are taking the test.
- If the instructions ask you to use no more than three words to complete an answer, do not write more than three words. You will lose points.
- Be careful not to confuse *True/False* with *Yes/No*. Many consider these to be the most difficult questions on the test. Practice them often so you will be confident during the test.

Writing Tips

- Don't underestimate the planning stage. It is very important to plan your writing carefully.
- Manage your time carefully. You should spend about 20 minutes on Task 1 and 40 minutes on Task 2. Leave about 5 minutes to proofread your work.
- Paraphrase the question in your introduction.
- Answer all parts of the question, and underline key points in it.
- Remember to indent your paragraphs.
- Learn the words and phrases used to link sentences and paragraphs.
- Add personal experiences and details whenever possible.
- Read as much and as often as you can so that you can become more familiar with the way writing is organized.
- Learn to look at your writing and estimate how many words it is. Don't waste precious time counting words.
- Write neatly and make your letters dark enough so that your writing can be easily read.
- Remember that you will be allowed to use a second sheet of paper if necessary.

Speaking Tips

- Imagine that the examiner is someone you know well.
- Practice introducing yourself and answering typical "getting to know you" questions.
- Don't waste preparation time writing out full sentences. Make notes of just your key ideas.
- Practice turning short notes into a short speech.
- Record your voice and listen to it.
- Practice giving opinions and supporting them with examples and details. You are being marked on your opinions and speaking abilities, not your knowledge.
- Pay attention to verb tenses. You may need to talk about the past, present, and future in the same topic.
- Ask the examiner to repeat or explain a question if the task is unclear.

Exam Day Tips

- Read all communication from the test center carefully. You may receive directions or advice on nearby hotels.
- Be early. Give yourself more than enough time to get to the test center. If you live far away, you may want to arrive the night before. Then you can relax without worrying about being late.
- Be comfortable. Don't wear clothes that don't fit or don't feel good.

- Don't take more than the necessary items with you to the testing center. The only things you will be allowed to take into the testing room are pencils and erasers (rubbers), your identification, and possibly a bottle of water. Everything else, including handbags, coats, jackets (even blazers or other jackets normally worn indoors), and cell (mobile) phones, will have to be left outside the testing room.
- You will have to bring identification with you to the testing site. The test administrators normally ask for a passport. You will be asked to arrive at the testing center at least 30 minutes ahead of time for check-in and identification check. Anyone who arrives late will not be admitted to the test.
- The Listening, Reading, and Writing parts of the test last about 3 hours altogether. You will have to remain in your seat in the testing room during this entire period of time, even if you finish the test early.
- You will be permitted to leave the room to go to the restroom if necessary. Raise your hand and quietly ask the person in charge for permission to leave the testing room. Do not disturb the other test-takers.
- The last part of the test is the Speaking part. It takes up to 20 minutes. This is a face-to-face interview, so each test-taker will be assigned a time for his or her interview. You probably won't know the time for your interview until the day of the test, so you need to be prepared to spend most of the day at the testing center.

LISTENING MODULE

- **QUICK STUDY**
  - Overview
  - Question Types
  - Listening Tips
  - Completing the Blanks
- **LISTENING SKILLS**
  - Target 1—Making Assumptions
  - Target 2—Understanding Numbers
  - Target 3—Understanding the Alphabet
  - Target 4—Listening for Descriptions
  - Target 5—Listening for Time
  - Target 6—Listening for Frequency
  - Target 7—Listening for Similar Meanings
  - Target 8—Listening for Emotions
  - Target 9—Listening for an Explanation
  - Target 10—Listening for Classifications
  - Target 11—Listening for Comparisons and Contrasts
  - Target 12—Listening for Negative Meaning
  - Target 13—Listening for Chronology

QUICK STUDY

Overview

There are four sections to the Listening module. There are 40 questions altogether. The audio will last approximately 30 minutes.

During the test, you will be given time to read the questions *before* you hear the audio. As you listen, you should write your answers in your test booklet. Do not wait until the end. The answers in the audio follow the order of the questions. If you hesitate and think about one question, you may miss the next question. The audio keeps going.

At the end of each section, you will be given 30 seconds to check your answers. You will have an additional 10 minutes to transfer your answers from your test booklet to the official answer sheet. You must transfer your answers. If you don't transfer your answers, your answers will not be counted. If you don't transfer your answers, you will not receive a listening score.

The Listening modules are the same for both the Academic and the General Training versions of the IELTS.

Listening Module

Sections	Topics	Speakers
1	General, everyday topics	Conversation between two people
2	General, everyday topics	One person
3	School or training-related topics	Conversation between two or more people
4	School or training-related topics	One person

Question Types

There are a variety of question types on the IELTS Listening module. You will find examples of these types in this chapter.

Multiple-choice
Short answer
Sentence completion
Chart completion
Flowchart completion
Graphs
Tables

Making notes
Summarizing[1]
Labeling[2] diagrams, plans, and maps
Classification
Matching
Selecting from a list

---

[1]BRITISH: Summarising
[2]BRITISH: labelling

Listening Tips

These tips will help you improve your listening score.

1. Learn and understand the directions now. Use your time during the test to study the questions, not the directions.
2. Study the different types of questions. Be prepared for what the question might ask you to do. Be prepared to complete a sentence, check[1] a box, or choose a letter.
3. Take notes in your question booklet as you listen. You can circle possible answers and change your mind later when you transfer your answers to the answer sheet.
4. If you don't know an answer, guess.
5. Anytime you have a chance, study the next set of questions. Make assumptions about what you think you will hear.
6. When you make assumptions, ask yourself: *Who? What? When? Where?* and *How?*
7. The correct answer is often repeated, but the words will not be written exactly as they are heard. The test will use paraphrases and synonyms.
8. A lot of information given in the conversations and lectures is not tested. Try to listen only for answers to the questions.
9. Don't get stuck on a question. If you didn't hear the answer, go on.
10. The answers are given in order. For example, if you hear the answer to Question 10, but didn't hear the answer for Question 9, you missed Question 9. You will not hear the answer later. Guess the answer to Question 9 and move on.
11. Be sure to read the instructions you receive from the test center. Some test centers supply pencils; some ask you to bring your own. If you are given an IELTS pencil at the start of the exam, you will probably not be allowed to bring your own pen or pencil into the examining room. You could bring a number 2 pencil, a soft lead pencil, to make sure you have something to write with. You may have to leave it outside the test center, but it's better to have a pencil than not.
12. When you write a word in a blank, you must spell the word correctly. It doesn't matter if you use British or American spelling. It must be spelled correctly. You will get a lower score if you did not spell correctly.

Completing the Blanks

Number of Words and Spelling

Many IELTS test-takers do not correctly complete the blanks. Some test-takers use more than the suggested number of words, or they do not spell the answer correctly.

If you make these mistakes, you will lose points. Be careful when you complete blanks. You may know the correct answer, but if you don't spell it correctly or if you add additional words, you will get a lower score.

[1]BRITISH: Tick a box

Number of Words

Complete the sentence below. Write NO MORE THAN THREE WORDS *for each answer.*

Incorrect: The scientists discovered *a new cure/treatment*.

Correct: The scientists discovered *a cure*.

> The incorrect answer above counts as four words. Four words will count against you. You can use fewer than three words, but you cannot use more than three words. Do not use a slash.

Number of Words

Complete the sentence below. Write NO MORE THAN THREE WORDS *for each answer.*

Incorrect: The scientists discovered *a new cancer treatment*.

Correct: The scientists discovered *a cancer treatment*.

> The incorrect answer above counts as four words. Four words will count against you. Use no more than three.

Spelling

Complete the sentence below. Write NO MORE THAN THREE WORDS *for each answer.*

Incorrect: The scientists discovered *a cancer treetment*.

Correct: The scientists discovered *a cancer treatment*.

> You must spell the words correctly. A misspelled word will count against you. You can use British or American spelling, but you must spell the word correctly.

> You can practice your spelling by taking dictation. Listen to the audio in this book. Write down everything you hear. Check your spelling in the audio script in the back of this book.

Questions 1–10

The following statements are not completed correctly. Write the correct answer. Write NO MORE THAN THREE WORDS *for each answer.*

1 The shelves were filled with *with fruits and fresh vegetables*.
The shelves were filled with *fruits and vegetables*.

> In the incorrect sentence, *with* is repeated, *fruits* is misspelled, the adjective *fresh* is not necessary to the statement, and there are five words instead of three.

2 Cynthia lives near *to the train stattion*.
Cynthia lives near ....

3 If you return a library book late, you must *pay a fine of 25 cents[1] a day*.
If you return a library book late, you must ....

4 Their trip was spoiled because of *they had very bad weather*.
Their trip was spoiled because of ....

---

[1]US Currency: 100 cents in one dollar.

5   The fountain is in the center of the *beautiful, sunny roses garden*.
    The fountain is in the center of the ....
6   Students *usually can to choose* the topic for their essay.
    Students .... the topic for their essay.
7   *More or less ten thousand of* visitors come to the museum each year.
    .... visitors come to the museum each year.
8   If you don't understand the assignment, you should *have to ask the professor* for help.
    If you don't understand the assignment, you should .... for help.
9   Roberto was excited about *about taking a trip to Alaska*.
    Roberto was excited about ....
10 Many northern song birds *spend the long witer* in Mexico.
    Many northern song birds .... in Mexico.

Gender and Number

The words you write in a blank must match the tense, gender, and number of the rest of the sentence. Don't use a singular verb when a plural verb is required. Don't use a singular noun when a plural noun is required. Don't use a masculine pronoun to refer to a feminine or neutral antecedent. You may know the correct answer, but if you don't use correct grammar, you will get a lower score.

Verb Agreement

Incorrect: The scientists at the research hospital *is looking* for a cure.
Correct: The scientists at the research hospital *are looking* for a cure.

The incorrect answer above uses a singular verb *is*. A plural verb *are* refers to the plural subject *scientists*. The singular noun *hospital* is the object of the preposition *at*, not the subject of the sentence.

Singular/Plural Noun

Incorrect: They ordered five *shirt*.
Correct: They ordered five *shirts*.

The incorrect answer above uses a singular noun *shirt*. A plural noun *shirts* is needed because of the plural number *five*.

Pronoun Agreement

Incorrect: The patients have confidence *in his doctors*.
Correct: The patients have confidence *in their doctors*.

The incorrect answer above uses a singular pronoun *his*. A plural pronoun *their* refers to the plural subject *patients*.

Questions 1–10

The following statements are not completed correctly. Write the correct answer. Write NO MORE THAN THREE WORDS *for each answer.*

1 Unlike most other ducks, wood ducks *build thier nest* in trees.
  Unlike most other ducks, wood ducks .... in trees.
2 The new compact laptop computer is very popular among *busines traveler*.
  The new compact laptop computer is very popular among ....
3 Bananas grow in *in a tropicale climates*.
  Bananas grow in ....
4 Fruit *cost moor* in the winter than in the summer.
  Fruit .... in the winter than in the summer.
5 Mrs. Smith donated *his old close* to charity.
  Mrs. Smith donated .... to charity.
6 Students in this class have to *must take two exam* this semester[1].
  Students in this class have to .... this semester.
7 The college professor bought *new house*.
  The college professor bought ....
8 Mr. and Mrs. Rodgers *took his vacations*[2] in August this year.
  Mr. and Mrs. Rogers .... in August this year.
9 Every house *have a garden* in the back.
  Every house .... in the back.
10 The female dragonfly *likes to lay their eggs* under water.
   The female dragonfly .... under water.

Articles

When completing a blank, you must use an article—*a, an, the*—if grammar requires it. An article counts as one word, just like any other word you may put in a blank.

When referring to something in general, you can use a plural noun without an article, or you can use a singular noun with *a* or *an*. If you use a non-count noun, do not use an article when speaking in general.

Incorrect: *Child needs* good nutrition to grow up healthy.
Correct: *Children need* good nutrition to grow up healthy.
Correct: *A child needs* good nutrition to grow up healthy.

When referring to specific people, places, or things, use *the* with a singular, plural, or non-count noun.

Incorrect: *Homework* in this class is very time consuming.
Correct: *The homework* in this class is very time consuming.

Questions 1–10

The following statements are not completed correctly. Write the correct answer. Write NO MORE THAN THREE WORDS *for each answer.*

1 We have to complete *all assignment* in this class before the end of the semester.
  We have to complete .... in this class before the end of the semester.

[1]BRITISH: term
[2]BRITISH: holiday

2 *A moth* usually fly at night.
.... usually fly at night.

3 The professor showed us a butterfly. *Butterfly* had beautiful colors.
The professor showed us a butterfly. .... had beautiful colors.

4 The old library building is too small, and it needs many repairs. Therefore, the City Council is talking about building *the new library* .
The old library building is too small, and it needs many repairs. Therefore, the City Council is talking about building ....

5 *The air pollution* is a serious problem in many large cities around the world.
.... is a serious problem in many large cities around the world.

6 *Animals* living near the Arctic has special adaptations for the cold climate.
.... living near the Arctic has special adaptations for the cold climate.

7 Keep your ticket with you at all times. To get a discount at the museum gift shop, show *a ticket* to the gift shop clerk.
Keep your ticket with you at all times. To get a discount at the museum gift shop, show .... to the gift shop clerk.

8 *An information* in this book will help you pass the course.
.... in this book will help you pass the course.

9 *The gold* is a precious metal that is valued by people everywhere.
.... is a precious metal that is valued by people everywhere.

10 *Pet parrot* requires a lot of care and attention.
.... requires a lot of care and attention.

Gerunds, Infinitives, and Base Form Verbs

When you write a verb, you must use the correct form. The main verb of a sentence has a verb tense. Other verbs in a sentence might be in the gerund, infinitive, or base form.

Gerunds *(verb + ing) can be used as the subject of a sentence. Gerunds follow certain verbs. They also follow prepositions.*

Incorrect: *Eat sweets* can cause weight gain and other health problems.
Correct: *Eating sweets* can cause weight gain and other health problems.

Incorrect: Many tourists *enjoy to visit* the museum.
Correct: Many tourists *enjoy visiting* the museum.

Incorrect: They are interested in *learn about history* .
Correct: They are interested in *learning about history* .

Infinitives *(* to + verb*) often follow adjectives. Infinitives also follow certain verbs.*

Incorrect: In the Antarctic climate, it is important *keeping warm* .
Correct: In the Antarctic climate, it is important *to keep warm* .

Incorrect: He expected *returning to school* in the autumn.
Correct: He expected *to return to school* in the autumn.

Base form verbs *follow modals.*

Incorrect: You can _to find information_ in the university library.
Correct: You can _find information_ in the university library.

Questions 1–10

The following statements are not completed correctly. Write the correct answer. Write **NO MORE THAN THREE WORDS** *for each answer.*

1 We will finish _read this novel_ before the end of the semester.
   We will finish .... before the end of the semester.
2 He _plans arrive_ in Chicago at 10:00.
   He .... in Chicago at 10:00.
3 She should _waiting for Jim_ at the health club.
   She should .... at the health club.
4 All visitors must _to have a ticket_ to enter the museum.
   All visitors must .... to enter the museum.
5 _Pay a deposit_ will secure the apartment for you.
   .... will secure the apartment for you.
6 It's easier _get reservations_ at the hotel during the winter season.
   It's easier .... at the hotel during the winter season.
7 Marvin felt nervous about _gave his report_ in front of the class.
   Marvin felt nervous about .... in front of the class.
8 You cannot _missing more than_ three classes during the semester.
   You cannot .... three classes during the semester.
9 Sarah failed the class because she was confused about _fulfills the lab_ requirement.
   Sarah failed the class because she was confused about .... requirement.
10 They hoped _saw alligators_ during their tour of the Everglades.
    They hoped .... during their tour of the Everglades.

LISTENING SKILLS

Target 1—Making Assumptions

In order to understand a conversation, you should focus on two things: the speakers and the topic. To score well on the IELTS, you should determine what you know and what you need to know.

As you listen to a conversation, you must make some assumptions about the speakers.

Who are they?
What is their relationship?
Where are they?
What do they plan to do?
What did they do?
What are their feelings?

You must also make some assumptions about the topic.

What are they talking about?
What happened?
What might happen?

You want to know *who*, *what*, *when*, *where*, *why*, and *how*.

To help you make these assumptions, you should scan the questions in your Listening Test booklet quickly and ask yourself: *Who? What? When? Where? Why?* and *How?* By looking for the answers to these general questions, you will discover what you know and what you need to know.

You will have about 20 seconds to look over these questions. Use that time to make assumptions about the listening passage. Read the question first. Then read the exercise on "Assumptions" on the following page. Do the exercises. Finally, listen to the conversation and test your assumptions.

SECTION 1—Questions 1–10

Questions 1–5

Complete the form below. Write NO MORE THAN THREE WORDS AND/OR A NUMBER for each answer.

Woodside Apartments[1]
Tenant Application Form

_____
EXAMPLE
_____

Type of apartment requested: *One bedroom*

Last name[2] **1** _____ First name <u>James</u>

Address 1705 **2** _____ Street, Apt. **3** _____

Phone: Home <u>721 - 0584</u>   Work: **4** _____

Date of birth **5** _____ 12, 1978[3]

Questions 6–8

Choose three letters, **A–G**.

What features will James get with his apartment?
   A   study
   B   balcony
   C   garage parking space[4]
   D   storage space
   E   exercise club
   F   fireplace
   G   washing machine

Questions 9–10

Complete the sentences. Write NO MORE THAN THREE WORDS for each answer.

9 The apartment will be ready next _____.

10 James will have to pay _____ of the first month's rent as a deposit.

[1]BRITISH: flats

[2]BRITISH: surname

[3]BRITISH: day month year; AMERICAN: month day, year

[4]BRITISH: parking place

ASSUMPTIONS

Find the answers to: Who? What? When? Where? Why? and How?

> Who are the speakers?
> What are they talking about?
> When is something happening?
> Where is something happening?
> Why are they having a conversation?

We know this:

James wants to rent an apartment at the Woodside Apartments. He is a prospective tenant. The apartment is not ready yet. He will have to pay a deposit.

Answer these questions. Write NO MORE THAN THREE WORDS for each answer.

> Who: *James*
> What: *renting an apartment*
> When: *Not ready*
> Where: *Woodside Apartments*
> Why: *apartment deposit*

Circle the clues in Questions 1–10 that help you make these assumptions.
James wants to rent a one-bedroom apartment at the Woodside Apartments.

> *How do we know his first name is James?*
> *How do we know he wants to rent?*
> *How do we know he wants a one-bedroom apartment?*
> *How do we know the name of the building?*

He is a prospective tenant.

> *How do we know he is a prospective tenant?*

The apartment is not ready yet.

> *How do we know the apartment is not ready?*

He will have to pay a deposit.

> *How do we know there is a deposit?*

We don't know this:

Write the number in Questions 1–10 next to the question you have to answer.

What is James' last name?	Question _____
What street does he live on?	Question _____
What is his work telephone number?	Question _____
What month was he born?	Question _____
What features will he get with his apartment?	Question _____
When will the apartment be ready?	Question _____
How much is the deposit?	Question _____

CD1
TRACK
1

Now listen to the conversation. Listen for the answers you don't know.

SECTION 2—Questions 11–20

Questions 11–13

Complete the information about the museum. Write NO MORE THAN THREE WORDS AND/OR A NUMBER for each answer.

Jamestown Museum of Art
Information for Visitors

Entrance Fees: Adults $ **11** _____
                      Children $ **12** _____
                      Entrance is free for senior citizens on **13** _____ .

Hours
Tues–Thur 11:00 A.M.–5:00 P.M.
Fri 11:00 A.M.–7:00 P.M.
Sat–Sun 10:00 A.M.–6:00 P.M.
Mondays and holidays closed

Questions 14–18

Fill in the missing information on the map of the museum. Write NO MORE THAN THREE WORDS for each answer.

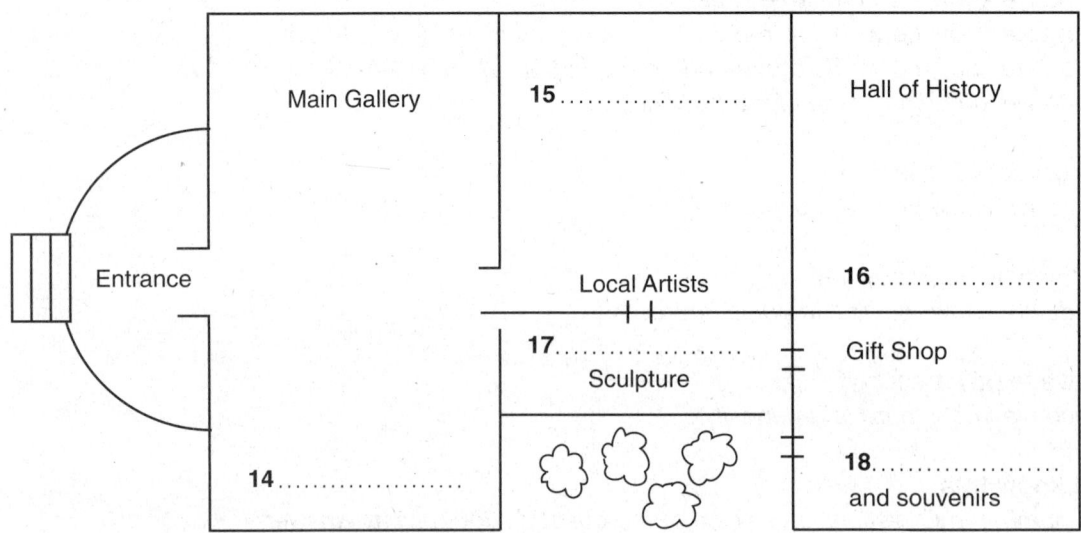

Questions 19–20

Complete the notice below. Write NO MORE THAN THREE WORDS for each answer.

Notice to museum visitors.

The following areas are restricted.

Hall of History: Closed for **19** _____ . Will reopen in April.

20 _____ : Museum staff offices. Employees only. All others must have an appointment.

ASSUMPTIONS

Find the answers to: Who? What? When? Where? and Why?

Who are the speakers?
What are they talking about?
When is something happening?
Where is something happening?
Why are they having a conversation?

We know this:

The Jamestown Museum of Art has varied hours of operation, but it is closed on Monday and holidays. There are four galleries. One gallery has local art. The other has sculpture. There is a gift shop. The Hall of History will reopen in April. The Museum staff offices are open only by appointment to non-staff members.

Answer these questions. Write NO MORE THAN THREE WORDS for each answer.

Who: _____
What:_____
When: _____
Where: _____
Why: _____

Circle the clues in Questions 11–20 that help you make these assumptions.

We do not know this:

Write the number in Questions 11–20 next to the question you have to answer.

What is the admission price for adults?   Question _____
What is the admission price for children?   Question _____
When is there no admission fee for senior citizens?   Question _____
What kind of art is in the Hall of History?   Question _____
In which gallery is local art located?   Question _____
What kind of art is in the Main Gallery?   Question _____
In which gallery is sculpture located?   Question _____
What besides souvenirs is sold in the gift shop?   Question _____
Why is the Hall of History closed?   Question _____
Where are the staff offices located?   Question _____

These questions are to help you focus your attention. No answers for them are provided in the Answer Key.

Now listen to the conversation. Listen for the answers you don't know.

Target 2—Understanding Numbers

Many of the questions on the IELTS Listening Module ask you to remember, identify, and/or write numbers that you hear. This is an easy skill to practice, but a difficult one to perfect.

EXAMPLE

You will see: *Write the number you hear.*
                 What is the flight number? ....

You will hear: Flight 33 leaves from Gate 13 Concourse C3.

Many numbers sound alike. Here are a few easily confused numbers.

3	13	30	33
4	14	40	44
6	16	60	66

   Try to use the context to make a guess about what you are hearing. When you look over the questions to make assumptions about the topic, pay attention to those questions that ask for specific numbers. Listen carefully for those numbers.

Questions 1–5

Listen for the numbers and answer the questions. Write a number in the blank or *choose the correct letter, **A**, **B**, or **C**.*

1

Credit Card Charge Form	
Card Holder:	Roger Wilcox
Address:	13 High Street
Card Number:	....

2   How many seats are there in the new theater?
   A   200
   B   250
   C   500

3

Name	Phone
Roberts, Sherry	....

4   How much will the woman pay for the hotel room?
   A $255
   B $265
   C $315

5

```
         Lost Luggage Report
Passenger name:  Richard Lyons
Flight number:  ..............................
```

Questions 6–10

Listen to these telephone numbers. Pay attention to the way three different speakers say the same number.

1   703–6588
2   744–1492
3   202–9983
4   671–4532
5   824–1561

Now write the numbers you hear.

6   ....
7   ....
8   ....
9   ....
10 ....

Target 3—Understanding the Alphabet

Many of the questions on the IELTS Listening module ask you to remember, identify, and/or write letters of the alphabet that you hear. This is a good skill to practice for the test and for real life.

EXAMPLE

You will see: *Write the name you hear.*
                  What is the person's name? ....

You will hear:
Speaker 1:   Is your name spelled[1] L - i - n or L - y - n - n?
Speaker 2:   Actually, it's Lynne with an e.

Questions 1–6

Circle the correct spelling of the name you hear.

1   Tomas   Thomas
2   Maine   Main
3   Patty   Patti
4   Roberts   Robertson
5   Springfield   Springvale
6   Nixon   Dixson

[1]BRITISH: spelt

CD1
TRACK
6

Questions 7–12

Complete the statements. Write NO MORE THAN THREE WORDS AND/OR A NUMBER for the answer.

7

> **Order Form**
>
> Name **A** .... *Green*
> Credit Card Number **B** ....

8

> **Telephone Directory**
>
> Barney's Discount Store   673–0982
> **A** .... Theater   **B**................

9

> **Hotel Serenity**
>
> Albert Street (Private Bag 91031)
> Auckland 1, New Zealand
> Tel: (9) 309-6445
>
> **Reservations**
>
> Name: *Roberta*   **A** ....
> Room number *304*
> Price   **B**   £.........................

10

> **Royale Theater**
> **Ticket Order Form**
>
> Name: *Peter Park* ....
> Address: *75*   **A**.................... *Street*
> City: *Riverdale* ....
> Seat number: **B** ....

11

> Professor: Dr.[1] **A** ....
> Office hours: T, Th 3:00–5:00
> Office number: **B** ....

12

> **Addresses**
>
> **W**
> Name: Wild Flower Society ....
> Address: **A** .... State Street
> City: **B** ....

[1]BRITISH: No period after Dr

Target 4—Listening for Descriptions

When you listen to a conversation or a lecture, you see in your mind what the speaker is discussing. If the speaker talks about a garden, you will see in your mind some plants, trees, and walkways. As the speaker continues and talks about a fountain in the garden, you will add a fountain in your mind's eye. You might think the fountain is made of cement, but the speaker describes one made of marble. You can change the image easily in your mind.

On the IELTS, you will have to listen to descriptions and match them to a drawing in your test booklet.

EXAMPLE

Look at the following houses. Write a short description of each.

A

B

C

*Now listen to the conversation. Where does the woman live? Choose the correct letter, **A**, **B**, or **C**.*

Questions 1–2

1 *Look at the following men. Write a short description of each.*

A   B   C

_____   _____   _____
_____   _____   _____

*Now listen to the news bulletin. Choose the letter that matches the description **A**, **B**, or **C**.*

2 *Look at the following women. Write a short description of each.*

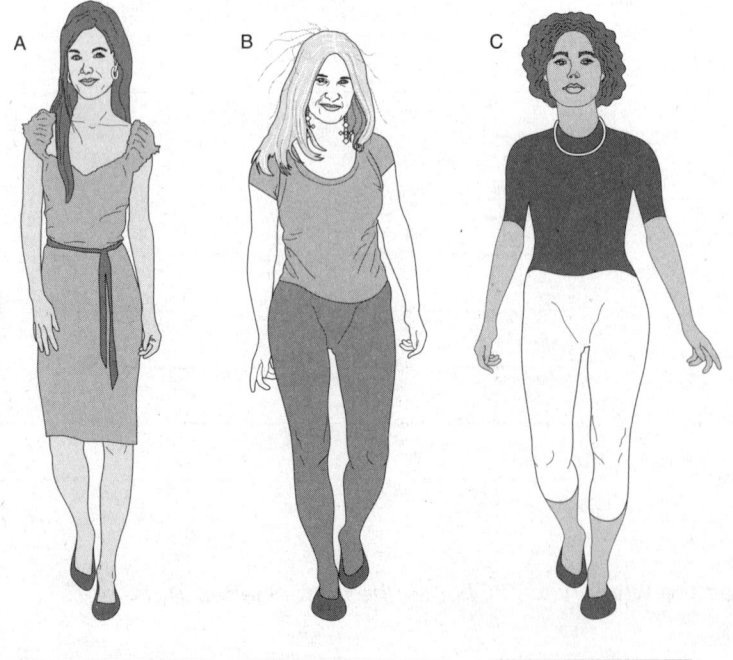

A   B   C

_____   _____   _____
_____   _____   _____

*Now listen to the conversation. Choose the letter that matches the description **A**, **B**, or **C**.*

Target 5—Listening for Time

Listening for time is a very important skill. You must know when something happened. You must listen for a date, a day, a month, a year, or a time.

EXAMPLE

You will see: *Choose the correct letter, **A**, **B**, or **C**.*

A      B      C

You will hear: The train was almost thirty minutes late. It didn't arrive until five o'clock.

Common Words and Phrases for Time

10:00 A.M. noon 5:00 P.M. Midnight	In January In February May 3 November 14	1912 1925 2005 2007	This week This month Next week Next month
At 4:00 Before 6:30 to 3:30 After 7:00 Half-past two Quarter-past three Quarter to four	March 5 of this year April 12 of next year	In the spring In the summer In the autumn[1]	On weekday mornings Any afternoon from 1:00
Sunday Monday Tuesday	On June 10th On August 3rd	Yesterday Tomorrow Day after tomorrow	

[1]AMERICAN: Fall

TIME—QUESTIONS 1–6

Listen for the correct time.

Questions 1 and 2

*Choose the correct letter, **A**, **B**, or **C**.*

1   What time does the class usually begin?
    A   2:00
    B   2:30
    C   4:00

2   What time will the final exam begin?
    A   1:45
    B   3:15
    C   4:05

Questions 3 and 4

*Choose the correct letter, **A**, **B**, or **C**.*

3   What time will the next train leave for Chicago?

4   What time will it arrive in Chicago?

Questions 5 and 6

Complete the schedule with the correct times.

Cindy's Schedule

Monday	
9:00	Spanish class
11:30	haircut
5.........	lunch with Jeannine
1:30	job interview
6.........	exercise class

DATE—QUESTIONS 1–6

Most of the world writes the date as day/month/year (dd/mm/yy). Americans write month/day/year (mm/dd/yy).

American:	May 15, 2010	April 23rd, 2009
International:	15 May 2010	23rd April 2009

Both forms are included in these exercises.

Listen for the correct date.

Questions 1 and 2

Complete these notes with the correct date and month.

> **Notes**
>
> *City Museum of Art*
> *Opened: August 1 ...., 1898*
> *Opening celebration: 2 .... 1, 1898*

Questions 3 and 4

Complete the form with the correct month and date.

> Insurance Application
>
> Applicant name: *Priscilla Katz* ....   Date of birth: **3** **22**
> Spouse: *Georges Katz* ....   Date of birth: *July* **4** ....

Questions 5 and 6

*Choose the correct letter, **A**, **B**, or **C**.*

5 Which is the most popular time to visit Silver Lake?
   A August
   B September
   C October

6 What day will the man leave for Silver Lake?
   A 7 November
   B 11 November
   C 17 November

DAY—QUESTIONS 1–6

Listen for the correct day.

Questions 1 and 2

Complete the schedule with the correct days.

> Class Schedule for <u>Jim McDonald</u>
>
> English: **1** .... and Wednesday ....
> History: **2** ....

Questions 3 and 4

Complete each sentence with the correct day.

There are tennis lessons at the club every **3** .... and Saturday.
The steam room is closed every **4** ....

Questions 5 and 6

*Choose the correct letter, **A**, **B**, or **C**.*

5 When is the final exam?
  A Thursday
  B Friday
  C Saturday

6 When is the essay due?
  A Monday
  B Tuesday
  C Wednesday

YEAR—QUESTIONS 1–6

Listen for the correct year.

Questions 1 and 2

Complete the time line with the correct year.

Life of John James Audubon

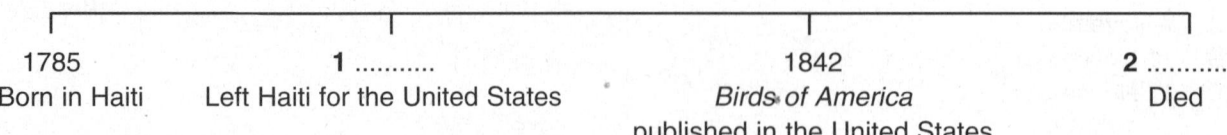

1785	1	1842	2 ....
Born in Haiti	Left Haiti for the United States	*Birds of America* published in the United States	Died

Questions 3 and 4

*Choose the correct letter, **A**, **B**, or **C**.*

3   When was Maria Mahoney born?
   A   1808
   B   1908
   C   1928

4   When did she become governor?
   A   1867
   B   1957
   C   1967

Questions 5 and 6

Complete the sentences with the correct years.

5   Library construction was begun in ....
6   The construction was finished in ....

SEASON—QUESTIONS 1–6

Listen for the correct season.

Questions 1 and 2

Complete the table with the correct seasons.

Season	Weather
1	cool, rainy
2	hot, dry

Questions 3 and 4

*Choose the correct letter, **A**, **B**, or **C**.*

3   When did Josh begin his hiking trip?
   A   Late winter
   B   Early spring
   C   Late spring

4   When did he finish his trip?
   A   Late summer
   B   Late autumn[1]
   C   Early winter

[1] AMERICAN: Fall or autumn

Questions 5 and 6

Complete the sentences with the correct years.

5   The busiest time of year at the language school is ....
6   The least busy time of year at the language school is ....

Target 6—Listening for Frequency

There are certain adverbs that tell you when something might happen. These two groups of adverbs will help you determine the time.

CD1
TRACK
13

EXAMPLE

You will see: *Choose the correct letter, **A**, **B**, or **C**.*
                  Sam goes to the gym
                  (A) every day.
                  (B) often.
                  (C) occasionally.

You will hear: Sam works out at the gym several days a week.

Common Adverbs of Frequency	**Common Adverbial Time Words or Phrases**
always usually often sometimes occasionally seldom hardly ever rarely never	every day daily twice a week once a month on occasion every year, yearly every other week from time to time once in a while

Questions 1–6

Listen to the conversations. Put a check[1] (✓) by the frequency of the action.

	always	often	sometimes	seldom	never
1					
2					
3					
4					
5					
6					

[1]BRITISH: tick

Questions 7–12

Listen to the conversations. Put a check (✓) by the frequency of the action.

	daily	twice a week	once a month	every other week	from time to time
7					
8					
9					
10					
11					
12					

Target 7—Listening for Similar Meanings

The words that you hear are not always the words that you see in your test booklet. You will have to listen for similar meanings. You could hear a synonym or you could hear a paraphrase.

EXAMPLE

You will see: *Write the answer.*

  Who are the <u>respondents</u>? ....

You will hear: The survey <u>participants</u> who wrote answers to the questions are all college graduates.

Questions 1–6

Look at the underlined words or phrases in the questions below. Listen to the audio. Write the synonym or paraphrase that you hear.

1   How many people are in the <u>group</u>?   ....
2   When is the work <u>corrected</u>?   ....
3   How <u>fast</u> is the population increasing?   ....
4   What happened to the <u>plants</u> in the region?   ....
5   When will the apartment be <u>ready</u>?   ....
6   What kind of <u>work</u> does the woman do?   ....

Target 8—Listening for Emotions

Can you tell if someone is excited to do something or is not looking forward to something? While listening, try to determine a speaker's emotion. How is that emotion expressed?

EXAMPLE

You will see: *Choose the correct letter, **A**, **B**, or **C**.*

What is Mark's attitude toward the debate?
A   He's nervous.
B   He's looking forward to it.
C   He's more excited than Jane.

You will hear: Jane: I can't wait to debate the team from Oxford.
              Mark: I'm more apprehensive than excited. In fact, I'm not looking forward to it at all.

Common Words That Express Emotion

afraid	ecstatic	nervous
angry	embarrassed	pleased
annoyed	exhausted	proud
ashamed	frustrated	sad
bored	happy	shocked
confused	jealous	surprised
disappointed	mad	unhappy
disgusted	miserable	upset
		worried

Questions 1–6

Listen to the conversations and answer the questions about emotions.

1   How did local residents feel about the millionaire's donation?
   A   angry
   B   surprised
   C   excited

2   How does the man feel about his science experiment?
   A   frustrated
   B   glad
   C   eager

3   What confuses students?
   A   foreign languages
   B   language lab equipment
   C   class assignments and tests

4 What is the man's attitude toward the contest?
  A He's upset.
  B He's disappointed.
  C He's indifferent.

5 How did people at the school feel about the mayor's visit?
  A They were surprised.
  B They were bored.
  C They were annoyed.

6 How does the woman feel about her research project?
  A nervous
  B bad
  C happy

Target 9—Listening for an Explanation

On the IELTS, a speaker may explain how something is done or made. You will have to listen and remember the steps of the process.

CD1
TRACK
17

EXAMPLE

You will see: *Match the letter in the diagram with one of these labels.*

1 _____ Electrical socket[1]
2 _____ Metal loops of wires
3 _____ Cord
4 _____ Appliance
5 _____ Your toast is ready to eat!
6 _____ Plug

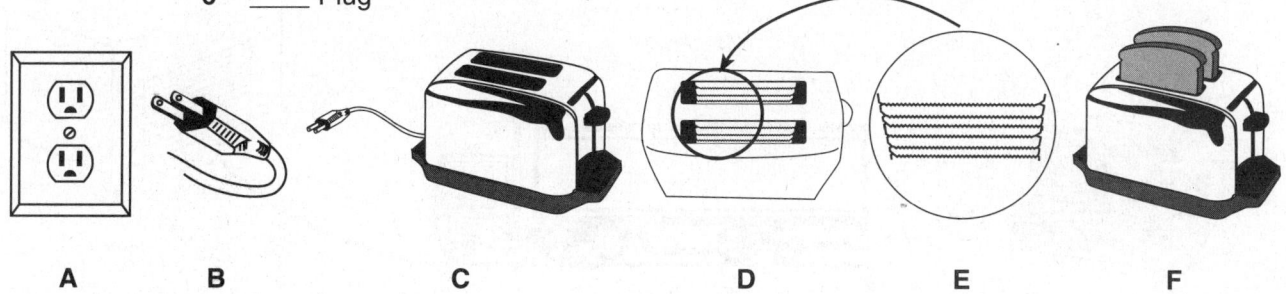

A   B   C   D   E   F

You will see: *Complete these sentences describing the process to make toast. Write* NO MORE THAN THREE WORDS *for each answer.*

7 Electricity runs from _____.
8 Electricity runs down _____.
9 Electricity runs to _____.
10 Electricity is slowed by _____.
11 When resistance to metal is high, metal will get _____.

[1]AMERICAN: outlet, also socket

12 The wires turn _____.
13 The bread _____.
14 You eat the _____.

You will hear: How does a toaster brown your toast every morning? Like all household appliances that heat up, a toaster works by converting electrical energy into heat energy. The electrical current runs from the electrical outlet in your kitchen wall, through the toaster plug, to the toaster cord. It travels down the cord to the appliance itself. Inside the toaster are wire loops. The wires are made of a special type of metal. Electricity passes slowly through this metal, creating friction. This friction causes the wires to heat up and glow orange. When the wires have sufficiently heated, your toast pops ready to eat.

Questions 1–12

Label the process diagram below based on what you hear.

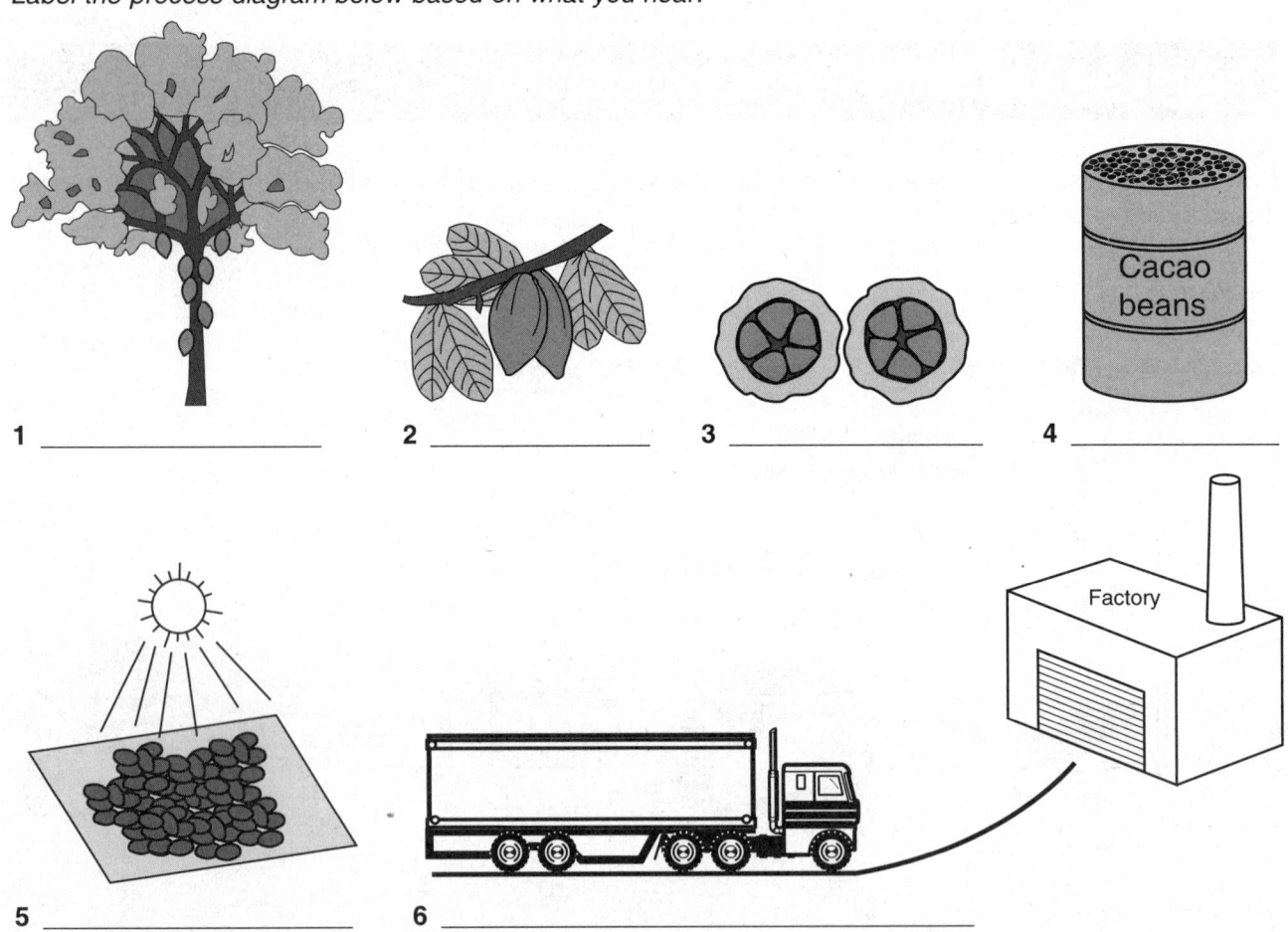

1 _____
2 _____
3 _____
4 _____

5 _____
6 _____

Complete the sentences. Write **NO MORE THAN THREE WORDS** *for each answer.*

7   When the fruit is ripe, it ....
8   Then the seeds ....
9   The cocoa[1] beans are fermented in vats for ....
10   Then the beans .... in the sun.
11   The cocoa beans .... the factory.
12   At the factory, the cacao beans are turned into ....

[1]Cacao refers to the tree. Cocoa is the drink. Cocoa is often used for both the tree and the beverage.

Target 10—Listening for Classifications

You will have to group similar objects or ideas on the IELTS Listening section. You will have to determine how to classify objects or ideas.

CD1 TRACK 18

EXAMPLE

You will see: *When would these courses most likely be offered? Write them under the appropriate program[1] below.*

Project Management   Literature of the 21st Century
History of Africa   Labor[2] Negotiations
The Art of Negotiating   International Relations
Creativity in the Workplace   Introduction to Philosophy

Course Offerings

1 .... Program	2 ....
Introduction to Art	Organizational[3] Behavior
Basic Chemistry	Commercial Law
Beginning Spanish	Compensation and Benefits
....	....
....	....
....	....
....	....

You will hear: The school offers two types of courses. One during the day is designed for students who are pursuing their academic degree full time. The night courses are designed for students who work during the day and are taking specific courses for an advanced business certificate.

These words and phrases are often used when classifying something.

Classification Words and Phrases

Can be divided into	Types
Can be categorized[4] as	Kinds
Can fit into this category	Ways

[1]BRITISH: programme
[2]BRITISH: labour
[3]BRITISH: organisational
[4]BRITISH: categorised

Questions 1–5

Complete the classifications below based on what you hear.

1   *Which of the following are offered to first-class passengers only? Choose three letters, A–E.*
   A   pillows and blankets
   B   snacks
   C   full meals
   D   magazines
   E   free movies

2   *Complete the chart. Write ONE WORD for each answer.*

Royal Theater	Deluxe Theater
War films	**B** .... films
A .... films	Classic films

3   *Complete the chart. Write ONE WORD for each answer.*

	A	**B** ....
Time to fly	Day	Night
Wing position	Folded back	Horizontal
Antennae	Thin	Feathery

4   *Check the things that the woman has already done to get ready for the party.*

> To Do List
> **A**   Clean house __
> **B**   Cook __
> **C**   Go shopping __
> **D**   Plan decorations __
> **E**   Mail invitations __

5   *Complete the chart. Write NO MORE THAN THREE WORDS for each answer.*

Tree Type	Description
A	Beautiful flowers, interesting leaves
B	Tall, broad leaves
C	Cones, needles

Target 11—Listening for Comparisons and Contrasts

Speakers often compare or contrast objects or ideas to help describe something. On the IELTS Listening section, you will have to determine what is being compared and what is being contrasted.

CD1 TRACK 19

EXAMPLE

You will see: Put a check (✓) to show if these items are alike or different.

		Same	Different
A	Nationality		
B	Sex		
C	Age		
D	Given name		
E	Present occupation		
F	Future occupation		
G	Sports		
H	Love of dancing		

You will hear:

Speaker 1: I've been corresponding by letter with a French student.

Speaker 2: In English? You don't speak French, do you?

Speaker 1: No, unfortunately, but she writes English well. We have a lot in common.

Speaker 2: Like what, your age?

Speaker 1: Well, I'm actually about two years older than she is. But we do have the same first name.

Speaker 2: And you're both students.

Speaker 1: Yes, and we both are studying to be doctors, although she wants to be a pediatrician[1], and I want to be a neurosurgeon.

Speaker 2: It seems the only similarities are your sex and your given name.

Speaker 1: Well, we both like to swim. She likes to dance, too, but you know how little I like dancing.

These words and phrases are often used with comparison and contrast.

Comparison		Contrast	
almost the same as	in common	although	more than
also	just as	but	nevertheless
as	like, alike	differ from	on the other hand
at the same time as	neither/nor	different from	otherwise
correspondingly	resemble	even though	still
either/or	similar to	however	unlike
in a like manner	similarly	in contrast to	while
in the same way	than	instead	yet
		less than	

[1]BRITISH: paediatrician

Questions 1–4

Complete the chart below based on what you hear.
Put a check (✓) to show if these items are alike or different.

1 Jobs

	Alike	Different
A Salary		
B Schedule		
C Responsibilities		
D Location		
E Transportation		

2 Libraries

	Alike	Different
A Location		
B Size		
C Parking facilities		
D Number of books		
E Services		

3 Club Memberships

	Alike	Different
A Cost		
B Use of club facilities		
C Access to fitness classes		
D Locker room privileges		
E Individual fitness plan		

4 Frogs and Toads

	Alike	Different
A Place for babies to live		
B Place for adults to live		
C Type of skin		
D Shape		
E Way to make sounds		

Target 12—Listening for Negative Meaning

On the IELTS, you may have to determine whether a statement is positive or negative. Listen to the statement carefully to determine whether the sense of the statement is positive or negative.

CD1
TRACK
20

EXAMPLE

You will see: *Choose the correct letter, **A**, **B**, or **C**.*

What does the woman say about the book?
A   She couldn't read it.
B   She was able to read it.
C   She enjoyed reading it.

You will hear: It was a very dense book, but it wasn't impossible to read.

A negative prefix can contradict the word it joins. This usually results in a negative meaning. For example, *unfriendly* contradicts *friendly* and has the negative meaning *not friendly*. But when a negative meaning is added to a negative word, the resulting meaning can be positive. For example, *unselfish* contradicts *selfish* and has the positive meaning *not selfish*.

You can also put a negative word before a verb or clause to change the meaning of the sentence.

These are common negative markers.

Before verbs/clauses	Before nouns/phrases	Negative prefixes	Positive meanings from negative prefixes	
not isn't/can't/won't/shouldn't/ couldn't/hasn't/mustn't rarely/only rarely hardly scarcely seldom never barely not since not until and neither	no nowhere nothing at no time not at this time in no case by no means	un im il in non	undone impossible illegal indefinite nonsense	unlimited unparalleled invaluable nonrestrictive nonviolent

Questions 1–6

Put a check (✓) next to the correct paraphrase of each sentence.

1 I can't wait to start the class.

__ **A** I'm looking forward to the class.

__ **B** I'm not looking forward to the class.

2 The teacher is not only my favorite[1] teacher, she's also my neighbor[2].

__ **A** I like my teacher a lot.

__ **B** I don't like my teacher very much.

3 I can't say that it was a particularly comfortable hotel.

__ **A** The hotel was comfortable.

__ **B** The hotel wasn't comfortable.

4 We'll never find a book as interesting as this.

__ **A** The book is very interesting.

__ **B** The book isn't very interesting.

5 That was not an illegal action.

__ **A** The action was legal.

__ **B** The action wasn't legal.

6 We could scarcely understand him.

__ **A** It was easy to understand him.

__ **B** It wasn't easy to understand him.

Questions 7–12

*Listen to the conversation. Choose the correct letter, **A**, **B**, or **C**.*

7 What describes the weather in the region?

A rainy

B dry

C cloudy

8 When taking the exam, the students can

A take as much time as they need.

B use a dictionary.

C bring several things into the testing room.

9 When will the car be fixed?

A today

B before the end of the week

C on the weekend[3]

---

[1]BRITISH: favourite

[2]BRITISH: neighbour

[3]BRITISH: at the weekend

10 What is the woman's opinion of the restaurant?
   A   The food is good.
   B   The service is bad.
   C   The wait is too long.

11 Which type of flower is not common in the area?
   A   violets
   B   roses
   C   irises

12 What homework does the man have to do this week?
   A   write papers and read books
   B   write papers only
   C   study for exams

Target 13—Listening for Chronology

Listening for the order in which events occur is an important skill. You will need to listen to what happened first, second, and so on.

CD1
TRACK
21

EXAMPLE

You will see: *Complete the Class Assignment Sheet, putting the assignments in the correct order. Write*
NO MORE THAN THREE WORDS *for each answer.*

> Class Assignment Sheet
>
>   A. **1**   ....
>   B. **2**   ....
>   C. Papers submitted
>   D. Student Presentations
>   E. **3**   ....

You will hear: Before you do your research, we'll have an orientation session in the library so you can become familiar with the various sources of information available there. Each student will give a presentation on his or her research topic after all the papers have been submitted. All of this will have to be completed prior to the date of the final exam.

Common Words and Phrases That Indicate Chronological Order

before	at birth, in childhood, in infancy, as an adult,
after	in adulthood, in old age
while	simultaneously, at the same time as
during	former, latter
between ____ and ____	previous
in (year)	previously
on (day)	prior to
at (time)	first, second, third, etc.
since _____	in the first place, second place
later	to begin with
earlier	next, then, subsequently
formerly	in the next place
every (number) (years, months, days)	at last
at the turn of the century (decade)	in conclusion
in the first half of the century	finally
in the 20s, 1980s, . . .	

Questions 1–5

*Listen to the audio and put these actions in the correct chronological order. Write **1** for the first action, **2** for the second, and so forth.*

1
____ Fill in application
____ Submit application
____ Get references
____ Pay a deposit
____ Receive notification of apartment
____ Sign lease

2
____ Leopold Mozart published a book.
____ Wolfgang Mozart began to compose music.
____ Leopold began taking Wolfgang on tours of Europe.
____ Wolfgang Mozart settled in Vienna.
____ Wolfgang's mother died.

3
____ Left home
____ Had picnic
____ Made sandwiches
____ Went swimming
____ Checked into motel

4
____ Find partner
____ Choose topic
____ Get professor's approval
____ Design research
____ Start research

5
____ Walk through rose garden
____ Show tickets
____ View pond area
____ Visit greenhouse
____ Photograph butterfly garden

READING MODULE

- **QUICK STUDY**
  - Overview
  - Question Types
  - Reading Tips
- **READING SKILLS**
  - Target 1—Using the First Paragraph to Make Predictions
  - Target 2—Using the Topic Sentence to Make Predictions
  - Target 3—Looking for Specific Details
  - Target 4—Analyzing the Questions and Answers
  - Target 5—Identifying the Tasks

QUICK STUDY

Overview

The Reading module lasts 60 minutes. The reading passages and the questions will be given to you in a Question Booklet. You can write in the Question Booklet, but you can't take it from the room.

You will write your answers on the Answer Sheet. Unlike in the Listening module, you will have no time to transfer your answers. You will have only 60 minutes to read the passages, answer the questions, and mark your answers.

The Reading modules on the Academic and the General Training versions of the IELTS are different.

Reading Module: Academic Reading

Time	Tasks	Topics	Sources
60 minutes	Read three passages and answer 40 questions	General interest topics written for a general audience	Journals, magazines, books, newspapers

Reading Module: General Training Reading

Time	Tasks	Topics	Sources
60 minutes	Read three passages and answer 40 questions	Basic social English Training topics General interest	Notices, flyers, timetables, documents, newspaper articles, instructions, manuals

Question Types

There are many types of questions used in the Reading module. You should be familiar with these types.

Multiple-choice questions
Short-answer questions
Completing sentences
Completing notes, summary, tables, flowcharts
Labeling a diagram
Choosing headings for paragraphs or sections
   of a text

Locating information
Identifying points of view
Identifying writer's claims
Classifying information
Matching lists or phrases

You will have a chance to practice the tasks of these different question types in Target 5.

Reading Tips

BEFORE YOU TAKE THE TEST

1. Read as much as you can in English.
2. Read a variety of topics from a variety of sources, for example, tourist information brochures, government reports, scientific research reports, health and safety brochures, newspapers, news and special interest magazines, information from colleges and universities.
3. Keep a notebook of the words you learn.
4. Try to write these words in a sentence. Try to put these sentences into a paragraph.
5. Learn words in context—not from a word list. Don't be afraid to guess meanings.
6. Know the types of questions found on the IELTS.
7. Know the type of information asked about on the IELTS.
8. Know how to make predictions.
9. Know how to skim and scan, to look quickly for information.

DURING THE TEST

1. Read the title and any headings first. Make predictions about the topic.
2. Look over the questions quickly. Make predictions about content and organization.
3. Read the passage at a normal speed. Don't get stuck on parts or words you don't understand.
4. When you answer the questions, don't spend too much time on the ones you don't feel sure about. Make a guess and go on.
5. After you have answered all the questions, you can go back and check the ones you aren't sure about.
6. Don't spend more than 20 minutes on each passage.
7. The last passage is longer and more complex than the first two, so remember to save time for it.
8. Be sure to write your answers on the answer sheet before the 60 minutes are up. You will NOT have extra time to transfer your answers.

READING SKILLS

In order to understand a reading passage, you need to understand the context of a passage. You need to have a clue about the topic. When you pick up a paper to read, you scan the headlines and choose an article that interests you. The clues in the newspaper (headlines, graphics, photos, captions) catch your eye and give you a context.

A passage on the IELTS is given to you; you did not choose to read it. There are few clues. You do not know what it is about. It may or may not interest you. Yet in order to understand it, you need some clues to help you understand the passage. Without the clues, you will not understand it very well. To score well on the IELTS, you should determine what you know and what you need to know.

When you look at a passage, you must make some predictions about the passage.

What is the passage about?
What is the main idea?
Who are the characters?
When are things taking place?
Where is it happening?
Why is it important?

You want to know *who*, *what*, *when*, *where*, and *why*.

In this section you will learn how the following can give you the answers to: *Who? What? When? Where?* and *Why?*

Using the first paragraph
Using the topic sentences
Using specific details
Using the questions and answers

Target 1—Using the First Paragraph to Make Predictions

The first paragraph of a passage can help you make predictions about the context of a passage.

The first paragraph often contains

the topic sentence (a summary of the main idea of the passage)
a definition of the topic
the author's opinion
clues to the organization of the passage

If you understand the first paragraph, you will understand the topic, the author's opinion (if any), and where to look for information within the passage.

Read this first paragraph of a passage on the illness, obsessive-compulsive disorder.

Obsessive-compulsive disorder (OCD) is clinically diagnosed as an anxiety disorder. This disorder affects up to 4 percent of adults and children. People who suffer from this debilitating disorder have distressing and obsessive thoughts, which usually cause them to perform repetitive behaviors[1] such as counting silently or washing their hands. Though OCD sufferers understand that their obsessions are unrealistic, they find it stressful to put these intrusive thoughts out of their minds. Those who suffer from obsessive-compulsive disorder develop strict behavioral[1] patterns that become extremely time-consuming and begin to interfere with daily routines. Many people with OCD delay seeking treatment because they are ashamed of their own thoughts and behavior.

Topic Sentence
Obsessive-compulsive disorder (OCD) is clinically diagnosed as an anxiety disorder.

Definition of Topic
People who suffer from this debilitating disorder have distressing and obsessive thoughts, which usually cause them to perform repetitive behaviors.

Author's Opinion
None given.

[1]BRITISH: Behaviour/behavioural

Organizational Clues

The author may discuss

- Obsessive behavior,
- Stress of sufferers, and/or
- Treatment.

PRACTICE 1

Read these introductory paragraphs of other passages. Make predictions about the topics using these first paragraphs.

1 The spread of wildfire is a natural phenomenon that occurs throughout the world and is especially common in forested areas of North America, Australia, and Europe. Locations that receive plenty of rainfall but also experience periods of intense heat or drought are particularly susceptible to wildfires. As plant matter dries out, it becomes brittle and highly flammable. In this way, many wildfires are seasonal, ignited by natural causes, most specifically lightning. However, human carelessness and vandalism also account for thousands of wildfires around the globe each year. To gain a clear understanding of how wildfires spread, it is necessary to analyze what it takes to both create and control these fires.

2 The term "bird brain" has long been a common means of expressing doubts about a person's intelligence. In reality, birds may actually be a great deal more intelligent than humans have given them credit for. For a long time, scientists considered birds to be of lesser intelligence because the cerebral cortex, the part of the brain that humans and other animals use for intelligence, is relatively small in size. Now scientists understand that birds actually use a different part of their brain, the hyperstriatum, for intelligence. Observations of different species of birds, both in the wild and in captivity, have shown a great deal of evidence of high levels of avian intelligence.

3 In 1834, a little girl was born in New Bedford, Massachusetts. She would grow up to become one of the richest women in the world. Her name was Hetty Green, but she was known to many as the Witch of Wall Street.

Target 2—Using the Topic Sentence to Make Predictions

Every paragraph has a key sentence called a topic sentence. This topic sentence explains what a paragraph is about. It is the general idea of a paragraph. If you understand the general idea, you can look for the specific details which support the idea.

Read the second paragraph of the passage on OCD. The first sentence happens to be the topic sentence.

OCD sufferers experience worries that are both unreasonable and excessive and that act as a constant source of internal stress. Fear of dirt and contamination are very common obsessive thoughts. The obsession with orderliness and symmetry is also common. In other cases, persistent thoughts are centered on doubts, such as whether or not a door is locked or a stove is turned off. Impulses, such as the urge to swear in public or to pull a fire alarm, are other types of OCD symptoms. In order to be diagnosed with OCD, a sufferer must exhibit obsessions and/or compulsions that take up a considerable amount of time (at least one hour per day).

Topic Sentence
OCD sufferers experience worries that are both unreasonable and excessive and that act as a constant source of internal stress.

Questions to Ask Yourself
What are unreasonable worries?
What are excessive worries?

PRACTICE 2

Read these paragraphs. Underline the topic sentence. Ask one or two questions about the topic sentence.

1   To combat excessive thoughts and impulses, most OCD sufferers perform certain repetitive rituals that they believe will relieve their anxiety. These compulsions can be either mental or behavioral in nature. Common rituals include excessive checking, washing, counting, and praying. Over time, OCD sufferers attach strict rules to their compulsions. For example, a woman who is obsessed with cleanliness might wash her hands three times before having a meal in order to get the thought of the dirty dishes or silverware out of her mind. However, in many cases, the compulsions aren't related to the obsession at all. A man obsessed with the image of dead animals might count silently up to 500 or touch a specific chair over and over in order to block the images. Holding onto objects that would normally be discarded, such as newspapers and empty containers, is another common compulsion.

2   OCD symptoms generally begin between the ages of 10 and 24 and continue indefinitely until a person seeks treatment. A child's upbringing does not seem to be part of the cause of the disorder, though stress can make the symptoms stronger. The underlying causes of OCD have been researched greatly and point to a number of different genetic factors. While studies show that OCD and its related anxiety disorders are often passed down through families, the specific symptoms for each family member are rarely the same. For example, a mother who is obsessed with order may have a son who can't stop thinking about a single word or number.

3   Research on OCD sufferers has found certain physiological trends. In particular, many studies show an overactivity of blood circulation in certain areas of the brain. As a result of this increase in blood flow, the serotoninergic system, which regulates emotions, is unable to function effectively. Studies have also shown that OCD sufferers have less serotonin than the average person. This type of abnormality is also observed in Tourette syndrome and Attention Deficit Hyperactive Disorder. People who developed tics as children are found to be more susceptible to OCD as well. Many reports of OCD point to infections that can trigger the disorder, namely streptococcal infections. It is believed that a case of childhood strep throat can elicit a response from the immune system that produces certain neuropsychiatric disorders, such as OCD.

Target 3—Looking for Specific Details

When you read, you first want to know the general idea. Next you read for specific ideas. The author supplies specific details to support his or her ideas. Knowing where to look for these supporting statements will help you answer questions on the IELTS.

When you identified the topic sentences in Practice 2, you found the general idea of the paragraph. When you asked your questions about the topic sentence, you expected the specific details would be the answers.

Read the second paragraph of a passage. The specific details follow the topic sentence.

> OCD sufferers experience worries that are both unreasonable and excessive and that act as a constant source of internal stress. Fear of dirt and contamination are very common obsessive thoughts. The obsession with orderliness and symmetry is also common. In other cases, persistent thoughts are centered on doubts, such as whether or not a door is locked or a stove is turned off. Impulses, such as the urge to swear in public or to pull a fire alarm, are other types of OCD symptoms. In order to be diagnosed with OCD, a sufferer must exhibit obsessions and/or compulsions that take up a considerable amount of time (at least one hour per day).

Topic Sentence
OCD sufferers experience worries that are both unreasonable and excessive and that act as a constant source of internal stress.

Questions to Ask Yourself
What are unreasonable worries?
What are excessive worries?

Supporting Details
Fear of dirt and contamination
The obsession with orderliness and symmetry
Persistent doubts
Impulses

PRACTICE 3

Read the three paragraphs from Practice 2 again. Pay attention to the topic sentence. Underline the details that support the topic sentence.

Target 4—Analyzing the Questions and Answers

You made predictions about the content based on the first paragraph, the topic sentences, and the specific details. Now let's look at how the questions or statements in your Reading test booklet can help you narrow these predictions and choose the correct answer.

To help you answer the questions in your Reading test booklet, take a few seconds to look over the questions or statements. Sometimes the questions are before the passage; sometimes they come after the passage. Ask yourself: *Who? What? When? Where?* and *Why?* By looking for the answers to these general questions, you will discover what you know and what you need to know. When you read the passage, you can test the predictions you made.

As you look at the question or statement and answer options, look for the key words. Key words may give you a clue to the context. They may help you predict what the passage is about.

Look at these typical IELTS comprehension questions in Practice 4. First identify the key words. (These are circled below to help you.) Then look for these words in the passage. You will know where to look because you have made predictions using topic sentences and specific details.

Notice the words close to the circled words in the passage. Do they help you complete the summary below?

PRACTICE 4

Questions 1–8

Complete the summary of the reading passage below.

Choose your answers from the box below and write them in boxes 1–8 on your answer sheet. There are more words than spaces so you will not use them all.

People who suffer from obsessive-compulsive disorder have 1 .... (thoughts), (doubts), and (fears) that they cannot 2 .... OCD sufferers (develop) certain ways of (acting) in order to 3 .... their fears. For example, being afraid of dirt is a (common) 4 ...., which may lead to (excessive) hand washing. Or, an OCD sufferer who worries about a locked door may engage in excessive 5 .... Some OCD sufferers (keep things) that other people would 6 .... Research shows that OCD may be a disorder that is 7 ...., though (members) of the same (family) don't always show the same symptoms. It is also possible that certain (infections) may 8 .... the disorder.

checking
doctor
upbringing
inherited
reduce
cause
treatment
throw away
unreasonable
obsession
control
compulsive
diagnosis
counting

Identify the key words in these questions and circle them in the questions and in the reading passage on pages 61–62. Notice the words close to the circled words in the passage. Do they help you complete the questions below?

Questions 9–16

Do the following statements agree with the information in the reading passage?

In boxes 9–16 write

TRUE	if the statement is true according to the passage
FALSE	if the statement contradicts the passage
NOT GIVEN	if there is no information about this in the passage

9 OCD often results from the way a child is raised.

10 Stress can have an effect on OCD.

11 OCD sufferers are deficient in serotonin.

12 Obsessive-compulsive disorder usually begins after the age of 17.

13 Many OCD patients prefer psychotherapy to medication.

14 OCD is very difficult to treat.

15 Many OCD sufferers keep their problem a secret.

16 Antibiotics can be used to treat OCD.

You should spend 20 minutes on Questions 9–16, which are based on the reading passage below.

Obsessive-Compulsive Disorder

Obsessive-compulsive disorder (OCD) is clinically diagnosed as an anxiety disorder and affects up to 4 percent of adults and children. People who suffer from this debilitating disorder have distressing and obsessive thoughts, which usually cause them to perform repetitive behaviors such as counting silently or washing their hands. Though OCD sufferers understand that their obsessions are unrealistic, they find it stressful to put these intrusive thoughts out of their minds. Those who suffer from obsessive-compulsive disorder develop strict behavioral patterns that become extremely time-consuming and begin to interfere with daily routines. Many people with OCD delay seeking treatment because they are ashamed of their own thoughts and behavior.

OCD sufferers experience worries that are both unreasonable and excessive and that act as a constant source of internal stress. Fear of dirt and contamination are very common obsessive thoughts. The obsession with orderliness and symmetry is also common. In other cases, persistent thoughts are centered on doubts, such as whether or not a door is locked or a stove is turned off. Impulses, such as the urge to swear in public or to pull a fire alarm, are other types of OCD symptoms. In order to be diagnosed with OCD, a sufferer must exhibit obsessions and/or compulsions that take up a considerable amount of time (at least one hour per day).

To combat excessive thoughts and impulses, most OCD sufferers perform certain repetitive rituals that they believe will relieve their anxiety. These compulsions can be either mental or behavioral in nature. Common rituals include excessive checking, washing, counting, and praying. Over time, OCD sufferers attach strict rules to their compulsions. For example, a woman who is obsessed with cleanliness might wash her hands three times before having a meal in order to get the thought of the dirty dishes or silverware out of her mind. However, in many cases, the compulsions aren't related to the obsession at all. A man obsessed with the image of dead animals might count silently up to 500 or touch a specific chair over and over in order to block the images. Holding onto objects that would normally be discarded, such as newspapers and empty containers, is another common compulsion.

OCD symptoms generally begin between the ages of 10 and 24 and continue indefinitely until a person seeks treatment. A child's upbringing does not seem to be part of the cause of the disorder, though stress can make the symptoms stronger. The underlying causes of OCD have been researched greatly and point to a number of different genetic factors. While studies show that OCD and its related anxiety disorders are often passed down through families, the specific symptoms for each family member are rarely the same. For example, a mother who is obsessed with order may have a son who can't stop thinking about a single word or number.

Research on OCD sufferers has found certain physiological trends. In particular, many studies show an over-activity of blood circulation in certain areas of the brain. As a result of this increase in blood flow, the serotonin-ergic system, which regulates emotions, is unable to function effectively. Studies have also shown that OCD sufferers have less serotonin than the average person. This type of abnormality is also observed in Tourette syndrome and Attention Deficit Hyperactive Disorder. People who developed tics as children are found to be more susceptible to OCD as well. Many reports of OCD point to infections that can trigger the disorder, namely streptococcal infections. It is believed that a case of childhood strep throat can elicit a response from the immune system that produces certain neuropsychiatric disorders, such as OCD.

Because OCD sufferers tend to be so secretive about their symptoms, they often put off treatment for many years. The average OCD sufferer waits about 17 years before receiving medical attention. As with many anxiety disorders, early diagnosis and proper medication can lessen many of the symptoms and allow people to live fairly normal lives. Most treatment plans for OCD involve a combination of medication and psychotherapy. Both cognitive and behavioral therapies are used to teach patients about their disorder and work through the anxiety. Serotonin reuptake inhibitors are prescribed to increase the brain's concentration of serotonin. This medication successfully reduces the symptoms in many OCD sufferers in a short amount of time. For cases when OCD is linked to streptococcal infection, antibiotic therapy is sometimes all that is needed.

Target 5—Identifying the Tasks

There are many types of questions on the IELTS Reading test. It is important to know what the question is asking you to do.

Question types:

    Multiple-choice questions
    Short-answer questions
    Completing sentences
    Completing notes, summary, tables, flowcharts
    Labeling a diagram
    Choosing headings for paragraphs or sections of a text
    Choosing three or four answers from a list
    Yes, No, True, False, or Not Given questions
    Classifying information
    Matching lists or phrases

The questions for the practice reading passages on pages 63–64 are labeled. Be familiar with the question types so you can quickly complete the task and answer the question correctly.

PRACTICE 5

READING PASSAGE 1

Read the passage and answer the questions. Use your predicting skills. Note the type of questions.

Zulu Beadwork

The South African province of KwaZulu-Natal, more commonly referred to as the Zulu Kingdom, is named after the Zulu people who have inhabited the area since the late 1400s. KwaZulu translates to mean "Place of Heaven." "Natal" was the name the Portuguese explorers gave this region when they arrived in 1497. At that time, only a few Zulu clans occupied the area. By the late 1700s, the AmaZulu clan, meaning "People of Heaven," constituted a significant nation. Today the Zulu clan represents the largest ethnic group in South Africa, with at least 11 million people in the kingdom. The Zulu people are known around the world for their elaborate glass beadwork, which they wear not only in their traditional costumes but as part of their everyday apparel. It is possible to learn much about the culture of the Zulu clan through their beadwork.

The glass bead trade in the province of KwaZulu-Natal is believed to be a fairly recent industry. In 1824, an Englishman named Henry Francis Fynn brought glass beads to the region to sell to the African people. Though the British are not considered the first to introduce glass beads, they were a main source through which the Zulu people could access the merchandise they needed. Glass beads had already been manufactured by the Egyptians centuries earlier around the same time when glass was discovered. Some research points to the idea that Egyptians tried to fool South Africans with glass by passing it off as jewels similar in value to gold or ivory. Phoenician mariners brought cargoes of these beads to Africa along with other wares. Before the Europeans arrived, many Arab traders brought glass beads down to the southern countries via camelback. During colonization[1], the Europeans facilitated and monopolized[2] the glass bead market, and the Zulu nation became even more closely tied to this art form.

The Zulu people were not fooled into believing that glass beads were precious stones but, rather, used the beads to establish certain codes and rituals in their society. In the African tradition, kings were known to wear beaded regalia so heavy that they required the help of attendants to get out of their thrones. Zulu beadwork is involved in every realm of society, from religion and politics to family and marriage. Among the Zulu women, the craft of beadwork is used as an educational tool as well as a source of recreation and fashion. Personal adornment items include jewelry, skirts, neckbands, and aprons. Besides clothing and accessories, there are many other beaded objects in the Zulu culture, such as bead-covered gourds, which are carried around by women who are having fertility problems. Most importantly, however, Zulu beadwork is a source of communication. In the Zulu tradition, beads are a part of the language with certain words and symbols that can be easily read. A finished product is considered by many artists and collectors to be extremely poetic.

The code behind Zulu beadwork is relatively basic and extremely resistant to change. A simple triangle is the geometric shape used in almost all beaded items. A triangle with the apex pointing downward signifies an unmarried man, while one with the tip pointing upward

[1]BRITISH: colonisation
[2]BRITISH: monopolised

is worn by an unmarried woman. Married women wear items with two triangles that form a diamond shape, and married men signify their marital status with two triangles that form an hourglass shape. Colors are also significant, though slightly more complicated since each color can have a negative and a positive meaning. Educated by their older sisters, young Zulu girls quickly learn how to send the appropriate messages to a courting male. Similarly, males learn how to interpret the messages and how to wear certain beads that express their interest in marriage.

The codes of the beads are so strong that cultural analysts fear that the beadwork tradition could prevent the Zulu people from progressing technologically and economically. Socio-economic data shows that the more a culture resists change the more risk there is in a value system falling apart. Though traditional beadwork still holds a serious place in Zulu culture, the decorative art form is often modified for tourists, with popular items such as the beaded fertility doll.

MATCHING

Questions 1–3

Match each definition in List A with the term it defines in List B.

*Write the correct letter **A–E** in boxes 1–3 on your answer sheet. There are more terms than definitions, so you will not use them all.*

List A	Definitions
1	It means *Place of Heaven*.
2	It is the Portuguese name for southern Africa.
3	It means *People of Heaven*.

List B	Terms
A	Phoenician
B	Natal
C	AmaZulu
D	Explorer
E	KwaZulu

SHORT-ANSWER QUESTIONS

Questions 4–6

Answer the questions below.

Write NO MORE THAN THREE WORDS for each answer.

Write your answers in boxes 4–6 on your answer sheet.

4 Which country does the Zulu clan reside in?

5 When did the Portuguese arrive in KwaZulu-Natal?

6 How many members of the Zulu kingdom are there?

TRUE–FALSE–NOT GIVEN QUESTIONS

Questions 7–11

Do the following statements agree with the information given in the passage? In boxes 7–11 on your answer sheet, write

TRUE if the statement is true according to the passage
FALSE if the statement contradicts the passage
NOT GIVEN if there is no information about this in the passage

7 The British were the first people to sell glass beads in Africa.

8 Henry Frances Flynn made a lot of money selling glass beads to the Zulu people.

9 The Zulu people believed that glass beads were precious stones.

10 The Zulu people use glass beads in many aspects of their daily lives.

11 Zulu women believe that bead-covered gourds can help them have babies.

LABELING A DIAGRAM

Label the diagram below. Choose one or two words from the reading passage for each answer. Write your answers in boxes 12–15 on your answer sheet.

Zulu Beadwork Code

12 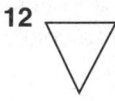   13 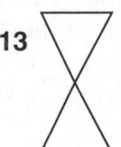   14 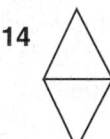   15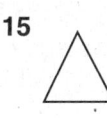

READING PASSAGE 2

Read the passage and answer the questions. Use your predicting skills. Note the type of questions.

CHOOSING HEADINGS

Questions 1–5

*The following reading passage has five sections, **A–E**.*

Choose the correct heading for each section from the list of headings on the next page.

*Write the correct number **i–viii** in boxes 1–5 on your answer sheet. There are more headings than sections, so you will not use them all.*

1   Section **A**

2   Section **B**

3   Section **C**

4   Section **D**

5   Section **E**

List of Headings	
i	Colorblindness[1] in Different Countries
ii	Diagnosing Colorblindness
iii	What Is Colorblindness?
iv	Curing Colorblindness
v	Unsolved Myths
vi	Animals and Colorblindness
vii	Developing the Ability to See Color
viii	Colorblindness and the Sexes

TEST TIP

If the test uses lower case Roman numerals, then you should, too.

Colorblindness

A

Myths related to the causes and symptoms of "colorblindness" abound throughout the world. The term itself is misleading, since it is extremely rare for anyone to have a complete lack of color perception. By looking into the myths related to colorblindness, one can learn many facts about the structure and genetics of the human eye. It is a myth that colorblind people see the world as if it were a black and white movie. There are very few cases of complete colorblindness. Those who have a complete lack of color perception are referred to as monochromatics, and usually have a serious problem with their overall vision as well as an inability to see colors. The fact is that in most cases of colorblindness, there are only certain shades that a person cannot distinguish between. These people are said to be dichromatic. They may not be able to tell the difference between red and green, or orange and yellow. A person with normal color vision has what is called trichromatic vision. The difference between the three levels of color perception have to do with the cones in the human eye. A normal human eye has three cones located inside the retina: the red cone, the green cone, and the yellow cone. Each cone contains a specific pigment whose function is to absorb the light of these colors and the combinations of them. People with trichromatic vision have all three cones in working order. When one of the three cones does not function properly, dichromatic vision occurs.

B

Some people believe that only men can be colorblind. This is also a myth, though it is not completely untrue. In an average population, 8% of males exhibit some form of colorblindness, while only 0.5% of women do. While there may be some truth to the idea that more men have trouble matching their clothing than women, the reason that color vision deficiency is predominant in males has nothing to do with fashion. The fact is that the gene for color blindness is located on the X chromosome, which men only have one of. Females have two X chromosomes, and if one carries the defective gene, the other one naturally compensates. Therefore, the only way for a female to inherit colorblindness is for both of her X chromosomes to carry the defective gene. This is why the incidence of color deficiency is sometimes more prevalent in extremely small societies that have a limited gene pool.

C

It is true that all babies are born colorblind. A baby's cones do not begin to differentiate between many different colors until the baby is approximately four months old. This is why many of the modern toys for very young babies consist of black and white patterns or primary colors, rather than traditional soft pastels. However, some current research points to the importance of developing an infant's color visual system. In 2004, Japanese researcher Yoichi Sugita of the Neuroscience Research Institute performed an experiment that would suggest that color vision deficiency isn't entirely genetic. In his experiment, he subjected a group of baby monkeys to monochromatic lighting for one year. He later compared their vision to normal monkeys who had experienced the colorful world outdoors. It was found that the test monkeys were unable to perform

[1]BRITISH: colour, colourblindness, colourful

the color-matching tasks that the normal monkeys could. Nevertheless, most cases of colorblindness are attributed to genetic factors that are present at birth.

D

Part of the reason there are so many inconsistencies related to colorblindness, or "color vision deficiency" as it is called in the medical world, is that it is difficult to know exactly which colors each human can see. Children are taught from a very young age that an apple is red. Naming colors allows children to associate a certain shade with a certain name, regardless of a color vision deficiency. Someone who never takes a color test can go through life thinking that what they see as red is called *green*. Children are generally tested for colorblindness at about four years of age. The Ishihara Test is the most common, though it is highly criticized[1] because it requires that children have the ability to recognize[2] numerals. In the Ishihara Test, a number made up of colored dots is hidden inside a series of dots of a different shade. Those with normal vision can distinguish the number from the background, while those with color vision deficiency will only see the dots.

E

While many of the myths related to colorblindness have been disproved by modern science, there are still a few remaining beliefs that require more research in order to be labeled as folklore. For example, there is a longstanding belief that colorblindness can aid military soldiers because it gives them the ability to see through camouflage. Another belief is that everyone becomes colorblind in an emergency situation. The basis of this idea is that a catastrophic event can overwhelm the brain, causing it to utilize[3] only those receptors needed to perform vital tasks. In general, identifying color is not considered an essential task in a life or death situation.

MULTIPLE-CHOICE QUESTIONS

Questions 6–8

*Choose the correct letter, **A, B, C**, or **D**. Write your answers in boxes 6–8 on your Answer Sheet.*

6 People who see color normally are called

    A monochromatic.
    B dichromatic.
    C trichromatic.
    D colorblind.

7 Children usually begin to see a variety of colors by the age of

    A one month.
    B four months.
    C one year.
    D four years.

8 Children who take the Ishihara Test must be able to

    A distinguish letters.
    B write their names.
    C read numbers.
    D name colors.

[1]BRITISH: criticised
[2]BRITISH: recognise
[3]BRITISH: utilise

COMPLETING A SUMMARY

Questions 9–12

Complete the summary using words from the box below.

Write your answers in boxes 9–12 on your Answer Sheet. There are more answers than spaces, so you will not use them all.

It is a common **9** .... that only men suffer from colorblindness. On average **10** .... than ten percent of men have this problem. Women have two **11** .... For this reason it is **12** .... for a woman to suffer from color-blindness.

myth	a little less
X chromosomes	defective genes
fact	slightly more
exactly	less likely
more probable	

READING PASSAGE 3

Read the passage and answer the questions. Use your predicting skills. Note the type of question.

Antarctic Penguins

Though penguins are assumed to be native to the South Pole, only four of the seventeen species have evolved the survival adaptations necessary to live and breed in the Antarctic year round. The physical features of the Adelie, Chinstrap, Gentoo, and Emperor penguins equip them to withstand the harshest living conditions in the world. Besides these four species, there are a number of others, including the yellow feathered Macaroni penguin and the King penguin that visit the Antarctic regularly but migrate to warmer waters to breed. Penguins that live in Antarctica year round have a thermoregulation system and a survival sense that allows them to live comfortably both on the ice and in the water.

In the dark days of winter, when the Antarctic sees virtually no sunlight, the penguins that remain on the ice sheet sleep most of the day. To retain heat, penguins huddle in communities of up to 6,000 of their own species. When it's time to create a nest, most penguins build up a pile of rocks on top of the ice to place their eggs. The Emperor penguin, however, doesn't bother with a nest at all. The female Emperor lays just one egg and gives it to the male to protect while she goes off for weeks to feed. The male balances the egg on top of his feet, covering it with a small fold of skin called a brood patch. In the huddle, the male penguins rotate regularly so that none of the penguins have to stay on the outside of the circle exposed to the wind and cold for long periods of time. When it's time to take a turn on the outer edge of the pack, the penguins tuck their feathers in and shiver. The movement provides enough warmth until they can head back into the inner core and rest in the warmth. In order to reduce the cold of the ice, penguins often put their weight on their heels and tails. Antarctic penguins also have complex nasal passages that prevent 80 percent of their heat from leaving the body. When the sun is out, the black dorsal plumage attracts its rays and penguins can stay warm enough to waddle or slide about alone.

Antarctic penguins spend about 75 percent of their lives in the water. A number of survival adaptations allow them to swim through water as cold as –2 degrees Celsius. In order to stay warm in these temperatures, penguins have to keep moving. Though penguins don't fly in the air, they are often said to fly through water. Instead of stopping each time they come up for air, they use a technique called "porpoising," in which they leap up for a quick breath while swiftly moving forward. Unlike most birds that have hollow bones for flight, penguins have evolved hard solid bones that keep them low in the water. Antarctic penguins also have unique feathers that work similarly to a waterproof diving suit. Tufts of down trap a layer of air within the feathers, preventing the water from penetrating to the penguin's skin. The pressure of a deep dive releases this air, and a penguin has to rearrange the feathers through a process called "preening." Penguins also have an amazing circulatory system, which in extremely cold waters diverts blood from the flippers and legs to the heart.

While the harsh climate of the Antarctic doesn't threaten the survival of Antarctic penguins, overheating can be a concern, and therefore, global warming is a threat to them. Temperate species have certain physical features such as fewer feathers and less blubber to keep them cool on a hot day. African penguins have bald patches on their legs and face where excess heat can be released. The blood vessels in the penguin's skin dilate when the body begins to overheat, and the heat rises to the surface of the body. Penguins who are built for cold winters of the Antarctic have other survival techniques for a warm day, such as moving to shaded areas, or holding their flippers out away from their bodies.

CLASSIFYING INFORMATION

Questions 1–5

Classify the following facts as applying to
- **A**   Antarctic penguins
- **B**   Temperate-zone penguins

Write the appropriate letter, **A** or **B**, in boxes 1–5 on your answer sheet.

1   stand in large groups to keep warm

2   spend about three-quarters of their time in the water

3   have feathers that keep cold water away from their skin

4   have areas of skin without feathers

5   have less blubber

TEST TIP

Think of alternate ways to represent numbers and symbols (e.g., 75 percent—three-quarters).

COMPLETING SENTENCES

Questions 6–9

Complete each of the following sentences with information from the reading passage. Write your answers in boxes 6–9 on your Answer Sheet. Write NO MORE THAN THREE WORDS for each answer.

6 Most penguins use .... to build their nests.

7 While the male Emperor penguin takes care of the egg, the female goes away to ....

8 A .... is a piece of skin that the male Emperor penguin uses to protect the egg.

9 Penguins protect their feet from the cold of the ice by resting on their ....

TEST TIP

Remember to spell correctly.
Copy spelling from the passage or questions when possible.

CHOOSING ANSWERS FROM A LIST

Questions 10–13

The article mentions many facts about penguins.

Which four of the following features are things that enable them to survive in very cold water?

Write the appropriate letters A–H in boxes 10–13 on your Answer Sheet.

A They move through the water very quickly.

B They hold their flippers away from their bodies.

C They choose shady areas.

D When necessary, their blood moves away from the flippers and toward the heart.

E They breathe while still moving.

F The blood vessels in their skin dilate.

G They waddle and slide.

H Their feathers hold in a layer of air near the skin.

WRITING MODULE

- **QUICK STUDY**
  - Overview
  - Question Types
  - Writing Tips
- **WRITING SKILLS**

Responding to the Task
- Target 1—Writing for a Specific Audience
- Target 2—Completing the Task
- Target 3—Determining the Task

Coherence and Cohesion
- Target 4—Developing a Thesis Statement
- Target 5—Organizing Your Writing
- Target 6—Writing the Introduction
- Target 7—Writing a Paragraph
- Target 8—Stating Your Opinion
- Target 9—Writing the Conclusion

Lexical Resource
- Target 10—Transition: Connecting and Linking
- Target 11—Synonyms
- Target 12—Writing with Variety

Grammatical Range and Accuracy
- Target 13—Pronouns
- Target 14—Parallel Structures
- Target 15—Coherence
- Target 16—Sentence Types
- Target 17—Voice

Revision
- Target 18—Using a Revision Checklist
- Target 19—Checking the Spelling
- Target 20—Checking the Punctuation

QUICK STUDY

Overview

There are two writing tasks in both the Academic and General Training Writing modules.

Academic Writing Module

Task	Number of Minutes	Number of Words	General Tasks
1	20	150	Describe a chart, graph, or table. Explain a diagram or a machine, a device, or a process.
2	40	250	Write about a given topic.

General Training Writing Module

Task	Number of Minutes	Number of Words	General Tasks
1	20	150	Write a letter. • Request information. • Give information. • Explain a problem.
2	40	250	Discuss information presented about a point of view, argument, or problem.

Question Types

You should be familiar with the variety of tasks and the writing style in both the Academic and General Training Writing modules. The following activities will help you become more familiar with the tasks and styles.

Academic Writing Module

Task	Style	Specific Tasks
1	Academic	Describe facts or figures presented in one or more charts, graphs, or tables.
2	Semi-formal/Neutral Formal	Present an argument giving examples to support the ideas.

General Training Writing Module

Task	Style	Specific Tasks
1	Informal (writing to a friend) Semi-formal (writing to an older person) Formal (writing to an official)	Cover all three bullet points in tasks. Ask for general factual information. Express needs, wants, likes, or dislikes. Express opinions or complaints. Make requests, suggestions, or recommendations.
2	Semi-formal/Neutral	Provide general factual information. Outline and/or present a solution. Justify an opinion. Evaluate evidence and ideas.

ACADEMIC WRITING

There are two principal tasks in the Academic Writing module. In Task 1 you will be asked to describe something and in Task 2 you will be asked to make an argument and support your opinion.

Look at the following examples.

Task 1—Describe Something

Example

You should spend about 20 minutes on this task.

> *The chart below shows the results of a survey that sampled a cross-section of travelers at a major metropolitan airport about the purpose of their trip. The survey was carried out during four different months.*
>
> *Summarize the information by selecting and reporting the main features, and make comparisons where relevant.*

Write at least 150 words.

Purpose of Travel

	March	June	September	December
Business	73%	29%	53%	34%
Holiday	18%	54%	31%	35%
Visit family	6%	13%	11%	26%
Other	3%	4%	5%	5%

Task 2—Support Your Opinion

Example

You should spend about 40 minutes on this task.

Write about the following topic:

> *Most schools offer some type of physical education program to their students. Why is physical education important? Should physical education classes be required or optional?*

Give reasons for your answer and include any relevant examples from your own knowledge or experience.

Write at least 250 words.

Writing Tips

1. Make sure you organize[1] your writing *before* you begin. Use the back of your test booklet to create a concept map.
2. The examiners judge your writing on its clarity. Make sure you have supported your ideas with specific details.
3. You can write more than 150 words for Task 1 or more than the 250 words for Task 2, but you can't write less. You will lose points if you have less than the assigned number of words in your essay.
4. In the introductory paragraph, paraphrase your ideas. Do not use the exact words in the introduction that you use in the body of the essay. This gives your writing more variety and more interest.
5. You must answer the question completely. Do not leave any part out or you will lose points.
6. Organize your time carefully. Leave time for planning, writing, and revising.
7. Write your essays in the correct place. Task 1 needs to be written on pages 1 and 2 of your writing test booklet. Task 2 needs to be written on pages 3 and 4.
8. Don't forget to indent.
9. Write clearly and legibly. Make sure the ink in your pen is dark enough.
10. Cross out changes neatly or erase thoroughly.
11. Leave some time at the end to check for and correct spelling and grammar mistakes.

WRITING SKILLS

RESPONDING TO THE TASK

Target 1—Writing for a Specific Audience

You write for someone to read what you write. You match your tone or style to your purpose and to your reader. These styles of writing are part of IELTS.

An **academic** style is used when writing to a large audience about a topic. Academic writing may describe, explain, or inform. A **semi-formal/neutral** style is used when writing to a colleague or associate. It is also used when writing to someone who is older or in a different social group.

[1]BRITISH: organise

Academic	Semi-formal/Neutral
• contractions and abbreviations not used • passive voice frequently used • high percentage of longer, multi-syllable words, particularly words of Latin and Greek origin • phrasal verbs generally less common • longer sentences with more complex grammatical structures • *which* and *who* rather than *that* in restrictive clauses • *whom* in object position, though not universally used • full clauses as opposed to reduced clauses (e.g., optional *that* more likely) • *one, one's, oneself* instead of second person (*you*) forms • first person (*I*) forms avoided • longer, more formal transition words and connectors such as *consequently, therefore, whereas, nonetheless* • transitions such as *firstly, secondly, lastly,* but *first, second, last* equally acceptable • variety of vocabulary strongly preferred • semi-colons used frequently; exclamation points rare	• use of contractions varies depending on purpose of writing • word choices generally neutral (highly informal or highly academic generally avoided) • slang normally avoided, but idioms sometimes used to make a point • mix of single and phrasal verbs, especially when the single verb may be perceived as too academic/formal • variety of sentence lengths; both reduced and unreduced clauses • *that* or *which* in restrictive clauses • all pronoun forms used, though *one, one's, oneself* somewhat less frequent • *whom* in object position rare • variety of transition words and connectors • exclamation points and semi-colons rare

A **formal** style is used when writing to someone in a position of authority. An **informal** style is used when writing to a friend or someone you know well.

Formal	Informal
• avoidance of gender-specific words such as *spokesman* or *sir* and *he* as the neutral pronoun unless the gender of the recipient is known • occasional use of *whom* in object position • adherence to correct business letter form and punctuation for greetings and closings • variety of transition words and connectors • exclamation points and semi-colons rare • contractions used infrequently	• contractions used frequently • high frequency of informal language, including slang and idioms • frequent use of phrasal verbs • shorter words preferred over longer, multi-syllable words • shorter sentences with more reduced clauses • *that* rather than *which* in restrictive clauses • *who* rather than *whom* in object position • *you* and *I* forms used • common transition words and connectors such as *first, next, then, and, but, or, because* as opposed to *firstly, lastly, consequently, therefore, whereas* • exclamation points common; semi-colons rare

PRACTICE 1

Put a check (✓) to indicate the style you might use in each case. One or more styles may be possible.

Purpose/Reader	Academic	Informal	Neutral	Formal
1. a letter of complaint to the mayor of your town				
2. some suggestions to your friend for his vacation				
3. an article for a professional journal				
4. an e-mail inviting your cousin to visit				
5. a letter to a hotel manager about a problem with your bill				
6. a notice reminding students not to use the faculty parking lot				
7. your opinion on how money should be spent in public schools				
8. an e-mail to your parents' friends asking to stay at their house				
9. a letter to a company inquiring about possible positions				
10. a description of a new computer for a technical magazine				
11. an explanation of the advantages and disadvantages of cell (mobile) phones				
12. a report on the effects of TV on society				

PRACTICE 2

Each of the following passages is written in a different style. In each passage, circle the correct words to match the indicated style.

Academic

It has been proven in (1) *numerous/many* studies that television has (2) *bad/negative* effects on academic achievement. A recent study by National University recorded the television viewing habits of primary school children. (3) *They found/It was found* that children watching two hours or less of television a day had higher grades in school than their peers. Children (4) *who/that* watched more than three hours of television a day tended to do poorly in school. The type of television programs viewed also affected children's performance in school. Viewing educational programs correlated with higher academic achievement, while viewing programs (5) *that/which* showed violence correlated with lower academic achievement. (6) *So/Therefore*, it can be concluded that television influences children's school performance.

Informal

Dear Lee,

I'm so happy about your visit. I (7) *can't wait/am eager* to see you. I have planned a lot of things for us to do while (8) *you are/you're* here. We'll have (9) *lots /a great deal* of fun. (10) *First/Firstly*, there's a party at my friend's house the day after you get here. Then we'll go horseback riding the next day, if you like that. (11) *On the other hand/Or*, we can go bike riding instead. It's up to you. There are also some good movies in town we can see. There's so much to do, we'll be busy every day from the time we (12) *awaken/get up* until the time we go to bed. I hope you weren't planning to rest too much! See you soon.

Your cousin,
Maya

Neutral

Dear Mr. and Mrs. Smith,

First, (13) *I'd/I would* like to thank you for letting me stay at your (14) *residence/house* last week. I also hope you will accept my sincere apologies for the trouble I caused. I am very sorry I broke your vase. That was out of line. People (15) *whom/who* you invite to your house should treat your things with respect. (16) *You don't/One doesn't* normally expect guests to break things. I am prepared to (17) *pay you back/reimburse you* for the vase I broke. Please let me know the cost, and I will send you a check right away.

Sincerely,
Joe Thornton

Formal

Cell phones are widely used these days. In fact, statistics show that close to 85% of the urban population uses cell phones on a regular basis (18) *!/.* Certainly, cell phones have many advantages, but there are disadvantages as well. One disadvantage is cost. Eager (19) *salespeople/salesmen* get customers to sign up for plans that they (20) *can't/cannot* afford. The customer who suddenly finds (21) *their/his or her* cell phone unexpectedly disconnected because of unpaid bills is certainly at a disadvantage.

Target 2—Completing the Task

It is very important that you do the task completely. For each task, you will be given a limited amount of time and a minimum number of words. Do not spend more than the given time, and do not write fewer than the minimum number of words. You can write more words, but be careful that you work within the time limit.

These are the instruction lines for each task.

Task 1
- You should spend about 20 minutes on this task.
- You should write at least 150 words.

Task 2
- You should spend about 40 minutes on this task.
- You should write at least 250 words.

PRACTICE

Complete this table.

	Time	**Words**
Task 1		
Task 2		

Target 3—Determining the Task

You must complete a task. Do not forget any of the parts of the task. You may have to describe the main features of a chart or graph, describe a process, describe a problem and solution, give an invitation, describe the advantages and disadvantages of an issue, or explain your opinion.

Read the following tasks and answer the questions.

ACADEMIC TASK 1

1.
You should spend about 20 minutes on this task.

> *The charts below show how average middle-income families spent their household budget in two different years.*
>
> *Summarize the information by selecting and reporting the main features, and make comparisons where relevant.*

Write at least 150 words.

Household Budget Allocation—Middle Income

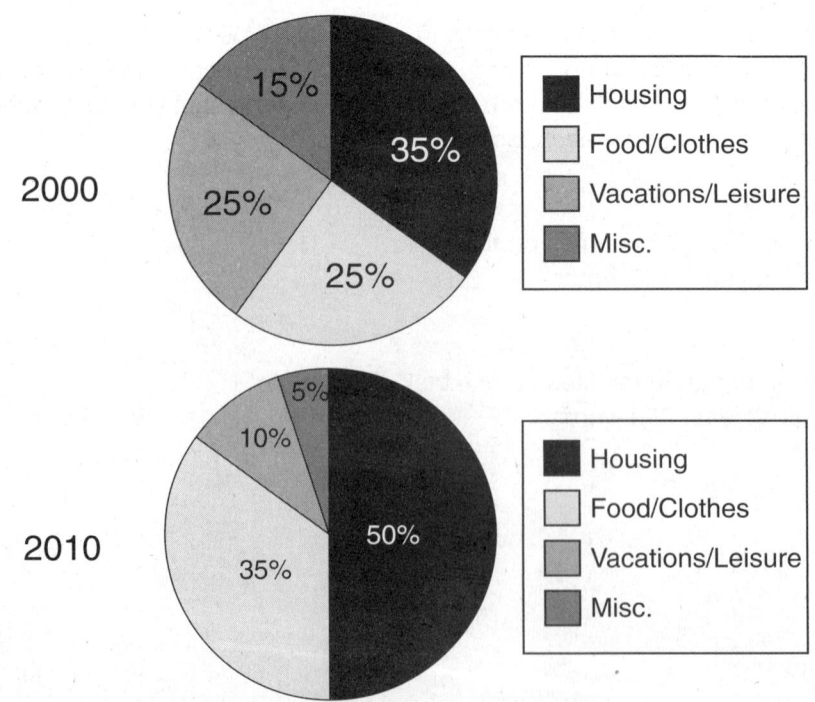

1.1 How long can I spend writing the answer?
1.2 How many words will I write?
1.3 Will I summarize a chart or explain a process?
1.4 What is the topic?
1.5 What do I have to compare?

2.
You should spend about 20 minutes on this task.

> *The diagram below shows the steps in the process of making maple syrup from the sap of the sugar maple tree.*
>
> *Summarize the information by selecting and reporting the main features, and make comparisons where relevant.*

Write at least 150 words.

Making Maple Syrup from the Sugar Maple Tree

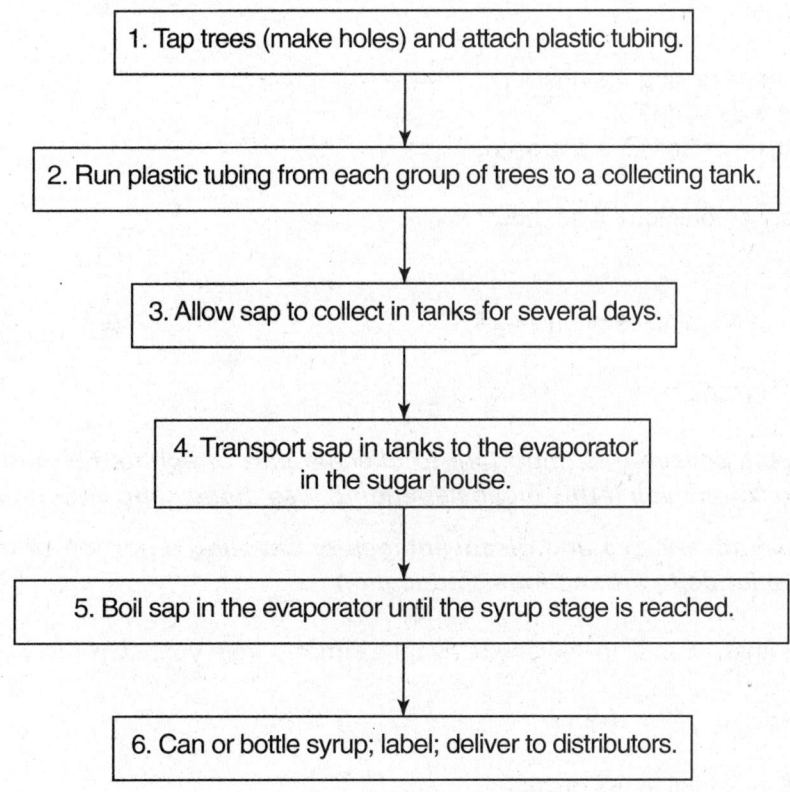

```
┌─────────────────────────────────────────────────┐
│ 1. Tap trees (make holes) and attach plastic tubing. │
└─────────────────────────────────────────────────┘
                        │
                        ▼
┌─────────────────────────────────────────────────────────┐
│ 2. Run plastic tubing from each group of trees to a collecting tank. │
└─────────────────────────────────────────────────────────┘
                        │
                        ▼
┌─────────────────────────────────────────────┐
│ 3. Allow sap to collect in tanks for several days. │
└─────────────────────────────────────────────┘
                        │
                        ▼
┌─────────────────────────────────────────────┐
│ 4. Transport sap in tanks to the evaporator      │
│    in the sugar house.                            │
└─────────────────────────────────────────────┘
                        │
                        ▼
┌──────────────────────────────────────────────────────┐
│ 5. Boil sap in the evaporator until the syrup stage is reached. │
└──────────────────────────────────────────────────────┘
                        │
                        ▼
┌─────────────────────────────────────────────────┐
│ 6. Can or bottle syrup; label; deliver to distributors. │
└─────────────────────────────────────────────────┘
```

Note: It takes 40 gallons of sap to make one gallon of syrup.

2.1 How long can I spend writing the answer?
2.2 How many words will I write?
2.3 Will I summarize a chart or outline a process?
2.4 What is the topic?
2.5 What kind of information do I have to explain?

ACADEMIC TASK 2

3.
You should spend about 40 minutes on this task.

Write about the following topic:

> *A successful person is one who has earned a lot of money.*
>
> *To what extent do you agree or disagree?*

Give reasons for your answer and include any relevant examples from your own knowledge or experience.

Write at least 250 words.

3.1 How long can I spend writing the answer?
3.2 How many words will I write?
3.3 Will I give an opinion or describe a process?
3.4 What is the topic?
3.5 Do I have to justify an opinion? If so, how?

4.
You should spend about 40 minutes on this task.

Write about the following topic:

> *Some people believe it is important to allocate part of school resources for art and music education even if this means spending less money and time on academics.*
>
> *Discuss the advantages and disadvantages of devoting a portion of the school day and school funds to art and music education.*

Give reasons for your answer and include any relevant examples from your own knowledge or experience.

Write at least 250 words.

4.1 How long can I spend writing the answer?
4.2 How many words will I write?
4.3 Will I summarize information or explain two sides of an issue?
4.4 What is the topic?
4.5 Do I have to give factual information?

GENERAL WRITING TASK 1

1.
You should spend about 20 minutes on this task.

> **You feel that the evening programs on a local television station are uninteresting.**
>
> **Write a letter to the manager of the television station. In your letter**
>
> • **explain why you don't like the current programs**
> • **describe what kinds of programs you would like to see instead**
> • **explain why these programs are better**

Write at least 150 words.

You do NOT need to write any addresses.

Begin your letter as follows:

Dear Sir or Madam:

1.1 How long can I spend writing the answer?
1.2 How many words will I write?
1.3 What is the topic?
1.4 What three things do I have to include?
1.5 Do I have to present a solution or provide facts?

2.
You should spend about 20 minutes on this task.

> **You just bought a new house and are planning a party to celebrate.**
>
> **Write a letter to a friend inviting him or her to the party. In your letter**
>
> • **explain the reason for the party**
> • **tell when and where the party will take place**
> • **describe some things that will happen at the party**

Write at least 150 words.

You do NOT need to write any addresses.

Begin your letter as follows:

Dear ....,

2.1 How long can I spend writing the answer?
2.2 How many words will I write?
2.3 What is the topic?
2.4 What three things do I have to include?
2.5 Do I have to make a complaint or provide facts?

GENERAL WRITING TASK 2

3.
You should spend about 40 minutes on this task.

Write about the following topic:

> *In the past, it was common for older people to live with their children and grand-children so that their relatives could take care of them as they grew older. Nowadays, it is common in many places for older people to live away from their families, in special homes for the elderly.*
>
> *Discuss the advantages and disadvantages of special homes for the elderly.*

Give reasons for your answer and include any relevant examples from your own knowledge or experience.

Write at least 250 words.

3.1 How long can I spend writing the answer?
3.2 How many words will I write?
3.3 What is the topic?
3.4 Do I have to justify an opinion?
3.5 Do I have to describe two sides of an issue?

4.
You should spend about 40 minutes on this task.

Write about the following topic:

> *In many parts of the world, people are relying more and more on prepared food from grocery stores or restaurants because they are too busy to cook at home. This is a bad idea because home-cooked food is much better for us.*
>
> *To what extent do you agree or disagree?*

Give reasons for your answer and include any relevant examples from your own knowledge or experience.

Write at least 250 words.

4.1 How long can I spend writing my answer?
4.2 How many words will I write?
4.3 What is the topic?
4.4 Do I have to give factual information?
4.5 Do I have to explain a problem or justify an opinion?

COHERENCE AND COHESION

Target 4—Developing a Thesis Statement

Before you begin writing, you must think about your thesis statement. A thesis statement is your main idea. It will set the stage for the rest of your writing. You have a thesis statement both for descriptions and for opinions.

GIVE A DESCRIPTION

Example

Write about the following topic:

The following diagram explains the process of heating water with an indirect solar water heating system.

Summarize the information by selecting and reporting the main features, and make comparisons where relevant.

Write at least 150 words.

Indirect Solar Water Heating System

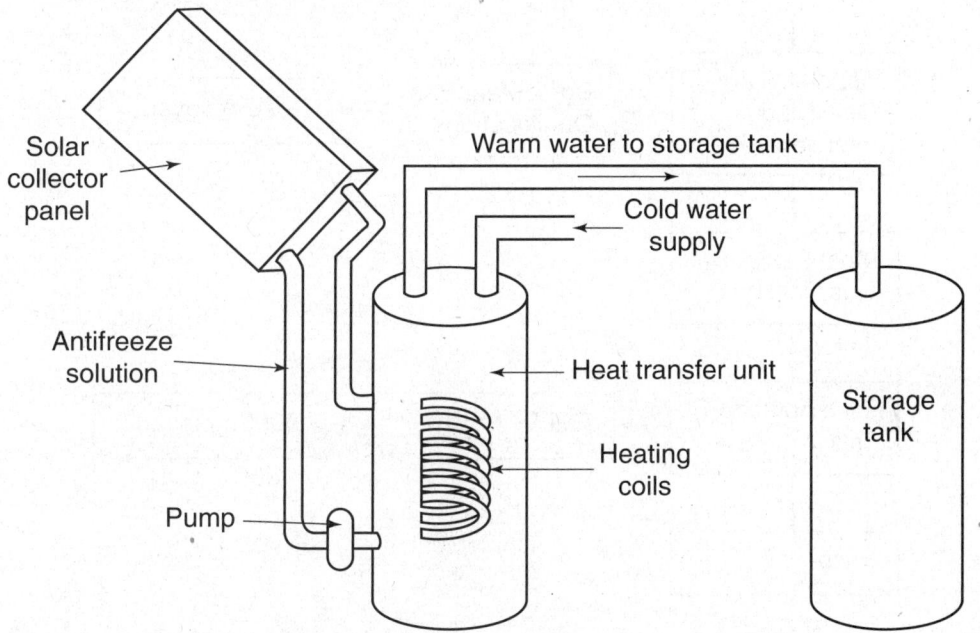

1. Pump moves antifreeze solution to the solar collector
2. Solution moves through solar collector
3. Warmed antifreeze solution moves to heat-transfer unit
4. Cool water moves through heat-transfer unit for warming
5. Warm water moves to storage tank
6. Antifreeze solution is pumped back to solar collector

POSSIBLE THESIS STATEMENTS

An indirect solar water heating system is a method of transferring the heat of the sun to household water.

An indirect solar water heating system does not heat the water directly, but uses a special solution to move heat from solar collectors to water.

A system that uses antifreeze solution to collect solar heat and transfer it to water is called an indirect solar water heating system.

ACME CORPORATION—RECRUITMENT PROCESS

Example

Write about the following topic:

> *The diagram on the next page shows the steps in the hiring process at a large corporation.*
>
> *Summarize the information by selecting and reporting the main features, and make comparisons where relevant.*

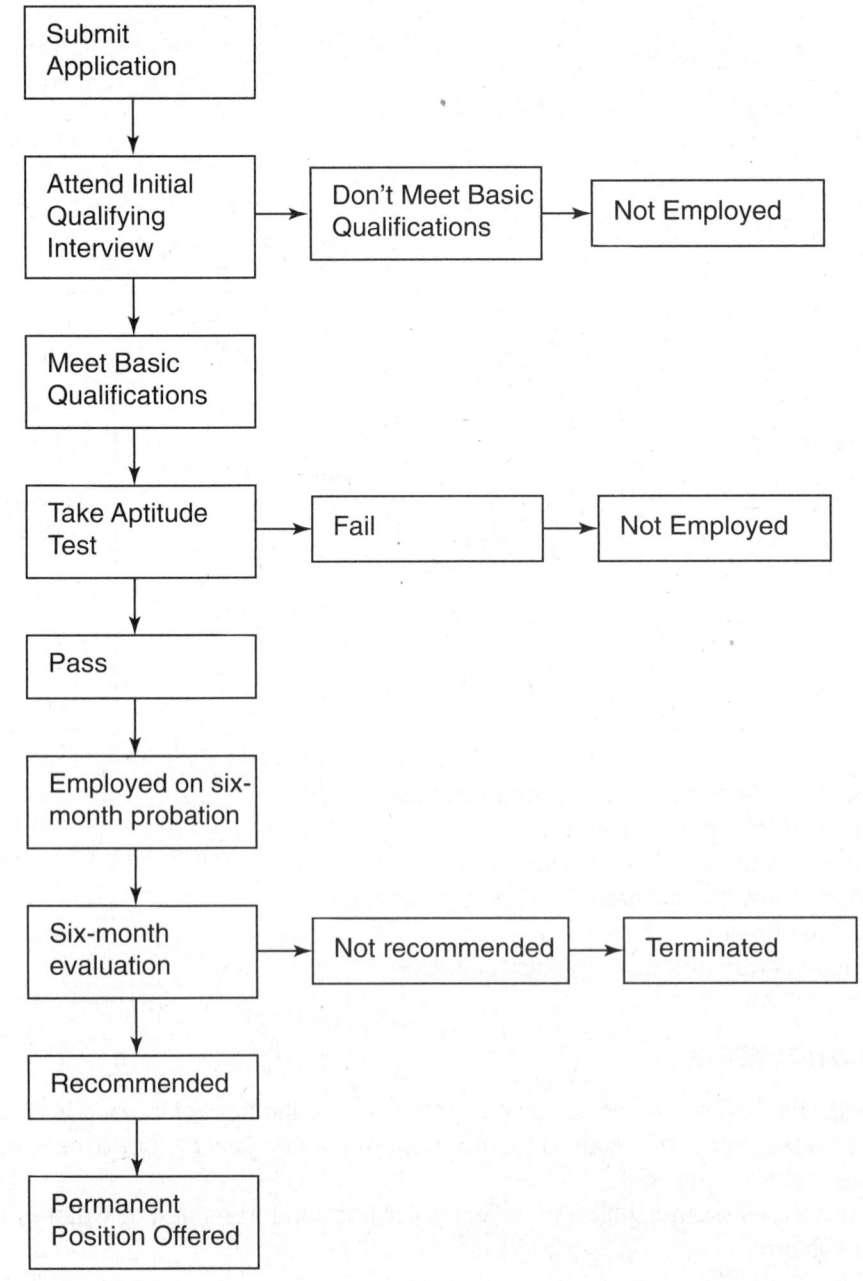

Possible Thesis Statements

1. There are several steps one must go through before being employed by the Acme Corporation.
2. Getting a job at the Acme Corporation is not a simple process.
3. The Acme Corporation wants to make sure that all potential employees are well-qualified before being offered a permanent position at the company.

SUPPORT YOUR OPINION

Example

Write about the following topic:

> *More and more fathers are taking a break from their careers so that they can stay home and take care of their children while their wives work. This is better for the family than having both parents work full-time. To what extent do you agree or disagree.*

Give reasons for your answer and include any relevant examples from your own knowledge or experience.

Possible Thesis Statements

1. Changing customs have made it possible for men to take on roles in the family that once were considered to be only for women.
2. Many modern couples are beginning to recognize[1] that it is better to have a parent at home to take care of the children, rather than relying on a full-time babysitter or pre-school.
3. Changing views of women in the professions have made it possible for many women to earn a salary that is high enough to support a family.

PRACTICE

First, identify the task. Then, choose the thesis statement or statements that are appropriate to the topic. There can be more than one thesis statement.

Topic 1

> *There should be laws to control the amount and type of violence shown on television programs.*
>
> *To what extent do you agree or disagree with this statement?*

Give reasons for your answer and include any relevant examples from your own knowledge and experience.

Task
(A) Give a description.
(B) Support your opinion.
(C) Explain a problem and ask for a solution.

[1]BRITISH: recognise

Thesis Statement

(A) There are many types of programs on television, and each person is free to choose which programs he or she wants to watch.

(B) I enjoy watching police and detective programs on television.

(C) We can learn a lot from television, but it's not a good idea to spend more than an hour a day watching it.

Topic 2

More and more families have computers in their homes, and children spend a great deal of their free time using their home computers.

Discuss the advantages and disadvantages of this situation, and give your own opinions.

Give reasons for your answer and include any relevant examples from your own knowledge and experience.

Task

(A) Give a description.

(B) Support your opinion.

(C) Explain a problem and ask for a solution.

Thesis Statement

(A) Computers have become very inexpensive in recent years.

(B) Computers can contribute a lot to a child's education, but they can be overused.

(C) Computers today can do much more than the computers of just a few years ago.

Topic 3

The graphs on the next page show the figures for population distribution in the Northwest region of the U.S. for 1900–2050.

Summarize the information by selecting and reporting the main features, and make comparisons where relevant.

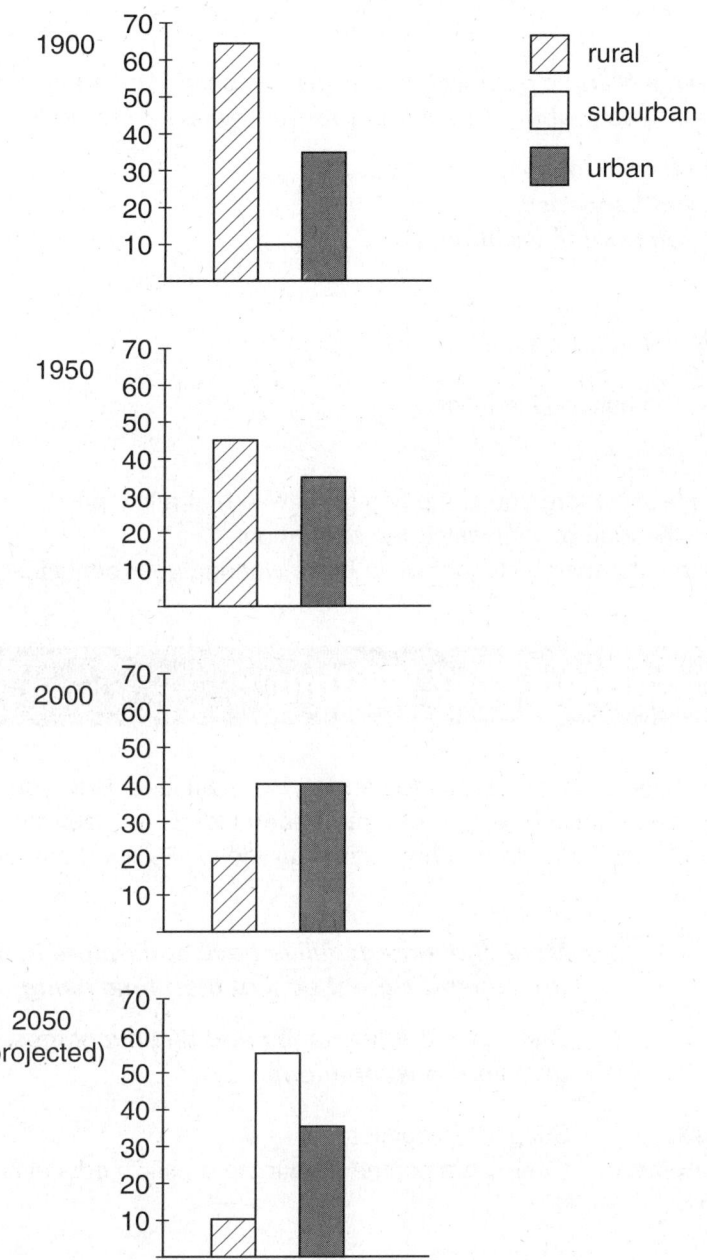

Task
(A) Give a description.
(B) Support your opinion.
(C) Explain a problem, and ask for a solution.

Thesis Statement
(A) Although the cost of living is high in urban areas, cities also have many advantages.
(B) Some people like to live in rural areas because they offer a peaceful and pleasant way of life.
(C) Over the past century, the population in the Northwest region of the U.S. has been shifting from largely rural to mostly suburban and urban.

Topic 4

You borrowed a friend's gold watch to wear to a party. Unfortunately, the watch fell off your wrist and you lost it. Write a letter to the owner of the watch. In your letter

- ***apologize for the loss***
- ***explain what happened***
- ***tell what you want to do about it***

Task

(A)   Give a description.

(B)   Support your opinion.

(C)   Explain a problem, and ask for a solution.

Thesis Statement

(A)   There are several places where you can buy a good watch at a low price.

(B)   I greatly appreciate the loan of your watch the other night.

(C)   An unfortunate thing happened last night while I was wearing your beautiful gold watch.

Target 5—Organizing Your Writing

Your writing needs a main idea. Your thesis statement is your main idea. Now you have to support your main idea with general ideas. You should have two or three general ideas for each topic.

You can use concept maps to help you organize your ideas. Follow these steps to help you organize your writing.

1. Read the topic.	***More and more families have computers in their homes, and children spend a great deal of their time using their home computers.*** ***Discuss the advantages and disadvantages of this situation and give your own opinions.***
2. Determine the task.	Support an opinion.
3. Write a thesis statement.	Computers contribute a lot to a child's education.
4. Add general ideas.	

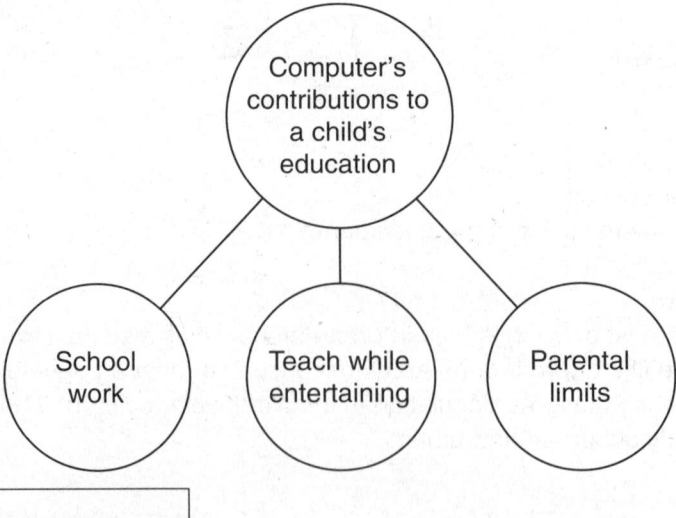

TEST TIP

Everything you write in your answer must be relevant to the question.

5. Add supporting details.

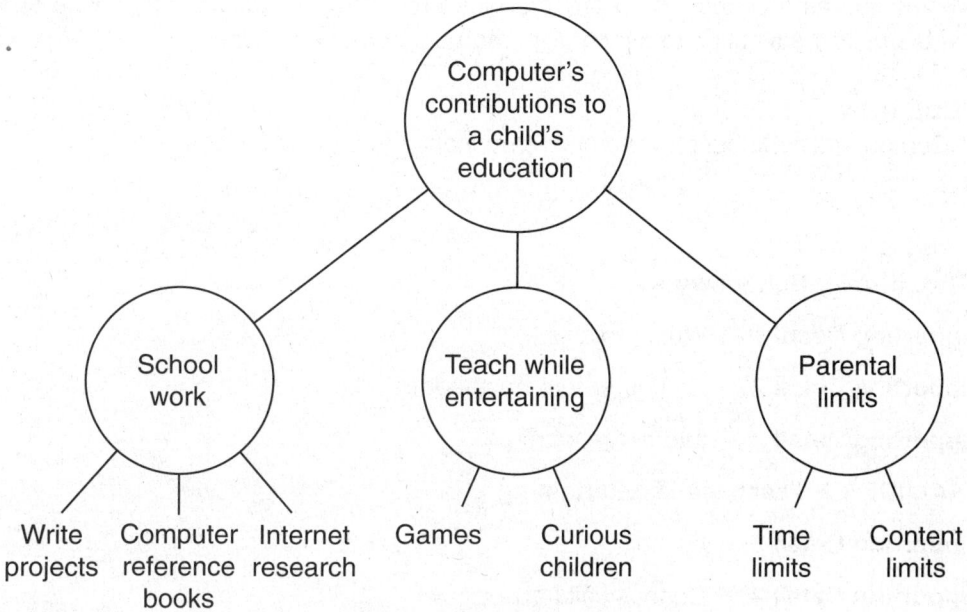

Compare this passage with the concept map above.

Home computers offer many advantages to the average family. One of the most important of these is the contribution computers can make to a child's education. With parental guidance, children can learn a lot by using a computer.

A computer is a useful tool for school work. Computers make it very easy to keep notes and write up school projects. Reference books on computer CDs make it convenient for children to research their school projects. In addition, the Internet makes research on any subject possible from the comfort of one's own home. Children can do all this work independently, without asking their parents to take them to the library or buy expensive reference books for them.

Computers keep children entertained in an educational way. There are many computer games that both attract children and teach them something. The Internet offers the curious child a way to find information about anything that he or she is interested in. A child can stay gainfully occupied for hours at a time with a computer.

Parents don't need to limit their children's computer time, although they should pay close attention to what a child does with a computer. Using a computer is not a passive activity like watching television is. The more time a child spends on a computer, the more the child can learn. However, parents should control which websites their children visit and which computer games they play. Then the computer is a safe learning tool for children.

Computers contribute a lot to a child's education. Every family should have one.

Instead of using a concept map to organize your information, you can use an outline. An outline contains the same information as a concept map but in a different format. Compare this outline of the essay about computers and a child's education to the concept map on the previous page.

INTRODUCTION
TOPIC Computer's contributions to a child's education

BODY

GENERAL IDEA 1 School work

> **Supporting Detail 1**   Write projects
>
> **Supporting Detail 2**   Computer reference books
>
> **Supporting Detail 3**   Internet research

GENERAL IDEA 2 Teach while entertaining

> **Supporting Detail 1**   Games
>
> **Supporting Detail 2**   Curious children

GENERAL IDEA 3 Parental limits

> **Supporting Detail 1**   Time limits
>
> **Supporting Detail 2**   Content limits

Practice 1

This exercise will help you learn the steps to organize your writing. Look at the concept map. Read the essay. Complete the missing parts of the map.

1. Read the topic.   **There should be laws to control the amount and type of violence shown on television programs.**

To what extent do you agree or disagree with this statement?

2. Determine the task.   Support an opinion.
3. Write a thesis statement.   We are free to choose the shows we watch. Laws are not necessary to help us decide what to watch.

4. Add general ideas.

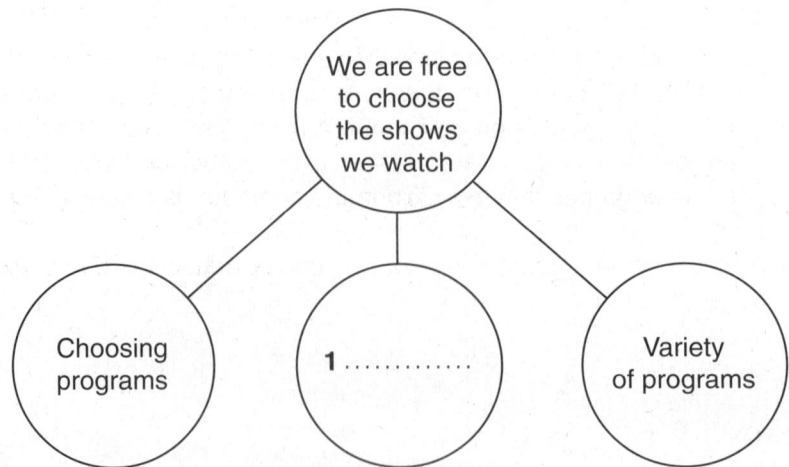

5. Add supporting details.

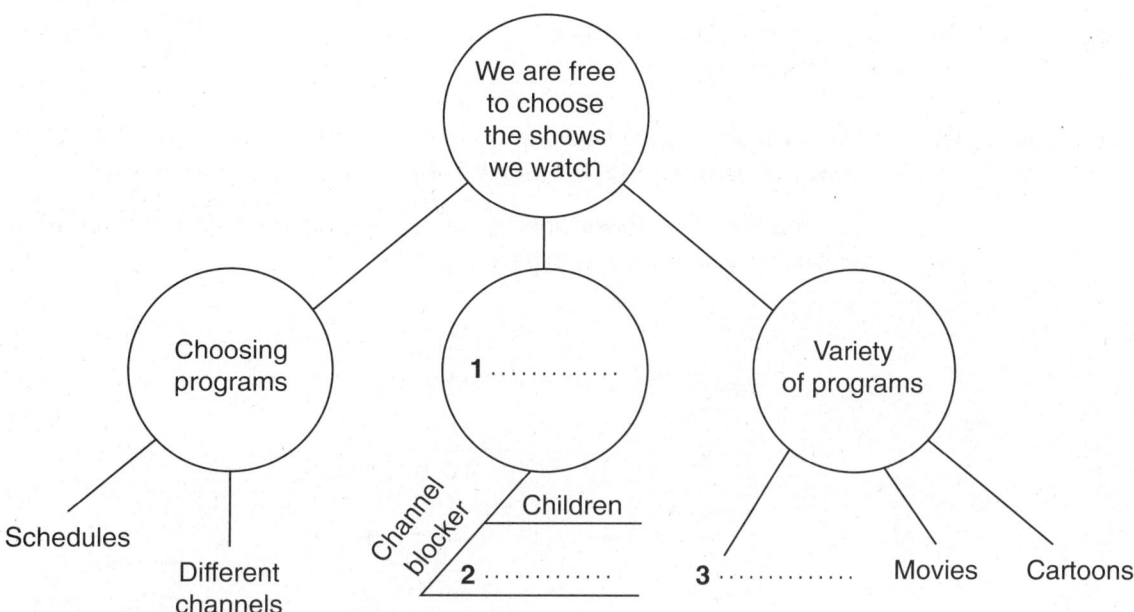

While it is true that there is violence on television, each individual has his or her own idea about how much is too much. Fortunately, we are all free to choose which TV programs we want to watch. Laws are not necessary to help us decide.

It isn't difficult to find out which programs are on TV at any given time. Most newspapers publish a schedule of TV programs every day. Also, anyone who watches TV regularly knows which programs she likes and which she doesn't like. She knows what kinds of programs each different channel tends to have. Because of this, it's easy for everyone to avoid violent programs if they want to.

Modern technology has given us a tool for controlling the TV programs we see. Most TVs can be programmed to block certain channels. Thus, parents have a way to protect their children from seeing shows[1] that are too violent. Adults can also use this technology to avoid seeing programs that they don't want to see.

The best thing about TV is that there is a variety of programs. There are news programs for serious people. There are films and cartoons for people who want to be entertained. The variety of TV programs needs to be protected, even if that means allowing some of them to show violence.

We each have our own ideas about what is too violent and what isn't. It would be difficult to make laws about violence on TV that would satisfy everybody. It is better to let each individual make his or her own choice about what to watch.

TEST TIP

You may use *she* for variety (rather than *he*) or you may use *he or she* but be consistent in the essay.

---

[1]BRITISH: programmes

PRACTICE 2

This exercise will help you learn the steps to organize your writing. Look at the outline. Read the essay. Complete the missing parts of the outline.

1. **Read the topic.**   **The 3 maps below show Palm Grove, a coastal town about 450 kilometers from the nearest city. It has recently become a major resort.**

           Summarize the information by selecting and reporting the main features, and make comparisons where relevant.

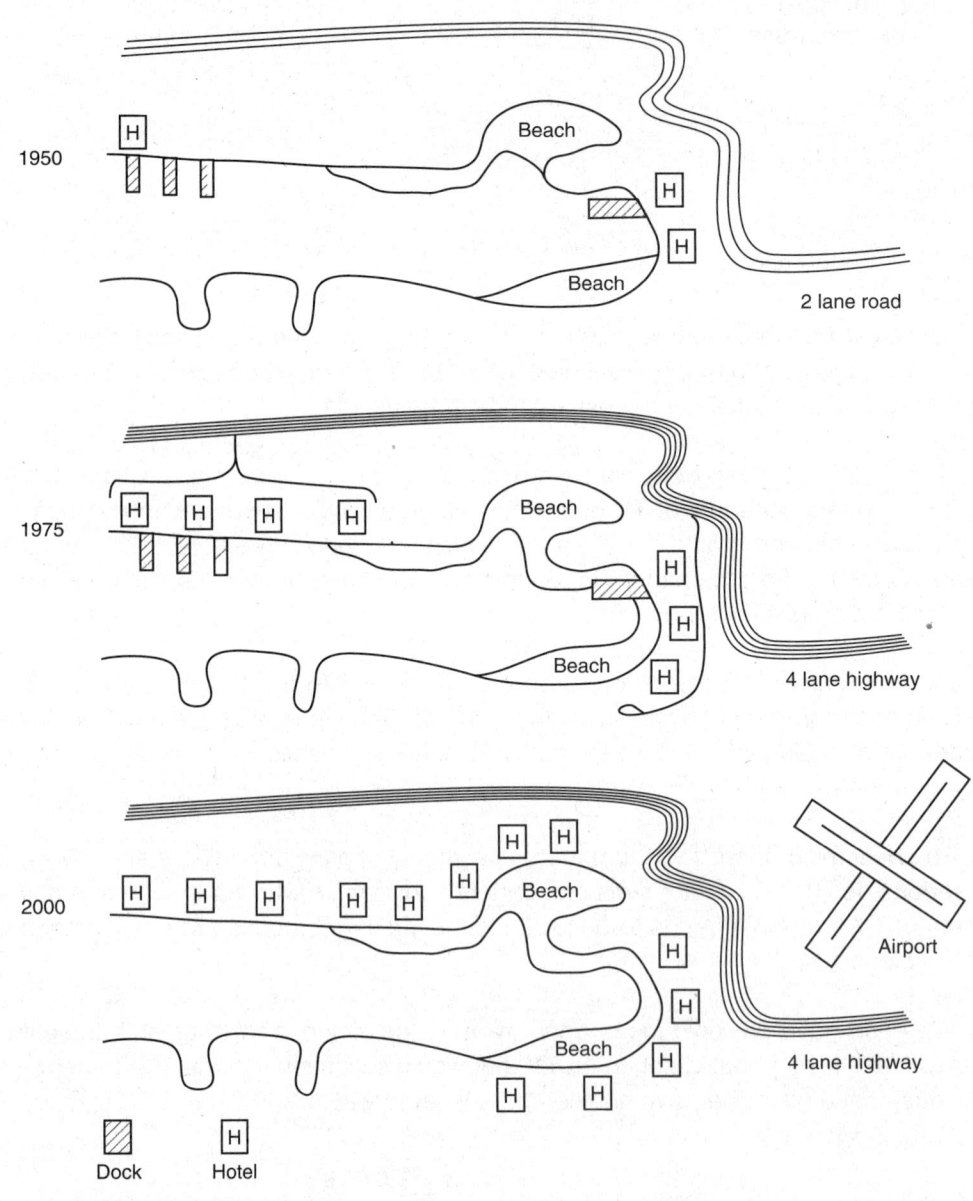

2. **Determine the task.**   Describe something.
3. **Write a thesis statement.** Palm Grove became a resort when accessibility from the outside improved.
4. **Add general ideas.**

INTRODUCTION
TOPIC Accessibility brings tourists

BODY

GENERAL IDEA 1	**1950—Poor access**
GENERAL IDEA 2	_____
GENERAL IDEA 3	**2000—Airport**

5. **Add supporting details.**

INTRODUCTION
TOPIC Accessibility brings tourists

BODY

GENERAL IDEA 1	**1950—Poor access**
Supporting Detail 1	fishing docks
Supporting Detail 2	_____
GENERAL IDEA 2	_____
Supporting Detail 1	_____
Supporting Detail 2	more hotels
GENERAL IDEA 3	**2000—Airport**
Supporting Detail 1	no fishing docks
Supporting Detail 2	_____

The three maps representing changes in Palm Grove between 1950 and 2000 show that the town became a resort as accessibility from the outside improved.

In 1950, Palm Grove was a small fishing village with few hotels. It lies 450 kilometers from the nearest city. Since the only access to the village in 1950 was by a two-lane road[1], most tourists probably didn't want to make the long trip to get there.

By 1975, a new four-lane highway had brought changes to Palm Grove. It was still a fishing village, but it appears that the new road made it easier for tourists to get there. Several new hotels had been built for them along the beach.

By 2000, an airport had been built just outside Palm Grove. This apparently changed the town into a resort. The hotel district was greatly expanded and the fishing docks removed. Probably most local residents now work in the tourist industry.

[1]BRITISH: Single carriageway or two-way traffic. In America a four-lane highway (road) is, in England, a dual carriageway.

PRACTICE 3

Identify the tasks for the following topics. Create a concept map or outline for each. On a separate piece of paper, write an essay or letter using the concept map or outline as a guide. Compare your essays or letters with those in the Answer Key.

Topic 1

Most schools offer some type of physical education program to their students. Why is physical education important? Should physical education classes be required or optional?

Task: _____

Thesis Statement: _____

Concept Map:

Students'
mental health

Topic 2

You have had a credit card with the same company for several years, and you always pay your bill on time. Your most recent bill included a $35 charge for late payment because, according to the company, you didn't pay the previous month. You know that you paid on time.

Write a letter to the credit card company. In your letter

- **explain the problem**
- **tell how you feel about it**
- **say what you would like the credit card company to do about it**

Task: _____

Thesis Statement: _____

Outline:

INTRODUCTION
TOPIC _____.

BODY

GENERAL IDEA 1 _____
    Supporting Detail 1   _____
    Supporting Detail 2   _____
    Supporting Detail 3   _____

GENERAL IDEA 2 _____
    Supporting Detail 1   _____
    Supporting Detail 2   _____
    Supporting Detail 3   _____

Topic 3   *The graph below shows the figures for population distribution in the Northwest region of the U.S. for 1900–2050.*

Summarize the information by selecting and reporting the main features, and make comparisons where relevant.

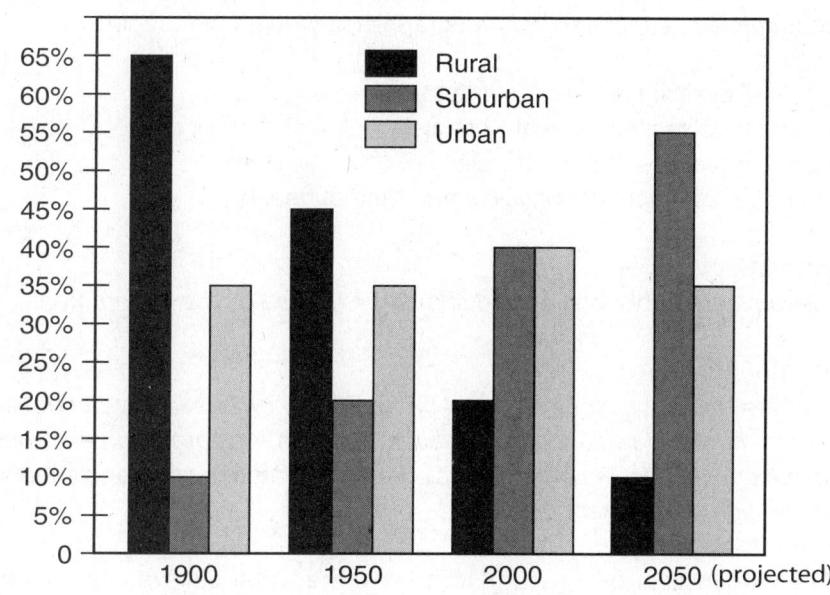

Population Distribution in the Northwest Region

Task: _____

Thesis Statement: _____

Concept Map: (Use a separate sheet of paper for your concept map.)

Target 6—Writing the Introduction

The introduction to your essay guides the reader. It is like a map. It tells the reader how you plan to develop your topic. The topic sentences you develop from the general ideas in your concept map or outline can be summarized in the introduction.

Compare these introductions:

Weak Introduction

In my opinion, physical education is important. It's better for children to have it than not.

Strong Introduction

Physical education is an important part of every child's education. In the first place, children learn better if they spend part of each day getting some physical exercise. Additionally, physical education teaches children important skills such as teamwork. Also, it contributes to their overall physical and mental health.

The first introduction tells us the writer's opinion, but not much about it. Why does the writer feel this way? We need to know the reasons for the opinion so that we can be ready to follow the supporting details in the body of the essay.

The second introduction outlines three specific reasons why the writer thinks physical education is important. We can expect that each paragraph in the body of the essay will explain one of these reasons more thoroughly. We will be able to follow the writer's ideas because we know what to look for as we read. These reasons (or general ideas) provide a focus to the paragraph. They guide the reader.

Thesis	Physical education is important.
General Idea	It helps children learn better.
General Idea	It teaches important skills.
General Idea	It contributes to physical and mental health.

Weak Introduction

Art museums are public places and should be funded by the government.

Strong Introduction

I don't agree that art museums should be funded by private instead of public money. It is difficult to raise enough private money to run a museum well. In addition, charging high entrance fees will keep many people away from museums. Most important, art is a valuable part of culture and should receive support from society as a whole through government funding.

With the first introduction, the reader knows what the writer believes, but not why. The second introduction gives detailed reasons to support the writer's opinion, and the reader can expect to read about these reasons in the body of the essay.

Thesis	Art museums should be funded with public money.
General Idea	It's difficult to raise private money.
General Idea	High entrance fees keep people away.
General Idea	Art is a valuable part of culture.

PRACTICE 1

Read the following introductions, based on questions from Targets 3 and 4. Tell the topic of the essay or letter and what the general idea or focus of each paragraph will be.

1. Many modern couples are beginning to recognize that it is better to have a parent at home to take care of the children, rather than relying on a full-time babysitter or pre-school. I agree that this is a good idea. First, no one can care for a child as well as his own parents. Parents also have to face the fact that child care costs are very high. Finally, it is my belief that family life is better when one of the spouses devotes his or her time to maintaining the home and family.

    Topic   _____
    General Idea   _____
    General Idea   _____
    General Idea   _____

2. Maple syrup is a tasty treat that many people enjoy eating on their pancakes. It is made from the sap of the sugar maple tree, and the process involves a number of steps. The sap has to be gathered from the trees, it has to be transported to the sugar house, and it has to be boiled before it is finally ready for distribution.

    Topic   _____
    General Idea   _____
    General Idea   _____
    General Idea   _____

3. Dear John,
    I have some unfortunate news to tell you. I am very sorry to have to tell you that I lost the watch you lent me. It disappeared while I was at a party last night. I hope you will let me pay you for it.

    Topic   _____
    General Idea   _____
    General Idea   _____

4. These days, people around the world use the Internet to get news and information. There are both advantages and disadvantages to this situation. On the one hand, the Internet has many advantages because it provides instant access to huge amounts of information that might be difficult to get otherwise. On the other hand, the Internet has certain problems, including the fact that much of the information you find there is unreliable.

    Topic   _____
    General Idea   _____
    General Idea   _____

PRACTICE 2

Read these topics. Determine the task. Write your thesis statement. Do a concept map. Write your topic sentences. (You can have between two and four topic sentences.) Then write the introduction to your essay. Be sure you answer all parts of the topic.

Topic 1

Some people believe that the best way to learn anything is "learning by doing." Others would rather learn through books and from teachers. Think of learning a language. Which way do you think is a better way to learn a language?

Task: _____

Thesis Statement: _____

Concept Map: Use a separate sheet of paper to draw a web concept map if you need more space.

Topic Sentences: 1.1 _____

1.2 _____

1.3 _____

1.4 _____

Introduction:

_____

_____

_____

_____

_____

_____

Topic 2

In many parts of the world and throughout history, governments have moved their capitals. Why would they do this? What are the potential problems and benefits? Would you vote for moving your capital?

Task: _____

Thesis Statement: _____

Concept Map: Use a separate sheet of paper to draw a web concept map if you need more space.

Topic Sentences: 2.1 _____

                   2.2 _____

                   2.3 _____

Introduction:

_____

_____

_____

_____

_____

_____

Target 7—Writing a Paragraph

In Target 4, you learned to write your thesis statement. The thesis statement is what your essay or letter is about. An essay is made up of paragraphs. Each paragraph has a topic sentence and supporting details.

A topic sentence tells what each paragraph is about. A topic sentence can come at the start of a paragraph, in the middle, or at the end. It can introduce a paragraph or it can summarize a paragraph.

When you made each concept map and outline, you wrote two or three general ideas in words or phrases. Turn those general ideas into a sentence and you have a topic sentence for a paragraph. It is important to write a good topic sentence. It helps the reader follow your line of thinking. It makes your intentions clear. A topic sentence gives your essay or letter clarity.

In your concept maps and outlines, each general idea (topic sentence) is connected to or followed by supporting details. These specific details support your general idea. They help the reader understand your intentions. A topic sentence with supporting details gives your letter or essay clarity.

Look at this outline:

Topic Accessibility brings tourists

Paragraph 1
General Idea 1950—Poor access
   Supporting Detail 1   fishing docks
   Supporting Detail 2   few hotels

Paragraph 2
General Idea 1975—Four-lane highway
   Supporting Detail 1   fishing docks still present
   Supporting Detail 2   more hotels

Paragraph 3
General Idea 2000—Airport
   Supporting Detail 1   no fishing docks
   Supporting Detail 2   greatly expanded hotel district

Read the paragraph for the general idea "Four-lane highway."

> By 1975, a new four-lane highway had brought changes to Palm Grove. It was still a fishing village, but it appears that the new road made it easier for tourists to get there. Several new hotels had been built for them along the beach.

Topic Sentence   By 1975, a new four-lane highway had brought changes to Palm Grove.

Supporting Details   It was easier for tourists to get there.
                        Several new hotels had been built.

Look at these examples.

Example 1

A computer is a useful tool for school work. Computers make it very easy to keep notes and write up school projects. Reference books on computer CDs make it convenient for children to research their school projects. In addition, the Internet makes research on any subject possible from the comfort of one's own home. Children can do all this work independently, without asking their parents to take them to the library or buy expensive reference books for them.

Topic Sentence   A computer is a useful tool for school work.

Supporting Details   Computers make it very easy to keep notes and write up school projects.

Reference books on computer CDs make it convenient for children to research their school projects.

In addition, the Internet makes research on any subject possible from the comfort of one's own home.

Example 2

It isn't difficult to find out which programs are on TV at any given time. Most newspapers publish a schedule of TV programs every day. Also, anyone who watches TV regularly knows which programs she likes and which she doesn't like. She knows what kinds of programs each different channel tends to have. It's easy for everyone to avoid violent programs if they want to.

Topic Sentence   It isn't difficult to find out which programs are on TV at any given time.

Supporting Details   Most newspapers publish a schedule of TV programs every day.

Also, anyone who watches TV regularly knows which programs she likes and which she doesn't like.

She knows what kinds of programs each different channel tends to have.

PRACTICE

Read the following paragraphs. Write the topic sentence and the supporting details.

1. Modern technology has given us a tool for controlling the TV programs we see. Most TVs can be programmed to block certain channels. Parents use this technology to protect their children from seeing shows that are too violent. Adults can also use this technology to avoid seeing programs that they don't want to see.

   Topic Sentence: 1.1 _____

   Supporting Details: 1.2 _____

   1.3 _____

   1.4 _____

2. The best thing about TV is that there is a variety of programs. There are news programs for serious people. There are films and cartoons for people who want to be entertained. The variety of TV programs needs to be protected, even if that means allowing some of them to show violence.

Topic Sentence: 2.1 _____

Supporting Details: 2.2 _____

2.3 _____

2.4 _____

3. Physical education classes teach children important skills that they need in life. They teach children how to work together on a team. They teach children how to set a goal and work to achieve it. They teach children about the importance of looking after their health.

Topic Sentence: 3.1 _____

Supporting Details: 3.2 _____

3.3 _____

3.4 _____

Target 8—Stating Your Opinion

For Writing Task 2 on both the Academic and General Training tests, you will probably be asked for your opinion. The introduction to your essay should tell the reader what your opinion is. There is no right or wrong opinion. Whatever your opinion is, the reader will look to see how you express it. You can use certain set phrases, verbs, adjectives, and adverbs to express your opinion.

Set Phrases	Verbs	Adjectives	Adverbs
In my opinion	agree	certain	definitely
From my point of view	believe	positive	doubtless
In my view	think	convinced	certainly
To my way of thinking	understand	sure	probably
To my mind	suppose	persuaded	conceivably
It seems to me that	guess	confident	maybe
To me	hope		perhaps
It is my opinion that	imagine		possibly
			seemingly

TEST TIP

Set phrases that are prepositional phrases and most adverbs are followed by a comma at the beginning of a sentence.

Examples

It seems to me that fathers can take care of children just as well as mothers can.
I suppose that some children could benefit from art and music education.
I am certain that over-reliance on cars has led to many problems in our society.

Parents should definitely put limits on their children's television viewing.
People are probably less polite now than they used to be.

PRACTICE 1

Give your opinion about these topics. Use the words and phrases suggested.

1. Violence on television (is/is not) very harmful for children.
   It is my opinion that _____

2. Parents (should/should not) monitor their children's computer use.
   In my view, _____

3. Home-cooked food (is/is not) better for the health of the family.
   I understand that _____

4. Dependence on private automobiles (causes/doesn't cause) many problems in our daily lives.
   I think that _____

5. Learning about art (is/is not) a good way to spend part of the school day.
   I am sure that _____

6. Children (learn/ don't learn) better when they have friendly relationships with their teachers.
   I am convinced that _____

7. People (spend/ do not spend) too much money on stylish clothes.
   Perhaps _____

8. Taking a train (is/ is not) just as convenient as driving a car.
   Certainly, _____

GENERALIZING AND QUALIFYING

Certain phrases can be used to make a general statement about how you feel about something. Others can be used to qualify your opinion, showing that what you state is not completely true.

Generalizing	Qualifying
all in all	in a way
as a rule	more or less
basically	so to speak
by and large	for all intents and purposes
for the most part	to some extent
generally	up to a point
in general	
on the whole	

Examples

All in all, children learn better when they have a more formal relationship with their teacher.
Generally, people pay too much attention to fashion.

Up to a point, parents should let their children choose their own television programs.
For all intents and purposes, the Internet is a valid educational tool.

Practice 2

Give your opinion about these topics. Use the phrases suggested to make a general statement or qualify your opinion.

1. Children (learn/ don't always learn) better when they spend part of each day getting physical exercise.
   As a rule, _____

2. Job security (is/is not) a thing of the past.
   On the whole, _____

3. Family ties (are/ are not) weaker now than they were in the past.
   For the most part, _____

4. Art and music classes (equal/ do not equal) academic classes in importance.
   To some extent, _____

5. A train (is/ is not) as convenient a form of transportation as a private car.
   In a way, _____

Target 9—Writing the Conclusion

A good essay has a good conclusion. The conclusion briefly supports your thesis and reminds the reader of your intentions. It returns to the ideas you presented in your introduction and uses them to conclude with a summary, generalization, prediction, question, or recommendation. Look at the following examples, noticing the relationship between the introduction and conclusion:

RESTATEMENT

In your conclusion, you can restate your thesis or topic sentence.

Introduction:

Maple syrup is a tasty treat that many people enjoy eating on their pancakes. It is made from the sap of the sugar maple tree, and the process involves a number of steps. The sap has to be gathered from the trees, it has to be transported to the sugar house, and it has to be boiled before it is finally ready for distribution.

Conclusion:

Making maple syrup involves several steps, and the result is a tasty treat that is well worth the effort.

GENERALIZATION

You can use all the information you provided and make a generalization about it.

Introduction:

Many modern couples are beginning to recognize that it is better to have a parent at home to take care of the children, rather than relying on a full-time babysitter or pre-school. I agree that this is a good idea. First, no one can care for a child as well as his own parents. Parents also have to face the fact that child care costs are very high. Finally, it is my belief that family life is better when one of the spouses devotes his or her time to maintaining the home and family.

Conclusion:

All in all, I would have to say that life is better for families when one parent stays home with the children. Both the parents and the children benefit.

PREDICTION

You can summarize the information in your essay and use it to suggest what might happen next.

Introduction:

These days, people around the world use the Internet to get news and information. There are both advantages and disadvantages to this situation. On the one hand, the Internet has many advantages because it provides instant access to huge amounts of information that might be difficult to get otherwise. On the other hand, the Internet has certain problems, including the fact that much of the information you find there is unreliable.

Conclusion:

In the future we will rely on the Internet for quick access to all of our news and information. This will bring us many benefits as long as we remain aware of the potential pitfalls.

RECOMMENDATION

You can suggest that your readers do something, based on the information you presented in your essay.

Introduction:

Dear John,

I have some unfortunate news to tell you. I am very sorry to have to tell you that I lost the watch you lent me. It disappeared while I was at a party last night. I hope you will let me pay you for it.

Conclusion:

I hope that you will not let this unfortunate incident affect our friendship and that you will accept my offer of payment. However, if you are uncomfortable about any of this, please let me know.

QUESTION

You can conclude your essay with a question. The question is not really asking for an answer. The answer is contained in the question.

Introduction:

Physical education is an important part of every child's education. In the first place, children learn better if they spend part of each day getting some physical exercise. Additionally, physical education teaches children important skills such as teamwork. Also, it contributes to their overall physical and mental health.

Conclusion:

Physical education is an essential part of any educational program. What would happen to our children's energy level if they didn't get a chance to be active every day? How would they learn to be part of a team if they didn't play sports? How would they stay healthy? Physical education meets all of these needs.

PRACTICE

Read each of the following conclusions and decide whether it is a restatement, generalization, prediction, recommendation, or question.

1. We each have our own ideas about what is too violent and what isn't. It would be difficult to make laws about violence on TV that would satisfy everybody. It is better to let each individual make his or her own choice about what to watch.

    _____

2. In the next 25 years, tourism in Palm Grove could grow if the airport is expanded, providing even greater accessibility from the outside. Then more hotels will be built and Palm Grove will no longer have any resemblance to the fishing village that it once was. ·

    _____

3. If art museums are funded by public money, then everyone will have access to them. What would our world be like without any art? What would bring beauty into our lives and give us a greater understanding of who we are? Art museums are a valuable part of our society.

    _____

4. On the whole, people prefer watching family-oriented TV shows in the evenings. Dramas, mysteries, and police shows are better left for late at night when the children are asleep.

    _____

5. I hope to see you at my party next Friday. We'll enjoy a good time dancing and eating with our friends.

    _____

LEXICAL RESOURCE

In a well-written essay, the writer makes good use of vocabulary. Certain vocabulary words can be used to make the ideas clearer and easier to follow. Vocabulary can be varied to make the writing more interesting to read and to express ideas more precisely.

Target 10—Transition: Connecting and Linking

You can use transition words and phrases in your writing to connect your ideas. They help your reader follow your ideas from one sentence to the next or from one paragraph to the next. Transition words can show time, degree, comparison and contrast, and cause and effect. They can also be used to add more information or to refer to previously mentioned subjects.

Time	Degree	Cause and Effect
before	most important	so
after	first	thus
since	primarily	for this reason
next	principally	as a result
then	above all	because
soon	in the first place	because of
at the same time	less important	since
while	second	due to
meanwhile	in the second place	therefore
	to a lesser degree	consequently
		owing to
		so that

Examples

After the new highway was built, the village of Palm Grove began to grow. People still worked in the fishing industry. *At the same time*, a few new hotels were built. *Then*, more and more tourists started arriving to spend their vacation time at the beach. *Soon*, the village was crowded with visitors from other places.

Family life is better when one of the parents stays home with the children. *Above all*, the children feel secure when they know one of their parents is always available to them. *To a lesser degree*, a parent at home helps the household run more smoothly. But *primarily*, having one parent whose job is to take care of the home and family helps everyone feel safer and happier.

I was honored when you offered to lend me your watch *because* I know how much you value it. *Consequently*, I was very careful with it while I had it on. Unfortunately, the buckle seems to have been broken. *As a result*, the watch fell off my wrist while I was at the party.

Comparison	Contrast
similar to	different from
similarly	nevertheless
just as	although/even though
like	unlike
likewise	yet
in the same way	but
at the same time as	in contrast to
also	however

Example

Many people believe that art and music classes are just as important as academic classes. *Although* there is validity to this point of view, I disagree with it. Art and music are important, *but* academics are even more important. Academic classes give children knowledge that they will need in their future professions. *Likewise*, academics teach children important cognitive skills. Art and music classes, *on the other hand*, do not help children develop professional skills unless they are planning to become artists or musicians.

Explanation	Adding More Information
in other words	in addition
such as	moreover
to clarify	besides
like	furthermore
for instance	also
for example	as well as
that is	what's more
to illustrate	
namely	

Examples

The first step in the process is tapping the trees, *that is*, making holes in them so the sap can come out. There are different ways to collect the sap, *for example*, using old-fashioned buckets or using modern plastic tubing. Using buckets is more time consuming, so most people nowadays use plastic tubing. *In other words*, people prefer using the more efficient method.

Home-cooked meals are generally more nutritious than store-bought or restaurant meals. They *also* tend to be tastier. *Furthermore*, preparing meals at home contributes to the improvement of family relationships.

PRACTICE

Read the following paragraphs. Choose the appropriate transition word or expression to complete each sentence. Add capital letters where necessary.

likewise   furthermore   as a result   in other words

By the year 2000, the population distribution had shifted a great deal. Many more people had moved to urban and suburban areas and (1) _____, the rural population was much smaller. (2) _____, the suburban population had grown since 1950. The urban population had (3) _____ increased. (4) _____, there were now fewer people living in the countryside and more living in the cities and suburbs.

then   unlike   such as   moreover

I know you will have a good time at the party. (5) _____ most parties we go to, at this one I plan to have live music. (6) _____, the band I have hired plays your favorite kind of music. My sister-in-law is planning to prepare some really good dishes (7) _____ seafood soup and roast beef. Come early so that you can enjoy the food, and (8) _____ you can dance all night!

in addition   but   above all   in other words

Physical education classes help children develop in numerous ways. Academics strengthen children's minds, (9) _____ physical education strengthens their bodies. (10) _____, it contributes to their good health. (11) _____, physical education classes help children learn about winning and losing. This is an important life skill. (12) _____, in physical education classes, children have the opportunity to learn about teamwork. This might be one of life's most important skills.

> **TEST TIP**
>
> Try using a range of vocabulary instead of repeating the same words and phrases.

Target 11—Synonyms

Using a variety of vocabulary in your essay rather than repeating the same words over and over helps to hold the reader's attention. You can do this by using synonyms—words that are similar in meaning. Synonyms help to keep your writing interesting, and they provide coherence by connecting ideas that are closely related. Read the paragraph below. Look for synonyms of *choose* and *choice*.

Verbs	Nouns
choose	choice
select	selection
opt	option
pick	alternative

There is a wide variety of television programs to *choose* from. I don't believe that television programming should be regulated, but that individuals should be allowed to *select* for themselves what they want to watch. However, in the case of children, the issue is a bit different. In my opinion, parents should be the ones to *pick* which programs their children see. Children may be attracted to programs that aren't appropriate for them. It is the parents' responsibility to guide their children toward *alternatives* that are more suitable to their age. Television channels have many *options* that actually offer positive contributions to a child's development.

PRACTICE

In each of the following groups of sentences, the underlined words are used twice. Choose a synonym from the list in place of the second mention of each underlined word.

Synonyms

curious	alone	easy	supervision
regulate	engaged	ration	

Children like to feel that they can do things <u>independently</u>. They gain self-confidence when they know they can complete their homework assignments <u>independently</u>, without asking their parents for help every step of the way.

1. independently   synonym: _____

Parents should pay attention to what their children do on the computer, and they should <u>control</u> which websites their children visit. Children have a safer experience on the Internet when their parents <u>control</u> their computer use.

2. control   synonym: _____

Children are naturally <u>interested</u> in many things. The Internet provides <u>interested</u> children with a wide range of information to satisfy their hungry minds.

3. interested   synonym: _____

It is not necessary for parents to <u>limit</u> the amount of time their children spend on the computer. When parents <u>limit</u> computer time too much, children don't have the chance to learn to manage their own time.

4. limit   synonym: _____

A computer can be a good way to keep children gainfully <u>occupied</u> for long periods of time. There are many worthwhile things children can do on the computer. They can spend hours <u>occupied</u> in educational activities.

5. occupied   synonym: _____

Children need a certain amount of <u>guidance</u> from their parents. With parental <u>guidance</u>, children can learn to choose computer activities that educate as well as entertain.

6. guidance   synonym: _____

A computer is a useful tool for school work. Computers make it very <u>convenient</u> to keep notes and write up school projects. Reference books on computer CDs make it <u>convenient</u> for children to research their school projects.

7. convenient   synonym: _____

Target 12—Writing with Variety

You can know about and read the topic, determine the task, map out your organization, create topic sentences, and write an introduction. You've done the hard part. Writing the body of the essay is easy.

However, you need to show you have command of a variety of styles of written English and can choose the appropriate one for the task. You need to show that you can write cohesively and accurately.

In this section, we will examine different approaches for these tasks.

Task	Approach
Describe something	Chronological order Spatial order Classification Definition
Support an opinion	Comparison and contrast Cause and effect Prediction

DESCRIBE SOMETHING

Chronological Order

Chronological order organizes your writing around the sequence of time. You write about what happens first, then what happens second, what happens after that, and what finally happens.

Useful words for time

after	in conclusion
at *(time)*	in the 20s, 1980s . . . .
at birth, in childhood, in infancy, as an adult, in adulthood, in old age	in the first half of the century
at last	in the first place, second place
at the turn of the century (decade)	in the next place
before	later
between ____ and ____	next, then, subsequently
during	on *(day)*
earlier	previous
every *(number) (years, months, days)*	previously
finally	prior to
first, second, third, etc.	simultaneously, at the same time as
former, latter	since _____
formerly	to begin with
in *(year)*	while

PRACTICE 1

Combine the pairs of sentences using after, while, *or* before. *There may be more than one way to combine these sentences. You may have to change pronouns and verb tenses.*

1. The audience left the concert hall. The orchestra played the last note.

2. Look at the menu. Order your meal.

3. The lights went out. We lit a candle.

4. We were waiting for you in the coffee shop. You were waiting for us at the bookstore.

5. They filled the car with gas¹. The car ran out of gas.

PRACTICE 2

Put these sentences into chronological order.

1. __ In the future, the town hopes to build an art museum next to the old factory.

2. __ Once the factory opened, river traffic increased, bringing raw materials to the factories and taking munitions downstream to the major river port at the mouth of the river.

3. __ In the early 1900s, Winston on Hudson was just a small town on the Hudson River.

4. __ Soon, Winston on Hudson became a tourist destination.

5. __ Today, the town's munitions factory has been turned into artist studios.

6. __ Nothing happened in the town until after the start of the First World War when a munitions factory opened.

7. __ Within ten years, cargo boats were followed by passenger boats bringing weekend sightseers.

PRACTICE 3

Write the sentences in Practice 2 as a paragraph. Circle the words that show chronological order.

_____

_____

_____

_____

_____

_____

¹BRITISH: petrol; filled up with petrol.

PRACTICE 4

Write several paragraphs about your life, describing the important dates and times of events in your life.

_____

_____

_____

_____

_____

_____

_____

_____

_____

_____

_____

Spatial Order

Spatial order organizes your writing around the position of things. You write about where things are in relation to one another.

Useful Words for Spatial Relations

across	adjacent
across from	midpoint
where	halfway
in which, to which, from which	interior
under	diagonal
over	edge
inside	limit
beside	parallel, parallel to
on top of	perpendicular to
along	opposite
through	overlapping
as far as	exterior
north, south, east, west	intersection
northern, southern, eastern, western	rectangle
to the left/on the left-hand side	square
to the right/on the right-hand side	circle
to the north	vertical
in back/in the back of the _____ /behind the	horizontal
in front/in front of the _____	
in the middle	

PRACTICE 5

Look at this diagram of the first floor of a suburban house. Complete the blanks with these prepositions of place.

around	east	north
behind	in front of	right
beside	left	south
between	next to	west

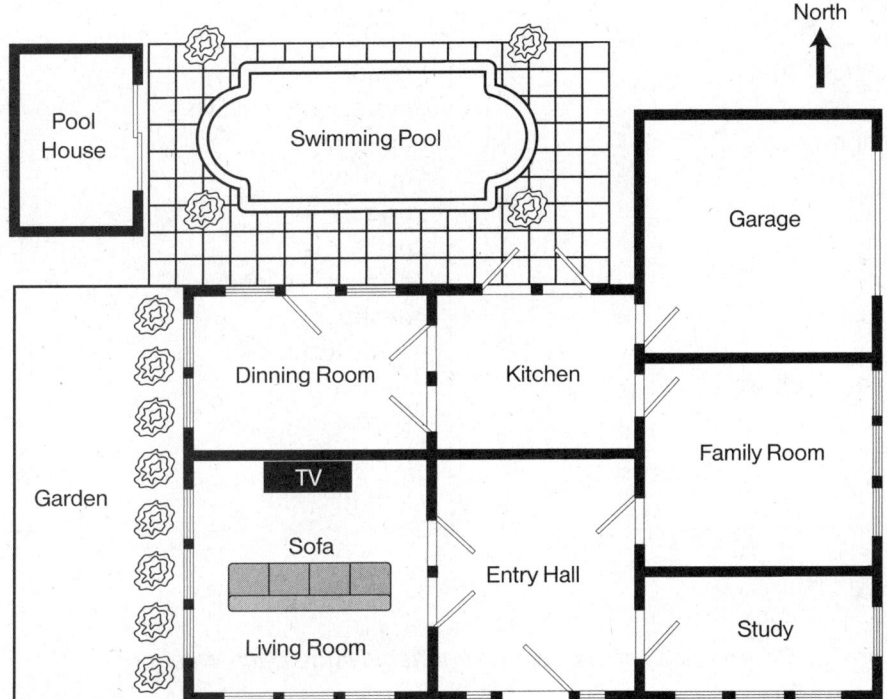

1. The entry hall is _____ the living room and the study.

2. The dining room is _____ the kitchen.

3. The garage is to the _____ of the house.

4. The pool house is _____ the garden.

5. The living room sofa is _____ the TV.

6. The garden is on the _____ side of the house.

7. The living room windows are on the _____ and _____ walls.

8. The swimming pool is _____ the house.

9. The family room is _____ the kitchen.

10. There are trees _____ the swimming pool.

Classification

Classification organizes your writing around the grouping or classification of things. You write about how things are similar to one another.

Useful Words for Classification

aspects	important
attributes	insignificant
bases	kinds of
basic kinds of	main kinds of
categories	methods
characteristics	minor
classes	mutually exclusive
classifications	opposing
classify	opposite
contradictory	origins
contrasting	parts
dissimilar	primary, secondary
distinguishable	qualities
divide	significant
divided into __ classes	similar
factors	sources
falls into	types of
fundamental	unimportant

PRACTICE 6

Classify the lists below. Divide each list into two categories. Name each category.

Word List	_____	_____
table		
boy		
frog		
car		
chair		
butterfly		
pencil		
teacher		

Word List		
doctor		
nurse		
contractor		
hospital		
building plans		
plumber		
patient		
architect		

PRACTICE 7

There are both positive and negative values. What some people see as positive values others see as negative. Match these values with the example sentences. Then, classify these values as either positive or negative. Finally, write a paragraph about either a positive or negative value, using the phrases as examples.

Positive Values	Negative Values

A	anger	**E**	greed	**I**	kindness
B	charity	**F**	hope	**J**	laziness
C	envy	**G**	humility	**K**	patience
D	gluttony	**H**	justice	**L**	pride

1 _____ I am proud that I am richer than my friends.

2 _____ I am kind to everyone, even those who hate me.

3 _____ I wish I had a house as big as a palace.

4 _____ I eat even though I am not hungry.

5 _____ I do not have to be the first in every line[1].

6 _____ It makes me mad when I don't win.

[1]BRITISH: queue

7 _____   I will never have enough money.

8 _____   I never brag about myself.

9 _____   Tomorrow is another day.

10 _____   It's too hot to work.

11 _____   I always look on both sides of an argument.

12 _____   I give 10 percent of my income to the poor.

Definition

You can write a simple definition of an object like a mobile phone in one sentence. To define a more abstract term like *virtue*, you may need several sentences, perhaps several paragraphs.

Useful Words for Definition

aspect	explain
category	explanation
characteristic	form
clarification	in other words
clarify	kind
class	method
condition	paraphrase
define	type
definition	

PRACTICE 8

Concrete objects like a computer can be defined in one sentence. Abstract objects like humility *may take several sentences. Classify these words.*

Words	Concrete	Abstract
printer		
success		
loyalty		
sidewalk		
freedom		
love		
black		
swimming		

PRACTICE 9

Write a definition for each concrete term and each abstract term. Try to be very specific in each. When defining abstract terms, it is helpful to use concrete terms as examples.

EXAMPLES

A printer (either laser or ink jet) is a computer peripheral that enables you to have a paper record of the data in your computer.

Success to me is defined as my own 30-seat jet plane and a ten-bedroom yacht.

SUPPORT AN OPINION

Comparison and Contrast

You can define an object or describe a person by comparing or contrasting the object with something else. You can define a pear by comparing it with a peach or contrasting it with a banana. This is a very useful way to organize your material.

Useful Words for Comparison and Contrast

Comparison	Contrast
almost the same as	different from
common with	differ from
correspond to	even so
in the same way	however
just as	in contrast to
like, alike	in opposition to
resemblance	less than
resemble	more than
similar to	otherwise
similarly	slower than, etc.
to be parallel to	still

PRACTICE 10

Read these questions. Write CON if it's a question asking for contrast. Write COMP if it's a question asking for comparison.

1. _____ How is greed different from envy?
2. _____ How does a mobile[1] phone differ from a landline phone?
3. _____ How are dogs and cats alike?
4. _____ In what ways are trains and planes different?
5. _____ What are the similarities between a chair and a stool?
6. _____ Can you list three ways a restaurant and a cafeteria are alike?
7. _____ What are the differences between classical music and hip hop?
8. _____ How are Japan and Madagascar the same?

[1]AMERICAN: cell or mobile

PRACTICE 11

Complete the blanks with words that show comparison or contrast. Use the words in the list below. Some words may be used more than once. Don't forget to add capitals where necessary.

A

Landline phones and cell phones are devices used for communicating with people in other places. The biggest _____**(1)**_____ between a landline phone and a mobile phone is that a landline phone stays in one place _____**(2)**_____ a mobile phone can go everywhere. A landline phone always stays in your home or office. A mobile phone, _____**(3)**_____, can go wherever you go. There is a disadvantage to this. You always know where your landline phone is—on your desk, on the kitchen wall, by the bed, or wherever you keep it. _____**(4)**_____ a landline phone, a mobile phone is easily misplaced[1].

> in contrast to
> while
> difference
> however

B

A restaurant is a place where you order food and it is brought to your table. A cafeteria is _____**(5)**_____ a restaurant, except that in a cafeteria you serve yourself. There are several ways in which a restaurant and a cafeteria are _____**(6)**_____. In _____**(7)**_____ places you can eat a good meal without cooking it yourself. In a restaurant you select your meal from a menu. In a cafeteria you can also choose your meal from among several different possibilities, _____**(8)**_____ in a restaurant. Finally, in _____**(9)**_____ a restaurant and a cafeteria, you have to pay for what you eat.

> both
> alike
> similar to
> just as

PRACTICE 12

When you write a compare/contrast paragraph, you begin by defining one item and then comparing or contrasting it with the other item.

Read the example below, then write a passage comparing dogs and cats.

EXAMPLE

A greedy person is someone who wants more of what he or she already has. An envious person is someone who wants what someone else has. For example, I may envy your car, but a greedy person will want a bigger car than you have plus a big garage to put the car in.

---

[1]BRITISH: mis-placed

PRACTICE 13

Look at the graph and table below. Describe them by comparing and contrasting the information.

1. The graph below shows the average cost of housing in three different areas.

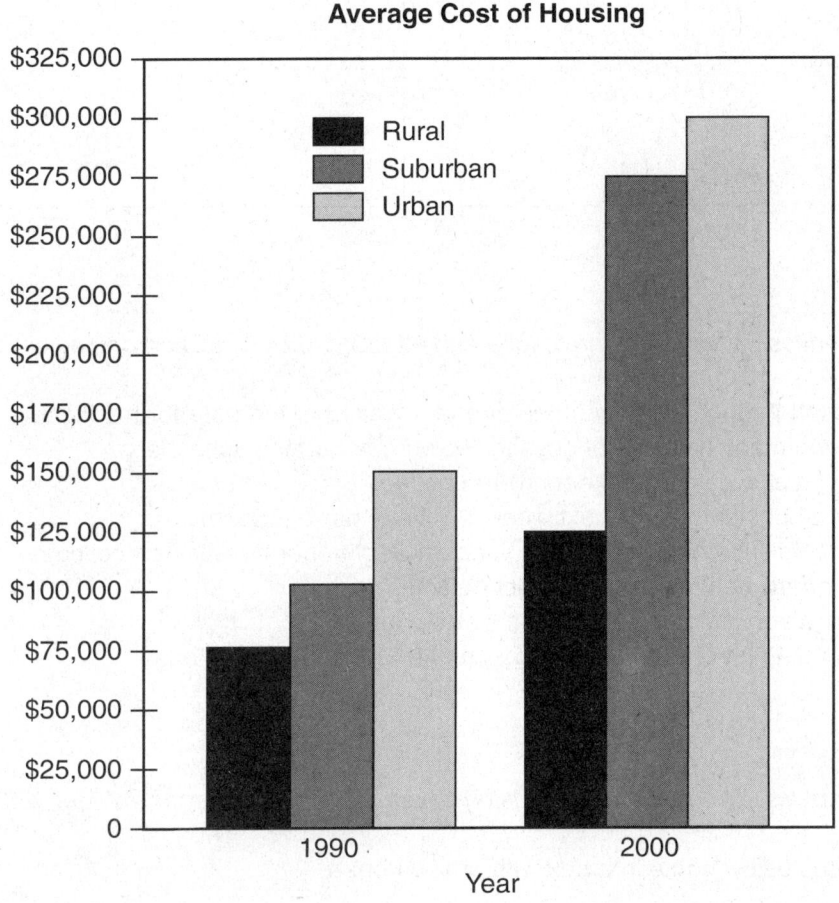

Average Cost of Housing

2. The table below shows information about three different types of restaurants.

	Sit-Down Restaurant	**Cafeteria**	**Fast-Food Restaurant**
Average cost of lunch	$10.00	$7.00	$4.50
Average time spent eating lunch	45 min.	30 min.	20 min.
Average cost of dinner	$17.00	$9.50	$5.00
Average time spent eating dinner	60 min.	45 min.	20 min.

Cause and Effect

A cause and effect relationship is a very useful organizational style. Something happens because something else happened. I turned on the air conditioner and the room became cooler.

Cause and effect is similar to chronological order. First something happens followed by something else. But in cause and effect, there is a definite relationship between the two.

Useful Words for Cause and Effect

accordingly	have an effect on
as a result	hence
because	owing to
because of	reason for
consequently	since
due to	so
for this reason	therefore
	thus

PRACTICE 14

Read these sentences. Write if they are cause *and* effect *(c/e) or simply* chronological order *(co).*

1. _____ I passed through security at the airport. I waited at the gate for my flight.
2. _____ I ate too many helpings of dessert. Now I have a stomachache.
3. _____ It rained all week. The streets were flooded.
4. _____ My mother's birthday is next week. I will buy her a present.
5. _____ James finished high school last June. In September he will start college.
6. _____ I put on my coat and scarf. I went outside.
7. _____ It was a very cold day. I put on a warm coat.
8. _____ Sarah got home after midnight last night. She's very tired today.

PRACTICE 15

Look at these graphics. Write a paragraph using cause *and* effect *to organize your writing.*

1. The instructions below come in a box with a new iron.

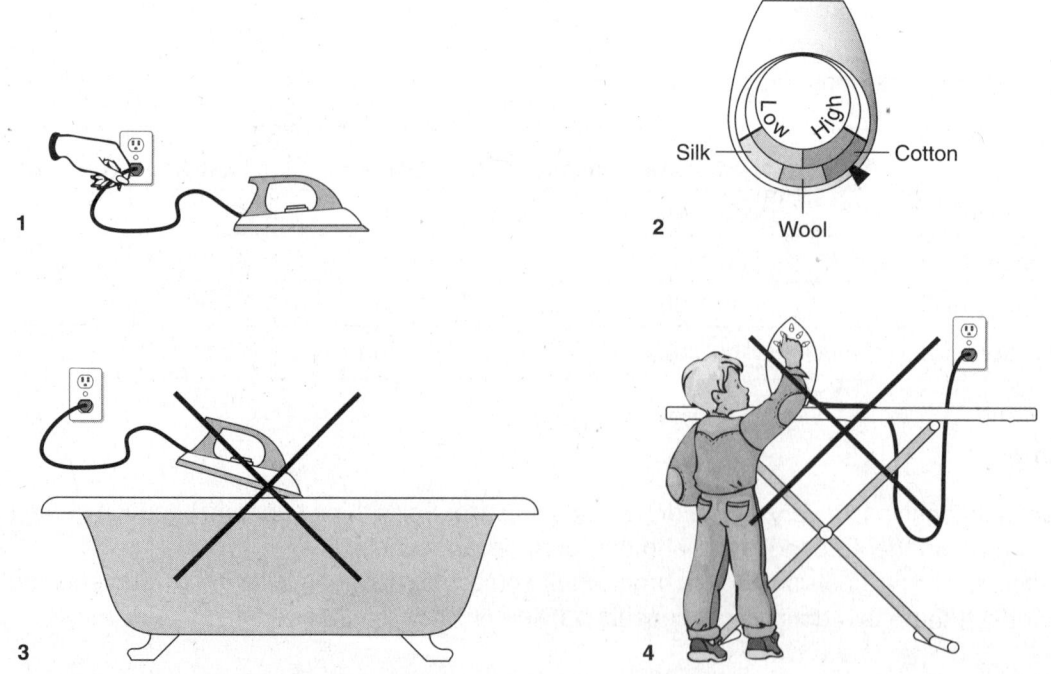

2. The graph below shows the average salaries earned by people with different levels of education.

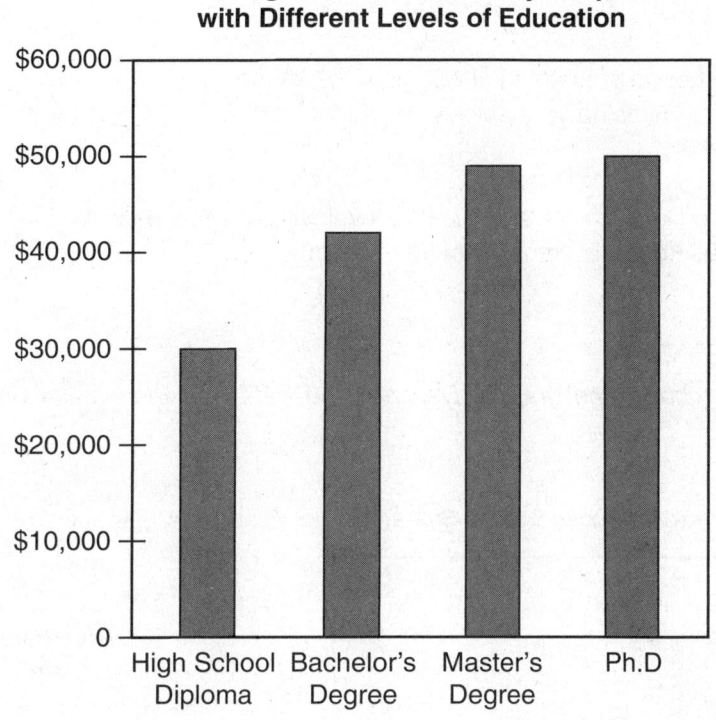

Average Salaries Earned by People with Different Levels of Education

Prediction

A prediction is your guess about what will happen in the future. You base this prediction on the facts you know. A prediction is similar to an inference. It is an educated guess that you deduced from the evidence.

Useful Words for Prediction

forecast	predict
foresee	predictable
future	presume
in the future	probable result
infer	projection
likely	the end result
make a prediction about	the future implications of
most likely	the most likely outcome
plan	the next step
plan to	

PRACTICE 16

Complete these sentences with the appropriate predictions.

Statements
1. If governments do not do something about global warming, _____.
2. The cost of gasoline[1] is rising very quickly. In the future, _____.

Predictions
A. The ice shelves are likely to melt and the sea level will probably rise.
B People may start using public transportation more often.

PRACTICE 17

Look at the following charts and graphs. Describe the data and then make predictions about what will happen next.

1.

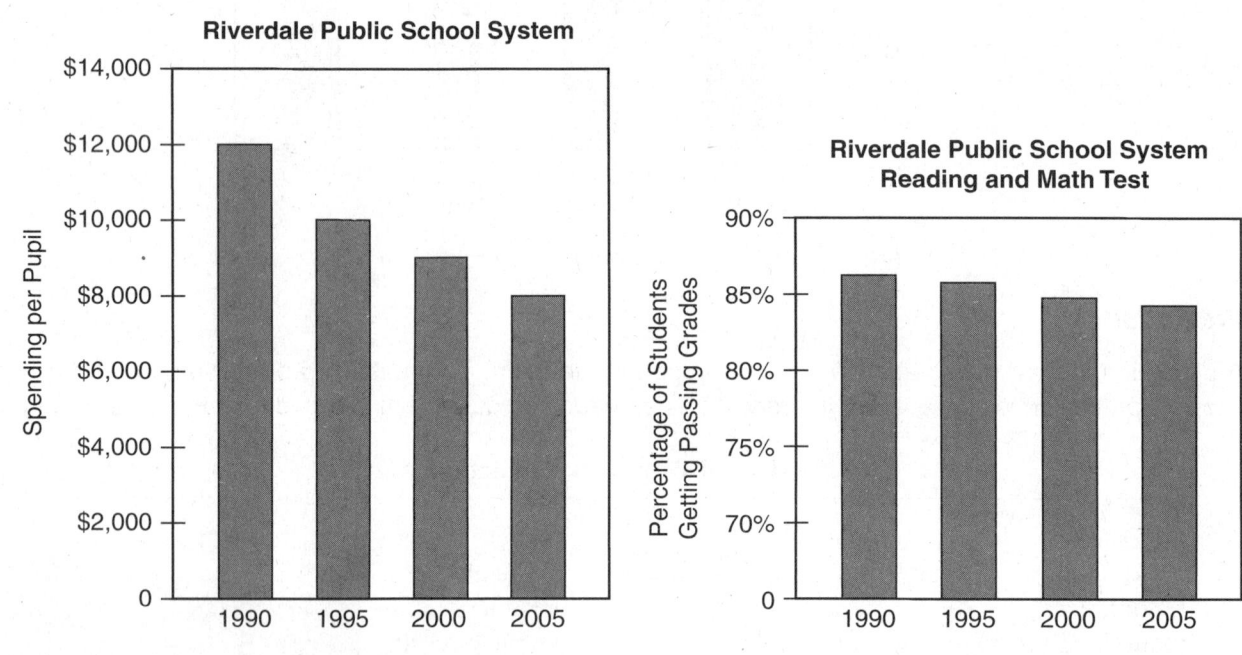

By 2010, the schools will likely _____ .

By 2010, the pupils will probably _____ .

2.

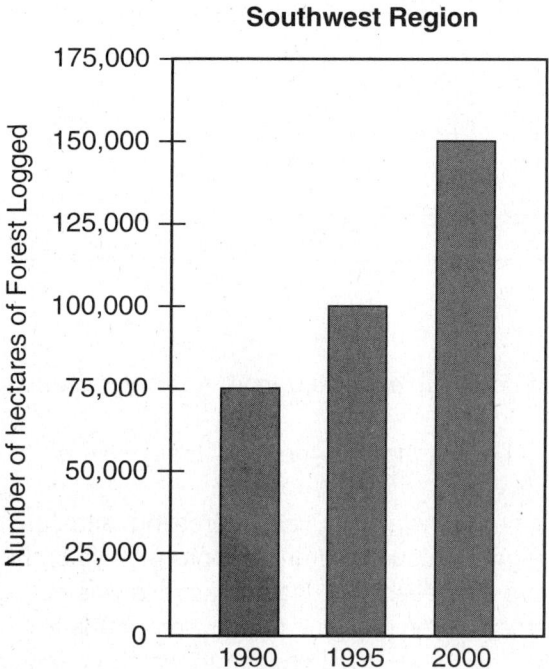

Number of Forest-Dwelling Species in the Southwest

Animals	*1998*	*2002*
Mammals	3	2
Birds	7	5
Amphibians	5	3

By 2005, the number of hectares of forest logged will likely_____ .

By 2007, the number of forest-dwelling species will likely _____ .

GRAMMATICAL RANGE AND ACCURACY

In addition to good organization of ideas and variety of vocabulary, a well-written essay has well-written sentences. It has variety of sentence structure and sentence length that holds the reader's interest and helps make the ideas clear. Naturally, correct grammatical structures are used.

Target 13—Pronouns

Pronouns are used to replace or refer to nouns so that you don't have to keep repeating the same word over and over.

Pronouns

Subject:	he this	she that	it these	they those
Object:	his this	her that	it these	them those
Possessive:	his	her	its	their

PRACTICE

Choose the correct pronoun to complete each sentence. Add capital letters where necessary.

> her   they   them   their   this   it

I feel that your evening TV programs are not very interesting, and I am sure that few people watch (1) __ _____. For example, last night I watched a drama program on your channel. (2) _____ was one of the most boring programs I have ever seen. The leading actress was not very inspiring, and (3) _____ voice made me want to fall asleep. If you continue to show programs like (4) _____, you will probably lose most of your viewers. (5) _____ will choose to watch channels with more interesting programs instead. Then your advertisers may well decide that (6) _____ advertising money would be better spent on channels that have a larger audience.

Target 14—Parallel Structures

Parallel structures are structures that follow the same pattern. When you write with parallel structures, your writing has a rhythm that is easy to follow. It helps make your ideas easier to understand.

EXAMPLES

Parallel subjects   Play and study are two ways children can use a computer.
                            Playing and studying are two ways children can use a computer.
In both of the above examples the subjects are parallel. In the first example, they are two simple nouns. In the second example, they are two gerunds.

Not parallel   Playing and study are two things children can use a computer for.
In this example, one word is a gerund and the other is not. The words are not parallel, and the sentence is awkward.

Parallel verbs   I reached out my hand, grabbed a glass, and noticed that the watch was gone.
                         The village is growing and becoming more prosperous.
The verbs in each of these examples are parallel because they are all in the same tense. It is not necessary to repeat an auxiliary verb (such as the verb *be* in a continuous tense) to keep verbs parallel within a clause.

Not parallel   Maple syrup is a popular treat and also tastes good.
This example is grammatically correct, but it is not parallel. It uses an adjective, *popular*, and a verb, *tastes*, to describe maple syrup.

Parallel adjectives   Maple syrup is a <u>popular</u> and <u>tasty</u> treat.
This example is parallel because it uses two similar words, that is, two adjectives, to describe maple syrup.

Not parallel   The house <u>was painted</u>, and we<u> repaired</u> the roof.
Parallel verbs   The house <u>was painted</u> and the roof <u>was repaired</u>.
The first example uses passive voice in the first clause and active voice in the second clause. The grammar is correct, but the sentence is not parallel. The second example uses passive voice in both clauses. It is parallel.

PRACTICE

Look at the two underlined words and phrases in each sentence or set of sentences below. Change the second one to make it parallel with the first.

1. Many children like <u>looking</u> for information on the Internet and <u>to play</u> online games.

2. People watch TV for <u>entertainment</u> and <u>to be informed</u>.

3. I <u>will be</u> in your neighborhood tomorrow and <u>am going to bring</u> you the check then.

4. A life that is all <u>work </u>and no <u>playing</u> is a very dull life indeed.

5. The TV programs I am recommending <u>are very amusing</u> and <u>also educate</u>.

6. Now, the citizens of Palm Grove <u>can earn </u>a good living from tourism, but they <u>are no longer able to enjoy</u> the simple, peaceful life they once had.

7. <u>Home-cooked meals are</u> more nutritious, and <u>I like the taste</u> better, too.

8. The hotel district <u>was expanded</u>, and <u>people removed</u> the fishing docks.

Target 15— Coherence

In a well-written essay, there is a clear relationship between sentences and between ideas. They all fit together well. This is coherence. Repeating words and rephrasing ideas are two ways to provide coherence to an essay.

Repeating

Repeating words and phrases adds rhythm to a paragraph and links similar ideas. In the paragraph below, notice how the phrase *It gives* is used several times.

    Physical education teaches children much more than the rules to a few sports. *It gives* children the opportunity to learn some important life skills. *It gives* them experience with teamwork. *It gives* them the chance to know how it feels to win and to lose. These are things that have importance in all areas in life, not just on a sports field.

Rephrasing

When you rephrase an idea, you say it again in a different way. This gives the reader a second chance to understand your idea and helps connect one idea to the next. Using synonyms is one way to rephrase.

One problem that *older people face is isolation*. Many of them are widowed, and their children are no longer living with them. Serious physical and mental health problems can arise when *people feel lonely*.

Notice how the two italicized phrases in the paragraph above essentially mean the same thing. Now look at another example, noticing the meaning of the two italicized phrases.

Family members can provide much-needed *companionship*. Even if an elderly parent does not live with his or her grown children, they can all *spend important time together*.

PRACTICE

Choose which phrase or sentence best completes the paragraph and makes it cohesive. Use the italicized phrases to guide you in your choices.

The best thing about TV is that there is a variety of programs. *There are news programs for serious people. There are films and cartoons for people who want to be entertained.* (1) _____ _____ The variety of TV programs needs to be protected even if it means allowing some of them to show violence.

1. (A) People also enjoy watching baseball and soccer games.
   (B) There are baseball and soccer games for people who enjoy sports.
   (C) We can see baseball and soccer games, too.

I am responsible about my finances. Your records will show that I have always paid my credit card bills *on time.* (2) My _____ makes me a desirable customer, and I am sure you wouldn't want to lose my business.

2. (A) punctuality
   (B) financial know-how
   (C) honesty

By the year 2050, the suburban population will have *increased* to almost 60% of the population of the entire region. This (3) _____ will put heavy *demands* on public services. The regional government will have to start making adjustments now in order to meet the (4) _____ of the future.

3. (A) area   4. (A) people
   (B) number   (B) needs
   (C) growth   (C) services

Art brings beauty into our lives. It enriches us in many ways. *It nourishes our minds. It nourishes our spirits.* (5) _____. Without access to art, our lives would be greatly impoverished.

5. (A) It is good for our bodies, too.
   (B) It also contributes to our physical health.
   (C) You could even say it nourishes our bodies.

Target 16—Sentence Types

Using variety in your sentences keeps your writing lively and interesting. It also shows the range of your writing ability. One way you can vary your sentences is by using a variety of sentence types. There are four types of sentences: simple, compound, complex, and compound-complex.

Simple Sentence

A simple sentence has one subject and one verb.

> Television offers a variety of programs.
> subject verb

Compound Sentence

A compound sentence has two or more simple sentences linked by the conjunctions *and*, *or*, and *but*.

> Some people are not bothered by violent TV programs, but others avoid them.
>   simple sentence 1   simple sentence 2

Complex Sentence

A complex sentence is made up of a simple sentence (an independent clause) and one or more subordinate clauses.

> If we don't like a particular TV program, we can easily change the channel.
>   subordinate clause   simple sentence

Compound-Complex Sentence

A compound-complex sentence has two or more simple sentences and one or more subordinate clauses.

> While many people avoid watching violent TV programs, others don't mind them and
>   subordinate clause   simple sentence 1
>
> they watch them frequently.
>   simple sentence 2

PRACTICE

Read the following essay and label the sentences by their type.
Simple = S   Compound = C   Complex = Cx   Compound-Complex = C-Cx

1. _____	The three maps representing changes in Palm Grove between 1950 and 2000 show that the town became a resort as accessibility from the outside improved.
2. _____ 3. _____ 4. _____	In 1950, Palm Grove was a small fishing village with few hotels. It lies 450 kilometers from the nearest city. Since the only access to the village in 1950 was by a two-lane road, most tourists probably didn't want to make the long trip to get there.

5. _____ 6. _____ 7. _____	By 1975, a new four-lane highway had brought changes to Palm Grove. It was still a fishing village, but it appears that the new road made it easier for tourists to get there. Several new hotels had been built for them along the beach.
8. _____ 9. _____ 10. _____ 11. _____	By 2000, an airport had been built just outside Palm Grove. This apparently changed the town into a resort. The hotel district was greatly expanded, and the fishing docks were removed. Probably most local residents now work in the tourist industry.

Target 17—Voice

There are two voices in English: active and passive. You can vary your writing by varying the voice you use. Some students think it is more impressive to use a lot of passive voice. This isn't necessarily true. The active voice is often clearer.

Choose the voice that bests suits your purpose. Active voice emphasizes the doer while passive voice emphasizes the action itself or the recipient of the action. We often use passive voice when it is not clear or important who or what the doer is.

Active Voice

Parents should limit their children's computer time.

In this example, the focus is on the parents—it is they, not teachers, babysitters, or somebody else, who should limit children's computer time.

Passive Voice

Children's computer time should be limited.

In this example, the focus is on children's computer time—not on their playtime, study time, or any other way they may spend their time.

PRACTICE

Choose the active sentence that has the same meaning as the passive sentence.

1. Delicious and nutritious food can be prepared at home with the help of the entire family.
   (A) Delicious and nutritious food prepares the family to be at home.
   (B) Preparing delicious and nutritious food at home helps the entire family.
   (C) The entire family can help to prepare delicious and nutritious food at home.

2. The price of the watch was estimated for me by a jeweler in town.
   (A) A jeweler in town gave me an estimate for the price of the watch.
   (B) I estimated the price of the watch by looking at jewelry in town.
   (C) Prices at the jeweler's in town are close to what I estimated.

3. These programs do not enjoy wide popularity and are watched by only a small audience.
    (A) The audience widely enjoys watching these programs.
    (B) Only a small audience watches these unpopular programs.
    (C) The audience popularizes these programs by watching and enjoying them.

4. Elderly parents should be cared for by their own family members, who love them more than a paid caretaker can.
    (A) Family members should pay caretakers to care for their parents because they love them.
    (B) Family members should be the ones to take care of their elderly parents because they love them more than any paid caretaker can.
    (C) Family members should love their elderly parents more than any paid caretaker can.

5. When art is taught in schools, children learn to appreciate creativity and beauty.
    (A) Teachers teach about creativity and beauty to children who study in art schools.
    (B) Schools teach art to children who are creative and beautiful.
    (C) Children learn appreciation for creativity and beauty when teachers teach them about art.

REVISION

Target 18—Using a Revision Checklist

When you respond to the writing tasks, you need to leave a few minutes at the end of each task to revise your writing. You need to check that you responded to all parts of the task. You need to make sure that your ideas are well organized and that you used correct language and punctuation. Here is a checklist that you can use to guide your revision.

REVISION CHECKLIST

RESPONDING TO THE TASK
- ❑ Did I complete the task?
- ❑ Did I write enough words?
- ❑ Did I complete the task on time?

COHERENCE AND COHESION
- ❑ Did I write a thesis statement?
- ❑ Did I write a topic sentence for each paragraph?
- ❑ Did I write supporting details in each paragraph?
- ❑ Did I write a conclusion?

LEXICAL RESOURCE
- ❑ Did I use transition words?
- ❑ Did I use a variety of vocabulary?

GRAMMATICAL RANGE AND ACCURACY
- ❑ Did I use parallel structures?
- ❑ Did I use a variety of sentence patterns?
- ❑ Did I use correct spelling and punctuation?

Look at the following model writing task and response from Target 5. Notice how the response can be checked against the revision checklist.

Academic Task 2

You should spend about 40 minutes on this task.

> **There should be laws to control the amount and type of violence shown on television programs.**
>
> **To what extent do you agree or disagree with this statement?**

Give reasons for your answer and include any relevant examples from your own knowledge or experience.

Write at least 250 words.

> While it is true that there is violence on television, each individual has his or her own idea about how much is too much. Fortunately, we are all free to choose which TV programs we want to watch. Laws are not necessary to help us decide.
>
> It isn't difficult to find out which programs are on TV at any given time. Most newspapers publish a schedule of TV programs every day. Also, anyone who watches TV regularly knows which programs she likes and which she doesn't like. She knows what kinds of programs each different channel tends to have. Because of this, it's easy for everyone to avoid violent programs if they want to.
>
> Modern technology has given us a tool for controlling the TV programs we see. Most TVs can be programmed to block certain channels. Thus, parents have a way to protect their children from seeing shows that are too violent. Adults can also use this technology to avoid seeing programs that they don't want to see.
>
> The best thing about TV is that there is a variety of programs. There are news programs for serious people. There are movies and cartoons for people who want to be entertained. The variety of TV programs needs to be protected, even if that means allowing some of them to show violence.
>
> We each have our own ideas about what is too violent and what isn't. It would be difficult to make laws about violence on TV that would satisfy everybody. It is better to let each individual make his or her own choice about what to watch.

Responding to the Task

REVISION CHECKLIST

RESPONDING TO THE TASK

☑ Did I complete the task?

☑ Did I write enough words?

☑ Did I complete the task on time?

Did I Complete the Task?

The task asks the writer to agree or disagree with the statement. The last sentence of the first paragraph, *Laws are not necessary to help us decide*, states the writer's disagreement. The task also asks for reasons and examples. The second, third, and fourth paragraphs each explain a reason for the writer's opinion, and they include examples to explain and support the reasons.

Did I Write Enough Words?

This passage is 262 words, 12 more than the minimum required.

Did I Complete the Task on Time?

The task was completed in less than 40 minutes.

Coherence and Cohesion

REVISION CHECKLIST

COHERENCE AND COHESION
- ☑ Did I write a thesis statement?
- ☑ Did I write a topic sentence for each paragraph?
- ☑ Did I write supporting details in each paragraph?
- ☑ Did I write a conclusion?

Did I Write a Thesis Statement?

The last two sentences of the first paragraph, *Fortunately, we are all free to choose which TV programs we want to watch. Laws are not necessary to help us decide*, are the thesis statement. They state the writer's opinion, which is explained and supported in the body of the essay.

Did I Write a Topic Sentence for Each Paragraph?

The first sentence of each paragraph in the body of the essay (paragraphs 2, 3, and 4) is the topic sentence.

Did I Write Supporting Details in Each Paragraph?

Each topic sentence is followed by details that support it.

Did I Write a Conclusion?

The last paragraph is the conclusion. In this paragraph the reader is reminded of the thesis, that laws about violence on television are not necessary, and there is a recommendation: *It is better to let each individual make his or her own choice about what to watch.*

Lexical Resource

REVISION CHECKLIST

LEXICAL RESOURCE

- ☑ Did I use transition words?
- ☑ Did I use a variety of vocabulary?

Did I Use Transition Words?

This passage uses appropriate transition words, for example:

Paragraph 2: *also*—adds information
because of—shows cause and effect

Paragraph 3: *thus*—shows cause and effect
also—adds information

Did I Use a Variety of Vocabulary?

This passage does not have too many repetitions of words. It uses a variety of ways to state similar ideas, for example, *block*, *protect*, and *avoid* are used to convey the idea of *not watching* certain programs.

Grammatical Range and Accuracy

REVISION CHECKLIST

GRAMMATICAL RANGE AND ACCURACY

☑ Did I use parallel structures?

☑ Did I use a variety of sentence structures?

☑ Did I use correct spelling and punctuation?

Did I Use Parallel Structures?

The fourth paragraph uses parallel structures: *There are news programs for serious people. There are movies and cartoons for people who want to be entertained.*

Did I Use a Variety of Sentence Structures?

This passage uses a variety of sentence structures, for example:

Complex: *While it is true that there is violence on television, each individual has his or her own idea about how much is too much.*

There are movies and cartoons for people who want to be entertained.

Simple: *Most newspapers publish a schedule of TV programs every day.*

There are news programs for serious people.

Compound-complex: *We each have our own ideas about what is too violent and what isn't.*

Did I Use Correct Spelling and Punctuation?

This passage has no spelling or punctuation errors.

PRACTICE 1

Complete each essay by answering the questions that follow.

Academic Task 1

The diagram below shows the steps in the process of making maple syrup from the sap of the sugar maple tree.

Summarize the information by selecting and reporting the main features, and make comparisons where relevant.

Making Maple Syrup from the Sugar Maple Tree

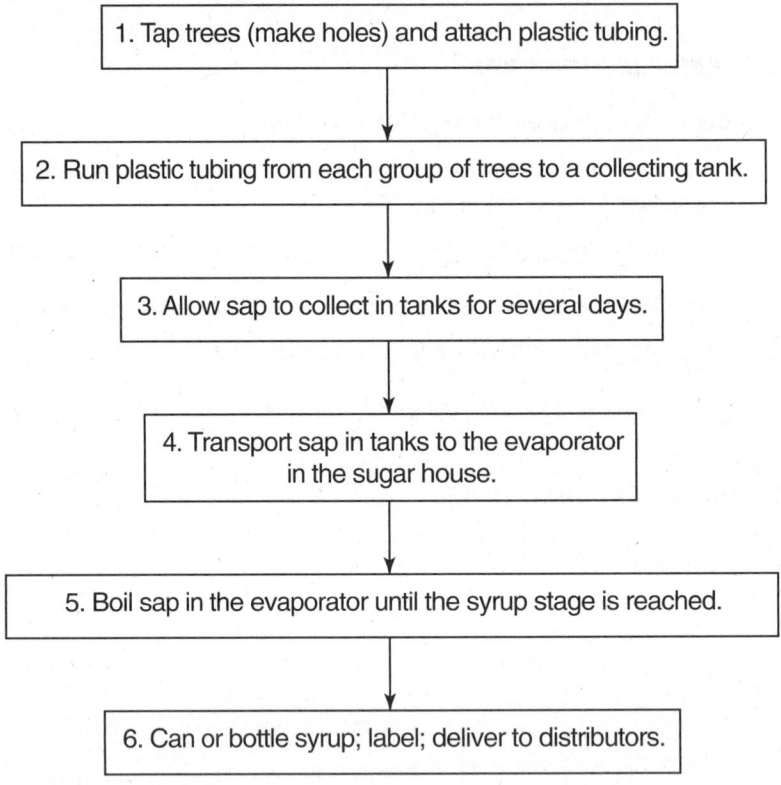

1. Tap trees (make holes) and attach plastic tubing.

2. Run plastic tubing from each group of trees to a collecting tank.

3. Allow sap to collect in tanks for several days.

4. Transport sap in tanks to the evaporator in the sugar house.

5. Boil sap in the evaporator until the syrup stage is reached.

6. Can or bottle syrup; label; deliver to distributors.

Note: It takes 40 gallons of sap to make one gallon of syrup.

Maple syrup is made from the sap of the sugar maple tree. (1) _____.
The sap has to be collected, boiled, and prepared for distribution.

(2) _____ This is done by tapping the trees, or making holes in them, and connecting plastic tubing to the holes. The plastic tubing from each group of trees are run to a collecting tank. The sap drips through the tubes and collects in the tank over a period of several days.

After the sap has collected in the tank, the full tank is transported to the sugar house and put into the evaporator. (3) _____ the sap is boiled until it reaches the syrup stage. A lot of sap has to be boiled because it takes 40 gallons of it to make just one gallon of syrup.

The syrup is put into cans or bottles and labeled. (4) _____

_____

It takes a lot of work to make maple syrup. However, it is a tasty treat that is well worth the effort.

1. Choose the best thesis statement.
   (A) It is a sweet syrup that people enjoy eating on their pancakes and waffles.
   (B) The syrup maker has to collect 40 gallons of sap for each gallon of syrup.
   (C) It is a process that involves several steps.

2. Choose the best topic sentence for this paragraph.
   (A) First, the sap has to be collected from the tree.
   (B) First, sugar maple trees have to be identified.
   (C) First, the sap has to be cooked for a long time.

3. Choose the best transition word for this sentence.
   (A) For example,
   (B) Then
   (C) Therefore,

4. Choose the missing supporting detail.
   (A) The syrup maker's name is always on the label.
   (B) These are then delivered to the distributor for sale.
   (C) Tourists enjoy buying cans of maple syrup to use as gifts.

General Training Task 1

> **You borrowed a friend's gold watch to wear to a party. Unfortunately, the watch fell off your wrist and you lost it. Write a letter to the owner of the watch. In your letter**
>
> - **apologize for the loss**
> - **explain what happened**
> - **tell what you want to do about it**

Dear John,

I have some unfortunate news to tell you. I am very, very sorry that I lost the beautiful gold watch that you were so kind to lend me. It fell off my wrist while I was at a party last night. (5) _____

(6) _____ It must have fallen off while I was dancing, (7) _____ I didn't notice it at the time. When I went to get a drink, I reached out my hand, grabbed a glass, and then noticed that the watch was no longer on my wrist.

I plan to repay you for the watch. (8) _____ I know the watch has sentimental value that is irreplaceable, but at least I can send you some money.

Again, I apologize for losing something that I know you value highly. I hope you won't let this get in the way of our friendship.

Your friend,
George

5. Choose the best general idea to complete the introduction.
   (A) I would like to send you a check for the full value of the watch.
   (B) I enjoyed wearing the watch before I lost it.
   (C) I stayed too late at the party and was very tired when I got home.

6. Choose the best topic sentence for this paragraph.
   (A) I wish I had a nice gold watch of my own.
   (B) The watch looked very nice with my new suit.
   (C) As you know, I wore your gold watch at my cousin's graduation party.

7. Choose the best transition word for this sentence.
   (A) for example
   (B) then
   (C) although

8. Choose the missing supporting detail.
   (A) It's a good idea to have a nice watch to wear on special occasions.
   (B) Please let me know its value, and I will send you a check.
   (C) I have a very nice watch, but it isn't made of gold.

General Training Task 2

In many parts of the world, people are relying more and more on prepared food from grocery stores or restaurants because they are too busy to cook at home. This is a bad idea because home-cooked food is much better for us.

To what extent do you agree or disagree?

(9) _____ In the first place, it is more nutritious than store-bought or restaurant food. It is also less expensive. In addition, preparing and eating home-cooked food helps strengthen family bonds.

Home-cooked food has higher nutritional value than prepared food. A lot of prepared food is high in sugar and fat. It is also not very fresh, so it has lost nutritional value while sitting on the shelf waiting to be bought. (10) _____, it often contains highly refined products, such as white flour, which are not as good for our health as whole grain products are.

(11) _____ A restaurant meal, even at a fast-food restaurant, is more expensive than a meal at home. Additionally, you have to tip the server and pay for transportation to and from the restaurant. Buying a pre-packaged meal at a grocery store is not any better. It costs a lot more than buying the ingredients and preparing the meal yourself.

Family ties grow stronger when family members cook and eat meals together. When family members prepare a meal together, they spend time together. They have the chance to share ideas and discuss problems. (12) _____ They have fun as a family. Their relationships are stronger.

Home-cooked food is good for our health, our wallets, and our family relationships. There is no reason to eat prepared food on a regular basis.

9. Choose the best thesis statement.
    (A) Home-cooked food is better for us than prepared food in several ways.
    (B) Home-cooked food takes time to prepare, but it tastes very good.
    (C) Home-cooked food requires following several steps.

10. Choose the best transition word for this sentence.
    (A) However
    (B) In addition
    (C) For instance

11. Choose the best topic sentence for this paragraph.
    (A) Eating at a restaurant is not as simple as it looks.
    (B) Many people enjoy eating at restaurants.
    (C) It costs a lot of money to buy prepared food.

12. Choose the missing supporting detail.
    (A) They prepare healthy meals.
    (B) They learn to communicate with each other.
    (C) They may have a large or small family.

PRACTICE 2

Read the following essay and use the revision checklist below to identify what is missing or incorrect. Then rewrite the essay, adding the missing parts and correcting the errors.

REVISION CHECKLIST

RESPONDING TO THE TASK
❑ Did I complete the task?
❑ Did I write enough words?
❑ Did I complete the task on time?

COHERENCE AND COHESION
❑ Did I write a thesis statement?
❑ Did I write a topic sentence for each paragraph?
❑ Did I write supporting details in each paragraph?
❑ Did I write a conclusion?

LEXICAL RESOURCE
❑ Did I use transition words?
❑ Did I use a variety of vocabulary?

GRAMMATICAL RANGE AND ACCURACY
❑ Did I use parallel structures?
❑ Did I use a variety of sentence patterns?
❑ Did I use correct spelling and punctuation?

Academic Task 2

A successful person is one who has earned a lot of money.

To what extent do you agree or disagree?

To a large extent. Having money can be one part of success. Having good relationships is another very important part of success. So is feeling fulfilled.

Everybody needs money, but the amount of money necessary depend on each person's goals. For example, one person may want a lot of material things, like fancy cars and big houses. For this person, a lot of money is important.

Everybody needs to have good relationships. Even a multi-millionaire is not successful if he or she does not have close connections with other people. If a woman always fights with her husband, if a man's children refuse to speak to him, when adult children might never see their parents, they cannot be considered successful people.

It is important to develop skills and talents and pursue interests. It is important to spend time doing things that are enjoyable or meaningful. A person who is unhappy at work, in addition, cannot be considered successful no matter how big his salary is. A person who spends evenings and weekends just sitting in front of the TV cannot be considered successful, either.

Money and the material things it can by may be one part of success, but non-material things like relationships and self-fulfillment are just as important.

Missing items:

Paragraph 1: _____

Paragraph 2: _____

Paragraph 3: _____

Paragraph 4: _____

Paragraph 5: _____

Grammar and vocabulary errors:

Paragraph 1: _____

Paragraph 2: _____

Paragraph 3: _____

Paragraph 4: _____

Paragraph 5: _____

Target 19—Checking the Spelling

When you revise your response to a writing task, one thing you will have to check is the spelling. You will be expected to know how to spell common English words correctly. Check your writing carefully to make sure that you haven't left out any letters, added extra letters, reversed the order of letters, or made other sorts of spelling mistakes.

PRACTICE

Read the following sentences and find the spelling errors. Rewrite each sentence with correct spelling.

1. It was fond that most middle-income families spent 50 percent of there household buget on housing expenses in 2010.

   _____

   _____

2. I thnk you must have a lott of money in order to be consedered successfull.

   _____

   _____

3. Spendin money on art and musick edacation gives children a big advantag that will help then in the future.

   _____

   _____

4. I feel that this type of television program is not of intrest to most poeple and will cause you to lose a large portion of your adience.

   _____

   _____

5. I no that you will enjay the party, and I hope you will be able to atend.

   _____

   _____

Target 20—Checking the Punctuation

As well as spelling correctly, you will also be expected to use correct punctuation. You must use capital letters in the correct places and use punctuation marks such as periods, commas, and question marks correctly. It is also important to indent each paragraph.

Indent	This is done at the beginning of each paragraph.
Capital letters	These are used at the beginning of each sentence and for proper nouns.
Period, question mark, exclamation point	One of these is always used at the end of a sentence.

Commas are used in the middle of sentence in certain situations:

- In a list of three or more things
  Home-cooked food is nutritious, tasty, and inexpensive.
  I reached out my hand, grabbed a glass, and noticed that the watch was gone.

- To separate transition words from the rest of the sentence
  Additionally, physical education teaches children important skills such as teamwork.
  Children, however, should not be exposed to these violent television programs.

- Between two independent clauses
  I watch television every evening, and I know what kinds of programs are being shown.
  Art and music classes are important, but academic classes are even more important.

- To separate a non-restrictive clause
  Parents, who are responsible for the well being of their children, should carefully monitor their children's computer time.
  Maple syrup, which is made from the sap of the sugar maple tree, is an expensive but tasty treat.

- After a subordinate clause at the beginning of a sentence
  If I had been more careful, I wouldn't have lost the watch.
  Although one can find information about almost anything on the Internet, the information isn't always reliable.

> **TEST TIP**
>
> Don't forget to indent at the beginning of each paragraph.

PRACTICE

Read the following paragraphs and check for punctuation errors. Then copy each paragraph on a separate piece of paper, correcting the punctuation as follows: indent, add capital letters and commas, and change periods to question marks where necessary.

1.
many families enjoy watching television together during the early evening hours. therefore programs shown during this time should be suitable for children. do you really think it is appropriate for children to see programs that involve shooting fistfights and other forms of violence. most parents do not and they change the channel when such programs are shown.

2.
it is important for children to know how to use computers but it is also important for them to spend time on other activities. when children spend a lot of time at the computer they spend less time playing outside. they spend less time interacting with other people. they miss out on activities that are important for their physical and emotional development.

3.
i have a lot of fun activities planned for your visit. john who is my next-door neighbor has promised to take us white-water rafting. have you ever done that before. it's a lot of fun and you will surely enjoy it. however there are plenty of other things we can do if you don't want to go rafting. we can ride bikes go to the movies or just relax at home.

4.

tourism which brings a lot of money to the town of palm grove is an important part of the local economy. tourist dollars pay the salaries of hotel employees restaurant servers and airport workers. all of these people earn a lot more money from tourism than they ever did from fishing. in addition they now have steady jobs with a steady income.

Writing Samples

Sample responses to the IELTS writing tasks with scores can be seen at **www.ielts.org** under Teacher Resources.

SPEAKING MODULE

- **QUICK STUDY**
  - Overview
  - Question Types
  - Speaking Tips
- **SPEAKING SKILLS**

Part 1: Introduction and Interview
  - Target 1—Identifying Yourself
  - Target 2—Giving Information

Part 2: Long Turn
  - Target 3—Organizing a Topic
  - Target 4—Discussing a Topic
  - Target 5—Verb Tenses
  - Target 6—Sequence
  - Target 7—Comparing and Contrasting
  - Target 8—Explaining
  - Target 9—Describing
  - Target 10—Responding to Follow-up Questions

Part 3: Discussion
  - Target 11—Explaining an Issue in Depth
  - Target 12—Describing an Issue in Depth
  - Target 13—Comparing and Contrasting an Issue in Depth
  - Target 14—Giving an In-Depth Opinion

General Speaking Skills
  - Target 15—Asking for Clarification
  - Target 16—Delay Tactics
  - Target 17—Avoiding Short Answers
  - Target 18—Word Families and Stress
  - Target 19—Sentence Stress
  - Target 20—Transition Words and Intonation
  - Target 21—Lists and Intonation

QUICK STUDY

Overview

There are three parts to the Speaking module, which lasts between 11 and 14 minutes. You will be alone in a room with one examiner, who will ask you questions and ask you to talk on certain topics. The interview will be recorded. You will be able to make notes in Part 2 only.

The Speaking modules are the same for both the Academic and the General Training versions of the IELTS. Topics include discussions about you, your family, etc.

Speaking Module

Part	Time	Tasks
1	4–5 minutes	Answer questions about yourself and your activities
2	3–4 minutes: 1 minute, preparation 1–2 minutes speaking 1 minute follow-up questions	Talk on a topic presented on a task card
3	4–5 minutes	Discuss with examiner issues related to the topic in Part 2

Question Types

There are a variety of questions and prompts the examiner will use to get you to talk during the IELTS Speaking module. You should be familiar with these types.

Part 1   *Wh-* questions
         Yes/No questions

Part 2   Describe and explain
         Wh- questions
         Yes/No questions

Part 3   *Wh-* questions
         Yes/No questions

The following activities will help you become familiar with these question types.

Part 1

PRACTICE A

Write the answers to the examiner's questions for Part 1.

1. What is your name?

   _____

2. How do you spell it?

   _____

3. Do you have your proof of identification? May I see it?

   _____

4. Let's talk about where you live. Can you describe your neighborhood?

   _____

5. What is an advantage of living there?

   _____

6. What is a disadvantage of living there?

   _____

7. Let's talk about jobs. What kind of job do you have?

   _____

8. What is the best thing about your job?

   _____

9. Let's talk about free time. What is one activity you enjoy doing in your free time?

   _____

10. How did you become interested in this activity?

   _____

PRACTICE B

Pretend you are taking the Speaking module. The examiner asked you the questions in Practice A. Now give your answers aloud to the examiner's questions for Part 1.

Part 2

PRACTICE C

Make notes to answer the questions on the Task Card for Part 2. Try to do this in one minute.

Task card

> Describe a place that you like to go.
>
> You should say:
> where the place is
> how you get there
> what it looks like
>
> and explain why you like this place.

Notes:
Place _____
Location _____
Transportation _____
Appearance _____

Why I like it _____

_____

PRACTICE D

Pretend you are taking the Speaking module. The examiner gave you the Task Card in Practice C. Now give your answers out loud to the examiner's questions for Part 2.

PRACTICE E

Write the answers to the examiner's follow-up questions for Part 2.

1. Do you go on your own to this place?

_____

2. Are there similar places you like to go?

_____

PRACTICE F

Pretend you are taking the Speaking module. The examiner asked you the questions in Practice E. Now give your answers out loud to the examiner's questions for Part 2 follow-up.

Part 3

PRACTICE G

Write the answers to the examiner's questions for Part 3. Note that these questions are related to the theme of Part 2.

1. Let's consider why people need to vary their surroundings.
   - What kinds of vacations[1] do most people take?
   - Are these different places than people used to go in the past?

   _____

   _____

   _____

2. Finally, let's talk about leisure time.
   - Why is leisure time important?

   _____

   _____

   _____

Speaking Tips

TIPS TO HELP YOU WHILE TAKING THE TEST

1. **Focus on the task.** Think what the examiner is asking you. Respond precisely to the question or topic.
2. **Speak clearly.** Sit up straight. Talk directly to the examiner. Do not be afraid to make eye contact.
3. **Speak loudly.** Make sure you are heard, but do not yell.
4. **Bring a watch.** You will have one minute to prepare your answer for Part 2. Glance at your watch to make sure you have enough time to complete your task.
5. **Laugh.** Do this before you meet the examiner. Before the speaking test begins, tell yourself a joke or think of something funny. Start to laugh. Laugh harder. Laugh louder. Laughter will make you feel better and more relaxed. It will also push air into your lungs and help you speak better. People around you may think you're crazy[2], but you're there to do well on the IELTS, not to impress people with your sanity.
6. **Smile.** Smile at the examiner. This will put both of you at ease and make you both more comfortable.
7. Don't they to memorize answers in advance.

TIPS TO HELP YOU STUDY FOR THE SPEAKING TEST

1. **Talk to yourself.** When you walk down the street, pay attention to the things around you. What do the buildings look like? Is there a lot of traffic? How is the weather? Is this a typical day and scene in your city? In your mind, describe the scene to someone in English. Imagine a person who has never visited your city, and describe the scene to that person.

   You can do the same thing at school, at work, or anywhere you go. Imagine describing the scene to a person from another country. Explain the customs of people in your country: how they dress, act, and talk in the different situations that you describe.

[1]BRITISH: holidays

[2]BRITISH: mad

2. **Make up stories.** Use your imagination. Look around you on the street, on the bus, on the elevator, wherever you are. Who are those people? Where are they going and why? What are they carrying? What will they do with what they are carrying? Imagine yourself in the story. What would you say to these people?

   Ask yourself questions about everything and everyone you see. How did it get here? Why is it here? What will happen to it next?

3. **Make your daily plans.** Do you talk to yourself about your plans for the day when you get up in the morning? Do this in English. If you have to decide what clothes to wear, what to have for breakfast, if you will walk or take the bus, think about these decisions in English. If you make a shopping list or a reading list or a list of chores, you can do this in English too.

4. **Think about your job.** Imagine you are at a job interview. Talk about your educational and work background. What kind of training and experience do you have? What can you do well? How do you see your future? In your mind, try to sell yourself to a future employer by talking about your strengths and good qualities.

5. **Explain your interests.** Choose a hobby or free time interest that you have. Imagine that you are teaching another person how to do it. Explain everything step by step. Describe any equipment or tools that are needed. Then pick another hobby and do it again.

6. **Read books, watch movies and TV.** Think about a book, film, or TV show that you really enjoy. In your mind, tell another person what it is about and why you like it. Think about a book, film, or TV show that you dislike. Explain why you don't like it.

7. **Read about the news.** When you read the newspaper or watch the news on TV, think about it in English. How could you explain it to another person in English? How could you explain your own opinions or feelings about particular news events?

8. **Talk to everyone you meet.** Talk to cashiers, bus drivers, neighbors—everyone!

What the Examiner Measures

FLUENCY AND COHERENCE

When you answer the examiner's questions or talk about a topic, your speech must be fluent and cohesive. This means the words you use must fit the situation, and these words must come quickly. You must address the topic fully, and your ideas must be tied together.

It is important to speak for a least one full minute during Part 2. You can speak up to two minutes if you can. There is no penalty for speaking over one minute. The examiner will tell you to stop and will then ask a question related to the topic.

ACCURACY

Accuracy is very important. An examiner will listen to your vocabulary, your grammar, and your pronunciation. She or he will want to make sure that you have a large enough vocabulary to express yourself easily and be understood completely.

The examiner will want to make sure that the grammar you use is varied and appropriate to what you want to say.

The examiner will, of course, be paying close attention to your pronunciation. Your speech must be comprehensible. You can have an accent, but the words must be intelligible.

SPEAKING SKILLS

PART 1: INTRODUCTION AND INTERVIEW

Target 1—Indentifying Yourself

There are three ways you can talk about yourself—factual, physical, and emotional. Look at these model introductions. When introducing yourself to the examiner, you will only use factual words.

Factually—My name is Jose Maria Menendez. My first name is spelled J-O-S-E and my last name ends in "Z" not "S." People often have trouble when spelling my name. My identity number is C-9870-667.

Physically—I am almost 6 feet tall. My hair color is brown, the same color as my eyes.

Emotionally—I'm a serious student, but I like to laugh, too. I spend a lot of time studying, but on weekends, I like to go out with my friends.

TEST TIP

When you say a string of numbers, use the single-digit number. For example, for C-9870-667, don't say: C-ninety-eight seventy sixty-six seven. You'll be less likely to make a mistake by keeping it simple: C nine eight seven zero six six seven.

Useful Factual Words

first name	begins with
last name	employer
surname	occupation
ends with	date of birth

PRACTICE 1

Complete this form about yourself. This will help you organize your personal information.

Personal Information Form

First Name _____

Middle Name _____

Last Name[1] _____

Age _____

Address _____

_____

Nationality _____

Native Language _____

Other Languages _____

Occupation _____

Name of Employer _____

Name of School _____

Forms of Identification:

Passport Number _____

Driver's License Number _____

Other ID Number _____

Write five sentences about yourself. Use the examples as models. Then, without looking at the form or sentences, describe yourself out loud. Record your description and listen to it. Record yourself speaking about the topic in different ways. Vary the vocabulary that you use and the order that you present the information. You only get one chance during the exam. This is your time to practice.

1. _____

2. _____

3. _____

4. _____

5. _____

[1]BRITISH: surname

Target 2—Giving Information

YOUR FAMILY

When talking about your family, it is simpler to talk about them factually.

EXAMPLE 1

I have a very small family. There is only my mother, father, and me. I'm an only child.

EXAMPLE 2

I have a very large family. I have three brothers and two sisters. I am the youngest. One of my brothers still lives with my parents; my other siblings have all married and moved to their own homes.

EXAMPLE 3

My father died when I was ten. I was brought up by my mother and grandparents. My mother and two sisters and I still live with my grandfather.

TEST TIP

You don't have to tell the examiner everything. She or he is not judging you. Just provide some basic information. If you don't want to talk about your family, talk about someone else's family.

Useful Words

parents	married	live with
relations	single	die/passed away
youngest/oldest	divorced	moved out
middle child	widowed	raised by
only child		

PRACTICE 1

Complete this form about your family. This will help you organize your personal information.

Family Information Form

	Relationship to You	Name	Age	Marital Status	Occupation	Other Information
Parents	mother					
	father					
Siblings						
Other Relatives						

Write four sentences about your family. Use the examples as a model. Then, without looking at the form or sentences, describe your family out loud. Record your description and listen to it. Record it over and over until you are satisfied with your presentation.

1. _____

2. _____

3. _____

4. _____

YOUR HOME AND HOMETOWN

You may be asked to talk about your home, your neighborhood, or your hometown. You can talk generally about these, or you can talk more personally. Try to have a lot of specific details prepared. This will help your answers be more cohesive and fluent.

Home
We live in a flat[1] in the old section of the city. It was once a large home that was converted to several flats. Now, five families live in this home. We have two bedrooms: one for me and one for my parents. There is a large living room and a kitchen with a small balcony overlooking the street. The streets are very narrow, and there are no trees.

---

[1]AMERICAN: apartment

Neighborhood[1]
I was born in Beijing. Even though it is a very large city and the capital, we live in a part that is like a small village. We know everyone here. On the corner of my street, there is a small grocery store. Across from that, there is a dry cleaner. Next to the dry cleaner is a big clothing store. On the corner opposite the grocery store, there is a bus stop so we can easily go anywhere in the city.

Useful Words

Type	Relation	Description
balcony	across from	large/small
one-bedroom	along	spacious
kitchen	behind	airy
section/area	beside	narrow
grocery store	corner	old/new
park	end	lots
post office	facing	a lot of
department store	in back/front/middle of	big
taxi stand/rank	left-hand/right-hand side	
clothing store	near	
dry cleaner	next to	
park	overlooking	

PRACTICE 2

Complete these forms about your home and neighborhood. This will help you organize your personal information.

Home Information Form

Size _____
Age _____
Number of bedrooms _____
Other rooms _____
Garden/yard _____
Special features _____

My Bedroom:
Size _____
Furniture _____
Colors _____
Art _____
Other _____

Neighborhood Information Form

Name _____
Style of houses _____
Shops/businesses _____
Schools _____
Religious buildings _____
Other buildings _____
Transportation _____
Parks/gardens _____
Special characteristics _____

[1]BRITISH: neighbourhood

Write four sentences about your home. Use the examples as models. Then, without looking at the form or sentences, describe your home and hometown out loud. Record your description and listen to it. Record it over and over until you are satisfied with your presentation.

Home

1. _____

2. _____

3. _____

4. _____

Neighborhood

1. _____

2. _____

3. _____

4. _____

YOUR OCCUPATION OR SCHOOL

You may be asked to discuss how you spend your day. Do you work or do you study? Be prepared with specific details about your occupation or your school life.

Occupation
I'm an engineer. I've worked for the same company for three years. My specific job is working with the senior engineer and helping her prepare presentations for contractors and their clients. I'd like to get an advanced[1] degree. That's why I'm applying to study at an engineering school in Australia.

School
I'm a third-year student at National University. I'm studying psychology. I'm in class most of the day, and when I'm not in class I have to spend a lot of time working on my assignments. My goal is to become a research psychologist, so I'll have to get a doctorate degree. I have a lot of years of studying ahead of me.

Useful Words

boss	duties	qualified
co-workers	assignments	goal
clients	position	advanced degree
classmates	schedule	bachelor's degree
instructors	salary	master's degree
manager	hourly	doctorate degree

[1]BRITISH: higher degree

PRACTICE 3

Complete this form about your occupation or studies. This will help you organize your personal information.

Job Information Form

Company name _____

Job title _____

Length of time at this job _____

Duties _____

Training required for this job _____

Skills required for this job _____

Things I like about this job _____

Things I don't like about this job _____

Future career goals _____

Education Information Form

Name of college/university _____

Major/subject[1] _____

Classes I am taking now _____

Hours per week in class _____

Years to complete degree/certificate _____

Educational goals _____

Future career goals _____

Write four sentences about your occupation or your studies. Use the examples as models. Then, without looking at the form or sentences, describe your job or school out loud. Record your discussion and listen to it. Record it over and over until you are satisfied with your presentation.

My occupation _____ or My studies _____

1. _____

2. _____

3. _____

4. _____

YOUR HOBBIES

The examiner may ask you how you spend your free time. Do you like to read, go to the cinema, play sports? Do you have any hobbies like collecting stamps, bird watching, photography?

[1]BRITISH: doing a degree in

Hobby *(EXAMPLE 1)*

I enjoy bird watching. I often go to a park near my house in the early morning to watch the birds. I also belong to a bird watching club. Several times a year we take trips to other places. We try to find birds that we've never seen before. You don't need much equipment for bird watching, just a pair of binoculars and a pair of strong legs for walking. I enjoy this hobby because I like to be outside, and I'm fascinated by the natural world.

Hobby *(EXAMPLE 2)*

I like to play the guitar. I took lessons when I was a child. Some friends and I had a rock band once, a long time ago. We played at parties. Now I mostly play on my own at home, and sometimes I get together with friends to play. I'm thinking about taking lessons again. I'd like to learn how to play jazz guitar. I have a large collection of jazz CDs.

Useful Words

interested in	club	equipment
enjoy	get together	collect/collection
join	learn how	passion
belong to	lessons	fascinate/fascinated by

PRACTICE 4

Complete this form about your hobbies or general interests. This will help you organize your personal information.

Hobby/Free-Time Activity Information Form

Hobby/Activity #1 _____
How often do you do this hobby or activity? _____
Do you do it on your own or with other people? _____
Do you belong to a club related to this hobby/activity? _____
How did you learn how to do this hobby/activity? _____
Do you need special equipment for it? _____
What do you like most about it? _____

Hobby/Activity #2 _____
How often do you do this hobby or activity? _____
Do you do it alone or with other people? _____
Do you belong to a club related to this hobby/activity? _____
How did you learn how to do this hobby/activity? _____
Do you need special equipment for it? _____
What do you like most about it? _____

Write four sentences about how you spend your free time. Use the examples as models. Then, without looking at the form or sentences, describe your hobbies and general interests out loud. Record your description and listen to it. Record it over and over until you are satisfied with your presentation.

Hobby/Activity _____

1. _____

2. _____

3. _____

4. _____

PART 2: LONG TURN

Target 3—Organizing a Topic

The examiner will give you a task card. The card will have a topic and some questions to guide your discussion of the topic. You will have one minute to prepare your answer. The questions are very important. They will guide your organization. You must answer ALL the questions on the task card. You can make notes on paper provided by the examiner. Your discussion will be more cohesive if you can provide a sequence of events or actions for your topic.

EXAMPLE

Describe a museum that you have visited.

You should say:
where it is located and what kind of museum it is
what specific things you can see there
when and why you last visited it

and discuss how it compares to other museums you have visited.

Notes

Museum	Greenport Ship Museum
Location and type of museum	Greenport, a beach resort in Massachusetts; a museum about old whaling ships
Specific things seen	Parts of old ships, items used by sailors, explanations of shipbuilding methods, information about whaling, whale bone products
When and why visited	Last summer with niece and nephew to pass the time on a rainy day
Compare to other museums	Not like a city museum, smaller, simpler exhibits, but friendlier staff

TEST TIP

Answer the questions on the task card. Don't talk about a different topic.

PRACTICE

Make notes about these topics. Then, without looking at your notes, discuss the topics out loud. Be sure to address every question on each task card. Record your discussion and listen to it. Record your discussion over and over until you are satisfied with your presentation.

Make notes about these topics. Give short answers to the question. Pay attention to the tense.

Topic 1

> Talk about a pet that you or someone you know once had.
>
> You should say:
> what kind of animal it was
> what kind of care it needed
> what you liked/didn't like about it
>
> and explain why this is or is not a popular type of pet to own.

Pet _____

Kind of animal _____

Kind of care _____

Liked/didn't like _____

Why it is/isn't popular _____

Topic 2

> Describe a birthday celebration that you attended recently.
>
> You should say:
> whose birthday it was and that person's age
> who attended the party
> where the party took place
>
> and describe some activities that happened at the party.

Birthday _____

Name and age of celebrant _____

Who attended _____

Location _____

Activities _____

Topic 3

> Talk about a friend you had as a child or teenager.
>
> You should say:
> > when and how you first met this friend
> > what things you liked to do together
> > what things you had in common
>
> and explain why this friendship was important to you.

Friend _____

When and how met _____

Things did together _____

Things in common _____

Why important _____

Topic 4

> Describe a trip you have taken recently.
>
> You should say:
> > where you went
> > who went with you
> > why you went there
>
> and describe some things you saw and did on your trip.

Trip _____

Where _____

Who _____

Why _____

Activities _____

Target 4—Discussing a Topic

When you write, you state a general idea and then add supporting details. The same is true in speaking.

Topic   A museum you have visited

Question   Discuss how this museum compares to other museums you have visited.

Ideas for Response
General Idea The Greenport Ship Museum is different from a museum in the city.

Supporting Detail 1   It is smaller.
Supporting Detail 2   The exhibits are simpler.
Supporting Detail 3   The staff is friendlier.

TEST TIP
Your notes can be full sentences or phrases.

PRACTICE

For each question, write one general idea followed by three supporting details. Then, without looking at your notes, answer the questions out loud. Record your answers and listen to them. Record your answers over and over until you are satisfied with your presentation.

1. Topic   A TV program you enjoy
    Question   Explain why this is or is not a popular TV show.

    General Idea _____

        Supporting Detail 1 _____

        Supporting Detail 2 _____

        Supporting Detail 3 _____

2. Topic   A trip you have taken recently
    Question   Describe some things you saw and did on your trip.

    General Idea _____

        Supporting Detail 1 _____

        Supporting Detail 2 _____

        Supporting Detail 3 _____

3. Topic   A close friend you have now
    Question   Tell about some things you have in common with this friend.

    General Idea _____

        Supporting Detail 1 _____

        Supporting Detail 2 _____

        Supporting Detail 3 _____

4. Topic   A book you have read recently
    Question   Tell what the book is about.

    General Idea _____

    Supporting Detail 1 _____

    Supporting Detail 2 _____

    Supporting Detail 3 _____

TEST TIP

Pay attention to the intonation for lists. See the
practice exercises in the General Speaking Skills
section.

Target 5—Verb Tenses

You may be asked to talk about something that you experienced in the past, or about something that is still
true now. Be careful to use the correct verb tense.

Past Tenses

Simple past   Last summer, we <u>went</u> to the Greenport Ship Museum.
Past continuous   When we left the house, it <u>was raining</u>.
Past perfect   By the time we got there, the demonstration <u>had</u> already <u>begun</u>.

Present Tenses

Simple present   This program <u>appears</u> on TV once a week.
Present continuous   TV stations <u>are</u> still <u>showing</u> the program even though it was originally made over ten
                     years ago.
Present perfect   I <u>have enjoyed</u> this program since I was a child.

PRACTICE

*For each question, circle the verb tense you will mostly use in your answer. Then write three general ideas to
answer the question. Then, without looking at your notes, answer the questions out loud. Record your answers
and listen to them. Record your answers over and over until you are satisfied with your presentation.*

1. Topic   A popular tourist destination in your country
    Question   Explain why this is a popular place for tourists to visit.
    Verb Tense   Past   Present

    General Idea _____

    General Idea _____

    General Idea _____

2. Topic   Your favorite year in either primary or secondary school

    Question   Explain why you liked this year in school so much.

    Verb Tense   Past   Present

    General Idea   _____

    General Idea   _____

    General Idea   _____

3. Topic   A time your plane/train/bus was delayed

    Question   What did you do while you were waiting for the plane/train/bus to leave?

    Verb Tense   Past   Present

    General Idea   _____

    General Idea   _____

    General Idea   _____

4. Topic   A popular place to go shopping in your city

    Question   Describe the things you can see and do there.

    Verb Tense   Past   Present

    General Idea   _____

    General Idea   _____

    General Idea   _____

Target 6—Sequence

When you describe something that happened in the past, you can use certain words to show the sequence of events.

Useful Words

first/second	next	then
after	before	until
by the time	finally	at last
as soon as	when	

EXAMPLE

After we watched the shipbuilding demonstration, we looked at some of the exhibits. *Then* we had a snack in the café. We stayed at the museum *until* it closed.

PRACTICE

Choose the correct sequence words to complete each paragraph. Add capital letters where necessary.

until   finally   then   as soon as

I arrived at the train station at 10:00. (1)_____ I got there, I checked my luggage. (2)_____ I heard the announcement: the train was delayed. I sat in the café and drank coffee (3)_____ I heard the boarding announcement. I boarded the train at 12:30. (4)_____, the train left the station at 12:50.

by the time   before   first   then

Our last day in Vancouver was very busy. (5) _____, we spent several hours at the anthropology museum. (6) _____ we had seen all the exhibits, we were very hungry. We had a quick snack in the cafeteria, and (7) _____ we took the bus to Chinatown for lunch. We studied the menu carefully (8) _____ ordering lunch and chose a variety of delicious Chinese dishes. It was a very good restaurant, and we really enjoyed our meal.

Target 7—Comparing and Contrasting

You may be asked to compare the person, place, or event of your topic to another one.

Useful Words

same	different from	alike
like	unlike	more
less	similar to	as

Comparative and superlative adjectives are also used to compare and contrast.

EXAMPLE

The Greenport Ship Museum is not <u>like</u> city museums.
It is <u>smaller</u> and the exhibits are <u>simpler</u>.
But it is just <u>as</u> interesting <u>as</u> some of the <u>bigger</u> museums.

PRACTICE

Answer the following questions. First, write three general ideas for each answer. Use compare *and* contrast *words. Then, without looking at your notes, answer the questions out loud. Record your answers and listen to them. Record your answers over and over until you are satisfied with your presentation.*

1. Topic   A teacher you remember
   Question   Compare this teacher to other teachers you have had.

   General Idea   _____

   General Idea   _____

   General Idea   _____

2. Topic   A party you attended
      Question   Compare this party to other parties you have attended.

      General Idea   _____

      General Idea   _____

      General Idea   _____

3. Topic   A popular tourist destination in your country
      Question   Compare this place to other tourist destinations you have visited.

      General Idea   _____

      General Idea   _____

      General Idea   _____

4. Topic   A TV program you enjoy watching
      Question   Compare this program to other popular TV programs.

      General Idea   _____

      General Idea   _____

      General Idea   _____

Target 8—Explaining

You may be asked to explain *why*. For example, you may be asked why you like something or why something is important.

Useful Words

because (of)	since
for this reason	another reason
that's why	so

EXAMPLE

It's important to visit museums *because* they teach us about a lot of things.
Since museums show us things, they can help us understand concepts and facts better than books can.
Another reason is that museums are a representation of our culture.

PRACTICE

Answer the following questions. First, write three general ideas for each answer. Use explaining words. Then, without looking at your notes, answer the questions out loud. Record your answers and listen to them. Record your answers over and over until you are satisfied with your presentation.

1. Topic   A book you have read recently
    Question   Explain why you liked this book.

    General Idea _____

    General Idea _____

    General Idea _____

2. Topic   Your favorite year in primary or secondary school
    Question   Explain why this was your favorite year.

    General Idea _____

    General Idea _____

    General Idea _____

3. Topic   A popular tourist destination in your country
    Question   Explain why this is a popular place to visit.

    General Idea _____

    General Idea _____

    General Idea _____

4. Topic   A movie you have seen
    Question   Explain why you remember this movie.

    General Idea _____

    General Idea _____

    General Idea _____

Target 9—Describing

You may be asked to describe some activities or events. Don't just list activities. Think of something interesting to say about each one. For example, talk about how long it took, say why you liked it, give some details about what it involved, or use some adjectives to describe it.

EXAMPLE

Topic   A museum you visited recently
Question   Describe some things you did there.
Activities   (1) looked at exhibits, (2) watched a movie, (3) had a snack
Description We spent about an hour looking at exhibits about ships and whaling. Then we watched a short but interesting movie that showed how ships were built. After that, we were tired, so we had some snacks in the museum café and looked at the view of the harbor.

PRACTICE

For each question, choose three activities to describe. Write one sentence about each one. Then, without looking at your notes, answer the questions out loud. Record your answers and listen to them. Record your answers over and over until you are satisfied with your presentation.

1. Topic   A trip you took recently
   Question   Describe some things you did on your trip.
   Activities   _____
   Description   _____
     _____
     _____

2. Topic   A party you attended recently
   Question   Describe some activities that took place at the party.
   Activities   _____
   Description   _____
     _____
     _____

3. Topic   A holiday you enjoy
   Question   Describe some things you do to celebrate this holiday.
   Activities   _____
   Description   _____
     _____
     _____

TEST TIP

Answer the questions thoroughly and in detail to make sure your answers are long enough.

Target 10—Responding to Follow-up Questions

The examiner will ask you specific questions about your discussion of a topic.

Follow-up questions for the example task card in Target 3:

How often do you go to museums?
What kinds of museums do you generally prefer to visit? Why?
Is it important to take children to visit different kinds of museums?

Useful Words

According to my point of view	I believe	I'm in favor of _____ because _____
As far as I'm concerned	I don't know if	It seems to me
I agree with/disagree with	I don't know whether	Personally, I think
I'm certain/positive/sure that	I think it's a good idea because _____	The advantage of _____ is that
I assume	I'm against _____	The disadvantage of _____ is that

PRACTICE 1

Look at these follow-up questions for the task cards from the practice exercise in Target 3. Make notes for your response. Then, without looking at your notes, answer the questions out loud. Record your answers and listen to them. Record your answers over and over until you are satisfied with your presentation.

Topic 1

What are some of the most popular pets in your country? Why are they popular?
What animal do you think makes the best pet?
What animal do you think would not make a good pet?
What are some advantages and disadvantages to owning pets?

1. _____

2. _____

3. _____

4. _____

Topic 2

How do you like to celebrate your birthday?
In your country, what kinds of gifts are common to give for birthdays?
Do you think it is important to celebrate birthdays? Why or why not?
What other kinds of celebrations are important for you?

1. _____

2. _____

3. _____

4. _____

Topic 3

Are you still friends with this person? Why or why not?
How do you make new friends?
What are some things you like to do with your friends now?
Do you think it's better to have a lot of friends, or just a few good friends?

1. _____

2. _____

3. _____

4. _____

Topic 4

Would you visit this place again? Why or why not?
Where would you like to go on your next vacation?
When you travel, what kinds of places do you usually visit?
Do you like to travel? Why or why not?

1. _____

2. _____

3. _____

4. _____

PRACTICE 2

Write an answer for each follow-up question. Then, without looking at your notes or your sentences, respond to the question out loud. Record your answers and listen to them. Record them over and over until you are satisfied with your presentation.

Topic 1

1. _____

2. _____

3. _____

4. _____

Topic 2

1. _____

2. _____

3. _____

4. _____

Topic 3

1. _____

2. _____

3. _____

4. _____

Topic 4

1. _____

2. _____

3. _____

4. _____

PART 3: DISCUSSION

In the last part of the Speaking section of the test, the examiner will ask you some more questions and give you an opportunity to discuss in depth some of the issues related to the topic in Part 2.

Target 11—Explaining an Issue in Depth

You may be asked to explain more about your ideas on a topic.

Topic　　　　　　　A museum you visited recently (See Target 3 example for task card questions.)

Related Questions　What role do museums play in a society?
Why do people visit museums?
What can we learn from museums?
Is learning about art important? Why or why not?

Useful Words

for example	for instance
in other words	such as
to illustrate	that is

You can organize your ideas in terms of a general idea with supporting details.

Question

What role do museums play in a society?

Ideas for Response

General Idea Different roles
　　Supporting Detail 1　Education
　　Supporting Detail 2　Entertainment
　　Supporting Detail 3　Represent culture

Response

Museums have several different roles in society. They educate us about a wide range of things such as art, science, and history. They also provide us with entertainment, as going to a museum is a pleasant and interesting way to spend a day. Most of all, they are a representation of our culture. In other words, they reflect back to us the things that are considered to be valuable or important in our culture.

PRACTICE

Look at these questions on issues related to the topic on a task card from the practice exercise in Target 3. Make notes for your response. Use your notes to write some sentences about each issue. Then, without looking at your notes, discuss the issues out loud. Record your discussion and listen to it. Record your discussion over and over until you are satisfied with your presentation.

ISSUES FROM TOPIC 2

1. Are birthday celebrations important in your country? Why or why not?
2. How do people in your culture generally feel about their birthdays?
3. How are older people treated in your culture?
4. What other types of anniversaries are celebrated in your culture? Why are they important?

Notes

1. General Idea _____

    Supporting Detail 1 _____

    Supporting Detail 2 _____

    Supporting Detail 3 _____

2. General Idea _____

    Supporting Detail 1 _____

    Supporting Detail 2 _____

    Supporting Detail 3 _____

3. General Idea _____

    Supporting Detail 1 _____

    Supporting Detail 2 _____

    Supporting Detail 3 _____

4. General Idea _____

    Supporting Detail 1 _____

    Supporting Detail 2 _____

    Supporting Detail 3 _____

Sentences

1. _____
   _____
   _____

2. _____
   _____
   _____

3. _____
   _____
   _____

4. _____
   _____
   _____

> **TEST TIP**
>
> If you make a mistake, correct it if you can. If not, just relax and move on.

Target 12—Describing an Issue in Depth

You may be asked to describe more details about your topic.

Topic   A museum you visited recently

Related Questions What does a museum near you look like?
                       What kinds of objects are in a museum near you?
                       What are some different ways museums present information?
                       What are some ways that museums use technology?

Useful Words

also	generally
usually	additionally
in addition	another
first	

Again, you can think about your response in terms of a general idea with supporting details.

Question

What are some different ways museums present information?

Ideas for Response

General Idea Exhibits, films, and hands-on
    Supporting Detail 1   Different kinds of displays to see
    Supporting Detail 2   Films related to the exhibits
    Supporting Detail 3   Exhibits you can touch and workshops to make things

Response

Museums present information through exhibits, films, and different hands-on activities. Museums exhibit things in different ways. Art might hang on the wall, or a scene from history may be shown in a diorama. In addition, museums usually show films that are specially made to accompany the exhibits. Many museums also have hands-on activities. For example, they have exhibits that can be touched. They also often offer workshops where participants can learn to make things that are similar or related to the items in the museum's exhibits.

PRACTICE

Look at these questions on issues related to the topic on a task card from the practice exercise in Target 3. Make notes for your response. Use your notes to write some sentences about each issue. Then, without looking at your notes, discuss the issues out loud. Record your discussion and listen to it. Record your discussion over and over until you are satisfied with your presentation.

ISSUES FROM TOPIC 4

1. What are some different kinds of places people visit on their vacations?
2. In your country, how much annual vacation time do people generally get? Is this enough?
3. Describe your ideal vacation.
4. What are some transportation problems in your country?

Notes

1. General Idea
    Supporting Detail 1 _____
    Supporting Detail 2 _____
    Supporting Detail 3 _____

2. General Idea
    Supporting Detail 1 _____
    Supporting Detail 2 _____
    Supporting Detail 3 _____

3. General Idea
    Supporting Detail 1 _____
    Supporting Detail 2 _____
    Supporting Detail 3 _____

4. General Idea

   Supporting Detail 1 _____

   Supporting Detail 2 _____

   Supporting Detail 3 _____

Sentences

1. _____

   _____

   _____

2. _____

   _____

   _____

3. _____

   _____

   _____

4. _____

   _____

   _____

TEST TIP

Contractions will make your speech sound more natural.

Target 13—Comparing and Contrasting an Issue in Depth

You may be asked to compare and contrast issues related to your topic.

Topic   A museum you visited recently.

Related Questions How are small town museums different from museums in big cities?
                     What do museums offer in terms of education that books or other sources don't?
                     Which are more interesting, art museums or history museums? Why?
                     How will museums be different in the future?

Useful Words

Comparison	Contrast
similar to	different from
also	although/even though
like	but
the same as	on the other hand
both	less/more
as...as	however

Organize your ideas by thinking about similarities and differences.

Question

How will museums be different in the future?

Ideas for Response

Similarities A. similar type of content
B. some similar exhibits

Differences A. more use of computers
B. many exhibits online

Response

In the future, I think that museums will be both similar to and different from museums now. I think they will have similar content. There will still be art museums that show paintings and sculpture and natural history museums that show dinosaurs, for example. And I think some of the exhibits will be set up in similar ways, too. But I also think that museums in the future will make more use of technology. Computers will be used to make the exhibits more interactive. Most museums will probably also have exhibits online. Then it won't be necessary to actually visit the museums, at least in some cases.

PRACTICE

Look at these questions on issues related to the topic on a task card from the practice exercise in Target 3. Make notes for your response. Use your notes to write some sentences about each issue. Then, without looking at your notes, discuss the issues out loud. Record your discussion and listen to it. Record your discussion over and over until you are satisfied with your presentation.

ISSUES FROM TOPIC 3

1. How have your friendships changed as you've grown older?
2. What differences are there between men's and women's friendships?
3. Do you think the nature of friendship is changing?
4. What is the difference between a friend and an acquaintance?

Notes

1. Similarities
   A. _____
   B. _____
   C. _____

   Differences
   A. _____
   B. _____
   C. _____

2. Similarities
   A. _____
   B. _____
   C. _____

   Differences
   A. _____
   B. _____
   C. _____

3. Similarities
   A. _____
   B. _____
   C. _____

   Differences
   A. _____
   B. _____
   C. _____

4. Similarities
   A. _____
   B. _____
   C. _____

   Differences
   A. _____
   B. _____
   C. _____

Sentences

1. _____
_____
_____

2. _____
_____
_____

3. _____
_____
_____

4. _____
_____
_____

Target 14—Giving an In-Depth Opinion

You may be asked to give your opinion on issues related to your topic.

Topic   A museum you have visited recently

Related Questions   What type of museum do you prefer to visit? Why?
How important is it for parents to take their children to museums?
Do you agree or disagree: Museums should not be allowed to charge high admission
fees.
Do you agree or disagree: Schools should always include museum visits as part of
their program.

Useful Words

I believe that	I tend to think	I agree that
To my mind	From my point of view	If I had to choose
I would prefer to	To my way of thinking	In my opinion

Organize your ideas by thinking about your opinion and details to support it.

Question

Do you agree or disagree: Museums should not be allowed to charge high admission fees.

Ideas for Response

Opinion Agree—no high admission fees
    Supporting Detail 1   High fees keep people away.
    Supporting Detail 2   Even high fees don't provide funds.
    Supporting Detail 3   Government should fund museums.

Response

I agree that museums should not be allowed to charge high admission fees. In my opinion, museums should not charge any fees at all. Many people, especially families with children, cannot afford to pay to go to a museum, so admission fees just keep people away. In any case, admission fees provide only a very small part of the funds a museum needs, so no one really benefits from them. To my way of thinking, museums benefit the public, so the government should provide most or all of the funds for museums.

PRACTICE

Look at these questions on issues related to the topic on a task card from the practice exercise in Target 3. Make notes for your response. Use your notes to write some sentences about each issue. Then, without looking at your notes, discuss the issues out loud. Record your discussion and listen to it. Record your discussion over and over until you are satisfied with your presentation.

ISSUES FROM TOPIC 1

Do you agree or disagree: Some people spend too much money on their pets.
What kind of animal makes the best pet?
Do you prefer to have a pet or not? Why?
Is it important for children to have pets? Why or why not?

Notes

1. Opinion _____

    Supporting Detail 1 _____

    Supporting Detail 2 _____

    Supporting Detail 3 _____

2. Opinion _____

    Supporting Detail 1 _____

    Supporting Detail 2 _____

    Supporting Detail 3 _____

3. Opinion _____

    Supporting Detail 1 _____

    Supporting Detail 2 _____

    Supporting Detail 3 _____

4. Opinion _____

    Supporting Detail 1 _____

    Supporting Detail 2 _____

    Supporting Detail 3 _____

Sentences

1. _____

   _____

   _____

2. _____

   _____

   _____

3. _____

   _____

   _____

4. _____

   _____

   _____

GENERAL SPEAKING SKILLS

Target 15—Asking for Clarification

If you don't understand a question, ask for clarification. This will give you time to think a bit.

EXAMPLES

Do you mean the house I live in or my hometown?
Would you like me to describe the house generally or in great detail?

Useful Words

do you mean	would you like me to
do you want me to	generally or in great detail
could you explain what you mean by	should I
I'm not sure what you mean by	

PRACTICE

Read each question. Then complete the sentence asking for clarification.

1. Describe a friend who is important to you.
   _____ a friend I have now or a friend from the past?

2. Explain why you liked this movie.
   _____ explain it generally or in great detail?

3. In your opinion, what kinds of people make the best friends?
   _____ close friends or friends in general?

4. How will the role of older people change in the future?
   _____ older people?

5. In what different ways have animals been useful to people throughout history?
   _____ just pets or animals in general?

Target 16—Delay Tactics

You sometimes need time to think about what you are going to say. A short silence is OK, but a long one is not. You have only a short amount of time to show how well you speak English.

While you think, you can paraphrase the question.

Question: What kinds of books do you prefer to read?
Paraphrase: What are my favorite books?

You can also use certain phrases to provide transition and fill the silence.

Useful Phrases

That's an interesting question.	I've never heard that one before.
I've never thought about that before.	That's a complicated issue.
There are a lot of different reasons.	There are so many ways to answer that.

EXAMPLE

What are my favorite books? That's an interesting question.

PRACTICE

First, paraphrase these questions to keep the conversation moving. Then, add a filler expression. Say the sentences out loud.

1. Tell some things that you have in common with this friend.

   _____

2. Explain why this is a popular place for people to visit.

   _____

3. Describe some things you do to celebrate this holiday.

   _____

4. What kind of animal makes the best pet?

   _____

5. What kind of training did you need to get this kind of job?

   _____

Target 17—Avoiding Short Answers

The more you say, the more you can show your ability to use a variety of grammar and vocabulary. Try not to answer a question with a simple *yes* or *no*. Use a full sentence.

EXAMPLE

Question: Do you live in Mumbai?
Avoid: No.
Say: No, I don't live in Mumbai. I live in a suburb outside of Mumbai.

PRACTICE

Answer these yes/no questions with long answers.

1. Do you live with your parents?

   _____

2. Are you a student?

   _____

3. Do you like living in an apartment?

   _____

4. Is your family large?

   _____

5. Do you like your job?

   _____

Target 18—Word Families and Stress

Using word families shows your fluency in English. Be careful to pronounce the words correctly. Depending on what suffixes you add to a root word, the stress may or may not shift.

Some suffixes cause no change in stress.

-able	**com**fort—**com**fortable
-ive	sup**port**—sup**port**ive
-ful	**mean**ing—**mean**ingful
-ment	**gov**ern—**gov**ernment
-ize	**spe**cial—**spe**cialize
-ly	**hap**py—**hap**pily

Some suffixes cause the stress to shift to the syllable immediately preceding the suffix.

-ity	**un**iform—uni**form**ity
-ic	**al**cohol—alco**hol**ic
-ify	**sol**id—so**lid**ify
-ical	**his**tory—hi**stor**ical
-ian	**li**brary—li**brar**ian

Some suffixes cause the stress to shift to the first syllable of the suffix.

-ation/-ition/-ution	com**bine**—combi**na**tion

PRACTICE

Look at these word families. Read the words aloud. Underline the stressed syllable in each word. Read the words aloud again.

	Root Word	Noun	Verb	Adjective	Adverb
1.	politics	politician	politicize	political	politically
2.	imagine	imagination	imagine	imaginative	imaginatively
3.	beauty	beauty	beautify	beautiful	beautifully
4.	agree	agreement	agree	agreeable	agreeably
5.	acid	acid/acidity	acidify	acidic	acidly
6.	quote	quotation	quote	quotable	
7.	act	activity	act	active	actively
8.	energy	energy	energize	energetic	energetically
9.	civil	civility	civilize	civil	civilly
10.	rare	rarity	rarify	rare	rarely

Target 19—Sentence Stress

In a sentence there are words that carry meaning and words that are function words. The words that carry meaning are usually stressed.

Meaning	Function
nouns	articles
verbs	prepositions
adjectives	conjunctions
question words	pronouns
	relative pronouns
	auxiliaries

EXAMPLES

The **large museums** in **town** were **built** in the **late 1900s**.
People who **buy expensive things** for their **pets** are **wasting** their **money**.
It's a **romance novel** that **takes place** in the **1800s**.

PRACTICE

Read each sentence aloud. Underline the stressed words. Then read the sentence aloud again.

1. I live in one of the newer neighborhoods in my city.

2. I've been working at the same company for twelve years.

3. I generally don't like parties because I'm a quiet person.

4. There is an excellent view of the ships in the harbor.

5. A statue of the first president of our country stands in the center of the park.

Target 20—Transition Words and Intonation

A transition word has a rising intonation. The end of the sentence or clause has a falling intonation.

First, a museum is a fun place to *visit*.

However, not everyone likes paintings.

I have lived in the same house since I was born.

PRACTICE

Read each sentence aloud. Mark the intonation patterns for transition words. Then read the sentence aloud again.

1. Nevertheless, it's a pleasant place to live.

2. We took a boat ride after we finished at the museum.

3. Next, the birthday cake was served.

4. It's a position that pays well, unlike many jobs in my field.

5. A good friend also helps you when you are in need.

Target 21—Lists and Intonation

When you have a list of words in a sentence, there is a specific stress pattern.
The first words of a list have a rising intonation. The last word of a list has a falling intonation.

I always eat three vegetables a day: corn, carrots, and peas.

Near my home you can find a bakery, a bank, a laundry, and a restaurant.

PRACTICE

Read each sentence aloud. Mark the intonation pattern. Then read the sentence aloud again.

1. Cats are affectionate, clean, and smart.

2. In addition to English and my native language, I speak Chinese, Korean, and French.

3. I read a variety of things, such as novels, newspapers, magazines, and journals.

4. This TV program is well-written, well-acted, and funny.

5. We had a very active vacation and played tennis, golf, and volleyball.

IELTS MODEL TESTS

ACADEMIC
MODEL TEST 1

Model Test 1

Candidate Name _____

INTERNATIONAL ENGLISH LANGUAGE TESTING SYSTEM

LISTENING

TIME Approx. 30 minutes

INSTRUCTIONS TO CANDIDATES

Do not open this booklet until you are told to do so.

Write your name and candidate number in the space at the top of this page.

You should answer all questions.

All the recordings will be played ONCE only.

Write all your answers on the Question Paper.

At the end of the test, you will be given ten minutes to transfer your answers to an Answer Sheet.

Do not remove this booklet from the examination room.

INFORMATION FOR CANDIDATES

There are **40** questions on this question paper.

The test is divided as follows:

Section 1	Questions 1–10
Section 2	Questions 11–20
Section 3	Questions 21–30
Section 4	Questions 31–40

SECTION 1 QUESTIONS 1–10

Question 1

Match the time with the event. Write the correct number next to the letter.

A _2_ Today
B ___ Next week
C ___ Next summer

1 Winston will go to Japan
2 Winston will register at the World Language Academy
3 Winston will study Japanese

Questions 2 and 3

Choose TWO letters, A–F

2 What TWO classes are offered at the World Language Academy.

A Japanese for University Professors
B Japanese for Business Travelers
C Japanese for Tour Guides
D Japanese for Tourists
E Japanese for Language Teachers
F Japanese for Restaurant Workers

Choose TWO letters, A–F

3 In Japan, Mark Winston says he will probably

A go shopping.
B climb mountains.
C attend a business meeting.
D try Japanese cuisine.
E take a university course.
F study with a tutor.

Questions 4–8

Complete the schedule below.

Write NO MORE THAN TWO WORDS AND/OR A NUMBER for each answer.

Japanese Class Schedule

Morning	Days: Monday–Friday Time: **4** .... Level: Beginner
Afternoon	Days: Monday, Wednesday, Thursday Time: 1:00–3:00 Level: **5** ....
Evening	Days: Monday, Wednesday, Thursday Time: 5:30–7:30 Level: **6** .... Days: **7** .... Time: 7:30–9:30 Level: Advanced
8	Days: Saturday Time: 9:00–2:00 Level: Beginner

Questions 9 and 10

*Choose the correct letter, **A**, **B**, or **C***

9   Which class will Mark take?

A

B

C

10   How will he pay?

A

B

C

SECTION 2   QUESTIONS 11–20

CD1
TRACK
24

> Sumner Mansion
> Notice to Visitors
> The following activities are prohibited inside the mansion:
> - Talking on cell phones
> - **11** _____
> - **12** _____
> - **13** _____
> Thank you, and enjoy your visit!

Questions 14–18

Fill in the missing information on the map of Sumner Mansion. Write **no more than three words** for each answer.

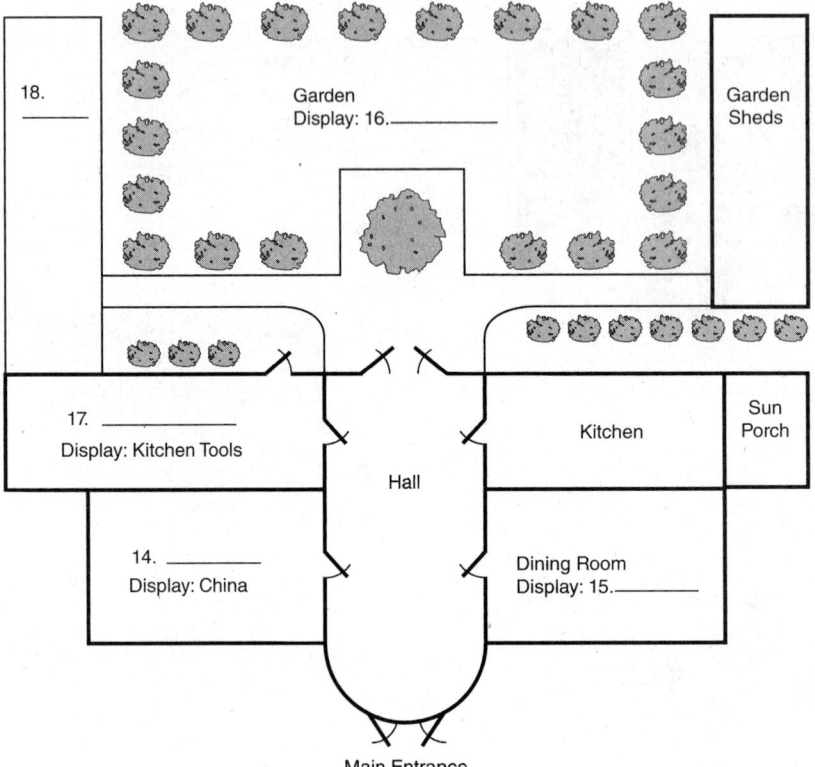

Questions 19–20

Complete the schedule below. Write no more than **three words and/or a number** for each answer.

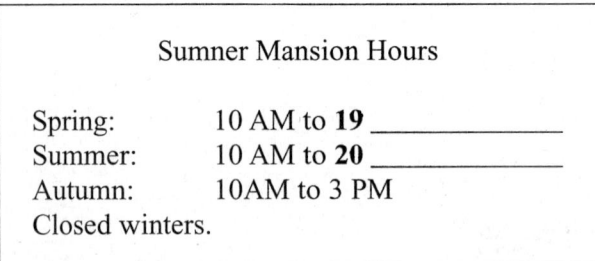

Sumner Mansion Hours

Spring: 10 AM to **19** _____
Summer: 10 AM to **20** _____
Autumn: 10AM to 3 PM
Closed winters.

SECTION 3   QUESTIONS 21–30

Questions 21–23

Complete the sentences below.

Write **NO MORE THAN THREE WORDS** for each answer.

21 There are high-speed trains in Japan and ....

22 The first high-speed train began operating in ....

23 High-speed trains can travel at speeds of .... kilometers an hour.

Questions 24–26

Complete the table below.

*Write **NO MORE THAN THREE WORDS** for each answer.*

Cause	Effect
We have better roads now than in the past.	**24** More people ....
Now we have plane service that is more **25**	More people use planes for long-distance travel.
There is a lot of **26**	We need to consider new forms of transportation.

Questions 27–30

*Choose **FOUR** letters, **A–G**.*

What are the advantages of trains over other types of transportation according to the people on the panel?

A   Less expensive than car trips

B   More relaxing than cars

C   Less polluting than cars

D   No traffic jams

E   Better security systems than planes

F   Larger capacity for passengers than planes

G   More frequent service than planes

SECTION 4   *QUESTIONS 31–40*

Questions 31–40

Complete the timeline below.

*Write **NO MORE THAN THREE WORDS AND/OR ONE NUMBER** for each answer.*

1879	Einstein was born in **31** _____
At age 12	Einstein began **32** _____
33 _____	Einstein's family moved to Italy
34 _____	Einstein graduated from high school
35 _____	Einstein met Mileva Maric
1900	Einstein **36** _____
1901	Einstein became **37** _____
1902	Einstein began work at the Swiss Patent Office
	Einstein **38** _____
39 _____	Einstein and Mileva Maric got married
40 _____	Einstein's first son was born

timeline

Model Test 1

Candidate Name _____

INTERNATIONAL ENGLISH LANGUAGE TESTING SYSTEM

ACADEMIC READING

TIME 1 hour

INSTRUCTIONS TO CANDIDATES

Do not open this booklet until you are told to do so.

Write your name and candidate number in the space at the top of this page.

Start at the beginning of the test and work through it.

You should answer all questions.

If you cannot do a particular question, leave it and go on to the next. You can return to it later.

All answers must be written on the Answer Sheet.

Do not remove this booklet from the examination room.

INFORMATION FOR CANDIDATES

There are **40** questions on this question paper.

The test is divided as follows:

Reading Passage 1 Questions 1–14
Reading Passage 2 Questions 15–27
Reading Passage 3 Questions 28–40

READING PASSAGE 1

*You should spend about 20 minutes on **Questions 1–14**, which are based on Reading Passage 1 below.*

The Value of a College Degree

The escalating cost of higher education is causing many to question the value of continuing education beyond high school. Many wonder whether the high cost of tuition, the opportunity cost of choosing college over full-time employment, and the accumulation of thousands of dollars of debt is, in the long run, worth the investment. The risk is especially large for low-income families who have a difficult time making ends meet without the additional burden of college tuition and fees.

In order to determine whether higher education is worth the investment, it is useful to examine what is known about the value of higher education and the rates of return on investment to both the individual and to society.

THE ECONOMIC VALUE OF HIGHER EDUCATION

There is considerable support for the notion that the rate of return on investment in higher education is high enough to warrant the financial burden associated with pursuing a college degree. Though the earnings differential between college and high school graduates varies over time, college graduates, on average, earn more than high school graduates. According to the Census Bureau, over an adult's working life, high school graduates earn an average of $1.2 million; associate's degree holders earn about $1.6 million; and bachelor's degree holders earn about $2.1 million (Day and Newburger, 2002).

These sizeable differences in lifetime earnings put the costs of college study in realistic perspective. Most students today—about 80 percent of all students—enroll either in public four-year colleges or in public two-year colleges. According to the U.S. Department of Education report, Think College Early, a full-time student at a public four-year college pays an average of $8,655 for in-state tuition, room, and board (U.S. Department of Education, 2002). A full-time student in a public two-year college pays an average of $1,359 per year in tuition (U.S. Department of Education, 2002).

These statistics support the contention that, though the cost of higher education is significant, given the earnings disparity that exists between those who earn a bachelor's degree and those who do not, the individual rate of return on investment in higher education is sufficiently high to warrant the cost.

OTHER BENEFITS OF HIGHER EDUCATION

College graduates also enjoy benefits beyond increased income. A 1998 report published by the Institute for Higher Education Policy reviews the individual benefits that college graduates enjoy, including higher levels of saving, increased personal/professional mobility, improved quality of life for their offspring, better consumer decision making, and more hobbies and leisure activities (Institute for Higher Education Policy, 1998). According to a report published by the Carnegie Foundation, nonmonetary individual benefits of higher education include the tendency for postsecondary students to become more open-minded, more cultured, more rational, more consistent, and less authoritarian; these benefits are also passed along to succeeding generations (Rowley and Hurtado, 2002). Additionally, college attendance has been shown to "decrease prejudice, enhance knowledge of world affairs and enhance social status" while increasing economic and job security for those who earn bachelor's degrees (Ibid.).

Research has also consistently shown a positive correlation between completion of higher education and good health, not only for oneself, but also for one's children. In fact, "parental schooling levels (after controlling for differences in earnings) are positively correlated with the health status of their children" and "increased schooling (and higher relative income) are correlated with lower mortality rates for given age brackets" (Cohn and Geske, 1992).

THE SOCIAL VALUE OF HIGHER EDUCATION

A number of studies have shown a high correlation between higher education and cultural and family values, and economic growth. According to Elchanan Cohn and Terry Geske (1992), there is the tendency for more highly educated women to spend more time with their children; these women tend to use this time to better prepare their children for the future. Cohn and Geske (1992) report that "college graduates appear to have a more optimistic view of their past and future personal progress."

Public benefits of attending college include increased tax revenues, greater workplace productivity, increased consumption, increased workforce flexibility, and decreased reliance on government financial support (Institute for Higher Education Policy, 1998). . . .

CONCLUSION

While it is clear that investment in a college degree, especially for those students in the lowest income brackets, is a financial burden, the long-term benefits to individuals as well as to society at large, appear to far outweigh the costs.

Questions 1–4

Do the following statements agree with the information in Reading Passage 1?

In boxes 1–4 on your Answer Sheet, write

TRUE	*if the statement is true according to the passage.*
FALSE	*if the statement contradicts the passage.*
NOT GIVEN	*if there is no information about this in the passage.*

1   The cost of a college education has remained steady for several years.

2   Some people have to borrow large amounts of money to pay for college.

3   About 80 percent of college students study at public colleges.

4   Public colleges cost less than private colleges.

Questions 5–9

Complete the fact sheet below.

*Choose **no more than three words** from the passage for each answer.*

Write your answers in boxes 5–9 on your Answer Sheet.

Financial Costs and Benefits of Higher Education

— The average high school graduate makes a little more than one million dollars in **5** ....

— The average person with an associate's degree earns **6** ....

— The average **7**................. makes over two million dollars.

— The average student at a four year college spends **8** $............... a year on classes, housing, and food.

— The average student at a two-year college spends $1,359 on **9** ....

Questions 10–13

The list below shows some benefits which college graduates may enjoy more of as compared to noncollege graduates.

Which four of these benefits are mentioned in the article?

*Write the appropriate letters **A–G** in boxes 10–13 on your Answer Sheet.*

A   They own bigger houses.

B   They are more optimistic about their lives.

C   They save more money.

D   They enjoy more recreational activities.

E   They have healthier children.

F   They travel more frequently.

G   They make more purchases.

READING PASSAGE 2

*You should spend about 20 minutes on **Questions 14–26,** which are based on Reading Passage 2.*

Less Television, Less Violence and Aggression

Cutting back on television, videos, and video games reduces acts of aggression among schoolchildren, according to a study by Dr. Thomas Robinson and others from the Stanford University School of Medicine.

The study, published in the January 2001 issue of the *Archives of Pediatric and Adolescent Medicine*, found that third- and fourth-grade students who took part in a curriculum to reduce their TV, video, and video game use engaged in fewer acts of verbal and physical aggression than their peers.

The study took place in two similar San Jose, California, elementary schools. Students in one school underwent an 18-lesson, 6-month program designed to limit their media usage, while the others did not.

Both groups of students had similar reports of aggressive behavior at the beginning of the study. After the six-month program, however, the two groups had very real differences.

The students who cut back on their TV time engaged in six fewer acts of verbal aggression per hour and rated 2.4 percent fewer of their classmates as aggressive after the program.

Physical acts of violence, parental reports of aggressive behavior, and perceptions of a mean and scary world also decreased, but the authors suggest further study to solidify these results.

Although many studies have shown that children who watch a lot of TV are more likely to act violently, this report further verifies that television, videos, and video games actually cause the violent behavior, and it is among the first to evaluate a solution to the problem.

Teachers at the intervention school included the program in their existing curriculum. Early lessons encouraged students to keep track of and report on the time they spent watching TV or videos, or playing video games, to motivate them to limit those activities on their own.

The initial lessons were followed by TV-Turnoff, an organization that encourages less TV viewing. For ten days, students were challenged to go without television, videos, or video games. After that, teachers encouraged the students to stay within a media allowance of seven hours per week. Almost all students participated in the Turnoff, and most stayed under their budget for the following weeks.

Additional lessons encouraged children to use their time more selectively, and many of the final lessons had students themselves advocate reducing screen activities.

This study is by no means the first to find a link between television and violence. Virtually all of 3,500 research studies on the subject in the past 40 years have shown the same relationship, according to the American Academy of Pediatrics.

Among the most noteworthy studies is Dr. Leonard D. Eron's, which found that exposure to television violence in childhood is the strongest predictor of aggressive behavior later in life—stronger even than violent behavior as children.

The more violent television the subjects watched at age eight, the more serious was their aggressive behavior even 22 years later.

Another study by Dr. Brandon S. Centerwall found that murder rates climb after the introduction of television. In the United States and Canada, murder rates doubled 10 to 15 years after the introduction of television, after the first TV generation grew up.

Centerwall tested this pattern in South Africa, where television broadcasts were banned until 1975.

Murder rates in South Africa remained relatively steady from the mid-1940s through the mid-1970s. By 1987, however, the murder rate had increased 130 percent from its 1974 level. The murder rates in the United States and Canada had leveled[1] off in the meantime.

Centerwall's study implies that the medium of television, not just the content, promotes violence, and the current study by Dr. Robinson supports that conclusion.

The Turnoff did not specifically target violent television, nor did the following allowance period. Reducing television in general reduces aggressive behavior.

Even television that is not "violent" is more violent than real life and may lead viewers to believe that violence is funny, inconsequential, and a viable solution to problems. Also, watching television of any content robs us of the time to interact with real people.

Watching too much TV may inhibit the skills and patience we need to get along with others without resorting to aggression. TV, as a medium, promotes aggression and violence. The best solution is to turn it off.

Questions 14–20

Complete the summary using words from the box below.

Write your answers in boxes 14–20 on your Answer Sheet.

A study that was published in January 2001 found that when children **14**........... less, they behaved less **15**........... . Students in a California elementary school participated in the study, which lasted **16**........... . By the end of the study, the children's behavior had changed. For example, the children's **17**........... reported that the children were acting less violently than before. During the study, the children kept a record of the **18**........... they watched TV. Then, for ten days, they **19**........... . Near the end of the study, the students began to suggest watching **20**........... .

parents	eighteen days
teachers	classmates
six months	nonviolent programs
violently	time of day
watched TV	number of hours
scared	avoided TV
less TV	favorite[2] programs

[1]BRITISH: levelled

[2]BRITISH: favourite

Questions 21–24

Do the following statements agree with the information in Reading Passage 2?

In boxes 21–24 write

> **TRUE**   *if the statement is true according to the passage.*
> **FALSE**   *if the statement contradicts the passage.*
> **NOT GIVEN**   *if there is no information about this in the passage.*

21 Only one study has found a connection between TV and violent behavior.

22 There were more murders in Canada after people began watching TV.

23 The United States has more violence on TV than other countries.

24 TV was introduced in South Africa in the 1940s.

Questions 25 and 26

*For each question, choose the correct letter **A–D** and write it in boxes 25 and 26 on your Answer Sheet.*

25 According to the passage,
    A   only children are affected by violence on TV.
    B   only violent TV programs cause violent behavior.
    C   children who watch too much TV get poor grades in school.
    D   watching a lot of TV may keep us from learning important social skills.

26 The authors of this passage believe that
    A   some violent TV programs are funny.
    B   the best plan is to stop watching TV completely.
    C   it's better to watch TV with other people than on your own.
    D   seven hours a week of TV watching is acceptable.

READING PASSAGE 3

*You should spend about 20 minutes on **Questions 27–40**, which are based on Reading Passage 3 below.*

Questions 27–30

*Reading Passage 3 has four sections (**A–D**). Choose the most suitable heading for each section from the list of headings below.*

*Write the appropriate numbers (**i–vii**) in boxes 27–30 on your Answer Sheet. There are more headings than sections, so you will not use all of them.*

	List of Headings
27 Section A	**i** Top Ocean Predators
	ii Toxic Exposure
28 Section B	**iii** Declining Fish Populations
	iv Pleasure Boating in the San Juan Islands
29 Section C	**v** Underwater Noise
	vi Smog in Large Cities
30 Section D	**vii** Impact of Boat Traffic

Issues Affecting the Southern Resident Orcas

A

Orcas, also known as killer whales, are opportunistic feeders, which means they will take a variety of different prey species. J, K, and L pods (specific groups of orcas found in the region) are almost exclusively fish eaters. Some studies show that up to 90 percent of their diet is salmon, with chinook salmon being far and away their favorite. During the last 50 years, hundreds of wild runs of salmon have become extinct due to habitat loss and overfishing of wild stocks. Many of the extinct salmon stocks are the winter runs of chinook and coho. Although the surviving stocks have probably been sufficient to sustain the resident pods, many of the runs that have been lost were undoubtedly traditional resources favored by the resident orcas. This may be affecting the whales' nutrition in the winter and may require them to change their patterns of movement in order to search for food.

Other studies with tagged whales have shown that they regularly dive up to 800 feet in this area. Researchers tend to think that during these deep dives the whales may be feeding on bottomfish. Bottomfish species in this area would include halibut, rockfish, lingcod, and greenling. Scientists estimate that today's lingcod population in northern Puget Sound and the Strait of Georgia is only 2 percent of what it was in 1950. The average size of rockfish in the recreational catch has also declined by several inches since the 1970s, which is indicative of overfishing. In some locations, certain rockfish species have disappeared entirely. So even if bottomfish are not a major food resource for the whales, the present low numbers of available fish increases the pressure on orcas and all marine animals to find food. (For more information on bottomfish see the San Juan County Bottomfish Recovery Program.)

B

Toxic substances accumulate in higher concentrations as they move up the food chain. Because orcas are the top predator in the ocean and are at the top of several different food chains in the environment, they tend to be more affected by pollutants than other sea creatures. Examinations of stranded killer whales have shown some extremely high levels of lead, mercury, and polychlorinated hydrocarbons. Abandoned marine toxic waste dumps and present levels of industrial and human refuse pollution of the inland waters probably presents the most serious threat to the continued existence of this orca population. Unfortunately, the total remedy to this huge problem would be broad societal changes on many fronts. But because of the fact that orcas are so popular, they may be the best species to use as a focal point in bringing about the many changes that need to be made in order to protect the marine environment as a whole from further toxic poisoning.

C

The waters around the San Juan Islands are extremely busy due to international commercial shipping, fishing, whale watching, and pleasure boating. On a busy weekend day in the summer, it is not uncommon to see numerous boats in the vicinity of the whales as they travel through the area. The potential impacts from all this vessel traffic with regard to the whales and other marine animals in the area could be tremendous.

The surfacing and breathing space of marine birds and mammals is a critical aspect of their habitat, which the animals must consciously deal with on a moment-to-moment basis throughout their lifetimes. With all the boating activity in the vicinity, there are three ways in which surface impacts are most likely to affect marine animals: (a) collision, (b) collision avoidance, and (c) exhaust emissions in breathing pockets.

The first two impacts are very obvious and don't just apply to vessels with motors. Kayakers even present a problem here because they're so quiet. Marine animals, busy hunting and feeding under the surface of the water, may not be aware that there is a kayak above them and actually hit the bottom of it as they surface to breathe.

The third impact is one most people don't even think of. When there are numerous boats in the area, especially idling boats, there are a lot of exhaust fumes being spewed out on the surface of the water. When the whale comes up to take a nice big breath of "fresh" air, it instead gets a nice big breath of exhaust fumes. It's hard to say how greatly this affects the animals, but think how breathing polluted air affects us (i.e., smog in large cities like Los Angeles, breathing the foul air while sitting in traffic jams, etc.).

D

Similar to surface impacts, a primary source of acoustic pollution for this population of orcas would also be derived from the cumulative underwater noise of vessel traffic. For cetaceans, the underwater sound environment is perhaps the most critical component of their sensory and behavioral lives. Orcas communicate with each other over short and long distances with a variety of clicks, chirps, squeaks, and whistles, along with using echolocation to locate prey and to navigate. They may also rely on passive listening as a primary sensory source. The long-term impacts from noise pollution would not likely show up as noticeable behavioral changes in habitat use, but rather as sensory damage or gradual reduction in population health. A new study at The Whale Museum called the SeaSound Remote Sensing Network has begun studying underwater acoustics and its relationship to orca communication.

Questions 31–32

For each question, choose the appropriate letter **A–D** and write it in boxes 31 and 32 on your Answer Sheet.

31 Killer whales (orcas) in the J, K, and L pods prefer to eat

   A   halibut.
   B   a type of salmon.
   C   a variety of animals.
   D   fish living at the bottom of the sea.

32 Some groups of salmon have become extinct because

   A   they have lost places to live.
   B   whales have eaten them.
   C   they don't get good nutrition.
   D   the winters in the area are too cold.

Questions 33–40

Complete the chart below.

Choose NO MORE THAN THREE WORDS for each answer.

Write your answers in boxes 33–40 on your Answer Sheet.

Cause	Effect
Scientists believe some whales feed **33**	These whales dive very deep.
Scientists believe that the area is being over fished.	Rockfish caught today is **34** .... than rockfish caught in the past.
Orcas are at the top of the ocean food chain.	**35** .... affects orcas more than it does other sea animals.
Orcas are a **36** .... species.	We can use orcas to make society aware of the problem of marine pollution.
People enjoy boating, fishing, and whale watching in the San Juan Islands.	On weekends there are **37** .... near the whales.
Kayaks are **38**	Marine animals hit them when they come up for air.
A lot of boats keep their motors running.	Whales breathe **39** ....
Boats are noisy.	Whales have difficulty **40** ....

Model Test 1

Candidate Name _____

INTERNATIONAL ENGLISH LANGUAGE TESTING SYSTEM

ACADEMIC WRITING

TIME 1 hour

INSTRUCTIONS TO CANDIDATES

Do not open this booklet until you are told to do so.

Write your name and candidate number in the space at the top of this page.

All answers must be written on the separate answer booklet provided.

Do not remove this booklet from the examination room.

INFORMATION FOR CANDIDATES

There are **2** tasks on this question paper.

You must do **both** tasks.

Underlength answers will be penalized.

WRITING TASK 1

You should spend about 20 minutes on this task.

The table below shows the sales at a small restaurant in a downtown business district.

Summarize the information by selecting and reporting the main features, and make comparisons where relevant.

Write at least 150 words.

Sales: week of October 7–13

	Mon.	Tues.	Wed.	Thurs.	Fri.	Sat.	Sun.
Lunch	$2,400	$2,450	$2,595	$2,375	$2,500	$1,950	$1,550
Dinner	$3,623	$3,850	$3,445	$3,800	$4,350	$2,900	$2,450

WRITING TASK 2

You should spend about 40 minutes on this task.

Write about the following topic:

As the world becomes technologically advanced, computers are replacing more and more jobs.

Describe some job positions that may be lost because of computers, and discuss at least one problem that may result.

Give reasons for your answer and include any relevant examples from your own knowledge or experience.

Write at least 250 words.

SPEAKING

Examiner questions:

Part 1

Tell about a sport that is interesting to you. What is it? Do you like to play this sport yourself? Do you
  follow professional teams?

Why do you like this sport?

Do you enjoy playing sports or doing other outdoor activities? Why or why not?

In your city or town, what kinds of places are available for sports and other outdoor activities?

What kinds of things do you enjoy doing on weekends?

Do you generally prefer to spend a day off from work or school at home, or do you like to go out to other
  places? Why?

Who do you like to spend time with on your days off?

Part 2

Describe a relative who you are like.

  You should say:
    who the relative is and how close you are to them
    what makes you and your relative alike
    why you think you and your relative have these shared qualities

You will have one to two minutes to talk about this topic.
You will have one minute to prepare what you are going to say.

Part 3

Do you enjoy spending time with relatives? Why or why not?

What types of traditions do you and your relatives have?

Do you think family members are more important than friends?

Do you think that having a good relationship with relatives is important to most people?

How do family members help each other?

Do you agree or disagree: families are not as important as they used to be.

How are families now different from families in the past?

How do you think families will change in the future?

ACADEMIC
MODEL TEST 2

Model Test 2

Candidate Name _____

INTERNATIONAL ENGLISH LANGUAGE TESTING SYSTEM

LISTENING

TIME Approx. 30 minutes

INSTRUCTIONS TO CANDIDATES

Do not open this booklet until you are told to do so.

Write your name and candidate number in the space at the top of this page.

You should answer all questions.

All the recordings will be played ONCE only.

Write all your answers on the Question Paper.

At the end of the test you will be given ten minutes to transfer your answers to an Answer Sheet.

Do not remove this booklet from the examination room.

INFORMATION FOR CANDIDATES

There are **40** questions on this question paper.

The test is divided as follows:

Section 1	Questions 1–10
Section 2	Questions 11–20
Section 3	Questions 21–30
Section 4	Questions 31–40

SECTION 1   QUESTIONS *1–10*

Questions 1–7

*Choose the correct letters, **A, B,** or **C.***

EXAMPLE

What is the man doing?
A   Shopping at the mall[1]
B   Asking shoppers questions
C   Looking for a certain shop

1   The interviewer wants to find out about
A   when the mall is open.
B   people's shopping habits.
C   the best stores[1] in the shopping center[2].

2   The interviewer wants to speak with
A   married women.
B   any shopper.
C   children.

3   What is the respondent's age?
A   18–25
B   26–35
C   36–45

4   How often does the respondent shop at the mall?
A   Less than once a month
B   Once a week
C   Two or more times a week

5   What does the respondent usually shop for?
A   Clothes
B   Books
C   Groceries

6   How much time does the respondent usually spend at the mall?
A   One hour or less
B   Between one and two hours
C   More than two hours

7   What method of transportation does the respondent use to get to the mall?
A   Car
B   Bus
C   Subway

[1]BRITISH: shops, shoppes
[2]BRITISH: shopping centre

Questions 8–10

Write NO MORE THAN THREE WORDS *for each answer.*

8 Why does the respondent like the shoe store?

_____

9 Why doesn't the respondent like the food court?

_____

10 What improvement does the respondent suggest?

_____

SECTION 2 QUESTIONS 11–20

Question 11

Choose the correct letter, **A, B, or C.**

11 The tour of the health club is for
   A people who want to become members of the club
   B people who are already members of the club
   C people who work at the club

Questions 12–14

Choose THREE letters, **A–F.**

What are three things that members can do at the club?
   A Learn to play tennis
   B Buy exercise equipment
   C Consult a nutrition expert
   D Exercise on a machine
   E Run on a track
   F Try out for the swim team

Questions 15–17

Choose THREE letters, **A–F**

What three things should club members bring with them to the locker room?
   A Towels
   B Soap
   C Shampoo
   D Hair dryers
   E Rubber sandals
   F Locks

Questions 18–20

Complete the notice below.

Write NO MORE THAN THREE WORDS for each answer.

Swimming Pool Rules

— Children must be accompanied **18**_____.

— No **19** _____ near the pool.

— Please **20** _____ before entering the pool.

SECTION 3 QUESTIONS 21–30

Questions 21–22

Write NO MORE THAN THREE WORDS for each answer.

21 How often will the students have to write essays?

_____

22 What should be the word length of each essay?

_____

Questions 23–26

Complete the chart below.

Write NO MORE THAN THREE WORDS for each answer.

Essay Type	Sample Topic
23 _____	How to change the oil in a car
24 _____	Three kinds of friends
25 _____	Student cafeteria food and restaurant food
Argumentative	The necessity of **26** _____

Questions 27–30

Choose the correct letters, **A, B,** or **C.**

27 How will the students get their essay topics?
   A The professor will assign them.
   B Students will choose them.
   C They will come from books.

28 When are the essays due?
   A Every Monday
   B Every Wednesday
   C Every Friday

29 The essays count for _____ percent of the final grade[1].

   A 15

   B 20

   C 65

30 The professor wants the students to

   A type their essays on a computer.

   B write their essays by hand.

   C photocopy their essays.

SECTION 4 QUESTIONS 31–40

CD2 TRACK 7

Questions 31–32

Answer the questions.

Write NO MORE THAN THREE WORDS for each answer.

31 What is the name of the class? _____

32 What day does the class meet? _____

Questions 33–36

Complete the notes below.

Write NO MORE THAN THREE WORDS for each answer.

In hunter-gatherer societies, gathering is done by **33** _____.

All humans lived in hunter-gatherer societies until **34** _____ ago.

Today we can find hunter-gatherer societies in the Arctic, **35** _____, and

36 _____.

CD2 TRACK 8

Questions 37–40

The following are characteristics of which types of society?

Check column A if it is a characteristic of hunter-gatherer societies.
Check column B if it is a characteristic of farming societies.

Characteristic	A	B
37 They usually stay in one place.		
38 They are nomadic.		
39 They have a higher population density.		
40 They have a nonhierarchical social structure.		

[1]BRITISH: mark

Model Test 2

Candidate Name _____

INTERNATIONAL ENGLISH LANGUAGE TESTING SYSTEM

ACADEMIC READING

TIME 1 hour

INSTRUCTIONS TO CANDIDATES

Do not open this booklet until you are told to do so.

Write your name and candidate number in the space at the top of this page.

Start at the beginning of the test and work through it.

You should answer all questions.

If you cannot do a particular question, leave it and go on to the next. You can return to it later.

All answers must be written on the Answer Sheet.

Do not remove this booklet from the examination room.

INFORMATION FOR CANDIDATES

There are **40** questions on this question paper.

The test is divided as follows:

READING PASSAGE 1

You should spend about 20 minutes on Questions 1–15, which are based on Passage 1 below.

Questions 1–5

*Reading Passage 1 has five paragraphs, **A–E**. Choose the most suitable heading for each paragraph from the list of headings below. Write the appropriate numbers **(i–viii)** on your Answer Sheet. There are more headings than paragraphs, so you will not use them all.*

		List of Headings
1	Paragraph A	i Glacial Continents
2	Paragraph B	ii Formation and Growth of Glaciers
3	Paragraph C	iii Glacial Movement
4	Paragraph D	iv Glaciers in the Last Ice Age
5	Paragraph E	v Glaciers Through the Years
		vi Types of Glaciers
		vii Glacial Effects on Landscape
		viii Glaciers in National Parks

Glaciers

A

Besides the earth's oceans, glacier ice is the largest source of water on earth. A glacier is a massive stream or sheet of ice that moves underneath itself under the influence of gravity. Some glaciers travel down mountains or valleys, while others spread across a large expanse of land. Heavily glaciated regions such as Greenland and Antarctica are called *continental glaciers.* These two ice sheets encompass more than 95 percent of the earth's glacial ice. The Greenland ice sheet is almost 10,000 feet thick in some areas, and the weight of this glacier is so heavy that much of the region has been depressed below sea level. Smaller glaciers that occur at higher elevations are called *alpine* or *valley glaciers.* Another way of classifying glaciers is in terms of their internal temperature. In *temperate glaciers*, the ice within the glacier is near its melting point. *Polar glaciers*, in contrast, always maintain temperatures far below melting.

B

The majority of the earth's glaciers are located near the poles, though glaciers exist on all continents, including Africa and Oceania. The reason glaciers are generally formed in high alpine regions is that they require cold temperatures throughout the year. In these areas where there is little opportunity for summer *ablation* (loss of mass), snow changes to compacted *firn* and then crystallized ice. During periods in which melting and evaporation exceed the amount of snowfall, glaciers will retreat rather than progress. While glaciers rely heavily on snowfall, other climactic conditions including freezing rain, avalanches, and wind, contribute to their growth. One year of below average precipitation can stunt the growth of a glacier tremendously. With the rare exception of *surging glaciers*, a common glacier flows about 10 inches per day in the summer and 5 inches per day in the winter. The fastest glacial surge on record occurred in 1953, when the Kutiah Glacier in Pakistan grew more than 12 kilometers in three months.

C

The weight and pressure of ice accumulation causes glacier movement. Glaciers move out from under themselves, via *plastic deformation* and *basal slippage*. First, the internal flow of ice crystals begins to spread outward and downward from the thickened snow pack also known as the *zone of accumulation*. Next, the ice along the ground surface begins to slip in the same direction. Seasonal thawing at the base of the glacier helps to facilitate this slippage. The middle of a glacier moves faster than the sides and bottom because there is no rock to cause friction. The upper part of a glacier rides on the ice below. As a glacier moves it carves out a U-shaped valley similar to a riverbed, but with much steeper walls and a flatter bottom.

D

Besides the extraordinary rivers of ice, glacial erosion creates other unique physical features in the landscape such as horns, fjords, hanging valleys, and cirques. Most of these landforms do not become visible until after a glacier has receded. Many are created by moraines, which occur at the sides and front of a glacier. Moraines are formed when material is picked up along the way and deposited in a new location. When many alpine glaciers occur on the same mountain, these moraines can create a *horn*. The Matterhorn, in the Swiss Alps is one of the most famous horns. *Fjords*, which are very common in Norway, are coastal valleys that fill with ocean water during a glacial retreat. *Hanging valleys* occur when two or more glacial valleys intersect at varying elevations. It is common for waterfalls to connect the higher and lower hanging valleys, such as in Yosemite National Park. A *cirque* is a large bowl-shaped valley that forms at the front of a glacier. Cirques often have a lip on their down slope that is deep enough to hold small lakes when the ice melts away.

E

Glacier movement and shape shifting typically occur over hundreds of years. While presently about 10 percent of the earth's land is covered with glaciers, it is believed that during the last Ice Age glaciers covered approximately 32 percent of the earth's surface. In the past century, most glaciers have been retreating rather than flowing forward. It is unknown whether this glacial activity is due to human impact or natural causes, but by studying glacier movement, and comparing climate and agricultural profiles over hundreds of years, glaciologists can begin to understand environmental issues such as global warming.

Questions 6–10

Do the following statements agree with the information in Passage 1? In boxes 6–10 on your Answer Sheet, write

TRUE	if the statement is true according to the passage.
FALSE	if the statement contradicts the passage.
NOT GIVEN	if there is no information about this in the passage.

6 Glaciers exist only near the north and south poles.

7 Glaciers are formed by a combination of snow and other weather conditions.

8 Glaciers normally move at a rate of about 5 to 10 inches a day.

9 All parts of the glacier move at the same speed.

10 During the last Ice Age, average temperatures were much lower than they are now.

Questions 11–15

Match each definition below with the term it defines.

*Write the letter of the term, **A–H**, on your Answer Sheet. There are more terms than definitions, so you will not use them all.*

11 a glacier formed on a mountain

12 a glacier with temperatures well below freezing

13 a glacier that moves very quickly

14 a glacial valley formed near the ocean

15 a glacial valley that looks like a bowl

Terms
A   fjord
B   alpine glacier
C   horn
D   polar glacier
E   temperate glacier
F   hanging valley
G   cirque
H   surging glacier

READING PASSAGE 2

You should spend about 20 minutes on Questions 16–28, which are based on Passage 2 below.

Irish Potato Famine

A

In the ten years following the Irish potato famine of 1845, over 750,000 Irish people died, including many of those who attempted to immigrate to countries such as the United States and Canada. Prior to the potato blight, one of the main concerns in Ireland was overpopulation. In the early 1500s, the country's population was estimated at less than three million, but by 1840 this number had nearly tripled. The bountiful potato crop, which contains almost all of the nutrients that a person needs for survival, was largely to blame for the population growth. However, within five years of the failed crop of 1845, the population of Ireland was reduced by a quarter. A number of factors contributed to the plummet of the Irish population, namely the Irish dependency on the potato crop, the British tenure system, and the inadequate relief efforts of the English.

B

It is not known exactly how or when the potato was first introduced to Europe; however, the general assumption is that it arrived on a Spanish ship sometime in the 1600s. For more than one hundred years, Europeans believed that potatoes belonged to a botanical family of a poisonous breed. It was not until Marie Antoinette wore potato blossoms in her hair in the mid-eighteenth century that potatoes became a novelty. By the late 1700s, the dietary value of the potato had been discovered, and the monarchs of Europe ordered the vegetable to be widely planted.

C

By 1800, the vast majority of the Irish population had become dependent on the potato as its primary staple. It wasn't uncommon for an Irish potato farmer to consume more than six pounds of potatoes a day. Families stored potatoes for the winter and even fed potatoes to their livestock. Because of this dependency, the unexpected potato blight of 1845 devastated the Irish. Investigators at first suggested that the blight was caused by static energy, smoke from railroad trains, or vapors from underground volcanoes; however, the root cause was later discovered as an airborne fungus that traveled from Mexico. Not only did the disease destroy the potato crops, it also infected all of the potatoes in storage at the time. Their families were dying from famine, but weakened farmers had retained little of their agricultural skills to harvest other crops. Those who did manage to grow things such as oats, wheat, and barley relied on earnings from these exported crops to keep their rented homes.

D

While the potato blight generated mass starvation among the Irish, the people were held captive to their poverty by the British tenure system. Following the Napoleonic Wars of 1815, the English had turned their focus to their colonial land holdings. British landowners realized that the best way to profit from these holdings was to extract the resources and exports and charge expensive rents and taxes for people to live on the land. Under the tenure system, Protestant landlords owned 95 percent of the Irish land, which was divided up into five-acre plots for the people to live and farm on. As the population of Ireland grew, however, the plots were continuously subdivided into smaller parcels. Living conditions declined dramatically, and families were forced to move to less fertile land where almost nothing but the potato would grow.

E

During this same period of colonization, the Penal Laws were also instituted as a means of weakening the Irish spirit. Under the Penal Laws, Irish peasants were denied basic human rights, such as the right to speak their own native language, seek certain kinds of employment, practice their faith, receive education, and own land. Despite the famine that was devastating Ireland, the landlords had little compassion or sympathy for tenants unable to pay their rent. Approximately 500,000 Irish tenants were evicted by their landlords between 1845 and 1847. Many of these people also had their homes burned down and were put in jail for overdue rent.

F

The majority of the British officials in the 1840s adopted the laissez-faire philosophy, which supported a policy of nonintervention in the Irish plight. Prime Minister Sir Robert Peel was an exception. He showed compassion toward the Irish by making a move to repeal the Corn Laws, which had been put in place to protect British grain producers from the competition of foreign markets. For this hasty decision, Peel quickly lost the support of the British people and was forced to resign. The new Prime Minister, Lord John Russell, allowed assistant Charles Trevelyan to take complete control over all of the relief efforts in Ireland. Trevelyan believed that the Irish situation should be left to Providence. Claiming that it would be dangerous to let the Irish become dependent on other countries, he even took steps to close food depots that were selling corn and to redirect shipments of corn that were already on their way to Ireland. A few relief programs were eventually implemented, such as soup kitchens and workhouses; however, these were poorly run institutions that facilitated the spread of disease, tore apart families, and offered inadequate food supplies considering the extent of Ireland's shortages.

G
Many of the effects of the Irish potato famine are still evident today. Descendants of those who fled Ireland during the 1840s are dispersed all over the world. Some of the homes that were evacuated by absentee landlords still sit abandoned in the Irish hills. A number of Irish descendents still carry animosity toward the British for not putting people before politics. The potato blight itself still plagues the Irish people during certain growing seasons when weather conditions are favorable for the fungus to thrive.

Questions 16–20

*The passage has seven paragraphs, **A–G**.*

Which paragraph contains the following information?

Write the correct letter in boxes 16–20 on your Answer Sheet.

16 the position of the British government towards the potato famine

17 a description of the system of land ownership in Ireland

18 early European attitudes toward the potato

19 explanation of the lack of legal protection for Irish peasants

20 the importance of the potato in Irish society

Questions 21–28

*Complete each sentence with the correct ending, **A–L** from the box at the top of the next page.*

Write the correct letter in boxes 21–28 on your Answer Sheet. There are more endings than sentences, so you won't use them all.

21 At first Europeans didn't eat potatoes

22 European monarchs encouraged potato growing

23 The potato blight was devastating to the Irish

24 Farmers who grew oats, wheat, and barley didn't eat these crops

25 Many Irish farmers lived on infertile plots

26 Many Irish farmers were arrested

27 Sir Robert Peel lost his position as prime minister

28 Soup kitchens and workhouses didn't relieve the suffering

Sentence Endings

A   because they couldn't pay the rent on their farms.

B   because railroad trains caused air pollution.

C   because potatoes were their main source of food.

D   because Charles Trevelyan took over relief efforts.

E   because they needed the profits to pay the rent.

F   because they weren't well-managed.

G   because there wasn't enough land for the increasing population.

H   because his efforts to help the Irish were unpopular among the British.

I   because they believed that potatoes were poisonous.

J   because the British instituted penal laws.

K   because it was discovered that potatoes are full of nutrients.

L   because Marie Antoinette used potato blossoms as decoration.

READING PASSAGE 3

You should spend about 20 minutes on Questions 29–40, which are based on Reading Passage 3.

Anesthesiology

Since the beginning of time, man has sought natural remedies for pain. Between 40 and 60 A.D., Greek physician, Dioscorides traveled with the Roman armies, studying the medicinal properties of plants and minerals. His book, *De materia medica*, written in five volumes and translated into at least seven languages, was the primary reference source for physicians for over sixteen centuries. The field of anesthesiology[1], which was once nothing more than a list of medicinal plants and makeshift remedies, has grown into one of the most important fields in medicine.

Many of the early pain relievers were based on myth and did little to relieve the suffering of an ill or injured person. The mandragora (now known as the mandrake plant) was one of the first plants to be used as an anesthetic[1]. Due to the apparent screaming that the plant made as it was pulled from the ground, people in the Middle Ages believed that the person who removed the mandrake from the earth would either die or go insane. This superstition may have resulted because the split root of the mandrake resembled the human form. In order to pull the root from the ground, the plant collector would loosen it and tie the stem to an animal. It was believed that the safest time to uproot a mandrake was in the moonlight, and the best animal to use was a black dog. In his manual, Dioscorides suggested boiling the root with wine and having a man drink the potion to remove sensation before cutting his flesh or burning his skin. Opium and Indian hemp were later used to induce sleep before a painful procedure or to relieve the pain of an illness. Other remedies such as cocaine did more harm to the patient than good as people died from their addictions. President Ulysses S. Grant became addicted to cocaine before he died of throat cancer in 1885.

[1]BRITISH: anaesthesiology/an anesthetic

The modern field of anesthetics dates to the incident when nitrous oxide (more commonly known as laughing gas) was accidentally discovered. Humphrey Davy, the inventor of the miner's lamp, discovered that inhaling the toxic compound caused a strange euphoria, followed by fits of laughter, tears, and sometimes unconsciousness. U.S. dentist, Horace Wells, was the first on record to experiment with laughing gas, which he used in 1844 to relieve pain during a tooth extraction. Two years later, Dr. William Morton created the first anesthetic machine. This apparatus was a simple glass globe containing an ether-soaked sponge. Morton considered ether a good alternative to nitrous oxide because the numbing effect lasted considerably longer. His apparatus allowed the patient to inhale vapors[1] whenever the pain became unbearable. In 1846, during a trial experiment in Boston, a tumor[2] was successfully removed from a man's jaw area while he was anesthetized with Morton's machine.

The first use of anesthesia in the obstetric field occurred in Scotland by Dr. James Simpson. Instead of ether, which he considered irritating to the eyes, Simpson administered chloroform to reduce the pain of childbirth. Simpson sprinkled chloroform on a handkerchief and allowed laboring[3] women to inhale the fumes at their own discretion. In 1853, Queen Victoria agreed to use chloroform during the birth of her eighth child. Soon the use of chloroform during childbirth was both acceptable and fashionable. However, as chloroform became a more popular anesthetic, knowledge of its toxicity surfaced, and it was soon obsolete.

After World War II, numerous developments were made in the field of anesthetics. Surgical procedures that had been unthinkable were being performed with little or no pain felt by the patient. Rather than physicians or nurses who administered pain relief as part of their profession, anesthesiologists became specialists in suppressing consciousness and alleviating pain. Anesthesiologists today are classified as perioperative physicians, meaning they take care of a patient before, during, and after surgical procedures. It takes over eight years of schooling and four years of residency until an anesthesiologist is prepared to practice in the United States. These experts are trained to administer three different types of anesthetics: general, local, and regional. General anesthetic is used to put a patient into a temporary state of unconsciousness. Local anesthetic is used only at the affected site and causes a loss of sensation. Regional anesthetic is used to block the sensation and possibly the movement of a larger portion of the body. As well as controlling the levels of pain for the patient before and throughout an operation, anesthesiologists are responsible for monitoring and controlling the patient's vital functions during the procedure and assessing the medical needs in the post-operative room.

The number of anesthesiologists in the United States has more than doubled since the 1970s, as has the improvement and success of operative care. In addition, complications from anesthesiology have declined dramatically. Over 40 million anesthetics are administered in the United States each year, with only 1 in 250,000 causing death.

[1]BRITISH: vapours
[2]BRITISH: tumour
[3]BRITISH: labouring

Questions 29–34

Do the following statements agree with the information in Passage 3? In boxes 29–34 on your Answer Sheet, write

TRUE	*if the statement is true according to the passage.*
FALSE	*if the statement contradicts the passage.*
NOT GIVEN	*if there is no information about this in the passage.*

29 Dioscorides' book, *De materia medica*, fell out of use after 60 A.D.

30 Mandragora was used as an anesthetic during the Middle Ages.

31 Nitrous oxide can cause the user to both laugh and cry.

32 During the second half of the 19th century, most dentists used anesthesia.

33 Anesthesiologists in the United States are required to have 12 years of education and training.

34 There are fewer anesthesiologists in the United States now than in the past.

Questions 35–40

Match each fact about anesthesia with the type of anesthetic that it refers to. There are more types of anesthetics listed than facts, so you won't use them all. Write the correct letter, **A–H** in boxes 35–40 on your Answer Sheet.

35 used by sprinkling on a handkerchief

36 used on only one specific part of the body

37 used by boiling with wine

38 used first during a dental procedure

39 used to stop feeling over a larger area of the body

40 used in the first anesthetic machine

Types of Anesthetic	
A	general anesthetic
B	local anesthetic
C	regional anesthetic
D	chloroform
E	ether
F	nitrous oxide
G	opium
H	mandrake

Model Test 2

Candidate Name _____

INTERNATIONAL ENGLISH LANGUAGE TESTING SYSTEM

ACADEMIC WRITING

TIME 1 hour

INSTRUCTIONS TO CANDIDATES

Do not open this booklet until you are told to do so.

Write your name and candidate number in the space at the top of this page.

All answers must be written on the separate answer booklet provided.

Do not remove this booklet from the examination room.

INFORMATION FOR CANDIDATES

There are **2** tasks on this question paper.

You must do **both** tasks.

Underlength answers will be penalized.

WRITING TASK 1

You should spend no more than 20 minutes on this task.

The diagram below shows the steps in the process of manufacturing yogurt.

Summarize the information by selecting and reporting the main features, and make comparisons where relevant.

Write at least 150 words.

Manufacturing Yogurt

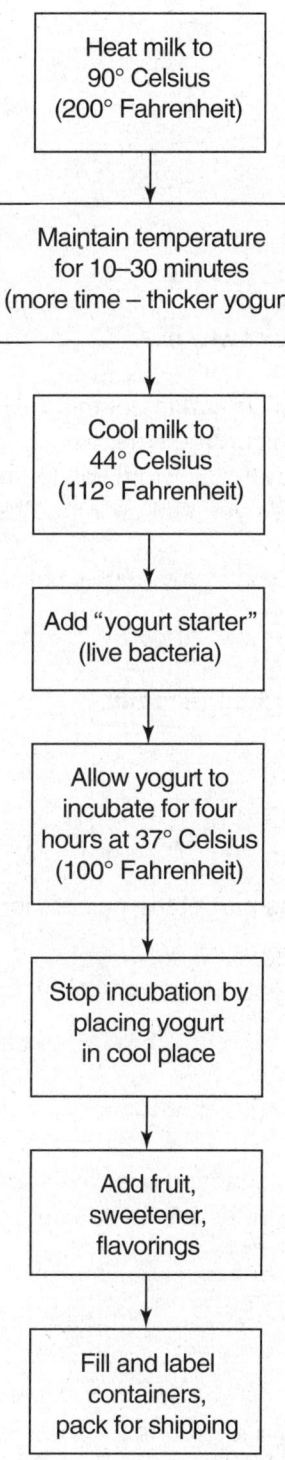

WRITING TASK 2

You should spend no more than 40 minutes on this task.

Write about the following topic:

> ***Families who do not send their children to government-financed schools should not be required to pay taxes that support universal education.***

To what extent do you agree or disagree with this statement? Give reasons for your answer, and include any relevant examples from your own knowledge or experience.

You should write at least 250 words.

SPEAKING

Examiner Questions:

Part 1

Do you have a job? Do you like it? Why or why not?

Why did you choose this job?

What kind of education or training did you need to get this job?

Describe an activity you enjoy doing in your free time.

How long have you been doing this activity? How did you learn it?

In your free time, do you prefer activities you can do with other people, or activities you can do alone? Why?

Is having a lot of free time important to you? Why or why not?

Part 2

Describe a holiday[1] that you have celebrated recently.

You should say:
    what the purpose of the holiday is
    who you celebrated with
    why this holiday is important to you

and describe some activities that you did as part of the celebration

You will have one to two minutes to talk about this topic.
You will have one minute to prepare what you are going to say.

Part 3

What are some important holidays in your country?

Why do people celebrate holidays?

Do you think holiday celebrations have changed over the years? Why or why not?

Do you think the importance of holiday celebrations has changed over the years? Why or why not?

How will holidays be different in the future?

[1]AMERICAN and BRITISH: A special day commemorating a religious, historical, social, or political event.

ACADEMIC
MODEL TEST 3

Model Test 3

Candidate Name _____

INTERNATIONAL ENGLISH LANGUAGE TESTING SYSTEM

LISTENING

TIME Approx. 30 minutes

INSTRUCTIONS TO CANDIDATES

Do not open this booklet until you are told to do so.

Write your name and candidate number in the space at the top of this page.

You should answer all questions.

All the recordings will be played ONCE only.

Write all your answers on the Question Paper.

At the end of the test, you will be given ten minutes to transfer your answers to an Answer Sheet.

Do not remove this booklet from the examination room.

INFORMATION FOR CANDIDATES

There are **40** questions on this question paper.

The test is divided as follows:

Section 1	Questions 1–10
Section 2	Questions 11–20
Section 3	Questions 21–30
Section 4	Questions 31–40

SECTION 1   QUESTIONS 1–10

Questions 1–4

Complete the form below. Write NO MORE THAN ONE WORD AND/OR A NUMBER *for each answer.*

Lost Item Report

Day item was lost:
Example *Monday*

Reported by:

Last Name <u>Brown</u>   First name **1** _____   Phones: Home <u>(not given)</u>
Address **2** _____   High Street, **3** _____ #5   Office <u>(not given)</u>
City <u>Riverdale</u>   **4** _____ 305–5938

Questions 5–10

Choose the correct letter, **A, B,** *or* **C.**

5   What do the woman's glasses look like?

A

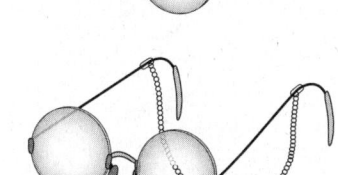

B

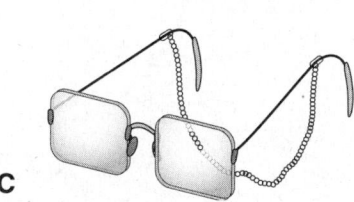

C

6   Where was the woman sitting when she lost her glasses?
  A   By the window
  B   Next to the door
  C   In the train station

7   What was the woman reading?
  A   A book
  B   A newspaper
  C   A magazine

8   Where was the woman going on the train?
  A   Home
  B   To work
  C   To visit her aunt

9   What time did the train arrive?
  A   5:00
  B   10:00
  C   10:30

10   Where did the woman find her glasses?

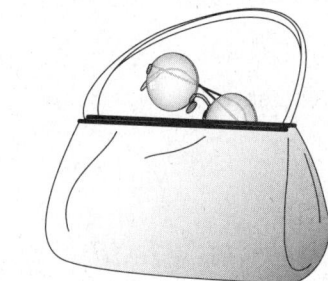

A

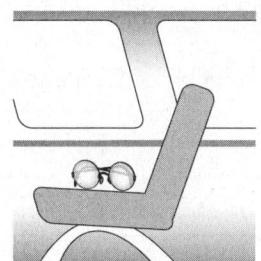

B

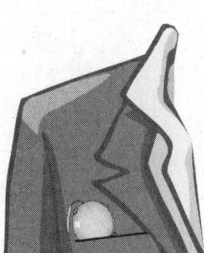

C

SECTION 2 *QUESTIONS 11–20*

Complete the notes. Write NO MORE THAN THREE WORDS for each answer.

<u>Places to look for housing</u>
Not recommended:

Near university	too expensive
Downtown[1]	**11** ....
	12 .... from the university

Recommended:

Uptown[2]	**13** ....
	a lot of buses go there
Greenfield Park	closer to the university
	you need **14** ....

<u>Places to look for ads[3]</u>
15 ....
University newspaper
16 ....
Internet

<u>Available at the Student Counseling Center[4]</u>
city maps
17 city ....
18 .... service
list of **19** ....
information about **20** .... plans

SECTION 3 *QUESTIONS 21–30*

Questions 21–25

Complete the table below. Write NO MORE THAN THREE WORDS for each answer.

Bicycles as Transportation: Advantages and Disadvantages

Advantages	Disadvantages
They are good for **21**	You can't ride in **24** ....
They are **22** .... cars	You can't ride if you have bad health
They don't cause **23**	You can't ride if your trip is **25** ....

[1]BRITISH: city centre

[2]BRITISH: area north of city centre

[3]BRITISH: advertisements/adverts

[4]BRITISH: centre

Questions 26–30

Complete the notes below. Write **NO MORE THAN THREE WORDS** *for each answer.*

<u>Encouraging Bicycle Riding</u>

Cities can:

26 .... on roads

make places to 27 .... at subway stations

provide 28 ....

<u>Bicycling Equipment</u>

Safety: wear a **29** ....

             reflective tape

Comfort: light clothes

             30 ....

SECTION 4   *QUESTIONS 31–40*

Questions 31–40

Complete the outline. Write **NO MORE THAN THREE WORDS** *for each answer.*

Writing a Research Paper

I.   Choose a topic

    A   Look at **31** ....

    B   Make topic more specific

    C   Get **32** ....

II.   **33** ....

    A.   Library

        1.   Reference and other types of books

        2.   Journals, **34** ....

        3.   Atlases and other similar sources

    B.   Internet

        1.   Online journals and newspapers

        2.   Online **35** ....

III.   **36** ....

IV.   Write an outline

    A.   Introduction

    B.   **37** ....

    C.   **38** ....

V.   **39** ....

VI.   Write first draft

VII. **40** ....

VIII. Type final draft

Model Test 3

Candidate Name _____

INTERNATIONAL ENGLISH LANGUAGE TESTING SYSTEM

ACADEMIC READING

TIME 1 hour

INSTRUCTIONS TO CANDIDATES

Do not open this booklet until you are told to do so.

Write your name and candidate number in the space at the top of this page.

Start at the beginning of the test and work through it.

You should answer all questions.

If you cannot do a particular question, leave it and go on to the next. You can return to it later.

All answers must be written on the Answer Sheet.

Do not remove this booklet from the examination room.

INFORMATION FOR CANDIDATES

There are **40** questions on this question paper.

The test is divided as follows:

Reading Passage 1   Questions 1–14
Reading Passage 2   Questions 15–27
Reading Passage 3   Questions 28–40

READING PASSAGE 1

You should spend about 20 minutes on Questions 1–14, which are based on Reading Passage 1 below.

Allergy Testing

Allergic reactions are triggered by the contact, inhalation, or ingestion of a number of different allergens. Some of the most common allergens are made up of proteins found in plants, mold, food, venom, animal skin, and medication. Symptoms of allergic reactions range from mild irritation such as itching, wheezing, and coughing to life-threatening conditions related to the respiratory and gastrointestinal organs. Serious allergic reactions are more likely to result from food, drugs, and stinging insects. A person does not become allergic to a particular substance until after the first exposure. However, in some cases, even trace amounts of a substance, such as peanuts or seafood in a mother's breast milk, can cause an allergic reaction in a subsequent exposure.

A variety of allergy tests are available for determining specific substances that trigger allergic reactions in individuals. Allergists, also known as immunologists, are trained in selecting the types of tests that are both safe and appropriate, depending on the suspected allergies. By using allergen extracts, tiny amounts of commonly bothersome allergens (usually in the form of purified liquid drops), immunologists are often able to isolate which substances cause reactions in allergy sufferers.

One of the most common types of environmental allergy tests is the skin-prick test. This technique involves placing small drops of potential allergen onto the skin of the forearm about one to two inches apart. After the drops are placed on the arm, a needle is used to puncture the skin at the site of each drop. (Though the procedure is virtually painless, this test is often done on the upper back of children to prevent them from seeing the needle.) If an allergy is present, an allergic antibody called *immunoglobulin* E (IgE) will activate a special cell called a *mast* cell. Mast cells release chemicals (also known as *mediators*) that cause itching and swelling. The most common mediator is *histamine.* Histamine is what causes the controlled hive known as a *wheal and flare.* The white wheal is the small raised surface, while the flare is the redness that spreads out from it. In an uncontrolled allergic reaction, wheals and flares can get much bigger and spread all over a person's body. Results from a skin test can usually be obtained within 20 to 30 minutes, while the reaction usually fades within a few hours.

Another test that is very similar to the skin-prick test is the intradermal allergy test. This involves placing the allergen sample under the skin with a syringe. The intradermal test involves more risk and is usually saved for use if the allergy persists even after a skin-prick test comes back negative. People who have experienced serious allergic reactions called anaphylactic reactions are not advised to have these types of tests. These allergy sufferers may be hypersensitive to even trace amount of the allergens when they are introduced into the blood. Anaphylaxis is an allergic reaction that affects the whole body and is potentially life-threatening. Hives on the lips and throat can become severe enough to block air passage. Anaphylactic shock occurs when enough histamine is released to cause the blood vessels to dilate and release fluid into the tissues. This lowers blood volume and can result in heart failure.

A blood test can be performed to safely isolate over 400 different allergies, including dangerous food and environmental allergens. The Radio Allergo Sorbent Test (RAST) measures specific IgE antibodies using a blood sample. IgE is normally found in very small amounts in the blood; it is created as a defense[1] mechanism when it senses an intruder. Separate tests are done for each potential allergen, and IgE results are graded from 0 to 6. For example, canine serum IgE will be high if a person has an allergy to dogs. The RAST is used if patients have pre-existing skin conditions or if patients cannot stop taking certain medications such as antidepressants or antihistamines for even a short period of time. (People must stop taking antihistamines several days prior to taking a skin allergy test because the medication can interfere with the results.) The RAST is a more expensive test that does not provide immediate results.

A number of other allergy tests are available, though many are considered unreliable according to The Academy of Allergy, Asthma, and Immunology. Applied kinesiology is a test that analyzes[2] the loss of muscle strength in the presence of potential allergens. Provocation and neutralization[3] testing involves injecting food allergens into the skin in different quantities, with the goal of determining the smallest dose needed to neutralize the symptoms. Sublingual provocation and neutralization is a similar test, except that the allergens are injected underneath the tongue. Cytotoxity testing involves watching for the reaction of blood cells after placing allergens on a slide next to a person's blood samples.

After using a reliable testing method, the cause of an allergic reaction is often identified, and a physician is able to help a patient develop a treatment plan with the goal of controlling or eliminating the allergic symptoms. Those who are allergic to furry pets, pollen, and plants are prescribed mild medication or taught how to control their reactions with simple lifestyle changes, while those with food allergies learn to safely remove certain foods from their diets. Allergy sufferers who are prone to anaphylactic reactions are educated about life-saving techniques such as carrying the drug epinephrine and wearing medical alert bracelets. As soon as people understand their allergies, they can begin to experience an improved quality of life.

Questions 1–7

The passage describes three different types of allergy tests. Which of the characteristics below belongs to which type of test? In boxes 1–7 on your Answer Sheet, write

A   if it is a characteristic of the skin-prick test.
B   if it is a characteristic of the intradermal test.
C   if it is a characteristic of the blood test.

1   A substance is inserted beneath the skin with a needle.

2   It is often done on a patient's back.

3   It is advisable for patients who have skin problems.

4   It is not advisable for patients who have had serious allergic reactions in the past.

5   It shows results within half an hour.

6   It can cause red and white bumps on the patient's skin.

7   It has a higher cost than other tests.

---

[1]BRITISH: defence

[2]BRITISH: analyses

[3]BRITISH: neutralisation/neutralise

Questions 8–14

Complete the summary of the reading passage below. Choose your answers from the box below, and write them in boxes 8–14 on your Answer Sheet. There are more words than spaces so you will not use them all.

Allergic reactions result from touching, breathing, or **8** .... certain substances called **9** .... Coughing or itching are two possible **10** .... of an allergic reaction. More serious allergic reactions may result from certain insect bites, foods, or **11** .... A severe allergic reaction is known as **12** .... It can result in loss of blood volume and heart failure. Doctors can use a variety of tests to **13** .... the source of an allergy. Treatment may include taking medication or **14** .... the substances that cause the allergic reaction.

mold	anaphylaxis	treat
avoiding	identify	signs
antihistamine	eating	
smelling	causes	
medicines	allergens	

READING PASSAGE 2

You should spend about 20 minutes on Questions 15–27, which are based on Reading Passage 2 below.

The Sacred Pipe

The sacred pipe was one of the most important artifacts of the indigenous people of North America. In almost every culture, the sacred pipe was considered a gift from The Great Spirit. The Cree believed that the pipe, the tobacco, and the fire were given as parting gifts from the Creator, while the Iowa Black Bear clan believed that the pipe bowl and later the pipe stem emerged from the earth as gifts to the earth's first bears. In most cases, the sacred pipe was considered a medium through which humans could pray to The Great Spirit, asking for guidance, health, and the necessities of life. In order for the prayers to reach the Great Spirit, they had to travel in the plumes of smoke from the sacred pipe. Because of its connection to the spiritual world, the pipe was treated with more respect than any human being, especially when the pipe bowl was joined to the stem.

Unlike the common pipe, which was used by average tribesmen for casual smoking purposes, the sacred pipe was built with precise craftsmanship. Before a pipe was carved, the catlinite (pipestone) was blessed and prayed over. The bowl of the traditional sacred pipe was made of red pipestone to represent the Earth. The wooden stem represented all that grew upon the Earth. In the Lakota Society, as in many Native American tribes, the people believed that the pipe bowl also represented a woman while the pipe stem represented a man. Joined together, the pipe symbolized the circle of love between a man and woman. The sacred pipe was the only object that was built by both genders; men carved the bowl and stem while women decorated the pipe with porcupine quills. In many tribes the man and woman held onto the sacred pipe during the marriage ceremony.

Cultivating the tobacco was the responsibility of certain members of the tribe. Generally, tobacco was mixed with herbs, bark, and roots, such as bayberry, mugwort, and wild cherry bark. These mixtures varied depending on the plants that were indigenous to the tribal area. Ceremonial tobacco was much stronger than the type that was used for everyday smoking. Rather than being inhaled, the smoke from the sacred pipe was puffed out the mouth in four directions.

In a typical pipe ceremony, the pipe holder stood up and held the pipe bowl in his left hand, with the stem held toward the East in his right hand. Before adding the first pinch of tobacco to the pipe bowl, he sprinkled some on the ground as an offering to both Mother Earth and the East. The East was acknowledged as the place where the morning star rose. Tribes believed that peace would evolve from wisdom if they prayed to the morning star.

Before offering a prayer to the South, the pipe holder again offered Mother Earth a sprinkling of tobacco and added another pinch into the bowl. The South was believed to bring strength, growth, and healing. While facing west the pipe holder acknowledged Mother Earth and prepared to thank the area where the sun sets. West was where the tribe believed the Spirit Helpers lived. At this time, they prayed for guidance from the spiritual world. The ceremony then proceeded to the North, which was thanked for blanketing Mother Earth with white snow, and for providing health and endurance.

After these four prayers, the pipe holder held the stem to the ground again and the tribe promised to respect and protect Mother Earth. Next, the stem was held up at an angle so that Father Sky could be thanked for the energy and heat he gave to the human body. Finally, the stem was held straight up and the tribe acknowledged The Great Spirit, thanking him for being the creator of Mother Earth, Father Sky, and the four directions.

After the pipe holder had worked his way around the four directions, he lit the pipe and passed it around the sacred circle in the same direction as the ceremonial prayers, starting from the East. Each member took a puff of smoke and offered another prayer. When the pipe had made a full circle, it was capped with bark, and the stem was removed. It was important for the stem and bowl to be stored in separate pockets in a pipe pouch. These pieces were not allowed to touch each other, except during a sacred pipe ceremony.

Pipestone, Minnesota, is considered hallowed ground for North American tribes. Regardless of their conflicts, tribes put their weapons down and gathered in peace in these quarries. According to the Dakota tribe, The Great Spirit once called all Indian nations to this location. Here the Spirit stood on the red pipestone and broke a piece away from the rock to make a giant pipe. He told his people that the red stone was their flesh and that it should be used to make a sacred pipe. He also said that the pipestone belonged to all native tribesmen and that the quarries must be considered a sacred place. Thus, people who had sacred pipes in their possession were considered caretakers, not owners.

Questions 15–19

Choose the correct letters, **A–C**, and write them in boxes 15–19 on your Answer Sheet.

15 The sacred pipe was important in native American cultures because
    A it was part of their spiritual practice.
    B it was used in gift exchanges between tribes.
    C it represented traditional handicrafts.

16 The pipe was made of
   A stone and wood.
   B bark and roots.
   C red clay from the Earth.

17 The pipe was sometimes used at
   A funerals.
   B births.
   C weddings.

18 During the pipe ceremony, tribe members smoked
   A plain tobacco.
   B a combination of plants.
   C only bark.

19 Pipestone, Minnesota, is an important place because it is
   A the site of a major battle.
   B the origin of the Dakota tribe.
   C source of stone for pipes.

Questions 20–27

Complete the flowchart about the pipe ceremony. Write **NO MORE THAN THREE WORDS** for each answer.

The pipe holder takes the **20** .... in his left hand and the **21** .... in his other hand.

↓

The pipe holder offers tobacco to Mother Earth and **22** .... , the place where the morning star rises, and then puts some in the pipe.

↓

The pipe holder prays to **23** .... to bring strength, growth, and healing and then prays to the remaining directions.

↓

The pipe holder points the pipe stem down and then up and prays to The Great Spirit, in appreciation for **24** ...., the sky, and **25** ....

↓

The pipe holder passes the pipe around the sacred circle, and all members of the circle **26** .... and pray.

↓

The bowl and stem are **27** .... because they can only touch each other during the ceremony.

READING PASSAGE 3

You should spend about 20 minutes on Questions 28–40, which are based on Reading Passage 3 below.

Bathymetry

The ocean floor is often considered the last frontier on earth, as it is a domain that remains greatly unexplored. Bathymetry, also known as seafloor topography, involves measuring and mapping the depths of the underwater world. Today much of the ocean floor still remains unmapped because collecting bathymetry data in waters of great depth is a time consuming and complex endeavor[1].

Two hundred years ago most people assumed that the ocean floor was similar to the beaches and coastlines. During the nineteenth century, attempts to produce maps of the seafloor involved lowering weighted lines from a boat and waiting for the tension of the line to change. When the handline hit the ocean floor, the depth of the water was determined by measuring the amount of slack. Each of these measurements was called a sounding, and thousands of soundings had to be done just to get a rough measurement of a small portion of the ocean floor. Besides estimating the depth, these surveys helped in identifying large shipping hazards, especially near the shoreline. A naval officer published the first evidence of underwater mountains in a bathymetric chart in 1855.

During World War I, scientists developed the technology for measuring sound waves in the ocean. Anti-Submarine Detection Investigation Committee (ASDICs) was the original name for these underwater sound projectors, but by World War II the term *sonar* was adopted in the United States and many other nations. Sonar, which stands for Sound, Navigation, and Ranging, was first used to detect submarines and icebergs. By calculating the amount of time it took for a sound signal to reflect back to its original source, sonar could measure the depth of the ocean as well as the depth of any objects found within it. The first sonar devices were passive systems that could only receive sound waves. By the 1930s, single-beam sonar was being used to transmit sound waves in a vertical line from a ship to the seafloor. The sound waves were recorded as they returned from the surface to the ship. However, this type of sonar was more useful in detecting submerged objects than mapping the seafloor. Throughout World War II, technology improved, and active sonar systems that both received and produced sound waves were being used. It was the invention of the acoustic transducer and the acoustic projector that made way for this modern sonar. The newer systems made it possible to identify certain material, such as rock or mud. Since mud absorbed a good portion of a sound signal, it provided a much weaker echo than rocks, which reflected much of the sound wave.

The multi-beam sonar, which could be attached to a ship's hull, was developed in the 1960s. With this type of sonar, multiple beams could be adjusted to a number of different positions, and a larger area of the ocean could be surveyed. Maps created with the aid of multi-beam sonar helped to explain the formation of ridges and trenches, including the Ring of Fire and the Mid-Ocean Ridge. The Ring of Fire is a zone that circles the Pacific Ocean and is famous for its seismic activity. This area, which extends from the coast of New Zealand to the coast of North and South America, also accounts for more than 75 percent of the world's active and dormant volcanoes. The Mid-Ocean Ridge is a section of undersea mountains that extends over 12,000 feet high and 1,200 miles wide. These mountains, which zigzag around the continents, are generally considered the most outstanding topographical features on earth.

---

[1]BRITISH: endeavour

The invention of the side-scan sonar was another modern breakthrough for the field of bathymetry. This type of sonar is towed on cables, making it possible to send and receive sound waves over a broad section of the seafloor at much lower angles than the multi-beam sonar. The benefit of the side-scan sonar system is that it can detect very specific features over a large area. The most modern form of bathymetry, which is also the least accurate, is done with data collected by satellite altimetry. This method began to be used in the 1970s. This type of mapping relies on radar altimeters that receive echoes from the sea surface. These signals measure the distance between the satellite and the ocean floor. Unfortunately, due to water vapor[1] and ionization, electromagnetic waves are often decelerated as they move through the atmosphere; therefore, the satellite receives inaccurate measurements. The benefit of using satellites to map the ocean is that it can take pictures of the entire globe, including areas that have not yet been measured by sonar. At this time, satellite altimetry is mainly used to locate areas where detailed sonar measurements need to be conducted.

Due to a constant flux of plate activity, the topography of the seafloor is ever-changing. Scientists expect bathymetry to become one of the most important sciences as humans search for new energy sources and seek alternate routes for telecommunication. Preserving the ocean's biosphere for the future will also rely on an accurate mapping of the seafloor.

Questions 28–33

Complete the table below. Write **NO MORE THAN THREE WORDS** for each answer. Write your answers in boxes 28–33 on your Answer Sheet.

Mapping the Ocean Floor

Method	First Used . . .	Used for . . .	How It Works
weighted line	**28**......................	measuring **29**......................	drop a line until it hits the bottom
30......................	1930s	detecting objects underwater	send **31**.................. to ocean floor
multi-beam sonar	**32**...................... ocean floor	mapping larger areas of the different directions	send multiple sound waves in
satellite altimetry	1970s	taking pictures of **33**......................	send signals from satellite

[1]BRITISH: vapour

Questions 34–37

Match each description below with the ocean region that it describes.

In boxes 34–37 on your Answer Sheet, write

    A if it describes the Ring of Fire
    B if it describes the Mid-Ocean Ridge

34 It is known for the earthquakes that occur there.

35 It is over one thousand miles wide.

36 It is a mountain range.

37 It contains the majority of the earth's volcanoes.

Questions 38–40

The list below gives some possible reasons for mapping the ocean floor.

Which three of these reasons are mentioned in the reading passage?

Write the appropriate Roman numerals i–iv in boxes 38–40 on your Answer Sheet.

    i   Predicting earthquakes
    ii Finding new fuel resources
    iii Protecting ocean life
    iv Understanding weather patterns
    v   Improving communications systems
    vi Improving the fishing industry

Model Test 3

Candidate Name _____

INTERNATIONAL ENGLISH LANGUAGE TESTING SYSTEM

ACADEMIC WRITING

TIME 1 hour

INSTRUCTIONS TO CANDIDATES

Do not open this booklet until you are told to do so.

Write your name and candidate number in the space at the top of this page.

All answers must be written on the separate answer booklet provided.

Do not remove this booklet from the examination room.

INFORMATION FOR CANDIDATES

There are **2** tasks on this question paper.

You must do **both** tasks.

Underlength answers will be penalized.

WRITING TASK 1

You should spend no more than 20 minutes on this task.

> *The charts below show the percentage of their food budget the average family spent on restaurant meals in different years. The graph shows the number of meals eaten in fast-food restaurants and sit-down restaurants.*

Summarize[1] the information by selecting and reporting the main features, and make comparisons where relevant.

You should write at least 150 words.

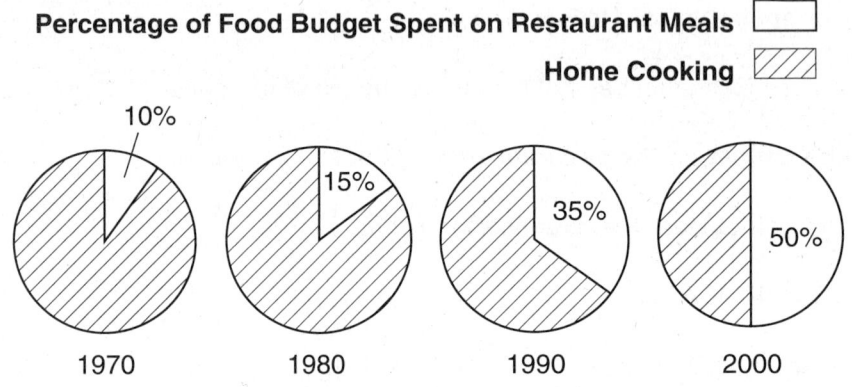

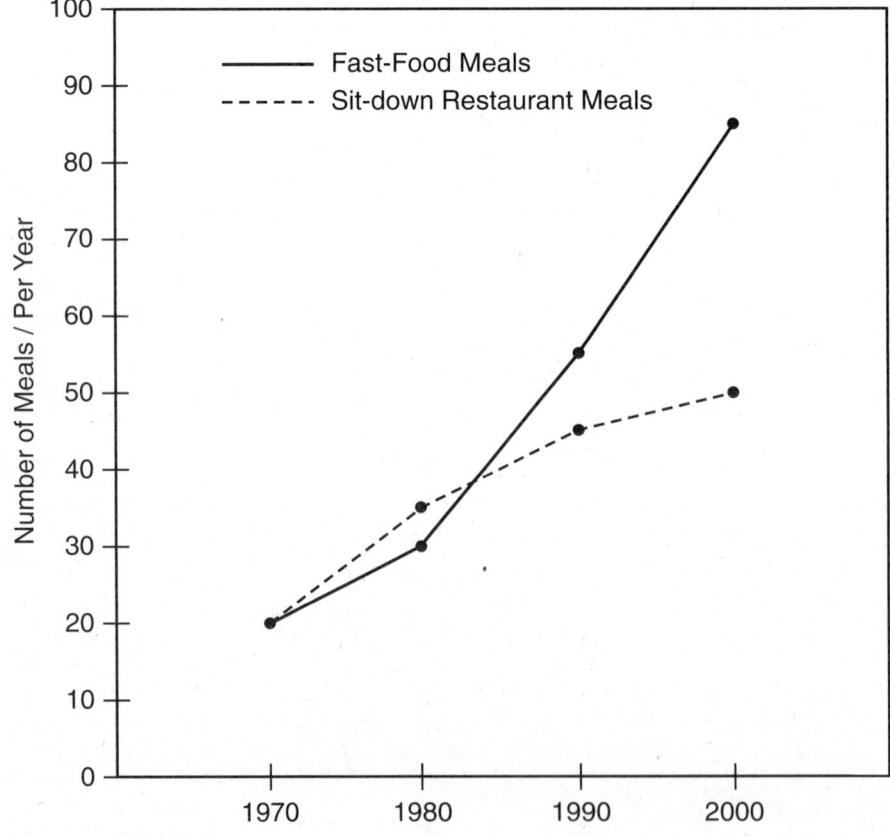

WRITING TASK 2

You should spend no more than 40 minutes on this task.

Write about the following topic.

> *By punishing murderers with the death penalty, society is also guilty of committing murder. Therefore, life in prison is a better punishment for murderers.*

To what extent do you agree or disagree with this statement?

Give reasons for your answer and include any relevant examples from your own knowledge or experience.

You should write at least 250 words.

SPEAKING

Examiner Questions:

Part 1

    What kind of food do you enjoy eating?
    What are some kinds of food you never eat? Why?
    Do you generally prefer to eat at home or at a restaurant? Why?
    What are some reasons that people eat at restaurants?
    Describe some things you enjoy doing with your friends.
    Do you think it's better to have a large group of friends or a few close friends? Why?
    How do people choose their friends?
    Have you remained friends with people from your childhood? Why or why not?

Part 2

Describe a teacher from your past that you remember.

    You should say:
        what class the teacher taught you and how old you were
        what the teacher's special qualities and characteristics were
        why you remember this teacher

You will have one to two minutes to talk about this topic.
You will have one minute to prepare what you are going to say.

Part 3

    What kind of person makes a good teacher?
    Why do you think people choose to become teachers?
    Which is more important for a teacher—to be an expert in the subject he or she teaches, or to be very skilled at explaining things and motivating students to learn?
    How are schools different now from when you were young? How do you think they will be different in the future?

ACADEMIC
MODEL TEST 4

Model Test 4

Candidate Name _____

INTERNATIONAL ENGLISH LANGUAGE TESTING SYSTEM

LISTENING

TIME Approx. 30 minutes

INSTRUCTIONS TO CANDIDATES

Do not open this booklet until you are told to do so.

Write your name and candidate number in the space at the top of this page.

You should answer all questions.

All the recordings will be played ONCE only.

Write all your answers on the Question Paper.

At the end of the test, you will be given ten minutes to transfer your answers to an Answer Sheet.

Do not remove this booklet from the examination room.

INFORMATION FOR CANDIDATES

There are **40** questions on this question paper.

The test is divided as follows:

Section 1	Questions 1–10
Section 2	Questions 11–20
Section 3	Questions 21–30
Section 4	Questions 31–40

SECTION 1 QUESTIONS 1–10

Questions 1–2

*Choose the correct letter, **A**, **B**, or **C**.*

EXAMPLE

Where will the man get the information he needs?
A The information desk
B The ticket office
Ⓒ The Special Events Department

1 What does the man want to do?
A Look at art
B Hear a lecture
C Listen to music

2 What day will he get tickets for?
A Thursday
B Saturday
C Sunday

Questions 3–5

Complete the form.

```
┌─────────────────────────────────────────────────┐
│                Ticket Order Form                  │
│                                                   │
│  Customer name: Steven 3 ...........................  │
│  Credit card number: 4 ...............................  │
│  Number of tickets: 2                             │
│  Amount due: 5 £............................        │
└─────────────────────────────────────────────────┘
```

Questions 6–10

Label the map below. Write the correct place names in boxes 6–10 on your Answer Sheet.

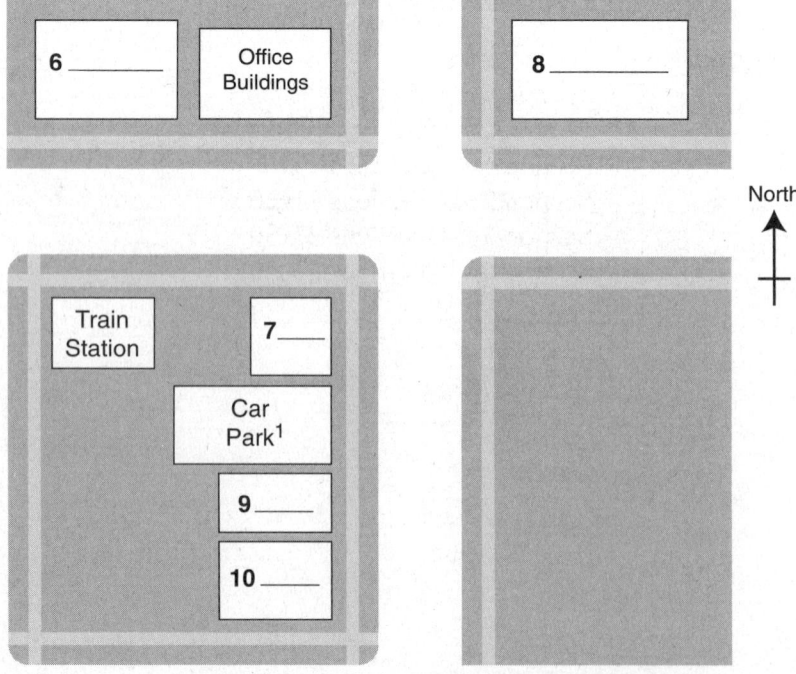

[1]AMERICAN: parking garage

SECTION 2   *Questions 11–20*

Questions 11–17

Complete the table comparing the two towns. Write **NO MORE THAN THREE WORDS** for each answer.

	Ravensburg	Blackstone Beach
Population	**11** _____	12,000
Summer climate	average temp: **12** _____ weather: sunny	average temp: **13** _____ weather: **14** _____
Advantage	**15** _____	good seafood
Disadvantage	crowded in summer	**16** _____
Distance from airport	25 kilometers	**17** _____

Questions 18–20

Which three of the following do tourists usually shop for on Raven Island?

Write the correct letters, **A–F**, in boxes 18–20 on your Answer Sheet.

    A   native handicrafts
    B   native music
    C   perfume
    D   jewelry[1]
    E   fish
    F   fishing gear[2]

SECTION 3   *Questions 21–30*

Questions 21–23

Write **NO MORE THAN THREE WORDS** for each answer.

21 When is the research project due?

22 What percentage of the final grade[3] does it count for?

23 What topic did Janet choose?

[1]BRITISH: jewellery
[2]BRITISH: tackle
[3]BRITISH: mark

Questions 24–30

Complete the chart showing the steps Janet took to complete her research project.

Write NO MORE THAN THREE WORDS for each answer.

A. Choose topic

B. Do **24**_____

C. Choose **25** _____

D. Submit research **26** _____

E. Choose subjects

F. **27** _____

G. Send out **28** _____

H. **29** _____ and graphs

I. Write a **30** _____

SECTION 4 *QUESTIONS 31–40*

Questions 31–34

According to the talk, in which parts of the world do crows live? Choose four places and write the correct letters, A–F in boxes 31–34 on your Answer Sheet.

A North America
B South America
C Antarctica
D Hawaii
E Europe
F Asia

Questions 35–40

Complete the table with information about the American crow.

Write NO MORE THAN THREE WORDS AND/OR A NUMBER for each answer.

Length	**35** _____ centimeters
Color	**36** _____
Favorite food	corn
Nest material	**37** _____
Nesting place	**38** _____
Number of eggs	**39** _____
Days to hatch	18
Days to fly	**40** _____

Model Test 4

Candidate Name _____

INTERNATIONAL ENGLISH LANGUAGE TESTING SYSTEM

ACADEMIC READING

TIME 1 Hour

INSTRUCTIONS TO CANDIDATES

Do not open this booklet until you are told to do so.

Write your name and candidate number in the space at the top of this page.

Start at the beginning of the test and work through it.

You should answer all questions.

If you cannot do a particular question, leave it and go on to the next. You can return to it later.

All answers must be written on the Answer Sheet.

Do not remove this booklet from the examination room.

INFORMATION FOR CANDIDATES

There are **40** questions on this question paper.

The test is divided as follows:

Reading Passage 1   Questions 1–14
Reading Passage 2   Questions 15–27
Reading Passage 3   Questions 28–40

READING PASSAGE 1

You should spend about 20 minutes on Questions 1–13, which are based on Reading Passage 1.

One Hundred Days of Reform

Since the early 1800s, the term *one hundred days* has represented a political phrase, refer-ring to a short period of concentrated political reform. In most cases, this period comes immediately after a new leader takes over a nation. The original Hundred Days took place between March and June of 1815, when Napoleon escaped from Elba, and King Louis XVIII reclaimed his throne. This was one of the results of the Battle of Waterloo. The Hundred Days of Reform in China (also known as the Wuxu Reform) was inspired by a similar event. After losing the Sino-Japanese war, the Emperor Guwangxu found his country to be in a major crisis. Desperate for change, the emperor hired the help of a young political activist named K'ang Yu-wei. At the age of only 27, K'ang had graduated with the highest degree (chin-shih), written two books on reform, and initiated several of his own political reform movements. K'ang impressed the court and convinced the emperor that China, like Japan, should form a constitutional government and do away with its monarchy.

On June 11, 1898, Emperor Guwangxu entrusted the reform movement to K'ang and put the progressive scholar–reformer in control of the government. Immediately, K'ang, with the help of a few other reformers, began work on changing China into a more modern society. Within days, the imperial court issued a number of statutes related to the social and political structure of the nation. First, K'ang planned to reform China's education system. The edicts called for a universal school system with an emphasis on practical and Western studies rather than Neo-Confucian orthodoxy. The new government also wanted to modernize[1] the country's examination systems and send more students abroad to gain firsthand knowledge of how technology was developing in other countries. K'ang also called for the establishment of a national parliamentary government, including popularly elected members and ministries. Military reform and the establishment of a new defense[2] system as well as the modernization of agriculture and medicine were also on the agenda.

These edicts were threatening to Chinese ideologies and institutions, especially, the army, which at the time was controlled by a few governor–generals. There was intense opposi-tion to the reform at all levels of society, and only one in fifteen provinces made attempts to implement the edicts. The Manchus, who considered the reform a radical and unrealistic idea, suggested that more gradual changes needed to be made. Just three months after the reform had begun, a coup d'etat was organized by Yuan Shikai and Empress Dowager Cixi to force Guangxu and the young reformers out of power and into seclusion. A few of the reformer's chief advocates who refused to leave were executed. After September 21st, the new edicts were abolished, and the conservatives regained their power.

Many Chinese civilians felt that the aftermath of the One Hundred Days of Reform was more detrimental to China than the short-lived failed attempt at reform. Immediately following the conservative takeover, anti-foreign and anti-Christian secret societies tore through north-ern China, targeting foreign concessions and missionary facilities. The violence of these "Boxer bands" provoked retaliation from the offended nations, and the government was forced to declare war on the invaders. By August, an Allied force made up of armies from nine European nations as well as the United States and Japan entered Peking. With little

[1]BRITISH: modernise
[2]BRITISH: defence

effort, north China was occupied, and foreign troops had stationed themselves inside the border. The court was ordered to either execute or punish many of its high officials under the Protocol of 1901. Rather than dividing up the occupied territory among the powers, the Allies settled on an "open door" trade policy. Within a decade, the court ordered many of the original reform measures, including the modernization of the education and military system.

The traditional view of the One Hundred Days of Reform depicted Emperor Guwangxu and K'ang Yu-wei as heroes and Empress Dowager Cixi as the villain who refused to reform even though the change was inevitable. However, since the *One Hundred Days* has turned into a cliché related to political failures, historians in the 20th century often portray the Wuxu Reform as an irrational dream. The fact that the reforms were implemented in a matter of decades, rather than months, suggests that the conservative elites may have been more opposed to the immediacy of the proposed edicts rather than the changes themselves.

Questions 1–4

*What were some of the reforms planned during the One Hundred Days of Reform in China? Choose four answers from the list below, and write the correct letters, **A–G** in boxes 1–4 on your Answer Sheet.*

A   Modernization of the school system
B   Establishment of a parliament
C   Focus on the study of Confucianism
D   Reorganization of the military
E   Abolition of elections
F   Improvement of farming
G   Initiation of foreign trade

Questions 5–13

Complete the sentences about the reading passage below.

Choose your answers from the box below, and write them in boxes 5–13 on your Answer Sheet. There are more choices than spaces, so you will not use them all.

5   China _____ with Japan.

6   Emperor Guwangxu put K'ang Yu-wei _____.

7   After June 11, 1898, the reforms _____.

8   People throughout China _____.

9   Yuan Shikai and Empress Dowager Cixi _____.

10 The reforms _____ after September 21st.

11 Secret societies attacked _____.

12 European, U.S., and Japanese troops _____.

13 Eventually, the reforms _____.

A	overthrew the government
B	in charge of the reform movement
C	were voted in
D	in prison
E	were abolished
F	lost a war
G	began trade
H	foreigners in China
I	were executed
J	reform supporters
K	occupied China
L	were initiated
M	opposed the reforms
N	were reestablished

READING PASSAGE 2

You should spend about 20 minutes on Questions 14–27, which are based on Reading Passage 2.

Sleep Apnea

Sleep apnea is a common sleeping disorder. It affects a number of adults comparable to the percentage of the population that suffers from diabetes. The term *apnea* is of Greek origin and means "without breath." Sufferers of sleep apnea stop breathing repeatedly while they sleep. This can happen hundreds of times during the night, each gasp lasting from 10 to 30 seconds. In extreme cases, people stop breathing for more than a minute at a time.

There are three different types of sleep apnea, with obstructive sleep apnea being the most common. Obstructive sleep apnea (OSA), which affects 90 percent of sleep apnea sufferers, occurs because of an upper airway obstruction. A person's breathing stops when air is somehow prevented from entering the trachea. The most common sites for air to get trapped include the nasal passage, the tongue, the tonsils, and the uvula. Fatty tissue or tightened muscles at the back of a throat can also cause the obstruction. Central sleep apnea has a different root cause, though the consequences are the same. In central sleep apnea, the brain forgets to send the signal that tells the muscles that it's time to breathe. The term *central* is used because this type of apnea is related to the central nervous system rather than the blocked airflow. The third type of sleep apnea, known as mixed apnea, is a combination of the two and is the most rare form. Fortunately, in all types of apnea, the brain eventually signals for a person to wake up so that breathing can resume. However, this continuous pattern of interrupted sleep is hard on the body and results in very little rest.

Sleep apnea is associated with a number of risk factors, including being overweight, male, and over the age of forty. However, like many disorders, sleep apnea can affect children and in many cases is found to be the result of a person's genetic makeup. Despite being so widespread, this disorder often goes undiagnosed. Many people experience symptoms for their whole lives without realizing they have a serious sleep disorder. Oftentimes, it is not the person suffering from sleep apnea who notices the repetitive episodes of sleep interruption, but a partner or family member sleeping nearby. The air cessation is generally accompanied by heavy snoring, loud enough to rouse others from sleep. Those who live alone are less likely to receive early diagnosis, though other symptoms such as headaches, dizziness, irritability, and exhaustion may cause a person to seek medical advice. If left untreated, sleep apnea, which is a progressive disorder, can cause cardiovascular problems, increasing the risk of heart disease and stroke. Sleep apnea is also blamed for many cases of impaired driving and poor job performance.

In order to diagnose sleep apnea, patients are generally sent to a sleep center for a polysomnography test. This test monitors brain waves, muscle tension, breathing, eye movement, and oxygen in the blood. Audio monitoring for snoring, gasping, and episodic waking is also done during a polysomnogram. Nonintrusive solutions for treating sleep apnea involve simple lifestyle changes. In many cases, symptoms of sleep apnea can be eliminated when patients try losing weight or abstaining from alcohol. People who sleep on their backs or stomachs often find that their symptoms disappear if they try sleeping on their sides. Sleep specialists also claim that sleeping pills interfere with the natural performance of the throat and mouth muscles and suggest patients do away with all sleep medication for a trial period. When these treatments prove unsuccessful, sleep apnea sufferers can be fitted with a CPAP mask, which is worn at night over the mouth and nose, similar to an oxygen mask. CPAP stands for Continuous Positive Airway Pressure.

In extreme cases, especially when facial deformities are the cause of the sleep apnea, surgery is needed to make a clear passage for the air. Many different types of surgeries are available. The most common form of surgery used to combat sleep apnea is uvulo-palato-pharyngoplasty (UPPP). This procedure involves removing the uvula and the excess tissue around it. UPPP helps about 50 percent of patients who undergo the procedure, while the other half continue to rely on the CPAP machine even after the surgery. Another type of surgery called mandibular myotomy involves removing a piece of the jaw, and adjusting the tongue. By reattaching[1] the tongue to a position about ten millimeters forward, air is able to flow more freely during sleep. This delicate procedure is performed only by surgeons with expertise in facial surgery and is almost always successful in eliminating the air obstruction. The latest surgical procedures use radio frequencies to shrink the tissue around the tongue, throat, and soft palate.

Questions 14–18

The passage describes three different types of sleep apnea. Which of the characteristics below belongs to which type of sleep apnea? In boxes 14–18 on your Answer Sheet, write

- **A** if it is a characteristic of obstructive sleep apnea.
- **B** if it is a characteristic of central sleep apnea.
- **C** if it is a characteristic of mixed apnea.

14 Its root cause is a blockage at the trachea.

15 It is connected exclusively with the nervous system.

16 It involves blocked airflow and a brain malfunction.

17 It is the most unusual type of sleep apnea.

18 It is the most common form of sleep apnea.

Questions 19–23

Do the following statements agree with the information in Reading Passage 2?

In boxes 19–23 on your Answer Sheet, write

TRUE	*if the statement is true according to the passage.*
FALSE	*if the statement contradicts the passage.*
NOT GIVEN	*if there is no information about this in the passage.*

19 Sleep apnea only affects men over 40.

20 Most people with sleep apnea have the problem diagnosed.

[1]BRITISH: re-attaching

21 Often a relative of the sleep apnea sufferer is the first to notice the problem.

22 Sleep apnea is more common in Greece than in other countries.

23 Sleep apnea can cause problems at work.

Questions 24–27

Which treatments for sleep apnea are mentioned in the passage?

*Choose four answers from the list below, and write the correct letters, **A–G,** in boxes 1–4 on your Answer Sheet.*

A getting surgery
B wearing a mask
C taking sleeping pills
D reducing one's weight
E massaging the throat muscles
F sleeping on one's side
G drinking moderate amounts of alcohol

READING PASSAGE 3

You should spend about 20 minutes on Questions 28–40, which are based on Reading Passage 3.

Adult Intelligence

Over 90 years ago, Binet and Simon delineated two different methods of assessing intelligence. These were the psychological method (which concentrates mostly on intellectual processes, such as memory and abstract reasoning) and the pedagogical method (which concentrates on assessing what an individual knows). The main concern of Binet and Simon was to predict elementary school performance independently from the social and economic background of the individual student. As a result, they settled on the psychological method, and they spawned an intelligence assessment paradigm, which has been substantially unchanged from their original tests.

With few exceptions, the development of adult intelligence assessment instruments proceeded along the same lines of the Binet-Simon tests. Nevertheless, the difficulty of items was increased for older examinees. Thus, extant adult intelligence tests were created as little more than upward extensions of the original Binet-Simon scales. The Binet-Simon tests are quite effective in predicting school success in both primary and secondary educational environments. However, they have been found to be much less predictive of success in post-secondary academic and occupational domains. Such a discrepancy provokes fundamental questions about intelligence. One highly debated question asks whether college success is actually dependent on currently used forms of measured intelligence, or if present measures of intelligence are inadequately sampling the wider domain of adult intellect. One possible answer to this question lies in questioning the preference of the psychological method over the pedagogical method for assessing adult intellect. Recent research across the fields of education, cognitive science, and adult development suggests that much of adult intellect is indeed not adequately sampled by extant intelligence measures and might be better assessed through the pedagogical method (Ackerman, 1996; Gregory, 1994).

Several lines of research have also converged on a redefinition of adult intellect that places a greater emphasis on content (knowledge) over process. Substantial strides have been made in delineating knowledge aspects of intellectual performance which are divergent from traditional measures of intelligence (e.g., Wagner, 1987) and in demonstrating that adult performance is greatly influenced by prior topic and domain knowledge (e.g., Alexander et al., 1994). Even some older testing literature seems to indicate that the knowledge measured by the Graduate Records Examination (GRE) is a comparable or better indicator of future graduate school success and post-graduate performance than traditional aptitude measures (Willingham, 1974).

Knowledge and Intelligence

When an adult is presented with a completely novel problem (e.g., memorizing a random set of numbers or letters), the basic intellectual processes are typically implicated in predicting which individuals will be successful in solving problems. The dilemma for adult intellectual assessment is that the adult is rarely presented with a completely novel problem in the real world of academic or occupational endeavors[1]. Rather, the problems that an adult is asked to solve almost inevitably draw greatly on his/her accumulated knowledge and skills—one does not build a house by only memorizing physics formulae. For an adult, intellect is better conceptualized by the tasks that the person can accomplish and the skills that he/she has developed rather than the number of digits that can be stored in working memory or the number of syllogistic reasoning items that can be correctly evaluated. Thus, the content of the intellect is at least as important as the processes of intellect in determining an adult's real-world problem-solving efficacy.

From the artificial intelligence field, researchers have discarded the idea of a useful general problem solver in favor[2] of knowledge-based expert systems. This is because no amount of processing power can achieve real-world problem-solving proficiency without an extensive set of domain-relevant knowledge structures. Gregory (1994) describes the difference between such concepts as "potential intelligence" (knowledge) and "kinetic intelligence" (process). Similarly, Schank and Birnbaum (1994) say that "what makes someone intelligent is what he [/she] knows."

One line of relevant educational research is from the examination of expert–novice differences which indicates that the typical expert is found to mainly differ from the novice in terms of experience and the knowledge structures that are developed through that experience rather than in terms of intellectual processes (e.g., Glaser, 1991). Additional research from developmental and gerontological perspectives has also shown that various aspects of adult intellectual functioning are greatly determined by knowledge structures and less influenced by the kinds of process measures, which have been shown to decline with age over adult development (e.g., Schooler, 1987; Willis & Tosti-Vasey, 1990).

Shifting Paradigms

By bringing together a variety of sources of research evidence, it is clear that our current methods of assessing adult intellect are insufficient. When we are confronted with situations in which the intellectual performance of adults must be predicted (e.g., continuing education or adult learning programs), we must begin to take account of what they know in addition to the traditional assessment of intellectual processes. Because adults are quite diverse in their knowledge structures (e.g., a physicist may know many different things than a carpen-

[1]BRITISH: endeavours

[2]BRITISH: favour

ter), the challenge for educational assessment researchers in the future will be to develop batteries of tests that can be used to assess different sources of intellectual knowledge for different individuals. When adult knowledge structures are broadly examined with tests such as the Advanced Placement [AP] and College Level Exam Program [CLEP], it may be possible to improve such things as the prediction of adult performance in specific educational endeavors, the placement of individuals, and adult educational counseling.

Questions 28–34

Complete the sentences about the reading passage below.

Choose your answers from the box below, and write them in boxes 28–34 on your Answer Sheet. There are more choices than sentences so you will not use them all.

28 The psychological method of intelligence assessment measures _____.

29 Binet and Simon wanted to develop an assessment method that was not influenced by the child's ____ _____.

30 The Binet-Simon tests have been successfully used to predict _____.

31 The Binet-Simon tests are not good predictors of _____.

32 According to _____, the pedagogical method is the best way to assess adult intelligence.

33 The pedagogical method is a better measure of adult intelligence because most problems that adults encounter in real life are not completely_____.

34 In the area of artificial intelligence, _____ systems are preferred.

A tests	H thought processes
B psychological issues	I Ackerman and Gregory
C new	J social class
D potential for achievement in school	K recent research
E knowledge-based	L future job performance
F knowledge	M problem solving
G Binet and Simon	

Questions 35–39

Do the following statements agree with the information in Reading Passage 3?

In boxes 35–39 on your Answer Sheet, write

TRUE	*if the statement is true according to the passage.*
FALSE	*if the statement contradicts the passage.*
NOT GIVEN	*if there is no information about this in the passage.*

35 The Binet-Simon tests have not changed significantly over the years.

36 Success in elementary school is a predictor of success in college.

37 Research suggests that experts generally have more developed intellectual processes than novices.

38 Knowledge structures in adults decrease with age.

39 Better methods of measuring adult intelligence need to be developed.

Question 40

*Choose the correct letter, **A–C**, and write it in box 40 on your Answer Sheet.*

40 The Advanced Placement and College Level Exam Program tests measure
   A thought processes.
   B job skills.
   C knowledge.

Model Test 4

Candidate Name _____

INTERNATIONAL ENGLISH LANGUAGE TESTING SYSTEM

ACADEMIC WRITING

TIME 1 hour

INSTRUCTIONS TO CANDIDATES

Do not open this booklet until you are told to do so.

Write your name and candidate number in the space at the top of this page.

All answers must be written on the separate answer booklet provided.

Do not remove this booklet from the examination room.

INFORMATION FOR CANDIDATES

There are **2** tasks on this question paper.

You must do **both** tasks.

Underlength answers will be penalized.

WRITING TASK 1

You should spend about 20 minutes on this task.

Write about the following topic:

> *The table below shows the sales made by a coffee shop in an office building on a typical weekday.*
>
> *Summarize the information by selecting and reporting the main features, and make comparisons where relevant.*

You should write at least 150 words.

	Coffee	Tea	Pastries	Sandwiches
7:30–10:30	265	110	275	50
10:30–2:30	185	50	95	200
2:30–5:30	145	35	150	40
5:30–8:30	200	75	80	110

WRITING TASK 2

You should spend no more than 40 minutes on this task.

Write about the following topic.

> *More and more people are relying on the private car as their major means of transportation.*
>
> *Describe some of the problems overreliance on cars can cause, and suggest at least one possible solution.*

Give reasons for your answer and include any relevant examples from your own knowledge or experience.

You should write at lest 250 words.

SPEAKING

Examiner Questions:

Part 1

Describe the place you live in now.
Do you think it's better to live in a house or in an apartment? Why?
Describe your neighborhood.
How do people choose their place to live?
Describe your family. Are you married? Do you have children? Brothers and sisters?
What are some things you enjoy doing with other members of your family?
Who in your family are you particularly close to? Why?
Do you spend more time with your family or with friends? Why?

Part 2

Describe a gift you have received that was important to you.

You should say:
    who gave it to you and for what occasion
    what it looks like and how you use it
    why it is important to you

You will have one to two minutes to talk about this topic.
You will have one minute to prepare what you are going to say.

Part 3

Do you think people generally enjoy giving and receiving gifts? Why or why not?
In your country, when do people usually give gifts?
What kind of gifts do they give?
Do you agree or disagree: The price of a gift shows how much the giver cares about the recipient.

IELTS MODEL TESTS

GENERAL TRAINING: READING WRITING MODEL TEST 1

General Training Model Test 1

Candidate Name _____

INTERNATIONAL ENGLISH LANGUAGE TESTING SYSTEM

GENERAL TRAINING READING

TIME 1 hour

INSTRUCTIONS TO CANDIDATES

Do not open this booklet until you are told to do so.

Write your name and candidate number in the space at the top of this page.

Start at the beginning of the test and work through it.

You should answer all questions.

If you cannot do a particular question, leave it and go on to the next. You can return to it later.

All answers must be written on the answer sheet.

Do not remove this booklet from the examination room.

INFORMATION FOR CANDIDATES

There are **40** questions on this question paper.

The test is divided as follows:

Section 1	Questions 1–14
Section 2	Questions 15–27
Section 3	Questions 28–40

SECTION 1   QUESTIONS *1–14*

You are advised to spend 20 minutes on questions 1–14.

Questions *1–7*

Look at the five apartment advertisements **A–E**.

Write the letters of the appropriate advertisements in boxes 1–7 on your answer sheet. You may use any letter more than once.

Which apartment is appropriate for a person who

1   owns a car?

2   is a university student?

3   has children?

4   likes to swim?

5   usually uses public transportation?

6   wants to rent for two months only?

7   often entertains large groups of people?

A   Sunny 1 bedroom, central location, washer/dryer in building. Storage space, parking included in rent. One year lease required. Call 837–9986 before 6 P.M.

B   Cozy one bedroom with study available in elevator building[1]. Near City Park. Amenities include exercise room, pool, and party room. Other apartments also available. One- and two-year leases. Call 592–8261.

C   Small one-bedroom, reasonable rent, near shopping, bus routes, university. References required. No pets. Call Mr. Watkins 876–9852.

D   Don't miss this unique opportunity. Large two-bedroom plus study, which could be third bedroom. Quiet neighborhood. Walk to elementary and high school, park, shops. Small pets allowed.

E   Furnished flats[2], convenient to central business district. Studios, one-, and two-bedrooms. Weekly and monthly rentals available. Call our office 376–0923 9–5 M–F.

[1]BRITISH: Building with lift

[2]AMERICAN: apartments

Questions 8–14

Thank you for buying a Blau Automatic Coffeemaker. If you use and maintain your Blau product correctly, you will enjoy it for years to come.

A   Preparing Coffee with Your Blau Coffeemaker
Your coffeemaker is guaranteed to make a perfect cup of coffee every time. First, fill the reusable coffee basket with coffee grounds, adding two tablespoons of grounds per cup. Next, fill the reservoir with eight ounces of water for each cup of coffee. Place the coffee pot under the coffee basket, making sure that it is directly underneath the drip spout. Press the "on" button located on the coffeemaker's base.

B   Built-in Convenience
Your Blau Coffeemaker is equipped with a built-in timer. You can set the timer so that your coffee is ready when you get up in the morning, when you return from work in the evening, or at any other time you choose. Just follow the directions above for preparing your coffee. Then set the timer by pushing the button underneath the clock at the front of the coffeemaker. Push twice to put the clock in timer mode. The minutes will flash. Push the button until the minutes are set. Push twice again and the hours will flash. Push the button until the hours are set. Push twice to return the timer to clock mode.

C   Maintaining Your Coffeemaker
Monthly cleaning will keep your coffeemaker functioning properly and your coffee tasting fresh. Just follow these easy steps. Fill the reservoir with a small bottle of vinegar. Turn your coffeemaker on and let the vinegar run through it, filling the coffeepot. Then fill the reservoir with fresh water and let it run through the coffeemaker. Do this twice to make sure all traces of vinegar are removed.

D   Really Fresh Coffee
If your Blau Coffeemaker came equipped with a coffee grinder, then you can enjoy extra fresh coffee every day. Simply add whole beans to the grinder compartment, being careful not to pass the "full" line below the rim. Make sure the lid is securely in place, then press the "grind" button.

E   Our Guarantee
Your Blau Coffeemaker has a lifetime guarantee. If your coffeemaker suffers any type of malfunction, just call our toll-free customer service line at 888–936–8721, 24 hours a day. If we are unable to help you over the phone, you may have to mail the coffeemaker to us for service.

Questions 8–11

Match each picture below with the appropriate section in the instructions.

Write the correct letter, **A–E** in boxes 8–11 on your Answer Sheet.

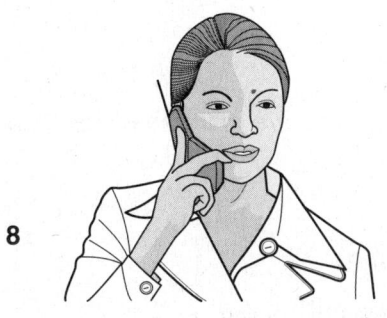

8

9

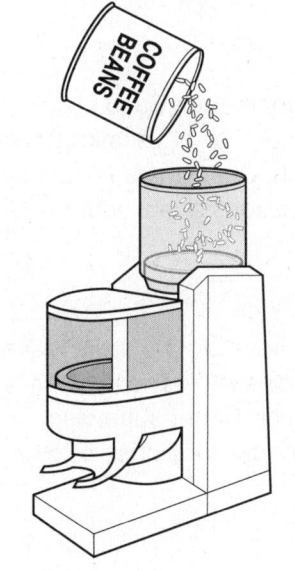

10

11

Questions 12–14

Answer the questions using **NO MORE THAN THREE WORDS** for each answer. Write your answers in boxes 12–14 on your Answer Sheet.

12 How much water should you use to make one cup of coffee?

13 How often should you clean the coffeemaker?

14 When can you call the company for assistance?

SECTION 2 *Questions 15–27*

You are advised to spend 20 minutes on questions 15–27.

Questions 15–20

Look at the information from a company's employee manual.

There are six paragraphs, **A-F**.

Choose the most suitable heading for each paragraph from the list below.

*Write the appropriate numbers (**i–viii**) in boxes 15–20 on your Answer Sheet. There are more headings than paragraphs, so you won't need to use them all.*

15 Paragraph **A**

16 Paragraph **B**

17 Paragraph **C**

18 Paragraph **D**

19 Paragraph **E**

20 Paragraph **F**

> **List of Headings**
>
> **i** Vacation and Sick Day Policy
> **ii** Cafeteria Schedule
> **iii** Getting Paid
> **iv** Employee Discounts
> **v** Use of Conference Rooms
> **vi** Work Schedule
> **vii** Office Supplies
> **viii** Budgets and Accounting

**The Mayberry Company
Employee Manual**

A

Department heads distribute checks[1] on the first and fifteenth of every month. Each check is accompanied by a statement which shows wages earned and the number of vacation[2] and sick days taken so far for the year. Overtime hours are also indicated. Checks are issued by the accounting department. Please contact them if you have any questions about your check or to report errors.

B

All new employees are entitled to two weeks of annual leave. The number of annual leave days increases with each year of employment at the company. The dates when this leave may be taken are left to the decision of the employee in consultation with his or her supervisor. In addition, employees are entitled to take five days of paid leave per year for illness or other unexpected emergencies.

C

Our normal hours of operation are 8:30 to 5:30 Monday-Friday. Any employee wishing to modify his or her hours of work must have prior approval from his or her supervisor. All employees are entitled to a daily one hour lunch break to be taken between 11:00 A.M. and 2:00 P.M.

---

[1] BRITISH: cheque
[2] BRITISH: holiday

D

Rooms 101 and 102 may be reserved if extra space is needed for meetings or presentations. Please see the office manager to schedule this. The company cafeteria can provide snacks or lunches for your event with one week's notice.

E

Paper, envelopes, pens and pencils, ink cartridges, and other similar items are stored in the closet in the coffee break room. This closet is kept unlocked, and any employee may enter it at any time to take what is needed. If you cannot find what you need there, let your supervisor know. Department heads have a budget for ordering any extra materials you may need.

F

Company employees are entitled to purchase lunch at a reduced rate in the company cafeteria. The local health club has special reduced-rate memberships available for interested employees.

Questions 21–27

Read the information about applying for a job.

Employment at XYZ, Inc.

We are always interested in hearing from qualified applicants interested in working at XYZ, Inc. You must apply for a specific position as we do not accept general applications. Review the job openings listed on our website. If you see a position you are interested in, complete the Application for Employment form. Please do not apply for more than one position at a time.

We ask that you do not call or e-mail us after submitting your application. We receive a large number of applications and cannot personally reply to them all. Be assured that we will read your application and, if we feel you are qualified for the position you have applied for, we will contact you by e-mail. You can expect to hear from us within four weeks of receipt of your application. At that time, we will ask you to make an appointment for an interview. All interviews are conducted at our downtown office.

When you come in for your interview, please dress in appropriate business attire and bring the names of references who are familiar with your business experience and qualifications. Depending on the type of position you are applying for, you may be asked to return at a later date to take a language, office skills, or other type of test. Arrangements for this will be made at the time of your interview. Thank you for your interest in XYZ, Inc. We look forward to hearing from you.

Complete the summary of information about applying for a job at XYZ, Inc.

Choose NO MORE THAN THREE WORDS from the text for each answer.

First, look at the **21** .... online. Then fill out **22** .... If you qualify for the position, the company will send you **23** .... You may have to wait **24** .... before you hear from the company. You will need to go to **25** .... for your interview. During your interview, you will be asked for **26** .... who know you and your work. Some job applicants may have to **27** .... This depends on the kind of job you apply for.

SECTION 3 *QUESTIONS 28–40*

You should spend 20 minutes on Questions 28–40, which are based on the reading passage below.

Questions 28–33

Reading Passage 3 has six sections, **A–F**.

*Choose the correct heading for sections **A–F** from the list of headings below.*

*Write the correct number **i–ix** in boxes 28–33 on your Answer Sheet.*

28 Section **A**

29 Section **B**

30 Section **C**

31 Section **D**

32 Section **E**

33 Section **F**

List of Headings
i   Newer Subway[1] Systems
ii   Early Subways in the Americas
iii Asian Subway Systems
iv   A New Device
v   The Longest Subway
vi   Subway Art
vii Europe's First Subways
viii The World's Largest Subways
ix   The Moscow Metro

A

People have been traveling by subway for well over a hundred years. The first subway systems began operating in Europe in the second half of the nineteenth century. London's subway system, known as "The Underground" or "The Tube," opened in early 1863. In 1896, subways began running in both Budapest, Hungary and Glasgow, Scotland. The Budapest subway ran from the center of the city to City Park and was just under four kilometers long. The city of Paris, France began operating its subway system in 1900. Its famous name, Metro, is short for *Chemin de Fer Metropolitan* or Metropolitan Railway. Many other cities have since adopted the name Metro for their own subways.

B

The city of Boston, Massachusetts boasts the oldest subway system in the United States, beginning operations in 1897. It had only two stations when it first opened. The New York City Subway, now one of the largest subway systems in the world, began running in 1904. The original line was 14.5 kilometers long and ran from City Hall in downtown Manhattan to 145th Street. The city of Philadelphia opened its first subway line in 1907. The oldest subway in Latin America began operations in Buenos Aires, Argentina in 1913. It is called the *subte*, short for *subterraneo* or underground.

[1]BRITISH: underground

C

The second half of the twentieth century saw new subway systems constructed in cities around the world. Many Korean cities have modern subway systems, the largest one in the capital city of Seoul, with 287 kilometers of track. The first subway in Brazil opened in the city of Sao Paulo in 1974. Since then subways have been built in a number of other Brazilian cities, including Rio de Janeiro and the capital, Brasilia. Washington, DC began running the Washington Metro in 1976. Hong Kong opened its subway in 1979. This system includes four lines that run under Victoria Harbour. In 2000, a 17-mile long subway system was completed in Los Angeles, a city infamous for its traffic problems and resulting smog. Construction of this system took fourteen years to complete.

D

With a total of 468 stations and 656 miles of passenger service track, the New York City Subway is among the largest subway systems in the world. If the tracks in train yards, shops, and storage areas are added in, the total track length of the New York Subway comes to 842 miles. Measured by number of riders, the Moscow Metro is the world's largest system, with 3.2 billion riders annually. Other cities with busy subways include Tokyo, with 2.6 billion riders a year, and Seoul and Mexico City, both carrying 1.4 billion riders annually.

E

In some cities, the subway stations are famous for their architecture and artwork. The stations of the Moscow Metro are well-known for their beautiful examples of socialist-realist art. The Baker Street station in London honors the fictional detective, Sherlock Holmes, who supposedly lived on Baker Street. Decorative tiles in the station's interior depict the character, and a Sherlock Holmes statue sits outside one of the station exits. Each of the stations of the new Los Angeles subway system contains murals, sculptures, or other examples of decorative artwork.

F

A new feature now often included in the construction of new subway stations is the Platform Screen Door (PSD). The Singapore subway was the first to be built with the inclusion of PSDs. The original purpose was to reduce high air-conditioning costs in underground stations. Since then, there has been more and more focus on the safety aspects of this device, as it can prevent people from accidentally falling or being pushed onto the track. PSDs also keep the station platforms quieter and cleaner and allow trains to enter stations at higher rates of speed. The subway system in Hong Kong was the first to have PSDs added to an already existing system. They are becoming more common in subway systems around the world. Tokyo, Seoul, Bangkok, London, and Copenhagen are just some of the cities that have PSDs in at least some of their subway stations. PSDs are also often used with other forms of transportation, such as monorails, light rail systems, and airport transportation systems.

Questions 34–41

Look at the following descriptions (Questions 33–40) of some of the subway systems mentioned in Reading Passage 3.

Match the cities (**A–L**) listed below with the descriptions of their subway systems.

Write the appropriate letters **A–L** in boxes 34–41 on your Answer Sheet.

34 has a station celebrating a storybook character	**A** Hong Kong
	B Paris
35 is the busiest subway system in the world	**C** Washington, DC
	D Sao Paulo
36 has lent its name to subway systems around the world	**E** London
	F Tokyo
37 has several lines running under water	**G** Seoul
	H Buenos Aires
38 was the first subway system constructed with PSDs	**I** Singapore
	J Budapest
39 has a total length of 287 kilometers	**K** Moscow
	L New York
40 was the first subway built in Latin America	

41 opened in 1976

GENERAL TRAINING Model Test 1

Candidate Name _____

INTERNATIONAL ENGLISH LANGUAGE TESTING SYSTEM

GENERAL TRAINING WRITING

TIME 1 hour

INSTRUCTIONS TO CANDIDATES

Do not open this booklet until you are told to do so.

Write your name and candidate number in the space at the top of this page.

All answers must be written on the separate answer booklet provided.

Do not remove this booklet from the examination room.

INFORMATION FOR CANDIDATES

There are **2** tasks on this question paper.

You must do **both** tasks.

Underlength answers will be penalized[1].

---

[1]BRITISH: penalised

WRITING TASK 1

You should spend about 20 minutes on this task.

> *You are going to spend your vacation in a city in a foreign country. You have never been there before. Your cousin has a friend who lives there. Write a letter to the friend. In your letter*
> *- introduce yourself*
> *- say why you are making this trip*
> *- ask some questions about the city (e.g. places to see, things to do, things to bring)*

Write at least 150 words.

You do NOT need to write any addresses.

Begin your letter as follows:

Dear John,

WRITING TASK 2

You should spend about 40 minutes on this task.

Write about the following topic:

> *Modern technology, such as personal computers and the Internet, have made it possible for many people to do their work from home at least part of the time instead of going to an office every day. What are some of the advantages and disadvantages of this situation?*

Give reasons for your answer and include any relevant examples from your own knowledge or experience.

Write at least 250 words.

IELTS MODEL TESTS

GENERAL TRAINING: READING WRITING MODEL TEST 2

General Training Model Test 2

Candidate Name _____

INTERNATIONAL ENGLISH LANGUAGE TESTING SYSTEM

GENERAL TRAINING READING

TIME 1 hour

INSTRUCTIONS TO CANDIDATES

Do not open this booklet until you are told to do so.

Write your name and candidate number in the space at the top of this page.

Start at the beginning of the test and work through it.

You should answer all questions.

If you cannot do a particular question, leave it and go on to the next. You can return to it later.

All answers must be written on the answer sheet.

Do not remove this booklet from the examination room.

INFORMATION FOR CANDIDATES

There are **40** questions on this question paper.

The test is divided as follows:

Section 1	Questions 1–14
Section 2	Questions 15–27
Section 3	Questions 28–40

SECTION 1   QUESTIONS 1–13

You are advised to spend 20 minutes on Questions 1–13.

Questions 1–7

Read the notice below. Answer the questions below using NO MORE THAN THREE WORDS *for each answer. Write your answers in boxes 1–6 on your Answer Sheet.*

To all tenants of Parkside Towers:
Please be advised of the building painting schedule.

Dec. 1–4:   Main foyer. Please don't use the main entrance at this time. Use the parking garage entrance to access the building.

Dec. 5–8:   Garage stairway and elevator[1]. Please stay away from these areas at this time. If you park in the garage, you will have to walk outside to the front of the building to gain access through the main entrance.

Dec. 9–13:   East stairway and elevators. If your apartment is in the East Wing, please use the West Wing elevators or stairway at this time.

Dec. 14–21:   West and north stairways and elevators. If your apartment is in these areas of the building, please use the east stairway or elevator at this time.

Dec. 22–27:   Parking garage. The garage will not be available to tenants at this time. In order to avoid illegal on-street parking, spaces in the parking lot[2] across the street will be made available to all tenants.

We are sorry for the inconvenience. If you have any questions or complaints, please contact the building manager.

If you would like to schedule painting for your apartment[3], please fill out a painting request form, available in the main lobby.

---

1 It's December 3rd. Which part of the building is being painted?

2 It's December 7th. How can you enter the building?

3 It's December 12th. How can you reach a tenth floor apartment in the East Wing?

4 You live on the sixth floor in the North Wing. How can you reach your apartment on December 15th?

5 Where should you park your car on December 24th?

6 What should you do if you are unhappy about the painting schedule?

7 What should you do if you want to have your apartment painted?

[1]BRITISH: lift
[2]BRITISH: car park
[3]BRITISH: flat

Questions 8–13

Read the bill from the electric company and answer the questions.

Write NO MORE THAN THREE WORDS for each answer.

Write your answers in boxes 8–14 on your Answer Sheet.

EnviroElectric Company

Date: 2 August

Customer name:
Oswald Robertson
15A Peacock Lane
Mayfield

For: 1 July–31 July—	Total charges:	£35
	Previous bill:	£29
	Payment:	–£29
	Total due:	£35

We must receive your payment in full by 21 August or a late fee of £2.50 will be assessed. Please make out your check to EnviroElectric Company and mail it to:
EnviroElectric Company
PO Box 30682
East Bradfield

Or, pay by credit card:
Number: _____ Expiration date: _____

Signature: _____

Cash payments may be made by visiting any branch of the Bradfield Bank.

Account questions? Call (01 223) 385–9387
For repair service, call (01 223) 385–9856

---

8 How much did Mr. Robertson pay on his electric bill in June?

9 When is his July bill due?

10 What is the total amount Mr. Robertson will owe if he makes a late payment on his July bill?

11 Where is the EnviroElectric Company located?

12 If Mr. Robertson wants to pay cash, what should he do?

13 If Mr. Robinson thinks the company has charged him too much, what should he do?

SECTION 2   QUESTIONS 14–27

You are advised to spend 20 minutes on Questions 14–27.

Questions 14–20

Read the information about repetitive stress injury.

> Repetitive Stress Injury (RSI) is the irritation of muscles, nerves, or tendons resulting from repetitive motions. In other words, it is an injury that comes from making the same movements again and again. It is a particular problem in the modern office, where workers spend hours a day in front of computers. In fact, the most commonly reported RSIs are related to computer use. In the past, office tasks were more varied. People had to stand up to go to the copy machine or filing cabinet. Now, almost everything is done on computers and as a result, people spend hours a day sitting in the same position and repeating the same motions.

> Fatigue, numbness, and pain in the hands, arms, neck, or shoulders are signs of RSI. These symptoms arise during an activity which involves repetitive motion and often cease when the activity stops. If left untreated, however, the discomfort starts lasting longer and becomes more intense. The pain can eventually become so severe as to cause long-lasting damage.

> Some common causes of RSI in an office setting are poorly designed keyboards and chairs, spending long hours in the same position, and the use of a computer mouse. Computer keyboards force the user to continually hold the hands with the palms down. This is an unnatural position and causes strain on the hands, fingers, and wrists. Desk chairs often do not support the user's posture, but instead encourage slumping, which results in poor circulation. Holding a computer mouse causes strain on the hand muscles. In addition, using a mouse requires the repetitive motion of one finger.

> RSI can be a serious problem if ignored. Fortunately, it isn't difficult to prevent. The best form of prevention is to take frequent breaks from work. A minimum of five minutes every hour is recommended. This will give your hands, wrists, and back a chance to change position and rest. If you spend hours typing, a wrist rest for your computer keyboard will help protect your wrists from strain. You can also protect your wrists by holding your palms parallel to the keyboard and keeping your forearms in a horizontal position. You can support your posture by adding armrests to your chair. This will actually aid in supporting your back and help you maintain a good posture.

Complete the sentences about the reading passage below.

Choose your answers from the box on the next page, and write them in boxes 14–20 on your Answer Sheet. There are more choices than sentences so you will not use them all.

14 In the past, people moved around the office a lot, but now the average office employee _____ all day.

15 When RSI is not treated, the pain _____.

16 Computer keyboards cause users to hold their hands in a position that _____.

17 _____ causes repeated stress on one finger.

18 _____ often can help prevent serious problems.

19 Holding your hands and arms in the proper position _____.

20 Using armrests on your chair _____.

A	supports the back
B	isn't difficult to prevent
C	holding a computer mouse
D	protects the wrists
E	is never recommended
F	works on a computer
G	typing for long hours
H	uses a filing cabinet
I	taking a break
J	becomes serious and permanent
K	is not natural

Questions 21–27

Read the information about company policy

Comet Corporation
Vacation[1] and Sick Leave Policy
To all employees: Please read the following information carefully. If you have any questions, contact the Human Resources Department.

Vacation/Personal Leave

Employees may use their vacation days when they choose, with the permission of their supervisor. To apply for permission, Form 101A must be completed and submitted at least three weeks ahead of time. Forms are available in the Human Resources Department.

Sick Days

Sick days are to be used in the case of illness or for doctor's appointments only. They may not be used as extra vacation days. Permission is not required to use these days, but department heads should be notified as soon as possible about unexpected absences due to illness. Supervisors should also be informed in a timely manner when employees need to be absent to attend doctor's appointments. Supervisors may request written confirmation of appointments from the doctor's office if they desire.

Rolling Over Vacation Days

Any vacation days that are not used up by the end of the calendar year will not be lost. Instead, they may be rolled over and added to the vacation days for the following year. This policy does not apply to sick days.

[1]BRITISH: Holiday

Do the following statements agree with the information in the reading passage?

In boxes 21–27 on your Answer Sheet, write

TRUE	*if the statement is true according to the passage.*
FALSE	*if the statement contradicts the passage.*
NOT GIVEN	*if there is no information about this in the passage.*

21 Employees must get permission from the Human Resources Department to use vacation days.

22 All employees at the Comet Corporation get three weeks of vacation a year.

23 Employees may use some of their sick days in order to take a longer vacation.

24 An employee does not need to ask for permission before using a sick day.

25 Employees must have confirmation from a doctor in order to use a sick day.

26 An employee may use fewer vacation days one year in order to have more the next year.

27 Sick days that are not used before the end of the year may be used the following year.

SECTION 3 *QUESTIONS 28–40*

You should spend 20 minutes on Questions 28–40, which are based on the reading passage below.

Stonehenge

Approximately two miles west of Amesbury, Wiltshire, in southern England stands Stonehenge, one of the world's most famous megalithic monuments. The remains of Stonehenge consist of a series of stone structures arranged in layers of circular and horseshoe-like patterns. Theories and myths concerning this mysterious monument have flourished for thousands of years. The Danes, Egyptians, and Druids are just a few of the groups who have been credited with building Stonehenge. Some people have even made attempts to prove that aliens erected Stonehenge. Early historians believed that the monument was constructed as a memorial to nobles killed in combat, while other later theorists described Stonehenge as a place for sacrificial ceremonies. Regardless of who built the monument and why, all of the legends surrounding these megaliths are based on speculation. With the exception of archeological evidence, very little of what we understand about Stonehenge today can actually be called fact.

Stonehenge was constructed in three phases during the Neolithic and Bronze Age periods. Stonehenge period 1, also commonly referred to as Phase 1, is believed to have occurred sometime around 3000 B.C., during the middle Neolithic period. In this first step of the construction, picks made of deer antlers were used to dig a series of 56 pits. These pits were later named "Aubrey Holes" after an English scholar. Outside of the holes was dug a large circular henge (a ditch with an earthen wall). During this phase, a break, or entranceway was also dug on the northeast corner of the henge. Archeologists[1] today refer to this break as the Avenue. Two stones were set in the Avenue. The "Slaughter Stone" was placed just inside

[1]BRITISH: archaeologists

the circle, while the "Heel Stone" was placed 27 meters down the Avenue. The Heel Stone weighs about 35 tons and is made of natural sandstone, believed to have originated from Marlborough Downs, an area 20 miles north of the monument. The 35-foot-wide Avenue is set so that, from the center of Stonehenge, a person would be able to see the sunrise to the left of the heel stone. Just inside the henge, four other "Station Stones" were placed in a rectangular formation.

There is great debate over how long the first phase of Stonehenge was used and when the original alterations were made; however, the second phase is generally placed between 2900 B.C. and 2400 B.C. and accredited to the Beaker people. It is thought that many wooden posts were added to the monument during this phase. One of the problems archeologists have had with Phase 2 is that unlike stone or holes in the earth, wood does not hold up over thousands of years. The numerous stake holes in the earth tell the story of where these posts were positioned. Besides the ones in the center of the henge, six rows of posts were placed near the entrance. These may have been used to mark astronomical measurements, or to guide people to the center. The original Aubrey holes were filled in either with earth or cremation remains. Many archeologists believed that the Beaker people were sun worshipers[1], and that they may have purposely changed the main axis of the monument and widened the entrance during this phase in order to show their appreciation for the sun.

The final phase of Stonehenge is usually described in terms of three subphases, each one involving a setting of large stones. The first stones that arrived were bluestones, brought all the way from the Preseli Hills in Pembrokeshire, Wales. A horseshoe of paired bluestones was placed in the center of the henge, with a tall Altar Stone marking the end of the formation. In the next subphase, a 30-meter ring of sandstones called the Sarsen Circle was built around the bluestones. Only 17 of the original 30 stones remain. These sarasen stones were connected with lintel blocks, each precisely carved in order to fit end-to-end and form perfectly with the stone circle. Approximately 60 more bluestones were then added inside the original horseshoe.

How these enormous stones were transported and raised in Phase 3 remains a mystery. The fact that these monoliths were built before the wheel means an incredible amount of manual labor was used. It is believed that a pulley system using rollers still would have required at least one hundred men to operate. Raising the lintels and fitting them into one another would have been another major struggle without the use of machines. Stonehenge remains one of the world's greatest mysteries and one of England's most important icons.

[1]BRITISH: worshippers

Questions 28–31

Complete the labels on the diagram of Stonehenge below.

Choose your answers from the box at the right of the diagram, and write them in boxes 28–31 on your Answer Sheet. There are more words than spaces, so you will not use them all.

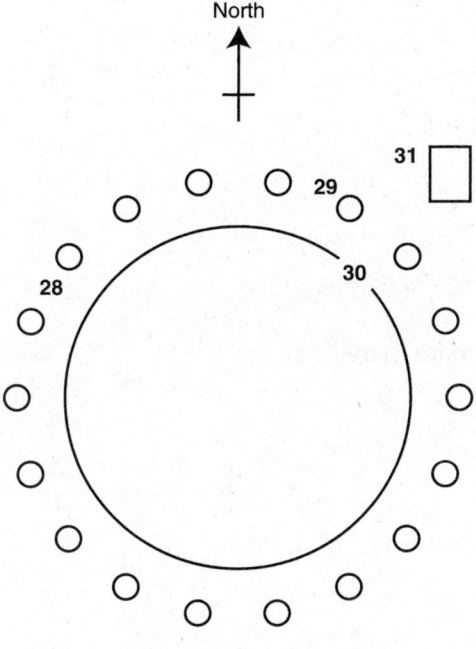

North

Stonehedge Phase 1

Aubrey Holes
Heel Stone
Marlborough Downs
Avenue
Henge
Station Stones

Questions 32–40

Stonehenge was built in three phases. During which phase did the following things occur? In boxes 32–40 on your Answer Sheet, write

A if it occurred during Phase 1.
B if it occurred during Phase 2.
C if it occurred during Phase 3.

32 The entrance was made wider.

33 The Slaughter Stone was erected.

34 Stones were placed in a horseshoe formation.

35 Wooden posts were set near the entrance.

36 Deer antlers were used to dig holes.

37 Bluestones were brought from a distant location.

38 A ring of sandstones was constructed.

39 Holes were filled with dirt.

40 The Altar Stone was erected.

GENERAL TRAINING Model Test 2

Candidate Name _____

INTERNATIONAL ENGLISH LANGUAGE TESTING SYSTEM

GENERAL TRAINING WRITING

TIME 1 hour

INSTRUCTIONS TO CANDIDATES

Do not open this booklet until you are told to do so.

Write your name and candidate number in the space at the top of this page.

All answers must be written on the separate answer booklet provided.

Do not remove this booklet from the examination room.

INFORMATION FOR CANDIDATES

There are **2** tasks on this question paper.

You must do **both** tasks.

Underlength answers will be penalized.

WRITING TASK 1

You should spend about 20 minutes on this task.

> *You stayed at a hotel last week. After you got home you realized that you had left your watch behind. Write a letter to the hotel manager, and explain what happened. Describe the watch, and ask them to help you find it.*

Write at least 150 words.

You do NOT need to write any addresses.

Begin your letter as follows:

Dear Sir or Madam:

WRITING TASK 2

You should spend about 40 minutes on this task.

Write about the following topic:

> *Children today spend more time watching television than they did in the past. Describe some of the advantages and disadvantages of television for children.*

Give reasons for your answer and include any relevant examples from your own knowledge or experience.

Write at least 250 words.

ANSWER KEYS
FOR THE MODULE
ACTIVITIES

- LISTENING MODULE
- READING MODULE
- WRITING MODULE
- SPEAKING MODULE

LISTENING MODULE

Completing the Blanks

Number of Words and Spelling

2. <u>the train station</u> The word *to* is unnecessary after *near*. The word *station* is misspelled[1].
3. <u>pay a fine</u> The other words are unnecessary and exceed the three-word limit.
4. <u>the weather</u> or <u>the bad weather</u> The expression *because of* must be followed by a noun, not by a clause. The words *very bad* are unnecessary.
5. <u>rose garden</u> The word *rose* must be singular because it serves as an adjective to describe *garden*. The words *beautiful, sunny* are not necessary and make the answer exceed the three-word limit.
6. <u>can choose</u> The word *usually* is not necessary. The word *can* is always followed by the base form of the verb, not the infinitive form.
7. <u>About ten thousand</u> Use *about* instead of *more or less* to stay within the three-word limit. The word *thousand* is misspelled. An exact number is not followed by *of*.
8. <u>ask the professor</u> The phrase *have to* cannot correctly follow *should* or any other modal.
9. <u>going to Alaska</u> or <u>traveling to Alaska</u> It is not necessary to repeat the word *about*. Using *going to* or *traveling to* instead of *his trip to* keeps the answer within the three-word limit. (BRITISH: travelling)
10. <u>spend the winter</u> The word *long* is not necessary and makes the answer exceed the three-word limit. The word *winter* is misspelled.

Gender and Number

1. <u>build their nests</u> The word *their* is misspelled and *nests* must be plural because it refers to many nests belonging to many ducks.
2. <u>business travelers</u> The word *business* is misspelled. The word *travelers* should be plural because *among* implies that there are many. (BRITISH: travellers)
3. <u>tropical climates</u> It isn't necessary to repeat the word *in*. The word *a* is incorrect before a plural noun. The word *tropical* is misspelled.
4. <u>costs more</u> The word *fruit* is a non-count noun and takes a singular verb. The word *more* is misspelled.
5. <u>her old clothes</u> The feminine possessive adjective *her* agrees with the feminine subject *Mrs. Smith*. The word *clothes* is misspelled.
6. <u>take two exams</u> Don't use *must* after *have to*—they have the same meaning. The word *exams* must be plural because there are *two*.
7. <u>a new house</u> The singular noun *house* must be preceded by an article.
8. <u>took their vacation</u> The plural adjective *their* agrees with the plural subject. The word *vacation* is singular. (BRITISH: took their holiday)
9. <u>has a garden</u> The verb *has* agrees with the singular subject *Every house*.
10. <u>lays her eggs</u> or <u>lays its eggs</u> The words *like to* are unnecessary and make the answer exceed the three-word limit. The possessive adjective must agree with the subject *female dragonfly—her* because the subject is female, or *its* because the subject is an animal.

[1]BRITISH: mis-spelt

Articles

1. *all the assignments* The article *the* is required because these are specific assignments—the ones in this class. The word *assignments* is plural because *all* implies that there are more than one.
2. *Moths* This sentence is a general statement, but the subject must be plural to agree with the plural verb *fly*.
3. *The butterfly* *The* is required because this refers to a specific butterfly—the one the professor showed us.
4. *a new library* A specific library is not referred to here, so the article *a* is used.
5. *Air pollution* This is a non-count, nonspecific noun.
6. *An animal* The sentence is a general statement, but the subject must be singular to agree with the singular verb *has*.
7. *the ticket* *The* is required because this refers to a specific ticket—*your ticket*.
   Keep your ticket with you at all times. To get a discount at the museum gift shop, show .... to the gift shop clerk.
8. *The information* *The* is required because this refers to the specific information *in this book*.
9. *Gold* This is a non-count, nonspecific noun.
10. *A pet parrot* The sentence is a general statement, but the subject must be singular to agree with the singular verb *requires*.

Gerunds, Infinitives, and Base Form Verbs

1. *reading this novel* The verb *finish* is followed by a gerund.
2. *plans to arrive* The verb *plan* is followed by the infinitive.
3. *wait for Jim* *Should* is a modal, so it is followed by base form.
4. *have a ticket* *Must* is a modal, so it is followed by base form.
5. *Paying a deposit* In this case, the gerund acts as the subject of the sentence.
6. *to get reservations* *Easier* is an adjective that is followed by the infinitive.
7. *giving his report* *About* is a preposition followed by a gerund.
8. *miss more than* *Cannot* is a modal, so it is followed by base form.
9. *fulfilling the lab* *About* is a preposition followed by a gerund.
10. *to see alligators* The verb *hope* is followed by the infinitive.

Listening Skills

Target 1—Making Assumptions

SECTION 1

1. Kingston
2. State
3. 7
4. 721-1127
5. December
6. C
7. D
8. F (Please note that answers for 6–8 can be in any order)
9. month
10. 50 percent

SECTION 2

11. 15
12. 11
13. Tuesday
14. Modern art
15. City Gallery
16. Portraits
17. East Room
18. art reproductions
19. repairs
20. Second floor

Target 2—Understanding Numbers

Example: 33

1. 8677532148	5. XY 538	8. 2876216
2. C	6. 6370550	9. 4553021
3. 575-3174	7. 2651811	10. 3058480
4. B		

Target 3—Understanding the Alphabet

Example: Lynne

1. Tomas	7. A. Miranda	10. A. String
2. Maine	B. 7043218	B. 15 B
3. Patti	8. A. Bijou	11. A. Willard
4. Roberts	B. 232–5488	B. 70
5. Springvale	9. A. Janson	12. A. 1705
6. Dixson	B. 335	B. Landover

Target 4—Listening for Descriptions

Example

A. It's a house with a flat roof. It's two floors high. On the first floor there is a large window and a door. On the second floor there is a row of windows.
B. It's a small house that's only one floor high. It has a door with a window on each side of it.
C. It's a single-story house for two families. It has two doors and one small window.

1. A. He's a short man with short hair and a mustache[1]. He's neither fat nor thin.
   B. He's a tall, thin man. He has long hair.
   C. He's a fat, bald man with a beard. He's neither short nor tall.
2. A. She's a young woman with long hair. She's very thin, and she's wearing earrings.
   B. She's a middle-aged woman with long grey hair. She's wearing earrings.
   C. She's a young woman with short, curly hair. She's wearing a necklace.
3. C
4. A

Target 5—Listening for Time

Example: A

TIME	DATE	DAY	YEAR	SEASON
1. B	1. 15	1. Monday	1. 1803	1. winter
2. A	2. December	2. Thursday	2. 1851	2. summer
3. C	3. September	3. Thursday	3. B	3. C
4. C	4. 7	4. Friday	4. C	4. B
5. 12:15	5. C	5. B	5. 1985	5. fall
6. 4:00	6. A	6. B	6. 1988	6. winter

[1]BRITISH: moustache

Target 6—Listening for Frequency

Example: B

1. sometimes	4. never	7. daily	10. from time to time
2. seldom	5. often	8. once a month	11. once a month
3. always	6. always	9. twice a week	12. every other week

Target 7—Listening for Similar Meanings

Example 1: college graduates	1. party	4. vegetation
Example 2: C	2. checks	5. available
Example 3: A	3. rate	6. occupation

Target 8—Listening for Emotions

Example: A

1. C	3. B	5. A
2. A	4. C	6. C

Target 9—Listening for an Explanation

Example

1. A
2. E
3. C
4. D
5. F
6. B
7. the electrical outlet/socket
8. the cord
9. the appliance
10. wires
11. hot
12. orange
13. turns brown
14. toast

Questions 1–12

1. cacao tree
2. cacao fruit
3. seeds/cocoa beans
4. vat for fermenting
5. drying trays
6. chocolate factory
7. is harvested
8. are removed
9. about a week
10. dry/are dried
11. are shipped/sent to
12. delicious chocolate treats

Target 10—Listening for Classifications

Example

Course Offerings

1 Academic Program	2 Business Program
Introduction to Art Basic Chemistry Beginning Spanish	Organizational Behavior/Behaviour Commercial Law Compensation and Benefits
History of Africa	Project Management
Literature of the 21st Century	The Art of Negotiating
International Relations	Creativity in the Workplace
Introduction to Philosophy	Labor/Labour Negotiations

Questions 1–5

1. A, C, E
2. (A) Horror, (B) Romantic
3. (A) Butterflies, (B) Moths
4. C, D
5. (A) Ornamental, (B) Shade, (C) Evergreen

Target 11—Listening for Comparisons and Contrasts

Example

A. Different	C. Different	E. Alike	G. Alike
B. Alike	D. Alike	F. Different	H. Different

1.	2.	3.	4.
A. Different	A. Alike	A. Different	A. Alike
B. Different	B. Different	B. Alike	B. Different
C. Alike	C. Different	C. Alike	C. Different
D. Different	D. Different	D. Different	D. Different
E. Alike	E. Alike	E. Different	E. Alike

Target 12—Listening for Negative Meanings

Example: B

1. A	4. A	7. B	10. A
2. A	5. A	8. A	11. C
3. B	6. B	9. C	12. A

Target 13—Listening for Chronology

Example

1. Orientation session
2. Do research
3. Final exam

Questions 1–5

1. 1,3,2,5,4,6
2. 1,2,3,5,4
3. 2,3,1,5,4
4. 2,1,4,3,5
5. 2,1,3,5,4

READING MODULE

Reading Skills

Target 1—Using the First Paragraph to Make Predictions

PRACTICE 1

1. **Topic Sentence.** The spread of wildfire is a natural phenomenon that occurs throughout the world and is especially common in forested areas of North America, Australia, and Europe.

   Definition of Topic. Locations that receive plenty of rainfall but also experience periods of intense heat or drought are particularly susceptible to wildfires.

   Author's Opinion. None given.

   Organizational Clues. Author may discuss
   - How wildfires start
   - How to control wildfires
   - Wildfires as a global problem

2. **Topic Sentence.** In reality, birds may actually be a great deal more intelligent than humans have given them credit for.

   Definition of Topic. For a long time, scientists considered birds to be of lesser intelligence because the cerebral cortex, the part of the brain that humans and other animals use for intelligence, is relatively small in size.

   Author's Opinion. None given.

   Organizational Clues. Author may discuss
   - Misunderstandings about the intelligence of birds
   - The anatomy of a bird's brain
   - Evidence of avian intelligence

3. **Topic Sentence.** She would grow up to become one of the richest women in the world.

   Definition of Topic. Her name was Hetty Green, but she was known to many as the Witch of Wall Street.

   Author's Opinion. None given.

   Organizational Clues. Author may discuss
   - Hetty Green's early years
   - How Hetty Green got rich
   - Why Hetty Green had a nickname

Target 2—Using the Topic Sentence to Make Predictions

PRACTICE 2

1. **Topic Sentence.** To combat excessive thoughts and impulses, most OCD sufferers perform certain repetitive rituals that they believe will relieve their anxiety.

   Questions to Ask Yourself
   What types of rituals do they perform?
   How does this help them?

2. **Topic Sentence.** A child's upbringing does not seem to be part of the cause of the disorder, though stress can make the symptoms stronger.

   Questions to Ask Yourself
   Is the disorder present at birth?
   Are there outside factors involved?
   What leads parents to seek treatment?

3. **Topic Sentence.** Research on OCD sufferers has found certain physiological trends.

   Questions to Ask Yourself
   What part of the body does it affect?
   What are some common trends?
   What can parents look for?

Target 3—Looking for Specific Details

PRACTICE 3

1. **Supporting Details**
   Compulsions can be mental or physical
   Examples include: checking, hand washing, disturbing images
   Compulsions and obsessions may or may not be related

2. **Supporting Details**
   Most cases are genetic
   Stress can add to the problem
   Many members of the family may have OCD

3. **Supporting Details**
   Over activity of blood in the brain
   Less serotonin
   Linked to other disorders such as Tourette syndrome and ADHD

Target 4—Analyzing the Questions and Answers

PRACTICE 4

Key Words in Statements 9–16: (Answers may vary.) child, stress, serotonin, age 17, psychotherapy, medication, treat, secret, antibiotics

1. *unreasonable.* Paragraph 1 states that, "OCD sufferers understand that their obsessions are unrealistic."
2. *control.* Paragraph 1 states that "they find it stressful to put these intrusive thoughts out of their minds."
3. *reduce.* The first sentence of paragraph 3 states: "To combat excessive thoughts and impulses, most OCD sufferers perform certain repetitive rituals that they believe will relieve their anxiety."
4. *obsession.* Paragraph 2 states that "Fear of dirt and contamination are very common obsessive thoughts."
5. *checking.* Paragraph 3 states that "Common rituals include excessive checking."
6. *throw away.* The last sentence in paragraph 3 states that, "Holding onto objects that would normally be discarded, such as newspapers and containers, is another common compulsion."
7. *inherited.* Paragraph 4 states that "a number of different genetic factors" have been found as underlying causes of the disease.

8. *cause*. Paragraph 5 gives an example of an illness (strep throat) that is thought to be the cause behind some OCD cases.

9. False. Paragraph 4 states: "A child's upbringing does not seem to be part of the cause of the disorder, though stress can make the symptoms stronger. The underlying causes of OCD have been researched greatly, and point to a number of different genetic factors."

10. True. Paragraph 4 states: "A child's upbringing does not seem to be part of the cause of the disorder, though stress can make the symptoms stronger."

11. True. Paragraph 5 states: "Studies have also shown that OCD sufferers have less serotonin than the average person."

12. False. Paragraph 4 states: "OCD symptoms generally begin between the age of 10 and 24 and continue indefinitely until a person seeks treatment."

13. Not Given. Paragraph 6 mentions both psychotherapy and medication but does not discuss which one patients prefer.

14. False. Paragraph 6 discusses different treatment options, and states that, "early diagnosis and proper medication can lessen many of the symptoms and allow people to live fairly normal lives."

15. True. Paragraph 6 begins with this sentence: "Because OCD sufferers tend to be so secretive about their symptoms, they often put off treatment for many years."

16. True. The final sentence in Paragraph 6 indicates that antibiotics can be used in special cases of OCD: "For cases when OCD is linked to streptococcal infection, antibiotic therapy is sometimes all that is needed."

Target 5—Identifying the Tasks

PRACTICE 5

Topic Sentence. The South African province of KwaZulu-Natal, more commonly referred to as the Zulu Kingdom, is named after the Zulu people who have inhabited the area since the late 1400s.

Questions to Ask Yourself
Who are the Zulu people?
What is the history behind this clan?
What are they known for?

Supporting Details
Large South African ethnic group
Region explored by Europeans
Zulu wear traditional jewelry/jewellry and clothing
Beadwork is important to the culture

Analyzing the Questions
1. Where?
2. Where?
3. Who?
4. Where?
5. When?
6. How many?
7. Who? Where? **Key Words:** British
8. What? **Key Words:** Henry Frances Flynn
9. What? **Key Words:** precious stones
10. What? Why? **Key Words:** daily lives
11. What? Why? **Key Words:** gourds

PASSAGE 1

1. (E) Paragraph 1 states: "KwaZulu translates to mean 'Place of Heaven'."
2. (B) Paragraph 1 states: "'Natal' was the name the Portuguese explorers gave this region when they arrived in 1497."
3. (C) Paragraph 1 states: "By the late 1700s, the AmaZulu clan, meaning 'People of Heaven,' constituted a significant nation."
4. *South Africa*. The first sentence of Paragraph 1 states that KwaZulu-Natal is a South African province.
5. *1497*. Paragraph 1 states: "Portuguese explorers . . . arrived in 1497."
6. *11 million*. Midway through paragraph 1 the passage states: "Today the Zulu clan represents the largest ethnic group in South Africa, with at least 11 million people in the kingdom."
7. *False*. Paragraph 2 talks about how the Egyptians were the first to bring beads to the area, though the British later facilitated the trade.
8. *Not Given*. Paragraph 2 states that Henry Frances Flynn brought glass beads to the region, but it doesn't state anywhere that he earned a lot of money doing this.
9. *False*. Paragraph 3 states: "The Zulu people were not fooled into believing that glass beads were precious stones but, rather, used the beads to establish certain codes and rituals in their society."
10. *True*. Paragraphs 3 discusses how beads are used for adornment, education, recreation, and communication.
11. *True*. Paragraph 3 discusses how bead-covered gourds are carried around by women who are having fertility problems. "Fertility problems" means *difficulty becoming and staying pregnant.*
12. *unmarried man*. Paragraph 4 states: "A triangle with the apex pointing downward signifies an unmarried man."
13. *married man*. Paragraph 4 states that "married men signify their marital status with two triangles that form an hourglass shape."
14. *married woman*. Paragraph 4 states: "Married women wear items with two triangles that form a diamond shape."
15. *unmarried woman*. Paragraph 4 states that a triangle "with the tip pointing upward is worn by an unmarried woman."

PASSAGE 2

Note: Alternative spellings: colour blindness, colour, colourful

1. iii. What is colorblindness? Paragraph A discusses what people think color blindness is, and what it really is. In the middle of the paragraph it states, "The fact is that in most cases of colorblindness, there are only certain shades that a person cannot distinguish between. These people are said to be dichromatic."
2. viii. Colorblindness and the Sexes. Paragraph B discusses the fact that men are more prone to colorblindness than women, and states the genetic reasons why this is the case.
3. vii. Developing the Ability to See Color. Paragraph C discusses the fact that babies are all born colorblind and that they do not develop the ability to see colors until they are a few months old. This paragraph also discusses the possibility that infants may require a colorful environment in order to develop proper color vision.
4. ii. Diagnosing Colorblindness. Paragraph D discusses the reasons why colorblindness is difficult to diagnose. It also discusses the Ishihara Test, which distinguishes those who are colorblind from those who have normal color vision.
5. v. Unsolved Myths. Paragraph E mentions two beliefs about colorblindness that haven't been proven as myths: that colorblindness can aid military soldiers and that everyone is colorblind in an emergency.
6. (C) The second to the last sentence of Paragraph A states that: "People with trichromatic vision have all three cones in working order."

7. (B) The second sentence in Paragraph C states that: "A baby's cones do not begin to differentiate between many different colors until the baby is approximately four months old."

8. (C) Paragraph D states the main downfall of the Ishihara Test: "The Ishihara Test is the most common, though it is highly criticized because it requires that children have the ability to recognize numerals."

9. *myth*. Paragraph B introduces the idea that although color vision deficiency is predominant in males, it is still possible for females to be colorblind.

10. *a little less*. Paragraph B states: "In an average population, 8% of males exhibit some form of colorblindness."

11. *X chromosomes*. Paragraph B states: "Females have two X chromosomes."

12. *less likely*. Paragraph B explains that it is less likely for women to be colorblind, because if one of their X chromosomes "carries the defective gene, the other one naturally compensates."
   "Compensate" means *to make up for another's weakness*.

PASSAGE 3

1. (A) Paragraph 2 discusses how Antarctic penguins "huddle in communities" to keep warm.

2. (A) The first sentence of Paragraph 3 states: "Antarctic penguins spend about 75 percent of their lives in the water."

3. (A) Paragraph 3 discusses the unique feathers of Antarctic penguins that work similarly to a waterproof diving suit: "Tufts of down trap a layer of air within the feathers, preventing the water from penetrating to the penguin's skin."

4. (B) Paragraph 4 states: "Temperate species have certain physical features such as fewer feathers and less blubber to keep them cool on a hot day."

5. (B) Paragraph 4 discusses the bald patches of a temperate species called African penguins.

6. rocks. Paragraph 2 states: "When it's time to create a nest, most penguins build up a pile of rocks on top of the ice to place their eggs."

7. feed/eat. Paragraph 2 discusses the Emperor penguin's gender roles: "The female Emperor lays just one egg and gives it to the male to protect while she goes off for weeks to feed."

8. brood patch. Paragraph 2 explains how the male Emperor penguin takes care of the egg: "The male balances the egg on top of his feet, covering it with a small fold of skin called a brood patch."

9. heels and tails. Toward the end of paragraph 2 the text states: "In order to reduce the cold of the ice, penguins often put their weight on their heels and tails."

10. (A) Paragraph 3 states that penguins have to keep moving to stay warm. Their swimming is compared to flight.

11. (D) The last sentence in Paragraph 3 describes the penguin's circulatory system: "Penguins also have an amazing circulatory system, which in extremely cold waters diverts blood from the flippers and legs to the heart."

12. (E) Paragraph 3 describes "porpoising" which penguins do in order to be able to breathe without having to stop swimming.

13. (H) Paragraph 3 describes how feathers keep Antarctic penguins dry: "Tufts of down trap a layer of air within the feathers, preventing the water from penetrating to the penguin's skin."
   Choice (B), (C), and (F) are incorrect because these are all of examples of how penguins stay cool.

WRITING MODULE

Target 1—Writing for a Specific Audience

PRACTICE 1

Purpose/Reader	Academic	Informal	Neutral	Formal
1. a letter of complaint to the mayor of your town			x	x
2. some suggestions to your friend for his vacation		x		
3. an article for a professional journal	x			
4. an e-mail inviting your cousin to visit		x		
5. A letter to a hotel manager about a problem with your bill			x	x
6. a notice reminding students not to use the faculty parking lot			x	
7. your opinion on how money should be spent in public schools	x			x
8. an e-mail to your parents' friends asking to stay at their house			x	
9. a letter to a company inquiring about possible positions				x
10. a description of a new computer for a technical magazine	x		x	
11. an explanation of the advantages and disadvantages of cell (mobile) phones	x		x	
12. your point of view on the effects of TV on society	x		x	

PRACTICE 2

1. numerous
2. negative
3. It was found
4. who
5. which
6. Therefore
7. can't wait
8. you're
9. lots
10. First
11. Or
12. get up
13. I would

14. house
15. who
16. You don't
17. pay you back
18. . (period)
19. salespeople
20. cannot
21. his or her

Target 2—Completing the Task

PRACTICE

	Time	Words
Task 1	20 minutes	150
Task 2	40 minutes	250

Target 3—Determining the Task

ACADEMIC TASK 1

1.1 This is Task 1, so I will have 20 minutes.
1.2 This is Task 1, so I will write at least 150 words.
1.3 I will summarize the information from two charts.
1.4 The topic is how average middle-income families spent their household budgets in two different years.
1.5 I have to compare how the budget was spent in the year 2000 with how it was spent in the year 2010.

2.1 This is Task 1, so I will have 20 minutes.
2.2 This is Task 1, so I will write at least 150 words.
2.3 I will explain the steps in a process.
2.4 The topic is how to make maple syrup.
2.5 I have to explain the steps followed to get sap from maple trees and make it into maple syrup.

ACADEMIC TASK 2

3.1 This is Task 2, so I will have 40 minutes.
3.2 This is Task 2, so I will write at least 250 words.
3.3 I have to explain my opinion about success and money.
3.4 The topic is whether or not money equals success.
3.5 Yes, I have to justify my opinion with reasons and examples from my own life and experience.

4.1 This is Task 2, so I will have 40 minutes.
4.2 This is Task 2, so I will write at least 250 words.
4.3 I will explain two sides of an issue.
4.4 The topic is whether or not it is a good idea to spend school resources for art and music education.
4.5 I do not have to give factual information. I have to explain my own ideas.

GENERAL WRITING TASK 1

1.1 This is Task 1, so I will have 20 minutes.

1.2 This is Task 1, so I will write at least 150 words.

1.3 The topic is TV programs that I don't like.

1.4 I have to explain why I don't like the current programs, say which kinds of programs I prefer, and tell why these programs are better.

1.5 I have to present a solution by suggesting better programs to replace the current ones.

2.1 This is Task 1, so I will have 20 minutes.

2.2 This is Task 1, so I will write at least 150 words.

2.3 The topic is a party to celebrate my new house.

2.4 I have to mention the reason for the party, the time and place of the party, and some things that will happen at the party.

2.5 I have to provide facts about the party.

GENERAL WRITING TASK 2

3.1 This is Task 2, so I will have 40 minutes.

3.2 This is Task 2, so I will write at least 250 words.

3.3 The topic is living situations for older people.

3.4 No, I don't have to justify an opinion.

3.5 Yes, I have to describe the advantages and disadvantages of special homes for the elderly.

4.1 This is Task 2, so I will have 40 minutes.

4.2 This is Task 2, so I will write at least 250 words.

4.3 The topic is home-cooked food versus prepared food from restaurants or grocery stores.

4.4 No, I don't have to explain factual information. I have to explain my own ideas.

4.5 I have to justify an opinion. The question asks me what I believe and to explain why I believe this.

Target 4—Developing a Thesis Statement

PRACTICE

Topic 1

Task
(B) Support your opinion. You are asked your opinion about violence on television and whether laws are needed. This answer must be related to the content of television programs.[1]

Thesis Statement
(A) There are many types of programs[1] on television, and each person is free to choose which programs he or she wants to watch.

Topic 2

Task
(B) Support your opinion. You are asked for your opinion regarding home computers. You must talk about their advantages and disadvantages for children.

Thesis Statement
(B) Computers can contribute a lot to a child's education, but they can be overused.

[1]BRITISH: programmes

Topic 3

Task

(A) Give a description. You are asked to describe the information shown in the table, reporting on the main features and making comparisons.

Thesis Statement

(C) Over the past century, the population in the Northwest region of the U.S. has been shifting from largely rural to mostly suburban and urban.

Topic 4

Task

(C) Explain a problem, and ask for a solution. You are asked to write about a problem. The problem is that you have lost your friend's watch. Then explain the solution, what you want to do about the loss.

Thesis Statement

(C) An unfortunate thing happened last night while I was wearing your beautiful gold watch. (C) is the best choice because the writer is clearly leading into explaining a problem. Some students might also select (B). With (B), the letter could talk about the problem. On the other hand, it might not. For this reason, (C) is the correct answer.

Target 5—Organizing Your Writing

PRACTICE 1

4. **Add general ideas.** The top circle shows the idea from paragraph 1, the introduction. The bottom three circles contain the ideas in the body paragraphs. The second body paragraph mentions "Modern technology."
   1. Technology

5. **Add supporting details.** These lines show the supporting details for each paragraph. Each line matches one of the body paragraphs. There are three body paragraphs in this essay. The answer "for adults" is expressed in the line, "Adults can also use this technology to avoid seeing programs/programmes that they don't want to see." The answer "news" is found in the statement: "There are news programs for serious people."
   1. Technology
   2. Channel blocker for children (for adults)
   3. News

PRACTICE 2

4. **Add general ideas**. The topic is the idea expressed in the thesis statement. Each general idea represents the main idea of one of the three body paragraphs. Body paragraph 2 describes the village in 1975, and the writer mentions "a new four-lane highway."
   General Idea 2: 1975—Four-lane highway

5. **Add supporting details**. The supporting details describe the changes to the village in each of the years covered.

Paragraph 1, supporting detail 2	few hotels
Paragraph 2, supporting detail 1	fishing docks still present
Paragraph 3, supporting detail 2	greatly expanded hotel district

PRACTICE 3

Topic 1

Task: Support your opinion.

Thesis Statement: Physical education classes are so important that schools must require them.

Concept Map:

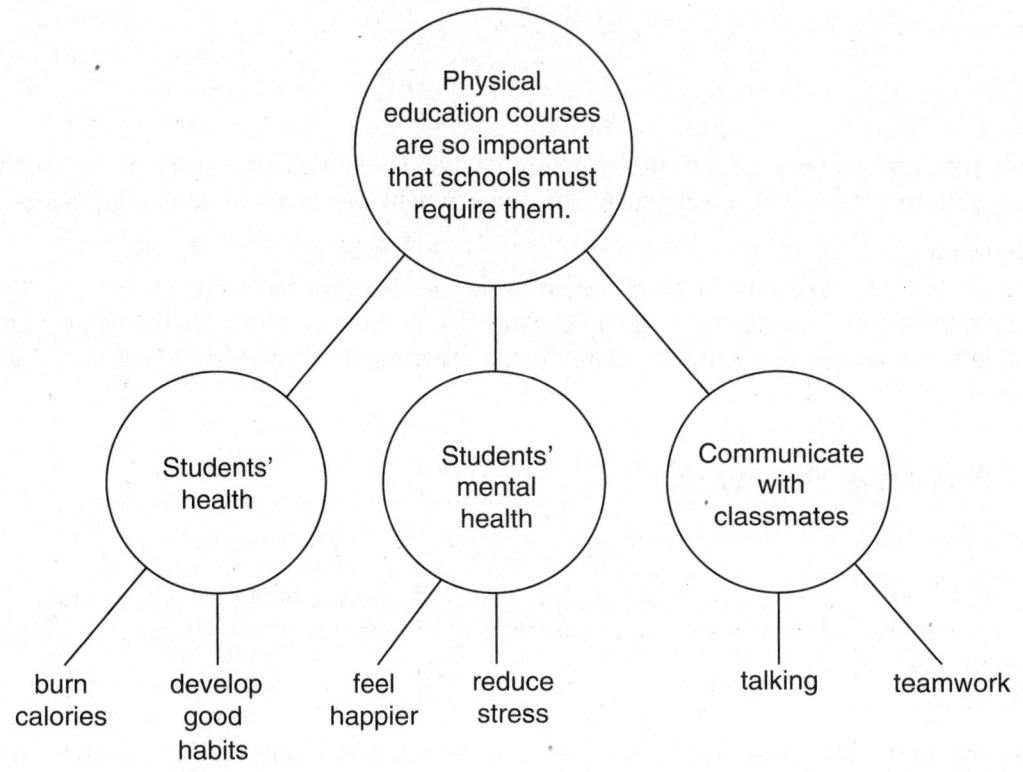

Some students hate exercising. They'd rather play computer games or talk to their friends. They would never take physical education classes if they had a choice. Physical education classes are so important that schools must require them.

These classes improve students' health, now and in the future. Students burn calories, and this helps them to maintain a healthy weight. The classes' regular exercise develops good habits for the present and the future. People who exercise as children are more likely to continue exercising when they're adults. This reduces the risk of heart disease, diabetes, and other serious illnesses.

Physical education also improves students' mental health. It can be difficult to sit in class all day. Students can exercise and then relax after their physical activity. This helps them to feel happier and more comfortable at school. The classes also include activities that help with stress reduction. Walking, stretching, and yoga are just a few of the exercises that reduce stress.

The students' favorite part of physical education classes may be the opportunity to communicate with their classmates. They enjoy talking to their friends while they play games. The students also learn how to work in teams. Teamwork is an important skill that they will use when playing sports or even at their jobs in the future.

We know that some students really don't like physical education. We also know that there are many advantages to taking physical education classes. There are so many benefits that schools must require students to take these classes.

Topic 2

Task: Explain a problem and ask for a solution.

Thesis Statement: My bill for this month contained an incorrect late payment charge.

Outline

INTRODUCTION
TOPIC: Incorrect late payment charge

BODY
GENERAL IDEA 1 Noticed the late payment charge
    Supporting Detail 1   checked my records
    Supporting Detail 2   called the bank

GENERAL IDEA 2 Remove the charge
    Supporting Detail 1   feel concerned
    Supporting Detail 2   remove the late charge
    Supporting Detail 3   corrected error within 30 days

Dear National Credit Card Company:

My bill for this month contained an incorrect late payment charge. I was surprised to read this. My last payment was definitely made on time. To be sure, I checked my records. They show that I wrote and mailed a check to you fifteen days before it was due. Next I called my bank and they checked their records. They say that your company cashed the check five days before the payment was due.

I am very concerned about this mistake. Please remove this late charge from my credit card. I would like to have your mistake corrected as soon as possible and within the next 30 days. I always make my payments on time, so seeing this charge upsets me.

Please contact me immediately if you have any questions about this letter. I want to be sure that my credit record with your company continues to be excellent.

Sincerely,

Michel Danel

Topic 3

Task: Describe something.

Thesis Statement: Over the past century, the population in the Northwest region of the U.S. has been shifting from largely rural to mostly suburban and urban.

Concept Map:

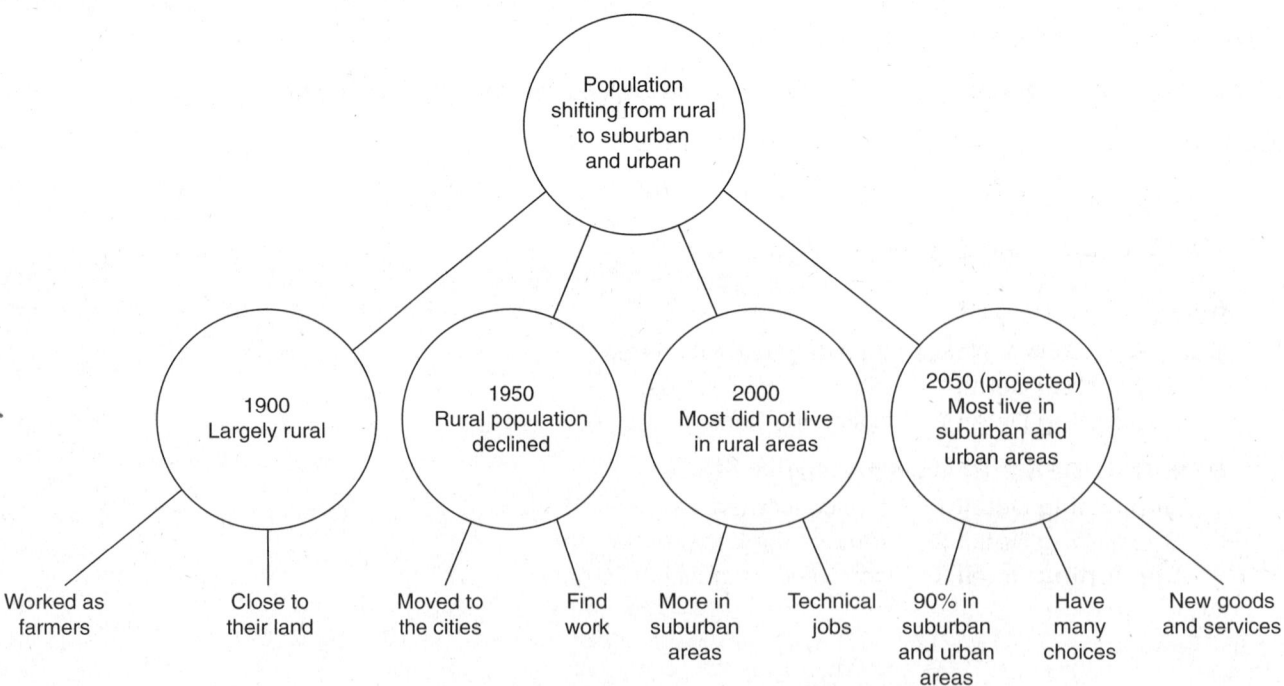

Over the past century, the population in the Northwest region of the U.S. has been shifting from largely rural to mostly suburban and urban.

In 1900, the Northwest region's population was largely rural. Many people worked as farmers. They needed to be close to their land. So, most people lived and worked at the same place, at their farm in the countryside.

By 1950, the rural population declined. Some people moved to the cities to be closer to them. They wanted to find work. More job opportunities were available outside of the rural regions.

By 2000, most people lived in suburban and urban areas. They worked in the city's technical jobs. Even fewer people worked as farmers.

For 2050, it is projected that 90 percent of people will live in suburban and urban areas. They will have many choices in the city. They will be involved with all of the new goods and services developed there.

Target 6—Writing the Introduction

PRACTICE 1

1. Topic   Parents stay at home to take care of children
  General Idea Parents are the best caretakers
  General Idea High cost of child care
  General Idea Better family life

2. Topic   Making maple syrup from sugar maple sap
  General Idea Gathering the sap
  General Idea Transporting the sap
  General Idea Boiling the sap

3. Topic   Unfortunate news about lost watch
  General Idea Disappearance of watch
  General Idea Payment for watch

4. Topic   Advantages and disadvantages of the Internet
  General Idea Advantages of the Internet
  General Idea Disadvantages of the Internet

PRACTICE 2

Topic 1

Task: Make an argument and support an opinion.

Thesis Statement: "Learning by doing" is a better way to learn a language.

Concept Map:

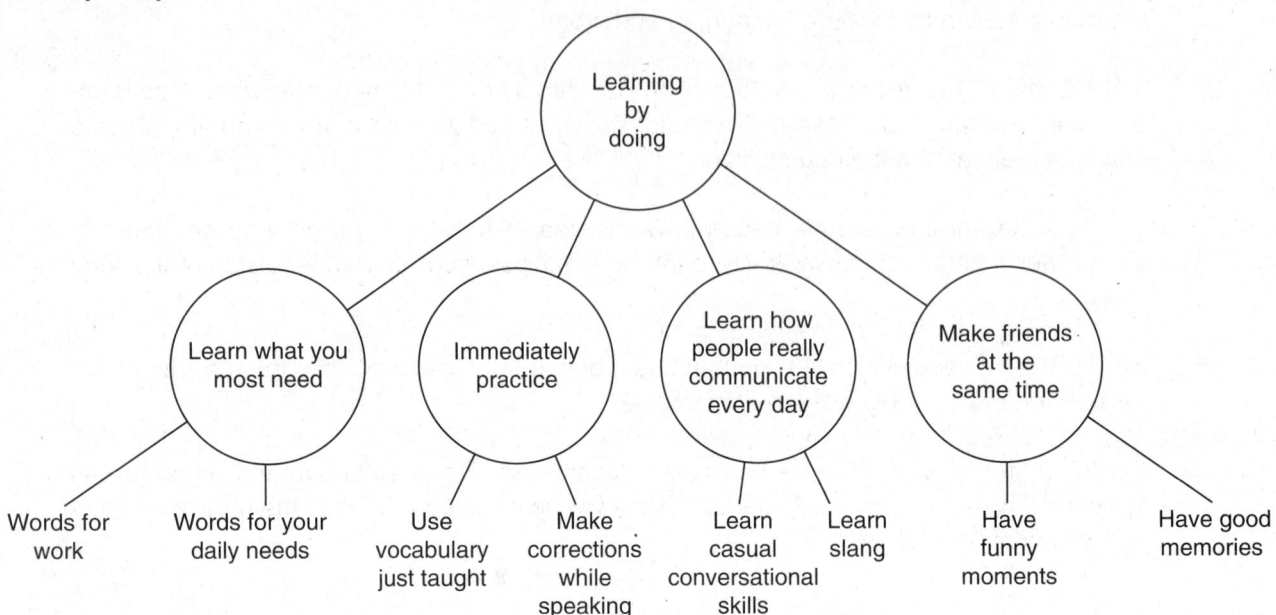

Topic Sentences:

1.1 You learn the most important words, the ones that you most need in order to communicate.

1.2 You immediately practice what you have learned.

1.3 You learn how people really communicate every day, instead of formal language that may only be used at school.

1.4 You make friends and learn a language at the same time.

Introduction: People often discuss what the best way is to learn languages: "learning by doing" or from books and teachers. In "learning by doing," you learn the most important words that you need. You immediately practice what you have learned. You learn how people really communicate every day, instead of formal language that may only be used at school. You make friends and learn a language at the same time. "Learning by doing" is a better way to learn language.

Topic 2

Task: Make an argument and support your position.

Thesis Statement: Because of the tremendous challenges caused by this change, I would vote against moving my capital.

Concept Map:

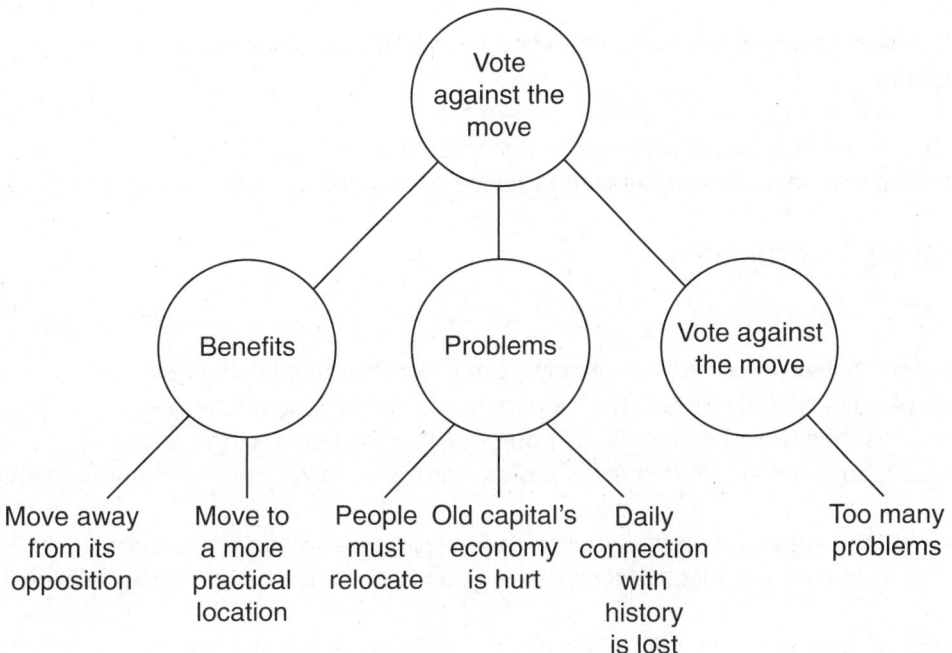

Topic Sentences:

2.1 A government may move its capital because of the benefits.

2.2 However, there are also some problems to consider.

2.3 If I were asked to move my capital, I would definitely vote against it.

Introduction: Perhaps you have never thought about moving your government's capital. However, it has happened worldwide and for hundreds of years. A government may move its capital because of the benefits. However, there are also some problems to consider. Because of the tremendous challenges caused by this change, I would vote against moving my capital.

Target 7—Writing a Paragraph

PRACTICE 1

1.

Topic Sentence:

1.1 Modern technology has given us a tool for controlling the TV programs[1] we see.

Supporting Details:

1.2 Most TVs can be programmed to block certain channels.

1.3 Parents use this technology to protect their children from seeing shows that are too violent.

1.4 Adults can also use this technology to avoid seeing programs that they don't want to see.

2.

Topic Sentence:

2.1 The best thing about TV is that there is a variety of programs.

Supporting Details:

2.2 There are news programs for serious people.

2.3 There are movies and cartoons for people who want to be entertained.

2.4 The variety of TV programs needs to be protected, even if that means allowing some of them to show violence.

[1]BRITISH: programmes

3.
Topic Sentence:
3.1 Physical education classes teach children important skills that they need in life.
Supporting Details:
3.2 They teach children how to work together on a team.
3.3 They teach children how to set a goal and work to achieve it.
3.4 They teach children about the importance of taking care of their health.

Target 8—Stating Your Opinion

PRACTICE 1

1. It is my opinion that violence on television is (is not) very harmful for children.
2. In my view, parents should (should not) monitor their children's computer use.
3. I understand that home-cooked food is (is not) better for the health of the family.
4. I think that dependence on private automobiles causes (doesn't cause) many problems in our daily lives.
5. I am sure that learning about art is (is not) a good way to spend part of the school day.
6. I am convinced that children learn (don't learn) better when they have friendly relationships with their teachers.
7. Perhaps people spend (do not spend) too much money on stylish clothes.
8. Certainly, taking a train is (is not) just as convenient as driving a car.

PRACTICE 2

1. As a rule, children learn (don't always learn) better when they spend part of each day getting physical exercise.
2. On the whole, job security is (is not) a thing of the past.
3. For the most part, family ties are (are not) weaker now than they were in the past.
4. To some extent, art and music classes equal (do not equal) academic classes in importance.
5. In a way, a train is (is not) as convenient a form of transportation as a private car.

Target 9—Writing the Conclusion

PRACTICE

1. recommendation
2. prediction
3. question
4. generalization
5. restatement

Target 10—Transition: Connecting and Linking

PRACTICE

1. as a result
2. Furthermore
3. likewise
4. In other words
5. Unlike
6. Moreover
7. such as
8. then

9. but
10. In other words
11. In addition
12. Above all

Target 11—Synonyms

PRACTICE

1. alone
2. regulate
3. curious
4. ration
5. engaged
6. supervision
7. easy

Target 12—Writing with Variety

CHRONOLOGICAL ORDER

PRACTICE 1

1. Before the audience left the concert hall, the orchestra played the last note.
2. After looking at the menu, you can order your meal.
   While looking at the menu, you can order your meal.
3. After the lights went out, we lit a candle.
   Before the lights went out, we lit a candle.
4. While we were waiting for you in the coffee shop, you were waiting for us at the bookstore.
5. Before they filled/filled up the car with gas/petrol, the car ran out of gas/petrol.

PRACTICE 2

1. 7	3. 1	5. 6	7. 4
2. 3	4. 5	6. 2	

PRACTICE 3

In the early 1900s, Winston on Hudson was just a small town on the Hudson River. Nothing happened in the town until after the start of the First World War when a munitions factory opened. Once the factory opened, river traffic increased, bringing raw materials to the factories and taking munitions downstream to the major river port at the mouth of the river. Within ten years, cargo boats were followed by passenger boats bringing weekend sightseers. Soon, Winston on Hudson became a tourist destination. Today, the town's munitions factory has been turned into artist studios. In the future, the town hopes to build an art museum next to the old factory.

PRACTICE 4

Answers will vary. Here is one example:

On December 22, 1990, I was born. I am my parents' first child. I started school when I was six years old, in 1996. Later, my parents had another baby, my brother. He was born in 1998. I was going to school then and enjoyed taking science classes. I won an award in 2004, "Best Science Student of the Year." That inspired me to study science seriously. In 2006, I decided to earn a chemistry degree at a university in an English-speaking country. Now I am studying English to prepare for my studies and my future career.

SPATIAL ORDER
PRACTICE 5

1. between
2. next to/beside
3. north
4. behind
5. in front of

6. west
7. south and west
8. behind/next to/beside
9. beside/next to
10. around/beside/next to

CLASSIFICATION
PRACTICE 6

Word List	Things That Are Not Alive	Things That Are Alive
table	table	boy
boy	car	frog
frog	chair	butterfly
car	pencil	teacher
chair		
butterfly		
pencil		
teacher		

Word List	People	Things
doctor	doctor	hospital
nurse	nurse	building plans
contractor	contractor	
hospital	plumber	
building plans	patient	
plumber	architect	
patient		
architect		

PRACTICE 7

Positive Values	Negative Values
B. charity	A. anger
F. hope	C. envy
G. humility	D. gluttony
H. justice	E. greed
I. kindness	J. laziness
K. patience	L. pride

1. L	4. D	7. E	10. J
2. I	5. K	8. G	11. H
3. C	6. A	9. F	12. B

Answers will vary. Here is one example:

People who say, "Tomorrow is another day," have hope. This is a positive virtue. Hope is good because it motivates us. After a bad day, it can be difficult thinking about the next day to come. Sometimes we want everything to stop. People with hope believe that tomorrow might be better. So, they continue because they believe in positive change. Sometimes we just need to survive a bad day and look ahead to tomorrow. Hope gives us the strength we need during the difficult times.

DEFINITION

PRACTICE 8

Words	Concrete	Abstract
printer	printer	success
success	sidewalk/pavement/curb	loyalty
loyalty	black	freedom
sidewalk	swimming	love
freedom		
love		
black		
swimming		

PRACTICE 9

Loyalty to me is defined as my family and knowing that they will always love me.

A sidewalk is a place to walk along the side of a street. It is usually paved, so the walkway is smooth and hard.

Freedom to me is defined as being able to choose what I want to do, such as my type of job.

Love to me is defined as the strong feelings of caring that I have for my parents.

Black is a very dark color.

Swimming is to move through the water by moving your arms and legs or if you're a fish, by moving your fins and tail.

COMPARISON AND CONTRAST

PRACTICE 10

1. CON	3. COMP	5. COMP	7. CON
2. CON	4. CON	6. COMP	8. COMP

PRACTICE 11

A
1. difference
2. while
3. however
4. In contrast to

B
5. similar to
6. alike
7. both
8. just as
9. both

PRACTICE 12

Dogs and cats are alike because both of these animals make wonderful pets. Both dogs and cats show a great deal of affection for their owners. Dogs may jump on their owners and lick them. Cats may rub against their owners' legs and purr. While their ways of expressing affection are different, both dogs and cats love the people who care for them.

PRACTICE 13

1. In all three areas—urban, suburban, and rural—the housing costs increased from 1990 to 2000. However, the amount of the increase differed. The urban housing costs doubled. Similarly, the suburban costs increased a great deal. They more than doubled. In contrast to those soaring prices, the rural cost increase was smaller. Like the other areas, it increased, but not as much.
2. When comparing the costs at each restaurant, lunch is less expensive than dinner served at the same place. The meals' costs at these restaurants varies; however, they all have something in common. Customers take more time eating at the places where the food is more expensive. For example, a 20-minute dinner at a fast-food restaurant is only $5.00. This differs from a 60-minute dinner at a sit-down restaurant. That costs $17.00, so it is more than three times more expensive. People who are looking for the cheapest option should eat lunch at the fast-food restaurant.

CAUSE AND EFFECT

PRACTICE 14

1. CO
2. C/E
3. C/E
4. C/E
5. CO
6. CO
7. C/E
8. C/E

PRACTICE 15

1. These instructions show how to use your new iron. Take the iron out of its package/box. As a result of plugging the cord into the outlet/socket, the iron will be turned on. Adjust the temperature gauge. This picture shows high/cotton. Because of the hot temperature used, be careful. The high/cotton setting will have a bad effect on silk. Be careful not to drop the iron into the water, since this is very dangerous. Also, you do not want small children to burn themselves. For this reason, keep them away from the iron. Following these directions will help you to enjoy your iron for many years.
2. Each level of education resulted in a higher average salary. Therefore, if you want to earn more money, you should go back to school. You may be able to request a higher salary as a result of a more advanced educational level.

PREDICTION

PRACTICE 16

1. A
2. B

PRACTICE 17

1. By 2010, the schools will likely <u>spend at least $1,000 less per pupil</u>.
   By 2010, the students will probably <u>decrease their test scores, at least 2%</u>.
2. By 2005, the number of acres of forest logged will likely <u>increase, to between 75,000 and 100,000 acres</u>.
   By 2007, the number of forest-dwelling species will likely <u>decrease, for every type of animal</u>.

Target 13—Pronouns

PRACTICE

1. them
2. It
3. her
4. this
5. They
6. their

Target 14—Parallel Structures

PRACTICE

1. playing
2. information
3. will bring
4. play
5. educational
6. can no longer enjoy
7. they taste
8. the fishing docks were removed

Target 15—Coherence

PRACTICE

1. B
2. A
3. C
4. B
5. C

Target 16—Sentence Types

PRACTICE

1. Cx
2. S
3. S
4. Cx
5. S
6. C-Cx
7. S
8. S
9. S
10. C
11. S

Target 17—Voice

PRACTICE

1. C
2. A
3. B
4. B
5. C

Target 18—Using a Revision Checklist

PRACTICE 1

1. C
2. A
3. B
4. B
5. A
6. C
7. C
8. B
9. A
10. B
11. C
12. B

PRACTICE 2

Missing items:
Paragraph 1: thesis statement
Paragraph 2: supporting ideas
Paragraph 3: none
Paragraph 4: topic sentence
Paragraph 5: none

Grammar and vocabulary errors:

Paragraph 1: none

Paragraph 2: the amount of money necessary <u>depends</u>

Paragraph 3: <u>if</u> adult children <u>never see</u> (parallel structures)

Paragraph 4: unhappy at work, <u>for example</u>

Paragraph 5: it can <u>buy</u>

Revised Essay

Added and corrected parts are underlined.

<u>I believe that success has many facets.</u> Having money can be one part of success. Having good relationships is another very important part of success. So is feeling fulfilled.

Everybody needs money, but the amount of money necessary <u>depends</u> on each person's goals. For example, one person may want a lot of material things, like fancy cars and big houses. For this person, a lot of money is important. <u>Another person may need money to pay for food and shelter so that she is then free to do the things she enjoys doing. For this person, the amount of money required is much less.</u>

Everybody needs to have good relationships. Even a multi-millionaire is not successful if he or she does not have close connections with other people. If a woman always fights with her husband, if a man's children refuse to speak to him, <u>if adult children never see</u> their parents, they cannot be considered successful people.

<u>Everybody needs to feel fulfilled.</u> It is important to develop skills and talents and pursue interests. It is important to spend time doing things that are enjoyable or meaningful. A person who is unhappy at work, <u>for example</u>, cannot be considered successful no matter how big his salary is. A person who spends evenings and weekends just sitting in front of the TV cannot be considered successful, either.

Money and the material things it can <u>buy</u> may be one part of success, but non-material things like relationships and self-fulfillment are just as important.

Target 19—Checking the Spelling

PRACTICE

Corrected words are underlined.

1. It was <u>found</u> that most middle-income families spent 50 percent of <u>their</u> household <u>budget</u> on housing expenses in 2010.
2. I <u>think</u> you must have a <u>lot</u> of money in order to be <u>considered</u> <u>successful</u>.
3. <u>Spending</u> money on art and <u>music education</u> gives children a big <u>advantage</u> that will help <u>them</u> in the future.
4. I feel that this type of television program is not of <u>interest</u> to most <u>people</u> and will cause you to lose a large portion of your <u>audience</u>.
5. I <u>know</u> that you will <u>enjoy</u> the party, and I hope you will be able to <u>attend.</u>

Target 20—Checking the Punctuation

PRACTICE

Corrections are underlined. Each paragraph has been indented.

1.

   <u>M</u>any families enjoy watching television together during the early evening hours. Therefore<u>,</u> programs shown during this time should be suitable for children. <u>D</u>o you really think it is appropriate for

children to see programs that involve shooting, fistfights, and other forms of violence? Most parents do not, and they change the channel when such programs are shown.

2.

It is important for children to know how to use computers, but it is also important for them to spend time on other activities. When children spend a lot of time at the computer, they spend less time playing outside. They spend less time interacting with other people. They miss out on activities that are important for their physical and emotional development.

3.

I have a lot of fun activities planned for your visit. John, who is my next-door neighbor, has promised to take us white-water rafting. Have you ever done that before? It's a lot of fun, and you will surely enjoy it. However, there are plenty of other things we can do if you don't want to go rafting. We can ride bikes, go to the movies, or just relax at home.

4.

Tourism, which brings a lot of money to the town of Palm Grove, is an important part of the local economy. Tourist dollars pay the salaries of hotel employees, restaurant servers, and airport workers. All of these people earn a lot more money from tourism than they ever did from fishing. In addition, they now have steady jobs with a steady income.

SPEAKING MODULE

Quick Study—Question Types

Part 1

PRACTICE A

Answers will vary. Possible answers are given.

1. *What is your name?*
   My name is Mary.

2. *How do you spell it?*
   I spell it M-A-R-Y.

3. *Do you have your identity card? May I see it?*
   Yes, I do. Of course, you may see it.

4. *Let's talk about where you live. Can you describe your neighborhood/neighbourhood?*
   My neighborhood/neighbourhood has lots of apartment buildings. We have a school and a playground. There is also a park in my neighborhood/neighbourhood.

5. *What is an advantage of living there?*
   It's a quiet neighborhood/neighbourhood. That's an advantage.

6. *What is a disadvantage of living there?*
   It is not close to the bus stop or to the train station.

7. *Let's talk about jobs. What kind of job do you have?*
   My job is an office job. I work as a secretary.

8. *What is the best thing about your job?*
   I like the people at my office. They're very friendly.

9. *Let's talk about free time. What is one activity you enjoy doing in your free time?*
   I enjoy cooking in my free time.

10. *How did you become interested in this activity?*
    My mother taught me how to cook. I have loved it since I was a little girl.

PRACTICE B

Answers will vary.

Part 2

PRACTICE C

Possible answers:

Place: the park
Location: in my neighborhood, 2 blocks away/2 streets away
Transportation: walking or riding my bike
Appearance: green grass and playground equipment
Why I like it: It's peaceful. I like watching the children playing and families having fun.

PRACTICE D

Answers will vary.

PRACTICE E

Possible answers:
1. *Do you go alone to this place?*
   Yes, usually I go alone/on my own. Sometimes a friend comes with me.

2. *Are there similar places you like to go?*
   There is a park in another neighborhood. Sometimes I go there, too.

PRACTICE F

Answers will vary.

Part 3

PRACTICE G

Possible answers:
1. Most people take vacations to the beach/take holidays by the seaside, a famous city, or a unique location. Many of the places are the same. But now people can travel far away with less trouble. In the past, this was more difficult or impossible.
2. Leisure time is important. It gives people the chance to relax. It refreshes them. It helps people to be ready to do more work in the future.

Target 1—Describing Yourself

PRACTICE 1

Answers will vary.

Personal Information Form

First Name *Stefan*
Middle Name *Andreas*
Last Name *Holsen*
Age *25*
Address *15 Harbor View Avenue, apt. 101, Portsmouth, ME*

Nationality *German*
Native Language *German*
Other Languages *English, Italian*

Occupation *Physician's Assistant*
Name of Employer *University Hospital*
Name of School *not applicable*

Forms of Identification:
Passport Number *300-098-0988*
Driver's License Number *5596847*
Other ID Number *887-A45 (hospital employee ID)*

---

1. My name is Fatma Aksay.
2. My first name is spelled F-A-T-M-A and my last name is spelled A-K-S-A-Y.
3. My name, Fatma, was also my grandmother's name.
4. I work as a software engineer.
5. My passport number is B2319875.

Target 2—Giving Information

PRACTICE 1

Answers will vary.

Family Information Form

	Relationship to You	Name	Age	Marital Status	Occupation	Other Information
Parents	mother	Juana	49	married	librarian	
	father	Eduardo	52	married	accountant	
Siblings	younger brother	Teodoro	22	single	student	has a girlfriend
	younger sister	Dora	19	single	student	likes studying languages
Other Relatives	uncle (Dad's brother)	Miguel	47	single	store manager	
	grandparents (all have passed on)					

1. I have four people in my immediate family.
2. I am the oldest child.
3. I have two younger siblings, my brother and my sister.
4. I have an uncle, Miguel, who is my dad's brother.

PRACTICE 2

Home Information Form	
Size	*medium*
Age	*fifty years*
Number of bedrooms	*four*
Other rooms	*kitchen, living room, dining room, 2 bathrooms*
Garden/yard	*large size, lots of flowers*
Special features	*attic*
My Bedroom:	
Size	*medium*
Furniture	*wood, painted brown, have a desk and a bed*
Colors	*white/cream paint on the walls*
Art	*posters of favorite musicians*
Other	*computer*

Neighborhood[1] Information Form	
Name	*Flower Valley*
Style of houses	*older, family homes*
Shops/businesses	*restaurant, small grocery store/shop, drycleaner, gas/petrol station*
Schools	*one school for children*
Religious buildings	*church and a mosque*
Other buildings	*none*
Transportation	*bus stop, train stop*
Parks/gardens	*one park with a playground*
Special characteristics	*friendly neighborhood, very comfortable*

Home
1. Our home is medium-sized. It is about fifty years old.
2. We have four bedrooms, 2 bathrooms, and some other rooms.
3. Our yard is large, with lots of flowers.
4. We have an attic that we use for storage.

Neighborhood
1. We live in a neighborhood called Flower Valley.
2. The neighborhood's homes are older.
3. Many of the homes are large and usually families live in them.
4. We have some stores in the neighborhood, so shopping is convenient.

[1]BRITISH: neighbourhood

PRACTICE 3

Answers will vary.

Job Information Form

Company name *Translational International*

Job title *Japanese translator*

Length of time at this job *2 years*

Duties *translate technical materials*

Training required for this job *computer training, using software, training in technical language*

Skills required for this job *language skills in English and Japanese, computer skills*

Things I like about this job *using language*

Things I don't like about this job *can be tiring; requires a lot of concentration*

Future career goals *manage a large translation project*

Education Information Form

Name of college *City University*

Major/subject *English literature*

Classes I am taking now *Structure of English, World Literature*

Hours per week in class *8*

Years to complete degree/certificate *2*

Educational goals *master's degree*

Future career goals *teach English and write a book*

My occupation: Japanese translator

1. I work as a Japanese translator at Translation International.
2. I have worked there for two years.
3. My main duty is translating technical materials.
4. I like using language skills for my work, but sometimes it can be very tiring. Working as a translator requires a lot of concentration.

PRACTICE 4

Answers will vary.

Hobby/Free-Time Activity Information Form

Hobby/Activity #1 *playing computer games*
How often do you do this hobby or activity? *almost every day*
Do you do it on your own or with other people? *both*
Do you belong to a club related to this hobby/activity? *no*
How did you learn how to do this hobby/activity? *from friends and from the instructions that come with games*
Do you need special equipment for it? *yes, a computer and an Internet connection*
What do you like most about it? *fun and I can do it any time of the day or night*

Hobby/Activity #2 *cooking*
How often do you do this hobby or activity? *twice a week*
Do you do it alone or with other people? *alone/on my own*
Do you belong to a club related to this hobby/activity? *no*
How did you learn how to do this hobby/activity? *watching other people, including TV shows/programmes*
Do you need special equipment for it? *yes, some cooking equipment*
What do you like most about it? *I like trying a new recipe and eating the food.*

Hobby/Activity: playing computer games

1. I like playing computer games almost every day.
2. I can play games by myself, or I can go online and play against people who live all over the world.
3. I started playing computer games when I was 10 years old.
4. I like being able to play any time. The computer graphics improve every year, and that makes the games more fun.

Target 3—Organizing a Topic

PRACTICE

Answers will vary.

Topic 1

Pet	Parrot
Kind of animal	An African grey parrot named Sammy
Kind of care	Needed a lot of companionship, twice daily feeding, frequent baths, daily cage cleaning
Liked/didn't like	Liked—he was funny and smart and could talk, and he was affectionate. Didn't like—he was noisy and messy.
Why it is/isn't popular	Not popular—hard to care for and expensive to buy, noisy and messy

Topic 2

Birthday	Maria's party last month
Name and age of celebrant	Maria Montalvo, 23 years old
Who attended	Maria's brothers and cousins, some of our old high school friends, some of Maria's work colleagues
Location	Maria's parents' house because they have a pool and a large garden and patio
Activities	Swimming and water games, dancing, eating, jokes and funny speeches, opening presents

Topic 3

Friend	Karl
When and how met	First day of preschool, we were classmates.
Things did together	Played childhood games, as we grew up did school work together, played soccer, hiking, some traveling
Things in common	Being outdoors, science classes, traveling, grew up together and went to school together
Why important	Friends since early childhood, we know each other very well, know each other's families, rely on each other for support.

Topic 4

Trip	Vancouver last June
Where	Vancouver, BC, Canada, a major Canadian city with many interesting tourist activities
Who	Husband and kids
Why	To visit sister and her family; we visit them every year
Activities	Relaxed and talked together; cooked some big meals, bike riding in the park; walked around Chinatown and Gas Town; anthropology museum

Target 4—Discussing a Topic

PRACTICE

Answers will vary.

1. General Idea	TV show is funny
Supporting Detail 1	The actors are excellent comedians.
Supporting Detail 2	The actors are good at physical comedy.
Supporting Detail 3	The story lines make everyone laugh.
2. General Idea	We went camping in the woods.
Supporting Detail 1	We slept in tents.
Supporting Detail 2	We cooked over a fire.
Supporting Detail 3	We saw beautiful views and lots of wildlife.
3. General Idea	We grew up in the same place, and we enjoy the same activities.
Supporting Detail 1	We went to all the same schools.
Supporting Detail 2	We have many of the same friends.
Supporting Detail 3	We like the same music, books, and movies.

4. General Idea   It's a romance novel that takes place in the 1800s.
   Supporting Detail 1   A wealthy woman and a poor man fall in love.
   Supporting Detail 2   Their families keep them apart.
   Supporting Detail 3   In the end they get married.

Target 5—Verb Tenses

PRACTICE

Answers will vary.

1. Present
   People like to visit the house where our first president grew up because it is important to the history of our country.
   The style of architecture is also very interesting.
   People also enjoy learning about daily life 300 years ago.

2. Past
   My first year of secondary school was my favorite because I felt grown up.
   I studied a lot of interesting subjects that year that were new to me.
   I participated in several activities such as the chess club and the student government.

3. Past
   I really hate waiting, so I tried to forget about the delay.
   I went to a nearby café and ordered a big meal.
   I bought a newspaper and read almost every article in it.

4. Present
   Since Center City Mall is one of the biggest malls in the country, you can see hundreds of stores there.
   It also has a fountain on each level, and each fountain is surrounded by pretty plants.
   Besides shopping, you can eat a meal, go to the movies, and even visit a doctor or dentist.

Target 6—Sequence

PRACTICE

1. As soon as
2. Then
3. until
4. Finally
5. First
6. By the time
7. then
8. before

Target 7—Comparing and Contrasting

PRACTICE

Answers will vary.

1. I think she was the nicest teacher I have ever had.
   She had a lot more patience than many teachers have.
   She also had a more interesting way of explaining things.

2. This party was the same as most parties I go to with my friends.
   The food was similar to the food that is served at most parties.
   The music was exactly the same music my friends and I listen to all the time at home or at school.

3. Unlike many other tourist destinations, this one has no admission charge.
   That's what makes it one of the most popular places to visit.
   But it's also one of the most crowded.

4. I think this program is a lot funnier than most other programs you can see on TV.
   The actors are more talented, and the jokes are better.
   It also has a different style of humor from other programs.

Target 8—Explaining

PRACTICE

Answers will vary.

1. I liked this book because I enjoy romance stories. They help me escape from the stresses of everyday life. This was a particularly good book because of the strong characters and the romantic setting in the African jungle.

2. This was my favorite year in school because it was the year I learned to read. Since all my older brothers and sisters could already read, I wanted to read, too. For this reason, I was very proud the day I came home from school and read an entire book (a very short one) to my parents.

3. This area has some of the most beautiful beaches in the world, so people come from all over to enjoy them. They enjoy the beaches because of the warm, calm water and the beautiful tropical scenery. Another reason tourists visit this area is the exciting nightlife.

4. I remember this movie because it's one of the scariest I have ever seen. I couldn't sleep well for several nights because of the nightmares the movie gave me. I don't like being scared, so I don't think I will see another movie like this one.

Target 9—Describing

PRACTICE

Answers will vary.

1. Activities: relaxed on the beach, took walks, ate great meals
   Description: Most days, we spent the whole morning relaxing on the beach. In the afternoons, we walked around the town and enjoyed looking at the houses and the boats in the harbor. We ate lots of tasty meals, including fresh fish and different kinds of tropical fruit.

2. Activities: danced, ate, talked to friends
   Description: There was good music, and we danced all night. We ate a big birthday cake with chocolate frosting all over it, and there were five or six kinds of ice cream. We had fun talking with friends we hadn't seen in a long time.

3. Activities: cook, clean house, visit with relatives
   Description: Usually I help my mother cook a kind of spicy soup, which is a traditional food for this holiday. Then we spend all morning cleaning the house and decorating it with special holiday decorations. In the afternoon, our relatives come over for a visit, and we talk about everything we've done since the last time we got together.

Target 10—Responding to Follow-up Questions

PRACTICE 1

Answers will vary.

NOTES

Topic 1

1. Dogs and cats—good companions—familiar to everyone
2. Fish—easy to care for—not demanding
3. Rabbit—makes a mess—not friendly
4. Advantage—children have responsibility. Disadvantage—parents do work if children don't

Topic 2

1. Celebrate with family and friends, at home or go out
2. flowers, cards, clothes
3. Yes—share with people you love—more important for children
4. Celebrating the new year

Topic 3

1. No—different cities—different lives
2. School, with other friends, sports
3. Fix our cars, eat, watch sports
4. A few good friends, so we're closer

Topic 4

1. Yes—more to see there—yearly visit to family
2. beach—relax, be in warm climate
3. Warm weather, different from where I live
4. Yes, so I can experience new things. Meet people, learn language and culture

PRACTICE 2

Answers will vary.

Topic 1

1. The most popular pets in my country are dogs and cats. Both of these animals make good companions. Also everyone is familiar with them, so when they think about getting a pet, it's usually a dog or cat that comes to mind.
2. I think fish make the best pets. They are very easy to care for. You just feed them and once in a while clean out the aquarium. They aren't demanding animals like dogs and cats are.
3. I think a rabbit would not make a good pet. Rabbits can be messy and they chew everything. On top of that, they aren't particularly friendly animals.
4. The advantage of pets is that children learn responsibility when they own pets. The disadvantage is that sometimes parents must care for the pets.

Topic 2

1. I like to celebrate my birthday by enjoying the day with my family and friends. We might stay at home or go out, but we must be together.
2. We usually give simple gifts on birthdays. Flowers and cards are very common. If it's the birthday of a relative or a close friend, then it is common to give gifts of clothes.
3. Yes, I think birthdays are important. They are a special occasion to share with the people you love. I think a birthday celebration is especially important for a child. It makes him or her feel special and loved.
4. I also like to celebrate the beginning of a new year. It is a good way to start the year.

Topic 3

1. No, we aren't friends anymore. We live in different cities, and we have very different lives. We don't have many opportunities to see each other any more.
2. Most of the new friends I make are at school because that's where I spend most of my time. I also meet people through friends that I already have. The other place I make friends is at my soccer games.
3. I like to fix our cars, eat, and watch sports.
4. Personally I think it's better to have just a few good friends. I want to be closer to a few people. When you have a lot of friends, you don't know each person as well.

Topic 4

1. Yes, because I go there every year to see my relatives. There are many more things to see there that I haven't seen yet, so I always have something new and interesting to do when I go there.
2. If I could, I would like to spend my next vacation at the beach. I would love to relax by the ocean and to be in a place where the weather is warm.

3. I'm in favor/favour of visiting places that have warm weather. I live in a cold place, so I like to go to a different climate.

4. As far as I'm concerned, traveling/travelling is a wonderful way to spend time. I like to experience new things. I meet new people and learn about their language and culture.

Target 11—Explaining an Issue in Depth

Practice

Answers will vary.

Topic 2

Notes

1. **General Idea** Important for children
   Supporting Detail 1   They feel special
   Supporting Detail 2   Helps them grow up

2. **General Idea** Birthdays are for children.
   Supporting Detail 1   Children want to grow up.
   Supporting Detail 2   Adults don't want to get old.
   Supporting Detail 3   Landmark birthdays

3. **General Idea** Loved but not always respected
   Supporting Detail 1   Families
   Supporting Detail 2   Work
   Supporting Detail 3   TV and movies

4. **General Idea** Wedding anniversaries; graduations
   Supporting Detail 1   Marriage central to society
   Supporting Detail 2   Graduation = rite of passage, like birthdays

Sentences

1. In my country, we believe that birthdays are important for children. A child's birthday is the day he gets to feel special and be the center of attention. Birthdays also help children feel like they are growing up and encourage them to act older.

2. Generally, we feel birthdays are for children but not for adults. Children want to grow up. In other words, they want to feel older. Adults, on the other hand, don't want to get old, and a birthday is just a reminder that we are getting older and older. Adults sometimes celebrate landmark birthdays, such as their 30th, 40th, or 50th birthdays. For some adults, those are important birthdays.

3. In my country, older adults may be loved, but they are not always respected. Within a family, for example, the parents and grandparents are loved and cared for. Outside of the family, it is different. At work, people may feel that older people can't do the job as well because their minds are old or because they can't keep up with new technology and work methods. Also, the images we see on TV and in the movies show us that youth is valued over old age.

4. It is common to celebrate wedding anniversaries and school graduations in my country. I think wedding anniversaries are important because marriage is an institution that is central to our society. Graduations from high school and university are not really anniversaries, but they are a celebration of an individual, like birthdays are. And like birthdays, they are a rite of passage into the next phase of life.

Target 12—Describing an Issue in Depth

PRACTICE

Answers will vary.

Topic 4

Notes

1. **General Idea** Beautiful or interesting places
    Supporting Detail 1 Beautiful places—beach, lake
    Supporting Detail 2 Interesting places—cities, old towns

2. **General Idea** Two weeks—not enough
    Supporting Detail 1 Need time to rest
    Supporting Detail 2 Need time for self and family

3. **General Idea** Camping
    Supporting Detail 1 Far from city
    Supporting Detail 2 Enjoy nature
    Supporting Detail 3 Hiking

4. **General Idea** Too many cars
    Supporting Detail 1 Crowded roads
    Supporting Detail 2 Pollution
    Supporting Detail 3 Need public transportation

Sentences

1. I think people generally choose either beautiful or interesting places to visit on their vacations. Some people like to go to beaches or lakes because they are pretty and pleasant places to spend time. Other people like to visit interesting places like cities, where there are a lot of different things to do. They might also visit old towns, where they can see interesting things from the past and learn about history.

2. In my country it is customary to give employees two weeks of vacation time a year, and I think this is not enough. First, people need more than just two weeks out of the whole year to rest and relax. Additionally, people need time away from work when they are not thinking about their jobs and can focus on themselves and their families. Two weeks is a very short amount of time for this.

3. I would spend my ideal vacation camping. The most important reason is that it would take me far away from the city. Also, I like to be in the middle of nature and feel wildlife all around me. I enjoy hiking, too, and I could do a lot of hiking on a camping trip.

4. The major transportation problem in my country is that there are too many cars. One result of this is that the roads are usually very crowded. The traffic moves slowly, and it takes a long time to get anywhere. In addition, the large number of cars causes pollution, which contributes to global warming. This is a very serious problem. One big reason we have this problem with cars is that we don't have adequate public transportation. If we had a better public transportation system, people wouldn't have to drive cars.

Target 13—Comparing and Contrasting an Issue in Depth

PRACTICE

Answers will vary.

Topic 3

1. **Similarities**
   A. Still have lots of friends
   Differences
   A. Spend less time with them
   B. Not as close
   C. Mostly about our children

2. **Similarities**
   A. Friendships—important
   Differences:
   A. Women—talk
   B. Men—do

3. **Similarities**
   A. Friendships—always important
   B. Support
   C. Companionship
   Differences
   A. Less face-to-face time
   B. More communication through technology

4. **Similarities**
   (none)
   Differences
   A. Circumstances vs. choice
   B. Common interests
   C. Depth of conversation

Sentences
1. Just the same as when I was younger, I still have lots of friends now. However, my friendships are differ-ent. I spend less time with my friends now than I did in the past. Also, the friendships of my youth were closer than they are now. Now my friendships center mostly on our children. My friends and I plan activi-ties that we can do together with the children.
2. I think that for both men and women friendships are important. However, men's and women's friendships are about different things. Women's friendships are about talking, sharing problems and experiences. Men's friendships, on the other hand, are about doing things together.
3. In some ways, friendships are still the same as they have always been. It is still important to have friends. We still rely on our friends for companionship. We still need their support. But, the way we interact with our friends is different. Now we spend less face-to-face time with our friends. We communicate with them more through technological means such as cell phones and the Internet.
4. An acquaintance and a friend are two completely different kinds of people. An acquaintance is someone you know through circumstance—you go to the same school or work for the same company or something like that. A friend, on the other hand, is someone you choose to know because you like that person. The interests you have in common with an acquaintance are superficial, but with a friend you share much more important and meaningful interests. Also, the conversations you have with an acquaintance are never as deep as the conversations you have with a friend.

Target 14—Giving an In-Depth Opinion

PRACTICE

Answers will vary.

Topic 1

1. **Opinion** Disagree—pets are important
   Supporting Detail 1   Deserve nice things
   Supporting Detail 2   Deserve good medical care

2. **Opinion** Best pet is cat
   Supporting Detail 1   Affectionate
   Supporting Detail 2   Easy to care for

3. **Opinion** I prefer to have a pet
   Supporting Detail 1   Companionship
   Supporting Detail 2   Good for children
   Supporting Detail 3   Help us with certain things

4. **Opinion** Children should not have pets
   Supporting Detail 1   Too much responsibility for child
   Supporting Detail 2   Lose interest quickly
   Supporting Detail 3   Might be dangerous

Sentences

1. I disagree that some people spend too much money on their pets. Pets are important, and it is impossible to spend too much on them. To my mind, pets are like another member of the family. They deserve to have nice things and to eat good food, just like anybody else in the family. They also deserve good medical care. It might be expensive to take a pet to the vet, but I believe that if we love our pets, it's worth the money.

2. If I had to choose the best pet, I would choose a cat. The first reason is that cats are very affectionate. They like to sit in your lap and be petted. Additionally, cats are the easiest pets to take care of in my opinion. You only have to feed them once a day and maybe brush them once in a while. They don't require a lot of attention like some other pets do.

3. I prefer to have a pet. To my way of thinking, pets are very important because they provide us with companionship. I also believe that pets are good for children. They help children learn about responsibility and compassion. In addition, pets can help us with certain things. For example, cats chase mice and dogs warn us of danger.

4. In my opinion, children should not have pets, in most cases. In the first place, caring for a pet is too big a responsibility for most young children. In the second place, as much as a child may beg for a pet, it is quite likely that he or she will lose interest in it before too long. This is the nature of children. Additionally, some pets can be dangerous for children. Dogs bite and cats scratch and children don't always understand when they should get out of an irritated animal's way.

Target 15—Asking for Clarification

PRACTICE

Answers will vary.

1. Do you mean a friend I have now or a friend from the past?
2. Should I explain it generally or in great detail?
3. Do you want me to talk about close friends or friends in general?
4. Could you explain what you mean by older people?
5. Would you like me to discuss just pets or animals in general?

Target 16—Delay Tactics

PRACTICE

Answers will vary.

1. How are my friend and I alike? I've never thought about that before.
2. Why do people like to go there? There are a lot of different reasons.
3. What special things do we do on this day? There are a lot of different ways to answer that.
4. What's a good kind of pet? That's a complicated issue.
5. How did I learn my profession? That's an interesting question.

Target 17—Avoiding Short Answers

PRACTICE

Answers will vary.

1. Yes, I do because I'm still a student. When I finish school and get a job, I will look for my own apartment.
2. No, I finished school last year and now I work for an engineering firm.
3. Yes. I think it's a lot easier to maintain than a house, and the location is very convenient.
4. No, not really. I just have one brother and one sister.
5. Yes. I'm learning a lot from my work, but in another year or so I would like to get a job with more responsibilities.

Target 18—Word Families and Stress

PRACTICE

1.	po<u>li</u>tics	pol<u>i</u>tician	po<u>li</u>ticize	po<u>li</u>tical	po<u>li</u>tically
2.	im<u>a</u>gine	imag<u>i</u>nation	im<u>a</u>gine	im<u>a</u>ginative	<u>i</u>maginatively
3.	<u>beau</u>ty	<u>beau</u>ty	<u>beau</u>tify	<u>beau</u>tiful	<u>beau</u>tifully
4.	a<u>gree</u>	a<u>gree</u>ment	a<u>gree</u>	a<u>gree</u>able	a<u>gree</u>ably
5.	<u>ac</u>id	acid/a<u>ci</u>dity	a<u>ci</u>dify	a<u>ci</u>dic	<u>ac</u>idly
6.	<u>quote</u>	quo<u>ta</u>tion	<u>quote</u>	<u>quo</u>table	
7.	<u>act</u>	ac<u>ti</u>vity	<u>act</u>	<u>ac</u>tive	<u>ac</u>tively
8.	<u>ener</u>gy	<u>ener</u>gy	<u>ener</u>gize	ener<u>ge</u>tic	ener<u>ge</u>tically
9.	<u>civ</u>il	ci<u>vil</u>ity	<u>civ</u>ilize	<u>civ</u>il	<u>civ</u>illy
10.	<u>rare</u>	<u>rar</u>ity	<u>rar</u>ify	<u>rare</u>	<u>rare</u>ly

Target 19—Sentence Stress

PRACTICE

1. I live in one of the newer neighborhoods in my city.
2. I've been working at the same company for twelve years.
3. I generally don't like parties because I'm a quiet person.
4. There is an excellent view of the ships in the harbor.
5. A statue of the first president of our country stands in the center of the park.

Target 20—Transition Words and Intonation

PRACTICE

1. Nevertheless, it's a pleasant place to live.

2. We took a boat ride after we finished at the museum.

3. Next, the birthday cake was served.

4. It's a position that pays well, unlike many jobs in my field.

5. A good friend also helps you when you are in need.

Target 21—Lists and Intonation

PRACTICE

1. Cats are affectionate, clean, and smart.

2. In addition to English and my native language, I speak Chinese, Korean, and French.

3. I read a variety of things, such as novels, newspapers, magazines, and journals.

4. This TV program is well-written, well-acted, and funny.

5. We had a very active vacation and played tennis, golf, and volleyball.

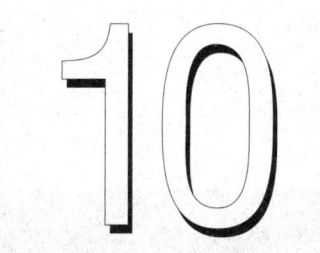

EXPLANATORY ANSWERS FOR THE IELTS MODEL TESTS

- **ACADEMIC**
  - Model Test 1
  - Model Test 2
  - Model Test 3
  - Model Test 4
- **GENERAL TRAINING**
  - Model Test 1
  - Model Test 2

ACADEMIC
MODEL TEST 1

Listening

1. 2.—(A) In Winston's first full exchange, he says he would like to *sign up now* which means he would like to *register for a class today*.

   3.—(B) In the same exchange, he says he wants to register for the classes that begin *next week*.

   1.—(C) Winston says, "I'm planning to take a vacation/holiday in Japan next summer . . ."

2. (B) and (D) either order. The receptionist mentions only three types of courses offered at World Language Academy—Japanese for Tourists, Japanese for Business Travelers, and Japanese for University Students. Two of these courses are included in the answer possibilities (B) and (D). Choice (A) is incorrect because a course is for university students, not professors. Choice (C) is incorrect because the course is for tourists, not tour guides. Choice (E) is incorrect because the speaker talks about native teachers of Japanese as teachers. Choice (F) is incorrect because this type of course is not offered, and Mark is planning on eating, not working in Japanese restaurants.

3. (A) and (D) either order. The student's reasons for learning Japanese are to order food in a restaurant and go shopping. Winston says, "I just want to learn enough to order food in restaurants and go shopping and things like that." Choice (B) *climbing mountains* is mentioned by the receptionist about what she had done in Japan and is therefore incorrect. Choices (C) and (E) confuse *business meeting* and *university course* with the topics of classes offered at the academy. Choice (F) is incorrect because the student does not want to learn with a tutor. Studying with a tutor is mentioned only as a possibility of how he can achieve his goal of learning basic Japanese.

The schedule for Japanese classes is as follows:

Beginner: Monday, Tuesday, Wednesday, Thursday 9:00–10:00 A.M.
Intermediate: Monday, Wednesday, Thursday 1:00–3:00
Advanced: Tuesday, Thursday 7:30–9:30
Japanese for Tourists: Monday, Wednesday, Thursday, 5:30–7:30

Morning	Days: Monday–Friday Time: **4** 9:00–10:00 Level: Beginner
Afternoon	Days: Monday, Wednesday, Thursday Time: 1:00–3:00 Level: **5** Intermediate
Evening	Days: Monday, Wednesday, Thursday Time: 5:30–7:30 Level: **6** Beginner Days: **7** Tuesday, Thursday Time: 7:30–9:30 Level: Advanced
8 Weekend	Days: Saturday Time: 9:00–2:00 Level: Beginner

9. (B) Choice (B) is the correct answer because the student decided to take the Saturday class. It meets from 9:00 to 2:00, and the receptionist says it will have only four or five people in it. Choice (A) is incorrect because the student only has evenings and weekends free, but the student cannot take the night classes they offer because the level is too advanced. Choice (C) is incorrect because the student says that a private class is too expensive for him.

10. (A) Choice (A) is correct because the student asks if he can pay by check, and the receptionist says he can. Choice (B) is incorrect because the student decides to pay by check. The receptionist does say that payment *can* be made by credit card or check.

11–13. *Taking photographs. Eating. Drinking.* The tour guide says: "...we ask that you not take photographs inside the building, and please turn off your cell phones during the tour. Also we request that you refrain from eating as well as drinking inside the mansion."

14. *Living room.* The living room is to the left of the main entrance and is the place where the china that was used for tea parties is displayed.

15. *Art.* The Sumner art collection is displayed in the dining room, to the right of the main entrance.

16. *Roses.* The tour guide explains: "Right now you can see a spectacular display of roses."

17. *Café.* The café is behind the living room and contains a display of kitchen tools.

18. *Parking area.* The tour guide explains: "Remember that the parking area is just beyond the café."

19. *5 PM* "The grounds close at five PM as we are still on our spring schedule."

20. *8 PM* "If you come back next week, the summer schedule will have started and we'll be open a full ten hours a day from ten in the morning until eight in the evening."

21. *several European countries/Europe.* These trains are having a great deal of success in Japan and in several European countries, as well.

22. *1964.* "They've actually been around for a while—since 1964, in fact."

23. *200.* "We usually call a train high speed if it's capable of traveling at 200 kilometers/kilometres an hour or faster."

24. *drive (cars).* "Cars and highways were improved, so more and more people started driving cars."

25. *frequent and affordable.* "Plane service is more frequent and affordable now than it was in the past, so planes, like cars, have become more convenient for people."

26. *congestion.* "But with everybody driving cars and taking planes, we have a lot of congestion."

27–30. (B), (D), (F), and (G) are correct.

      (B) "But, a train trip is much more relaxing than a car trip. You can read, sleep, eat, whatever, while the train carries you to your destination."

      (D) "And of course you're never delayed by traffic jams."

      (F) "Also trains can carry more passengers than planes."

      (G) "They can also offer more frequent service."

      (A) is incorrect because the speaker says that train trips are sometimes more expensive than car trips. (C) is incorrect because the speaker does not discuss pollution from trains or other forms of transportation. (E) confuses security systems on trains with going through security at the airport.

31. *Germany.* Paragraph 2: "Albert Einstein was born in Germany in 1879."

32. *studying math(s)/mathematics.* Paragraph 3: "He didn't even begin to study mathematics until he was 12."

33. *at age 15.* Paragraph 5: "When Einstein was 15, his family moved to Italy."

34. *1896.* Paragraph 5: " Soon after that, his parents sent him to Switzerland, where in 1896 he finished high school."

35. *1898.* Paragraph 7: "Meanwhile, in 1898, between graduating from high school and getting his job at the Patent Office, Einstein met and fell in love with a young Serbian woman, Mileva Maric."

36. *received/got teaching diploma.* Paragraph 5: "After graduating from high school, he enrolled in a Swiss technological institute. He received a teaching diploma from the institute in 1900."

37. *a Swiss citizen.* Paragraph 5: "He remained in Switzerland and eventually became a Swiss citizen, in 1901."

38. *had a daughter.* Paragraph 7: "They had a daughter in 1902."

39. *1903.* Paragraph 7: "but unusual for the time even for geniuses, they didn't get married until 1903."

40. *1904.* Paragraph 6: "they didn't get married until 1903. Their first son was born the following year."

Reading

Passage 1—The Value of a College Degree

1. False. Paragraph 1 states: "The escalating cost of higher education is causing many to question the value of continuing education beyond high school."

2. True. Paragraph 1 states: "the accumulation of thousands of dollars of debt is, in the long run, worth the investment."

3. True. (Paragraph 4 states: "Most students today—about 80 percent of all students—enroll either in public four-year colleges or in public two-year colleges."

4. Not Given. There is no information about the contrast of public and private colleges.

5. *a lifetime.* Paragraph 3: "According to the Census Bureau, over an adult's working life, high school graduates earn an average of $1.2 million."

6. *$1.6 million/1.6 million dollars.* Paragraph 3: "associate's degree holders earn about $1.6 million"

7. *bachelor's degree holder.* Paragraph 3: "and bachelor's degree holders earn about $2.1 million."

8. *8,655.* Paragraph 4: "a full-time student at a public four-year college pays an average of $8,655 for in-state tuition, room, and board."

9. *tuition.* Paragraph 4: "A full-time student in a public two-year college pays an average of $1,359 per year in tuition."

(C), (D), (E), and (G) are correct.

(C) Paragraph 6 "graduates enjoy, including higher levels of saving"

(D) Paragraph 6 "graduates enjoy . . . more hobbies and leisure activities"

(E) Paragraph 7: "In fact, 'parental schooling levels (after controlling for differences in earnings) are positively correlated with the health status of their children" and "increased schooling" (and higher relative income) are correlated with lower mortality rates for given age brackets.'"

(G) Paragraph 9: "Public benefits of attending college include . . . increased consumption."

Choices (A), (B) and (F) are incorrect. The text does not include a discussion of house size (A), or travel (F). (B) is incorrect because the text gives many reasons why a graduate degree has a positive impact on people ("improved quality of life . . . more open-minded, more cultured, rational greater productivity") but it does not *say* that people are more optimistic about their lives.

Passage 2—Less Television and Less Violence

14. *watched TV*. Paragraph 2: The study found that the third- and fourth-grade students "engaged in fewer acts of verbal and physical aggression than their peers" when they watched less TV.

15. *violently*. Paragraph 2: The study found that the third- and fourth-grade students "engaged in fewer acts of verbal and physical aggression than their peers" when they watched less TV.

16. *6/six months*. Paragraph 3: "18-lesson, 6-month program"

17. *parents*. Paragraph 6: "parental reports of aggressive behavior, and perceptions of a mean and scary world also decreased"

18. *number of hours*. Paragraph 8: "Early lessons encouraged students to keep track of and report on the time they spent watching TV or videos, or playing video games, to motivate them to limit those activities on their own."

19. *avoided TV*. Paragraph 9: "For ten days, students were challenged to go without television, videos, or video games."

20. *less TV*. Paragraph 10 states that "students themselves [began to] advocate reducing screen activities."

21. False. Paragraph 11 states that "This study is by no means the first to find a link."

22. True. Paragraph 14 states that "In the United States and Canada, murder rated doubled."

23. Not Given. Paragraph 14 discusses TV and violence in the United States and Canada, but there is no discussion about which country has more, or if the United States has more than other countries.

24. Not Given. Regarding South Africa, we are given information about how long TV was banned—until 1975 (Paragraph 15)—and that murder rates were steady in the 1940s, but the text does not say when TV was introduced in South Africa.

25. (D) In the second to last paragraph, the text states that "watching television of any content robs us of the time to interact with real people," which can be seen as learning an important social skill. (A), (B), and (C) are incorrect because the text does not address the role of TV for adults (A), does not suggest that TV is the *only* cause of violence (B), and does not make any comparisons between the United States and other countries (C).

26. (B) In the last line, the authors suggest that "[t]he best solution is to turn it [the TV] off." Choice (A) is incorrect because the authors do not discuss humor[1] in TV programs. Choice (C) is incorrect because they do not talk about watching TV alone or with company. Choice (D) is incorrect because the text says in paragraph 9 that the children were encouraged to keep their TV watching time to under seven hours, but that is not suggested as an ideal amount for the reader.

---

[1]BRITISH: humour

Passage 3—Issues Affecting the Southern Resident Orcas

27. iii—Declining Fish Populations is the correct answer. Section A discusses the decrease of fish populations which affect the diet of the orcas. In the last line of the first paragraph, "This may be affecting . . .", *this* refers to declining fish populations. In addition, there is no other heading listed that can describe the idea of Section A.

28. ii—Toxic Exposure is the correct answer. The first line of Section B starts with "Toxic substances accumulate . . . ," which indicates that the section is about toxic substances. Further reading of the section shows supporting evidence for the topic sentence. Heading (i) is mentioned in the section, but it is not the central idea of the section.

29. vii—Impact of Boat Traffic is the correct answer. Again, the first line of Section C states: "waters around the San Juan Islands are extremely busy due to international commercial shipping, fishing, whale watching, and pleasure boating," and the section goes on to talk about the dangers of various types of boats. The fourth paragraph in Section C mentions "smog" as being similar to the exhaust of idle boat traffic. Also, heading (iv) describes *one* type of boating mentioned in the section.

30. v—Underwater Noise is the correct answer. The first line introduces the idea of "acoustic pollution," suggesting the theme of noise. In the section, there are five additional mentions of "noise," or synonyms of noise: noise, sound, listening, noise, acoustics. Choice (v) is the only logical heading for this section.

31. (B) In section A the text states "90 percent of their [orcas'] diet is salmon." (A) and (D) are both secondary choices for the orcas if there are no salmon, and the orcas must eat from the bottom of the ocean and (C) is true for all orcas, but not for the pods specified in the question—J, K, and L—who eat mostly fish, and the fish they prefer is salmon.

32. (A) Section A states that "salmon have become extinct due to habitat loss." Whales only eat the surviving stocks of salmon after they have already decreased in numbers, so (B) is incorrect; it is *whales* and not the *salmon* that have poor nutrition, making (C) incorrect. Choice (D) assumes that the "winter" is a temperature indicator when it is actually a seasonal adjective and does not describe temperature as being cold.

33. *on bottomfish*. Section A, paragraph 2: "whales may be feeding on bottomfish" becomes "they believe the whales *feed* on bottomfish."

34. *smaller*. Section A says: "their size has decreased" = "they are smaller." The grammar compels you to use the comparative form.

35. *Pollution*. Section B states that orcas are affected more by pollutants than other creatures because they are at the top of the food chain.

36. *(so) popular*. The last sentence of section B says: "because orcas are so popular."

37. *numerous boats/vessels*. Paragraph 1 in section C states that: "On a busy weekend day in the summer, it is not uncommon to see numerous boats in the vicinity of the whales as they travel through the area."

38. *(so) quiet*. Paragraph 3 of section C says: "Kayakers even present a problem here because they're so quiet."

39. *exhaust fumes*. Paragraph 4 of section C says that whales "get a nice big breath of exhaust fumes."

40. *communicating*. Section D discusses how noise pollution contributes to orca communication.

Writing

Answers will vary:

Writing Task 1

The sales at this small restaurant during the week of October 7 to 13th followed a fairly set pattern from Monday to Friday, and then showed a notable shift on the weekend. The lunch and dinner sales during the week peaked on Friday and then dipped down as the weekend set in.

During the week of October 7–13, the lunch sales averaged approximately $2,400. The highest lunch sales occurred on Friday, and the lowest occurred on Sunday. Sunday's lunch sales were approximately $1,000 less than the average lunch sales during the rest of the week.

Dinner sales, which generated at least $1,000 to $1,500 more a day than lunch sales, also remained steady during the week. Just like the lunch sales, the dinner sales peak on Friday and dipped down for the weekend.

Excluding Wednesday and Thursday, the lunch and dinner sales from October 7–11 rose gradually until the end of the business week. Midweek, on Wednesday and Thursday, the sales were slightly lower than they were on Tuesday.

According to the sales report, this restaurant has a steady lunch and dinner crowd. The most profitable day during the second week of October was Friday. Sunday, was the least profitable day, with the full day's sales totaling/totalling less than the Friday dinner sales. These numbers are reflective of a restaurant that is located in a business/financial district where business hours are Monday through Friday.

Writing Task 2

When computers first made their way into the business sector, everyone believed that they would make people's jobs easier. What was not expected was that computers would eliminate jobs. Besides contributing to unemployment, these automated workers often exhibit inadequate job performance.

A number of jobs have been lost as a direct result of new computer technology. Ticket agents in various transportation facilities, from subway/underground stations to airports are virtually nonexistent these days. Bank tellers have been greatly reduced due to automated bank machines. In addition, many call centers/centres that have help lines are almost entirely computerized/computerised. A few years ago I worked as a helper in our local library. Today this position does not exist, because six new computers have been installed. The number of positions lost to computers grows exponentially, and unemployment continues to get worse.

While a computer may easily achieve the main tasks of these jobs, most computers fall short when customers have a unique request or problem. A pre-paid ticket booth does not have insight about the entertainment district and cannot offer friendly directions to a tourist. Similarly, an automated bank machine cannot provide assistance and reassurance to a customer who has just had his credit card stolen. And, more often than not, automated telephone operators cannot answer the one question that we have, and we end up waiting on the line to speak with someone anyway. Every time I go into the library where I worked I notice elderly people who don't know how to use the computers and can't find anyone to help.

In the future, I believe a new business trend will evolve. As computers eliminate jobs, new positions will have to be invented. More and more people will go into business for themselves, and hopefully put the personal touch back into business. I believe that the human workforce will demonstrate that it is more valuable than computers.

Speaking

Part 1

Tell about a sport that is interesting to you. What is it? Do you like to play this sport yourself? Do you follow professional teams?
Figure skating is a sport that's interesting to me. I don't do it myself, it's much too hard, but I enjoy watching professional skaters. I often watch the national and regional competitions.

Why do you like this sport?
I like it because it takes a lot of skill and grace. It's beautiful to see. And I really admire the skaters. It takes a lot of discipline to be a champion skater.

Do you enjoy playing sports or doing other outdoor activities? Why or why not?
I don't play sports much. I like watching skating, but I don't skate myself. I'm not really interested in soccer or other ball sports. I like to go bike riding, though. I guess that's my sport. Whenever the weather is nice, I try to get outside on my bike. It feels good to be outside and get some exercise. It makes me feel relaxed and healthy.

In your city or town, what kinds of places are available for sports and other outdoor activities?
We have a lot of parks and most of them have a soccer field or a baseball diamond or a basketball court, or something like that. They also have walking trails and biking trails. The city also runs a few public swimming pools, though they can get very crowded. If you take a short trip outside of the city, you can find lots of opportunities for hiking and biking.

What kinds of things do you enjoy doing on weekends?
I'm so busy during the week that on weekends I just want to relax. I like to have a lot of unscheduled time to just rest, maybe read, take a walk, talk to friends, just little things like that.

Do you generally prefer to spend a day off from work or school at home, or do you like to go out to other places? Why?
Generally, I prefer to spend my days off at home. It's easier to relax that way. But I like to go out, too, to see my friends. Sometimes we meet at a café or at the movies. If I can relax at home all day, then it's fun to go out in the evening with my friends.

Who do you like to spend time with on your days off?
I like to spend time with some of my close friends. I'm not married and my family isn't nearby, but I have some close friends that I enjoy spending time with. We have a favorite restaurant that we like to go to. We usually eat there on Saturdays.

Part 2

Everyone says I'm a lot like my dad, because we look a lot alike. But, truthfully, I'm a lot more like my mom. Part of the reason my mom and I are so similar is that we spend so much time together. Besides spending one year abroad, I've lived with my mom for my whole life. My parents split up ten years ago, and ever since then my mom and I became very close.

My mom and I have the same taste in a lot of things, such as food, fashion, and literature. We both love to eat spicy food, and we both love to bake sweets. Oh, and neither of us ever start the day without our morning cup of green tea. It was weird when I first realized/realised that I could borrow my mom's clothes. I guess she's always just kept up with modern fashion unlike some of my friends' mothers. We both like long skirts and warm sweaters and neither of us ever wear jeans. My mom and I both like to read as well. Ever since I was little my mother always read to me before bed. Sometimes she still reads out loud to me just for fun.

I guess its natural for a person to share some of the same qualities as one or both of their parents. But I also think that part of the reason we are so alike is just that we became dependent on each other. I'm an only child, so my mom always had lots of time to spend with me.

Part 3

Do you enjoy spending time with relatives? Why or why not?
Yes, I love getting together for family functions because it's nice to catch up on each other's lives and see how people have changed.

What types of family traditions do you and your relatives have?
We used to have a lot more traditions when were kids. For example, every New Year, we would have a big party at my grandfather's house, and all of the kids would collect a lot of money. We also used to have a big summer picnic for all of the birthdays that happened in the summer. I miss those traditions.

Do you think family members are more important than friends?
I think it depends on where you are at in life. At some points in my life, my mom has been the most important person, and at other times I have been closer to one of my friends.

Do you think that having a good relationship with relatives is important to most people?
I think that depends on the individual person. I know some people who are very close to their cousins or their siblings or their parents. I know other people who always fight with their relatives and don't like to spend time with them. Some of my friends see their grandparents or uncles and aunts often, and others don't. But even though people have different kinds of relationships with their relatives, I think everybody feels that it's important to know that you have a family who cares about you. You may spend a lot or a little time with your relatives, but it's important to know that they are there.

How do family members help each other?
Family members can help each other in many ways, both emotionally and materially. Older family members serve as role models for younger family members. Parents, older siblings, and family members can provide guidance and advice to their younger relatives. Family members provide each other with companionship. They can also help each other with material things, like lending money or offering a place to stay, or helping to find a job. Grandparents sometimes help take care of their grandchildren. There are a lot of different ways that family members help each other.

Do you agree or disagree: families are not as important as they used to be.
I disagree. I think families are more important now than ever. These days we have so many choices and so many decisions to make. We have to decide what to study and where. We might have to think about moving to another city or country to take a good job. These are hard decisions and if you don't have the support of your family, who will help you? We might make the decision to go to another country, for example, and that would be far away from the family, but still, it's important to know that your family cares about you and will help you.

How are families now different from families in the past?
Families don't always live close together now, and that makes a big difference. I think in the past, the members of an extended family were always around each other and they always helped each other with daily things. If someone didn't have enough money or a place to live or needed help with the children, there was always a relative who could help out. Now that people often go to other places to live, it's harder for family members to help each other because they are farther apart. They still care each other and provide support, but it has to be in a different way. For example, maybe they can give advice, but it's harder to help care for a sick relative. Also they spend less time together so they don't know each other as well.

How do you think families will change in the future?
I think families will be even farther apart in the future. Kids growing up today don't know their extended family very well because they live apart from them. By the time they are adults, they might not know their cousins and aunts and uncles at all. They won't have family members that they can ask for support. People will depend even more on the nuclear family, on their spouses and children, because that will be all the family they have.

ACADEMIC MODEL TEST 2

Listening

Example. (B) Choice (B) is correct because the man is "conducting a survey of shoppers at this mall." He also wants to learn about "people's habits when they shop at the mall." Choice (A) is incorrect because the man is not shopping at the mall; he is conducting a survey. Choice (C) is incorrect because he is not looking for a shop.

1. (B) The man wants to learn about "people's habits when they shop at the mall." The other choices—(A) and (C)—are not mentioned during their conversation.
2. (A) Choice (A) is correct because the man is "interviewing married women, that is women with husbands and children who shop for their families." Choice (B) is incorrect because the man won't talk to "any shopper." Choice (C) is incorrect because the man does not want to speak to children.
3. (B) Choice (B)—26–35—is correct because she says, "I'm 34", which fits into that range. Choices (A) and (C) give numeric ranges that do not match her age.
4. (C) Choice (C) is correct because she says, "I'm here at least twice a week." This statement is the equivalent of choice (C)—two or more times a week. Choice (A)—less than once a month—is incorrect because it is a time period that the man mentions, but the woman does not select that time period. Choice (B)—once a week—is incorrect. It is never mentioned during their conversation.
5. (C) Choice (C) is correct because she says, "The reason I come here so often is for food. I told you I have a large family. I buy all our food at the supermarket here." Choice (A) is incorrect because the woman says, "The clothing stores are quite nice," but she doesn't say that she usually shops for clothes. Choice (B) is incorrect because she says, "I like the bookstore," but she doesn't say that she usually shops for books.
6. (B) Choice (B) is correct because she spends "about an hour and a half or so." Choice (A)—one hour or less—is incorrect because she doesn't say that she ever spends that amount of time at the mall. Choice (C)—more than two hours—is incorrect because she says, "I'm hardly ever here for more than two hours." So, she is not usually at the mall for that amount of time . . . and the question asks for her usual length of time.
7. (A) Choice (A) is correct because the woman says, "I always drive." Choice (B)—bus—is provided by the man as an option, which she doesn't select. Choice (C)—subway—is incorrect. It is never mentioned.
8. Multiple possible answers:
   (a) Employees are polite
   (b) Give good service
   (c) Very good service
   (d) Polite employees
   The woman likes the shoe store because, "the employees there are so polite. They give very good service."

9. The correct answer is "it's very expensive." The woman says, "[the food] is very expensive. It shouldn't cost so much."

10. Multiple possible answers
    (a) add more parking
    (b) more parking spaces/places
    (c) add parking spaces/places
    (d) add parking
    The woman says, "You should add more parking spaces."

11. (A) Choice (A) is correct because the purpose of the tour is to let people "become familiar with the different activities available at the club." The goal of the tour is to have everyone "decide to become members." Choice (B) is incorrect because the club members already have a membership. They don't need to be convinced to join again. Choice (C) is incorrect because the people who work at the club already know about all of the club's activities.

12–14. Choices (A), (D), and (F) are correct.
    Choice (A)—learn to play tennis—is correct because the club does "offer tennis lessons." Choice (D) is correct because the club has "the most modern exercise machines." Choice (F) is correct because club members "have the opportunity to try out for the swim team."
    Choice (B) is incorrect because their club store offers only "snacks or drinks." Choice (C) is incorrect because the only expert mentioned is a fitness and technology expert, but not a nutrition expert. Choice (E) is incorrect because "run on a track" is never mentioned.

15–17. Choices (C), (E), and (F) are correct.
    Choice (C) is correct because they are told to "supply your own shampoo." Choice (E) is correct because people are told that everyone must "wear rubber sandals in the changing rooms" and since they aren't told where to get the sandals, it is understood that you need to bring your own. Choice (F) is correct because people are told "to supply your own lock."
    Choices (A) and (B) are incorrect because the club's locker/changing rooms are kept "well-stocked with basic necessities such as towels and soap." Choice (D) is incorrect because "There are plenty of . . . hair dryers."

18. *by an adult.* "Children must be accompanied by an adult at all times."

19. Multiple possible answers.
    (a) *running.* "No running near the pool."
    (b) *children alone* (see #18).

20. *shower.* People are told, "we ask everyone to shower before entering the pool."

21. *weekly/once a week/every week.* The professor says, "You'll have to write one essay each week." Also, she says, "Every week I'll assign a different type of essay."

22. *350 to 400.*

Essay Type	Sample Topic
23 Process	How to change the oil in a car
24 Classification	Three kinds of friends
25 Compare and contrast	Student cafeteria food and restaurant food
Argumentative	The necessity of **26** homework

27. (B) Choice (B) is correct because the professor tells the students that she wants them to "pick your own topics." Choices (A) and (C) are incorrect because the professor says that students will pick their own topics. The professor mentions books, but only when telling students that the topics must be original: "I want them [the topics] to come out of your own heads, not out of any book on essay writing."

28. (C) Choice (C)—Friday—is correct because the professor says each student will "hand [it] in to me the following Friday." Choice (A) is incorrect—Monday—because that is the day that the essay assignment is given, not when it is due. Choice (B)—Wednesday—is incorrect because that day is never mentioned.

29. (C) Choice (C) is correct because the professor says that "your essays will count for 65 percent of your final grade[1]." Choice (A) is incorrect because it doesn't refer to essays: "Other class work will count for 15 percent." Choice (B) is incorrect because it doesn't refer to essays: "Your tests will be 20 percent of the final grade."

30. (A) Choice (A) is correct because the professor tells them, "Please type your essays on a computer." Choice (B) is incorrect because the professor says, "Handwritten essays are not acceptable," which has the same meaning as Choice (B)—write their essays by hand. Choice (C) is incorrect because the professor says, "I don't want to receive any photocopied work."

31. *Introduction to Anthropology.* "This class is Introduction to Anthropology."

32. *Tuesday.* "This class meets every Tuesday evening."

33. *women.* "The men's job is to hunt . . . while the women gather plants . . ."

34. *twelve thousand years.* "Before 12,000 years ago, all humans lived as hunter-gathers."

35. *some desert areas/deserts.* "Today hunter-gather societies still exist in the Arctic, in some desert areas, and in tropical rainforests."

36. *rainforests/tropical rainforests.* (see #35).

Characteristic	A	B
37 They usually stay in one place.		XX
38 They are nomadic.	XX	
39 They have a higher population density.		XX
40 They have a nonhierarchical social structure.	XX	

37. (B) Choice (B) is correct because the professor says that farmers are more likely to be sedentary. They can't move often because they need to plant their crops. Choice (A) is incorrect because the hunter-gatherers "travel from place to place."

38. (A) Choice (A) is correct because the professor says that they tend to be nomadic. Choice (B) is incorrect because farmers can't move often because they need to plant their crops.

39. (B) Choice (B) is correct because "Farming can support much higher population densities than hunting and gathering can because farming results in a larger food supply." Choice (A) is incorrect because "hunter-gatherer societies generally have lower population densities." Also, the farming society's population density is higher than theirs.

40. (A) Choice (A) is correct because hunter-gatherer societies "tend not to have hierarchical social structures." Choice (B) is incorrect because farming societies had "hierarchical social structures begin to develop."

Reading

Passage 1—Glaciers

1. vi—Types of Glaciers is the correct answer. Paragraph A defines the term *glacier* and describes four specific types of glaciers.

[1]BRITISH: mark

2. ii—Formation and Growth of Glaciers is the correct answer. Paragraph B describes the reason why glaciers generally form in the high alpine regions—because "they require cold temperatures throughout the year." The paragraph also describes the retreat of glaciers during periods when melting and evaporation exceed the amount of snowfall.

3. iii—Glacial Movement is the correct answer. Paragraph C begins with a clear topic sentence: "The weight and pressure of ice accumulation causes glacier movement." The rest of the paragraph then provides details about this movement.

4. vii—Glacial Effects on Landscape is the correct answer. Like the previous paragraph, paragraph D begins with a clear topic sentence directly related to the topic: "glacial erosion creates other unique physical features in the landscape such as horns" and so on. Each feature is described in the following sentences.

5. v—Glaciers Through the Years is the correct answer. Paragraph E refers to the glaciers from the Ice Age, the past century, and even looks into the future by referring to studies that glaciologists can conduct now and in the future.

6. False. Paragraph B, first sentence states: "glaciers exist on all continents," and Paragraph B, last sentence states: "The fastest glacial surge on record occurred in . . . the Kutiah Glacier in Pakistan," which is not at the poles.

7. True. Paragraph B, middle sentence states: "While glaciers rely heavily on snowfall, other climatic conditions including freezing rain, avalanches, and wind, contribute to their growth."

8. True. Paragraph B, second to the last sentence states: "With the rare exception of *surging glaciers,* a common glacier flowers about 10 inches per day in the summer and 5 inches per day in the winter." This fits the 5–10 inch range.

9. False. Paragraph C states: "The middle of a glacier moves faster than the sides and bottom because there is no rock to cause friction."

10. Not Given. Paragraph E refers to the last Ice Age and the percentage of glaciers that covered the earth's surface. However, no mention is made of the temperatures then.

11. (B) Paragraph A explains: "Smaller glaciers that occur at higher elevations are called *alpine* or *valley glaciers.*" Paragraph D refers to "alpine glaciers [occurring] on the same mountain."

12. (D) Paragraph A states: "*Polar glaciers* . . . always maintain temperatures far below melting." Therefore, these temperatures are freezing, and D is the correct answer.

13. (H) Paragraph B says: "With the rare exception of *surging glaciers*, a common glacier flows about 10 inches per day in the summer and 5 inches per day in the winter. The fastest glacial surge on record occurred in 1953." So the reader can infer that the term surging glacier is related to the speed of the glacier's movement.

14. (A) Paragraph D explains: "*Fjords* . . . are coastal valleys that fill with ocean water." Therefore, the reader assumes that fjords form near the ocean and term A (fjord) is selected as the correct answer.

15. (G) Paragraph D states: "A cirque is a large bowl-shaped valley that forms at the front of a glacier."

Passage 2—Irish Potato Famine

16. (F) Paragraph F begins by stating the British government's political policy toward Ireland during the famine: "The majority of the British officials in the 1840s adopted the laissez-faire philosophy." The rest of the paragraph provides details about the British government's action (or lack of action) to help Ireland and the impact that had on Ireland.

17. (D) Paragraph D describes the British tenure system, including how British landowners charged rent and people lived on smaller and smaller parcels of land.

18. (B) Paragraph B describes how Europeans changed their attitude about potatoes, from saying it "belonged to a botanical family of a poisonous breed" to having the European monarchs order the wide planting of the vegetable.

19. (E) Paragraph E examines the Penal Laws and the many rights those laws denied the Irish peasants.

20. (C) Paragraph C describes Ireland's dependence on the potato—as a crop and as a stored food item.

21. (I) Paragraph B states: "Europeans believed that potatoes belonged to a botanical family of a poisonous breed."
22. (K) Paragraph B states: "By the late 1700s, the dietary value of the potato had been discovered, and the monarchs of Europe ordered the vegetable to be widely planted."
23. (C) Paragraph C states: "By 1800, the vast majority of the Irish population had become dependent on the potato as its primary staple."
24. (E) Paragraph C states: "Those who did manage to grow things such as oats, wheat, and barley relied on earnings from these exported crops to keep their rented homes."
25. (G) Paragraph D states: "As the population of Ireland grew, however, the plots were continuously subdivided . . . families were forced to move to less fertile land where almost nothing but the potato would grow."
26. (A) Paragraph E states: "Approximately 500,000 Irish tenants were evicted. . . . Many of these people . . . were put in jail for overdue rent."
27. (H) Paragraph F states: "Sir Robert Peel . . . showed compassion toward the Irish by making a sudden move to repeal the Corn Laws. . . . For this hasty decision, Peel quickly lost the support of the British people and was forced to resign."
28. (F) Paragraph F states: "A few relief programs were eventually implemented, such as soup kitchens and workhouses; [but] these were poorly run institutions."

Passage 3—Anesthesiology

29. False. Paragraph 1 states that his book "was the primary reference source for physicians for over sixteen centuries," so it did not fall out of use after 60 A.D.
30. True. Paragraph 2 states: "The mandragora . . . was one of the first plants to be used as an anesthetic." Then the paragraph refers to its use in the Middle Ages.
31. True. Paragraph 3 explains nitrous oxide caused "a strange euphoria, followed by fits of laughter, tears, and sometimes unconsciousness."
32. Not Given. Paragraph 3 refers to laughing gas being used in 1844 to relieve pain during a tooth extraction. However, no details are given about anesthesia/anaesthesia being used for the remainder of the century.
33. True. Paragraph 5 states: "It takes over eight years of schooling and four years of residency until an anesthesiologist is prepared to practice in the United States."
34. False. Paragraph 6 states: "The number of anesthesiologists in the United States has more than doubled since the 1970s."
35. (D) Paragraph 4 states: "Simpson sprinkled chloroform on a handkerchief."
36. (B) Paragraph 5 states: "Local anesthetic is used only at the affected site."
37. (H) Paragraph 2 states: "Dioscorides suggested boiling the root [of mandrake] with wine."
38. (F) Paragraph 3 states: "laughing gas [also known as nitrous oxide], which he used in 1844 to relieve pain during a tooth extraction."
39. (C) Paragraph 5 states: "Regional anesthetic is used to block the sensation and possibly the movement of a larger portion of the body."
40. (E) Paragraph 3 states that the first anesthetic machine contained an ether-soaked sponge.

Writing

Answers will vary:

Writing Task 1

Several steps are involved in the process of manufacturing yogurt and preparing it for sale.

First, milk has to be heated to the proper temperature, which is 93° Celsius, or 200° Fahrenheit. The milk is kept at this temperature for at least ten minutes. The longer this temperature is maintained, the thicker the yogurt will be. Thirty minutes is generally the maximum time.

Next, the milk is cooled to 44° Celsius, or 112° Fahrenheit. Yogurt starter, or live bacteria, is added. The yogurt is kept at a temperature of 37° Celsius, or 100° Fahrenheit, while it incubates for four hours. After four hours, incubation is stopped by putting the yogurt in a cool place.

Now the yogurt is ready to have things added to it, usually fruit, sweetener, and different flavorings. Then it is put into containers. The containers are labeled and packed for shipping. Soon, the yogurt will show up in your neighborhood grocery store.

Writing Task 2—Agree

Families who do not send their children to government-financed[1] school should not be required to pay taxes that support universal education.

When families send their children to non-public[1] (that is, parochial and private) schools, they must pay tuition and other school expenses. Spending additional money to pay taxes creates an even greater financial hardship for these families. They must make sacrifices, trying to have enough money to pay for school in addition to other bills. For example, my friend Amalia is a single mother with an eight-year-old son, Andrew. Because they survive solely on her income, money is tight. Amalia works at least 10 hours of overtime each week to cover Andrew's school expenses. This gives Amalia and Andrew less time to spend together, and she is always so tired that she is impatient with him when they do have family time. Clearly, this extra expense is an unfair burden for hard-working parents like Amalia.

While some people may consider parochial or private school to be a luxury, for many families it is essential because their community's public schools fail to meet their children's needs. Unfortunately, due to shrinking budgets, many schools lack well-qualified, experienced educators. Children may be taught by someone who is not a certified teacher or who knows little about the subject matter. Some problems are even more serious. For example, the public high school in my old neighborhood/neighbourhood had serious safety problems, due to students bringing guns, drugs, and alcohol to school. After a gang-related shooting occurred at the high school, my parents felt that they had no choice but to enroll me in a parochial school that was known for being very safe.

Unfortunately, even when families prefer public schools, sometimes they can't send their children to one. These families are burdened not only by paying expenses at another school, but also by being forced to pay taxes to support a public school that they do not use.

Writing Task 2—Disagree

Families who do not send their children to public school should be required to pay taxes that support public education.

[1]American public schools are government-financed, i.e., paid for by local taxpayers.

Every child in my country is required to attend school, and every child is welcome to enroll at his/her local public school. Some families choose to send their children to other schools, and it is their prerogative to do so. However, the public schools are used by the majority of our children and must remain open for everyone. For example, my uncle sent his two children to a private academy for primary school. Then he lost a huge amount of money through some poor investments and he could no longer afford the private school's tuition. The children easily transferred to their local public school and liked it even more than their academy. The public schools supported their family when they had no money to educate their children.

Because the public schools educate so many citizens, everyone in my country—whether a parent or not—should pay taxes to support our educational system. We all benefit from the education that students receive in public school. Our future doctors, firefighters, and teachers—people whom we rely on every day—are educated in local public schools. When a person is in trouble, it's reassuring to know that those who will help you—such as firefighters—know what they're doing because they received good training in school and later. Providing an excellent education in the public school system is vital to the strength of our community and our country.

Our government must offer the best education available, but it can only do so with the financial assistance of all its citizens. Therefore, everyone—including families who do not send their children to public school—should support public education by paying taxes.

Speaking

Part 1

Do you have a job? Do you like it? Why or why not?

Yes, I have a job. I work as an enrollment manager for a university. I recruit new students into the program. I like it a lot because I can help people, and I get to meet a lot of new and interesting people. Also I have the opportunity to travel a lot.

Why did you choose this job?

I chose this job because I enjoy travel, and I like meeting people. I have to travel at least 25 percent of the time for my job. I am always talking to people, e-mailing them, or writing articles about our university. It's really interesting.

What kind of education or training did you need to get this job?

I have my MBA (Masters in Business Administration) and that's the same program that I recruit students into. So, having that education really helped me to get this job, because I know what the students need to succeed in our program. Also, I've taken courses in public speaking so I'm comfortable giving presentations about our university.

Describe an activity you enjoy doing in your free time.

One of my favorite free time activities is painting with watercolors. I especially like to paint outdoor scenes, so when the weather is nice, I go outside and paint.

How long have you been doing this activity? How did you learn it?

I've been painting since I was in high school. I learned how to use watercolors in one of my classes and I really liked it and I've been painting ever since. Sometimes I take a painting class at the local community center, but mostly I learn by doing.

In your free time, do you prefer activities you can do with other people, or activities you can do alone? Why?
It really depends on the activity. Painting is something I usually do alone, although sometimes I go to a park or other pretty place with some other painters I know and we paint together. But if I want to go to the movies or go shopping, those things are always much more fun when you do them with other people.

Is having a lot of free time important to you? Why or why not?
I like having a lot of free time because I always have so much to do. I have my painting and then I want to spend time with my family, of course. I think family is really the most important reason to have free time. It's important to do things with your family.

Part 2

I recently celebrated New Year's Day. The purpose of this day is to welcome the New Year. I think people celebrate it just about everywhere in the world. I celebrated with my cousins. We try to get together every year to celebrate this holiday, even though some of us live far away now. They're like my brothers and sisters; we grew up together. And that's the reason why this holiday is important to me, because I know I will see my cousins then. We're still young, so we did what young people do. We went to some clubs and stayed out all night dancing. We also met up with some old school friends, so it was like a reunion. We stayed out really late, until about 5:00 in the morning. The next day we went to my aunt's house and had a big family dinner with all the aunts and uncles and cousins, everyone in the family of all ages. We ate/had my country's traditional food and told stories and played games. It was a traditional family party. We do it every year.

Part 3

What are some important holidays in your country?
Some important holidays in my country are New Year's Day, National Day, and Children's Day.

Why do people celebrate holidays?
Holidays are a time to remember important dates and people from our past and to practice our traditions. They're also a time to be with our families, and to relax and enjoy good food.

Do you think holiday celebrations have changed over the years? Why or why not?
Holiday celebrations haven't changed much over the years. The dates are the same, and the reason for each day hasn't changed. Families and friends still meet and spend time together.

Do you think the importance of holiday celebrations has changed over the years? Why or why not?
No, I don't think that the importance of holiday celebrations has changed. These days are still special for everyone. But sometimes it's difficult for people to have time to really enjoy the holiday.

How will holidays be different in the future?
In the future, we may have some new holidays. Also, with so many busy families, some of the holiday traditions may change. Instead of eating home-cooked food on holidays, I think that more and more families will go to restaurants. Then they can do less work and still enjoy the holiday together.

ACADEMIC MODEL TEST 3

Listening

1. *Patty.* In line 9 of the dialogue she says, "It's Patty, that's P-A-T-T-Y."
2. *17.* In line 11, she says, "I live at 17 High Street" and in line 13 she emphasizes this, "SevenTEEN."
3. *apartment.* In line 15, she says, "It's an apartment."/flat."
4. *cell.* In line 19, she says, "It's my cell/mobile phone."
5. (B) In line 23, when asked to describe her glasses, the woman says, "They're round. And they have a chain attached." (A) is incorrect because it only mentions the shape of the glasses, and doesn't say anything about the chain. (C) is incorrect because it indicates square reading glasses, and hers were round.
6. (A) In line 25, the woman says that she "had a window seat." So, she was by the window when she lost her glasses. (B) is incorrect because she was not near a door: "the door [was] at the other end of the car." (C) is incorrect because she "was sitting on the train reading," not in the station.
7. (C) In line 27, she "was [reading] a fascinating article in that new magazine." (A) and (B) are incorrect because those choices are never mentioned.
8. (C) In line 29 she says, "I've come here to visit my aunt." (A) is incorrect because she wasn't going home. In fact, she "left home at five o'clock this morning." (B) is incorrect because she wasn't going to work. She took "a whole week off work to make this trip."
9. (B) In line 31 she says, "At ten o'clock, I think. Yes, that's right." (A) is incorrect because that is the time she left home that morning. (C) is incorrect because in line 31 she says that her train arrived "just about 30 minutes ago. At ten o'clock." So her train arrived at 10 and she is making the lost report at 10:30.
10. (C) In lines 34 and 35, the man asks about what is in her coat pocket, and she finds her glasses then. (A) is incorrect because they were not in her purse/handbag. She does say, "I had my handbag," but her glasses weren't there. (B) is incorrect because she says, "I checked my seat to see if I had left anything on it, but I hadn't."
11. *mainly commercial area.* The downtown is described as "mainly a commercial area."
12. *too far.* The downtown is described as "rather far from the university."
13. *prices are low.* The speaker says that in uptown "The prices there are quite low."
14. *a car.* The speaker says, "you'll need a car if you choose to live there" (in uptown).
15. *University's Student Center/Student Center wall.* The speaker says, "look . . . at the university's Student Center. There is a wall there devoted to apartment ads."
16. *Local newspaper/The Greenfield Times.* He mentions, "The local city newspaper, *The Greenfield Times,* . . . lists apartment for rent ads."
17. *bus schedules.* He says the Student Counseling[1] Center (SCC) has "city bus schedules."
18. *roommate matching.* He says the SCC has a "roommate[2] matching service."
19. *inexpensive furniture stores.* He says the SCC can provide "a list of inexpensive furniture stores."
20. *meal.* He mentions that students can sign up "for a meal plan on campus" and that SCC has several different plans.
21. *your health.* The speaker says, "First, bicycling is good for your health."
22. *cheaper than.* The speaker says, "Bicycles are a lot cheaper to use than cars."
23. *pollution.* The speaker says, "Bicycles don't cause pollution like cars and buses do."

[1]BRITISH: counselling

[2]BRITISH: flatmate

24. *bad weather*. The speaker talks about rain and the cold. She says, "So bad weather would be a problem."
25. *a long distance*. The speaker says, "It's difficult to ride your bike if your trip is a long distance."
26. *make bike lanes*. The woman says, "I think the biggest thing is making bicycle lanes on roads."
27. *lock up bikes/lock bikes*. The woman says, "They need a safe place to lock up their bikes."
28. *bicycling maps*. The woman says, "Some cities provide bicycling maps."
29. *helmet*. The woman says, "For safety you should wear a helmet."
30. *waterproof clothes*. The woman says, "For comfort you need . . . waterproof clothes when it rains."
31. *suggested topics list*. In paragraph 1, the professor says, "I have a list of suggested topics . . . and I'd like you to look over it."
32. *final approval/professor's approval*. At the end of paragraph 1, the professor says, "You'll need to get my final approval on your topic."
33. *Gather information*. In paragraph 2, the professor says, "The next thing you'll do is gather information on your topic."
34. *magazines, and newspapers*. In paragraph 2 the professor mentions the "journals, magazines, and newspapers."
35. *encyclopedias/encyclopaedias*. In paragraph 2, the professor refers to the "online encyclopedias."
36. *Write thesis statement*. In paragraph 3 the professor says, "the next step is to write a thesis statement."
37. *body*. Midway through paragraph 4, the professor explains there is an introduction and "then the body."
38. *conclusion*. At the end of paragraph 4, the professor explains there is "finally the conclusion."
39. *Organize/organise your notes*. At the beginning of paragraph 5, the professor says, "you can start organizing your notes."
40. *Revise your draft*. In paragraph 7 the professor says, "the next thing to do is revise your draft."

Reading

Passage 1

1. (B) In paragraph 4, it states that the intradermal allergy test "involves placing the allergen sample under the skin with a syringe."
2. (A) In paragraph 3, it says that the "test is often done on the upper back of children."
3. (C) In paragraph 5, it says that a blood test (the RAST) "is used if patients have pre-existing skin conditions."
4. (B) In paragraph 4 about the intradermal allergy test, the text states, "People who have experienced serious allergic reactions called anaphylactic reactions are not advised to have these types of tests."
5. (A) In paragraph 3 about the skin-prick test, the text says, "Results from a skin test can usually be obtained within 20 to 30 minutes."
6. (A) In paragraph 3 about the skin-prick test, the text discusses a controlled hive known as a wheal and flare. "The white wheal is the small raised surface, while the flare is the redness that spreads out from it."
7. (C) In paragraph 5 about the blood test, the text states, "The RAST is a more expensive test."
8. *eating*. In paragraph 1, the text states: "Allergic reactions are triggered by the contact, inhalation, or *ingestion* . . . ."
9. *allergens*. In paragraph 1, the text states: "Allergic reactions are triggered by the contact, inhalation, or ingestion of a number of different *allergens*."

10. *signs.* In paragraph 1, the text states: "*Symptoms* of allergic reactions range from mild irritation such as itching, wheezing, and coughing."

11. *medicines.* In paragraph 1, the text states: "Serious allergic reactions are more likely to result from food, *drugs,* and stinging insects."

12. *anaphylaxis.* In paragraph 4, the text states: "*Anaphylaxis* is an allergic reaction that affects the whole body and is potentially life threatening." This sentence expresses that anaphylaxis is an allergic reaction, and a very severe one.

13. *identify.* In paragraph 7, the text states: "After using a reliable testing method, the cause of an allergic reaction is often *identified.*"

14. *avoiding.* In paragraph 7, the text states: "while those with food allergies learn to safely *remove* certain foods from their diets."

Passage 2

15. (A) Choice (A) is correct because paragraph 1 explains: "the sacred pipe was considered a medium through which humans could pray to The Great Spirit." The text mentions the pipe's "connection to the spiritual world." Choice (B) is incorrect because the reading passage mentions "a gift from the Great Spirit" and "gifts to the earth's first bears," but it does not describe using the sacred pipe in gift exchanges. Choice (C) is incorrect because paragraph 2 says that, "the sacred pipe was built with precise craftsmanship." But there is no mention of it representing traditional handicrafts.

16. (A) Choice (A) is correct because paragraph 2 states: "The bowl of the traditional sacred pipe was made of red pipestone. . . . The wooden stem." Paragraph 8 elaborates on the red pipestone by explaining that "the quarries must be considered a sacred place" and these quarries, where the pipestone was found, indicate that pipestone is a rock. Choice (B) is incorrect because those are the substances used in mixing tobacco–paragraph 3. Choice (C) is incorrect because there is no mention of red clay in this reading passage.

17. (C) Choice (C) is correct because paragraph 2 states, "In many tribes the man and woman held onto the sacred pipe during the marriage ceremony." Choices (A) and (B) are incorrect because funerals and births are not mentioned.

18. (B) Choice (B) is correct because paragraph 3 states: "tobacco was mixed with herbs, bark, and roots. . . . These mixtures varied depending on the plants that were indigenous to the tribal area." So, the tobacco combined a variety of herbs as well as other plant life. Choice (A) is incorrect because this ceremonial tobacco was not plain. Choice (C) is incorrect because bark was only one of the ingredients in the mixture.

19. (C) Choice (C) is correct because paragraph 8 describes Pipestone, Minnesota. The text refers to its quarries, so this is a source of stone for pipes. Choice (A) is incorrect because there were no battles here. The text states, "Regardless of their conflicts, tribes put their weapons down and gathered in peace in these quarries." Choice (B) is incorrect because the text says that "According to the Dakota tribe, The Great Spirit once called all Indian nations to this location." No mention is made of the Dakota tribe originating from there.

20. *pipe bowl/bowl.* Paragraph 4 states: "In a typical pipe ceremony, the pipe holder stood up and held the pipe bowl in his left hand."

21. *pipe stem/stem.* Paragraph 4 states: "In a typical pipe ceremony, the pipe holder stood up . . . with the stem held toward the East in his right hand."

22. *the East.* Paragraph 4 states: "he sprinkled some on the ground as an offering to both Mother Earth and the East. The East was acknowledged as the place where the morning star rose."

23. *the South.* Paragraph 5 states: "Before offering a prayer to the South. . . . The South was believed to bring strength, growth, and healing."

24. *Mother Earth*

25. *the four directions.* Paragraph 6 explains: "Finally, the stem was held straight up and the tribe acknowledged The Great Spirit, thanking him for being the creator of Mother Earth, Father Sky, and the four directions."

26. *smoke.* Paragraph 7 states: "Each member took a puff of smoke and offered another prayer."

27. *stored separately.* Paragraph 7 explains: "It was important for the stem and bowl to be stored in separate pockets in a pipe pouch. These pieces were not allowed to touch each other, except during a sacred pipe ceremony."

Passage 3

28. *19th century/1800s.* Paragraph 2 states: "During the nineteenth century attempts to produce maps of the seafloor involved lowering weighted lines from a boat."

29. *depth.* Paragraph 2 says: "When the handline hit the ocean floor, the depth of the water was determined."

30. *single-beam sonar.* Paragraph 3 focuses on sonar and says it "was first used to detect submarines and icebergs." So, it was used for detecting objects underwater. The text explains, "By the 1930s, single-beam sonar was being used."

31. *sound waves.* Paragraph 3 states that "By the 1930s single-beam sonar was being used to transmit sound waves in a vertical line from a ship to the seafloor."

32. *1960s.* According to paragraph 4, "The multi-beam sonar . . . was developed in the 1960s."

33. *the entire globe/the world/Earth.* Paragraph 5 says: "The benefit of using satellites to map the ocean is that it can take pictures of the entire globe."

34. (A) Choice (A) is correct because paragraph 4 says: "The Ring of Fire . . . is famous for its seismic activity."

35. (B) Choice (B) is correct because paragraph 4 states: "The Mid-Ocean Ridge is . . . 1,200 miles wide."

36. (B) Choice (B) is correct because paragraph 4 explains: "The Mid-Ocean Ridge is a section of undersea mountains."

37. (A) Choice (A) is correct because paragraph 4 says: "This area [the Ring of Fire] . . . accounts for more than 75 percent of the world's active and dormant volcanoes."

38–40. (ii) (iii), (v) are correct. Choice (ii) is correct because paragraph 6 states: "Scientists expect bathymetry to become one of the most important sciences as humans search for new energy sources." Choice (iii) is correct because paragraph 6 says: "Preserving the ocean's biosphere for the future will also rely on an accurate mapping of the seafloor." Choice (v) is correct because paragraph 6 states: "Scientists expect bathymetry to become one of the most important sciences as humans . . . seek alternate routes for telecommunication."

Writing

Answers will vary:

Writing Task 1

Over the past 30 years, the average family has dramatically increased the number of meals that they eat at restaurants. The percentage of the family's food budget spent on restaurant meals steadily climbed. Just 10 percent of the food budget was spent on restaurant meals in 1970 and 15 percent in 1980. That percentage more than doubled in 1990, to 35 percent, and rose again in 2000 to 50 percent.

Where families eat their restaurant meals also changed during that 30-year period. In 1970, families ate the same number of meals at fast-food and sit-down restaurants. In 1980, families ate slightly more frequently at sit-down restaurants. However, since 1990, fast-food restaurants serve more meals to the families than do the sit-down restaurants. Most of the restaurant meals from 2000 were eaten at fast-food restaurants. If this pattern continues, eventually the number of meals that families eat at fast-food restaurants could double the number of meals they eat at sit-down restaurants.

Writing Task 2—Agree

"Do as I say, not as I do." This is what society tells us when it punishes murderers with the death penalty. Society tells us that murder is wrong, and in our legal system, murder is against the law. Yet we still see our society kill murderers, and thus we are committing murder ourselves. For this reason, the death penalty should end, and instead murderers should be punished with life in prison.

Society needs to show a positive model of how our lives should be and how people should act. We should always strive to improve our situation, to be at peace and in harmony with others. However, when we kill murderers, we are not working to improve our society. Instead, we are stooping to the criminals' level.

It makes me think about the revenge that came when playing games with my brother. When we were kids/children, my brother would take my toys, so I would hit him and take my toys back. Then he would hit me harder and take the toys again. Thinking of the death penalty, I imagine a murderer kills someone. Society takes revenge by killing the murderer. This leaves behind the murderer's family and friends, who have tremendous anger inside of them, which they may release onto society. The cycle of killing goes on and on.

Society should not condemn people who are taking the same action that society is taking. Society tells us not to kill, and yet society kills when it exercises the death penalty. Because of this contradiction, we should end the death penalty and instead punish murderers by sentencing them to life in prison.

Writing Task 2—Disagree

I strongly support the death penalty for murderers. In today's society, life is very violent. There are many mentally ill people committing crimes and almost nothing will stop them. We have interviewed captured criminals who say, "I was going to kill him, but I knew that I could get the death penalty if I did. So I just left him there." Obviously, having the death penalty saves lives and that makes a positive difference to society.

If a criminal does murder someone and then gets the death penalty, that isn't society's fault. Everyone knows about the death penalty as a punishment for murder. So, the person who murders is really killing himself at the same time he is killing his victim. The murderer has made the choice to die.

It is important to remember that the death penalty is used only for people who have committed very serious crimes. For example, a woman shot a police officer when she was trying to escape from jail. She was already a convicted criminal when she committed murder, and she deserves the death penalty.

People need to accept responsibility for their actions. Punishing murderers with the death penalty is one way that society can help people to realize/realise the consequences of their decisions.

Speaking

Part 1

What kind of food do you enjoy eating?
Most of the time, I enjoy healthy food. I like fish, salad, and vegetables. Sometimes I like something sweet.

What are some kinds of food you never eat? Why?
I never eat fast food. It's so unhealthy that I can't enjoy eating it. Well, sometimes I will eat French fries.

Do you generally prefer to eat at home or at a restaurant? Why?
I usually like to eat at home. It's less expensive than a restaurant, and I can make all of the food exactly the way I like it.

What are some reasons that people eat at restaurants?
Most of all, it's convenient. It's so nice to have someone make the food and clean up everything afterwards.

Describe some things you enjoy doing with your friends.
When I get together with my friends on weekends, we often have dinner together or we have a picnic lunch at a park. Most of us have young children, so that's really the easiest way to spend time together, because the children enjoy it too.

Do you think it's better to have a large group of friends or a few close friends? Why?
I like having a large group of friends. There's more variety that way. You don't always see the same people or talk about the same thing. And if you have a large group of friends, there's always somebody who has time to spend with you or who feels like doing what you feel like doing.

How do people choose their friends?
I think we choose our friends based on a comfortable feeling. You know, sometimes people just understand each other so easily and the conversation just flows. Of course, there's usually one thing that people have in common when they become friends such as work or school, or maybe their children are classmates.

Have you remained friends with people from your childhood? Why or why not?
No, I haven't really. I live in a different city now, so I'm not near any of my childhood friends. There are one or two I see when I go home to visit my family, but that's all. I don't think I have much in common with my childhood friends any more.

Part 2

There is one teacher that I remember very well. I went to school at age five, and she was my first teacher. She read stories to us and taught us our letters and numbers. She taught us a lot of nice songs, too. She taught us all the things that kindergarten children need to learn. I think she had a very good personality for a kindergarten teacher. She was a very kind person. She cared about all of us. She was very warm. I think these qualities are very important for a kindergarten teacher because kindergarten children are so young.

Sometimes it's hard for them to spend all those hours away from home. This teacher was also very patient. When we made a lot of noise or had disagreements or anything like that, she never yelled at us. She always helped us solve our problems in a calm way. I remember her because she was my first teacher and because she was so nice. I think it was because I had a good experience with my first teacher that I learned to like school. I learned that school was a nice place to be and that learning was fun and interesting.

Part 3

What kind of person makes a good teacher?
A person who is smart and caring makes a good teacher. Also, the person should like talking to other people and presenting information.

Why do you think people choose to become teachers?
There are many reasons, but I think that most teachers want to make a positive difference in others' lives. Many teachers have family members who were teachers.

Which is more important for a teacher—to be an expert in the subject he or she teaches, or to be very skilled at explaining things and motivating students to learn?
I think it's more important for a teacher to be an expert in the subject matter. How can you teach a subject if you don't know it very well? You have to know it in order to explain it. You have to be able to answer any questions the students ask. Anybody can read a book on any subject, but the subject matter expert is the one who can explain it well.

How are schools different now from when you were young? How do you think they will be different in the future?
When I was a child in school, we didn't have so much technology. We had computers, but they weren't in every classroom and a lot of the teachers didn't know how to use them. So I had a more traditional education. Now I believe computers are often used in schools. Children use the Internet now for research. That makes a very big difference. They can have access to a lot of information they didn't have before. In the future, I think there might not be any schools at all. Children will just stay home and do all their learning through the Internet.

ACADEMIC MODEL TEST 4

Listening

Example: (C) Line 3 has a woman ask, "Tickets? That's our Special Events Department. Let me transfer you." She directs the phone call to that number.

1. (C) Choice (C) is correct because in lines 5 and 7, the man says, "I'm interested in the series you have going on now . . . Actually, I meant the concert series." Choice (A) is incorrect because in line 6, the woman thinks he is interested in the "lecture series on the history of art", but he isn't. Choice (B) is incorrect because he's interested in listening to music at the concert, not attending a lecture.
2. (A) All three choices are mentioned. Choice (A) is correct because in lines 8–11, the woman explains: "there's still a concert tomorrow, that's Thursday." The man asks, "The one tomorrow, is that when they'll be playing the Mozart concerto?" and the woman answers, "Yes, it is." Choice (B) and (C) are incorrect because the man does not want to attend the concert on those days, even though there are performances. In line 8, the woman says, "There's also one [concert] on Saturday, and then the last one is on Sunday."
3. *Milford.* In line 13, he provides his name, "It's Steven Milford. That's M-i-l-f-o-r-d."
4. *1659798164.* In line 17, he gives his credit card number, "1659798164."
5. *32.70.* In line 20, she says: "At 16.35 a piece that comes out to a total of 32 pounds and 70 p/pence."
6. Library

7. Bank
8. Post Office
9. Museum
10. Hotel
11. *56,000*. In paragraph 1, Sheila says: "Ravensburg is the major city on the island, though with a population of only 56,000."
12. *26*. In paragraph 2, Sheila says: "Summer in the city of Ravensburg is warm with average temperatures reaching 26 degrees."
13. *23*. In paragraph 2, Sheila says: "Summer at Blackstone is a bit cooler, with average temperatures of around 23 degrees."
14. *windy*. In paragraph 2, Sheila says: "the weather is often windy because, of course, it's located on the coast."
15. *entertainment*. In paragraph 3, Sheila says: "so if entertainment is what you're looking for, Ravensburg has the advantage there."
16. *very quiet*. At the end of paragraph 3, Sheila says about Blackstone: "It's a very quiet town, which is a disadvantage if you're looking for excitement."
17. *75 kilometers*. In paragraph 4, Sheila says: "Travelers[1] to Blackstone Beach also use the Ravensburg airport, which is about 75 kilometers away."
18. (C) Sheila says, "Some very good deals can be found, however, in the perfume shops."
19. (D) Sheila says, "Jewelry[2] is also popular among tourists, and jewelry shops abound."
20. (E) Sheila says, "Since fishing is the major island industry, no tourist goes home without a package of smoked fish."
    For this section, choice (A) is incorrect because Sheila says, "Well, contrary to what one might think, native handicrafts are not a popular item." Choice (B) is incorrect because Sheila says, "there are not many CDs available of the native music, and the ones that are available are quite expensive." Choice (F) is incorrect because Sheila says, ". . . be sure to bring your own fishing gear[3]. Believe it or not, it's difficult and expensive for tourists to buy it on the island."
21. *next Thursday*. In line 6, Janet says, "It's due next Thursday."
22. *40*. In line 8, Janet says, "And it counts for 40 percent of our final semester grade[4]."
23. *TV watching habits/ people's TV habits*. In line 10, Janet says, "I did my research about people's TV watching habits."
24. *library research*. In line 14, Janet says, "Well, after I decided my topic, I went to the library and did some research. I mean, I read about other studies people had done about TV watching."
25. *research method*. In line 16, Janet says, "So after I did the library research, I chose my research method."
26. *questionnaire*. In line 18, Janet says, "Well, I could do either interviews or just send around a paper questionnaire. I decided to use the questionnaire." In line 20, Janet says, "I made up the questions for the questionnaire."
27. *Submit*. In line 23, Harry asks, "So then you just went around and asked people the questions?" Janet answers, "Well, first I had to submit my research design to Professor Farley. He had to make sure it was OK before I went ahead with the research."
28. *Send out questionnaires*. In line 26, Janet says, "So then I had to send out the questionnaire."
29. *Make charts*. After collecting the information, in line 28, Janet says, "I made charts and graphs."
30. *report*. In line 32, Janet says, "Well, I'll have to write a report, too, of course."
31. (A) In paragraph 2, the professor says, "You'll find crows in North America."
32. (D) In paragraph 2, the professor says, "There are several species of crows, for example, in Hawaii."

---

[1]BRITISH: Travellers

[2]BRITISH: Jewellery

[3]BRITISH: tackle

[4]BRITISH: end of term mark

33. (E) In paragraph 2, the professor says, "And of course you'll find them in other parts of the world, Europe, Asia, and so on."

34. (F) In paragraph 2, the professor says, "And of course you'll find them in other parts of the world, Europe, Asia, and so on."
    Choice (B) is incorrect because in paragraph 2, the professor says, "You'll find crows in North America, although interestingly enough, not in South America." Choice (C) is incorrect because in paragraph 2, the professor says, "There are none in Antarctica."

35. *39–49*. In paragraph 3, the professor says, "[It measures] 39 to 49 centimeters in length."

36. *black*. In paragraph 3, the professor says, "the American crow is completely black, including the beak and feet."

37. *sticks*. In the first sentence of paragraph 4, the professor says, "Crows build large nests of sticks."

38. *trees/bushes/trees and bushes*. In the first sentence of paragraph 4, "Crows build large nests of sticks, usually in trees or sometimes in bushes."

39. *3 to 6*. In paragraph 4, the professor says, "The female lays from three to six eggs at a time."

40. *35*. In paragraph 4, the professor says, "Generally, 35 days after hatching they have their feathers and are ready to fly."

Reading

Passage 1

1–4. (A), (B), (D), and (F) are correct. Choice (A) is correct because in paragraph 2, line 5, it says, "First, K'ang planned to reform China's education system." Choice (B) is correct because in paragraph 2, line 9, it says, "K'ang also called for the establishment of a national parliamentary government, including popularly elected members and ministries." Choice (D) is correct because paragraph 2 says, "Military reform and the establishment of a new defense[1] system . . . were also on the agenda." Choice (F) is correct because paragraph 2 says, "Military reform . . . as well as the modernization[2] of agriculture and medicine were also on the agenda."
     Choice (C) is incorrect because paragraph 2 says, "The edicts called for a public school system with an emphasis on practical and Western studies rather than Neo-Confucian orthodoxy." So, the study of Confucianism was not a focus. Choice (E) is incorrect because paragraph 2 says, "K'ang also called for the establishment of a national parliamentary government, including popularly elected members and ministries." K'ang called for the addition of elections, not the abolition (or end) of elections. Choice (G) is incorrect because there is no mention in the reading passage about initiating foreign trade.

5. (F) Choice (F) is correct because paragraph 1 states: "After losing the Sino-Japanese war, the Emperor Guwangxu found his country to be in a major crisis." So, China lost the war with Japan.

6. (B) Choice (B) is correct because paragraph 2 states: "On June 11, 1898, Emperor Guwangxu entrusted the reform movement to K'ang and put the progressive scholar–reformer in control of the government."

7. (L) Choice (L) is correct because paragraph 2 states, "On June 11, 1898, Emperor Guwangxu entrusted the reform movement to K'ang." The text states, "Within days, the imperial court issued a number of statutes related to the social and political structure of the nation."

8. (M) Choice (M) is correct because paragraph 3 states: "There was intense opposition to the reform at all levels of society, and only one in fifteen provinces made attempts to implement the edicts."

9. (A) Choice (A) is correct because paragraph 3 states: "a coup d'etat was organized by Yuan Shikai and Empress Dowager Cixi to force Guangxu and the young reformers out of power and into seclusion."

[1]BRITISH: defence

[2]BRITISH: modernisation

10. (E) Choice (E) is correct because paragraph 3 states: "After September 21st, the new edicts were abolished."
11. (H) Choice (H) is correct because paragraph 4 states: ". . . anti-foreign and anti-Christian secret societies tore through northern China targeting foreign concessions and missionary facilities."
12. (K) Choice (K) is correct because paragraph 4 states: "an Allied force made up of armies from nine European nations as well as the United States and Japan entered Peking. With little effort, north China was occupied."
13. (N) Choice (N) is correct because paragraph 4 states: "Within a decade, the court ordered many of the original reform measures, including the modernization of the education and military system."

Passage 2

14. (A) Choice A is correct because paragraph 2 states: "A person's breathing stops when air is somehow prevented from entering the trachea."
15. (B) Choice (B) is correct because paragraph 2 states: "The term *central* is used because this type of apnea is related to the central nervous system rather than the blocked airflow." Immediately before this sentence, the passage is describing central sleep apnea.
16. (C) Choice (C) is correct because paragraph 2, states: "The third type of sleep apnea, known as mixed apnea, is a combination of the two."
17. (C) Choice (C) is correct because paragraph 2 states: "The third type of sleep apnea, known as mixed apnea, is a combination of the two and is the most rare form."
18. (A) Choice (A) is correct because paragraph 2 states: "There are three different types of sleep apnea, with obstructive sleep apnea being the most common."
19. False. Paragraph 3, states: "However, like many disorders, sleep apnea can affect children and in many cases is found to be the result of a person's genetic makeup." The paragraph does include risk factors related to sleep apnea, "including being overweight, male, and over the age of forty." So, people with those factors may be more likely to have sleep apnea, but all people can be affected by the disorder.
20. False. Paragraph 3, states: "Despite being so widespread, this disorder often goes undiagnosed."
21. True. Paragraph 3 states: "Often times, it is not the person suffering from sleep apnea who notices the repetitive episodes of sleep interruption, but a partner or family member sleeping nearby."
22. Not Given. This topic is not addressed in this reading passage.
23. True. Paragraph 3 states: "Sleep apnea is also blamed for many cases of impaired driving and poor job performance."
24–27. (A), (B), (D), and (F). Choice (A) is correct because paragraph 5 states: "In extreme cases, especially when facial deformities are the cause of the sleep apnea, surgery is needed to make a clear passage for the air." Choice (B) is correct because paragraph 4 states: "When these treatments prove unsuccessful, sleep apnea sufferers can be fitted with a CPAP mask." Choice (D) is correct because paragraph 4 states: "In many cases, symptoms of sleep apnea can be eliminated when patients try losing weight." Choice (F) is correct because paragraph 4 states: "People who sleep on their backs or stomachs often find that their symptoms disappear if they try sleeping on their sides."
Choice (C) is incorrect because paragraph 4 states: "Sleep specialists also claim that sleeping pills interfere with the natural performance of the throat and mouth muscles and suggest patients do away with all sleep medication for a trial period." Choice (E) is incorrect because the passage includes surgery as a treatment, but massage is not mentioned. Choice (G) is incorrect because paragraph 4 states: "In many cases, symptoms of sleep apnea can be eliminated when patients try losing weight or abstaining from alcohol." This means that the patient will not drink any alcohol, even moderate amounts as included in item (G).

Passage 3

28. (H) Choice (H) is correct because paragraph 1 states: "the psychological method [which concentrates mostly on intellectual processes, such as memory and abstract reasoning]."
29. (J) Choice (J) is correct because paragraph 1 states: "The main concern of Binet and Simon was to predict elementary school performance independently from the social and economic background of the individual student."
30. (D) Choice (D) is correct because paragraph 2 states: "The Binet-Simon tests are quite effective in predicting school success."
31. (L) Choice (L) is correct because paragraph 2 states: "However, they have been found to be much less predictive of success in post-secondary academic and occupational domains."
32. (I) Choice (I) is correct because paragraph 3 states: "Recent research across the fields of education, cognitive science, and adult development suggests that much of adult intellect is indeed not adequately sampled by extant intelligence measures and might be better assessed through the pedagogical method (Ackerman, 1996; Gregory, 1994)."
33. (C) Choice (C) is correct because paragraph 4 states: "The dilemma for adult intellectual assessment is that the adult is rarely presented with a completely novel problem in the real world of academic or occupational endeavors.[1]"
34. (E) Choice (E) is correct because paragraph 5 states: "From the artificial intelligence field, researchers have discarded the idea of a useful general problem solver in favor[2] of knowledge-based expert systems."
35. True. Paragraph 1 states: "they spawned an intelligence assessment paradigm which has been substantially unchanged from their original tests."
36. False. Paragraph 2, states: "The Binet-Simon tests are quite effective in predicting school success in both primary and secondary educational environments. However, they have been found to be much less predictive of success in post-secondary academic and occupational domains." So, even though the tests predict elementary school success, we cannot make a connection between that predictor and a student's college success.
37. False. Paragraph 6 states: "the typical expert is found to mainly differ from the novice in terms of experience and the knowledge structures that are developed through that experience rather than in terms of intellectual processes (e.g., Glaser, 1991)."
38. False. Process structures, not knowledge structures, decline with age. Paragraph 6 states: "various aspects of adult intellectual functioning are greatly determined by knowledge structures and less influenced by the kinds of process measures, which have been shown to decline with age over adult development (e.g., Schooler, 1987; Willis & Tosti-Vasey, 1990)."
39. True. Paragraph 7 states: "By bringing together a variety of sources of research evidence, it is clear that our current methods of assessing adult intellect are insufficient."
40. (C) Choice (C) is the correct answer because paragraph 7 states: "When adult knowledge structures are broadly examined with tests such as the Advanced Placement [AP]."

Writing

Answers will vary:

Writing Task 1

Analyzing/analysing the coffee shop's sales report reveals some clear trends in the customers' buying habits. On a typical weekday, the usual morning foods and drinks are bought. More coffee, tea, and pastries are purchased from 7:30 to 10:30 in the morning than

[1]BRITISH: endeavours
[2]BRITISH: favour

at any other time. At 10:30, fewer of these items are purchased; however, the number of sandwiches sold quadruples. The most sandwiches are sold from 10:30 to 12:30.

Later in the day, all items reach their lowest selling point. Three of the four items: coffee, tea, and sandwiches sell their smallest amounts during the 2:30–5:30 block. The fewest pastries are sold from 5:30 to 8:30. However, the sandwiches and drinks sell more briskly from 5:30 to 8:30. It is their second-highest selling time period. This increase occurs when people are leaving work for the day or are working overtime and need to eat something convenient. By reviewing this table, it is clear that the office workers are using the coffee shop throughout the day and following a typical schedule.

Writing Task 2

More and more people rely on their private car as their typical means of transportation. This overreliance on cars causes problems with safety, pollution, and dependence on oil. Solutions to these problems need to be found.

As more people use their own cars, the number of vehicles on the road continues to increase. Greater numbers of vehicles and drivers leads to unsafe driving conditions. People want to reach their destinations quickly, but with so many people on the road, driving quickly can be unsafe. Yesterday, my car was almost hit by a truck/lorry driving much faster than the speed limit.

Another problem is pollution. Instead of having thirty people ride the bus together, each person drives a car. This leads to thirty vehicles spewing pollution into the air. The environment can't handle this large amount of dirty air. Our cities now have smog because the air pollution hangs in the sky.

A third problem is that we depend on oil, but oil is a fossil fuel. When we use all of the world's oil, it will be gone forever. As we drive more vehicles, we use more oil, and eventually none will be left.

To solve these problems, it would be wonderful if people would start to use more busses and trains instead of their private cars. People like their cars' convenience, but if the busses and trains are comfortable and inexpensive, people might use them instead. We also need to investigate how to use fuel more efficiently. Some people are buying hybrid cars, which use gasoline/petrol and electricity, and smaller cars, which have greater fuel efficiency. By identifying the problems and suggesting solutions, we can work to reduce people's overreliance on cars.

Speaking

Part 1

Describe the place you live in now.
I live in a small apartment that isn't far from the university. It has two bedrooms, and I share it with a classmate.

Do you think it's better to live in a house or in an apartment? Why?
For me, it's better to live in an apartment/flat. A house is too expensive. Anyway, even if I had the money for a house, I wouldn't have the time to care for it.

Describe your neighborhood.
The neighborhood/neighbourhood is in a good location. We're close to the bus and train. We have some good restaurants, and it's easy to buy food here. We're downtown/in the city centre, but it's safe.

How do people choose their place to live?
They choose where to live based on location, money, and what is available. If they need a roommate/flatmate like me, they also need to think about that.

Describe your family. Are you married? Do you have children? Brothers and sisters?
I'm not married yet. I have a younger brother who still lives at home with my parents. I have an older sister who got married recently. I don't live with my family now because I'm studying in a different city.

What are some things you enjoy doing with other members of your family?
When my brother and I are together, we always like to play soccer. We play it a lot at the park near my parents' house. We watch soccer matches on TV, too. Sometimes when I visit my sister, we cook a meal together, or we sit around and talk about old times.

Who in your family are you particularly close to? Why?
This might sound funny, but I am close to my mother. She is someone I can always count on. If I have a problem at school, I can tell her about it and she helps me figure out a solution. My father isn't like that. It's harder to talk to him.

Do you spend more time with your family or with friends? Why?
Right now I spend more time with my friends because I'm living away from home. Also, I have a lot in common with them. We take a lot of the same classes, so we help each other study. When we have free time, we enjoy doing the same things, like going to the movies or going to parties.

Part 2

NOTE: Gift/present

A really special gift I received was a set of cuff links and a key chain. My sister gave them to me when she got married. I helped a lot with the wedding arrangements. I helped organize everything, and I arranged for my friends' band to play the music at the reception. My sister gave me the cuff links and key chain to thank me for all my help. They are made of silver with a modern design, and the key chain has my initials on it. I use the key chain every day. I wear the cuff links on special occasions. They're really only for formal wear. I wore them at my best friend's wedding last fall, for example. Occasionally I go to a formal dance, and I wear the cuff links then. This gift is important to me because it has a personal meaning. I was happy to be able to help my sister on an important day in her life, and this gift reminds me of that. It reminds me of how important my sister is to me.

Part 3

Do you think people generally enjoy giving and receiving gifts? Why or why not?
Some people might enjoy giving gifts, but I think it has become an obligation in many cases. If it's a birthday or some other occasion, you have to get a gift. You may not have the time and money to spend shopping for a gift and wrapping it up, but you have to do it anyway. I think children like getting gifts, but adults don't always. Often the gift you get is something you really don't like and can't use. But gift-giving is a custom, it's a tradition, so we have to do it.

In your country, when do people usually give gifts?
In my country, the most important time to give gifts is on birthdays. This is especially true for children, but we often give birthday gifts to adults, too. Another important gift-giving occasion is weddings. If you are invited to a wedding, you have to bring a gift to help the couple start their new life. In everyday life, if you are invited to a special dinner, you might bring a small gift to the host and hostess. If you spend several days at someone's house, you definitely should give a gift to your hosts.

What kind of gifts do they give?
The kind of gift depends on the occasion and the people involved. Children, of course, get toys and sometimes clothes. For a wedding, you are supposed to give something for the couple's new home. If you are a close relative or friend, it is expected that you will give something more expensive. You might give a silver dish, for example, or an expensive appliance. For a host and hostess gift, you can give flowers or a bottle of wine or something small for the house. Grandparents and parents often give money to their children for birthdays or weddings. Everyone can give a gift of money for a graduation present.

Do you agree or disagree: The price of a gift shows how much the giver cares about the recipient.
I have to say that I disagree. Some people try to make an impression by spending a lot of money, but anybody can spend money. It's not hard to do! I think just the fact of thinking to give someone a gift shows that you care about the person. If you can find a gift that the person really likes, that will show that you really care. But it's hard to do that. I think that's why people buy expensive gifts. It's easier than figuring out exactly what would be the best gift for that particular person.

GENERAL TRAINING MODEL TEST 1

Reading

NOTE: apartment/flat

1. (A) This apartment includes parking.
2. (C) This apartment is near the university.
3. (D) This apartment is big enough for a family and is close to elementary and high schools.
4. (B) This apartment has a pool.
5. (C) This apartment is near the bus lines/routes.
6. (E) This flat offers weekly and monthly rentals.
7. (B) This apartment has a party room.
8. (E) This section says that if there are any problems with the coffeemaker a customer can call the free service line.
9. (C) This section demonstrates how to clean the coffeemaker with vinegar.
10. (D) This section contains the warning that one should only pour coffee beans up to the "full" line.
11. (B) This section states that the coffeemaker comes with a built-in timer for convenience.
12. *Eight ounces.* Section A states: "fill the reservoir with eight ounces of water for each cup of coffee."
13. *Once a month.* Section C states: "Monthly cleaning will keep your coffeemaker functioning properly and your coffee tasting fresh."
14. *Any time.* Section E states that the customer service line is open 24 hours a day.
15. iii. Getting Paid. This paragraph gives information about paychecks.
16. i. Vacation and Sick Day Policy. This paragraph gives information about taking time off from work for annual leave (vacation) and for illness (sick days).

17. **vi. Work Schedule.** This paragraph explains the hours that employees are expected to work.
18. **v. Use of Conference Rooms.** This paragraph discusses the rooms used for meetings and presentations, normally called conference rooms.
19. **vii. Office Supplies.** This paragraph deals with paper, pens and pencils, ink cartridges, and other supplies used for office work.
20. **iv. Employee Discounts.** This paragraph describes discounts employees can get at the cafeteria and health club.
21. *job openings.* Applicants are asked to review, or look at, the job openings on the website.
22. *an application form.* Applicants are asked to "complete an Application for Employment form."
23. *an e-mail.* If you are qualified, the company will "contact you by e-mail."
24. *four weeks.* Applicants are told that they can expect to hear from the company within four weeks.
25. *the downtown office.* At the end of paragraph 2, it is explained that interviews take place at the downtown office.
26. *names of references.* In the third paragraph, applicants are asked to bring "names of references who are familiar with your business experience and qualifications."
27. *take a test.* Some applicant may have to take a language, office skills, or other type of test.
28. **vii** Paragraph A describes the first subways/underground systems built in Europe in the cities of London, Budapest, Glasgow, and Paris.
29. **ii** Paragraph B describes the first subways in the USA and South America.
30. **i** Paragraph C describes subways built in the second half of the twentieth century.
31. **viii** Paragraph D describes the largest subway systems in the world, measured in terms of total track length and numbers of riders.
32. **vi** Paragraph E gives examples of several subway systems known for the art in their stations.
33. **iv** Paragraph F describes Platform Screen Doors, a safety device now becoming more and more common in subway stations around the world.
34. **E** The Baker Street Station in London honors the fictional detective Sherlock Holmes.
35. **K** The Moscow Metro has more riders than any other subway system.
36. **B** Many subway systems have adopted the name Metro from the Paris Metro.
37. **A** The subway in Hong Kong has four lines that run under Victoria Harbour.
38. **I** The subway in Singapore was the first to be built with Platform Screen Doors. The subway in Hong Kong was the first to add PSDs to a system that was already built.
39. **G** The subway in Seoul has 287 kilometers of track.
40. **H** Buenos Aires has the oldest subway in Latin America.
41. **C** The Washington, DC Metro began running in 1976.

General Training Writing

Writing Task 1

Dear John,

Hello, my name is Irma. I'm Jake Vandelft's cousin. When Jake told me that he had a friend who lived in Toronto, I was excited. I'm hoping to visit Toronto in the summer. I hope you don't mind that I asked for your address. Jake said you probably wouldn't mind answering some questions if I wrote to you.

When I found out that I would get three weeks for a vacation/holiday this summer, I decided I wanted to go to a foreign country/abroad. I've always dreamed of going to Canada. I love watching baseball and I would love to see a major league game in Toronto. The Toronto Blue Jays are my favorite team.

Where should I stay when I visit Toronto? I think it is probably too expensive to stay in a hotel downtown/in the city centre for more than a week. Do you know of any youth hostels? Also, could you tell me about the weather in the summer? I don't know what to pack!

I look forward to hearing from you if you have time to write back. Maybe we can meet for lunch.

Best wishes,
Irma Klein

P.S. Jake said to say hello.

Writing Task 2

On average, today's businessmen and women work more hours than ever. However, modern technology has made the office less of a necessity. Rather than spending every working hour in the office, people can work at home on their personal computers. There are advantages and disadvantages to home offices for both the family and the employer.

The home office gives employees more flexibility with childcare. When a child is sick from school, a parent can put in a few hours of work at home instead of going into the office. Flex-time also allows parents to leave work early enough to be home for the children to come home from school. Employees can make up time for their employers by putting in an extra hour or two in the morning or evening from home.

The home office eliminates transportation problems. Sometimes poor weather can make it difficult to get to work. The time it takes for some employees to commute could be better spent on deadlines for their employers from home. When a personal vehicle breaks down or a public service gets shut down, the home office takes the stress out of getting to work.

The home office can be very distracting. Some people find it difficult not to answer personal calls. Others can't explain to relatives or neighbors/neighbours that, even though they are home, they are actually "on the clock." Young children can't be expected to understand the concept of their mother being at work when she is actually in the home, especially if it only happens once in a while. And, when a young child is home, the parent's job is to be a caretaker.

Used sparingly, the home office is a convenient alternative to working at the office. It relieves the stress on busy parents and sometimes saves money and time for the employer. However, rather than killing two birds with one stone, oftentimes neither the job nor the parenting is done adequately out of the home. Even today, the office is really where the work gets done.

GENERAL TRAINING MODEL TEST 2

Reading

1. *The main foyer*. From Dec. 1–4, the Main foyer is being painted.
2. *The main entrance*. From Dec. 5–8, tenants cannot enter the building from the garage.
3. *West Wing elevator/lift*. From Dec. 9–13, the East stairway is being painted. To reach the tenth floor one would have to take an elevator.
4. *East Wing elevator*. From Dec. 14–21, the west and north stairways and elevators are blocked. The east stairway or elevator must be used.
5. *Across the street*. From Dec. 22–27, the parking garage is unavailable. Tenants will get fined if they park on the street, but there is a parking lot/car park across the street that will be made available.
6. *Contact building manager*. Near the bottom of the notice it says, "If you have any questions or complaints, please contact the building manager."
7. *Get a form*. At the end of the notice it says that tenants can request a painting form if they want their apartments/flats painted.
8. *$29*. The invoice shows the last payment made. This bill is for the month of July, so the last bill was for June.
9. *August 21st*. The invoice says: "We must receive your payment in full by August 21st."
10. *£37.50*. EnviroElectric Company charges a £2.50 late fee. The total due is £35. If the payment is not made on time, the late fee will be added to the total due.
11. *East Bradfield*. The mailing address for this company is given below the late fee information.
12. *Visit Bradfield Bank*. The invoice states: "Cash payments may be made by visiting any branch of the Bradfield Bank."
13. Call 385–9387. This number is given for any customer who has questions about a bill.
14. (F) Paragraph 1 states: "It is a particular problem in the modern office, where workers spend hours a day in front of computers" and "Now, almost everything is done on computers...."
15. (J) Paragraph 2: "The pain can eventually become so severe as to cause long-lasting damage."
16. (K) Paragraph 3 states: "Computer keyboards force the user to continually hold the hands with the palms down. This is an unnatural position...."
17. (C) Paragraph 3 states: "In addition, using a mouse requires the repetitive motion of one finger."
18. (I) Paragraph 4 states: "RSI can be a serious problem if ignored. Fortunately, it isn't difficult to prevent. The best form of prevention is to take frequent breaks from work."
19. (D) Paragraph 4 states: "You can also protect your wrists by holding your palms parallel to the keyboard and keeping your forearms in a horizontal position."
20. (A) Paragraph 4 states: "You can support your posture by adding armrests to your chair. This will actually aid in supporting your back and help you maintain a good posture."
21. False. Employees must get permission from their supervisors. The Human Resources Department has information and forms but doesn't give permission.
22. Not Given. There is no information about the amount of vacation time employees get.
23. False. Paragraph 3 explicitly states that employees may not do this.
24. True. Paragraph 3 says that permission is not required for sick days.
25. False. Conformation from a doctor is not required for sick days but may be requested for doctor's appointments.
26. True. Paragraph 4 states that unused vacation days can be added to vacation days for the following year.

27. False. Paragraph 4 explicitly states that this is not allowed.
28. *Henge*. Paragraph 2 states that a large circular ditch called the henge was located around the Aubrey Holes.
29. *Aubrey Holes*. Paragraph 2 talks about the series of holes called Aubrey Holes that were dug with deer picks.
30. *Avenue*. Paragraph 2 says that archeologists called the entrance way the "Avenue."
31. *Heel Stone*. Paragraph 2 describes the Heel Stone as being placed along the Avenue.
32. (B) The last sentence in paragraph 3 states that the Beaker people likely, "widened the entrance during this phase in order to show their appreciation for the sun."
33. (A) Halfway through Paragraph 2 is the description of the Slaughter Stone addition in Phase 1.
34. (C) Paragraph 4 contains the description of the bluestones being placed in a horseshoe formation.
35. (B) The second sentence in paragraph 3 describes the wooden posts being added.
36. (A) Paragraph 2 states that the Aubrey Holes were dug with picks made of deer antlers.
37. (C) The second sentence in paragraph 2 states that the bluestones came "all the way from the Preseli Hills." The expression "all the way" means *a long distance*.
38. (C) In the middle of paragraph 4, the addition of the sandstone ring is described.
39. (B) Toward the end of the third paragraph is a description of the Aubrey Holes being filled in: "The original Aubrey Holes were filled in either with earth or cremation remains."
40. (C) In the middle of paragraph 4, the addition of the Altar Stone is described.

Writing

Writing Task 1

September 15/15 September

Dear Sir or Madam:

My friend and I were guests in your hotel last week. We stayed in Room 401 from September the 4th until September the 9th. When I arrived home in Taiwan on the 11th, I realized/realised that I didn't have my watch. The last time I saw my watch was in the hotel room on the morning that we left. I think I may have accidentally left it on the bed.

My lady's watch has a chrome wristband. There is a yellow moon on the face of the watch with a bluish-black background. The brand of the watch is TIMEOUT.

This piece of jewelry/jewellery is not worth a lot of money, but it has sentimental value to me. It was the last gift my grandmother gave me before she passed away. I was wondering if you could ask your staff if they have seen it. Perhaps you could also check in the hotel's lost and found/lost property in case I left it at the hotel restaurant or in a public washroom. Please call me if you find it. I will send you a check to pay for the postage.

Thank you for your help.

Sincerely,

Theresa Lim

Writing Task 2

In the past, children amused themselves without a television. Toys and books kept children occupied, as did the outdoors. Many children today are happy sitting inside and watching TV. Though television is a teaching tool, it also isolates children from important activities.

Children used to get information from books, but now they learn more from TV. Children are often called sponges. They love to learn. Before television became so popular, children learned new words and concepts through storybooks. My mother said I could recite a few books by the time I was two. Some television shows/programmes are designed specifically to teach kids these same things. Though they keep children interested in learning, they don't require children to learn how to read. My little cousins are almost five, and they still can't write their names.

The television keeps children entertained on a rainy day. In the past, children sometimes ran out of ideas if their friends were away or the weather wasn't pleasant. Today they can just flip through the TV channels until something interesting comes on. My uncle says the TV is great because the children never complain they are bored. However, a child that is always entertained has no need to expand his imagination or learn to be creative. My cousins don't have hobbies, and they don't like sports like my brother and I did.

These days, children spend more time with the television than they do their own parents. In busy families, parents turn on the TV to distract their kids so that they can get other things done. My aunt has two jobs, and she is going to school. When she gets home, she doesn't have time to sit and play or read with the kids. Sitting in the same room and watching a program/programme while a parent reads the newspaper isn't my idea of spending quality time together as a family.

The television has changed the way children learn. Though there are plenty of educational shows on television, they don't require active participation from the child. No matter how entertaining a television may be, this machine should never replace books, play, or parenting.

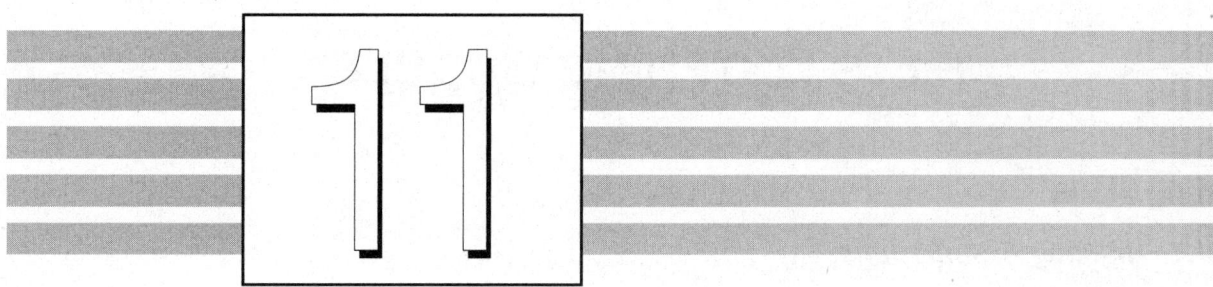

APPENDIX

AUDIOSCRIPT FOR THE LISTENING SECTIONS
- IELTS Listening Module
- Model Test 1
- Model Test 2
- Model Test 3
- Model Test 4

ANSWER SHEETS
- Listening Module
- Reading Module
- Writing Module

IELTS LISTENING MODULE

Listening Skills

Target 1—Making Assumptions

SECTION 1

Example

W1:   Good morning. How may I help you?

M1:   Yes, I was wondering, do you have any one-bedroom apartments available?

W1:   Yes, we do. Were you looking for yourself?

M1:   Yes, it's for me.

Narrator: James asks if there are any one-bedroom apartments available, so the correct answer is "one bedroom." Now we shall begin. You should answer the questions as you listen because you will not hear the recording a second time.

Questions 1–10

W1:   Good morning. How may I help you?

M1:   Yes, I was wondering, do you have any one-bedroom apartments available?

W1:   Yes we do. Were you looking for yourself?

M1:   Yes, it's for me.

W1:   Let me just get some information from you then, for our application form. May I have your name?

M1:   Yes. It's Kingston. James Kingston.

W1:   And what's your current address?

M1:   I live over on State Street. Number 1705 State Street, apartment seven.

W1:   And your phone number?

M1:   My home phone? It's 721-0584.

W1:   Work phone?

M1:   721-1127.

W1:   Great. I need to know just one more thing. What is your date of birth?

M1:   December 12, 1978.

W1:   Thank you. Now, you're interested in a one-bedroom apartment, correct?

M1:   That's right.

W1:   Did you want just a one-bedroom, or a one-bedroom with a den? We have several of those available, and a study is really nice. Having that extra room gives you space for a small home office or you can use it as a guest room.

M1:   I don't think so. I live alone. I don't need an extra room.

W1:   Right. Then I'll put you down for a simple one bedroom. With a balcony?

M1:   No, I don't need that. I'll tell you what I do need, though, is a parking space.

W1:   We have garage parking spaces available for a low monthly fee.

M1:   Great. I really need that. Oh, and something else. I need an apartment with lots of closets for storage.

W1:   We actually have storage areas in the basement. You can rent your own storage space by the month.

M1:   Hmmm. That sounds like a good idea.

W1:   All right. So I'll put you down for a storage space in the basement.

M1:   Sounds good.

W1:   Are you interested in our exercise club? We have an exercise room with several pieces of equipment as well as a sauna.

M1:   Is it included in the rent?

W1:   It's a available for a small extra fee.

M1:   Then I don't think so. I can always go for a walk for free.

W1:   All right then, one bedroom, no balcony. . . . I have several apartments you might like. One of them has a fireplace. Would you be interested in that?

M1:   Do I have to pay extra for it?

W1:   Actually no. That apartment is slightly smaller than our other one bedrooms, so even though it has a fireplace, the rent isn't any higher.

M1:   OK then I'll take the fireplace.

W1:   There is one drawback to that apartment. It doesn't have a washing machine. You'll have to go out to a laundromat.[1]

M1:   Oh. Well, I suppose that doesn't matter. Can I see the apartment today?

W1:   Certainly. I can show it to you now. However, we're still painting it, so it won't be available until next month.

M1:   I was hoping to move next week, but . . . . maybe I can wait.

W1:   And I'll need a small deposit to hold it for you, just 50 percent of the first month's rent.

SECTION 2

Questions 11–20

> Now turn to Target 1, Making Assumptions, Section 2, Questions 11–20.

> Section 2. You will hear a recording of a tour of an art museum.
> Listen carefully and answer the questions.

Female tour guide:

> Good afternoon, everyone. I'm Lucy and I'll be your guide for today's two o'clock tour of the Jamestown Museum of Art. As a reminder, if you haven't purchased your ticket yet, please do so now. It's 15 dollars for adults, and for children twelve and under it costs just 11 dollars. If you're a senior, today's your lucky day because it's Tuesday. That's Senior Citizens Day, so admission is free for all people over 65. However, you'll still need to get a ticket before the tour starts.

> All right now, does everyone have a ticket? Yes? Good, then, let's go. We begin our tour here in the Main Gallery. Here you can see our collection of modern art. We're quite proud of this collection, which includes some minor works by major artists, for example, you'll see over there a small Picasso. And on this wall you'll see works by some other well-known modern painters.

> Moving ahead to the next room, now we're in the City Gallery. This is the room where we feature local artists, who have painted a variety of subjects. You'll notice here some local scenes, in addition to a few portraits, and right over there you'll see some abstract works. Most of these works are modern, although we have a few older paintings in this room as well.

> Straight ahead is the Hall of History. In that room we have a wonderful collection of portraits of famous figures in our city's history. The oldest paintings date back to the 17th century, and there are some quite modern paintings in there as well, including a portrait of our current governor, who was born in this city. Unfortunately, the Hall is closed right now, so we won't be able to visit it today.

[1] BRITISH: laundrette.

Here to our right is the East Room. Isn't this a beautiful room? The view of the garden is just lovely. You'll see there are no paintings in here because this room is devoted entirely to sculpture. That large sculpture in the center is by a well-known local artist, and over here you'll see several pieces by a modern European sculptor. You can see we have quite a number of lovely pieces in this room.

Just beyond the East Room is the gift shop. You may want to visit it after you have finished looking at the galleries. You can buy reproductions of art in the museum's collections, as well as souvenirs of the city, and many other lovely things as well.

All right then, we've visited all the open galleries in the museum. If you would like to return to any area of the museum now and look at the exhibits more carefully, please do so. Remember, the Hall of History is closed for repairs, but it should be open again next month. Also, please don't go up to the second floor. There's nothing up there but offices, and the area is off limits to visitors. Thank you for coming to the museum. Don't forget to visit the gift shop on your way out.

Target 2—Understanding Numbers

Example

M1:   Flight 33 leaves from Gate 13 Concourse C3.

Questions 1–5

Question 1

W1:   Now, Mr. Wilcox, you can send us a check[1] or, if you pay now by credit card, I can process your order right away.
M1:   I'll pay by credit card.
W1:   Great. May I have your credit card number then?
M1:   It's 8 6 double 7 5 3 2 1 4 8.
W1:   2 1 4 8. All right then, you should have your order within four business[2] days.

Question 2

M1:   The university is very proud of its new theater, which is equipped with a state-of-the-art light and sound system and has a much greater seating capacity than the old one. The old theater had seats for just 250 people while the new one can seat an audience of 500.

Question 3

W1:   I'm updating my phone list. Do you know Sherry's phone number by any chance?
M1:   I know it by heart. It's 575-3174.
W1:   Great. Thanks.

---

[1] BRITISH: cheque.

[2] BRITISH: working.

Question 4

M1:   That room is only three hundred and fifteen dollars a night if you stay for three nights.

W1:   Wow! Do you have anything more, uh, economical?

M1:   Let me see . . . for next week . . . . Yes, I have another room that is just two hundred and sixty-five dollars a night. For a minimum three-night stay of course.

W1:   That's still a lot of money, but I'll take it.

Question 5

M1:   Is this the lost luggage office?

W1:   Yes. How may I help you?

M1:   How can you help me? By finding my luggage that your airline lost.

W1:   All right, sir. Calm down. May I have your name and your flight number, please?

M1:   My name is Richard Lyons and my flight number is X Y 5 3 8.

Examples

1. S1:   seven oh three six five double eight
    S2:   seven oh three six five eight eight
    S3:   seven zero three sixty-five eighty-eight

2. S1:   seven double four one four nine two
    S2:   seven four four one four nine two
    S3:   seven forty-four fourteen ninety-two

3. S1:   two oh two double nine eight three
    S2:   two oh two nine nine eight three
    S3:   two zero two ninety-nine eighty-three

4. S1:   six seven one four five three two
    S2:   six seven one four five three two
    S3:   six seventy-one forty-five thirty-two

5. S1:   eight two four one five six one
    S2:   eight two four one five six one
    S3:   eight twenty-four fifteen sixty-one

6. S1:   six three seven oh double five oh
    S2:   six three seven oh five five oh
    S3:   six thirty-seven zero fifty-five zero

7. S1:   two six five one eight double one
    S2:   two six five one eight one one
    S3:   two sixty-five eighteen eleven

8. S1:   two eight seven six two one six
    S2:   two eight seven six two one six
    S3:   two eighty-seven sixty-two sixteen

9.	S1:	four double five three oh two one
	S2:	four five five three oh two one
	S3:	four fifty-five thirty twenty-one

10.	S1:	three oh five eight four eight oh
	S2:	three oh five eight four eight oh
	S3:	three zero five eighty-four eighty

Target 3—Understanding the Alphabet

Example

	M1:	Is your name spelled L - i - n or L - y - n - n?
	W1:	Actually, it's Lynne with an e.

Questions 1–6

1.	M1:	My name is Tomas, t-o-m-a-s. I use the Spanish spelling.
	W1:	Oh, without the h.

2.	W1:	I live at 534 Maine Avenue. That's Maine with an "e" on the end.
	M1:	With an e. Not like Main Street with no e.

3.	M1:	Is that Patty, p-a-t-t-y?
	W1:	No, with an i. P-a-t-t-i.

4.	W1:	Excuse me. You spelled my family name wrong. It's Roberts. The last letter is s.
	M1:	Oh, I'm sorry. I thought you said Robertson.

5.	M1:	All right then, and you live in the city of Springfield.
	W1:	No, that's Springvale, v-a-l-e.

6.	W1:	OK, that's Mr. Nixon, n-i-x . . .
	M1:	No, no, no. Dixson, d-i-x-s-o-n.

Questions 7–12

7.	M1:	If you're paying by credit card, I'll need your full name.
	W1:	Sure. It's Miranda Green. That's m-i-r-a-n-d-a.
	M1:	A-n-d-a. Great. And what's your credit card number?
	W1:	7-oh-4-3-2-1-8.
	M1:	2-1-8. OK, you wanted two tickets, right?

8.	W1:	I'm looking up the number of the Bijou Theater. How do you spell that? With a g?
	M1:	No, with a j. It's B-i-j-o-u.
	W1:	B-i-j . . . . Found it. Write this number down for me: 2-3-2-5-4-double 8.

9.	M1:	Let me just get your name. That was Miss Roberta Johnson.
	W1:	Not Johnson, Janson. With an a. J-a-n-s-o-n.

	M1:	S-o-n. Got it. Now I can give you room 203. It's small but has a nice view. That room is only 245 pounds a night.
	W1:	I'd really prefer a larger room. I don't mind paying for it.
	M1:	Room 304 is the biggest we have available at the moment. It's 335 pounds a night.
	W1:	That's fine. I'll take it.
10.	W1:	All right, Mr. Park. May I have your address?
	M1:	It's 75 String Street. That's String Street S-t-r-i-n-g.
	W1:	That's an unusual name for a street. Well, would you like a seat near the front or more towards the middle?
	M1:	I'd like to be as close to the front as possible. Row B or C would be best.
	W1:	I can give you row B. Seat number 15 B.
	M1:	Fifteen B. Perfect.
11.	W1:	Good evening, class. Welcome to Introduction to Economics. I'm your instructor, Dr. Willard. That's W-i-double l-a-r-d. Please don't hesitate to ask for help if you need it. My office hours are Tuesday and Thursday from three to five. My office is here in this building. It's office number 70, on the first floor.
12.	M1:	Thank you for the opportunity to speak tonight about my passion, wildflowers. If anyone in the audience would like to know more about the subject, I recommend contacting the Wildflower Society. They're at 17-oh-five State Street in Landover. That's L-a-n-d-o-v-e-r. Landover. They issue a number of interesting publications and also host several events each year for wildflower enthusiasts.

Target 4—Listening for Descriptions

Example

W1:	It's really easy to get here. Just take the bus to the corner of the High Street and Regent Avenue. Then it's the second house from the corner.
M1:	Second house from the corner, OK. It's not the two-story duplex with two doors, is it?
W1:	No, that's across the street. Mine's small, it's only one story. There's only one door, so knock or ring the bell. I'll be waiting for you.

Questions 1 and 2

Question 1

W1:	This is the noon news report for Friday, April 12. Several stores in the downtown area of Jamestown were robbed[1] early this morning. Police are on the lookout for the suspect, who is described as about 45 years of age, bald, somewhat overweight, with a beard. If you see anyone meeting this description, please contact the Jamestown police.

---

[1]BRITISH: shops in the city centre were burgled.

Question 2

W1:   May I help you?

M1:   Yes, I'm looking for a present for my girlfriend. It's her nineteenth birthday. I was thinking maybe some jewelry.

W1:   I can help you choose something that would look nice on her. What does she look like?

M1:   Well, she's very pretty. She has really long dark hair and she's very thin. She almost always wears earrings.

W1:   We have many nice earrings to choose from. Or, what about something different? Would she like a necklace?

M1:   I don't know. Maybe . . .

Target 5—Listening for Time

Example

M1:   The train was almost thirty minutes late. It didn't arrive until five o'clock.

TIME

Questions 1–6

Questions 1 and 2

M1:   Good afternoon class. There have been a number of questions about the time for our final exam. As you know, this class regularly meets from two thirty until four Wednesday and Friday. Some of you have realized that during exam week there is a different schedule, thence the questions. Our final exam will be on Wednesday of exam week. It is scheduled to start at one forty-five and should last about an hour and a half, so you'll be out of here at around three fifteen or so.

Questions 3 and 4

W1:   Could you tell me what time the train to Chicago leaves?

M1:   The next train is at five fifteen.

W1:   Hm. That's a long wait. It's only three now. What time does it arrive in Chicago?

M1:   The trip is a little over six hours. It arrives at 11:30.

Questions 5 and 6

W1:   Hi Cindy. I wanted to see if you could meet me for lunch tomorrow.

W2:   Let's see, tomorrow's Monday . . . . I have a Spanish class in the morning . . . . Yes, I think that's a good idea.

W1:   OK. Let's meet at twelve.

W2:   Well, I have a haircut at 11:30. Better make it quarter past.

W1:   Quarter past twelve, great.

W2:   I'm so glad we're getting together. I'll be really nervous because I have a job interview in the afternoon. You can help me get ready for it.

W1:   You know what's good for nerves? Exercise.

W2:   I have my exercise class tomorrow at four. That should help.

DATE

Questions 1–6

Questions 1 and 2

W1: The City Museum of Art was established in the year 1898. It first opened its doors to the public on August fifteenth of that year. There was a spectacular opening celebration, but it wasn't held until later in the year, on December first, to be exact. Now the reasons for the delayed celebration are very interesting . . .

Questions 3 and 4

M1: All right, Mrs. Katz. I need just a bit more information to complete your application. May I have your date of birth?
W1: It's twenty-second September.
M1: Your husband's name is Georges, correct?
W1: Yes, and he was born on seventh July.

Questions 5 and 6

W1: We're thinking about going to Silver Lake this year. When do you think is a good time to go?
M1: Well, most people don't like to go in July or August because it's so hot then. September is too. I think the most popular time to go is October.
W1: Is that when you plan to go?
M1: Actually, no. We can't get away till November this year. We've made our reservations[1] for then, and we're leaving on the seventh.

DAY

Questions 1–6

Questions 1 and 2

W1: Hey, Jim. Are you going to history class?
M1: No, I don't have history today. I have English.
W1: It's Monday. Are you sure you don't have history today?
M1: Yeah. I have English today and Wednesday. My history class is on Thursday.
W1: Just one day a week for history, huh? Not bad.

Questions 3 and 4

M1: We're very glad that you are considering becoming members of the Urban Exercise Club. I'm sure you'll want to sign up for membership after you've enjoyed this afternoon here. Since today's Thursday, you could have a tennis lesson. The tennis instructor is here twice a week, Saturday as well as Thursday. You're lucky it's not Friday. You'll be able to enjoy the steam room. It'll be closed for its weekly cleaning tomorrow.

---

[1] BRITISH: booking.

Questions 5 and 6

W1: Let me remind you of your assignments for next week. Don't forget that the final exam has been rescheduled, so it'll be on Friday instead of Thursday. And you have an essay due on Tuesday. You should have a lot to study over Saturday and Sunday. Don't forget that I have office hours on Monday afternoon, in case you have any questions.

YEAR

Questions 1–6

Questions 1 and 2

M1: John James Audubon, the famous naturalist and painter of birds, was born on the island of Haiti in 1785. In 1803, he went to live in the United States. He was a self-taught painter and supported himself for a while by painting portraits. His famous work, *Birds of America*, was first published in England. Later, in 1842, Audubon published a version of this work in the United States. He died in 1851.

Questions 3 and 4

W1: That was a really interesting lecture on Maria Mahoney. I really admire her for being the first woman governor of our state.
M1: Yes, she was an admirable person. Let's go over our notes. I put down that she was born in 1808.
W1: Not eighteen. Nineteen. She was born in 1908.
M1: Whoops! OK, then, but I have this right. She became governor in 1967.
W1: Are you sure? Wasn't it 1957?
M1: No, 1957 is when she first decided to run for office, but she didn't win an election until 1967.

Questions 5 and 6

M1: The university began construction of the library in 1985. It was expected to take just two years, but by the end of 1987, the library was only three-quarters completed. Finally, by the summer of 1988, construction was finished and the new library opened in August of that year.

SEASON

Questions 1–6

Questions 1 and 2

W1: Tourists visit the region only during certain times of the year. The winters are not harsh, but it rains a lot then and the temperatures are quite cool. Spring is quite a bit less rainy than winter, and the temperatures are warmer, so many tourists like to visit then. Summers are hot and dry, so hot that most tourists stay away. They return in the autumn when the weather is still dry but not as hot.

Questions 3 and 4

W1:   Wow, Josh, I can't believe you hiked the whole mountain range. When did you start your trip?

M1:   Well, you can't leave too early in the spring, because it's still late winter in the mountains then. Most hikers start in the late spring, and that's what I did too.

W1:   And then you hiked all summer. What's summer like in the mountains?

M1:   It's not too hot and you can see a lot of wild life, especially later in the summer when the birds start to migrate.

W1:   It must have been winter by the time you finished the trip.

M1:   Not quite. It was late in the autumn, which is almost as cold as winter in the mountains.

Questions 5 and 6

M1:   I'd like to sign up for the beginning Japanese class.

W1:   I'm sorry, all our Japanese classes are full. Fall is the busiest time of year here at the language school.

M1:   Hm. Well, then, maybe I'll wait until next summer to take a class.

W1:   That would be fine, but I recommend enrolling early. Summer is almost as busy as fall.

M1:   Really? Well, when is your least busy time of year?

W1:   Spring is a quieter time, but we have our lowest enrollment in the winter.

Target 6—Listening for Frequency

Example

W1:   Sam works out at the gym several days a week.

Questions 1–6

Question 1

M1:   Do you like dancing?

W1:   Yes , but I don't go very much.

M1:   No?

W1:   Well, I go about once a month or so.

Question 2

W1:   Do you smoke?

M1:   No, I don't.

W1:   Really? Not at all?

M1:   Mmmm, maybe once or twice a year.

Question 3

M1:   Another rainy day. Does it ever stop raining here?

W1:   It's the rain forest. It rains every day.

Question 4

W1:   Mike says he's a vegetarian. What does that mean?
M1:   It means he doesn't eat meat.
W1:   No meat at all? Not even on special occasions?
M1:   Not even then.

Question 5

M1:   How's your class?
W1:   It's really hard. The professor loves giving tests.
M1:   Really? Does he give a lot of tests?
W1:   Oh, yeah. We have one or two a week.

Question 6

W1:   Do these geese spend all summer here?
M1:   Yes, and all winter, too. They don't migrate.
W1:   So you can see them here any season of the year.

Questions 7–12

Question 7

W1:   For the first part of my research, I counted the number of shoppers who entered the store between 6 A.M. and 8 A.M.
M1:   And you did this every morning?
W1:   Yes, every morning for a week.

Question 8

W1:   Are you interested in joining the chess club?
M1:   Maybe. When does it meet?
W1:   On the last Sunday of every month.

Question 9

W1:   How often do you have your history class?
M1:   Every Tuesday and Thursday.

Question 10

M1:   Do you go to the movies much?
W1:   I go when I get the chance, but not as often as I'd like. Maybe once or twice a semester.

Question 11

W1:   How can I start managing my money better?
M1:   First, you need to make a monthly spending plan.

Question 12

M1:   While you're student teaching, I'll observe each one of you in the classroom several times.
W1:   How frequent will your visits be?
M1:   You'll get a visit from me once every two weeks.

Target 7—Listening for Similar Meanings

Example

M1:   The survey participants who wrote answers to the questions are all college graduates.

Questions 1–6

Question 1

M1:   How many tickets will you need?
W1:   There will be three adults and two children in our party.

Question 2

W1:   How's your French class? Do you like the instructor?
M1:   Yes, she's great, but she gives us a lot of work to do in class.
W1:   Then you have to wait weeks before you get your papers back, right?
M1:   No, she always checks our assignments on the same day we do them.

Question 3

M1:   I've heard that this area of the country is really growing.
W1:   Yes, the population is increasing at a rate of about 10,000 people a year.

Question 4

W1:   I understand that this area has suffered harsh weather conditions in recent years.
M1:   Yes, for example, last year a severe drought killed much of the vegetation in the region.
W1:   That must have had a devastating effect on agriculture.

Question 5

M1:   If I give you a check for the first month's rent right now, can I move in tomorrow?
W1:   I'm sorry, but the apartment won't be available until next week.

Question 6

M1:   Let's see . . . I got your address and phone number. Oh, I need to know your occupation.
W1:   Put computer programmer.

Target 8—Listening for Emotions

Example

W1:   I'm really excited about the chance to debate the team from Oxford.

M1:   I'm more apprehensive than excited. In fact, I'm not looking forward to it at all.

Questions 1–6

Question 1

W1:   We'll begin the tour of Roselands Park with a bit about the history of the park. Local residents were thrilled when millionaire Samuel Waters announced that he would donate land for the park, including his collection of prized rose bushes. Some of his heirs, quite naturally, were a bit angry when they learned[1] that he had given away so much family property.

Question 2

W1:   What's the matter with you? Yesterday you seemed really excited about your science experiment.

M1:   That was yesterday. Today I just can't seem to get it to work right.

W1:   Oh, don't worry about it. I'm sure it will be fine.

M1:   I don't know. I keep trying and trying, but it isn't working the way I planned.

Question 3

M1:   Our language lab is equipped with state-of-the-art equipment guaranteed to greatly improve your foreign language skills. Students are often confused when they first use our facilities because it seems complicated at first glance, but it's actually quite simple once you get used to it. Today I'll give you an orientation to the lab, and you'll see how easy it is to use this equipment to complete your class assignments and study for tests.

Question 4

W1:   You didn't win the essay contest? Aren't you upset?

M1:   Not really.

W1:   .I'd be really disappointed if I'd worked so hard and didn't even win second or third place.

M1:   It's just a contest. It doesn't really matter.

Question 5

W1:   In local news, children and teachers at Burnside Elementary School received an unexpected visit yesterday from Mayor Sharon Smith as part of her campaign to focus attention on the plight of city schools. Several school board members accompanied the Mayor. "We had no idea she was planning to visit us," said school principal[2] Roger Simmons. "But naturally we felt quite honored."

[1] BRITISH: learnt

[2] BRITISH: head master.

Question 6

M1:   How is your research project going?

W1:   Great. It's almost done.

M1:   I'm impressed. I always get nervous when I have a big project like that to do.

W1:   It's not so bad really. And I'm quite pleased with the results that I'm getting.

Target 9—Listening for an Explanation

Example

Listen to the explanation of how a toaster works.

M1:   How does a toaster brown your toast every morning? Like all appliances that heat up, a toaster works by converting electrical energy into heat energy. The electrical current runs from the electrical socket in your kitchen wall, through the toaster plug, to the toaster cord. It travels down the cord to the appliance itself. Inside the toaster are wire loops. The wires are made of a special type of metal. Electricity passes through this metal, creating friction. This friction causes the wires to heat up and glow orange. When the wires have sufficiently heated, your toast pops up ready to eat.

Questions 1–12

Listen to the explanation of how cacao beans are processed.

W1:   The rich flavor of chocolate that almost everyone loves comes from the cacao tree, which is grown in tropical regions around the world. The farmer harvests the ripe fruit of the cacao tree, then cuts it open to remove the seeds. These seeds are the cocoa beans from which chocolate is made. The beans are fermented in a large vat for about a week. Then they are placed on trays in the sun to dry. When the cocoa beans are ready, they are shipped off to the chocolate factory. At the chocolate factory, the cocoa beans are turned into all sorts of delicious chocolate treats.

Target 10—Listening for Classifications

Example

M1:   The school offers two types of courses. The one during the day is designed for students who are pursuing their academic degree full time. The night courses are designed for students who work during the day and are taking specific courses for an advanced business certificate.

Questions 1–5

Question 1

W1: It's easy to upgrade your ticket from economy class to first class. It costs just a little bit more, and it will enhance your travel experience in several ways. While we have roomy seats in both economy and first class, our first-class passengers are also offered pillows and blankets so they can nap in comfort. Snacks are served in economy class, while full meals are served to all first-class passengers. As an economy-class passenger you'll be offered the most current magazines for your entertainment, but you'll have to bring your own DVDs if you want to watch movies. In first class, we show complimentary first-run movies.

Question 2

M1: Do you want to go to the movies tonight? There's a great film showing at the Royal Theater.

W1: The Royal Theater? I never like the movies there. They only show violent types like horror and war movies.

M1: So what kind of movie do you like?

W1: Oh, romantic movies and classic movies, like the ones they show at the Deluxe Theater.

Question 3

M1: Although butterflies and moths look very similar, they aren't exactly alike. There are several ways to tell the difference between them. The most well-known difference is that butterflies fly during the day, while moths are night fliers. Additionally, when butterflies rest, they fold their wings back. Moths at rest hold their wings in a horizontal position. The antennae are different also. Butterflies have thin antennae, and moths often have feathery antennae.

Question 4

W1: I have so much to do to get ready for the party. I have to clean the house, cook . . .

M1: You've bought all the food already, haven't you?

W1: Yes, the shopping's done. And I've planned all the decorations, too.

M1: When did you mail[1] the invitations?

W1: Mail the invitations? Oh, no! I guess I'd better do that today.

Question 5

W1: Trees for landscaping your garden can be divided into three categories. Some trees we plant to add beauty to the yard. They are chosen for their beautiful flowers or interesting leaves. These are the ornamental trees. If you live in a sunny location, then you'll probably want to plant some shade trees. These are usually tall, broad-leafed trees. Finally we have the evergreens. Every garden should have at least one to provide a bit of green year round. Most evergreens are cone-bearing trees with needles instead of leaves.

[1]BRITISH: post.

Target 11—Listening for Comparisons and Contrasts

Example

F1:   I've been corresponding by mail with a French student.

F2:   In English? You don't speak French, do you?

F1:   No, unfortunately, but she writes English well. We have a lot in common.

F2:   Like what, your age?

F1:   Well, I'm actually about two years older than she is. But we do have the same first name.

F2:   And you're both students.

F1   Yes, and we are both studying to be doctors, although she wants to be a pediatrician[1], and I want to be a neurosurgeon.

F2:   It seems the only similarities are your sex and your given name.

F1:   Well, we both like to swim. She likes to dance, too, but you know how little I like dancing.

Questions 1–4

Question 1

W1:   How's your new job?

M1:   It's great. Much better than my old job.

W1:   Really? That's wonderful. You're earning more money now, aren't you?

M1:   Yeah, the salary's a lot higher, but I have to work more hours.

W1:   Too bad. I remember you had a really good schedule at your old job.

M1:   Yes, I miss that. But the job itself is pretty similar. I have the same kind of responsibilities that I had before.

W1:   That makes it easier. Are you still working in the same place?

M1:   No, now I have to go to the other side of town. But at least I can still take the bus like I did for my old job.

W1:   Well, that's convenient.

Question 2

W1:   The new Riverdale Library will have its grand opening next month. The new library, which has been under construction for the past two years, stands on the same site as the old library. But there the similarity ends. The new library is much larger than the old two-story building, boasting four floors of books and two floors of offices, as well as an underground parking garage, which everyone agrees will be a great improvement over the old outside parking lot. With so much space to fill, we have greatly expanded the size of our book collection. You will continue to enjoy the same services as before. Online book renewal, free Internet access, and the Ask-a-Librarian Hotline that you enjoyed at the old library will also be available at our new facilities.

Question 3

M1:   I'm interested in joining the health club, but I see you have two types of membership.

W1:   Yes, we have both full and associate memberships. The full membership costs almost twice as much as the associate, and many members feel it's worth the extra cost.

M1:   What's the difference between them?

[1]BRITISH: paediatrician.

W1:   With both types of membership you are entitled to the use of all our club facilities and you can take advantage of all our fitness classes as well. You also get use of the locker room[1] with both memberships, but full members get extra locker room privileges, such as your own locker exclusively for your use and laundry service as well. May I sign you up for a full membership today?

M1:   I'm not sure. The associate membership sounds fine to me.

W1:   Let me point out that with the full membership you also get a complimentary individualized fitness plan tailored just for you. Associate members may take advantage of this service as well, but they have to pay extra for it.

M1:   I'll have to think about it.

Question 4

M1:   Toads and frogs begin their lives in similar ways. The eggs hatch in or near water, and the babies, called tadpoles, spend the first part of their lives living in the water. When they become adults, frogs continue to live in the water, while adult toads usually live on the land. When you come across one of these animals, how can you tell whether it's a toad or a frog? The easiest way is to touch its skin. Frogs have smooth skin while the skin of toads is generally rough and bumpy. Their shape is somewhat different also, with toads being plumper and broader than frogs. What is a more typical sound on a summer evening than a chorus of croaking frogs or toads? Both these animals make their croaking sound by inflating a sac in their throat.

Target 12—Listening for Negative Meanings

Example

W1:   It was a very dense book, but it wasn't impossible to read.

Questions 7–12

Question 7

M1:   The flora and fauna of this region are adapted to the special climate. It hardly ever rains here, even in the winter. Most of the year, there is barely a cloud to be seen in the sky.

Question 8

W1:   Your essay writing exam is coming up tomorrow, so I'd like to review some of the testing rules with you now. The good news is that you'll have an unlimited amount of time to write your essay. You won't, however, be permitted to consult a dictionary while[2] writing the exam. Neither can you take anything else into the testing room with you except a pen.

Question 9

M1:   I'm in a bit of a hurry. Do you think you can fix the problem with my car today?

W1:   I'm sorry, but I'm behind schedule. I won't be able to get to it until the weekend.

M1:   Then I'll have to take a bus to work tomorrow.

---

[1]BRITISH: changing room

[2]BRITISH: whilst.

Question 10

W1:   What a restaurant! Never in my life have I tasted such delicious food.

M1:   You really think so? But don't you think the service was too slow?

W1:   Not a bit. I can't wait to go back there.

Question 11

M1:   Botanists and other flower lovers enjoy visiting this area in the spring and summer to see the abundant variety of wildflowers. In the early spring it isn't uncommon to find violets and, later in the season, there is a profusion of wild roses as well. Many also come here seeking the wild iris, although that is more rarely seen in these parts.

Question 12

M1:   I have so much homework this week. Not only do I have to write two papers, I have to read four books, too.

W1:   Wow. That's a lot.

M1:   Yeah, well, at least I don't have any exams to study for.

Target 13—Listening for Chronology

Example

W1:   Before you do your research, we'll have an orientation session in the library so you can become familiar with the various sources of information available there. Each student will give a presentation on his or her research topic after all the papers have been submitted. All of this will have to be completed prior to the date of the final exam.

Questions 1–5

Question 1

W1:   I'm interested in renting an apartment in this building.

M1:   OK, first you'll have to fill out[1] an application. Then, before you submit it, you'll need to get two references.

W1:   References?

M1:   Yes, from former landlords or your boss or someone like that who can vouch for your responsibility. All right, so you do that, then you'll have to have some money ready for a deposit. As soon as we have an available apartment, we'll notify you, and we'll ask that you pay a deposit to hold it for you.

W1:   I have to pay the deposit before signing the lease?

M1:   Well, of course we'll refund it if you decide not to take the apartment, but the deposit holds it for you while you look the apartment over and decide whether or not you want it.

---

[1]BRITISH: fill in.

Question 2

M1: Today we'll take a look at the life of classical composer Wolfgang Amadeus Mozart. Mozart was born in Austria in 1756. His father, Leopold, was a well-known music teacher and published an important textbook on violin playing shortly after Wolfgang's birth. Young Wolfgang showed his genius at an early age, beginning to write his own musical compositions at the age of 5. This was one factor that led to his father's decision to take Wolfgang and his sister on performing tours around Europe, beginning in 1762. After a childhood of touring Europe, Mozart visited Vienna in 1781 and decided to settle there. He had been greatly saddened during his tour of 1777 when his mother, who was accompanying him, died while they were abroad. He looked forward to a new life in Vienna.

Question 3

W1: How'd your trip to the beach go?

M1: Fantastic. Well, mostly. Of course, we had to leave home at five in the morning.

W1: Ouch! So early.

M1: Yeah, but, then, by lunchtime we were almost there.

W1: So where'd you have lunch? At that burger place, right?

M1: No, we just had a roadside picnic to save time. We'd made our sandwiches the night before we left.

W1: You're so organized.

M1: I guess. Whatever. So anyhow, back in the car after lunch we started arguing about a place to stay. We finally agreed on the White Sands Motel.

W1: I've been there. It's all right.

M1: Yeah, well, it's a good thing we left home early because by the time we got there, there was only one room left at the motel, so we were lucky to get it. We went swimming as soon as we'd checked in.

Question 4

W1: I have to do this research project for my sociology class, and I don't know how to begin.

W2: Is that Professor Miller's class? I took it last year. It's a great class.

W1: Really? Can you help me get started?

W2: Sure, well, I mean, I guess so. Well, I'd say the most important thing is get a partner. It's much easier working with someone else.

W1: So the first thing is to get a partner?

W2: You probably should choose a research topic first, then find a classmate who's also interested in your topic. Then you need the professor's approval.

W1: Approval for what?

W2: No, wait. OK first you and your partner design your research, I mean you write up your question-naire and decide whom you will interview and all that.

W1: *Then* we get the professor's approval for our research design?

W2: Yes. And then you can start your research.

Question 5

W1: Welcome to Waterside Gardens. We'll begin our tour by walking through the rose garden, just as soon as everyone has shown me his or her tickets. Following the rose garden, we'll view the pond area. We'll visit the greenhouse after everyone who so desires has had a chance to photograph the butterfly garden. It is our most picturesque area. And that's it. I hope you'll enjoy the tour.

MODEL TESTS

MODEL TEST 1

Narrator: IELTS Listening. Model Test 1.

You will hear a number of different recordings, and you will have to answer questions on what you hear. There will be time for you to read the instructions and questions, and you will have a chance to check your work. All the recordings will be played once only.

The test is in four sections. Write all your answers in the Listening Question booklet. At the end of the test you will be given ten minutes to transfer your answers to an answer sheet.

Now turn to Section 1 on page 188.

Section 1. You will hear a conversation between Mark Winston who wants to learn Japanese, and Kathy Green who is a receptionist at the World Language Academy.

First you have some time to look at Questions 1 to 3 on page 188.

Listen carefully and answer Questions 1 to 3.

Questions 1–3

Narrator: You will see that there is an example which has been done for you. On this occasion only, the conversation relating to this will be played first.

Kathy Green: Good morning. May I help you?
Mark Winston: Yes, I'm Mark Winston and I . . .

(Telephone rings)

Oh, Excuse me, Mr. Winston. World Language Academy. This is Kathy Green. May I help you? (pause). No this is a private language school, not a travel agency. (pause) No problem at all. Good-bye. I'm sorry, Mr. Winston. Now, may I help YOU?

Mr. Winston: Yes, I hope you can. I'd like to sign up now for a Japanese class next week.

Narrator: The man says he'd like to **"sign up now"** which means "register today" for a language class. The number 2 has been written in the blank. You should answer the questions as you listen because you will not hear the recording a second time. Listen carefully and answer questions 1 to 3.

Kathy Green: Good morning. May I help you?

Mark Winston: Yes, I'm Mark Winston and I . . .

(Telephone rings)

Oh, Excuse me, Mr. Winston. World Language Academy. This is Kathy Green. May I help you? (pause). No this is a private language school, not a travel agency. (pause) No problem at all. Good-bye. I'm sorry, Mr. Winston. Now may I help YOU?

Mr. Winston: Yes, I hope you can. I'd like to sign up now for a Japanese class next week.

Kathy Green: Classes start next week, and we have lots of Japanese classes to choose from. Have you studied Japanese before?

Mark Winston: No, I haven't. I'm a beginner. I'm planning to visit Japan next summer so I want to learn a bit of the language.

Kathy Green: That's great. Japan is a wonderful place to visit. I spent a month in Tokyo last year, actually, and I even climbed Mount Fujiyama.

Mark Winston: Really? That's too much activity for me. I'm just planning to visit Tokyo. I think I'll find plenty to do there.

Kathy Green: You certainly will. All right then, let me tell you a bit about our classes. They're all taught by native speakers, and they are all specialists in their field. You can choose a Japanese for Tourists class, Japanese for Business Travelers, or Japanese for University Students. You're not studying at a university, are you?

Mark Winston: No, I graduated a few years ago.

Kathy Green: Well, then, the tourist class is probably best for you.

Mark Winston: Yes, I think you're right. I just want to learn enough to order food in restaurants and go shopping and things like that. When does the Japanese for Tourists class begin?

Kathy Green: Let's see. We have a class for beginners that starts next week. I think there are still a few spaces left. You're in luck . . . we have 15 students enrolled, and there's room for three more.

Narrator: Before you hear the rest of the conversation, you have some time to look at questions 4 to 10 on pages 188 and 189.

Now listen and answer questions 4 to 10.

Questions 4–10

Mark Winston: When does that class meet?

Kathy Green: Every Monday, Wednesday, and Thursday from 5:30 until 7:30.

Mark Winston: That's a bit early for me. I work until 6:00. Don't you have a class that starts later in the evening?

Kathy Green: No . . . not for beginners. Let's see . . . we have an afternoon class on Monday, Wednesday, and Thursday, from one to three. Oh, but that's an intermediate class. What about mornings? We have a beginner's class that meets five days a week, Monday through Friday, from 9 A.M. until 10 A.M. Could you do that?

Mark Winston: No, I work all day. I only have evenings and weekends free.

Kathy Green:	The advanced class is Tuesday and Thursday from 7:30 to 9:30, but you've never studied Japanese before, have you?
Mark Winston:	No, I don't know anything about it.
Kathy Green:	Well, we have a beginner's class on Saturday from 9 in the morning until 2 in the afternoon.
Mark Winston:	Nine until two? That's a long class.
Kathy Green:	We also have private tutors. Actually, I usually recommend private tutors because they give you individualized attention. You are the only student in the class, so the tutor teaches you according to your specific needs. It really is the best way to learn a language.
Mark Winston:	It sounds great! I'd learn a lot that way, wouldn't I?
Kathy Green:	You really would. And it's very convenient. You can arrange to meet with your tutor at whatever time suits you.
Mark Winston:	Fantastic.[1] How do I sign up?
Kathy Green:	Well, how many hours a week do you want to study? We usually recommend three to five hours a week for a minimum of four weeks.
Mark Winston:	OK. I'll start with three hours a week.
Kathy Green:	Great. You can send us a check to cover the first week of classes, or you can pay now by credit card. Three hours of private classes comes out to 300 dollars, plus a 25-dollar registration fee.
Mark Winston:	Three hundred dollars? That's 100 dollars a class!
Kathy Green:	And it's certainly worth it. You'll be studying with a native speaker of Japanese. And all our tutors are professionally trained in the latest teaching methods. You'll be getting the best instruction money can buy.
Mark Winston:	But 100 dollars a class! That's over one thousand dollars for a month of classes. I'm sorry, but I just can't do that.
Kathy Green:	Then take the Saturday class. It's only $300 a month. And it's small. There will be only four or five students in it.
Mark Winston:	Great. I'll take that class. Can I pay by check?
Kathy Green:	Yes. Just bring your check to the first class. See you next Saturday at 9:00.

(Audio fades as last speaker continues to speak.)

Narrator:	That is the end of Section 1. You now have half a minute to check your answers.
	Now turn to Section 2 on page 189.
	Section 2. You will hear a guided tour of an old mansion.
	First, you have some time to look at questions 11 to 13 on page 189.
	As you listen to the first part of the talk, answer questions 11 to 13.

[1]BRITISH: Brilliant.

Questions 11–13

Barbara Wilson: Good afternoon. My name is Barbara Wilson, and I will be your guide for today's tour of Sumner Mansion. As a reminder before we begin, we ask that you not take photographs inside the building, and please turn off your cell phones during the tour. Also we request that you refrain from eating as well as drinking inside the mansion. Refreshments will be available at the end of the tour in the café next to the garden.

Narrator: Before you hear the rest of the tour, you have some time to look at questions 14–20 on page 190.

Questions 14–20

Now, to begin. Here we are at the main entrance. You will notice the elaborate Italian frieze installed by the original owner when the mansion was built in 1810. To the left of the entrance is the main living room. This was used by the Sumner family for entertaining guests, particularly for their tea parties. They were famous for the tea parties that they gave in this room. Here on display you can see the elegant chinaware they used for their parties. There are several sets of china imported from abroad.

Let's go over to the other side now. This room to the right of the main entrance is the dining room. Of course the family meals were served here, but the most interesting thing abut this room is the art. The Sumners collected a lot of art, and some of the finest pieces of their art collection are displayed in this room. On that wall opposite, you can see a large painting of a garden. Mr. Sumner bought that on a trip to China in 1825. You will also notice several smaller pieces of Chinese art as well as some portraits of the family.

Behind the mansion are the famous Sumner gardens. Right now you can see a spectacular display of roses. The tea roses are especially nice, and there are many other varieties of roses, as well. The guided tour will not continue into the garden. You can enjoy it on your own. Don't forget to stop in at the café before you go home for some tasty hot or cold tea and pastries. You enter it through the garden, but it's just behind the living room. There is also a small display there of kitchen tools used in the original mansion kitchen, which I am sure you will enjoy viewing. If you feel disoriented after walking around the gardens, don't worry. Remember that the parking area is just beyond the café, so it's a short walk back to your car.

Also, please remember that the grounds close at five <u>p.m.</u> as we are still on our spring schedule. If you come back next week, the summer schedule will have started and we'll be open a full ten hours a day from ten in the morning until eight in the evening. Thank you for visiting, and come back anytime. We're open seven days a week.

Narrator: That is the end of Section 2. You now have half a minute to check your answers.

Now turn to Section 3 on page 190.

Section 3. You will hear a panel discussion between the panel moderator and two panelists, Dr. Karen Akers and Dr. Fred Williams, both transportation consultants. In the first part of the discussion, they are talking about the future of public transportation.

First, you will have some time to look at questions 21 to 26 on page 190.

Now listen carefully and answer the questions 21 to 26.

Questions 21–26

Moderator:	Dr. Williams and Dr. Akers, I want to thank both of you for coming today and sharing your thoughts on the future of public transportation.

(Simultaneous thanks)

Dr. Akers:	Glad to be here.
Dr. Williams:	Thank You.
Moderator:	Let me ask you first, Dr. Williams, traffic congestion is becoming more and more of a problem, and it's spreading. We're used to traffic jams in cities, but now we find traffic problems on many major highways[1] that run between cities. What solutions do you see for the future of transportation?
Dr. Williams:	Many transportation experts, myself included, are excited about the potential of high-speed trains. These trains are having a great deal of success in Japan and in several European countries, as well. They've actually been around for a while—since 1964, in fact. The first high-speed train was put into operation that year.
Moderator:	What would the speed be exactly of a high-speed train? How would you define "high-speed" train?
Dr. Williams:	We usually call a train high speed if it's capable of traveling at 200 kilometers an hour or faster.
Moderator:	That's very fast. It would seem to open up a lot of possibilities for transportation between cities.
Dr. Akers:	Yes, that's right. Fifty years ago or more, conventional trains were the major form of transportation between cities. Of course, they weren't high-speed trains, but nobody expected that then. Those old trains provided frequent, reliable, and affordable long-distance transportation, and most people used them. Then things changed. Cars and highways were improved, so more and more people started driving cars.
Dr. Williams:	Cars are a great form of transportation. Everybody loves them because they're so convenient. But we usually use cars for local trips . . . shopping, and going to work, and things like that.
Dr. Akers:	That's true. For long-distance trips, most people nowadays rely on planes. Plane service is more frequent and affordable now than it was in the past, so planes, like cars, have become more convenient for people. Meanwhile, trains have more or less fallen by the wayside as a common means of transportation.
Moderator:	But with everybody driving cars and taking planes, we have a lot of congestion. And not just on the roads. Airports have become very crowded, too.
Dr. Williams:	Exactly. We have congestion everywhere now, so we need to look at new forms of transportation.

[1]BRITISH: motorways.

Narrator: Before you hear the rest of the conversation, you have some time to look at questions 27 to 30 on page 191.

Now listen and answer questions 27 to 30.

Questions 27–30

Dr. Akers: And that's where high-speed trains come in. They offer several advantages over both cars and planes. When you take everything into consideration—getting to the train station, boarding the train, and all that—a high-speed train gets you to your destination just about as quickly as a car. So speed isn't really an advantage. Cost isn't always, either. Depending on how many people are traveling with you, a train trip could be more expensive than a car trip. But, a train trip is much more relaxing than a car trip. You can read, sleep, eat, whatever, while the train carries you to your destination. And of course you're never delayed by traffic jams. To my mind, these are great advantages.

Moderator: Yes, I can really see the advantage of the train over the car. But what about planes? Planes are much faster than cars, so that's a big plus for planes.

Dr. Williams: Not necessarily. For trips shorter than 650 kilometers, high-speed trains can actually be faster. Checking in at the airport and going through security takes a long time. You don't have that kind of delay with a train. Also trains can carry more passengers than planes. They can also offer more frequent service. So for your medium-distance trips, they really are faster than planes.

Narrator: That is the end of Section 3. You now have half a minute to check your answers.

Now turn to Section 4 on page 191.

Section 4. You will hear a lecture on Albert Einstein. First you have some time to look at the questions 31 to 40 on page 191.

Now listen carefully and complete the timeline in questions 31 to 40.

Questions 31–40

Lecturer: Today I want to talk about the early life of a man whose name is synonymous with genius—Albert Einstein. He is well known, of course, for his work in physics, especially his theory of relativity. This is a term that everyone has heard, but few lay people, . . . and I do not mean to include you in this group, . . . but few non-physicists understand. Equally incomprehensible to most people is why Einstein the genius did so poorly at school. There are some questions, actually misconceptions about his early life, particularly about his lack of success in school that I want to try to clear up for you. Let's look now at some true facts about the life of this famous man.

Albert Einstein was born in Germany in 1879. As a child in school, he had a reputation as a slow learner. Now there were a couple of theories about why he could not keep pace with his classmates. He may have had some sort of learning disability; we don't know for sure. Another theory about his slow learning is that he may have suffered from a condition related to autism.

Whether it was a learning disability or not, Einstein himself believed that his slowness actually helped him develop his theory of relativity. He said that he ended up thinking about time and space at a later age than most children, at a time when his intellect was more developed. He didn't even begin to study mathematics until he was 12. There are popular rumors that he failed his math classes, but this is actually not true.

Mathematics was a late passion; his first was the violin. Like many intellectuals, Einstein had a passion for music. He started his study of the violin during elementary school and continued playing the violin for the rest of his life.

When Einstein was 15, his family moved to Italy. Soon after that, his parents sent him to Switzerland, where in 1896 he finished high school. After graduating from high school, he enrolled in a Swiss technological institute. He received a teaching diploma from the institute in 1900. He remained in Switzerland and eventually became a Swiss citizen, in 1901.

Einstein had a hard time finding a teaching job. In fact he never did find one. A friend's father helped him get a job at the Swiss Patent Office. He began working there in 1902. His job involved reviewing inventors' applications for patents. When he looked over the applications, he often found faults in the applicants' drawings. He would make suggestions so they could improve their designs and better their chances for receiving a patent.

Meanwhile, in 1898, between graduating from high school and getting his job at the Patent Office, Einstein met and fell in love with a young Serbian woman, Mileva Maric. Maric was a mathematician, and Einstein considered her his intellectual equal. They had a daughter in 1902 but unusual for the time even for geniuses, they didn't get married until 1903. Their first son was born the following year. There is no record of whether the two children inherited their father's learning disability.

Narrator: That is the end of Section 4. You now have half a minute to check your answers.

You will now have 10 minutes to transfer your answers to the listening answer sheet.

This is almost the end of the test. You now have one more minute to check all your answers.

That is the end of the Listening section of Model Test 1.

MODEL TEST 2

Narrator: IELTS Listening. Model Test 2

You will hear a number of different recordings, and you will have to answer questions on what you hear. There will be time for you to read the instructions and questions, and you will have a chance to check your work. All the recordings will be played once only.

The test is in four sections. Write all your answers in the Listening Question booklet. At the end of the test you will be given ten minutes to transfer your answers to an answer sheet.

Now turn to Section 1 on page 207.

Section 1. You will hear a conversation between an interviewer and a woman shopper.

First you have some time to look at Questions 1 to 7 on page 207.

You will see that there is an example which has been done for you. On this occasion only, the conversation relating to this will be played first.

Example

M1:   Excuse me. Could I have a few minutes of your time?

W1:   What do you need?

M1:   First, welcome to Lougheed (Lawheed) Mall, the largest shopping center in Vancouver. We're conducting a survey of the shoppers at this mall. We want to learn about when and how often people shop, the stores they prefer, in general, people's habits when they shop at the mall. Would you mind answering a few questions about your shopping?

Narrator: The man says he is conducting a survey of shoppers, so B has been circled. Now we shall begin. You should answer the questions as you listen because you will not hear the recording a second time. Listen carefully and answer questions 1 to 7.

Questions 1–7

M1:   Excuse me, ma'am. Could I have a few minutes of your time?

W1:   What do you need?

M1:   First, welcome to Lougheed (Lawheed) Mall, the largest shopping center in Vancouver. We're conducting a survey of the shoppers at this mall. We want to learn about when and how often people shop, the stores they prefer, in general, people's habits when they shop at the mall. Would you mind answering a few questions about your shopping?

W1:   Not at all.

M1:   Thank you. Today we're interviewing married women, that is women with husbands and children who shop for their families. So the first question is, do you fit this category?

W1:   Yes, I do.

M1:   Wonderful. Now, I need to know your age. Are you between the ages of 18 and twenty-five, twenty-six and . . . ?

W1:   (interrupting) I'm 34.

M1:   Great. OK. Now, how often do you shop here? Less than once a month, at least once a month, once a . . .

W1:   I have a big family. I have to buy a lot of things. I'm here at least twice a week.

M1:   Well that's just fine. You must be very familiar with the stores here.

W1:   I certainly am.

M1:   All right then. The next question concerns the things that you buy. What do you usually shop for here?

W1:   Just about everything. I've been in all the stores at one time or another. The clothing stores are quite nice, though, frankly, their prices are a bit high, and I like the bookstore too, but . . .

M1:   What I need to know, though is, what is the one type of thing you shop for most often? Would it be books?

W1:   Oh, no. That's only occasionally. The reason I come here so often is for food. I told you I have a large family. I buy all our food at the supermarket here.

M1:   OK. So, the next question is how much time do you usually spend at the mall?

W1:   What do you mean? Do you mean every week?

M1:   I mean, each time you come here, how long do you spend?

W1:   Oh, I'd say about an hour and a half or so. Maybe a little longer, but I'm hardly ever here for more than two hours.

M1:   Now there's one last question in this section. How do you usually come to the mall? Do you take the bus, the . . . ?

W1:   I always drive.

Narrator: Before you hear the rest of the conversation, you have some time to look at questions 8 to 10 on page 208.

Now listen and answer questions 8 to 10.

Questions 8–10

M1:   Fine. OK, the next part of the questionnaire concerns your opinions. You say you've been in all the stores in the mall. In general, in which store would you say you've had the best shopping experience?

W1:   That's easy. The shoe store.

M1:   That's a big store, isn't it? They have a huge selection of shoes.

W1:   They do, but I consider it a good store because the employees there are so polite. They give very good service.

M1:   Now, you may have had a chance to eat at our new food court.

W1:   Yes, I have, but I don't think I'll eat there again.

M1:   Why not?

W1:   Well, the food tastes fine, but it's very expensive. It shouldn't cost so much.

M1:   I have just one last question. Do you have any suggestions for improvements to the mall?

W1:   Yes. You should add more parking spaces. I can never find a place to park. It's really annoying sometimes when . . .

(Audio fades as last speaker continues to speak.)

Narrator: That is the end of Section 1. You now have half a minute to check your answers.

Now turn to Section 2 on page 208.

Section 2. You will hear a recording of a tour of a health club.

First, you have some time to look at questions 11 to 14 on page 208.

Now listen carefully and answer questions 11 to 14.

Questions 11–14

Good afternoon. Welcome to the Riverside Health Club. The purpose of today's tour is to let you become familiar with the different activities available at the club. I hope that by the end of the tour all of you will decide to become members.

When you become a member of the health club, you will have the opportunity to participate in a wide range of fitness activities. Over here we have our indoor tennis courts. There are three of them, and if you don't know how to play, we offer tennis lessons throughout the week. Right here next to the courts is the club store. It's quite small, you see, but we have it as a convenience. So if you need snacks or drinks after exercising, you can buy them here.

OK, now this is the exercise room. It's the most well-equipped exercise facility in the city. You won't find old-fashioned weights for lifting here. We have only the most modern exercise machines. All the machines are electronic. They automatically adjust to your weight and fitness level, so you get the workout that's just right for you. The exercise room is run by Peter Jones, who's an expert in both fitness and technology, so he can help you become familiar with the machines. Once you learn how to use them, and Peter makes that easy, they're really great. I work out on them myself just about every day.

OK. In here we have the swimming pool. We offer different types and levels of swimming lessons. Also you'll notice that the pool is Olympic size, so it's well-suited for competitions. In fact, our swimming team is well-known throughout the city. As a club member, you would have the opportunity to try out for the swim team if you're interested.

Narrator: Before you hear the rest of the tour, you have some time to look at questions 15 to 20 on pages 208 and 209.

Now listen and answer questions 15 to 20.

Questions 15–20

Over there at the other end are the locker rooms where you can change from your business clothes to your swimsuit or whatever. You can look in them later if you wish. They're very comfortable. We keep them well-stocked with the basic necessities such as towels and soap. You'll have to supply your own shampoo, however. There are plenty of showers, so you'll never have to wait your turn. We also have hairdryers for you to use. For safety reasons, we ask that everyone wear rubber sandals in the changing rooms. What else? Oh, you'll have to supply your own lock, of course. That's for your security.

Before we leave the pool area, I'd like to make you aware of some of our rules. The pool is the most popular place in the club, and it's often crowded, so we have rules for everyone's comfort and safety. The most important one, if you have children, please be aware that they are not allowed in the pool area alone. Children must be accompanied by an adult at all times. Naturally, there is no running near the pool. The floor is very wet, and it would be easy to get hurt. One last thing, for sanitary reasons, we ask everyone to shower before entering the pool.

All right, I hope you've enjoyed the tour. Are there any questions?

Narrator: That is the end of Section 2. You now have half a minute to check your answers.

Now turn to Section 3 on page 209.

Section 3. You will hear a professor and her students discussing class assignments.

First, you will have some time to look at questions 21 to 26 on page 209.

Now listen carefully and answer questions 21 to 26.

Questions 21–26

W1:   In this class we focus on developing writing skills, so one of the most important things we do is practice those skills by writing essays. Today we'll go over the requirements for your essay assignments. You'll have to write one essay each week. They're not very long essays, just about 350 to 400 words apiece. Every week I'll assign a different type of essay, so I thought today we'd go over some of the important essay types. The first type of essay I'll assign will be an essay describing a process. So you'll need to choose something that you can describe step-by-step. Yes, Mr. Smith?

M1:   Is that a "how to" essay? I mean, would a topic be something like "How to fix a car?"

W1:   Well, you should be more specific. Remember, you have a limited number of words. A better example would be "How to change the oil in a car." Yes?

W2:   How about friendship as a topic? "How to make friends." Would that be a topic for a process essay?

W1:   It could be, but actually friendship is a better topic for a classification essay, which is the second type I'll assign. In a classification essay you present your idea by organizing it into categories. "Three types of friends" would be a good topic for a classification essay. The third essay type you'll write is compare and contrast. So, obviously, for your topic you'll pick two or more things to compare.

M2:   (*laughing*) Like comparing the food in the student cafeteria to the food in a real restaurant.

W1:   Why not? That could actually be quite a good topic. But it really doesn't matter which topic you choose, as long as you develop your argument well. The next essay type is argumentative, in which you'll present an opinion and prove or defend it.

M1:   I like to argue.

W1:   Then you should do quite well with an argumentative essay. When writing this type of essay, be sure to state your opinion in a clear, straightforward sentence. For example "Homework is necessary" could be a thesis statement. Yes?

Narrator: Before you hear the rest of the conversation, you have some time to look at questions 27 to 30 on pages 209 and 210.

Now listen carefully and answer questions 27 to 30.

Questions 27–30

W2:   Will you give us the topics, or do we pick our own?

W1:   I'd like you to pick your own topics. That way you can write about things that interest you. But be sure your topics are original. I want them to come out of your own heads, not out of any book on essay writing. So, any original topic is fine as long as it fits the assigned essay type. Are there any more questions? Yes?

M2:   When are the essays due?

W1:   Every Monday I'll make a new essay assignment, which you'll have to hand in to me the following Friday. Another question?

W2:   Will the essays count toward the final grade?

W1:   Of course. The essays are the most important thing we do in this class. All together your essays will count for 65 percent of your final grade. Other class work will count for 15 percent and your tests will be 20 percent of the final grade. One more thing. Please type your essays on a computer. Handwritten essays are not acceptable, and I don't want to receive any photocopied work either.

Narrator: That is the end of Section 3. You now have half a minute to check your answers.

Now turn to Section 4 on page 210.

Section 4. You will hear a professor give a lecture. First you have some time to look at questions 31 to 36 on page 210.

Now listen carefully and answer questions 31 to 36.

Questions 31–36

Good evening. I'm Professor Williams and this class is Introduction to Anthropology. This class meets every Tuesday evening from 6:45 until 8:15. Please be on time for each class session. This evening we'll begin with a discussion of hunter-gatherer societies. This is an important topic because at one time all humans were hunter-gatherers. What are hunter-gatherer societies? They are groups of people that survive by hunting animals and gathering plants to eat. Typically in these societies the men's job is to hunt large animals while the women both gather plants and hunt smaller animals. Before twelve thousand years ago, all humans lived as hunter-gatherers. Now there are relatively few groups of people living this way, but there are some. Experts estimate that in about 50 years or so all such groups will have disappeared. Today hunter-gatherer societies still exist in the Arctic, in some desert areas, and in tropical rainforests. These are areas where other forms of food production, namely agriculture, are too difficult because of the climate.

Narrator: Before you hear the rest of the conversation, you have some time to look at questions 37 to 40 on page 210.

Now listen carefully and answer questions 37 to 40.

Questions 37–40

In history, many hunter-gatherer societies eventually developed into farming societies. What are some of the basic differences between hunter-gatherers and farmers? The first is that hunter-gatherers tend to be nomadic. They travel from place to place. Once they have used up the food in one area, they have to move on to the next place to find more. Farmers, on the other hand, are more likely to be sedentary. They can't move often because, of course, they have to stay in one place long enough to plant their crops and harvest them.

Another difference is that hunter-gatherer societies generally have lower population densities. Farming can support much higher population densities than hunting and gathering can because farming results in a larger food supply. So you'll find smaller groups among hunter-gatherers. Another very important difference is in social structure. A characteristic of hunter-gatherer societies is that they tend not to have hierarchical social structures. They usually don't have surplus food, or surplus anything, and if they did they would have no place to keep it since they move around so often. So in a hunter-gatherer society, there is little ability to support full-time leaders. Everybody has to spend their time looking for food. These societies are more egalitarian than farming societies, where we see hierarchical social structures begin to develop.

Please bear in mind that everything I have said so far this evening is of a general nature. Next we will look at some specific examples of hunter-gatherer societies to see how these general concepts translate into reality.

Narrator: That is the end of Section 4. You now have half a minute to check your answers.

You will now have 10 minutes to transfer your answers to the listening answer sheet.

This is almost the end of the test. You now have one more minute to check all your answers.

That is the end of the Listening section of Model Test 2.

MODEL TEST 3

Narrator: IELTS Listening. Model Test 3.

You will hear a number of different recordings, and you will have to answer questions on what you hear. There will be time for you to read the instructions and questions, and you will have a chance to check your work. All the recordings will be played once only.

The test is in four sections. Write all your answers in the Listening Question booklet. At the end of the test you will be given ten minutes to transfer your answers to an answer sheet.

Now turn to Section 1 on page 225.

Section 1. You will hear a conversation between a lost and found agent and a woman who has lost something.

First you have some time to look at Questions 1 to 4 on page 225.

You will see that there is an example which has been done for you. On this occasion only, the conversation relating to this will be played first.

Example

W1:   (*excited and impatient*) Is this the lost and found department?
M1:   Yes, this is Lost Property. Did you lose something on the train?
W1:   Yes, I did. I lost something very valuable, and it's very important that I get it back.
M1:   All right, calm down. We'll fill in a lost item report form. Now, when did you lose the item?
W1:   Just now. Today. A few minutes ago.
M1:   Today's Monday, OK, right.

Narrator: The item was lost today, which is Monday, so "Monday" has been written in the space. Now we shall begin. You should answer the questions as you listen because you will not hear the recording a second time. Listen carefully and answer questions 1 to 4.

Questions 1–4

W1:   (*excited and impatient*) Is this the lost and found department?
M1:   Yes, this is Lost Property. Did you lose something on the train?
W1:   Yes, I did. I lost something very valuable, and it's very important that I get it back.
M1:   All right, calm down. We'll fill out a lost item report form. Now, when did you lose the item?
W1:   Just now. Today. A few minutes ago.
M1:   Today's Monday, OK, right.
W1:   Can't you hurry? Can't you send the police to look for it or something?
M1:   Now just relax. This will only take a minute. May I have your name, please?
W1:   It's Patty, that's P-A-T-T-Y, last name Brown, like the color.
M1:   Patty Brown. All right, Ms. Brown, your address?
W1:   I live at 17 High Street.
M1:   Seventy or seventeen?
W1:   SevenTEEN.
M1:   Is that a house or a flat?
W1:   Oh. It's a flat, an apartment. Number 5. And the city is Riverdale.

M1:   Just one more thing. I need a phone number.

W1:   305-5938.

M1:   Is that home or office or . . .

W1:   It's my mobile phone. That's the best number to use because you can always reach me there.

Narrator: Before you hear the rest of the conversation, you have some time to look at questions 5 to 10 on page 225.

          Now listen and answer questions 5 to 10.

Questions 5–10

M1:   OK. I'll need a description of the lost item. What exactly did you lose?

W1:   I lost my reading glasses. But you know I bought them in Italy, they're Italian designer glasses and very expensive.

M1:   I see. And can you describe them? Are they square or round or . . .

W1:   They're round. And they have a chain attached. You know, those chains on glasses so you can hang them around your neck.

M1:   Where were you when you last had them?

W1:   I was sitting on the train reading. I had a window seat. The train was just about to enter the station. I heard the door at the other end of the car open, so I looked up from the article I was reading to see what the noise was.

M1:   So you had your glasses on then because you were reading?.

W1:   Yes, that's right. It was a fascinating article in that new magazine, you know the one, I can't remember the name now but anyhow . . .

M1:   Which train were you on?

W1:   Oh, dear. I don't remember the number, but it was the train from Riverdale. I've come here to visit my aunt. I've taken a whole week off of work to make this trip. I left home at five o'clock this morning, and I'm very tired.

M1:   I'm sorry to hear that. Several trains have arrived from Riverdale this morning. What time did your train get here?

W1:   Oh, just about 30 minutes ago. At ten o'clock, I think. Yes, that's right.

M1:   So the last time you had your glasses was when you were reading on the train?

W1:   Yes, and when I got off the train, I had my hand bag and my suitcase, and I checked my seat to see if I had left anything on it, but I hadn't.

M1:   And what's that in your coat pocket?

W1:   What's what? Oh . . . oh, my glasses! Oh my goodness! I can't believe they were there the whole time.

(Audio fades as last speaker continues to speak.)

Narrator: That is the end of Section 1. You now have half a minute to check your answers.

          Now turn to Section 2 on page 226.

          Section 2. You will hear a recording of a talk about student housing.

          First, you have some time to look at questions 11 to 14 on page 226.

          Now listen carefully and answer questions 11 to 14.

Questions 11–14

M1:   Good morning. Welcome to Day 2 of Student Orientation Week. The subject of the first talk today will be off-campus housing. This is of interest to those of you who don't want to live in student housing and are not familiar with our city. I'll give you some tips about where to look for housing and how to go about it.

OK, first let's talk about where to look for an apartment. There are some places that I don't recommend. The obvious place to look, you might think, would be in the neighborhood of the university. However, that's probably not a very good idea because, unfortunately, this is one of the more expensive areas of the city to live in. The downtown area is a popular place to visit; however, that's not a good place to look for housing, either, because it's mainly a commercial area. There are very few apartments there. It's also rather far from the university. So where does that leave us? I can recommend a couple of good places to look. Many students rent apartments in the uptown neighborhoods. The prices there are quite low, and many buses go there, so it's very easy to get to the university from there. The Greenfield Park neighborhood is also popular. It's closer to the university, but not many buses run in that direction, so you'll need a car if you choose to live there.

Narrator: Before you hear the rest of the talk you have some time to look at questions 15 to 20 on page 226.

Now listen and answer the questions 15 to 20.

Questions 15–20

M1:   All right, so let's say you've decided on a neighborhood. Next you have to find out what apartments are available. There are a number of places where you can look for apartment ads. The best place to look is at the university's Student Center. There is a wall there devoted to apartment ads. You can also look in the university newspaper. It comes out every Friday, which gives you the weekend for apartment hunting. The local city newspaper, *The Greenfield Times*, also lists apartment for rent ads. Again, Friday and Saturday are the best days. That's when you'll find the most ads. Finally, of course, you can look on the Internet. There are several Internet sites devoted to apartment rental ads in this area.

The staff at the Student Counseling Center is always ready to help you in your apartment search. They have available city maps as well as city bus schedules to help you get around to the various neighborhoods. If you would like to find someone to share an apartment with you, the Counseling Center has a roommate matching service. Most students find that having roommates is the most economical way to rent an apartment. The Center can also provide you with a list of inexpensive furniture stores. We all know how expensive it can be to furnish an apartment, but it can also be done in a more economical way. Also you might want to consider signing up for a meal plan on campus. If you don't like to cook or are too busy, well, you still have to eat, right? If you live off campus you can still eat in the university student dining rooms. We have plans for buying meals by the week, month, or semester. The Student Counseling Center can give you all the necessary information on that.

Narrator: That is the end of Section 2. You now have half a minute to check your answers.

Now turn to Section 3 on page 226.

Section 3. You will hear two students talking about their assignment.

First, you will have some time to look at questions 21 to 25 on page 226.

Now listen carefully and answer the questions 21 to 25.

Questions 21–25

M1: Have you decided what you're going to write your paper on? The one for Professor Anderson's class?

W1: The topic is transportation, right? I've been thinking about writing about bicycles as a way to solve our transportation problems.

M1: Really? I usually think of bicycling as a sport or recreational activity.

W1: Around here, that's what most people think. But in some parts of the world bicycles are an important form of transportation for many people. I think we have a lot to learn from them.

M1: So, what are you going to say in your paper?

W1: I'm not sure. Maybe you can help me figure some of it out.

M1: Sure. OK, well, I'd say if you want to persuade people to use bicycles more often, you have to start by thinking about the advantages and disadvantages.

W1: You're right. Let's see . . . well, I think the advantages are obvious. First, bicycling is good for your health.

M1: Yes, that's true. And another thing is that bicycles are a lot cheaper to use than cars.

W1: Or any other form of transportation, when you think about it. You don't have to pay a fare every time you ride your bike, like you do when you take the bus or the train.

M1: OK, another one is that bicycles don't cause pollution like cars and buses do.

W1: Yeah, that's a really important one. Bicycles are a clean form of transportation.

M1: OK, so what about the other side? What are some disadvantages, some reasons why people might not want to use bicycles?

W1: One thing I thought of is weather. Who wants to ride a bike in the rain? Or if you live where the weather is cold all winter, it would be hard to use a bicycle regularly. So bad weather would be a problem.

M1: Bad health would be too. Some people just aren't strong enough to ride bikes very much. You have to be in good shape.

W1: Yes, especially if you live far from your job or wherever you have to go. So that would be another problem, distance. It's difficult to ride your bike if your trip is a long distance.

Narrator: Before you hear the rest of the conversation, you have some time to look at questions 26 to 30 on page 227.

Now listen and answer questions 26 to 30.

Questions 26–30

M1: OK, so using a bike might not work for everyone, but for a lot of people it would. How can people be encouraged to use bikes for transportation?

W1: I think there's a lot cities can do. I think the biggest thing is making bicycle lanes on roads. It's really dangerous riding a bike where there's a lot of traffic, so special lanes just for bicycles would make things a lot safer.

M1: That's a great idea.

W1: Yeah, they already do that in some cities. And another thing is to make safe places for people to leave their bikes. I mean like at subway stations. A lot of people ride to the subway station and then take the subway to work. They need a safe place to lock up their bikes all day so they don't get stolen.

M1: That seems important.

W1: Yes, and another thing I've read about is maps. Some cities provide bicycling maps that show all the good routes. They show people how easy it is to get around by bike.

M1: OK, but what about equipment? Don't you need a lot of special stuff to ride a bicycle?

W1:   I don't think so. For safety you should wear a helmet, and at night you should have lights or wear reflective tape so cars can see you. For comfort you need light clothes, and waterproof clothes when it rains. But that's all I can think of. Really, it's easy and inexpensive to get started riding a bike.

M1:   I think you'll write a great paper. You've already persuaded me to get a bike.

Narrator: That is the end of Section 3. You now have half a minute to check your answers.

Now turn to Section 4 on page 227.

Section 4. You will hear a professor explaining an assignment to the class. First you have some time to look at the questions 31 to 40 on page 227.

Now listen carefully and answer questions 31 to 40.

Questions 31–40

W1:   Good afternoon, everyone. Today we'll talk about the most important assignment you'll do in this class, which is write a research paper. I'll start by going over the process step-by-step so you'll know exactly what I expect of you. All right, let's begin at the beginning. The first step is to choose a topic. I have a list of suggested topics related to the content of this class, and I'd like you to look over it to find a topic that interests you. Then, since they are somewhat general, I'd like you to narrow your topic choice down to something more specific. You'll need to get my final approval on your topic before you begin your research.

The next thing you'll do is gather information on your topic. There are two major places to go for that. At the library you'll have reference books and other types of books available, as well as journals, magazines, and newspapers. Don't forget to look at atlases and other similar sources too. They contain a lot of useful information. Then of course there is the Internet, where you'll find online journals and newspapers, as well as online encyclopedias, and much more.

After you have gathered some information and had the chance to start thinking about your topic, the next step is to write a thesis statement. This is a critical part of the process because the bulk of the paper will be about using your information to defend your thesis statement. I will be happy to help you with this, and, actually, with any other part of your writing process if you need it.

Now then, let's say you have your thesis statement and you have your information. How do you get started writing? It can seem overwhelming with all your ideas and notes floating around. Writing an outline will help you to start getting focused. Make sure your outline includes three important things: first your introduction, where you state your thesis, then the body, which is the bulk of the paper and where you make the arguments to support your thesis, and finally the conclusion. Here you'll restate your thesis and summarize your arguments.

So now that you have your outline, you can start organizing your notes. Organize them according to the outline. As you go along you'll start seeing what information is important to emphasize, what information you may actually not want to include, what you need to find out more about, etc. So organizing your notes helps you understand your information better and start to analyze it.

The next step is to write your first draft. If you have developed a good outline and organized your notes well, then this should not be too difficult. Following your outline, present your information and analysis of it.

Then, of course, the next thing to do is revise your draft. Read it over carefully, checking to make sure that you have explained your ideas clearly and presented your information correctly. You may want to reorganize some of your information at this point, too.

Finally, you'll type your final draft on the computer. Make sure that you check it for punctuation and spelling errors before you hand it in.

OK, that's a general outline of how to go about writing a research paper. Now let's talk about the proper format for footnotes and bibliographic entries.

Narrator: That is the end of Section 4. You now have half a minute to check your answers.

You will now have 10 minutes to transfer your answers to the listening answer sheet.

This is almost the end of the test. You now have one more minute to check all your answers.

That is the end of the Listening section of Model Test 3.

MODEL TEST 4

Narrator: IELTS Listening. Model Test 4.

You will hear a number of different recordings, and you will have to answer questions on what you hear. There will be time for you to read the instructions and questions, and you will have a chance to check your work. All the recordings will be played once only.

The test is in four sections. Write all your answers in the Listening Question booklet. At the end of the test you will be given ten minutes to transfer your answers to an answer sheet.

Now turn to Section 1 on page 242.

Section 1. You will hear a man buying tickets over the phone.

First you have some time to look at Questions 1 to 5 on page 242.

You will see that there is an example which has been done for you. On this occasion only, the conversation relating to this will be played first.

Example

F1:   Good morning. Municipal Museum of Art. Information Desk.
M1:   Yes, I'd like to find out about tickets for . . .
F1:   Tickets? That's our Special Events Department. Let me transfer you.

Narrator: The woman says she will transfer him to the Special Events Department, so C has been circled. Now we shall begin. You should answer the questions as you listen because you will not hear the recording a second time. Listen carefully and answer questions 1 to 5.

Questions 1–5

F1:   Good morning. Municipal Museum of Art. Information Desk.
M1:   Yes, I'd like to find out about tickets for . . .
F1:   Tickets? That's our Special Events Department. Let me transfer you.

(*telephone ringing*)

F2:	Special Events.
M1:	Yes, hello. I'm interested in the series you have going on now . . .
F2:	Oh, you mean our lecture series on the history of art.
M1:	Actually, I meant the concert series.
F2:	Oh, yes, of course. It's already begun, but there's still a concert tomorrow, that's Thursday. There's also one on Saturday, and then the last one is on Sunday.
M1:	The one tomorrow, is that when they'll be playing the Mozart concerto?
F2:	Yes, it is.
M1:	Then I'd like two tickets for that, if they're still available.
F2:	Yes, we have some tickets left. Now, I'll need your name.
M1:	It's Steven Milford. That's M-i-l-f-o-r-d.
F2:	Since you want tickets for tomorrow there isn't time to mail in a check. You'll have to pay by credit card.
M1:	That's not a problem.
F2:	Then I'll need your credit card number.
M1:	Oh, of course. It's 1659798164.
F2:	. . . 8164. Got it. OK you wanted two tickets, right?
M1:	Yes.
F2:	At 16.35 apiece that comes out to a total of 32 pounds and 70 p. You can pick up your tickets at the door.

Narrator:	Before you hear the rest of the conversation, you have some time to look at questions 6 to 10 on page 242.
	Now listen and answer questions 6 to 10.

Questions 6–10

M1:	Fine. Um, could you tell me how to get there? We're coming by train.
F2:	Certainly. It's very easy. When you get out of the train station, you'll see the library right across the street. Just walk down to the corner . . .
M1:	Do I go right or left out of the train station?
F2:	Oh, sorry. Go right, walk down to the corner. Right there on the corner you'll see a bank and across the street on the opposite corner is the post office. There are some office buildings across the street, too. Anyhow, you just go right at the corner, pass the car park and you'll see the museum right there in the middle of the block. If you get to a hotel, you've gone too far.
M1:	So right at the corner and pass the car park but not the hotel. All right I think I've got it.
F2:	Great. Make sure you're here by 7:30.

(*Audio fades as last speaker continues to speak.*)

Narrator:	That is the end of Section 1. You now have half a minute to check your answers.
	Now turn to Section 2 on page 243.
	Section 2. You will hear a recording of a radio show about tourism to Raven Island.
	First, you have some time to look at questions 11 to 17 on page 243.
	Now listen carefully and answer questions 11 to 17.

Questions 11–17

M1:   Good afternoon and welcome to Travel Time. Our guest today is Sheila Farnsworth, director of Raven Tours travel agency. She'll talk to us about travel to Raven Island.

F1:   Thank you, George. Raven Island is becoming quite a popular tourist destination, and with good reason. The prices are still low, and there's so much to enjoy there. Most tourists to Raven Island usually spend their time in one of two places. Ravensburg is the major city on the island, though with a population of only 56,000, it's not large by most standards. But for those who enjoy a more urban-style vacation, Ravensburg is where they go. For those looking for a bit of peace and quiet, Blackstone Beach is a favorite destination. This town, located on the island's northern coast, has a population of just 12,000 people.

The weather on Raven Island is always nice, especially during the summer. Summer in the city of Ravensburg is warm with average temperatures reaching 26 degrees or higher, and the weather is always pleasantly sunny there during July and August. Summer at Blackstone is a bit cooler, with average temperatures of around 23 degrees, and the weather is often windy because, of course, it's located on the coast.

Ravensburg has a lot to offer visitors. Its clubs and theaters are well-known, so if entertainment is what you're looking for, Ravensburg has the advantage there. The disadvantage to this is that, particularly during the summer theater festival, the city can become quite crowded with entertainment seekers. Blackstone Beach, on the other hand, is famous for its many fine seafood restaurants, considered to be the best on the island. So if you like seafood, that's the place to go. Unfortunately, eating seafood is the major activity in Blackstone. It's a very quiet town, which is a disadvantage if you're looking for excitement.

How can you get there? The Ravensburg airport is actually located a bit out of town. It's 25 kilometers from the city, but frequent bus service, taxis, and car rentals make it quite easy to get downtown. Travelers to Blackstone Beach also use the Ravensburg airport, which is about 75 kilometers away. There are three buses a day from the airport to Blackstone or you can rent[1] a car, of course.

Narrator: Before you hear the rest of the talk, you have some time to look at questions 18 to 20 on page 243.

Now listen and answer the questions 18 to 20.

Questions 18–20

F1:   Because of the low prices on Raven Island, many tourists travel there with shopping on their minds. What are some of the best bargains available on the island? Well, contrary to what one might think, native handicrafts are not a popular item. And although Raven Island has a beautiful musical tradition, there are not many CDs available of the native music, and the ones that are available are quite expensive. Some very good deals can be found, however, in the perfume shops. Raven Island Scents, a local factory, produces several fashionable perfumes, which they sell at reasonable prices. Jewelry[2] is also popular among tourists, and jewelry shops abound. Since fishing is the major island industry, no tourist goes home without a package of smoked fish. If you want to try fishing yourself, however, be sure to bring your own fishing gear.[3] Believe it or not, it's difficult and expensive for tourists to buy it on the island.

[1]BRITISH: hire.
[2]BRITISH: jewellery.
[3]BRITISH: tackle.

Narrator: That is the end of Section 2. You now have half a minute to check your answers.

               Now turn to Section 3 on page 243.

               Section 3. You will hear two students talking about a class project.

               First, you will have some time to look at questions 21 to 23 on page 243.

               Now listen carefully and answer the questions 21 to 23.

Questions 21–23

M1:   Hi, Janet.

F1:   Harry. What's up?

M1:   You know that research project we have to do for Professor Farley's class? Have you started it yet?

F1:   Started it? I'm almost done.

M1:   Really? I'm having trouble. Do you think you could help me?

F1:   You're going to need a lot of help. It's due next Thursday.

M1:   I know.

F1:   And it counts for 40 percent of our final semester grade.

M1:   I know! So I could really use your help. So, what topic did you choose?

F1:   I did my research about people's TV watching habits.

M1:   You mean which programs they watch?

F1:   Yeah, and how often they watch. It was really interesting.

Narrator: Before you hear the rest of the conversation, you have some time to look at questions 24 to 30 on page 244.

               Now listen and answer questions 24 to 30.

Questions 24–30

M1:   So, how'd you get started?

F1:   Well, after I decided my topic, I went to the library and did some research. I mean, I read about other studies people had done about TV watching.

M1:   How did that help you?

F1:   Oh, it was really important. It gave me lots of ideas about what questions to ask. So after I did the library research, I chose my research method.

M1:   What did you choose?

F1:   Well, I could do either interviews or just send around a paper questionnaire. I decided to use the questionnaire because I could get information from a lot more people that way.

M1:   And then what?

F1:   I made up the questions for the questionnaire.

M1:   And who did you give it to?

F1:   Well, that's what I had to do next, choose my subjects. You have to think about if you want data from people of a certain age or certain professions and things like that. I decided to ask people like myself—university students.

M1:   So then you just went around and asked people the questions?

F1:   Well, first I had to submit my research design to Professor Farley. He had to make sure it was OK before I went ahead with the research.

M1:   Did he make you change anything?

F1:   No, he pretty much liked it the way it was. So then I had to send out the questionnaire. I just put it in all the students' mailboxes. A lot of them responded. I got a lot of results—pages and pages.

M1:   Well, what did you do with all that information?

F1: Well, I did what Professor Farley told us to do. I made charts and graphs. That helped me figure out what all that data meant.

M1: Charts and graphs, huh? Hmm, I'll have to look at my class notes.

F1: Yes, you'd better. The professor outlined the whole process for us.

M1: So then you'll just hand in those charts and graphs on Thursday?

F1: Well, I'll have to write a report, too, of course. I mean, the professor wants to see our interpretation of the results. That's the whole point, don't you see?

M1: Yeah, I guess. If I get started now, do you think I'll finish on time?

F1: Maybe, if you don't have anything else to do this week.

Narrator: That is the end of Section 3. You now have half a minute to check your answers.

Now turn to Section 4 on page 244.

Section 4. You will hear a professor giving a lecture on the American crow. First you have some time to look at the questions 31 to 40 on page 244.

Now listen carefully and answer questions 31 to 40.

Questions 31–40

M1: Today I'll talk about the American crow, also known as the common crow. This bird has a bad reputation, and many people consider it to be a pest, but the American crow and many of its cousins in the corvid family are actually among the most intelligent of all the birds.

There are about 40 species in the crow family, and they can be found in most parts of the world. You'll find crows in North America, although interestingly enough, not in South America. While crows live in cold areas of the far north close to the Arctic region, there are none in Antarctica. They also like warm regions. There are several species of crows, for example, in Hawaii. And of course you'll find them in other parts of the world, Europe, Asia, and so on.

The American crow is one of the 15 species of crows found in North America and is also one of the most common. It's not a small bird, measuring 39 to 49 centimeters in length. Unlike some of its cousins—the magpie, for example, which is black and white, or the blue jay which is blue with white and black markings—the American crow is completely black, including the beak and feet. Because of their intensely dark color, some people dislike crows, or better said, fear them. Another reason people dislike crows is because they associate these birds with garbage. Crows love garbage and are often seen hanging around dumpsters behind restaurants and grocery stores. In addition to garbage left behind by humans, crows eat seeds, grains, eggs, fish, and carrion. They'll eat just about anything. One of their absolute favorite foods is corn.

Crows build large nests of sticks, usually in trees or sometimes in bushes. For safety reasons, they almost never nest on the ground. Mostly they nest alone, but in some places they have been seen nesting in colonies. The female lays from three to six eggs at a time. The eggs hatch in about 18 days. The babies stay in the nest for around a month. Generally, 35 days after hatching they have their feathers and are ready to fly.

Next we'll talk about some studies which have demonstrated the extreme intelligence of these animals.

Narrator: That is the end of Section 4. You now have half a minute to check your answers.

You will now have 10 minutes to transfer your answers to the listening answer sheet.

This is almost the end of the test. You now have one more minute to check all your answers.

That is the end of the Listening section of Model Test 4.

NOTE: Please photocopy the Answer Sheets on pages 407 to 412 to use for Model Tests.

IELTS Listening Answer Sheet

#		√ / X		#		√ / X
1		√ 1 X		21		√ 21 X
2		2		22		22
3		3		23		23
4		4		24		24
5		5		25		25
6		6		26		26
7		7		27		27
8		8		28		28
9		9		29		29
10		10		30		30
11		11		31		31
12		12		32		32
13		13		33		33
14		14		34		34
15		15		35		35
16		16		36		36
17		17		37		37
18		18		38		38
19		19		39		39
20		20		40		40
				Listening Total		

IELTS Reading Answer Sheet

Module taken:

Academic ▭   General Training ▭

1		✓ 1 ✗
2		▭ 2 ▭
3		▭ 3 ▭
4		▭ 4 ▭
5		▭ 5 ▭
6		▭ 6 ▭
7		▭ 7 ▭
8		▭ 8 ▭
9		▭ 9 ▭
10		▭ 10 ▭
11		▭ 11 ▭
12		▭ 12 ▭
13		▭ 13 ▭
14		▭ 14 ▭
15		▭ 15 ▭
16		▭ 16 ▭
17		▭ 17 ▭
18		▭ 18 ▭
19		▭ 19 ▭
20		▭ 20 ▭

21		✓ 21 ✗
22		▭ 22 ▭
23		▭ 23 ▭
24		▭ 24 ▭
25		▭ 25 ▭
26		▭ 26 ▭
27		▭ 27 ▭
28		▭ 28 ▭
29		▭ 29 ▭
30		▭ 30 ▭
31		▭ 31 ▭
32		▭ 32 ▭
33		▭ 33 ▭
34		▭ 34 ▭
35		▭ 35 ▭
36		▭ 36 ▭
37		▭ 37 ▭
38		▭ 38 ▭
39		▭ 39 ▭
40		▭ 40 ▭
	Listening Total	

Writing (Academic and General Training) Answer Sheet

Module: ACADEMIC ☐   GENERAL TRAINING ☐   (Tick as appropriate)

TASK 1

_____

_____

_____

_____

_____

_____

_____

_____

_____

_____

_____

_____

_____

_____

_____

_____

_____

_____

_____

_____

_____

_____

_____

-2-

Writing (Academic and General Training) Answer Sheet

TASK 2   -3-

-4-

NOTE:

The enclosed Audio CDs contain audio for the Listening Module exercises (Targets 1–13) and the Listening Modules in IELTS Model Tests 1, 2, 3, and 4.

CD Tracks:

CD#1:   Tracks 1 and 2:   Target 1—Making Assumptions

              Tracks 3 and 4:   Target 2—Understanding Numbers

              Tracks 5 and 6:   Target 3—Understanding the Alphabet

              Track 7:   Target 4—Listening for Descriptions

              Tracks 8–12:   Target 5—Listening for Time

              Tracks 13 and 14:   Target 6—Listening for Frequency

              Track 15:   Target 7—Listening for Similar Meanings

              Track 16:   Target 8—Listening for Emotions

              Track 17:   Target 9—Listening for an Explanation

              Track 18:   Target 10—Listening for Classifications

              Track 19:   Target 11—Listening for Comparisons and Contrasts

              Track 20:   Target 12—Listening for Negative Meanings

              Track 21:   Target 13—Listening for Chronology

              Tracks 22–29:   Model Test 1—Listening Module

CD#2:   Tracks 1–9   Model Test 2—Listening Module

              Tracks 10–17   Model Test 3—Listening Module

              Tracks 18–25   Model Test 4—Listening Module

BARRON'S

IELTS

PRACTICE EXAMS

with Audio CDs

Lin Lougheed
Ed.D., Teachers College
Columbia University

BARRON'S

All inquiries should be addressed to:
Barron's Educational Series, Inc.
250 Wireless Boulevard
Hauppauge, NY 11788
www.barronseduc.com

Library of Congress Catalog Card Number: 2010010641

ISBN-13: 978-0-7641-9798-7
ISBN-10: 0-7641-9798-3

Library of Congress Cataloging-in-Publication Data

Lougheed, Lin, 1946–
    IELTS practice exams : with audio cds / Lin Lougheed.
      p. cm.
    ISBN-13: 978-0-7641-9798-7
    ISBN-10: 0-7641-9798-3
    1. International English Language Testing System—Study guides. 2. English language—Textbooks for foreign speakers. 3. English language—Examinations—Study guides.
I. Barron's Educational Series, Inc. II. Title. III. Title: International English Language Testing System practice exams.
  PE1128.L6445   2010
    428.0076—dc22   2010010641

PRINTED IN THE UNITED STATES OF AMERICA

9 8 7 6 5 4

10%
POST-CONSUMER
WASTE
Paper contains a minimum
of 10% post-consumer
waste (PCW). Paper used
in this book was derived
from certified, sustainable
forestlands.

Contents

Introduction

WHAT IS IELTS?

The IELTS (International English Language Testing System) measures your English language proficiency for either academic or professional purposes. The Academic Module is for those planning to attend a university where English is the spoken language. The General Training Module is for those planning to live or work in an English-speaking country. The test is divided into four sections; each section tests a different language skill—Listening, Reading, Writing, and Speaking. The Listening and Speaking sections are the same for the Academic and General Training Modules, while the Reading and Writing sections differ.

Note

Audioscipts for the Listening section of each test can be found on pages 401–439. If you do not have access to an audio CD player, please refer to the audioscripts when prompted to listen to an audio passage.

HOW TO USE THIS BOOK

This book contains six complete practice tests for each training module; the tests match the level of the actual IELTS. Each practice test is divided into four sections: Listening, Reading, Writing, and Speaking. This follows the order the sections appear on the actual IELTS.

Although it is easier to work through the practice tests in that order, this is not necessary. You can study only those sections that you want to study. You can study them in any order.

STUDYING FOR THE ACADEMIC MODULE

If you plan to take the Academic Module, you can begin with an Academic Practice Test and complete all four parts of the test. (See the chart on page v.) You can check your answers by reading the Answer Explanations. You can check your answers at the end of each section or at the end of all four sections. The Answer Explanations will help you understand your incorrect responses.

If you are an Academic Module test taker, you do not have to take the General Training Module practice tests. The General Training Module does not contain anything you will see in the Academic Module of the IELTS. Of course, if you want more practice with English, you can learn more English by studying these sections. You can also improve your language skills and test-taking skills by studying *Barron's IELTS, 2nd Edition*.

Academic Module

Practice Test	Listening Pages	Reading Pages	Writing Pages	Speaking Pages
1	4–9	10–19	20–22	23
2	44–48	49–59	60–61	62
3	82–87	88–98	99–100	101
4	122–126	127–138	139–140	141
5	162–167	168–177	178–179	180
6	200–205	206–216	217–219	220

STUDYING FOR THE GENERAL TRAINING MODULE

If you plan to take the General Training Module, you should begin with an Academic Module, Listening section. The IELTS Listening section is the same for both Academic and General Training Modules.

After completing the Listening questions, go to a General Training Module Practice Test and complete the Reading and Writing questions. (See the chart below.) Then return to the Academic Practice Test to complete the Speaking questions. The IELTS Speaking section is the same for both Academic and General Training Modules.

By following this order, you will complete the practice test questions in the same order that you will complete them when you take the actual IELTS. You can check your answers by checking the Answer Key and reading the Answer Explanations that follow each test. You can do this at the end of each section or at the end of all four sections.

General Training Module

Practice Test	Listening Pages	Reading Pages	Writing Pages	Speaking Pages
1	4–9	242–251	252–253	23
2	44–48	268–277	278–279	62
3	82–87	294–305	306–307	101
4	122–126	322–331	332–333	141
5	162–167	348–358	359–360	180
6	200–205	374–385	386–387	220

USING THE ANSWER EXPLANATIONS

At the end of each test, you will find the Answer Explanations. By studying these explanatory answers, you will learn why your answer choice was correct or why it was wrong.

Of course, in the Writing and Speaking sections, there are many possible answers. In the Answer Explanations for the Writing section, you are shown a model answer that would receive a high band score.

The model answers for the Writing section demonstrate elements found in a high band score, including:

- addressing all parts of the task
- fluent cohesion of ideas
- well-developed paragraphs
- accurate use of a wide range of vocabulary
- fluent use of a wide variety of grammatical structures
- all paragraphs are indented
- no contractions
- no personal references except in personal letters or personal opinion tasks

In the Answer Explanations for the Speaking section, you are shown a sample of the type of answers that would successfully complete the task. However, these are only models. During the actual IELTS Speaking section, an examiner will guide you through a conversation. It will be a normal conversation, not a scripted performance.

The Answer Explanations for the Speaking section demonstrate elements found in a high band score, such as:

- appropriate use of a variety of vocabulary
- use of a variety of well-connected sentence structures with consistent accuracy
- ability to discuss a variety of topics fluently and developing the topics well
- natural and accurate use of idioms

American English vs. British English

This book uses American English spelling, pronunciation style, and vocabulary. There are footnotes if British spelling or grammar differ from American. You will not be penalized if you use American spelling when you write your answers on the IELTS.

When you answer the questions in the Speaking section of the IELTS, you will also be scored on your pronunciation and ability to speak clearly.

IELTS Study Contract

You must make a commitment to study English. Sign a contract with yourself. A contract is a promise. You should not break a contract, especially a contract with yourself.

- Print your name on the blank on the first line of the contract.
- On lines 5–9, write the amount of time you will spend each week studying English. Think about how much time you can study English every day and every week. Make your schedule realistic.

IELTS STUDY CONTRACT

I, _____, promise to study for the IELTS. I will begin my study with *Barron's Practice Tests for the IELTS*, and I will also study English on my own.

I understand that to improve my English I need to spend time on English.

I promise to study English _____ hours a week.

I will spend _____ hours a week listening to English.

I will spend _____ hours a week writing English.

I will spend _____ hours a week speaking English.

I will spend _____ hours a week reading English.

This is a contract with myself. I promise to fulfill the terms of this contract.

_____   _____

Signed   Date

- Sign your name and date the contract on the last line.
- At the end of each week, add up your hours. Did you meet the requirements of your contract?

Self-Study Activities

Here are some ways you can study English on your own. Check the ones you plan to try. Add some of your own ideas.

INTERNET-BASED SELF-STUDY ACTIVITIES

Listening

_____ Podcasts on the Internet
_____ News websites: ABC, BBC, CBS, CNN, NBC
_____ Movies and TV shows in English
_____ YouTube
_____ _____
_____ _____

Speaking

_____ Use Skype to talk to English speakers
_____ _____
_____ _____

Writing

_____ Write e-mails to website contacts
_____ Write a blog
_____ Leave comments on blogs
_____ Post messages in a chat room
_____ Use Facebook and MySpace
_____ _____
_____ _____

Reading

_____ Read news and magazine articles online
_____ Do web research on topics that interest you
_____ Follow blogs that interest you
_____ _____
_____ _____

OTHER SELF-STUDY ACTIVITIES

Listening

_____ Listen to CNN and BBC on the radio or on TV
_____ Watch movies and TV shows in English
_____ Listen to music in English
_____ _____
_____ _____

Speaking

_____ Describe what you see and what you do out loud
_____ Practice speaking with a conversation buddy

_____ _____

_____ _____

Writing

_____ Write a daily journal
_____ Write letters to an English speaker
_____ Make lists of the things you see every day
_____ Write descriptions of your family and friends

_____ _____

_____ _____

Reading

_____ Read newspapers and magazines in English
_____ Read books in English

_____ _____

_____ _____

EXAMPLES OF SELF-STUDY ACTIVITIES

Whether you read an article in a newspaper or a website, you can use that article in a variety of ways to practice reading, writing, speaking, and listening in English.

- Read about it.
- Make notes about it.
- Paraphrase, summarize, or write comments about it.
- Give a talk or presentation about it.
- Record or make a video of your presentation.
- Listen to or watch what you recorded. Write down your presentation.
- Find and correct your mistakes.
- Do it all again.

Plan a Trip

Go to *www.concierge.com*

Choose a city, choose a hotel, go to that hotel's website, and choose a room. Then choose some sites to visit (*reading*). Write a report about the city (*writing*). Tell why you want to go there. Describe the hotel and the room you will reserve. Tell what sites you plan to visit and when. Where will you eat? How will you get around?

Now write a letter to someone recommending this place (*writing*). Imagine you have to give a lecture on your planned trip. Make a video of yourself talking about this place (*speaking*). Then watch the video and write down what you said (*listening*). Correct any mistakes you made and record the presentation again. Then choose another city, and do this again.

Shop for an Electronic Product

Go to *www.cnet.com*

Choose an electronic product and read about it (*reading*). Write a report about the product (*writing*). Tell why you want to buy one. Describe its features.

Now write a letter to someone recommending this product (*writing*). Imagine you have to give a talk about this product. Make a video of yourself talking about this product (*speaking*). Then watch the video and write down what you said (*listening*). Correct any mistakes you made and record the presentation again. Then choose another product and do this again.

Discuss a Book or CD

Go to *www.amazon.com*

Choose a book or CD or any product. Read the product description and review (*reading*). Write a report about the product (*writing*). Tell why you want to buy one or why it is interesting to you. Describe its features.

Now write a letter to someone recommending this product (*writing*). Pretend you have to give a talk about this product. Make a video of yourself talking about this product (*speaking*). Then watch the video and write down what you said (*listening*). Correct any mistakes you made and record the presentation again. Then choose another product and do this again.

Discuss Any Subject

Go to *http://simple.wikipedia.org/wiki/Main_Page*

This website is written in simple English. Pick any subject and read the entry (*reading*).

Write a short essay about the topic (*writing*). Give a presentation about it. Record the presentation (*speaking*). Then watch the video and write down what you said (*listening*). Correct any mistakes you made and record the presentation again. Then choose another topic and do this again.

Discuss Any Event

Go to *http://news.google.com*

Google News has a variety of links. Pick one event and read the articles about it (*reading*).

Write a short essay about the event (*writing*). Give a presentation about it. Record the presentation (*speaking*). Then watch the video and write down what you said (*listening*). Correct any mistakes you made and record the presentation again. Then choose another event and do this again.

Report the News

Listen to an English language news report on the radio or watch a news program on TV (*listening*). Take notes as you listen. Write a summary of what you heard (*writing*).

Pretend you are a news reporter. Use the information from your notes to report the news. Record the presentation (*speaking*). Then watch the video and write down what you said (*listening*). Correct any mistakes you made and record the presentation again. Then listen to another news program and do this again.

Express an Opinion

Read a letter to the editor in the newspaper (*reading*). Write a letter in response in which you say whether you agree with the opinion expressed in the first letter. Explain why (*writing*).

Pretend you have to give a talk explaining your opinion. Record yourself giving the talk (*speaking*). Then watch the video and write down what you said (*listening*). Correct any mistakes you made and record the presentation again. Then read another letter to the editor and do this again.

Review a Book or Movie

Read a book (*reading*). Think about your opinion of the book. What did you like about it? What didn't you like about it? Who would you recommend it to and why? Pretend you are a book reviewer for a newspaper. Write a review of the book with your opinion and recommendations (*writing*).

Give an oral presentation about the book. Explain what the book is about and what your opinion is. Record yourself giving the presentation (*speaking*). Then watch the video and write down what you said (*listening*). Correct any mistakes you made and record the presentation again. Then read another book and do this again.

You can do this same activity after watching a movie (*listening*).

Summarize a TV Show

Watch a TV show in English (*listening*). Take notes as you listen. After watching, write a summary of the show (*writing*).

Use your notes to give an oral summary of the show. Explain the characters, setting, and plot. Record yourself speaking (*speaking*). Then watch the video and write down what you said (*listening*). Correct any mistakes you made and record the presentation again. Then watch another TV show and do this again.

PART 1

ACADEMIC MODULE

PRACTICE TEST 1

PRACTICE TEST 2

PRACTICE TEST 3

PRACTICE TEST 4

PRACTICE TEST 5

PRACTICE TEST 6

NOTE TO GENERAL TRAINING MODULE TEST-TAKERS
If you are studying for the General Training Module Test, you will take the Listening and Speaking sections in the Academic Module Practice Tests. The Listening and Speaking sections are the same for all test takers. See the charts on page v for page numbers.

ACADEMIC MODULE
PRACTICE TEST 1

Academic Module
Practice Test 1

Candidate Name and Number: _____

INTERNATIONAL ENGLISH LANGUAGE TESTING SYSTEM

LISTENING

TIME APPROX. 30 MINUTES

Instructions to Candidates

Do not open this booklet until you are told to do so.

Write your name and candidate number in the space at the top of this page.

You should answer all questions.

All the recordings will be played ONCE only.

Write all your answers on the test pages.

At the end of the test, you will be given ten minutes to transfer your answers to an Answer Sheet. (The answer sheet can be found on page 25.)

Do not remove the booklet from the examination room.

Information for Candidates

There are **40** questions on this question paper.

The test is divided as follows:

Section 1	Questions 1–10
Section 2	Questions 11–20
Section 3	Questions 21–30
Section 4	Questions 31–40

SECTION 1   QUESTIONS 1–10

Note

If you do not have access to an audio CD player, please refer to the audio-scripts starting on page 401 when prompted to listen to an audio passage.

Questions 1–4

Complete the schedule below.
Write **NO MORE THAN THREE WORDS** *for each answer.*

Example: *Globetrotters*   Language School
Class Schedule

Chinese
Level: Advanced

Days: **1** _____ evenings

Japanese

Level: **2** _____
Days: Tuesday and Thursday mornings

Level: **3** _____
Days: Monday, Wednesday, and Friday mornings

French
Level: Intermediate

Days: Friday **4** _____

Questions 5–8

Complete the information below.
Write **NO MORE THAN ONE NUMBER** *for each answer.*

Tuition Information

One week   **5** $ _____

Four weeks   **6** $ _____

Six weeks   **7** $ _____

Twelve weeks   **8** $ _____

Questions 9 and 10

Complete the sentences below.
*Write **NO MORE THAN THREE WORDS** for each answer.*

9 Students can register for a class by visiting _____.

10 _____ is in charge of student registration.

SECTION 2   QUESTIONS 11–20

Questions 11–15

Label the map below.
*Write the correct letter, **A–J**, next to questions 11–15.*

City Shopping District

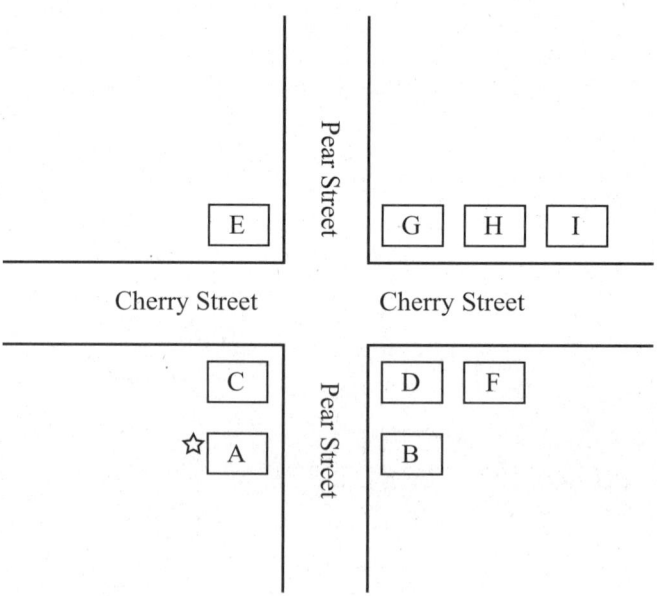

11 Harbor[1] View Bookstore

12 Pear Café

13 Souvenir Store

14 Art Gallery

15 Harbor Park

---

[1]*British: harbour*

Questions 16–20

Complete the sentences below.
Write **ONE WORD ONLY** *for each answer.*

Harbor Park

16 The park was built in _____.

17 A _____ stands in the center[2] of the park.

18 Take the path through the _____.

19 In the middle of the garden is a _____.

20 A _____ takes you down to the harbor and a view of the boats.

SECTION 3   QUESTIONS 21–30

Questions 21–24

Complete the information about the archives.
Write **NO MORE THAN THREE WORDS AND/OR A NUMBER** *for each answer.*

Welcome to City Archives

The following people may use the archives:

- University students with a valid **21** _____
- City residents with payment of **22** _____
- All others: Special permission from the director is required.

Hours:
Days: **23** _____ through _____
Hours: **24** 9:30 A.M. until _____ P.M.

---

[2]*British: centre*

Questions 25–30

What can be found on each floor¹ of the archives building?
*Write the correct letter, **A–G** next to questions 25–30.*

CITY ARCHIVES

A nineteenth-century documents
B maps
C personal papers
D photographs
E books about the city
F newspapers
G information about the woolen² mill

Floor of the building

25 basement   _____

26 ground floor   _____

27 second floor   _____

28 third floor   _____

29 fourth floor   _____

30 fifth floor   _____

SECTION 4   *QUESTIONS 31–40*

Questions 31–33

Complete the notes below.
*Write **NO MORE THAN TWO WORDS** for each answer.*

	Historical Uses of Wind Power
Ancient China	Windmills were used to **31** _____
Ancient Persia	Farmers used wind power to **32** _____
The Netherlands	People used windmills to **33** _____

---

¹*In the United States, the ground floor is considered the first floor; the next floor up is the second floor, and so on.*
²*British: woollen*

Questions 34–40

Complete the chart[1] below.
Write **NO MORE THAN TWO WORDS** *for each answer.*

Wind Power

Advantages	Disadvantages
Unlike oil and coal, wind power does not cause **34** _____	The cost of the initial investment is high.
There are limited supplies of oil and coal, but wind is a **35** _____	The **37** _____ of the wind is not constant.
It **36** _____ to generate electricity with the wind.	Wind turbines are usually located far from **38** _____
Wind turbines do not take up much land.	Wind turbines may spoil **39** _____
	Wind turbines are as **40** _____ as a high-speed car.

Take ten minutes to transfer your answers onto the Answer Sheet on page 25.

---

[1] *British: table*

Academic Module
Practice Test 1

Candidate Name and Number: _____

INTERNATIONAL ENGLISH LANGUAGE TESTING SYSTEM

ACADEMIC READING

TIME 1 HOUR

Instructions to Candidates

Do not open this booklet until you are told to do so.

Write your name and candidate number in the space at the top of this page.

Start at the beginning of the test and work through it.

You should answer all questions.

If you cannot do a particular question, leave it and go on to the next. You can return to it later.

All answers must be written on the Answer Sheet. (The answer sheet can be found on page 26.)

Do not remove the booklet from the examination room.

Information for Candidates

There are **40** questions on this question paper.

The test is divided as follows:

Reading Passage 1	Questions 1–13
Reading Passage 2	Questions 14–26
Reading Passage 3	Questions 27–40

READING PASSAGE 1

You should spend about 20 minutes on **Questions 1–13**, *which are based on Reading Passage 1 below.*

Odonata

Odonata is the order of insects that includes dragonflies and damselflies. To the human eye, their shining colors[1] and delicate-looking wings make them beautiful creatures to behold. In the natural world, however, they are fearsome predators. Dragonflies and damselflies get their name from the powerful serrated jaws they use to tear apart their prey. The word *odonata* means "toothed jaw."

Dragonflies and damselflies are often confused with each other because they are very similar. Close observation reveals the differences between them. The most obvious difference is the way they hold their wings while at rest. Dragonflies hold their wings out to the side while damselflies fold their wings back. Dragonflies have very large eyes that seem to cover the entire face because they are so close together that they touch each other. Damselflies' eyes are smaller, and there is a space between them. Dragonflies are larger and stronger animals than damselflies and fly longer distances. Thus, they can be found in woods and fields away from the water. Damselflies are not such strong fliers and are most often seen around the edges of ponds and streams since they do not normally fly far from the water.

The largest odonata living today are the Hawaiian endemic dragonfly and the Central American damselfly, each of these species having a wingspan of 19 centimeters. The smallest is the libellulid dragonfly, native to east Asia, with a wingspan of just 20 millimeters. Fossils have been discovered that prove that dragonflies have been in existence for over 300 million years. The largest dragonfly fossil ever found belongs to the now-extinct *meganeura monyi*, which lived 300 million years ago and had a wingspan of 75 centimeters. This giant was a fearsome predator indeed, which feasted on small amphibians as well as on other insects.

Dragonflies and damselflies both lay their eggs on or just below the surface of the water in a pond or stream. Some species lay their eggs on the stem of an aquatic plant. The babies emerge from the eggs in the form of nymphs. They live underwater, breathing through gills and preying upon water insects, tadpoles, small fish, and even other nymphs. They hunt by hiding in the shadows at the bottom of a pond or stream, waiting for prey animals to swim by. They have a special lip that they can extend far forward in order to grab their prey when it comes close. Depending on the species, they live this way for several months or even several years. As the nymph grows, it sheds its skin several times. Finally, it leaves the water and sheds its skin one last time. The adult emerges, ready to live the next few weeks or months on land and in the air. The adults do not live for more than four months, and many species live as adults for only a few weeks.

---

[1] *British: colours*

The exceptional visual abilities and flying skills of dragonflies and damselflies make them very adept hunters. Their special eyes give them a nearly 360-degree field of vision, and they can detect even the smallest movement or flash of light caused by other flying insects. They have two sets of wings that can move independently of each other. This gives them great maneuverability[1] in the air, which is important to these creatures because they catch their prey while flying. They can hover, make sharp turns, and fly backward. Some species of dragonflies can fly 60 kilometers an hour or more. Their prey consists of flying insects such as mosquitoes, deerflies, smaller dragonflies, and butterflies and moths. One species of dragonfly takes spiders out of their webs.

Bloodthirsty predators that they are, dragonflies and damselflies are prey for other animals in their turn. The nymphs are eaten by fish, frogs, toads, and other aquatic creatures. In the adult stage, they are hunted by birds, frogs, and larger dragonflies and damselflies. They might also be caught in a spider's web. What goes around comes around.

Questions 1–6

Which of the facts below are true of dragonflies, and which are true of damselflies, according to the information in the passage? On lines 1–6 on your answer sheet, write:

A if it is a fact about dragonflies only

B if it is a fact about damselflies only

C if it is a fact about both dragonflies and damselflies

1 They have sawlike jaws.

2 They hold their wings on their backs while resting.

3 Their eyes have a gap between them.

4 They can be seen in fields at a distance from ponds and streams.

5 The largest species has a wingspan of 19 centimeters.

6 The largest fossil has a wingspan of 75 centimeters.

[1] *British: manouevrability*

Questions 7–13

*Complete the notes about the life cycle of odonata below. Choose your answers from the box below and write the correct letters, **A–K**, on lines 7–13 on your answer sheet.*

The eggs are laid **7** _____. The young dragonflies and damselflies, called **8** _____, live underwater for a few **9** _____. They eat small water animals, catching their food **10** _____. When they are almost fully grown, they leave the water. The adults live for only a few **11** _____. They are skillful[1] **12** _____ and catch their prey **13** _____.

A	in the air
B	with their lips
C	tadpoles
D	fliers
E	near the water's surface
F	nymphs
G	at the bottom of a pond
H	months or years
I	weeks or months
J	swimmers
K	with their wings

READING PASSAGE 2

*You should spend about 20 minutes on **Questions 14–26**, which are based on Reading Passage 2 below.*

History of Fire Fighting and Prevention

More than two thousand years ago, Roman emperor Augustus organized[2] a group of watchmen whose job was mainly to look out for fires and sound an alarm in the event of one. For many centuries that followed, fire equipment was limited to buckets of water that got passed from person to person. The ax[3] was

---

[1]*British: skilful*

[2]*British: organised*

[3]*British: axe*

later found to be a useful tool both for removing fuel in large fires and for opening holes to allow smoke and flames to escape from burning buildings. Watchmen also learned to create firebreaks with long hooked poles and ropes in order to pull down structures that provided fuel for a fire. In 1066, in order to reduce the risk of fire in thatched-roof houses, King William the Conqueror made a ruling: Citizens had to extinguish their cooking fires at night. His term *couvre-feu,* meaning "cover fire," is the origin of the modern day term *curfew,* which no longer carries a literal translation.

The event that had the largest influence in the history of fire fighting was the Great Fire of London in 1666. The devastating blaze originated at the King's Bakery near the London Bridge. At the onset, Lord Mayor Bludworth showed little concern for the fire, assuming it would extinguish itself before he could organize a group of men to attend to it. However, the summer of 1666 had been uncharacteristically hot and dry, and the wooden houses nearby caught fire quickly. Within a short time, the wind had carried the fire across the city, burning down over 300 houses in its path. Although the procedure of pulling down buildings to prevent a fire from spreading was standard in Britain, the mayor grew concerned over the cost it would involve to rebuild the city and ordered that the surrounding structures be left intact. By the time the king ordered the destruction of buildings in the fire's path, the fire was too large to control. It was not until the Duke of York ordered the Paper House to be destroyed in order to create a crucial firebreak that the London fire finally began to lose its fuel.

When it became clear that four-fifths of the city had been destroyed by the fire, drastic measures were taken in London to create a system of organized fire prevention. At the hands of architects such as Christopher Wren, most of London was rebuilt using stone and brick, materials that were far less flammable than wood and straw. Because of the long history of fires in London, those who could afford to build new homes and businesses began to seek insurance for their properties. As insurance became a profitable business, companies soon realized[1] the monetary benefits of hiring men to extinguish fires. In the early years of insurance companies, all insured properties were marked with an insurance company's name or logo. If a fire broke out and a building did not contain the insurance mark, the fire brigades were called away and the building was left to burn.

The British insurance companies were largely responsible for employing people to develop new technology for extinguishing fires. The first fire engines were simple tubs on wheels that were pulled to the location of the fire, with water being supplied by a bucket brigade. Eventually, a hand pump was designed to push the water out of the tub into a hose with a nozzle. The pump allowed for a steady stream of water to shoot through a hose directly at the fire source. Before long, companies began to utilize water pipes made from hollowed tree trunks that were built under the roadway. By digging down into the road, firemen could insert a hole into the tree-trunk pipe and access the water to feed into the pump.

---

[1] *British: realised*

Fire fighting became a competitive business, as companies fought to be the first to arrive at a scene to access the water pipes. After a series of fires destroyed parts of London, fire-fighting companies were forced to reconsider their intentions. By the eighteenth century, fire brigades began to join forces, and in 1833 the Sun Insurance Company along with ten other London companies created the London Fire Engine Establishment. In 1865, the government became involved, bringing standards to both fire prevention and fire fighting and establishing London's Metropolitan Fire Brigade. Though the firemen were well paid, they were constantly on duty and thus obliged to call their fire station home for both themselves and their families.

New technology for fighting fires continued to develop in both Europe and the New World. Leather hoses with couplings that joined the lengths together were hand-sewn in the Netherlands and used until the late1800s, when rubber hoses became available. The technology for steam engine fire trucks was available in Britain and America in 1829, but most brigades were hesitant to use them until the 1850s. It was the public that eventually forced the brigades into putting the more efficient equipment to use. In the early 1900s, when the internal-combustion engine was developed, the trucks became motorized.[1] This was a timely advancement in fire-fighting history, as World War I put added pressure on brigades throughout the world.

Questions 14–20

Complete the chart below.
Use **NO MORE THAN THREE WORDS** *from the text for each answer. Write your answers on lines 14–20 on your answer sheet.*

Cause	Effect
Men used poles and ropes to pull down buildings near a fire.	The fire did not have **14** _____.
Thatched-roof houses burn down easily.	The King ordered people to **15** _____ their fires nightly.
At the time of the Great Fire of London, the weather was **16** _____.	The fire spread quickly.
The Mayor of London thought it would be too expensive to **17** _____.	He told people not to pull down buildings in the fire's path.
The Great Fire destroyed most of London.	People built new buildings out of **18** _____.
There had been many **19** _____ in London over time.	People started to buy insurance to protect their homes.
Insurance companies did not want to pay for rebuilding clients' houses destroyed by fire.	Insurance companies hired men to **20** _____.

---

[1] *British: motorised*

Questions 21–23

*Choose the correct letters, **A–C**, and write them on lines 21–23 on your answer sheet.*

21 The first fire engines

    A carried water to the site of the fire.
    B used hand pumps.
    C had very long hoses.

22 In 1865,

    A London was destroyed by a series of fires.
    B fire brigades began to join forces.
    C the Metropolitan Fire Brigade was established.

23 Firemen who worked for the Metropolitan Fire Brigade

    A earned low salaries.
    B lived at the fire station.
    C were not allowed to marry.

Questions 24–26

Do the following statements agree with the information in the reading passage? On lines 24–26 on your answer sheet, write:

YES	if the statement agrees with the views of the writer
NO	if the statement disagrees with the views of the writer
NOT GIVEN	if there is no information on this in the passage

24 Leather hoses for fire fighting were made by machine.

25 Steam engine fire trucks were used until the early 1900s.

26 Fires caused a great deal of damage in London during World War I.

READING PASSAGE 3

You should spend about 20 minutes on **Questions 27–40**, *which are based on Reading Passage 3 below.*

The Luddites

The term *Luddite* is used to refer to a person who is opposed to new technology. The word derives from the name Ned Ludd, a man who may or may not have actually existed. The original Luddites were textile workers in early nineteenth-century England who protested changes brought on by the industrial revolution. These weavers made lace and stockings by hand, carrying out their craft independently in their homes according to traditional methods. In the 1800s, automated power looms and stocking frames were introduced, radically changing the traditional work system. Weavers' work was moved from individual homes to factories; individuals could not afford to buy the new machines for themselves. The new machines were not difficult to run. They could be operated by unskilled workers and turned out an inferior product, but they produced large quantities cheaply, which was the aim of the new factory owners. The makers of finely crafted, handmade textiles could not compete with the new machines. Instead of continuing their tradition as skilled, independent workers, they would have to go to work in factories for low wages.

The industrial revolution was happening everywhere. In the textile-producing towns of England, workers focused on the new weaving machines as the source of their troubles. The height of Luddite activity occurred in the years 1811–1812. Groups of men, often in disguise, would arrive at a factory and make demands for higher wages and better working conditions. If these demands were not met, the group retaliated by smashing the factory machines. These groups often claimed that they were working under the command of General Ned Ludd, and thus came to be called Luddites.

Who was Ned Ludd? Rumors[1] about this mysterious person abounded. He came to be associated with that traditional champion of the poor, Robin Hood. The original Luddite activity was centered[2] around Nottingham, and many said that Ned Ludd hid out in nearby Sherwood Forest, just as the legendary Robin Hood had. According to another tradition, Ned Ludd was a weaver who had accidentally broken two stocking frames, and from that, came to be the one blamed any time an expensive piece of weaving equipment was damaged. Whoever Ned Ludd may or may not have been, riots protesting the new factories were carried out in his name throughout England's textile-producing region.

Workers' families suffered as wages fell and food prices rose. There were food riots in several towns, and Luddite activity spread. In the winter of 1812, the

---

[1] *British: rumours*

[2] *British: centred*

Frame-Breaking Act was passed, making the destruction of factory equipment a crime punishable by death. The government sent thousands of troops into areas affected by the riots. In the spring of that year, several factory owners were killed during Luddite riots, and a number of textile workers died as well. Following one of the largest incidents, when rioters set fire to a mill in Westhoughton, four rioters, including a young boy, were executed. In another incident that spring, a group of over a thousand workers attacked a mill in Lancashire with sticks and rocks. When they were beaten back by armed guards protecting the mill, they moved to the mill owner's house and burned it down. The wave of violence resulted in a crack down by the government. Suspected Luddites were arrested and imprisoned, and many of them were hanged.

By the summer of 1812, Luddite activity had begun to die down, although there continued to be sporadic incidents over the next several years. In 1816, a bad harvest and economic downturn led to a small revival of rioting. In June of that year, workers attacked two mills, smashing equipment and causing thousands of dollars worth of damage. Government troops were brought in to stop the violence. In the end, six of the rioters were executed for their participation. However, rioting never again reached the levels it had in 1811 and 1812.

The Luddites were short-lived, but they left an impressive mark. They were responsible for destroying close to one thousand weaving machines during the height of their activity in 1811–1812, as well as burning down several factories. Beyond the physical damage, however, they left their mark in people's minds. The famed English novelist Charlotte Brontë set her novel *Shirley* in Yorkshire at the time of the riots. This novel is still widely read today. In our present time of rapid technological change, people who are concerned about the pace of technological advance often call themselves Neo-Luddites. Although the responses to it may differ, concern about the changes brought on by technology continues.

Questions 27–32

*Match each cause in List A with its effect in List B. Write the correct letter, **A–H**, on lines 27–32 on your answer sheet. There are more effects in List B than you will need, so you will not use them all.*

List A Causes

27 The new weaving machines were expensive to buy.

28 The new weaving machines were easy to operate.

29 Workers' demands for better pay and conditions were not met.

30 Rioting spread to many towns.

31 A law was passed against destroying factory equipment.

32 Economic conditions worsened in 1816.

List B Effects

A Troops were sent into the area.

B Weavers stopped working at home and went to work in factories.

C Rioters often wore disguises.

D Workers destroyed factory equipment.

E Many rioters were hanged.

F Charlotte Brontë wrote a novel about the Luddites.

G Prices went up, and salaries went down.

H Factory owners did not need to hire skilled weavers.

I Luddite rioting resumed for a short while.

J People compared Ned Ludd to Robin Hood.

Questions 33–40

Do the following statements agree with the information given in the passage? On lines 33–40 on your answer sheet, write:

TRUE	if the statement agrees with the information
FALSE	if the statement contradicts the information
NOT GIVEN	if there is no information on this

33 A Luddite is a person who resists new technology.

34 Before the nineteenth century, weavers made lace by hand.

35 Factory owners as well as workers died as a result of Luddite rioting.

36 The Luddite movement did not spread beyond England.

37 Nobody knows for certain who Ned Ludd was.

38 Worker protests during the economic downturn of 1816 were nonviolent.

39 Luddite activity lasted for many years.

40 Neo-Luddites do not use computers.

Academic Module
Practice Test 1

Candidate Name and Number: _____

INTERNATIONAL ENGLISH LANGUAGE TESTING SYSTEM

ACADEMIC WRITING

TIME 1 HOUR

Instructions to Candidates

Do not open this booklet until you are told to do so.

Write your name and candidate number in the space at the top of this page.

All answers must be written on the separate answer booklet provided. (Answer sheets can be found beginning on page 27.)

Do not remove the booklet from the examination room.

Information for Candidates

There are **2** tasks on this question paper.

You must do **both** tasks.

Under-length answers will be penalized.[1]

---

[1] *British: penalised*

WRITING TASK 1

You should spend about 20 minutes on this task. Write at least 150 words.

The diagram below explains the process of making wood pellets, used to heat buildings.

Summarize[1] the information by selecting and reporting the main features, and make comparisons where relevant.

How Wood Pellets Are Made

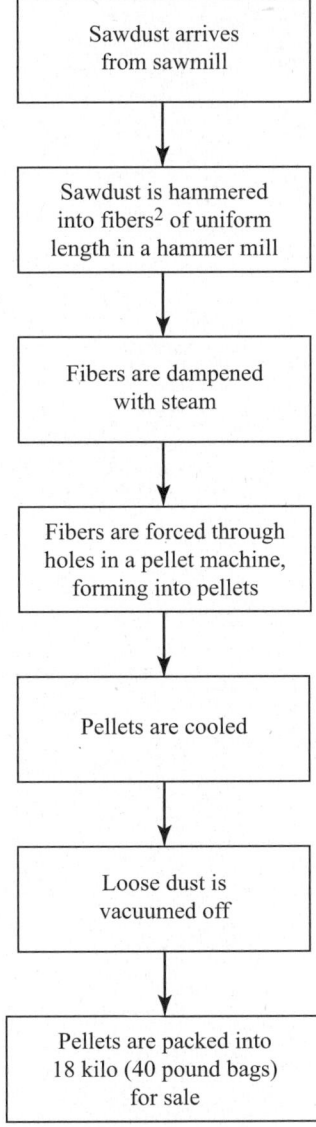

Wood pellets manufactured by this process are suitable for use in both pellet stoves and pellet furnaces.

---

[1] *British: Summarise*
[2] *British: fibres*

WRITING TASK 2

You should spend about 40 minutes on this task. Write at least 250 words.

Write about the following topic:

Everybody should be allowed admission to university study programs[1] regardless of their level of academic ability.

To what extent do you agree or disagree with this statement? Give reasons for your answer and include any relevant examples from your own knowledge or experience.

---

[1] *British: programmes*

SPEAKING

Examiner questions:

Part 1

Describe the neighborhood[1] where you live.

What do you like about living there?

What do you dislike about your neighborhood?

What kind of neighborhood would you like to live in?

Do you like walking? Why or why not?

Are there places you can walk near your house?

Do people in your country like walking? Why or why not?

What other kinds of exercise do you enjoy?

Part 2

Describe a friend who is important to you.

> You should say:
>
> > The name of your friend
> >
> > When and where you met this friend
> >
> > What kinds of things you and this friend like to do together and explain why this friend is important to you

> You will have one to two minutes to talk about this topic.
>
> You will have one minute to prepare what you are going to say.

Part 3

Generally, friendships are important to people?

How can friends help each other?

Do people spend more time with friends or with relatives?

How do our friendships change as we grow older?

---

[1] *British: neighbourhood*

Practice Test 1–Academic Module
IELTS LISTENING ANSWER SHEET

1. _____

2. _____

3. _____

4. _____

5. _____

6. _____

7. _____

8. _____

9. _____

10. _____

11. _____

12. _____

13. _____

14. _____

15. _____

16. _____

17. _____

18. _____

19. _____

20. _____

21. _____

22. _____

23. _____

24. _____

25. _____

26. _____

27. _____

28. _____

29. _____

30. _____

31. _____

32. _____

33. _____

34. _____

35. _____

36. _____

37. _____

38. _____

39. _____

40. _____

Practice Test 1–Academic Module
IELTS READING ANSWER SHEET

1. _____

2. _____

3. _____

4. _____

5. _____

6. _____

7. _____

8. _____

9. _____

10. _____

11. _____

12. _____

13. _____

14. _____

15. _____

16. _____

17. _____

18. _____

19. _____

20. _____

21. _____

22. _____

23. _____

24. _____

25. _____

26. _____

27. _____

28. _____

29. _____

30. _____

31. _____

32. _____

33. _____

34. _____

35. _____

36. _____

37. _____

38. _____

39. _____

40. _____

Practice Test 1–Academic Module
WRITING TASK 1

Writing Task 1 *continued*

Practice Test 1—Academic Module
WRITING TASK 2

Writing Task 2 *continued*

_____

_____

_____

_____

_____

_____

_____

_____

_____

_____

_____

_____

_____

_____

_____

_____

_____

_____

_____

_____

_____

_____

_____

Writing Task 2 *continued*

_____

_____

_____

_____

_____

_____

_____

_____

_____

_____

_____

_____

_____

_____

_____

_____

_____

_____

_____

_____

_____

Answer Key
PRACTICE TEST 1—ACADEMIC MODULE

Listening

1. Wednesday and Friday	11. A	21. identification card/ID	31. pump water
2. intermediate	12. C	22. an annual fee	32. grind grain
3. beginning	13. F	23. Tuesday; Sunday	33. drain lakes
4. mornings	14. H	24. 8:30	34. pollution
5. $125	15. I	25. D	35. renewable resource
6. $410	16. 1876	26. A	36. costs less
7. $575	17. statue	27. F	37. strength
8. $1,050	18. woods	28. B	38. cities
9. the school office	19. fountain	29. G	39. the scenery
10. Mr. Lindsay	20. staircase	30. C	40. noisy

Reading

1. C	11. I	21. A	31. E
2. B	12. D	22. C	32. I
3. B	13. A	23. B	33. True
4. A	14. fuel	24. No	34. True
5. C	15. put out	25. Yes	35. True
6. A	16. hot and dry	26. Not Given	36. Not Given
7. E	17. rebuild the city	27. B	37. True
8. F	18. stone and brick	28. H	38. False
9. H	19. fires	29. D	39. False
10. B	20. extinguish fires	30. A	40. Not Given

Answer Explanations

ACADEMIC MODULE—PRACTICE TEST 1

Listening

1. *Wednesday and Friday* evenings is when the advanced Chinese class meets, and the man can't take that class because he works evenings.

2. *intermediate.* This is the level of the Japanese class that meets Tuesday and Thursday mornings.

3. *beginning.* This is the level of the Japanese class that meets Monday, Wednesday, and Friday mornings.

4. *mornings.* The intermediate French class meets on Friday mornings.

5. *$125* is the cost if the student pays one week at a time.

6. *$410* is the cost of four weeks of classes.

7. *$575* is the cost for a six-week class.

8. *$1,050* is the cost of twelve weeks of classes.

9. *the school office.* "What you'll need to do is to visit the school office today or tomorrow."

10. *Mr. Lindsay.* "When you arrive, ask for Mr. Lindsay. He is in charge of student registration."

11. **(A)** The tour begins at the bookstore, marked with a star.

12. **(C)** The café is the next building up from the bookstore.

13. **(F)** On the corner is the clothing store, and the souvenir store is next to that.

14. **(H)** The art gallery is one building down from the corner and across the street from the souvenir store.

15. **(I)** Harbor Park is next to the art gallery.

16. *1876.* The speaker says, "Captain Jones designed the park himself, and it was built in 1876."

17. *statue.* The speaker says, "Exactly in the center of the park a statue of Captain Jones was erected, and it's still standing there today."

18. *woods.* The speaker says, "you can follow the path that goes through the woods just behind."

19. *fountain.* The speaker says, "It will lead you to a lovely garden, in the middle of which is a fountain."

20. *staircase.* The speaker says, "There, you'll find a wooden staircase, which will take you down to the harbor."

21. *identification card/ID* The librarian says, "All you need to do is show your university identification card . . . ."

22. *an annual fee.* The librarian says, "City residents pay an annual fee . . . ."

23. *Tuesday; Sunday.* The librarian says, "So you can come any day, Tuesday through Sunday . . . ."

24. *8:30.* The librarian says, we're open from nine thirty in the morning until eight thirty in the evening.

25. **(D)** The librarian says, "Yes, we store all the photographs in the basement."

26. **(A)** The librarian says, "Now, if you're interested in seeing documents from the nineteenth century, those are here on the ground floor."

27. **(F)** The librarian says, "No, all the newspapers from the earliest ones, in the eighteenth century, up to the current time, are on the second floor."

28. **(B)** The student mentions the room devoted to maps, and the librarian remarks that the room is on the third floor.

29. **(G)** The student asks, "What's this on the fourth floor—Ogden's Woolen Mill?"

30. **(C)** The librarian says, "The personal papers would be on the fifth floor, where we keep all the personal papers of famous residents of our city."

31. *pump water.* The speaker says, "In ancient China, farmers used a rudimentary sort of windmill to pump water."

32. *grind grain.* The speaker says, "In Persia, for example, farmers used wind-powered mills to grind their grain."

33. *drain lakes.* The speaker says, "During the Middle Ages in the Netherlands, people . . . used windmills to drain lakes, thereby creating more land for farming."

34. *pollution.* The speaker says, "Wind power, on the other hand, is clean. It causes no pollution . . . ."

35. *renewable resource.* The speaker says, "Another great advantage of wind power is that it's a renewable resource. Oil and coal reserves are limited, but we'll never run out of wind."

36. *costs less.* The speaker says, "Using the wind to generate electricity costs less, much less, than running other types of generators."

37. *strength.* The speaker says, "Wind doesn't blow at a constant strength."

38. *cities.* The speaker says, "Wind turbines usually have to be located in rural areas . . . . Their distance from cities, where the most electricity is needed, is another issue."

39. *the scenery.* The speaker says, "Rural residents often feel that the beautiful local scenery is spoiled by the sight of the wind turbines."

40. *noisy.* The speaker says, "In fact, one wind turbine can produce as much noise as a car traveling at highway speeds."

Reading

PASSAGE 1

1. **(C)** Paragraph 1: "Dragonflies and damselflies get their name from the powerful serrated jaws they use to tear apart their prey."

2. **(B)** Paragraph 2: "Dragonflies hold their wings out to the side while damselflies fold their wings back."

3. **(B)** Paragraph 2: "Damselflies' eyes are smaller, and there is a space between them."

4. **(A)** Paragraph 2: "Dragonflies are larger and stronger animals than damselflies and fly longer distances. Thus, they can be found in woods and fields away from the water."

5. **(C)** Paragraph 3: "The largest odonata living today are the Hawaiian endemic dragonfly and the Central American damselfly, each of these species having a wingspan of 19 centimeters."

6. **(A)** Paragraph 3: "The largest dragonfly fossil ever found belongs to the now-extinct *meganeura monyi,* which lived 300 million years ago and had a wingspan of 75 centimeters."

7. **(E)** Paragraph 4: "Dragonflies and damselflies both lay their eggs on or just below the surface of the water in a pond or stream."

8. **(F)** Paragraph 4: "The babies emerge from the eggs in the form of nymphs."

9. **(H)** Paragraph 4: "Depending on the species, they live this way for several months or even several years."

10. **(B)** Paragraph 4: "They have a special lip that they can extend far forward in order to grab their prey when it comes close."

11. **(I)** Paragraph 4: "The adults do not live for more than four months, and many species live as adults for only a few weeks."

12. **(D)** Paragraph 5: "They have two sets of wings that can move independently of each other. This gives them great maneuverability in the air . . . . They can hover, make sharp turns, and fly backward."

13. **(A)** Paragraph 5: "they catch their prey while flying."

PASSAGE 2

14. *fuel.* Paragraph 1: "Watchmen also learned to create firebreaks with long hooked poles and ropes in order to pull down structures that provided fuel for a fire."

15. *put out.* Paragraph 1: "In 1066, in order to reduce the risk of fire in thatched-roof houses, King William the Conqueror made a ruling: Citizens had to extinguish their cooking fires at night."

16. *hot and dry.* Paragraph 2: "However, the summer of 1666 had been uncharacteristically hot and dry . . . ."

17. *rebuild the city.* Paragraph 2: "the mayor grew concerned over the cost it would involve to rebuild the city and ordered that the surrounding structures be left intact."

18. *stone and brick.* Paragraph 3: "most of London was rebuilt using stone and brick, materials that were far less flammable than wood and straw."

19. *fires.* Paragraph 3: "Because of the long history of fires in London, those who could afford to build new homes and businesses began to seek insurance for their properties."

20. *extinguish fires.* Paragraph 3: "As insurance became a profitable business, companies soon realized the monetary benefits of hiring men to extinguish fires."

21. **(A)** Paragraph 4: "The first fire engines were simple tubs on wheels that were pulled to the location of the fire . . . ." Choice (B) is incorrect because hand pumps were added "eventually," that is, later. Choice (C) is incorrect because water was "supplied by a bucket brigade."

22. **(C)** Paragraph 5: "In 1865, the government became involved, ... establishing London's Metropolitan Fire Brigade. Choice (A) is mentioned in the same paragraph but not as something that occurred in 1865. Choice (B) is mentioned as something that happened in the eighteenth century or earlier.

23. **(B)** Paragraph 5: "Though the firemen were well paid, they were constantly on duty and thus obliged to call their fire station home . . . ." Choice (A) is incorrect because the paragraph mentions that firemen were well paid. Choice (C) is incorrect because the paragraph mentions firemen's families.

24. *No.* Paragraph 6: "Leather hoses with couplings that joined the lengths together were hand-sewn in the Netherlands . . . ."

25. *Yes.* Paragraph 6 explains that steam engine fire trucks were used from about the 1850s until the early 1900s, when the trucks became motorized.

26. *Not Given.* World War I is mentioned, but its particular effect on London is not.

PASSAGE 3

27. **(B)** Paragraph 1: "Weavers' work was moved from individual homes to factories; individuals could not afford to buy the new machines for themselves."

28. **(H)** Paragraph 1: "The new machines were not difficult to run. They could be operated by unskilled workers . . . ."

29. **(D)** Paragraph 2: "If these demands were not met, the group retaliated by smashing the factory machines."

30. **(A)** Paragraph 4: "Luddite activity spread . . . . The government sent thousands of troops into areas affected by the riots."

31. **(E)** Paragraph 4: "the Frame-Breaking Act was passed, making the destruction of factory equipment a crime punishable by death." Paragraphs 4 and 5 mention several incidents where rioters were imprisoned or executed.

32. **(I)** Paragraph 5: "In 1816, a bad harvest and economic downturn led to a small revival of rioting."

33. *True.* Opening sentence: "The term *Luddite* is used to refer to a person who is opposed to new technology."

34. *True.* Paragraph 1: "These weavers made lace and stockings by hand. . . . In the 1800s, automated power looms and stocking frames were introduced . . . ."

35. *True.* Paragraph 4: "In the spring of that year, several factory owners were killed during Luddite riots, and a number of textile workers died as well."

36. *Not Given.* The article describes Luddite activity in England but does not mention whether it occurred in other countries.

37. *True.* Paragraph 3 discusses possible explanations of who Ned Ludd was and implies that none of them is accepted as fact.

38. *False.* Paragraph 5: "In 1816, a bad harvest and economic downturn led to a small revival of rioting."

39. *False.* According to Paragraphs 2 and 5, most Luddite activity occurred in the years 1811 and 1812.

40. *Not Given.* Paragraph 6 describes Neo-Luddites as people concerned about technological advances but does not give any specifics about their activities.

Writing

These are models. Your answers will vary. See page vi in the Introduction to see the criteria for scoring.

WRITING TASK 1

Wood pellets are a type of fuel used for heating buildings. They are made from sawdust. The manufacturing process takes several steps and uses several different types of machines.

The first machine that is used is the hammer mill. When the sawdust arrives from the sawmill, it is put into the hammer mill. There, the sawdust is hammered into fibers. The fibers are all the same length. The fibers are then dampened with steam, and they are ready for the next machine. It is called the pellet machine. This machine forms the damp fibers into pellets by forcing them through holes.

After the pellets come out of the machine, they are cooled. The cool pellets are vacuumed to remove the loose dust. Finally, the finished pellets are packed into 18-kilo (40-pound) bags. They are then ready for sale. They can be burned in either a pellet stove or a pellet furnace to heat any kind of building.

WRITING TASK 2

I agree that everybody, no matter what his or her level of academic ability, should be admitted to university programs. In the first place, everyone has the right to an education and no one can take this away. Also, people are generally attracted to educational programs that fit their interests and abilities. Finally, there are different university programs designed to fit different kinds of students.

Everybody has the right to an education, and this includes education beyond high school. Some people choose to go to a university while others choose some other form of training. No matter what form of education a person chooses, no one else has the right to make that choice for him or her.

People tend to choose educational programs that fit their interests and abilities. They do not need someone else to tell them what they can and cannot do. If a person is interested in studying law, for example, it is probably because he or she feels it is something he or she likes and will do well at. Also, when students are interested in their program of study, they are motivated to work hard, even when some of the assignments are difficult for them.

There are all different kinds of university programs. There are programs that suit different interests, goals, and abilities. Because of this, there is no reason to deny a university education to anyone. There is something for everyone who wants it at the university level.

Everyone has the right to an education, including a university education if that is what he or she chooses. It should not be denied to anyone.

Speaking

These are models. Your answers will vary. See page vi in the Introduction to see the criteria for scoring.

PART 1

Describe the neighborhood where you live.
The neighborhood I live in is right outside of the city. It's almost like living in the city, except that it has houses instead of apartment buildings. The houses are small with small yards. People in the neighborhood really like to garden, so there are a lot of flowers and nice plants. It's very pretty. We are near a bus stop, so it's easy to get to the city. There are a few small stores that sell food and newspapers and things like that.

What do you like about living there?
What I like about my neighborhood is that it's close to the city. It's very easy to get to work. Also, it's not very expensive. I can afford to live there and not spend all my money on rent.

What do you dislike about your neighborhood?
My neighborhood is in a boring area. If I want to do something interesting like go to a movie or a concert or if I want to shop at good stores, I have to go to the city. It's quiet, so it's a good place to relax, but it's not a good place to have fun.

What kind of neighborhood would you like to live in?
When I start making more money, I'm going to move into the city. I would like to live in a city neighborhood that's full of activity. I'd like to live near restaurants and stores and clubs. I'd like to live in a place where I can walk out my front door and be right in the middle of everything.

Do you like walking? Why or why not?
I don't dislike walking, but I can't say that I particularly like it. I walk to the bus stop every day, and I often walk to the store because it's nearby. I walk to get places, but I never walk for fun. I don't think it's an interesting thing to do.

Are there places you can walk near your house?
There's a nice park not far from my house. It has pretty gardens and some walking trails through the woods. A lot of my neighbors go there to take walks. It's also easy to walk around my neighborhood because there are sidewalks everywhere.

Do people in your country like walking? Why or why not?
Walking is popular in my country. A lot of people walk for their health. In fact, there are walking clubs. Often, early in the mornings you can see groups of people walking around the neighborhood together. These are the walking clubs. They walk together every morning, I think.

What other kinds of exercise do you enjoy?
I never walk for exercise, but I enjoy bike riding. I often ride my bike on weekends. I go wherever I can find bike trails. There are a lot of them near where I live. When the weather is bad, I go to the gym and use the exercise machines there. I really like doing that. I like to play soccer, too. I play it with my friends every week.

PART 2

My friend's name is Bob. We've known each other most of our lives. We met in preschool when we were around four or five years old, and we've been friends ever since. We like to do a lot of things together. When we were little kids, we played a lot of different kinds of games together. In high school, we used to study together, but we don't do that anymore because Bob isn't studying business administration like I am. He's studying law. We're both busy with school and work, but we still get together often. It's easy because we're still living in the same city. We play soccer with some other friends at least once a week, and we go to soccer games together. When the weather's nice, we go to the beach or hang out in the park. We talk about things we're doing now, and these days we also talk a lot about the future, the things we hope to do after we finish school. Bob is an important friend because we've known each other all our lives. We grew up together. I guess you could say we know just about everything about each other. I know if I ever needed serious help or if I needed money or any kind of support, Bob would help me. And I would help him if he needed it. He's the kind of friend you can always count on. I think we'll always be friends, all our lives. I hope so.

PART 3

Generally, are friendships important to people?
I think friendships are important to most people. Nobody likes to be alone. Friends like to do the same things you like to do. Usually, they have ideas similar

to yours. Friends understand how you feel. Of course, friends don't always think alike or feel alike, but generally, they're similar to you in many ways.

How can friends help each other?
Friends can help each other at work and school. Close friends can help each other with personal problems, and they can be company for each other. That way you don't have to be alone.

Do people spend more time with friends or with relatives?
I think this depends on the time of life. Children and teenagers spend a lot of time with their friends. But when they get a little older and start their own families, then they spend more time with relatives. They spend time with their children because they have to take care of them, and they spend time with other relatives because they need their support. When the children are older and spending more time with their friends, then the parents might have time again for their own friendships.

How do our friendships change as we grow older?
As we grow older, our lives change, so our friendships change too. Children have a lot of time to play with their friends. When you get older and study or work, you don't have so much free time, so you might have fewer friends, maybe even just one or two close friends. When you start a family, then your family becomes more important than your friends. Your friends might be other parents and you help each other out with your children.

ACADEMIC MODULE
PRACTICE TEST 2

Academic Module
Practice Test 2

Candidate Name and Number: _____

INTERNATIONAL ENGLISH LANGUAGE TESTING SYSTEM

LISTENING

TIME APPROX. 30 MINUTES

Instructions to Candidates

Do not open this booklet until you are told to do so.

Write your name and candidate number in the space at the top of this page.

You should answer all questions.

All the recordings will be played ONCE only.

Write all your answers on the test pages.

At the end of the test, you will be given ten minutes to transfer your answers to an Answer Sheet. (The answer sheet can be found on page 63.)

Do not remove the booklet from the examination room.

Information for Candidates

There are **40** questions on this question paper.

The test is divided as follows:

Section 1	Questions 1–10
Section 2	Questions 11–20
Section 3	Questions 21–30
Section 4	Questions 31–40

SECTION 1   QUESTIONS 1–10

Questions 1–5

Complete the chart[1] below.
Write **NO MORE THAN TWO WORDS** *for each answer.*

Example	Plainfield <u>*Community Center*</u>[2]	
	Classes and Activities	
Days	**Class/Activity**	**Age Group**
Wednesday, Saturday	1 _____	children, teens
2 _____	Tennis	3 _____
Tuesday, Thursday	4 _____	children, teens, adults
Friday	Book club	5 _____

Questions 6–10

Complete the notes below.
Write **NO MORE THAN THREE WORDS AND/OR A NUMBER** *for each answer.*

Membership fees **6** $_____ (individual)

                 7 $_____ (family)

Located at 107 **8** _____ Street

Parking is located **9** _____

The Center is closed on **10** _____

SECTION 2   QUESTIONS 11–20

Questions 11–15

Choose **FIVE** *letters, A–J.*
Which **FIVE** *things should hikers take on the hiking trip?*

A	sleeping bag	**F**	backpack
B	tent	**G**	walking poles
C	food	**H**	maps
D	dishes	**I**	jacket
E	hiking boots	**J**	first-aid kit

---

[1] British: table
[2] British: Centre

Questions 16–20

Complete the sentences below.
Write **NO MORE THAN TWO WORDS** *for each answer.*

Safety Rules for Hiking

Always stay ahead of the **16** _____.
Stop and wait at any **17** _____.
Don't try to climb **18** _____.
Don't **19** _____ wild animals.
Always carry **20** _____ with you.

SECTION 3   *QUESTIONS 21–30*

Questions 21–24

Choose **FOUR** *letters* **A–G***.*
Which **FOUR** *of the following are required of student teachers?*

A   weekly journal
B   sample lesson plans
C   meetings with other student teachers
D   observing other teachers
E   evaluation from supervising teacher
F   portfolio
G   final exam

Question 25

Choose the correct letter, **A***,* **B***, or* **C***.*

25 Who has to sign the agreement form?

A the student teacher
B the supervising teacher
C the advisor

Questions 26–30

Complete the schedule below.
Write **NO MORE THAN THREE WORDS** *for each answer.*

First week	26 _____ due
Fourth week	27 _____ meeting
Seventh week	28 _____
Fourteenth week	29 _____ due
Fifteenth week	30 _____

SECTION 4   QUESTIONS 31–40

Questions 31–35

Choose the correct letter, **A, B,** *or* **C.**

31 Retailers place popular items

    A in the back of the store.
    B near the front entrance.
    C at the end of the aisle.

32 Carpet patterns are used to

    A help shoppers feel comfortable.
    B appeal to shoppers' decorative sense.
    C encourage shoppers to walk in certain directions.

33 Retailers can keep customers in the store longer by

    A providing places to sit.
    B keeping the doors closed.
    C lowering the prices.

34 Music is used in stores to

    A entertain customers.
    B slow customers down.
    C make customers shop faster.

35 The scent of vanilla has been used in

    A ice cream shops.
    B bakeries.
    C clothing stores.

Questions 36–40

Complete the chart about the effects of color.[1]
Write **NO MORE THAN TWO WORDS** *for each answer.*

Color	Effect
Purple	encourages people to **36** _____
Orange	makes restaurant customers **37** _____
Blue	conveys a sense of **38** _____
Bright colors	appeal to **39** _____
Soft colors	appeal to **40** _____

Take ten minutes to transfer your answers onto the Answer Sheet on page 63.

---

[1] *British: colour*

Academic Module
Practice Test 2

Candidate Name and Number: _____

INTERNATIONAL ENGLISH LANGUAGE TESTING SYSTEM

ACADEMIC READING

TIME 1 HOUR

Instructions to Candidates

Do not open this booklet until you are told to do so.

Write your name and candidate number in the space at the top of this page.

Start at the beginning of the test and work through it.

You should answer all questions.

If you cannot do a particular question, leave it and go on to the next. You can return to it later.

All answers must be written on the Answer Sheet. (The answer sheet can be found on page 64.)

Do not remove the booklet from the examination room.

Information for Candidates

There are **40** questions on this question paper.

The test is divided as follows:

Reading Passage 1	Questions 1–13
Reading Passage 2	Questions 14–26
Reading Passage 3	Questions 27–40

Academic Module–Practice Test 2

READING PASSAGE 1

You should spend about 20 minutes on **Questions 1–13**, *which are based on Reading Passage 1 below.*

The Vikings' Wayfaring Ways

Perhaps best known as fierce warriors, the Vikings were also the most far-ranging of peoples. In fact, the term *Viking*, in Old Norse, means "to go on an expedition." From the late 700s until the eleventh century, Viking explorers journeyed from their native Norway, Denmark, and Sweden to many distant lands. They traveled[1] as far west as Newfoundland in present-day Canada, and as far east as Baghdad.

Those from Norway sailed west to the British Isles, and eventually across the Atlantic Ocean. During their first expedition, in 793, a force of Viking warriors sacked the famed abbey at Lindisfarne, on England's northeast coast. In the 800s, groups of raiders went on to occupy the Shetland Islands, north of the British Isles and west of Norway, and the Orkney Islands off northern Scotland.

By 870, the Vikings were settling Iceland. In 980, an Icelandic assembly found a man named Eric "the Red" Ericson guilty of murder and sent him into exile. Eric the Red responded by sailing to a large island to the west, which he called "Greenland." An Icelandic saga mentions that people would be attracted to go to Greenland if it had a favorable[2] name. Around 998, Eric the Red's son, Leif "the Lucky" Ericson, and a small Viking fleet sailed west to North America. There they established the first European settlement in the New World, called "Vinland."

Vikings from Denmark, meanwhile, ravaged large swaths of England and France. In 866, a Viking "Great Army" landed in England, occupying much of the country's north and east. They forced the English king to acknowledge their control of much of England under the so-called Danelaw. To the west, they conquered coastal portions of Ireland, and in 841 founded Dublin, today a major Irish city, but originally a Viking fort. The Vikings remained a major power in Ireland until the early eleventh century.

To the south, the Vikings conquered France, moving swiftly up rivers in long boats, powered by oar and sail. From 845 to 886, they surged up the Seine to attack Paris three times. To stop the raids, French King Charles III the Simple in 911 offered the Viking chief Rollo territories in northwest France, called Normandy, after the Normans or "Northmen." There they set up a powerful kingdom and, in 1066, under William, Duke of Normandy, defeated King Harold at the battle of Hastings in England.

Farther south, in 844, the Vikings had raided Portugal and Spain, then largely controlled by Arab Moors. A fleet of 100 Viking ships seized Lisbon and boldly

---

[1] *British: travelled*
[2] *British: favourable*

sailed up the Guadalquivir River to occupy Seville. However, the Moors dealt them a rare defeat. The Moors catapulted flaming projectiles onto the Viking vessels, forcing a retreat.

Still other Vikings sailed much farther, to raid Morocco, then to the eastern Mediterranean and beyond. Many of these Vikings enlisted with the military forces of the Byzantine Empire, the Greek-speaking successors to the Roman Empire. Vikings made up the Byzantine Emperor's elite Varangian Guard. In 902, hundreds of Varangians served as marines during a Byzantine naval assault on the island of Crete. Varangians battled Arab forces in Syria in 955, and even fought in Jerusalem. So many men left Scandinavia for the Byzantine Empire that, to stem the outflow, Sweden passed a law denying inherited property to anyone serving under the Byzantines.

The Vikings of Sweden, meanwhile, were moving out of Scandinavia to the east and south. They journeyed through the Baltic Sea, then built inland trading posts in Germany and Poland. In time, they struck out across Central and Eastern Europe, down the Vistula River in Poland, and the Dnieper, Volga, and Don Rivers in Russia. Their vessel of choice was the "knar," a cargo ship with a deep draft and wide hull. Viking merchants on horseback penetrated far into the Asian heartland, trading with towns on the Caspian and Black seas.

The most significant settlements were in Russia and Ukraine. In 862, Vikings settled in the town of Novgorod, in northwestern Russia. It became the capital of a country called Rus, after the Finnish name for the Swedes. Rus came from the word *Rutosi*, meaning "rowers." Rus formed the foundation of Russia, as the Russian and Viking leaders of Rus intermarried, converted to Christianity, and steadily expanded their territory. And after lucrative trade relations were established with the Byzantines and with Muslim lands, the Rus moved their capital southward to Kiev, later the capital of Ukraine.

Another important Viking market town was Bulgar, on the Volga River. There, merchants peddled honey, wax, amber, and steel swords. The Viking's most common commodity may have been skins: they dealt in horse, beaver, rabbit, mink, ermine, and sable skins. They also traded hazelnuts, fish, cattle, and falcons. Another commodity was slaves, many of them Slavs from Eastern Europe. The merchants eagerly exchanged their goods for Arab silver coins. In Sweden, archeologists[1] have excavated about 100,000 such coins, minted in such distant cities as Cairo and Tashkent.

Like their Danish and Norwegian relatives, the Swedish Vikings traveled to the most exotic realms. They took part in the Silk Road trade with India and China. Archeological evidence shows that Viking traders even traveled by camel caravan to Baghdad.

Given the wide-ranging travel of the Vikings, it is fitting the Anglo-Saxons gave them the nickname "Færgenga"—"Far Going."

---

[1] *British: archaeologists*

Questions 1–5

Answer the questions below.
*Choose **ONE NUMBER ONLY** from the text for each answer.*
Write your answers on lines 1–5 on your answer sheet.

1 When did Viking warriors raid an abbey on the coast of England?

2 When was Eric the Red convicted of a crime?

3 When did Vikings establish a fort in Ireland?

4 When was a Viking chief granted lands by a king of France?

5 When did Viking warriors defeat an English king?

Questions 6–13

*Complete the summary using the list of words, **A–O**, below. Write the correct letter, **A–O**, on lines 6–13 on your answer sheet.*

The people known as Vikings were given this name because they were **6** _____. Groups of Vikings from Norway traveled west to Britain, Iceland, and beyond. They were the first Europeans who **7** _____ North America. Groups from Denmark **8** _____ large areas of England and France. Other groups of Vikings raided areas of Portugal and Spain. The people of Seville, Spain, drove the Vikings away by throwing **9** _____ at them. Large numbers of Vikings left Scandinavia for the Byzantine Empire, and many of these joined the Byzantine military. At one point, they took part in **10** _____ on the Greek island of Crete. Groups of Swedish Vikings crossed the Baltic Sea to explore the lands beyond. They traveled down Russian rivers, then journeyed deep into Asia by **11** _____. After settling in northwest Russia, they expanded their territories toward the south. Kiev, Ukraine, eventually became the Vikings' territorial **12** _____. The Vikings also had an important **13** _____ in the town of Bulgar on the Volga River.

A warriors	**B** an attack	**C** capital	**D** explorers
E trade with	**F** conquered	**G** burning objects	**H** settled in
I ship	**J** oars	**K** market	**L** a parade
M archeologists	**N** silver coins	**O** horse	

READING PASSAGE 2

Dyslexia

Dyslexia, also referred to as "specific reading disability," predominantly affects a person's ability to read and write. Dyslexics have difficulty connecting visual symbols (i.e., letters) with their corresponding sounds. Many people who suffer from dyslexia also have trouble with enunciation, organization,[1] and short-term memory. Dyslexia is the most common learning disability in children. It is not related to intellectual ability, vision, or access to education. Approximately 5-10 percent of school-age children in North America suffer from the condition, with each case varying in severity. Children are generally diagnosed with dyslexia during the elementary school years when they are learning how to read and spell.

Determining the definite cause of dyslexia is a difficult task since studies of the morphology of the brain are generally conducted in an autopsy. One hypothesis suggests that dyslexic children suffer from "strabismus," the tendency of the eyes to focus on two different points. When reading, for example, one eye focuses on the beginning of the word and the other focuses on the end. This theory could explain why dyslexics have difficulty reading. Many dyslexic children read letters and words backwards, often mistaking a *b* for a *d* or reading *was* instead of *saw*. These reversals are normal for children under the age of six, but indicate a problem if they persist beyond the early elementary grades. Neurological research points to tiny flaws in the dyslexic brain called ectopias and microgyria. These flaws alter the structure of the cortex, the area of the brain that is responsible for connecting visual and audio processing. Genetic research, often in the form of twins studies, shows that dyslexia may be passed on in families.

Though most children are not diagnosed with dyslexia until they enter the school system, there are some early signs of the disability. Toddlers who talk much later than average, have difficulty learning new words, or do not understand the concept of rhyming may develop other dyslexic symptoms. As children begin school, teachers are trained to look for warning signs, such as an inability to recognize[2] letters or spaces between words on a page or difficulty following instructions given with more than one command at a time. Properly screening children for dyslexia is important since other factors can limit reading abilities, including vision or hearing impairment, anxiety, or other neurological problems.

---

[1] *British: organisation*

[2] *British: recognise*

Dyslexia is a type of learning disorder that can often be compensated for with therapy and motivational techniques. Phonological training, which involves identifying and separating sound patterns, is the most common form of therapy used in the school system. Depending on the severity of the disorder, dyslexic children are pulled from regular classroom activities in order to work one-on-one with a language specialist. Studies have shown that activity in the right temporoparietal cortex tends to increase after sufficient phonological training. Improvements in visual focus can sometimes be achieved when students are given an eye patch to wear while they learn to read. Encouraging children to use many senses while reading also has proven benefits. Some teachers find that having students listen to a book on tape before reading the text can help with information processing as well.

Though it is properly classified as a learning disability, dyslexia is commonly mistaken for a behavioral[1] disorder. Dyslexic children often exhibit behavior that seems abnormal but is caused by frustration at their own inability to perform at the same level as their peers. Some studies show that attention deficit disorder co-occurs with dyslexia in up to 50 percent of cases. In general, behavioral problems decline as dyslexic students are diagnosed and begin to receive treatment.

Other learning disabilities are neurologically linked to dyslexia, including dyscalculia, dysgraphia, and dyspraxia. People who suffer from dyscalculia can usually perform difficult mathematical tasks, but have trouble with formulas or basic addition and subtraction. Dysgraphia prevents people from writing in an organized manner. Dyspraxia impedes the performance of routine tasks that involve balance and fine motor skills.

The earlier children are diagnosed with dyslexia, the more likely they are to overcome their disabilities and progress to adult reading levels. Many studies show that children who are diagnosed after grade three have a much lower chance of eliminating the symptoms of dyslexia. Some dyslexics, especially those who are not diagnosed as children, naturally develop their own coping mechanisms such as an increased visual memory. In some instances, dyslexics develop keen spatial and visual abilities that prepare them for very specialized[2] careers.

---

[1] *British: behavioural*
[2] *British: specialised*

Questions 14–20

Do the following statements agree with the information in the reading passage? On lines 14–20 on your answer sheet write:

YES	if the statement agrees with the views of the writer
NO	if the statement disagrees with the views of the writer
NOT GIVEN	if there is no information on this in the passage

14 Dyslexia is a disorder related to intelligence.

15 Dyslexia is usually diagnosed during a child's first years of school.

16 People with dyslexia often read in reverse.

17 There is a tendency for dyslexia between twins.

18 Scientists are looking for a drug treatment for dyslexia.

19 Dyslexia in children is often accompanied by behavioral problems.

20 People with dysgraphia have difficulty with math.

Questions 21–23

*Which of the following are signs of dyslexia mentioned in the passage? Choose THREE answers from the list below and write the correct letters, **A–F**, on lines 21–23 on your answer sheet.*

A   learning to talk at a later than normal age
B   trouble with new vocabulary
C   leaving big spaces between words
D   problems following directions
E   difficulty turning the pages of a book
F   inability to give commands

Questions 24–26

*Which of the following are treatments for dyslexia mentioned in the passage? Choose THREE answers from the list below and write the correct letter, **A–F**, on lines 24–26 on your answer sheet.*

A   using special computers
B   learning to identify sounds
C   wearing eyeglasses
D   attending a special school
E   covering one eye while reading
F   listening to tapes

READING PASSAGE 3

*You should spend about 20 minutes on **Questions 27–40**, which are based on Reading Passage 3 below.*

Catastrophe Theory

A

In the late eighteenth and early nineteenth centuries, the popular theory among Earth scientists was that a number of major catastrophes had taken place over a relatively short period of time to give Earth its shape. French geologist Baron Georges Cuvier introduced this idea, which was later coined the "catastrophe theory." Proponents of the catastrophe theory used fossilized[1] creatures and the faunal changes in rock strata to support their beliefs that major events such as volcanoes had occurred on a worldwide scale. The catastrophe theory was used to support the notion that Earth's history was not a relatively long one.

B

In response to the catastrophe theory, a handful of Earth scientists searched for explanations that would provide a better scientific basis for Earth's geology. James Hutton, the father of geology, is best known for his gradualist theory, a paradigm that became known as "uniformitarianism." Hutton published *Theory of the Earth* in 1795, after which many other geologists including Charles Lyell, adopted the idea that small changes on Earth occurred over a large expanse of time. Uniformitarians rejected the idea that cataclysmic events could shape the Earth so quickly, and instead proposed the theory that the key to the present is the past. The term *deep time* was used to describe the span in which gradual geological processes occurred, especially the formation of sedimentary rock. Charles Darwin later based his work on the idea, by developing his theory of evolution.

C

The majority of paleontologists[2] and geologists adopted the gradualist theory of Earth's history for more than 100 years. In 1980, a discovery in Italy gave scientists a reason to reconsider the discarded theories of catastrophism. Geologist Walter Alvarez discovered a clay layer in the K-T boundary that intrigued him. The K-T boundary refers to the layer of Earth between the Cretaceous and Tertiary periods. The geologist with the help of his father Luis Alvarez, a prominent physicist, analyzed the clay for heavy metals. After careful examination, the clay was found to contain high levels of iridium. Samples taken from the K-T boundary in other parts of the world were examined, with the same findings.

---

[1] fossilised
[2] British: palaeontologists

D

The Alvarez group wrote a historic paper that applied the catastrophe theory to their discovery. According to their hypothesis, the iridium in the K-T boundary was caused by an asteroid or a comet that hit Earth near the end of the Cretaceous period, over 65 million years ago. They also proposed that the impact would have raised enough dust to block the sun and cool Earth, which in turn would have prevented photosynthesis. This chain reaction would have led to the extinction of plants and animals. The main reason that the Alvarez theory took hold so quickly in both the world of science and the public realm, was that it could account for the extinction of the dinosaurs at the end of the Cretaceous period. The acceptance of this theory was widespread, even before the discovery in 1990 of a 180-kilometer[1] crater in Mexico's Yucatan Peninsula, a potential piece of evidence of the asteroid impact.

E

Events that have occurred on Earth in the last 100 years or more have proved to geologists that not all processes are gradual. Major rivers have flooded areas in a matter of days, and volcanoes have erupted, causing mass devastation. The eruption of Mount St. Helens was proof of how a catastrophe could easily change the Earth's landscape. Modern research on fossils even supports the theory of a marine catastrophe, not unlike the legends and stories among many peoples of great floods. Some scientists believe that animal remains found within the layers of sedimentary rock may have been casualties of such a flood. Sedimentary rock is made up of layers such as sandstone and limestone and is created by water movement. In addition, some scientists propose that the glacial ice sheet that once spread out across North America melted catastrophically rather than having a slow glacial retreat. Deep erosion up to 100 meters wide was discovered along the bottom of some of the Great Lakes. Within the gullies, layers of periodic sediment point to catastrophic melting.

F

Though there is little debate that catastrophic events caused the mass extinction of several of Earth's species, namely the dinosaurs, geologists still question whether asteroids, volcanoes, or other natural disasters were the cause. The idea that the moon was formed as a result of catastrophic events is a related field of study and one that has been debated for decades.

[1]*British: kilometre*

Questions 27–32

*Complete the notes using the list of words, **A–K**, below.*
*Write the correct letter, **A–K**, on lines 27–32 on your answer sheet.*

Catastrophe Theory

First introduced by **27** _____

Proposes that major **28** _____ have given Earth its shape.

Supports the idea that the Earth has a **29** _____ history.

Gradualist Theory

First introduced by **30** _____

Proposes that many **31** _____ changes in the shape of the

Earth happened over a **32** _____ period of time.

A	short
B	small
C	Charles Darwin
D	long
E	definite
F	disasters
G	James Hutton
H	mysterious
I	Walter Alvarez
J	evolution
K	Georges Cuvier

Questions 33–39

*The passage has six paragraphs, **A–F**. Which paragraph mentions the following information?*
*Write the correct letter, **A–F**, on lines 33–39 on your answer sheet. You may use any paragraph more than once.*

33 proof that not all changes on Earth have occurred gradually

34 a theory explaining the presence of iridium beneath Earth's surface

35 publication of a book about the gradualist theory

36 discovery of a large crater that could have been caused by an asteroid

37 evidence of the occurrence of a large flood in Earth's past

38 recurrence of interest in the catastrophe theory

39 ideas about how quickly ice age glaciers disappeared

Question 40

*Choose the correct letter, **A–C**, and write it on line 40 on your answer sheet.*

40 Most scientists now agree that

    A the gradualist theory is correct.
    B catastrophic events occur regularly on the moon.
    C a major catastrophe caused the dinosaurs to disappear.

Academic Module—Practice Test 2

Academic Module
Practice Test 2

Candidate Name and Number: _____

INTERNATIONAL ENGLISH LANGUAGE TESTING SYSTEM

ACADEMIC WRITING

TIME: 1 HOUR

Instructions to Candidates

Do not open this booklet until you are told to do so.

Write your name and candidate number in the space at the top of this page.

All answers must be written on the separate answer booklet provided. (Answer sheets can be found beginning on page 65.)

Do not remove the booklet from the examination room.

Information for Candidates

There are **2** tasks on this question paper.

You must do **both** tasks.

Under-length answers will be penalized.[1]

---

[1] *British: penalised*

WRITING TASK 1

You should spend about 20 minutes on this task. Write at least 150 words.

The graph below shows the percentage of urban/suburban and rural households in a European country that had Internet access between 1999 and 2004.

Summarize[1] the information by selecting and reporting the main features, and make comparisons where relevant.

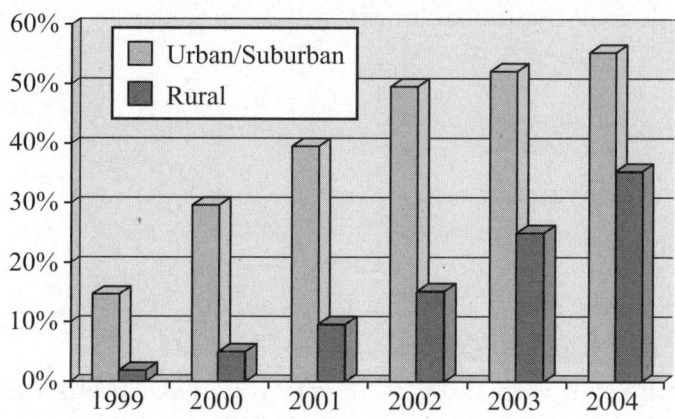

WRITING TASK 2

You should spend about 40 minutes on this task. Write at least 250 words.

Write about the following topic:

Because of the busy pace of modern life, many children spend most of their time indoors and have little exposure to the natural world.

How important is it for children to learn to understand and appreciate nature? Give reasons for your answer and include any relevant examples from your own knowledge or experience.

---

[1] *British: Summarise*

SPEAKING

Examiner questions:

Part 1

When and how much leisure time do you generally have in a week?

Who do you generally spend your leisure time with?

What are some activities you enjoy in your leisure time?

What do you like about these activities?

What kinds of music do you like listening to?

Have you learned to play a musical instrument? Why or why not?

Tell me about any traditional music in your country.

Do you think that traditional music will be popular in the future? Why or why not?

Part 2

Describe a movie that you saw recently.

You should say:

The title of the movie and what it was about

When and where you saw it

Who you saw it with and explain why you enjoyed/didn't enjoy seeing this movie

> You will have one to two minutes to talk about this topic.
>
> You will have one minute to prepare what you are going to say.

Part 3

What kinds of movies are popular these days? Why do you think they are popular?

What can we learn from watching movies?

How are movies different from live theater[1]?

How do you think movies will be different in the future?

---

[1] *British: theatre*

Practice Test 2—Academic Module
IELTS LISTENING ANSWER SHEET

1. _____
2. _____
3. _____
4. _____
5. _____
6. _____
7. _____
8. _____
9. _____
10. _____
11. _____
12. _____
13. _____
14. _____
15. _____
16. _____
17. _____
18. _____
19. _____
20. _____

21. _____
22. _____
23. _____
24. _____
25. _____
26. _____
27. _____
28. _____
29. _____
30. _____
31. _____
32. _____
33. _____
34. _____
35. _____
36. _____
37. _____
38. _____
39. _____
40. _____

Practice Test 2—Answer Sheet

Practice Test 2—Academic Module
IELTS READING ANSWER SHEET

1. _____
2. _____
3. _____
4. _____
5. _____
6. _____
7. _____
8. _____
9. _____
10. _____
11. _____
12. _____
13. _____
14. _____
15. _____
16. _____
17. _____
18. _____
19. _____
20. _____

21. _____
22. _____
23. _____
24. _____
25. _____
26. _____
27. _____
28. _____
29. _____
30. _____
31. _____
32. _____
33. _____
34. _____
35. _____
36. _____
37. _____
38. _____
39. _____
40. _____

Practice Test 2–Academic Module
WRITING TASK 1

Writing Task 1 *continued*

Practice Test 2—Academic Module
WRITING TASK 2

Writing Task 2 *continued*

Writing Task 2 *continued*

Answer Key

PRACTICE TEST 2—ACADEMIC MODULE

Listening

1. tutoring sessions	11. A	22. B	32. C
2. Sunday	12. D	23. D	33. A
3. teens, adults	13. E	24. F	34. B
4. Yoga	14. F	25. B	35. C
5. adults	15. I	26. term paper topic	36. spend money
6. 75	16. sweep/rear leader	27. first evaluation	37. leave faster
7. 225	17. intersection	28. student teacher	38. security
8. Eliot	18. rocks	conference	39. younger people
9. across the street/in	19. feed	29. term paper	40. older people
a garage	20. water	30. semester review	
10. Monday	21. A	31. A	

Reading

1. 793	11. O	21. A	31. B
2. 980	12. C	22. B	32. D
3. 841	13. K	23. D	33. E
4. 911	14. No	24. B	34. D
5. 1066	15. Yes	25. E	35. B
6. D	16. Yes	26. F	36. D
7. H	17. Not Given	27. K	37. E
8. F	18. Not Given	28. F	38. C
9. G	19. Yes	29. A	39. E
10. B	20. No	30. G	40. C

Answer Explanations

ACADEMIC MODULE—PRACTICE TEST 2

Listening

1. *tutoring sessions.* The man says, "during the school year, we have tutoring sessions for children and teens, in all subjects."

2. *Sunday.* The man says, "We have tennis lessons on Sunday mornings for teens and Sunday afternoons for adults."

3. *teens, adults.* The man says, "We have tennis lessons on Sunday mornings for teens and Sunday afternoons for adults."

4. *Yoga.* The man says, "Our yoga classes take place on Tuesday and Thursday evenings . . . there's one class for younger children, one for teens, and one for adults."

5. *adults.* The man says, "actually, that book club is for adults only."

6. *75.* The man says, "The yearly fee is seventy-five dollars for individuals and two hundred twenty-five dollars for families."

7. *225.* The man says, "The yearly fee is seventy-five dollars for individuals and two hundred twenty-five dollars for families."

8. *Eliot.* The man says, "It's at 107 Eliot Street."

9. *across the street/in a garage.* The man says, "You can park just across the street. There's a garage there."

10. *Monday.* The man says, "but don't come on Monday because we're closed . . . ."

11. **(A)** The speaker says, "First, you'll need a warm and comfortable sleeping bag."

12. **(D)** The speaker says, "We've found, though, that it's more efficient for each person to bring his or her own dishes . . . ."

13. **(E)** The speaker says, "Perhaps the most important item to put on your list is a comfortable pair of hiking boots."

14. **(F)** The speaker says, "a backpack is necessary for carrying your equipment."

15. **(I)** The speaker says, "And don't forget to bring a warm jacket."

16. *sweep/rear leader.* The speakers says, "At the end of the line will be the rear leader, or sweep. It's important to always stay ahead of this person while we're on the trail."

17. *intersection.* The speaker says, "When you come to any intersection of trails, stop and wait for the rest of the group to catch up."

18. *rocks.* The speaker says, "Don't be tempted to go off on your own and try to climb some rocks."

19. *feed.* The speaker says, "we'll encounter some large wild animals along the way. The last thing you want to do is try to feed any of them."

20. *water.* The speaker says, "you must always be sure to carry an adequate supply of water with you."

21. **(A)** The advisor says, "I require all my students to keep a journal about their teaching experience."

22. **(B)** The advisor says, "Another thing I'll want from you is a few sample lesson plans."

23. **(D)** The advisor says, "You will, however, have to observe some of the other teachers in the school, besides the teacher you'll be working with."

24. **(F)** The advisor says, "I'll base it on several things. One is your required portfolio . . . ."

25. **(B)** The student teacher asks about the person who will sign the agreement form, and the advisor explains that it is the supervising teacher. Choices (A) and (C) are the speakers.

26. *term paper topic.* The advisor says, "You should let me know your term paper topic by the end of the first week of the semester."

27. *first evaluation.* The advisor explains, "during the fourth week of the semester, we'll have our first evaluation meeting to discuss my observations."

28. *student teacher conference.* The student mentions the student teacher conference, and the advisor says, "The conference takes place, let me check, yes, the seventh week of the semester."

29. *term paper.* The advisor says, "The term paper is due by the end of the fourteenth week of the semester."

30. *semester review.* The advisor explains, "Then during the fifteenth and final week, we'll get together one last time for a semester review."

31. **(A)** The speaker says, "For example, a common practice among retailers is to place the store's best-selling merchandise near the back of the store." Choices (B) and (C) are mentioned in the talk but not as places where popular items are placed.

32. **(C)** The speaker says, "Carpets are also used to direct customers through particular areas of the store." Choices (A) and (B) are mentioned as reasons for having carpets, but not as reasons for the patterns on carpets.

33. **(A)** The speaker says, "One way to do this is to provide comfortable seating throughout the store, but not too close to the doors." Choice (B) is confused with the suggestion of putting seating "not too close to the doors." Choice (C) is plausible but is not mentioned.

34. **(B)** The speaker says, "Music . . . can slow the customers' pace through the store . . . ." Choice (A) is wrong because the speaker says it is not the reason for music. Choice (C) is the opposite of what the speaker says.

35. **(C)** The speaker says, "For example, the scent of vanilla has been used to increase sales in clothing stores." Choice (A) is associated with the scent of vanilla but is not mentioned. Choice (B) is mentioned with the scent of baking bread, not vanilla.

36. *spend money.* The speaker says, "People shopping in an environment where light purple is the predominating color seem to spend money more . . . ."

37. *leave faster.* The speaker says, "Orange . . . encourages customers to leave faster."

38. *security.* The speaker says, "Blue . . . gives customers a sense of security . . . ."

39. *younger people.* The speaker says, "Stores that cater to a younger clientele should use bold, bright colors, which tend to be attractive to younger people."

40. *older people.* The speaker says, "Stores that are interested in attracting an older clientele will have more success with soft, subtle colors . . . ."

Reading

PASSAGE 1

1. *793.* Paragraph 2: "During their first expedition, in 793, a force of Viking warriors sacked the famed abbey at Lindisfarne, on England's northeast coast."

2. *980.* Paragraph 3: "In 980, an Icelandic assembly found a man named Eric 'the Red' Ericson guilty of murder and sent him into exile."

3. *841.* Paragraph 4: "To the west, they conquered coastal portions of Ireland, and in 841 founded Dublin, today a major Irish city, but originally a Viking fort."

4. *911.* Paragraph 5: "French King Charles III the Simple in 911 offered the Viking chief Rollo territories in northwest France, called Normandy, after the Normans or 'Northmen . . . .'"

5. *1066.* Paragraph 5: "in 1066, under William, Duke of Normandy [they], defeated King Harold at the battle of Hastings in England."

6. **(D)** Paragraph 1: "In fact, the term *Viking*, in Old Norse, means 'to go on an expedition.'"

7. **(H)** Paragraph 3: "There they established the first European settlement in the New World, called 'Vinland.'"

8. **(F)** Paragraph 4: "Vikings from Denmark, meanwhile, ravaged large swaths of England and France."

9. **(G)** Paragraph 6: "The Moors catapulted flaming projectiles onto the Viking vessels, forcing a retreat."

10. **(B)** Paragraph 7: "In 902, hundreds of Varangians served as marines during a Byzantine naval assault on the island of Crete."

11. **(O)** Paragraph 8: "Viking merchants on horseback penetrated far into the Asian heartland, trading with towns on the Caspian and Black seas."

12. **(C)** Paragraph 9: "the Rus moved their capital southward to Kiev, later the capital of Ukraine."

13. **(K)** Paragraph 10: "Another important Viking market town was Bulgar, on the Volga River."

PASSAGE 2

14. *No.* Paragraph 1: "It is not related to intellectual ability . . . ."

15. *Yes.* Paragraph 1: "Children are generally diagnosed with dyslexia during the elementary school years when they are learning how to read and spell."

16. *Yes.* Paragraph 2: "Many dyslexic children read letters and words backwards . . . ."

17. *Not Given.* Genetic research with twins is mentioned, but a tendency for dyslexia between twins is not.

18. *Not Given.* There is no mention of drug treatment for dyslexia.

19. *Yes.* Paragraph 5: "Dyslexic children often exhibit behavior that seems abnormal but is caused by frustration at their own inability to perform at the same level as their peers."

20. *No.* Paragraph 6 explains that dysgraphia describes difficulty with writing; difficulty with math is called dyscalculia.

21. **(A)** Paragraph 3: "Toddlers who talk much later than average…may develop other dyslexic symptoms."

22. **(B)** Paragraph 3: "have difficulty learning new words . . . ."

23. **(D)** Paragraph 3: "As children begin school, teachers are trained to look for warning signs, such as an inability to recognize letters or spaces between words on a page or difficulty following instructions given with more than one command at a time."

24. **(B)** Paragraph 4: "Phonological training, which involves identifying and separating sound patterns, is the most common form of therapy . . . ."

25. **(E)** Paragraph 4: "Improvements in visual focus can sometimes be achieved when students are given an eye patch to wear while they learn to read."

26. **(F)** Paragraph 4: "Some teachers find that having students listen to a book on tape before reading the text can help with information processing as well."

PASSAGE 3

27. **(K)** Paragraph A: "French geologist Baron Georges Cuvier introduced this idea . . . ."

28. **(F)** Paragraph A: "the popular theory among Earth scientists was that a number of major catastrophes had taken place over a relatively short period of time to give Earth its shape."

29. **(A)** Paragraph A: "The catastrophe theory was used to support the notion that the Earth's history was not a relatively long one."

30. **(G)** Paragraph B: "James Hutton, the father of geology, is best known for his gradualist theory, ..."

31. **(B)** Paragraph B: "the idea that small changes on Earth occurred over a large expanse of time."

32. **(D)** Paragraph B: "the idea that small changes on Earth occurred over a large expanse of time."

33. **(E)** The topic sentence for paragraph E is "Events that have occurred on Earth in the last 100 years or more have proved to geologists that not all processes are gradual."

34. **(D)** "According to their hypothesis, the iridium in the K-T boundary was caused by an asteroid or a comet that hit Earth . . . ."

35. **(B)** "Hutton published *Theory of the Earth* in 1795 . . . ."

36. **(D)** "the discovery in 1990 of a 180-kilometer crater in Mexico's Yucatan Peninsula, a potential piece of evidence of the asteroid impact."

37. **(E)** "Some scientists believe that animal remains found within the layers of sedimentary rock may have been casualties of the flood."

38. **(C)** "In 1980, a discovery in Italy gave scientists a reason to reconsider the discarded theories of catastrophism."

39. **(E)** "In addition, some scientists propose that the glacial sheet that once spread out across North America melted catastrophically rather than having a slow glacial retreat."

40. **(C)** Paragraph F: "Though there is little debate that catastrophic events caused the mass extinction of several of Earth's species, namely the dinosaurs . . . ." Choice (A) is incorrect because paragraph E discusses evidence that this theory is not correct. Choice (B) is confused with the debate over whether the moon was formed through a series of catastrophic events.

Writing

These are models. Your answers will vary. See page vi in the Introduction to see the criteria for scoring.

WRITING TASK 1

The bar graph shows that in a certain country, Internet access in the home increased dramatically between the years 1999 and 2004. By the end of that time, over one half of urban and suburban households and one third of rural households had Internet access.

In 1999, relatively few households in the region had Internet access. Only 15 percent of homes in urban and suburban areas had access to the Internet, while less than 5 percent of rural homes had it. The following year, Internet access in urban and suburban households had doubled, and 30 percent of households had it. During that same time, Internet access in rural households increased only slightly, to around 5 percent.

Over the next few years, Internet access continued to increase in both urban and suburban and in rural households. Then, between 2002 and 2004, the percentage of households with Internet access remained more or less steady at close to 50 percent. Meanwhile, the percentage of rural households with Internet access continued to grow steadily and reached 35 percent by 2004.

While the percentage of households with Internet access increased in both urban and suburban as well as rural areas during the years shown on the graph, the percentage in urban and suburban areas continued to remain higher than the percentage in rural areas.

WRITING TASK 2

In my opinion, it is extremely important for children to learn to understand and appreciate nature. Without balance in the natural world, we would not survive. When people understand this, they are less likely to cause harm to our natural environment. If children have opportunities to enjoy and learn about the natural environment, they will grow up to appreciate and care for it.

We depend on nature for the food we eat, the air we breathe, and the materials we use to build our houses and make our clothing. Everything in the natural world is interdependent. If something goes wrong with one thing, it affects everything else in the environment. When nature is out of balance, animals start losing their food sources and habitat. This eventually affects our food sources and other natural resources that we depend on.

When we understand that air and water pollution destroy parts of the natural environment, we may be more careful about our actions. We may look for ways to drive cars less frequently. We may try to create less garbage. We might support laws that require industries to reduce the amount of pollution they create.

Parents and schools have the important task of helping children learn to understand and appreciate nature. Parents should encourage their children to play outside. They should encourage them to notice the wild plants and animals around them. Schools should devote part of the curriculum to environmental studies, starting with the earliest grades.

Adults need to show children that caring for our natural environment is important. Our future survival depends on it.

Speaking

These are models. Your answers will vary. See page vi in the Introduction to see the criteria for scoring.

PART 1

When and how much leisure time do you generally have in a week?
I have a normal work schedule, nine to five, Monday through Friday, so my leisure time is in the evenings and on the weekends.

Who do you generally spend your leisure time with?
I spend my evenings at home with my family. I rarely see other people during the week. On weekends we might get together as a family with other families that have children the same age as ours. Sometimes on weekends I have the chance to spend time with my own friends, without my family.

What are some activities you enjoy in your leisure time?
Sometimes I just like to sit and relax because I'm so tired after work. I also enjoy talking with my family and playing games with my children. On weekends we often enjoy going to the movies together. We also spend time at the park if the weather is nice.

What do you like about these activities?
For me, leisure time is important because it's my time to relax and be with my family. I like playing games with my children because it gives me the chance to know

them better and also to teach or guide them. Also, it's fun. I enjoy my children. After we've seen a movie together, we always talk about it. It's nice to share things like this with my family. It's interesting to hear what my children think about and how they understand things.

What kinds of music do you like listening to?
I listen to music to relax, so I generally like slow, quiet music. I often listen to classical music, and I like romantic music, too.

Have you learned to play a musical instrument? Why or why not?
When I was a child, I took piano lessons for about a year. I wasn't very good at it, though, so I wasn't motivated to continue or to try another instrument. I just don't think I have musical talent. But I like listening to other people play music.

Tell me about any traditional music in your country.
We mostly hear traditional music on holidays or at special festivals. It's played with guitar and some other string instruments. Some of the songs are very pretty. I like it, but I don't get the chance to hear it much since it's just for special occasions. There are some traditional dances that go with the music, but hardly anyone knows them anymore.

Do you think that traditional music will be popular in the future? Why or why not?
These days our traditional music is played only by certain musicians who specialize in it. Not many people know how to play it or know the songs. Children learn a few of the songs in school, but that's all. It's very nice music, but it isn't commonly played or listened to now, so I think in the future it will be even less common. Unfortunately, it may soon die out. I think in the near future there won't be anyone left who knows how to play our traditional music.

PART 2

I recently saw a movie called *The Secret Garden.* It takes place more than 100 years ago. It's about a lonely little girl who is an orphan. She goes to live with an elderly relative in a big house in the country. There she discovers a garden that no one is allowed to enter. The movie is about how she discovers the secret history of the garden, and how she makes some friends in the process and isn't lonely anymore. I saw the movie with my husband and children a few weeks ago. We saw it at the movie theater that's near our house, where we often go to see movies. I really enjoyed this movie. It's a nice story for children. It shows them some sad things in life—loneliness and loss, and some good things as well—friendship and gardens. It's a little bit scary but not too scary, and the ending is very happy. The characters seem very real, and the actors are very good. The movie didn't rely on special effects or fast action or loud music to hold children's attention. Rather, it was a well-done movie with a good story. My children enjoyed it too and it gave us a lot to talk about afterward.

PART 3

What kinds of movies are popular these days? Why do you think they are popular?
Romantic movies seem to be popular, and I think they always have been. Everybody dreams of romance, but since we often don't have it in real life, we enjoy seeing it in the movies. Action movies are popular, too, and I think for the same reason—we don't have much action in our lives, so we get it from watching movies.

What can we learn from watching movies?
From some movies we can learn about life in other places and other times, but we have to be careful about that because not all movies are factual. We can also learn about the same things we can learn from literature, themes like love, loss, overcoming difficulties, heroism, things like that.

How are movies different from live theater?
In the theater, everything takes place on the stage, so I think theater relies a lot more on the acting to convey the sense of place, the mood, things like that. A movie is filmed in a real setting and can use real scenery not only to tell the story but also to convey mood, foreshadow events, and other things. Watching live theater is quite different from watching a movie, but I enjoy them both.

How do you think movies will be different in the future?
I think in the future movies will make much more use of computers. There will probably be more animated films. Special effects will be more elaborate and will probably be used a lot more. However, I think that the types of movies made isn't going to change much. There will still be romance movies, action movies, sad movies, spy thrillers, all the same kinds of movies we enjoy now.

ACADEMIC MODULE
PRACTICE TEST 3

Academic Module
Practice Test 3

Candidate Name and Number: _____

INTERNATIONAL ENGLISH LANGUAGE TESTING SYSTEM

LISTENING

TIME APPROX. 30 MINUTES

Instructions to Candidates

Do not open this booklet until you are told to do so.

Write your name and candidate number in the space at the top of this page.

You should answer all questions.

All the recordings will be played ONCE only.

Write all your answers on the test pages.

At the end of the test, you will be given ten minutes to transfer your answers to an Answer Sheet. (The answer sheet can be found on page 103.)

Do not remove the booklet from the examination room.

Information for Candidates

There are **40** questions on this question paper.

The test is divided as follows:

Section 1	Questions 1–10
Section 2	Questions 11–20
Section 3	Questions 21–30
Section 4	Questions 31–40

SECTION 1 QUESTIONS 1–10

Note

If you do not have access to an audio CD player, please refer to the audio-scripts starting on page 414 when prompted to listen to an audio passsage.

Questions 1–4

Complete the form below.
*Write **NO MORE THAN TWO WORDS AND/OR A NUMBER** for each answer.*

Example: *Grandview* Hotel
                  Reservation Form

Arrival date: **1** _____ 13th. Number of nights: 2
Number of guests: **2** _____
Guest name: *Roxanne* **3** _____
Credit card number **4** _____

Questions 5–7

*Choose **THREE** letters, **A–G**.*
*Which **THREE** places will the caller visit?*

A art museum
B science museum
C shopping mall
D monument
E post office
F restaurant
G park

Questions 8–10

*Choose the correct letters, **A**, **B**, or **C**.*

8 When will the caller arrive at the airport?

   A In the morning
   B In the afternoon
   C At night

9 How will the caller get to the hotel?

   A Subway
   B Bus
   C Taxi

10 What time does the hotel front desk close?

   A 10:00
   B 12:00
   C 2:00

 SECTION 2 QUESTIONS 11–20

Questions 11 and 12

Complete the information below.
*Write **ONE NUMBER** for each answer.*

City Tours
Fare Information

Adult All-Day Pass: **11** $ _____

Children ages 5–12 All-Day Pass: **12** $ _____

Children under age 5:   Free

Questions 13–15

Label the map below.
*Write **NO MORE THAN TWO WORDS** for each answer.*

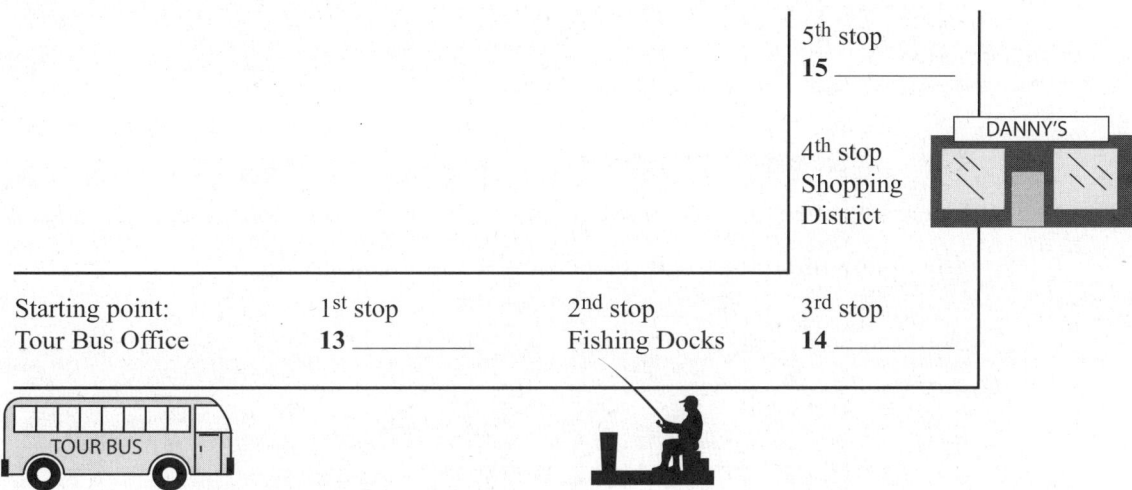

5ᵗʰ stop
15 _____

4ᵗʰ stop
Shopping
District

DANNY'S

Starting point:
Tour Bus Office

1ˢᵗ stop
13 _____

2ⁿᵈ stop
Fishing Docks

3ʳᵈ stop
14 _____

TOUR BUS

Questions 16–20

Complete the chart¹ below.
*Write **NO MORE THAN ONE WORD** for each answer.*

Place	Activity
First stop	Enjoy the **16** _____ of the bay
Second stop	Look at the **17** _____
Third stop	**18** _____ fish.
Fourth stop	Purchase **19** _____
Fifth stop	Visit the **20** _____

¹*British: table*

SECTION 3   *QUESTIONS 21–30*

> ### Questions 21–23
>
> *Answer the questions below.*
> *Write* **NO MORE THAN THREE WORDS AND/OR A NUMBER** *for each answer.*

21 When is the research project due? _____

22 Where will the students conduct the interviews? _____

23 How many interviews will they complete all together? _____

> ### Questions 24–30
>
> *Complete the outline showing the steps the students will take to complete their projects.*
> *Write* **NO MORE THAN THREE WORDS** *for each answer.*

A. Read **24** _____
B. **25** _____
C. Get **26** _____
D. **27** _____
E. Get together to **28** _____
F. Prepare **29** _____
G. Give **30** _____

SECTION 4   QUESTIONS 31–40

> *Questions 31–40*
>
> *Complete the timeline below. Write* **NO MORE THAN THREE WORDS AND/OR A NUMBER** *for each answer.*

1832	**31** _____
In her teens	Alcott worked to **32** _____
At age 17	Alcott wrote **33** _____
34 _____	Alcott enlisted as an army nurse.
35 _____	Alcott published her letters in a book called *Hospital Sketches*.
36 _____	Alcott returned from her trip to Europe.
37 _____	Alcott published *Little Women*.
1879	**38** _____ died.
39 _____	Alcott set up a home for her family in Boston.
1888	**40** _____

> Take ten minutes to transfer your answers onto the Answer Sheet on page 103.

Academic Module
Practice Test 3

Candidate Name and Number: _____

INTERNATIONAL ENGLISH LANGUAGE TESTING SYSTEM

ACADEMIC READING

TIME 1. HOUR

Instructions to Candidates

Do not open this booklet until you are told to do so.

Write your name and candidate number in the space at the top of this page.

Start at the beginning of the test and work through it.

You should answer all questions.

If you cannot do a particular question, leave it and go on to the next. You can return to it later.

All answers must be written on the Answer Sheet. (The answer sheet can be found on page 104.)

Do not remove the booklet from the examination room.

Information for Candidates

There are **40** questions on this question paper.

The test is divided as follows:

Reading Passage 1	Questions 1–13
Reading Passage 2	Questions 14–27
Reading Passage 3	Questions 28–40

READING PASSAGE 1

*You should spend about 20 minutes on **Questions 1–13**, which are based on Reading Passage 1 below.*

Questions 1–7

*The following reading passage has seven sections, **A–G**. Choose the correct heading for each section from the list of headings below. Write the correct number, **i–x**, on lines 1–7 on your answer sheet. There are more headings than sections, so you will not use them all.*

LIST OF HEADINGS

i	Scanning the Brain and Chest
ii	The Role of Computers
iii	The CT Scan Is Invented
iv	The High Cost of CT Scans
v	Risks Associated with CT Scans
vi	Emergency Room Care
vii	Faster and More Comfortable
viii	How Doctors Use CT Scans
ix	The Patient Is Photographed
x	Enhancing Scan Images with Dyes

1 Section A

2 Section B

3 Section C

4 Section D

5 Section E

6 Section F

7 Section G

The CT Scanner

A

The computed tomography scanner, better known as the CT scanner, was originally designed to provide cross-sectional images of the brain. The word *tomography* comes from the Greek word *tomos*, meaning "section," and *graphia*, meaning "picture." Godfrey Hounsfield developed the technique in 1972 and was later knighted and awarded the Nobel Peace Prize for his contribution to the medical field. Within four years of this development, CT scans, also called CAT scans (computed axial tomography), were restructured, allowing technicians to scan the entire body for evidence of tumors, injuries, and other abnormalities. Rather than taking a single picture as in an X ray, a CT scanner sends several beams into an area and takes photographs from many different angles.

B

While the original CT scans took Hounsfield several hours to reconstruct into a useful image, today's machines can produce an in-depth image in a fraction of a second. Creating a scanner that could produce images at a faster rate was crucial in the development of tomography, as it reduced the degree of distortion in an image caused when patients breathed and moved. As well as providing images with better resolution, today's scanners also provide more comfort for the patient.

C

During a CT scan, a patient must lie still on a special table while the radiology technician locates the specific area that needs to be photographed. The table slides into a round tunnel (gantry), where it can be rotated or moved forward and backward in order to obtain the necessary view. Inside the donut-shaped[1] machine, a number of X rays are taken, each producing a small slice of the image that doctors require. When passing through dense tissue such as a bone, the X-ray beams are weak and appear white in the CT images. Tissues such as those found in the brain are less dense and appear gray. Images that appear black denote organs such as lungs or others that can fill with air.

D

The CT scanner is made up of several computer systems, including the host computer, which organizes[2] the entire process. One of the computers converts the raw data into an image, while another allows the technician to control the rotation of the gantry. After the information is processed, it is displayed on a monitor for radiologists and physicians to analyze.[3] The information is also saved and printed to keep in a doctor's records and to share and discuss with patients and their family members.

E

Physicians order CT scans for a number of different reasons, including searching for and assessing tumors, cysts, kidney stones, and bone injuries. Without this technology, surgeons would have to perform many needless and costly operations. Brain, chest, and abdominal CT scans are the most common, though physicians also rely on the CT scanner to guide their needles while draining an abscess or performing a biopsy. Most emergency or shock-treatment centers contain a CT scanner in order to assess trauma victims. CT scans can pinpoint internal bleeding both in the brain and throughout the body.

F

In many cases, a patient must be given a contrast material before undergoing a CT scan. During "dynamic CT scanning," iodine dye is either injected into the blood or added to a drink that the patient must ingest approximately forty-five minutes

---

[1] *British: doughnut-shaped*
[2] *British: organises*
[3] *British: analyse*

before entering the scanner. The liquid X-ray dye makes it easier to see the organs and blood vessels when the pictures are developed. The intravenous contrast material is typically used for chest or pelvic scans, while oral-contrast material is used for abdominal scans. In some cases, physicians request that pictures be taken both before and after the contrast material enters the patient's body. Patients who receive contrast material in the arm often report feeling a warm sensation, and in rare cases an allergic reaction occurs. Contrast material causes water loss and is avoided when scanning patients who suffer from kidney failure.

G

The danger of radiation exposure caused by X-ray beams is generally considered minimal compared to the benefits that a CT scan can provide. In many cases, especially in the detection of tumors and internal bleeding, CT scans provide information that can save a person's life. Full-body scanning, which is saved for serious conditions such as coronary artery disease, remains a controversial procedure as prolonged exposure to radiation is linked to cancer. Pregnant women are excluded from receiving CT scans, as the X rays can be harmful to the fetus. When pregnant woman require an evaluation, most physicians favor using other procedures such as an ultrasound or an MRI.

Questions 8–10

*Which of the following are facts about the original CT scanner mentioned in the passage? Choose **THREE** answers from the list below and write the correct letters, **A–F**, on lines 8–10 on your answer sheet.*

A It made it difficult for patients to breathe.
B It was created to take pictures of the brain.
C It was much bigger than current CT scanners.
D It was developed in 1972.
E It took several hours to produce a completed image.
F It produced images in color.

Questions 11–13

*Which of the following are facts about contrast materials used for CT scans mentioned in the passage? Choose **THREE** answers from the list below and write the correct letters, **A–F**, on lines 11–13 on your answer sheet.*

A They are bright in color.
B They can be given by injection.
C They have a bitter taste.
D They might cause a feeling of warmth in the arm.
E They are administered only by a specially trained technician.
F They may cause allergies in a few patients.

READING PASSAGE 2

*You should spend about 20 minutes on **Questions 14–27**, which are based on Reading Passage 2 below.*

Nineteenth-Century Paperback Literature

A publishing craze that hit both America and England from the mid- to late nineteenth century attracted the readership of the semiliterate working class. In America, dime novels typically centered on tales of the American Revolution and the Wild West, while British penny bloods (later called penny dreadfuls) told serial tales of horror or fictionalized[1] versions of true crimes. These paperback novels were sold at newsstands and dry goods stores and succeeded in opening up the publishing market for both writers and readers. The industrial revolution facilitated the growth of literacy, making it easier to print and transport publications in large quantities, thus providing inexpensive entertainment for the masses.

Though Johann Gutenberg's printing press was designed in the fifteenth century, it was not until after the first newspapers began circulating in the eighteenth century that it became a profitable invention. Throughout the nineteenth century, commoners in England were becoming educated through normal schools, church schools, and mutual instruction classes, and by the 1830s, approximately 75 percent of the working class had learned to read. In 1870, the Forster Education Act made elementary education mandatory for all children. Though few children's books were available, penny dreadfuls were highly accessible, especially to male youths who created clubs in order to pool their money and start their own libraries. Similar to reading a newspaper, dime novels and penny dreadfuls were meant to be read quickly and discarded, unlike the hardbound high literature that was written in volumes and published for the elite. Struggling authors, many of whom had limited writing and storytelling skills, suddenly found an audience desperate to read their work. When the first typewriter became available in the 1870s, authors were able to maximize[2] their output. Successful authors, some of whom wrote over 50,000 words a month, were able to earn a decent living at a penny per word.

From the 1830s to 1850s, penny bloods featured tales of gore that often depicted the upper class as corrupt. One of the most beloved characters from the penny blood serials was Sweeney Todd. In the original story, *String of Pearls: A Romance*, published in 1846, Sweeney Todd was a demon barber who used his razor to torture his victims before turning them into meat pies. In 1847, hack-playwright George Dibdin Pitt adapted Thomas Prest's story for the stage,

---

[1] *British: fictionalised*
[2] *British: maximise*

renaming it *The String of Pearls: The Fiend of Fleet Street*. With no copyright laws, authors were always at risk of having their ideas pilfered. Pitt's play was released again one year later at one of London's "bloodbath" theaters[1] under the name *Founded on Fact*. The Sweeney Todd story also made its way into musicals and comedies. Controversy still exists over whether Thomas Prest's character was based on a real person. No records of a barber shop on Fleet Street, or a barber named Sweeney Todd have been found, though Thomas Prest was known for getting his inspiration from "The Old Bailey" of the *London Times*, a section devoted to real-life horror stories.

Despite the warning from Lord Shaftsbury that the paperback literature was seducing middle-class society into an unproductive life of evil, the penny bloods grew in popularity. They provided a literary voice for commoners at an affordable price. Eventually, penny bloods became known as penny dreadfuls and began to focus more on adventure than horror.

In 1860, Beadle and Adams was the first firm in the United States to publish a title that would be categorized[2] as a dime novel. *Malaeska: The Indian Wife of the White Hunter*, by Anne Stephens, had originally been published twenty years earlier as a series in a magazine. In novel form, approximately 300,000 copies of the story were sold in the first year, paving the way for the new fad in America. Many dime novels were written as serials with recurring characters, such as Deadwood Dick, Commander Cody, and Wild Bill. Originally, the paperbacks were intended for railroad travelers; however, during the Civil War, soldiers quickly became the most avid dime novel readers. Beadle dime novels became so popular that the company had to build a factory of hack writers to mass produce them. As urbanization[3] spread, stories of the Wild West were in less demand, and tales of urban outlaws became popular. At that time, dime novels were chosen for their illustrated covers rather than their sensational stories and characters. Despite their popularity, by the late 1880s dry goods stores were so full of unsold books that prices dropped to less than five cents per copy. Many titles that could still not sell were given away or destroyed. The International Copyright Law, passed by Congress in 1890, required publishers to pay royalties to foreign authors. Selling at less than five cents a copy, the paperback industry was doomed until the arrival of pulp paper.

---

[1] *British: theatres*
[2] *British: categorised*
[3] *British: urbanisation*

Questions 14–19

Which of the characteristics below belongs to which type of literature? On lines 14–19 on your answer sheet write:

> **A** if it is characteristic of penny bloods
>
> **B** if it is characteristic of dime novels
>
> **C** if it is characteristic of both penny bloods and dime novels

14 They were popular in America.

15 They were popular in Britain.

16 They showed members of the upper class as corrupt.

17 They were inexpensive.

18 They featured tales of the Wild West.

19 They were popular among members of the working class.

Questions 20–23

Match each year with the event that occurred during that year. Choose the correct event, A–F, from the box below and write the correct letter on lines 20–23 on your answer sheet. There are more events than years, so you will not use them all.

20 1870

21 1846

22 1860

23 1890

> **EVENTS**
>
> **A** The first dime novel was published in the United States.
>
> **B** Lord Shaftsbury warned people about the dangers of penny bloods.
>
> **C** if it is characteristic of both penny bloods and dime novels
>
> **D** A law was passed requiring children to attend school.
>
> **E** A law about copyrights was passed.
>
> **F** The first Sweeney Todd story was published.

Questions 24–27

Do the following statements agree with the information in the reading passage? On lines 24–27 on your answer sheet write:

YES	if the statement agrees with the views of the writer
NO	if the statement disagrees with the views of the writer
NOT GIVEN	if there is no information on this in the passage

24 The literacy rate in England rose in the nineteenth century.

25 Children's books were popular in the nineteenth century.

26 Most people agree that Sweeney Todd was based on a real person.

27 Dime novels were popular among Civil War soldiers.

READING PASSAGE 3

You should spend about 20 minutes on **Questions 28–40**, *which are based on Reading Passage 3 below.*

Cosmic Black Holes

In 1687, the English scientist Isaac Newton published his monumental work, *Philosophiae Naturalis Principia Mathematica (Mathematical Principles of Natural Philosophy)*, containing his theory of gravitation and the mathematics to support it. In essence, Newton's law of gravitation stated that the gravitational force between two objects, for example, two astronomical bodies, is directly proportional to their masses. Astronomers found that it accurately predicted all the observable data that science at that time was able to collect, with one exception— a very slight variation in the orbit of the planet Mercury around the sun.

It was 228 years before anyone was able to offer a refinement of Newton's law that accounted for the shape of Mercury's orbit. In 1915, Albert Einstein's general theory of relativity was published. Using the equations of general relativity, he calculated the shape of Mercury's orbit. The results predicted astronomical observations exactly and provided the first proof of his theory. Expressing it very simplistically, the general theory of relativity presumes that both matter and energy can distort space–time and cause it to curve. What we commonly call gravity is in fact the effect of that curvature.

Among other phenomena, Einstein's theory predicted the existence of black holes, although initially he had doubts about their existence. Black holes are areas in space where the gravitational field is so strong that nothing can escape them. Because of the immense gravitational pull, they consume all the light that comes near them, and thus they are "black." In fact, neither emitting nor reflecting light, they are invisible. Due to this, they can be studied only by inference based on observations of their effect on the matter—both stars and gases[1]—around them and by computer simulation. In particular, when gases are being pulled into a black hole, they can reach temperatures up to 1,000 times the heat of the sun and become an intensely glowing source of X rays.

Surrounding each black hole is an "event horizon," which defines the area over which the gravitational force of the black hole operates. Anything passing over the lip of the event horizon is pulled into the black hole. Because observations of event horizons are difficult due to their relatively small size, even less is known about them than about black holes themselves.

Black holes exist in three sizes. Compact ones, called star-mass black holes and which have been known to exist for some time, are believed to be the result of the death of a single star. When a star has consumed itself to the point that it no longer has the energy to support its mass, the core collapses and forms a black hole. Shock waves then bounce out, causing the shell of the star to explode. In a way that is not yet understood, the black hole may then reenergize[2] and create multiple explosions within the first few minutes of its existence. So-called super-massive black holes, also well documented, contain the mass of millions or even billions of stars. And just recently one intermediate black hole, with about 500 times the mass of the sun, has been discovered. Scientists have postulated that the intermediate black hole may provide a "missing link" in understanding the evolution of black holes.

Current scientific data suggest that black holes are fairly common and lie at the center of most galaxies. Based on indirect evidence gained using X-ray telescopes, thousands of black holes have been located in our galaxy and beyond. The black hole at the center of the Milky Way, known as Sagittarius A* (pronounced "A-star"), is a supermassive one, containing roughly four million times the mass of our sun. Astronomers suggest that orbiting around Sagittarius A*, 26,000 light years from Earth, may be as many as tens of thousands of smaller black holes. One possible theory to explain this is that a process called "dynamical friction" is causing stellar black holes to sink toward the center of the galaxy.

It is thought that the first black holes came into existence not long after the big bang. Newly created clouds of gases slowly coalesced into the first stars. As these early stars collapsed, they gave rise to the first black holes. A number of theories proposed that the first black holes were essentially "seeds," which then gravitationally attracted and consumed enormous quantities of matter found in adjacent gas clouds and dust. This allowed them to grow into the super-massive black holes that now sit in the centers of galaxies. However, a new computer

---

[1] *British: gasses*
[2] *British: reenergise*

simulation proposes that such growth was minimal. When the simulated star collapsed and formed a black hole, there was very little matter anywhere near the black hole's event horizon. Being in essence "starved," it grew by less than 1 percent over the course of its first hundred million years. The new simulations do not definitively invalidate the seed theory, but they make it far less likely. On the other hand, it is known that black holes a billion times more massive than our sun did exist in the early universe. Researchers have yet to discover how these super-massive black holes were formed in such a short time, and the origin of these giants poses one of the most fundamental questions in astrophysics.

It has become practically a hallmark of the research on black holes that with each new study, more is known, more theories are generated, and yet more questions are raised than answered.

Questions 28–34

*Complete each sentence with the correct ending, **A–N**, below.*
*Write the correct letter, **A–N**, on lines 28–34 on your answer sheet.*

28 Newton's law of gravitation

29 Einstein's theory of relativity

30 We define black holes as areas that have

31 Scientists study black holes

32 Gases that are pulled into a black hole

33 Event horizons are

34 Compact black holes occur

A	by observing the matter around them.
B	suggested the presence of black holes in outer space.
C	when a single star collapses.
D	difficult to study.
E	barely visible light.
F	an inescapable gravitational pull.
G	did not apply to most astronomical bodies.
H	by direct observation.
I	could not explain Mercury's path around the sun.
J	caused doubt about the existence of black holes.
K	lose visibility.
L	become very hot.
M	with large event horizons.
N	at the center of each black hole.

Questions 35 and 36

*Choose the correct letter, **A**, **B**, or **C**, in boxes 35 and 36 on your answer sheet.*

35 Black holes can be found

    A only in the Milky Way.
    B in most galaxies.
    C close to the sun.

36 Sagittarius A* is

    A a black hole located 26,000 light years from Earth.
    B one of thousands of black holes orbiting Earth.
    C a well-known compact black hole.

Questions 37–40

Do the following statements agree with the information given in the passage? On lines 37–40 on your answer sheet, write:

TRUE	if the statement agrees with the information
FALSE	if the statement contradicts the information
NOT GIVEN	if there is no information on this.

37 It is not certain when the big bang occurred.

38 According to the "seed" theory, the first black holes eventually became super-massive black holes.

39 The "seed" theory has been proven true by computer simulation.

40 The black holes that existed in the early universe were all compact black holes.

Academic Module
Practice Test 3

Candidate Name and Number: _____

INTERNATIONAL ENGLISH LANGUAGE TESTING SYSTEM

ACADEMIC WRITING

TIME 1 HOUR

Instructions to Candidates

Do not open this booklet until you are told to do so.

Write your name and candidate number in the space at the top of this page.

All answers must be written on the separate answer booklet provided. Answer sheets can be found beginning on page 105.

Do not remove the booklet from the examination room.

Information for Candidates

There are **2** tasks on this question paper.

You must do **both** tasks.

Under-length answers will be penalized.[1]

---

[1] *British: penalised*

WRITING TASK 1

> You should spend about 20 minutes on this task. Write at least 150 words.

The charts below show degrees granted in different fields at the National University in the years 1990, 2000, and 2010.

Summarize[1] the information by selecting and reporting the main features, and make comparisons where relevant.

Degrees Granted at the National University

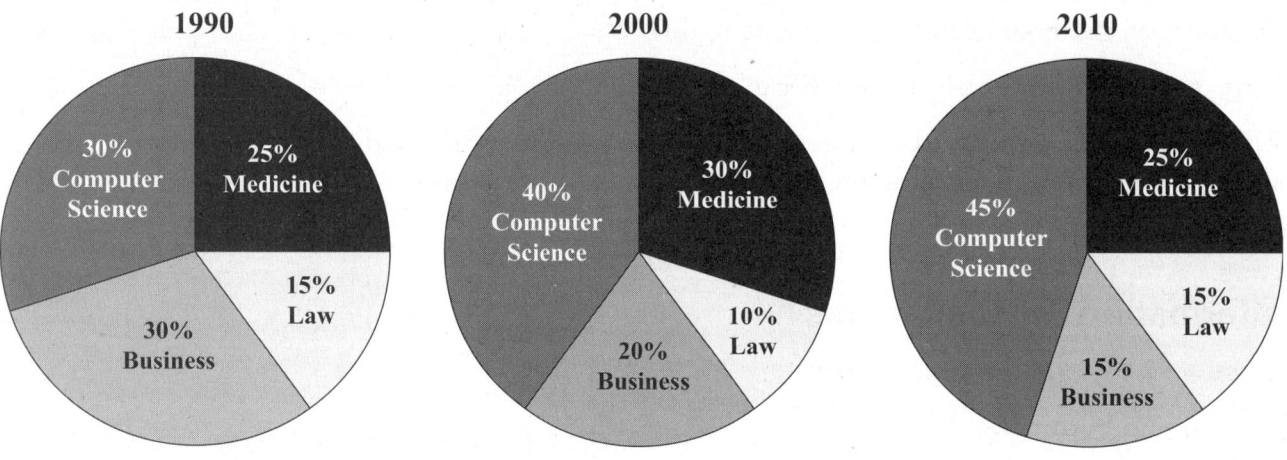

WRITING TASK 2

> You should spend about 40 minutes on this task. Write at least 250 words.

Write about the following topic:

> *All children should study a foreign language in school, starting in the earliest grades.*

To what extent do you agree or disagree with this statement? Give reasons for your answer and include any relevant examples from your own knowledge or experience.

---

[1] *British: Summarise*

SPEAKING

Examiner questions:

Part 1

Describe a place in your city or town where you like to go in your free time.

Why do you like to go there?

Is there anything you don't like about it?

Is it a popular place for people in your city? Why or why not?

Describe a park in your neighborhood or city.

What are some things people can do there?

Do you enjoy spending time there? Why or why not?

Are parks important? Why or why not?

Part 2

Describe a hobby you enjoy doing.

You should say:

What the hobby is

What materials or tools you need for it

How you learned to do it and explain why you enjoy it

> You will have one to two minutes to talk about this topic.
>
> You will have one minute to prepare what you are going to say.

Part 3

Why do people have hobbies?

Are there any hobbies you think are not worthwhile?

What can we learn from hobbies?

Is it important to teach hobbies to children? Why or why not?

Practice Test 3—Academic Module
IELTS LISTENING ANSWER SHEET

1. _____
2. _____
3. _____
4. _____
5. _____
6. _____
7. _____
8. _____
9. _____
10. _____
11. _____
12. _____
13. _____
14. _____
15. _____
16. _____
17. _____
18. _____
19. _____
20. _____

21. _____
22. _____
23. _____
24. _____
25. _____
26. _____
27. _____
28. _____
29. _____
30. _____
31. _____
32. _____
33. _____
34. _____
35. _____
36. _____
37. _____
38. _____
39. _____
40. _____

Practice Test 3—Academic Module
IELTS READING ANSWER SHEET

1. _____
2. _____
3. _____
4. _____
5. _____
6. _____
7. _____
8. _____
9. _____
10. _____
11. _____
12. _____
13. _____
14. _____
15. _____
16. _____
17. _____
18. _____
19. _____
20. _____

21. _____
22. _____
23. _____
24. _____
25. _____
26. _____
27. _____
28. _____
29. _____
30. _____
31. _____
32. _____
33. _____
34. _____
35. _____
36. _____
37. _____
38. _____
39. _____
40. _____

Practice Test 3–Academic Module
WRITING TASK 1

Writing Task 1 *continued*

Practice Test 3—Academic Module
WRITING TASK 2

Writing Task 2 *continued*

Writing Task 2 *continued*

Answer Key
PRACTICE TEST 3—ACADEMIC MODULE

Listening

1. February	12. 9	23. thirty	31. Alcott was born.
2. one	13. Hill Park	24. a government study	32. support her family.
3. Wilson	14. Bay Bridge	25. design the	33. her first novel/The
4. 2336189872	15. Green Street	questionnaire	Inheritance
5. C	16. view	26. professor's	34. 1862
6. F	17. boats	approval/approval for	35. after the war
7. G	18. eat	questionnaire	36. 1866
8. C	19. baskets	27. conduct interviews	37. 1868
9. A	20. theater	28. analyze the results	38. May died.
10. C	21. in three weeks	29. charts (showing results)	39. 1882
11. 18	22. a shopping mall	30. class presentation	40. Alcott died.

Reading

1. iii	11. B	21. F	31. A
2. vii	12. D	22. A	32. L
3. ix	13. F	23. E	33. D
4. ii	14. B	24. Yes	34. C
5. viii	15. A	25. No	35. B
6. x	16. A	26. No	36. A
7. v	17. C	27. Yes	37. Not Given
8. B	18. B	28. I	38. True
9. D	19. C	29. B	39. False
10. E	20. D	30. F	40. False

Answer Explanations

ACADEMIC MODULE—PRACTICE TEST 3

Listening

1. *February.* The man says, "So, that's February 13th and 14th," and the woman confirms this.

2. *one.* The man asks, "And how many guests will there be?" and the woman replies, "Just me," meaning she will be the only guest.

3. *Wilson.* The woman spells her last name.

4. *2336189872.* The woman gives her credit card number, and the man repeats the last four digits.

5. **(C)** The woman says she loves shopping, and the man directs her to a shopping mall.

6. **(F)** The woman asks about a place to eat lunch, and the man tells her about a nearby restaurant.

7. **(G)** The woman says that she will walk in the park after having lunch at the restaurant.

8. **(C)** The woman says that she will be arriving after 10:00 P.M. Choice (A) is confused with when she will have free time, "Friday morning." Choice (B) is not mentioned.

9. **(A)** The man says the subway runs late, and the woman then says, "Then I'll do that," meaning that she will take the subway.

10. **(C)** The man says, "The front desk stays open until two." Choice (A) is the time that the woman will arrive. Choice (B) is how late the subways run.

11. *18.* The speaker says, "The all-day bus pass costs eighteen dollars for adults."

12. *9.* The speaker says, "Children between the ages of five and twelve pay half the adult fare. . . ."

13. *Hill Park.* The speaker says, "the bus goes to the first stop, Hill Park."

14. *Bay Bridge.* The speaker says, "the bus goes on to the third stop, Bay Bridge. . . ."

15. *Green Street.* The speaker says, "then the fifth and last stop is at Green Street."

16. *view.* The speaker says, "At the first stop, you can enjoy a spectacular view of the bay. . . ."

17. *boats.* The speaker says, "At the second stop, you can walk around and look at the boats."

18. *eat.* The speaker says, "You can eat fresh fish here prepared in the traditional local way."

19. *baskets.* The speaker says, "Don't miss the opportunity to purchase some of our city's famous handmade baskets."

20. *theater.* The speaker says, "Finally, at the last stop on the tour, you can visit one of the oldest buildings in our city, the theater."

21. *in three weeks.* The two students start out by discussing when the project is due, and Student 2 says it's due in "only three more weeks."

22. *a shopping mall.* Student 1 suggests the shopping mall, and Student 2 agrees.

23. *thirty.* They will conduct fifteen interviews each to meet the required total of thirty.

24. *a government study.* The students discuss reading a government study so that they can compare their results to the government study results.

25. *design the questionnaire.* Student 2 says, "Yes, so we'd better read that first and then design our questionnaire."

26. *professor's approval/approval for questionnaire.* Student 1 says, "The professor said she had to approve our questionnaire first, before we actually conducted the interviews."

27. *conduct interviews.* Student 2 says, "So we'll get her approval and then conduct the interviews."

28. *analyze the results.* Student 2 says, "And let's also plan to get together the next day to analyze the results."

29. *charts (showing results).* Student 1 says, "Well, I think the obvious thing is to prepare some charts showing our results. . . ."

30. *class presentation.* Student 1 says, "All that will be left to do is give the class presentation."

31. *Alcott was born.* The speaker says, "She was born in 1832. . . ."

32. *support her family.* The speaker says, "As a teenager, she worked to support her family. . . ."

33. *her first novel/The Inheritance.* The speaker says, "She wrote her first novel when she was just seventeen years old. . . . It was called *The Inheritance.*"

34. *1862.* The speaker says, "In 1861, the Civil War broke out. . . . The following year, she enlisted as an army nurse."

35. *after the war.* The speaker says, "After the war, she turned the letters into a book which was published under the title *Hospital Sketches.*"

36. *1866.* The speaker says, "When she returned home from Europe in 1866. . . ."

37. *1868.* The speaker says, "Her big break came in 1868 with the publication of her first novel for girls, *Little Women.*"

38. *May died.* The speaker says, "In 1878, her youngest sister, May, got married. A year later, May died. . . ."

39. *1882.* The speaker says, "In 1882, Bronson Alcott suffered a stroke. Soon after that, Louisa Alcott set up a house for him, her niece, her sister Anna, and Anna's two sons in Boston."

40. *Alcott died.* The speaker says, "She died in March of 1888 at the age of 55."

Reading

PASSAGE 1

1. *iii.* Section A explains the origin and development of the CT scanner.

2. *vii.* Section B talks about how CT scanners were developed to work faster so that images were less distorted and patients were more comfortable.

3. *ix.* Section C explains the process of getting X-ray images of the patient.

4. *ii.* Section D explains the computer systems used for CT scans.

5. *viii.* Section E talks about the different circumstances for which CT scans are used.

6. *x.* Section F explains the use of dyes to make CT scan images easier to analyze.

7. *v.* Section G talks about possible dangers to patients receiving CT scans.

8. **(B)** Section A: "The computed tomography scanner, better known as the CT scanner, was originally designed to provide cross-sectional images of the brain."

9. **(D)** Section A: "Godfrey Hounsfield developed the technique in 1972. . . ."

10. **(E)** Section B: "While the original CT scans took Hounsfield several hours to reconstruct into a useful image. . . ."

11. **(B)** Section F: "During 'dynamic CT scanning,' iodine dye is either injected into the blood. . . ."

12. **(D)** Section F: "Patients who receive contrast material in the arm often report feeling a warm sensation. . . ."

13. **(F)** Section F: "in rare cases an allergic reaction occurs."

PASSAGE 2

14. **(B)** Paragraph 1: "In America, dime novels. . . ."

15. **(A)** Paragraph 1: "while British penny bloods (later called penny dreadfuls) told serial tales of horror or fictionalized versions of true crimes."

16. **(A)** Paragraph 3: "penny bloods featured tales of gore that often depicted the upper class as corrupt."

17. **(C)** Paragraph 1: "thus providing inexpensive entertainment for the masses."

18. **(B)** Paragraph 1: "dime novels typically centered on tales of the American Revolution and the Wild West. . . ."

19. **(C)** Paragraph 1: "A publishing craze that hit both America and England from the mid- to late nineteenth century attracted the readership of the semiliterate working class."

20. **(D)** Paragraph 2: "In 1870, the Forster Education Act made elementary education mandatory for all children."

21. **(F)** Paragraph 3: "In the original story, *String of Pearls: A Romance*, published in 1846, Sweeney Todd. . . ."

22. **(A)** Paragraph 5: "In 1860, Beadle and Adams was the first firm in the United States to publish a title that would be categorized as a dime novel."

23. **(E)** Paragraph 5: "The International Copyright Law, passed by Congress in 1890, required publishers to pay royalties to foreign authors."

24. *Yes.* Paragraph 2: "by the 1830s, approximately 75 percent of the working class had learned to read."

25. *No.* Paragraph 2: "Though few children's books were available. . . ."

26. *No.* Paragraph 3: "Controversy still exists over whether Thomas Prest's character was based on a real person."

27. *Yes.* Paragraph 5: "during the Civil War, soldiers quickly became the most avid dime novel readers."

PASSAGE 3

28. **(I)** Paragraph 1: "Astronomers found that it accurately predicted all the observable data . . ., with one exception—a very slight variation in the orbit of the planet Mercury around the sun."

29. **(B)** Paragraph 3: "Among other phenomena, Einstein's theory predicted the existence of black holes."

30. **(F)** Paragraph 3: "Black holes are areas in space where the gravitational field is so strong that nothing can escape them."

31. **(A)** Paragraph 3: "they can be studied only by inference based on observations of their effect on the matter—both stars and gases—around them and by computer simulation."

32. **(L)** Paragraph 3: "when gases are being pulled into a black hole, they can reach temperatures up to 1,000 times the heat of the sun. . . . "

33. **(D)** Paragraph 4: "Because observations of event horizons are difficult due to their relatively small size, even less is known about them than about black holes themselves."

34. **(C)** Paragraph 5: "Compact ones . . . are believed to be the result of the death of a single star."

35. **(B)** Paragraph 6: "Current scientific data suggest that black holes are fairly common and lie at the center of most galaxies." Choice (A) is contradicted by the information in paragraph 6. Choice (C) is confused with the mention of the sun, but it is used to describe the size, not the location, of a back hole.

36. **(A)** Paragraph 6 explains that Sagittarius A* is a black hole in the center of the Milky Way and 26,000 light years from Earth. Choice (B) uses words from the paragraph, but black holes do not orbit Earth. Choice (C) is incorrect because the paragraph tells us that Sagittarius A* is a super-massive, not a compact, black hole.

37. *Not Given.* The big bang is mentioned, but the time of its occurrence is not.

38. *True.* Paragraph 7: "A number of theories proposed that the first black holes were essentially "seeds," which then gravitationally attracted . . . matter . . . . This allowed them to grow into the super-massive black holes."

39. *False.* Paragraph 7: "The new simulations do not definitively invalidate the seed theory, but they make it far less likely."

40. *False.* Paragraph 7: "it is known that black holes a billion times more massive than our sun did exist in the early universe."

Writing

These are models. Your answers will vary. See page vi in the Introduction to see the criteria for scoring.

WRITING TASK 1

The three pie charts show the different kinds of degrees granted by the National University in three different years. The fields of study shown are Medicine, Law, Business, and Computer Science. The percentage of the total degrees granted for each field changes over the three years shown.

In 1990, Business and Computer Science were the most popular fields of study. Thirty percent of the degrees granted were in Business, and another 30 percent were in Computer Science. Medicine accounted for 25 percent of the degrees, and Law accounted for only 15 percent.

The figures changed somewhat in 2000. Computer Science had gained popularity, with 40 percent of the degrees granted in this field. Business had dropped to 20 percent, and Law had dropped to 10 percent. Medicine accounted for 30 percent of the degrees.

In 2010, an even greater percentage of students had earned Computer Science degrees, with 45 percent of the total degrees in this field. Business and Medicine had both lost popularity, dropping to 15 percent and 25 percent of the total degrees granted, respectively. Law, on the other hand, had gone back up to 15 percent of the total degrees granted. The only field that consistently grew in popularity in the time period shown was Computer Science.

WRITING TASK 2

I strongly agree that all children should study a foreign language in school, starting from their first day of school. Learning how to communicate with people in other countries is very important in the modern world, and we need to speak different languages in order to do this. Childhood is the best time to learn foreign languages.

Modern technology has made the world smaller. By airplane, we can travel to faraway countries in just a few hours. With the Internet, we can communicate instantly with people on the other side of the world. People do business with people in other countries, buy products from other countries, and, unfortunately, have wars with foreign countries. None of these activities are new, but they have become easier to do and more common because of modern technology. Therefore, it is now more important than ever to know how to speak one, two, or more foreign languages.

To learn a foreign language well, it is best to start in childhood. Children's brains are made for learning. Children are eager to absorb new information. Children can learn to speak foreign languages as well as their native language. It is difficult to learn a foreign language quite as well if you start studying it at a later age. Therefore, the best way to learn a foreign language is to start studying it during the first years of school.

The healthy future of our planet depends on people everywhere being able to communicate well. Teaching children to speak foreign languages from the first years of school will go a long way toward achieving this goal.

Speaking

These are models. Your answers will vary. See page vi in the Introduction to see the criteria for scoring.

PART 1

Describe a place in your city or town where you like to go in your free time.
There's a huge shopping mall just outside my city. It's one of the biggest in the country, and people come from all over, even from faraway places, to shop there. It has hundreds of stores of all different kinds. It also has restaurants, clubs, and movie theaters. It also has a couple of areas kind of like indoor parks where you can sit on benches and watch a water fountain. There's a lot you can do there.

Why do you like to go there?
I like to go there because there are so many different things to do. Whatever I may need to buy, I can buy it there. If I want to get together with my friends, it's a good place for us to meet. We have our choice of restaurants, movies, and clubs. It's kind of like a little city all under one roof. I especially like to go there in the winter when it's too cold to be outside.

Is there anything you don't like about it?
I can only think of one thing I don't like about it, and that's the parking situation. The parking garage is very crowded and sometimes I spend a long time driving around looking for an empty spot. That really annoys me. They should have a system to let people know where the empty spaces are so we can go right to them without driving around and around.

Is it a popular place for people in your city? Why or why not?
It's a very popular place for people in my city. The main reason is because there are so many different things to do and buy there. There's something for everyone. Another reason people like it is because it's all indoors. We live in a cold climate, and the winters can be very, very cold. No one likes to walk around outside then. If you go to the shopping mall, you don't have to go outside to get from place to place.

Describe a park in your neighborhood or city.

There's a small park at the end of my street. It has a fountain in the middle and a few benches where you can sit and relax. It also has a small garden. Some of the local neighbors plant flowers there every year.

What are some things people can do there?

It's a small park, so there's not much to do there. It's mostly there for looking pretty. You can sit on the benches and watch the water in the fountain. That's relaxing. You can enjoy the flowers. It's right next to the bus stop, so you can wait for the bus there, too.

Do you enjoy spending time there? Why or why not?

Yes, I like to go there when the weather is nice. After being inside all day at work, I like to go to the park on my way home. It's a way to be outside for a little while. Sometimes I run into friends there. I've gotten to know some of my neighbors by spending time in the park, so that's an advantage.

Are parks important? Why or why not?

Parks are very important in the city. Without parks, there wouldn't be any nice outdoor places to spend time in. Parks add beauty to the city because they're places where we can see trees and flowers. Larger parks also provide places for outdoor sports. Without parks, it would be difficult to do any outdoor activities in a city.

PART 2

A hobby I enjoy is painting. I can't say I'm very artistic, but I like painting. I do watercolor paintings, so the materials I need are paint and brushes, water, and special watercolor paper. I learned to paint by taking classes. Frankly, I can't remember how I got the idea to learn to paint, but once I decided I wanted to do it, I looked for classes at the local community center. I've taken several painting classes there, and I've learned a lot. I enjoy painting because it's very relaxing. When I paint, I can take my mind off my work and off personal problems. I just think about my painting. I also like the challenge. It's a challenge to try to make a painting look the way I want it to look. I work all the time to improve my technique. I've had a lot of frustrations, but when I feel like I've finally made a painting look the way I want it to look, I feel really happy. It's a satisfying feeling. Another thing I like about painting is that it gives me something to hang on the walls of my apartment! Of course, I only hang up the successful paintings.

PART 3

Why do people have hobbies?

I think the biggest reason people have hobbies is to relax. Another reason is that people have different kinds of interests, and hobbies give them a way to pursue those interests. For example, I like art, so I paint as a hobby. People who like music might learn to play the guitar or sing in a local choir. People who like flowers might garden as a hobby. Hobbies give people ways to express different aspects of their personalities and develop different abilities.

Are there any hobbies you think are not worthwhile?

I suppose some people think some things are a waste of time, but it's hard to make that decision for other people. I don't like building ship models, for example. I can't think of anything more boring than that, so for me that would be a real waste of time. But another person might get a lot out of an activity like that. So I think that as long as a hobby is enjoyable to the person who does it, and doesn't cost too much money, we can't say it's not worthwhile.

What can we learn from hobbies?

Depending on the hobby, we can learn different things. People who garden as a hobby can learn about botany. People who play musical instruments can learn about music theory. We can learn about a lot of different things, depending on what our interests are.

Is it important to teach hobbies to children? Why or why not?

Yes, I think it's important to teach hobbies to children. Childhood is a time of trying out different things. By pursuing different kinds of hobbies, children can learn how to do different kinds of things. They can learn about the kinds of things that interest them, and they can discover which things are boring to them. This helps them develop a better sense of who they are. Also, a child who develops hobbies will always have interesting ways to spend his or her time throughout his or her life.

ACADEMIC MODULE
PRACTICE TEST 4

Academic Module
Practice Test 4

Candidate Name and Number: _____

INTERNATIONAL ENGLISH LANGUAGE TESTING SYSTEM

LISTENING

TIME APPROX. 30 MINUTES

Instructions to Candidates

Do not open this booklet until you are told to do so.

Write your name and candidate number in the space at the top of this page.

You should answer all questions.

All the recordings will be played ONCE only.

Write all your answers on the test pages.

At the end of the test, you will be given ten minutes to transfer your answers to an Answer Sheet. (The answer sheet can be found on page 143.)

Do not remove the booklet from the examination room.

Information for Candidates

There are **40** questions on this question paper.

The test is divided as follows:

Section 1	Questions 1–10
Section 2	Questions 11–20
Section 3	Questions 21–30
Section 4	Questions 31–40

SECTION 1 *QUESTIONS 1–10*

Questions 1–10

Complete the form below.
*Write **NO MORE THAN TWO WORDS AND/OR A NUMBER** for each answer.*

Example:	ClearPoint *Telephone Company*
	Customer Order Form
Order taken by:	Ms. Jones _____
Name:	Harold **1** _____
Address:	**2** _____ Fulton Avenue, apartment 12
Type of service:	**3** _____
Employer:	Wrightsville Medical Group
Occupation:	**4** _____
Work phone:	**5** _____
Time at current job:	**6** _____
Special services:	**7** _____ **8** _____
Installation scheduled for:	Day **9** _____ Time of day **10** _____

CD 2 Track 1

SECTION 2   QUESTIONS 11–20

Questions 11–14

*Choose the correct letter, **A**, **B**, or **C**.*

11 The fair will take place at the

    A fairgrounds.
    B park.
    C school.

12 The fair will begin on Friday

    A morning.
    B afternoon.
    C evening.

13 The fair will begin with a

    A parade.
    B dance performance.
    C speech by the mayor.

14 There will be free admission on

    A Friday.
    B Saturday.
    C Sunday.

Questions 15–20

Complete the chart[1] below.
*Write **NO MORE THAN ONE WORD** for each answer.*

Day/Time	Event
Saturday afternoon	15 _____ show
Saturday evening	16 _____ by the lake
Sunday afternoon	17 _____ contest
All weekend	18 _____ food
	19 _____ for children
	20 _____ for sale

[1]*British: table*

SECTION 3   QUESTIONS 21–30

Questions 21–23

Complete the information below.
*Write **NO MORE THAN TWO WORDS** for each answer.*

How to get academic credit for work experience

First, read the **21** _____. Find courses that match your work experience. Then write **22** _____ of your work experience. Submit that together with a letter from your **23** _____ to the university admissions office.

Questions 24–28

Where can the items listed below be found?

A   admissions office

B   counseling center[1]

C   library

---

*Write the correct letter, **A**, **B**, or **C**, next to questions 24–28.*

24   university catalog[2]

25   application for admission form

26   requirements list

27   recommendation forms

28   job listings

---

[1] *British: counselling centre*
[2] *British: catalogue*

Questions 29 and 30

*Choose the correct letters, **A**, **B**, or **C**.*

29 What are full-time students eligible for?

 A Discounted books
 B The work-study program[1]
 C A free bus pass

30 How can a student get financial assistance?

 A Speak with a counselor[2]
 B Apply to the admissions office
 C Make arrangements with a bank

SECTION 4   QUESTIONS 31–40

Questions 31–35

Complete the chart with information about the black bear.
*Write **NO MORE THAN TWO WORDS** for each answer.*

Range	Lives in **31** _____ of North America
Diet	Ninety percent of diet consists of **32** _____.
	Also eats **33** _____
Cubs	Baby bear cubs are born in **34** _____.
Life span	Black bears live for about **35** _____ in the wild.

Questions 36–40

Which characteristics fit black bears and which fit grizzly bears?
*Write **A** if it is a characteristic of black bears. Write **B** if it is a characteristic of grizzly bears.*

36 Has a patch of light fur on its chest ⎯⎯⎯⎯⎯

37 Weighs 225 kilos ⎯⎯⎯⎯⎯

38 Has a shoulder hump ⎯⎯⎯⎯⎯

39 Has pointed ears ⎯⎯⎯⎯⎯

40 Has shorter claws ⎯⎯⎯⎯⎯

Take ten minutes to transfer your answers onto the Answer Sheet on page 143.

---

[1]British: programme
[2]British: counsellor

Academic Module
Practice Test 4

Candidate Name and Number: _____

INTERNATIONAL ENGLISH LANGUAGE TESTING SYSTEM

ACADEMIC READING

TIME 1 HOUR

Instructions to Candidates

Do not open this booklet until you are told to do so.

Write your name and candidate number in the space at the top of this page.

Start at the beginning of the test and work through it.

You should answer all questions.

If you cannot do a particular question, leave it and go on to the next. You can return to it later.

All answers must be written on the Answer Sheet. (The answer sheet can be found on page 144.)

Do not remove the booklet from the examination room.

Information for Candidates

There are **40** questions on this question paper.

The test is divided as follows:

Reading Passage 1	Questions 1–13
Reading Passage 2	Questions 14–27
Reading Passage 3	Questions 28–40

READING PASSAGE 1

*You should spend about 20 minutes on **Questions 1–13**, which are based on Reading Passage 1 below.*

The Gulf Stream and Global Warming

Labrador and London lie at about the same latitude, but Labrador is frigid and has only 30 miles of paved roads while London is one of the major centers[1] of civilization.[2] Why do two places, equidistant from the Arctic Circle, have such disparate climates? The Gulf Stream that flows by the British Isles makes all the difference: Its warm waters make northwestern Europe so abundant with life that palm trees can actually grow on the southern shores of England.

This life-giving Gulf Stream is warm, salty water, which travels along the surface of the Atlantic Ocean from the Caribbean, along the east coast of the United States, and then veers toward Europe. In the tropics, this water is warmed by the sun and becomes saltier because of the higher rate of evaporation in the heat. The Gulf Stream divides as it travels, but the majority of the stream moves north and east. As it travels past Europe, the Gulf Stream warms the atmosphere, and the prevailing westerly winds bring the warmed air to all of northwestern Europe, making the area suitable for intense agriculture. The Gulf Stream makes it possible for Europe to feed an increasingly large population.

After the Gulf Stream reaches southeast Greenland and western Iceland, much of the heat of the stream is gone, and the colder, denser water then sinks. The bulk of the Gulf Stream is carried down toward the ocean floor into as many as seven large vortices, called chimneys. They suck the Gulf Stream waters down over a mile deep, where the water is then drawn into another dynamic ocean current. Almost 2 miles below the surface, this cold water current flows in reverse, from the north southward. When this cold water nears the equator, it is again pulled up from the bottom of the ocean as the surface water is heated and starts its journey north. This upwelling brings with it minerals and food from the detritus at the bottom of the ocean to refresh food supplies for fish and other marine creatures.

This stream of water—the warm water traveling[3] north along the surface and the cold water traveling south along the floor—has become known as the Great Ocean Conveyor Belt. This flow of ocean currents has been extremely important in regulating the temperature of the globe and in making life possible. These currents in the North Atlantic are part of the Great Conveyor Belt that flows through all the oceans of the world. The least stable section of this global current is in the North Atlantic. The Gulf Stream is the most unstable of all.

---

[1] *British: centres*
[2] *British: civilisation*
[3] *British: travelling*

Predictions of the effects of global warming on the Gulf Stream are based on computer models, which differ to some extent. But several important facts are known. South of Greenland, there used to be as many as seven chimneys that pulled water from the Gulf Stream down toward the ocean floor. In the last several years, only one remained, and then, in 2007, that one disappeared. The causes for the demise of the chimneys may include the increase in fresh water from glacial melt. In recent winters, glacial melt has released record amounts of fresh water into the oceans. As the North Atlantic waters, including fresh water from rivers as well as the increased amount of glacial melt, mix with the Gulf Stream, the salt water is diluted. Because fresh water is not as dense as salt water, it does not sink, which impairs the natural mechanism for forming the chimneys. As the chimneys have disappeared, the Gulf Stream has slowed. About 30 percent of the water from the Gulf Stream that used to reach Europe travels elsewhere or is lost in the disintegration of the current, a loss of over six million tons of water flow every second. Without a strong Gulf Stream, the slow, cold water of the lower part of the conveyor belt fails to rise, which reduces the circulation of nutrients for marine life. The problem of warming then worsens: As less surface water, which is full of carbon dioxide from the atmosphere, siphons into the depths of the ocean, less carbon dioxide is removed from the atmosphere, thus increasing global warming.

Ocean sediments and glacial cores show that there have been global swings in temperature in the past. The last Ice Age, when much of North America and northern Europe were covered in glaciers 2 miles thick, occurred when the average temperature dropped about 5 degrees Celsius. That ice age ended about 20,000 years ago. The last "Little Ice Age," when the average temperature dropped only 1 to 2 degrees Celsius, occurred in the sixteenth and seventeenth centuries, hitting Europe hardest. At that time, the Gulf Stream had slowed to about half its usual rate.

Core samples also show that the changes in temperature have been abrupt, not gradual. There would be little time to prepare for the devastating changes resulting from the weakening of the Gulf Stream. The good news is that in the winters of 2008 and 2009, one of the chimneys off southeastern Greenland suddenly burst into action again, bringing the Gulf Stream waters down deep enough to be caught in the conveyor and to keep the ocean currents in the North Atlantic flowing.

Questions 1–7

*Write the correct letter, **A**, **B**, or **C**, on lines 1–7 on your answer sheet.*

1 Labrador and London are similar in

   A climate.
   B distance from the North Pole.
   C abundance of wildlife.

2 Europe can support a large population because

   A it has a lot of fresh water.
   B it is at the proper latitude.
   C it has a good climate for farming.

3 When the Gulf Stream reaches the North Atlantic, it sinks because

   A it has become colder.
   B it has become less salty.
   C it is blown by the winds.

4 Ocean currents help make life on Earth possible because they

   A enable marine life to travel.
   B maintain suitable temperatures.
   C regulate glacial melt.

5 In 2007, the number of vortices, or chimneys, that pulled the waters of the Gulf Stream down toward the ocean floor was

   A zero.
   B one.
   C seven.

6 During the most recent Little Ice Age,

   A the Gulf Stream slowed down significantly.
   B Europe was affected only slightly.
   C glaciers covered much of North America.

7 In the past, climate change has happened

   A at regular intervals.
   B gradually over time.
   C very quickly.

Questions 8–13

*The flow chart below shows a possible effect of global warming on the Gulf Stream. Complete the flow chart using the list of words, **A–L**, below.*

*Write the correct letter, **A–L**, on lines 8–13 on your answer sheet.*

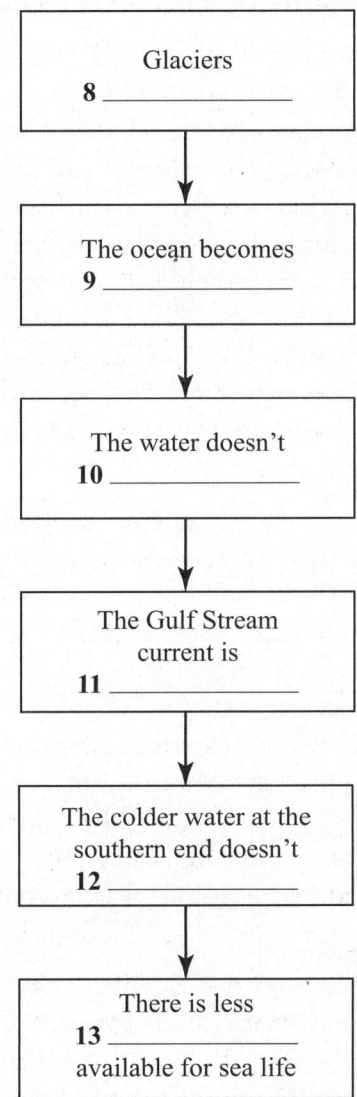

| Glaciers |
| 8 _____ |

↓

| The ocean becomes |
| 9 _____ |

↓

| The water doesn't |
| 10 _____ |

↓

| The Gulf Stream current is |
| 11 _____ |

↓

| The colder water at the southern end doesn't |
| 12 _____ |

↓

| There is less |
| 13 _____ |
| available for sea life |

A less salty	**B** colder	**C** warmer
D sink	**E** rise	**F** weakened
G strengthened	**H** heated	**I** food
J thaw	**K** air	**L** form

READING PASSAGE 2

*You should spend about 20 minutes on **Questions 14–27**, which are based on Reading Passage 2 below.*

Chocolate—Food of the Gods

The cacao plant is believed to have evolved at least 4,000 years ago. It is a small evergreen tree, 15–25 feet high, which grows in the tropical forest understory, where it is protected by the shade of larger trees. The scientific name for the cacao plant is *Theobroma*, which means "food of the gods." Native to the Amazon and Orinoco River basins, it requires a humid climate and regular rainfall. Small pink flowers grow directly on the trunk and older branches. The fruit, a cacao pod, is melon shaped and weighs roughly 1 pound when fully ripened. A mature tree may have as many as 6,000 flowers but will only produce about twenty pods. Each pod contains between twenty and sixty seeds, called beans. The beans have a 40–50 percent fat content, referred to as *cocoa butter*. (*Cacao* is the plant; *cocoa* is the edible derivative and the primary ingredient in chocolate.)

Chemical analysis of pottery vessels unearthed in Puerto Escondido, Honduras, and dating from around 3,100 years ago show traces of a compound that is found exclusively in the cacao plant. At that time, the plant was already being used as a beverage ingredient. However, it was not the cacao beans that were first used. Instead, the first cacao-based drink was probably produced by fermenting the pulp in the cacao pods to yield a beerlike beverage. Researchers speculate that the chocolate drink made from the cacao beans and known later throughout Mesoamerica may have arisen as an accidental by-product of the brewing process. In all, ten small, beautifully crafted drinking vessels were found at the Puerto Escondido site, suggesting that even then the cacao brew was not consumed on a frequent basis but was reserved for important feasts or ceremonial events.

The villagers of Puerto Escondido had likely been influenced by the great Olmec civilization,[1] which flourished for about 800 years beginning 3,200–2,400 years ago in the southern Gulf of Mexico region. Although centered in the modern Mexican states of Tabasco and Veracruz, Olmec influence reached as far south as El Salvador and Honduras. A majority of scholars concur that the Olmec people created the first civilization in the western hemisphere. They built large cities with significant architecture and established commerce extending over hundreds of miles. Relatively little is known about Olmec society because very little archeological[2] evidence has survived the damp

---

[1]*British: civilisation*
[2]*British: archaeological*

climate of the Gulf of Mexico. What is known, however, is that the later Mayan peoples, who did leave behind a great deal of cultural evidence, based much of their high culture on earlier Olmec traditions.

Mayan civilization flourished in southern Mexico and Central America from around 500 B.C.E.[1] to around 1500, and the word *cacao* comes from the Mayan word *Ka'kau'*. However, this is not a native Mayan word but is derived from the Olmec language. To the Mayans, the cacao pod symbolized[2] life and fertility. Many of the bas-reliefs carved on their palaces and temples show cacao pods. It is believed that the Mayans took the cacao tree from its native rain forest and began to cultivate it in plantations. After harvesting the seed pods, they scooped out the contents—the cacao beans embedded in a sticky, white flesh—and allowed it all to ferment until the seeds turned dark brown. The seeds were then roasted and ground into a thick chocolate paste.

From the paste, the Mayans made a hot chocolate drink. However, it was very different from contemporary hot chocolate. The basic drink was made by mixing the paste with water, chili powder, cornmeal, and other ingredients and heating it. Then the liquid was poured back and forth from one vessel held at arm's height to another resting on the ground. This created a chocolate drink with a thick head of dark foam—considered the best part of the drink. Among the Mayans, as the chocolate drink grew more popular and the ingredients more readily available, people from all levels of society enjoyed it at least on occasion.

The Maya preserved their knowledge of cacao use through stone carvings, some in jade and obsidian, pottery decorations, and written documents that detailed the use of cacao, described in Mayan as "food of the gods." Cacao was used in ceremonies, medical treatments, and daily life centuries before the discovery of the New World by Europeans. Certain recipes for cacao drinks included vanilla, nuts, honey from native bees, and various flowers.

Ek Chuah (meaning "black star" in Yucatec Maya) was the patron god of merchants and commerce. Because cacao seeds were light in weight, easily transported, and of great value, they were used as currency throughout Mesoamerica. Thus *Ek Chuah* also became the patron god of cacao. Each April, the Maya held a festival to honor[3] this deity. The celebration included offerings of cacao, feathers, and incense, the sacrifice of a dog with cacao-colored[4] markings, other animal sacrifices, and an exchange of gifts. Given that the chocolate drink could be made only through the direct destruction of currency, one can understand why it was called the "food of gods." The immortals could easily afford it, while for humans it was a precious commodity indeed.

---

[1] B.C.E. *is the abbreviation for "Before the Common Era," that is, before the year 0.*
[2] *British: symbolised*
[3] *British: honour*
[4] *British: coloured*

Questions 14–18

Do the following statements agree with the information in the passage? On lines 14–18 on your answer sheet, write:

TRUE	if the statement agrees with the information
FALSE	if the statement contradicts the information
NOT GIVEN	if there is no information on this

14 The cacao plant originated in the Gulf of Mexico region.

15 The cacao plant prefers wet weather.

16 Each flower on the cacao plant produces twenty pods.

17 Cacao drinks were originally made using the pulp from the pod.

18 In ancient Puerto Escondido, cacao drinks were served hot.

Questions 19–25

According to the information in Reading Passage 2, which ancient civilizations do the following phrases describe?
On lines 19–25 on your answer sheet, write:

A	if the phrase describes the ancient Olmec civilization only
B	if the phrase describes the ancient Mayan civilization only
C	if the phra both the Olmec and the Mayan civilizations

19 collapsed around 2,400 years ago

20 was located in Mexico

21 grew cacao on large farms

22 left behind little concrete evidence of their culture

23 influenced the ancient inhabitants of Puerto Escondido

24 carved images of cacao pods

25 made a drink by mixing cacao with chili powder and cornmeal

Questions 26 and 27

*Write the correct letter, **A**, **B**, or **C**, on lines 26 and 27 on your answer sheet.*

26 The ancient Maya used cacao seeds as

  A decorations.
  B a dye.
  C money.

27 In April, the ancient Maya celebrated

  A dogs.
  B a god.
  C stars.

READING PASSAGE 3

*You should spend about 20 minutes on **Questions 28–40**, which are based on Reading Passage 3 below.*

The Intelligence of Corvids

For hundreds of years humans thought that tool making was a uniquely human trait. In 1960, Jane Goodall observed chimpanzees using tools in the wild, a discovery to which Goodall's mentor Louis Leakey famously responded, "We must redefine tool, redefine man, or accept chimpanzees as human." It is now commonly accepted that various primates engage in tool making, and there is a growing body of evidence that many corvids, a group of bird species that includes crows, jays, rooks, ravens, and magpies, are also tool makers, and that they show many other signs of possessing high intelligence.

Scientists have observed wild New Caledonian crows making hooks out of twigs to pull grubs from tree holes that are too deep for their beaks. New Caledonian crows also sometimes use their beaks to create small spears from leaves for collecting insects. Because New Caledonian crows are highly social and because tool design varies from area to area, most researchers assume the birds' tool use is cultural; that is, the tool use is learned from other crows.

In 2002, however, three researchers at Oxford University reported in *Science* a startling new twist to tool making in corvids: A New Caledonian crow that had been captured in 2000 as a juvenile had invented a new tool from materials not found in her natural habitat without observing the behavior[1] in other crows. The crow, named Betty, shared space with a male crow named Abel. The researchers had set up an experiment in which both crows were presented with a straight wire

---
[1] *British: behaviour*

and a hooked wire and food that could most easily be retrieved with a hooked wire. When Abel flew away with the hooked wire, Betty bent the straight wire and successfully lifted the bucket of food with her hook. The researchers then set out to see whether they could get Betty to replicate the behavior. Ten times, they set out a single straight wire and food to be retrieved. Betty retrieved the food nine times by bending the wire; once she managed to retrieve the food with the straight wire. Alex Kacelnik, one of the researchers who worked with the crows, noted that she had solved a new problem by doing something she had never done before.

Professor John Marzloff, at the University of Washington in Seattle, demonstrated another interesting ability in American crows: recognizing[2] faces of individual humans. In 2005, he and other researchers each wore a caveman mask when they captured, tagged, and then released crows on campus. Then Marzloff and other researchers took turns wearing the mask and walking around campus. Over time, increasing numbers of crows flocked together and cawed at anyone wearing the caveman mask, regardless of the size, gender, and skin color of the mask wearer or whether the wearer was one of the researchers who had originally captured crows. When the same people did not wear the mask, they got no reaction from the crows. This showed that it was clearly the face that was identified as a threat to the flock. Crows that had not originally been captured were joining the harassment of the perceived threat. When Marzloff suggested that researchers try wearing the caveman mask upside down, some crows actually turned their heads upside down to better identify the face of the "enemy."

In their studies of western scrub jays published in *Science* in May 2006, Johann Dally, Nathan Emery, and Nicola Clayton showed that jays have the ability to remember whether a specific other jay saw them hide food for later use. When it became clear that a jay that observed the hiding might have access to the cache, the hiders retrieved their food and re-hid it when given the opportunity to do so without observation. They did not re-hide food when other jays were introduced to the situation. Similarly, ravens in the wild have been observed misleading other ravens by pretending to hide food in one location then flying off to hide it elsewhere when the other raven goes to investigate the false cache.

Corvids are also capable of fooling humans. Marzloff tells the story of a pair of crows that built a fake nest that they always flew to when researchers were in their area. The crows' actual nest with their young was nearby, but the humans never saw the crows actually fly to it.

In an experiment to test social cooperation in rooks, University of Cambridge researchers found that pairs of rooks quickly figured out how to pull on ropes at the same time to bring food that could not be gained through the individual effort of one rook.

Otto Koehler tested the ability of captive jackdaws to count, a skill apparently related to their communication often being based on the number of calls. First, Koehler trained jackdaws to expect five food rewards. Then the jackdaws were

---

[2]*British: recognising*

given a number of boxes, some of which contained food. They proceeded to open the boxes until they had found five pieces of food, at which point they stopped opening boxes because they knew they had reached five. In another experiment Koehler also trained jackdaws to choose a box with the same number of dots on the lid as the number of dots on a cue card.

Tool makers, tricksters, cooperators, mathematicians—the corvids are far from "bird brains." In fact, their intelligence, in many cases, appears to equal or even surpass that of many of our primate "cousins."

Questions 28–33

*Complete the summary using the list of words and phrases, **A–N**, below. Not all letters are used.*

*Write the correct letter, **A–N**, on lines 28–33 on your answer sheet.*

Jane Goodall's work in 1960 showed that **28** _____ were not the only ones to make tools. Since then, scientists have observed different kinds of animals making tools. New Caledonian crows, for example, make tools in order to retrieve the **29** _____ that they eat in the wild. Scientists believe that generally these birds **30** _____ how to make tools. In 2002, a captive New Caledonian crow named Betty invented a new tool. Scientists observed Betty use pieces of wire to make **31** _____, which she used to retrieve food. The interesting thing is that other crows did not **32** _____ the tools. Once the scientists saw Betty make a tool, they tried to get her to **33** _____ the behavior, which she did successfully.

A	learn from other birds	**H**	hooks
B	twigs	**I**	try to take away
C	humans	**J**	modify
D	repeat	**K**	chimpanzees
E	spears	**L**	grubs
F	are born knowing	**M**	teach her how to make
G	leaves	**N**	corvids

Questions 34–36

*Write the correct letter, **A**, **B**, or **C**, on lines 34–36 on your answer sheet.*

34 Researchers wore a mask when working with crows in order to

   A conceal their true identity from the crows.
   B find out whether crows would recognize the mask in another situation.
   C protect their faces from aggressive crows.

35 Crows harassed researchers wearing the mask because the researchers

   A had worn the mask when handling crows.
   B were of a size and skin color that crows feared.
   C took turns wearing the mask while walking around campus.

36 When researchers removed the mask,

   A the crows did not harass them.
   B they were attacked by the entire flock of crows.
   C they could more easily tag the crows.

Questions 37-40

Match each corvid action described by researchers below with the information it shows us about corvid intelligence.

*Write the correct letter, **A–F**, on lines 37–40 on your answer sheet. There are more types of information listed than actions, so you will not use them all.*

37 Birds opened boxes to obtain food.

38 Birds pulled ropes to get food.

39 Birds hid food from other birds.

40 Birds built a nest that was not real.

INFORMATION ABOUT CORVID INTELLIGENCE
A   Corvids can count.
B   Corvids recognize individual birds.
C   Corvids are good at discovering food sources.
D   Corvids can work together to achieve a goal.
E   Corvids protect themselves by tricking their enemies.
F   Corvids are skilled at remembering where they hid things.

Academic Module
Practice Test 4

Candidate Name and Number: _____

INTERNATIONAL ENGLISH LANGUAGE TESTING SYSTEM

ACADEMIC WRITING

TIME 1 HOUR

Instructions to Candidates

Do not open this booklet until you are told to do so.

Write your name and candidate number in the space at the top of this page.

All answers must be written on the separate answer booklet provided. (The answer sheet can be found beginning on page 145.)

Do not remove the booklet from the examination room.

Information for Candidates

There are **2** tasks on this question paper.

You must do **both** tasks.

Under-length answers will be penalized.[1]

---

[1] *British: penalised*

WRITING TASK 1

> You should spend about 20 minutes on this task. Write at least 150 words.

The diagram below explains the process of recycling plastic bottles for new uses.

Summarize[1] the information by selecting and reporting the main features, and make comparisons where relevant.

How Plastic Bottles Are Recycled

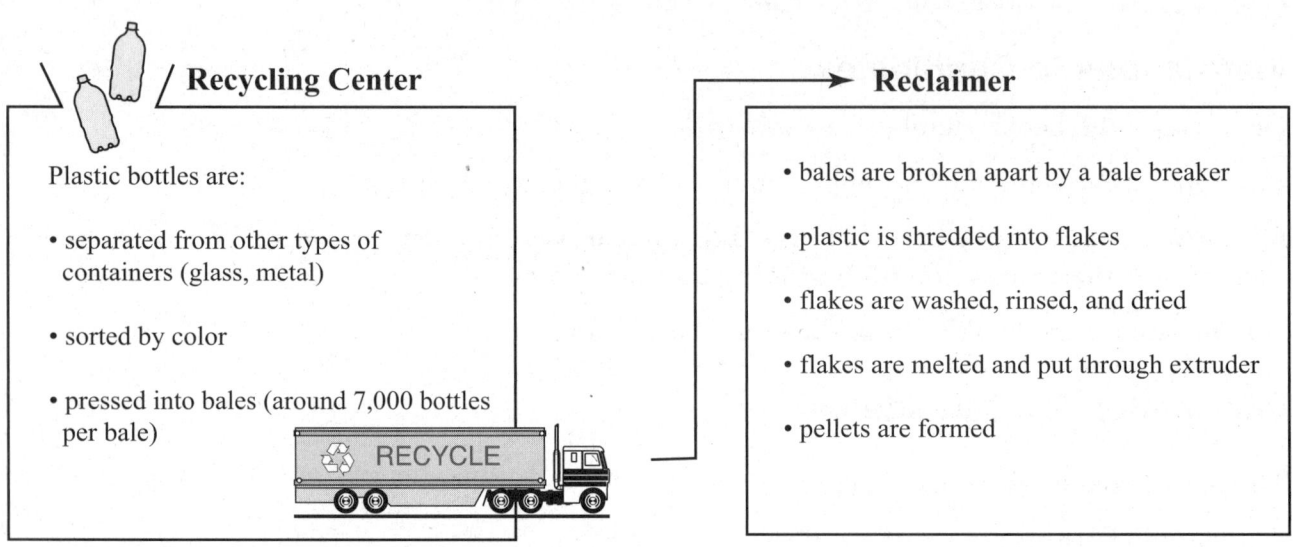

Recycling Center

Plastic bottles are:

• separated from other types of containers (glass, metal)

• sorted by color

• pressed into bales (around 7,000 bottles per bale)

RECYCLE

Reclaimer

• bales are broken apart by a bale breaker

• plastic is shredded into flakes

• flakes are washed, rinsed, and dried

• flakes are melted and put through extruder

• pellets are formed

The pellets are sold to manufacturers to be used to make fibers[2] for carpets and clothing, nonfood containers, and other products.

WRITING TASK 2

> You should spend about 40 minutes on this task. Write at least 250 words.

Write about the following topic:

> *The proliferation of private cars on the roads in many parts of the world has led to serious problems of pollution and may contribute to global warming. Some people think that governments should spend money for the development of public transportation systems in order to help alleviate this problem. Others think it is better to spend money for the development of electric and other types of cars that may cause less pollution.*

Do you think it is better for governments to spend money developing public transportation or developing new kinds of cars? Why or why not? Give reasons for your answer and include any relevant examples from your own knowledge or experience.

---

[1] *British: Summarise*
[2] *British: fibres*

SPEAKING

Examiner questions:

Part 1

How much time have you spent by the ocean?

Why do people like being near the ocean?

What do you like about the ocean?

Would you like to live near the ocean?

Do you prefer to spend your leisure time indoors or outdoors?

Is there anything you don't like about being indoors (outdoors)?

What are some activities you do indoors (outdoors)?

What do you enjoy about these activities?

Part 2

Describe a book you read recently.

You should say:

The title and author of the book

What the book was about

Why you decided to read it and explain why you enjoyed/didn't enjoy reading it?

> You will have one to two minutes to talk about this topic.
>
> You will have one minute to prepare what you are going to say.

Part 3

Why do people read?

How important do you think reading is?

What kinds of things are popular to read these days?

How do you think reading will be different in the future?

Practice Test 4—Academic Module
IELTS LISTENING ANSWER SHEET

1. _____

2. _____

3. _____

4. _____

5. _____

6. _____

7. _____

8. _____

9. _____

10. _____

11. _____

12. _____

13. _____

14. _____

15. _____

16. _____

17. _____

18. _____

19. _____

20. _____

21. _____

22. _____

23. _____

24. _____

25. _____

26. _____

27. _____

28. _____

29. _____

30. _____

31. _____

32. _____

33. _____

34. _____

35. _____

36. _____

37. _____

38. _____

39. _____

40. _____

Practice Test 4–Academic Module
IELTS READING ANSWER SHEET

1. _____

2. _____

3. _____

4. _____

5. _____

6. _____

7. _____

8. _____

9. _____

10. _____

11. _____

12. _____

13. _____

14. _____

15. _____

16. _____

17. _____

18. _____

19. _____

20. _____

21. _____

22. _____

23. _____

24. _____

25. _____

26. _____

27. _____

28. _____

29. _____

30. _____

31. _____

32. _____

33. _____

34. _____

35. _____

36. _____

37. _____

38. _____

39. _____

40. _____

Practice Test 4–Academic Module
WRITING TASK 1

Writing Task 1 *continued*

Practice Test 4—Academic Module
WRITING TASK 2

Writing Task 2 *continued*

Writing Task 2 *continued*

Answer Key
PRACTICE TEST 4—ACADEMIC MODULE

Listening

1. Kramer	11. B	21. university catalog	31. forested area
2. 58	12. C	22. a summary	32. plant foods
3. residential	13. B	23. work supervisor	33. insects/fish
4. office manager	14. A	24. C	34. the winter
5. 637-555-9014	15. clown	25. A	35. twenty-five years
6. nine years	16. concert	26. B	36. A
7. long distance	17. singing	27. A	37. B
8. Internet	18. international	28. C	38. B
9. Friday	19. games	29. B	39. A
10. morning	20. crafts	30. A	40. A

Reading

1. B	11. F	21. B	31. H
2. C	12. E	22. A	32. M
3. A	13. I	23. A	33. D
4. B	14. False	24. B	34. B
5. A	15. True	25. B	35. A
6. A	16. False	26. C	36. A
7. C	17. True	27. B	37. A
8. J	18. Not Given	28. C	38. D
9. A	19. A	29. L	39. B
10. D	20. C	30. A	40. E

Answer Explanations

ACADEMIC MODULE—PRACTICE TEST 4

Listening

1. *Kramer.* The man spells his name.

2. *58.* The man gives his address, "That would be number 58 Fulton Avenue, apartment 12."

3. *residential.* The woman asks, "Then the type of phone service you want is residential, not business?" Then the man confirms that it is for his home.

4. *office manager.* The woman asks about the man's occupation, and the man says, "I'm the office manager."

5. *637-555-9014.* The man gives his work phone number, and the woman repeats the last part of it.

6. *nine years.* The man thinks about it then says that he has been at his current job for nine years.

7. *long distance.* The speakers discuss the special services offered. The woman says, "Then I'll put you down for long-distance service."

8. *Internet.* The speakers discuss voicemail and Internet, and the man says, "Please put me down for Internet as well as phone service."

9. *Friday.* The woman suggests Friday, and the man says, "That would be fine."

10. *morning.* The man says, "Morning would be best."

11. **(B)** The woman says, "So we've moved the fair to City Park." Choice (A) is where the fair has been held in the past. Choice (C) is near the fairgrounds.

12. **(C)** The man mentions Friday morning, but the woman says, "it won't begin until that evening. . . ." Choice (A) is when the man thinks the fair will begin. Choice (B) is not mentioned.

13. **(B)** The woman says, "this year our opening event will be a special dance performance. . . ." Choice (A) is what the traditional opening event has been. Choice (C) mentions the mayor, who will participate in the dance performance, but a speech is not mentioned.

14. **(A)** The woman says, "The opening event on Friday. . .doesn't cost anything to attend. . . ." Choices (B) and (C) are incorrect because the woman mentions admission fees for those days.

15. *clown.* The woman says, "There are a number of events especially for children, including a clown show on Saturday afternoon."

16. *concert.* The woman says, "On Saturday evening we've got an event that can be enjoyed by the whole family—a concert by the lake."

17. *singing.* The woman says, "There will be a singing contest in the afternoon."

18. *international.* The woman says, "international food will be served."

19. *games.* The woman says, "There will also be special games for children at different locations around the fair."

20. *crafts.* The woman says, "We have a large area set aside where there will be crafts for sale."

21. *university catalog.* The advisor explains, "First, you'll need to read the university catalog to see if any of the course descriptions match your specific job experience."

22. *a summary.* The advisor explains, "You would write a summary of your work experience, relating it to specific courses we offer."

23. *work supervisor.* The advisor explains, "Submit that to the admissions office with a letter from your work supervisor confirming your experience."

24. **(C)** While discussing the university catalog, the advisor tells the student, "you can get one from the library for now."

25. **(A)** The advisor says, "Well, first you'll need to get an application-for-admission form. Those are available in the admissions office."

26. **(B)** The advisor says, "We have copies of the requirements lists for all university programs here in the counseling center."

27. **(A)** The advisor says, "The recommendation forms are available in the admissions office."

28. **(C)** The advisor says, "You can access the job listings from the computers in the library."

29. **(B)** After the student says that he wants to be a full-time student, the advisor says, "Then you'll qualify for the work-study program." Choice (A) is confused with the advisor saying that the student can apply for assistance to help pay for books, but a discount is not mentioned. Choice (C) is what the advisor says is not available.

30. **(A)** While discussing financial assistance, the advisor says, "You'll need to make an appointment with a counselor." Choice (B) is what the student thinks. Choice (C) is plausible but is not mentioned.

31. *forested areas.* The speaker says, "The black bear, or *Ursus americanus,* has a wide range, inhabiting forested areas of North America"

32. *plant foods.* The speaker says, "plant foods make up 90 percent of the bear's diet."

33. *insects/fish.* The speaker says, "The rest of its meals consist of animal foods such as insects and fish."

34. *the winter.* The speaker says, "but bear cubs aren't born until the following winter."

35. *twenty-five years.* The speaker says, "Wild black bears can live as long as twenty-five years."

36. **(A)** The speaker says, "Many black bears, however, have a patch of fur on their chests that's lighter in color than the rest of their fur."

37. **(B)** The speaker says, "grizzly bears are usually heavier, with an average weight of 225 kilos."

38. **(B)** The speaker explains that grizzly bears spend time digging so "The large muscles they need for this give them a distinct shoulder hump."

39. **(A)** The speaker says, "Black bears, on the other hand, have a straighter profile and longer, more pointed ears."

40. **(A)** In paragraph 3, the speaker says, "Black bears have shorter claws, which are better suited for climbing trees."

Reading

PASSAGE 1

1. **(B)** Paragraph 1: "Labrador and London lie at about the same latitude . . . two places, equidistant from the Arctic Circle. . . ." Choice (A) contradicts the information given in the paragraph. Choice (C) is confused with the mention of the abundance of palm trees on England's southern shores, but wildlife and Labrador are not mentioned.

2. **(C)** Paragraph 2: "the Gulf Stream warms the atmosphere, and the prevailing westerly winds bring the warmed air to all of northwestern Europe, making the area suitable for intense agriculture." Choices (A) and (B) are related to the discussion but are not given as reasons.

3. **(A)** Paragraph 3: "After the Gulf Stream reaches southeast Greenland and western Iceland, . . . the colder, denser water then sinks." Choices (B) and (C) are related to the discussion but are not given as reasons.

4. **(B)** Paragraph 4: "This flow of ocean currents has been extremely important in regulating the temperature of the globe and in making life possible." Choices (A) and (C) are plausible but are not given as conditions that make life possible.

5. **(A)** Paragraph 5: "there used to be as many as seven chimneys . . . in the last several years, only one remained, and then, in 2007, that one disappeared." Choices (B) and (C) were true prior to 2007.

6. **(A)** Paragraph 6: "At that time, the Gulf Stream had slowed to about half its usual rate." Choice (B) contradicts facts in the paragraph. Choice (C) was true during a previous ice age.

7. **(C)** Paragraph 7: "Core samples also show that the changes in temperature have been abrupt, not gradual." Choices (A) and (B) are plausible but not mentioned.

8. **(J)** Paragraph 5: "In recent winters, glacial melt has released record amounts of fresh water into the oceans."

9. **(A)** Paragraph 5: "As the North Atlantic waters, including fresh water from rivers as well as the increased amount of glacial melt, mix with the Gulf Stream, the salt water is diluted."

10. **(D)** Paragraph 5: "Since fresh water is not as dense as salt water, it does not sink, and the mechanism for forming the chimneys is impaired."

11. **(F)** Paragraph 5: "As the chimneys have disappeared, the Gulf Stream has slowed."

12. **(E)** Paragraph 5: "Without a strong Gulf Stream, the slow, cold water of the lower part of the conveyor belt fails to rise. . . ."

13. **(I)** Paragraph 5: "which reduces the circulation of nutrients for marine life."

PASSAGE 2

14. *False.* According to paragraph 1, the cacao plant is native to the Amazon and Orinoco River basins.

15. *True.* Paragraph 1: "it requires a humid climate and regular rainfall."

16. *False.* According to paragraph 1, the entire plant, with 6,000 flowers, produces only twenty pods.

17. *True.* Paragraph 2: "Instead, the first cacao-based drink was probably produced by fermenting the pulp. . . ."

18. *Not Given.* There is no mention of whether the drinks were served hot or cold.

19. **(A)** According to paragraph 3, the Olmec civilization lasted until around 2,400 years ago.

20. **(C)** According to paragraph 3, Olmec civilaztion was "centered in the modern Mexican states of Tabasco and Veracruz" and "Mayan civilization flourished in southern Mexico and Central America. . . ."

21. **(B)** Paragraph 4: "It is believed that the Mayans took the cacao tree from its native rain forest and began to cultivate it in plantations."

22. **(A)** Paragraph 3: "Relatively little is known about Olmec society because very little archeological evidence has survived. . . ."

23. **(A)** Paragraph 3: "The villagers of Puerto Escondido had likely been influenced by the great Olmec civilization. . . ."

24. **(B)** Paragraph 4: "Many of the bas-reliefs carved on their palaces and temples show cacao pods."

25. **(B)** Paragraph 5: "The basic drink was made by mixing the paste with water, chili powder, cornmeal, and other ingredients and heating it."

26. **(C)** According to paragraph 7, the ancient Mayans used cacao seeds as currency, or money. Choices (A) and (B) are plausible but are not mentioned.

27. **(B)** According to paragraph 7, the ancient Mayans held a festival in honor of the deity Ek Chuah every April. Choice (A) is the animal sacrificed during the festival. Choice (C) is part of the meaning of the deity's name.

PASSAGE 3

28. **(C)** Paragraph 1: "In 1960, Jane Goodall observed chimpanzees using tools in the wild. . . ."

29. **(L)** Paragraph 2: "Scientists have observed wild New Caledonian crows making hooks out of twigs to pull grubs from tree holes that are too deep for their beaks."

30. **(A)** Paragraph 2: "most researchers assume the birds' tool use is cultural; that is, the tool use is learned from other crows."

31. **(H)** Paragraph 3: "Betty bent the straight wire and successfully lifted the bucket of food with her hook."

32. **(M)** Paragraph 3: "invented a new tool from materials not found in her natural habitat without observing the behavior in other crows."

33. **(D)** Paragraph 3: "The researchers then set out to see if they could get Betty to replicate the behavior."

34. **(B)** Paragraph 4 explains the experiment. Researchers wore a mask when handling crows, an upsetting experience for the crows. When crows saw the mask later in other places, they attacked it, showing that they remembered and associated it with their bad experience. Choices (A) and (C) are plausible reasons but are not the correct answer.

35. **(A)** The crows associated the mask with the bad experience of being handled, so they attacked whoever was wearing it. Choice (B) is about features of the masks that had no effect on the crows. Choice (C) is true but is not the reason for the crows' behavior.

36. **(A)** Paragraph 4: "When the same people did not wear the mask, they got no reaction from the crows." Choice (B) is the opposite of what actually happened. Choice (C) is something the researchers did but was not related to the crow's reaction to the masks.

37. **(A)** Paragraph 8 describes the experiment where jackdaws, trained to expect five rewards, stopped opening boxes after they had found five that contained food.

38. **(D)** Paragraph 7 describes an experiment with pairs of rooks, which figured out that they had to pull ropes together, not alone, to get food.

39. **(B)** Paragraph 5 describes observations by researchers who saw scrub jays re-hide food when they noticed that another bird had seen the original hiding place.

40. **(E)** Paragraph 6 describes the observation of researchers who saw that a pair of crows always flew to a fake nest when the researchers were present, thus hiding the location of their true nest.

Writing

These are models. Your answers will vary. See page vi in the Introduction to see the criteria for scoring.

WRITING TASK 1

Plastic bottles can be recycled into plastic pellets, which can then be made into new products. The process begins at the recycling center and continues at the reclaimer. At the recycling center, plastic bottles are separated from other containers, such as glass jars and bottles and metal cans. Then the plastic is sorted by color and each separate color is pressed into a bale. Each bale is made up of about 7,000 plastic bottles.

From the recycling center, the plastic bales are transported to the reclaimer. There a machine called a bale breaker breaks up the bales of bottles, and then the plastic is shredded into flakes. The flakes are cleaned. Then they are melted and put through a machine called an extruder. From there, the plastic is formed into pellets. These pellets are used as the material for manufacturing fiber that is, in turn, used to make carpets and clothing. They can also be used to make nonfood containers and other products.

WRITING TASK 2

Pollution caused by cars is a serious problem in the modern world. Developing better public transport systems is one answer to this problem. However, I think it is even more important for governments to spend money on developing cars that pollute less. In the first place, I believe that most people enjoy having their own cars. In addition, any technology that is developed to improve cars can also improve public transportation.

Many people in the world these days have their own car, and many others aspire to have one. Owning a car is convenient. You can go anywhere you want whenever you want. You are not limited to the places the bus and subway routes take you. You do not have to rely on bus or subway schedules. Everyone enjoys the freedom a car gives. Better public transportation systems may be put in place, but I think people will still prefer driving their own cars.

The same technology that is developed to improve cars can also be used to improve public transportation. Buses can run on electricity or hydrogen as well as cars can. Any money spent to make cars less polluting can also be used to make public transportation less polluting, so the benefit is doubled. Then, people can choose to drive cars or ride buses and either way, pollution will be reduced.

It is a nice idea to improve public transportation systems, but I feel that it is unrealistic. People will always choose to drive their own cars whenever they can. Therefore, I think it is much wiser to spend money on improving cars. The benefit will be much greater.

SPEAKING

These are models. Your answers will vary. See page vi in the Introduction to see the criteria for scoring.

PART 1

How much time have you spent by the ocean?
When I was a child, I spent a great deal of time by the ocean. My family usually went to the ocean every summer. We spent two weeks there. Usually, my parents rented a small house for us right near the beach. We spent most of our time on the beach, swimming in the ocean and playing in the sand. Some of my best childhood memories are of those days we spent our vacations by the ocean. These days, unfortunately, I don't have much time to go to the ocean. I go when I can, but it's not very often.

Why do people like being near the ocean?

One reason people like the ocean is that it's very beautiful, no matter what the weather. When the day is calm, the ocean looks beautiful sparkling in the sun. When there's a storm, the waves and color of the ocean are dramatic. I think people also like being near the ocean because there are so many fun things to do. You can swim, fish, ride in a boat, or just relax in the sun.

What do you like about the ocean?

The thing I like most about the ocean is swimming. I love the feel of salt water, and I like the fun and the challenge of swimming in the ocean waves. It's so much better than swimming in a pool. The water in a pool is unnatural because it has chlorine, and the water is completely calm. It's very boring. The ocean, on the other hand, is natural and exciting. It's the best place to swim.

Would you like to live near the ocean?

Even though I love the ocean, I don't think I would like to live near it. For one thing, towns near the ocean are usually crowded with tourists on vacation. Tourists at the beach are always in a relaxed, party mood. I think that's fun sometimes, but I wouldn't like to live around it all the time. Also, in towns near the ocean there often isn't much to do besides go to the beach. I love the beach, but I prefer living in a city where there's a wide variety of things to do and many more opportunities for jobs and studies and things like that.

Do you prefer to spend your leisure time indoors or outdoors?

I definitely prefer to spend my leisure time outdoors. I work all week in an office, so when the weekend comes, I want to spend as much time as possible outdoors in the sun and fresh air. It feels good to be outdoors, and there are a lot of outdoor activities that I enjoy doing.

Is there anything you don't like about being outdoors?

I suppose sometimes it can be uncomfortable to be outdoors. I don't like it when the weather is bad. I don't like getting wet from the rain or too hot when the temperature is high. I don't like to be outdoors when it's mosquito season. That's a very uncomfortable time! But usually these things aren't much of a problem. Usually I feel very happy outdoors.

What are some activities you do outdoors?

I enjoy a lot of outdoor activities. I like walking, which is good because I live in a city and that's a great way to be outdoors in a city. There are so many places to walk. I also like to go to the park with my friends. Sometimes, we bring food and have a picnic, and sometimes we just hang out and relax. Another thing I like doing outdoors is playing tennis. I play several times a week when the weather is nice.

What do you enjoy about these activities?

The first thing I like about these activities is that they're outdoors. That's why I do them. Another thing I like is that they're relaxing. I can leave my worries behind at the office or at home and take a relaxing walk, or enjoy the nice weather in the park or a good tennis game. Also, they're a good way to spend time with my friends. We enjoy walking together or being in the park together. I think we enjoy each other's company more when we're in a pleasant outdoor place rather than being in some crowded, noisy indoor place like a shopping mall.

PART 2

A book I read recently was *Gone with the Wind* by Margaret Mitchell. This is a well-known novel written in the 1930s, and the main character, Scarlett O'Hara, is also well known. The novel takes place in the United States around the time of the Civil War. Partly it's a romance novel, and it's also about history and the effects of war. I decided to read it because I saw the movie, which is from the 1930s, too. I was going on vacation, and I always like to take along a nice, long novel to read when I travel. I really enjoyed the book at first. There are very interesting descriptions of life at that time, and it was also interesting to get an idea of what the Civil War was like, especially how it affected daily life. But I have to admit that after a while I got bored. I didn't really like the main character. She kept doing the wrong thing and ruining her happiness. Since I'd seen the movie, I knew what was going to happen, so I didn't finish the book.

PART 3

Why do people read?
People read for a lot of different reasons. Leisure time reading is to pass the time in a relaxing way. I think it also helps people escape from reality. Readers can imagine they're in the time and place they're reading about and forget their own problems. Of course, not everybody has the habit of reading for leisure. Most people read for information. They read newspapers, magazines, and certain websites to know about and understand what's going on in the world, what the news is. People also read books, manuals, or pamphlets to learn something they need to know for their jobs or to find out about something they need help with, for example, a health problem.

How important do you think reading is?
I think reading is extremely important. They say that people are reading less these days, and I think that's a serious problem. If people don't read, either they're uninformed, or they get their information from radio, TV, and the Web. I think it's also really important to read for information. The process of reading develops the mind, and reading forces you to think. I think that people are generally more analytical about all the information they receive if reading is part of their lives.

What kinds of things are popular to read these days?
As far as books go, I think light reading is very popular. People seem to be reading certain novels that are entertaining but not very deep. I think people also enjoy reading about the lives of famous people, especially different celebrities. A lot of movie stars and athletes have published memoirs recently. These are the types of light reading I see around a lot.

How do you think reading will be different in the future?
In the future, there may not be any books, magazines, or newspapers at all. Probably everything will be electronic. Most people will read things on the Internet, or they'll have electronic devices like those new electronic readers. This might mean that it will be easier for people to have access to a large variety of things to read, so maybe they'll read more.

ACADEMIC MODULE
PRACTICE TEST 5

Academic Module
Practice Test 5

Candidate Name and Number: _____

INTERNATIONAL ENGLISH LANGUAGE TESTING SYSTEM

LISTENING

TIME APPROX. 30 MINUTES

Instructions to Candidates

Do not open this booklet until you are told to do so.

Write your name and candidate number in the space at the top of this page.

You should answer all questions.

All the recordings will be played ONCE only.

Write all your answers on the test pages.

At the end of the test, you will be given ten minutes to transfer your answers to an Answer Sheet. (The answer sheet can be found on page 181.)

Do not remove the booklet from the examination room.

Information for Candidates

There are **40** questions on this question paper.

The test is divided as follows:

Section 1	Questions 1–10
Section 2	Questions 11–20
Section 3	Questions 21–30
Section 4	Questions 31–40

SECTION 1   *QUESTIONS 1–10*

Note

If you do not have access to an audio CD player, please refer to the audio-scripts starting on page 426 when prompted to listen to an audio passage.

Questions 1–4

Complete the form below.
*Write **NO MORE THAN ONE WORD AND/OR A NUMBER** for each answer.*

Example:	*Global* Bicycle Tours
Tour name:	*River Valley tour* Tour month: **1** _____
Customer Name:	**2** _____ *Schmidt*
Address:	*P.O. Box* **3** _____
	Manchester
Bicycle rental required?	___ Yes *X* No
Dietary restrictions:	**4** _____

Questions 5–7

*Choose the correct letters, **A**, **B**, or **C**.*

5 What size deposit does the caller have to pay?

   A 5 percent
   B 30 percent
   C 50 percent

6 When does the deposit have to be paid?

   A Two weeks from now
   B Four weeks from now
   C Six weeks from now

7 How will the luggage be carried?

   A By bus
   B By bicycle
   C By van

Questions 8–10

Choose **THREE** *letters,* **A–F.**
Which **THREE** *things should the caller take on the tour?*

A	raincoat	**D**	water bottle
B	spare tire	**E**	camera
C	maps	**F**	guide book

SECTION 2   QUESTIONS 11–20

Questions 11–15

What change has been made to each part of the health club?
Write the correct letter, **A–F** *next to questions 11–15.*

HARTFORD HEALTH CLUB

A installed a new floor
B repainted
C moved to a new location
D rebuilt
E enlarged
F replaced the equipment

Part of the health club

11 swimming pools   _____

12 locker rooms   _____

13 exercise room   _____

14 tennis court   _____

15 club store   _____

Questions 16–18

Complete the sentences below.
Write **NO MORE THAN TWO WORDS** *for each answer.*

16 Tomorrow, _____ for adults and children will start.

17 On Wednesday, there will be a _____.

18 A _____ is planned for next weekend.

Questions 19 and 20

Answer the questions below.
*Choose the correct letter, **A**, **B**, or **C**.*

19 How many months did it take to complete the renovation work?

   A three
   B nine
   C twelve

20 What project is planned for next year?

   A An indoor pool
   B An outdoor tennis court
   C An outdoor pool

SECTION 3   *QUESTIONS 21–30*

Questions 21–25

*Choose **FIVE** letters, **A–I**.*
*What **FIVE** things will the students do during their museum internship?*

A	art conservation	**F**	research
B	administrative duties	**G**	write brochures
C	guide tours	**H**	plan a reception
D	attend board meetings	**I**	meet artists
E	give classes		

Questions 26–30

Complete the notes below.
*Write **NO MORE THAN TWO WORDS AND/OR A NUMBER** for each answer.*

City Art Museum

The main part of museum was built in **26** _____

The **27** _____ was built sixty years later.

Collections: modern art, works by **28** _____, sculpture, European art.

Classes: **29** _____ classes for adults
         Arts and crafts workshops for children

Weekly **30** _____ in the fall and winter

SECTION 4   QUESTIONS 31–40

Questions 31–35

*Choose the correct letter, **A**, **B**, or **C**.*

31 The tomato originally came from

  A Mexico.
  B Spain.
  C Peru.

32 The original color[1] of the tomato was

  A red.
  B green.
  C yellow.

33 The Aztec word for *tomato* means

  A golden apple.
  B plump thing.
  C small fruit.

34 In the 1500s, people in Spain and Italy

  A enjoyed eating tomatoes.
  B used tomatoes as ornamental plants.
  C made medicine from tomatoes.

35 In the 1600s, the British

  A saw tomatoes as poisonous.
  B published tomato recipes.
  C ate tomato sauce daily.

[1] *British: colour*

Academic Module–Practice Test 5

Questions 36–40

Complete the timeline with information about the history of the tomato in the United States.
Write **NO MORE THAN TWO WORDS** *for each answer.*

1806   Tomatoes were mentioned as food in **36** _____

1809   Thomas Jefferson **37** _____ at his home in Virginia.

1820   A man proved that tomatoes were not poisonous by eating them **38** _____

1830s **39** _____ appeared in newspapers and magazines.

1930s People began to eat **40** _____

Take ten minutes to transfer your answers onto the Answer Sheet on page 181.

Academic Module
Practice Test 5

Candidate Name and Number: _____

INTERNATIONAL ENGLISH LANGUAGE TESTING SYSTEM

ACADEMIC READING

TIME 1 HOUR

Instructions to Candidates

Do not open this booklet until you are told to do so.

Write your name and candidate number in the space at the top of this page.

Start at the beginning of the test and work through it.

You should answer all questions.

If you cannot do a particular question, leave it and go on to the next. You can return to it later.

All answers must be written on the Answer Sheet. The answer sheet can be found on page 182.

Do not remove the booklet from the examination room.

Information for Candidates

There are **40** questions on this question paper.

The test is divided as follows:

Reading Passage 1	Questions 1–14
Reading Passage 2	Questions 15–27
Reading Passage 3	Questions 28–40

READING PASSAGE 1

*You should spend about 20 minutes on **Questions 1–14**, which are based on Reading Passage 1 below.*

Candle Making in Colonial America

The primary material used in making candles today is paraffin[1] wax, which is derived from petroleum. In the process of refining crude oil, refiners "crack" the oil, thereby separating it into different products such as gasoline, heating oil, and kerosene. Paraffin wax, originally produced by plants that lived 100 to 700 million years ago to protect their leaves, is inert and remains suspended in the decayed vegetable matter that eventually becomes crude oil. In the refining process, paraffin wax is separated out and sold as a by-product.

Paraffin was not discovered until the early 1800s. At that time, paraffin was derived by a process of distilling bituminous schist, now known as shale oil. In 1850, Dr. James Young, a Scottish industrial chemist, applied for a patent for obtaining paraffin oil and paraffin from bituminous coals. Shortly after that, under a license from Young, paraffin was being produced from coal on a large scale in the United States. Because petroleum is now readily available, Young's original process for obtaining parrafin is no longer profitable, and paraffin is currently produced from crude oil.

Before the discovery of paraffin, candle making had for centuries relied on different materials. Chemically, those materials were also hydrocarbons; however, they were derived directly from insects, animals, or plants.

In colonial times in America, beeswax was highly valued for making candles. Even today beeswax, though more expensive, is highly regarded because pure beeswax candles emit no smoke when burning, whereas paraffin candles produce a black, slightly oily soot. Beeswax is secreted only by female worker bees. As a worker bee eats honey, her wax glands exude the wax as oval flakes that form on the underside of her last four abdominal segments. The bee then removes the wax flakes and chews them, mixing the wax flakes with her saliva to soften them. When the wax is sufficiently pliable, she attaches it to the honeycomb. As the wax comb is built up, each pocket is filled with honey and then sealed with more wax.

Given the numerous uses and considerable value not only of honey but also of the bees themselves and their beeswax, beekeeping was an important part of American life in the seventeenth and eighteenth centuries. Many of the early settlers brought honeybee hives with them from Europe. Not indigenous to North America, the European honeybees nonetheless thrived and often escaped into the wild. In 1785, writing in *Notes on the State of Virginia*, Thomas Jefferson

---

[1] *This parrafin is different from the British word* parrafin, *which is called* kerosene *in the United States.*

observed, "The bees have generally extended themselves into the country, a little in advance of the white settlers. The Indians therefore call them the white man's fly, and consider their approach as indicating the approach of the settlements of the whites." Eventually, the Native Americans as well as the colonists used beeswax and honey in the frontier bartering system that grew up in the absence of readily available coinage.

Another source of colonial candle material was animal fat or tallow. Cattle and sheep were the most common sources of tallow. Pork fat was not used because candles made from it dripped too much and were dangerous. Additionally, the odor[1] of burning pork tallow was particularly offensive. Chicken and duck fat were too soft to make candles. The tallow was rendered—heated in a cauldron until the fat melted—and then strained numerous times to remove any gristle, meat fibers,[2] and as many impurities as possible. Straining reduced, but did not entirely eliminate, the extent to which the candles smoked and emitted a noxious odor. Tallow candles needed to be stored in tightly closed containers, usually made of tin or wood, to keep out rodents and other animals that might eat them.

In the New World, the colonists discovered a native plant high in a natural waxy substance that could be extracted and used for candle making. The plant is the bayberry shrub, also known as candleberry. Bayberry shrubs are dense and semievergreen. The plants are extremely hardy, grow to as much as nine feet high, and do well even in salt-laden, coastal soil unsuitable for other horticulture. In winter, the female plants bear clusters of blue–gray berries, which lend their color to the wax. The colonists boiled the berries to separate the waxy matter from the pulp and then skimmed the wax off the top. Although making bayberry candles was more labor[3] intensive than making tallow candles, bayberry candles were considerably superior, burning longer and producing less smoke. Further recommending them, they had a pleasing scent. Compared to beeswax, bayberries were available in greater quantities, and the colonists found that bayberry wax was harder than beeswax and thus also burned longer.

Because the bayberry clusters were harvested in winter and because making the candles was very time-consuming, the candles were often saved for special occasions, particularly Christmas and New Year's Eve. Eventually, they became a holiday tradition and gave rise to the saying, "Bayberry candles burned to the socket, puts luck in the home, food in the larder, and gold in the pocket." Fortunate indeed was the colonial household with brightly burning candles and a holiday feast.

---

[1] *British: odour*

[2] *British: fibres*

[3] *British: labour*

Questions 1–3

*Write the correct letter, **A**, **B**, or **C**, on lines 1–3 on your answer sheet.*

1 Paraffin is

   A a petroleum by-product.
   B found in rocks.
   C from a type of vegetable.

2 Paraffin was first obtained from

   A crude oil.
   B rotten vegetables.
   C bituminous coal.

3 James Young was

   A a candle maker.
   B an oil producer.
   C a scientist.

Questions 4–14

Classify the following as descriptive of

A	paraffin
B	beeswax
C	tallow
D	bayberry wax

*Write the correct letter, **A**, **B**, **C**, or **D**, in boxes 4–14 on your answer sheet.*

 4 was often made from the fat of cows

 5 is made from a bush that grows near the sea

 6 needs to be filtered before being made into candles

 7 was not used before the nineteenth century

 8 produces smokeless candles

 9 produced candles that were attractive to hungry mice and rats

10 is bluish in color

11 was brought to colonial America by European settlers

12 was often reserved for holiday use

13 has a pleasing aroma

14 was often used for trading in place of money

READING PASSAGE 2

*You should spend about 20 minutes on **Questions 15–27**, which are based on Reading Passage 2 below.*

Caffeine

Almost 200 years ago, a young German chemist named Friedrich Ferdinand Runge isolated a molecule from coffee beans; he named the substance *kaffein*. Today, scientists are still studying the properties of this bitter, white powder. More than sixty plants are known to produce caffeine, whose pungent taste helps protect them from insect predators.

Caffeine is probably the most widely used drug in the world. Humans have been consuming caffeine for hundreds of years, primarily in the form of coffee, tea, and cocoa. Today, it is also added to soft drinks and energy drinks and is a component of some over-the-counter medications. Many of the world's people, including children, ingest it in some form daily.

The body absorbs caffeine in less than an hour, and it remains in the system for only a few hours, passing from the gastrointestinal tract into the bloodstream within about ten minutes and circulating to other organs, including the brain. Caffeine molecules are small and soluble in fat, properties that allow them to pass through a protective shield known as the blood–brain barrier and directly target the central nervous system.

Caffeine acts on the body in many ways, some of them probably still unknown. However, caffeine accomplishes its principal action as a stimulant by inhibiting adenosine, a chemical that binds to receptors on nerve cells and slows down their activity. Caffeine binds to the same receptors, robbing adenosine of the ability to do its job and leaving caffeine free to stimulate nerve cells, which in turn release epinephrine (also known as adrenaline), a hormone that increases heart rate and blood pressure, supplies an energy boost, and in general makes people feel good.

For all its popularity, caffeine retains a somewhat negative image. It is, after all, a mildly habit-forming stimulant that has been linked to nervousness and anxiety and that causes insomnia. It affects most of the body's major organs. Recent research casts doubt on the magnitude of many of these seemingly undesirable effects and even suggests that a daily dose of caffeine may reduce the risk of some chronic diseases, while providing short-term benefits as well.

Daily caffeine consumption has been associated with lowered incidence of type II diabetes, Parkinson's disease, and Alzheimer's disease. How caffeine works to thwart diabetes, a condition characterized[1] by high levels of glucose in the blood, remains unknown, but glucose tolerance or more efficient glucose metabolism may be involved. Parkinson's disease, a central nervous system

---

[1] British: *characterised*

disorder that causes tremor and joint stiffness, is linked to insufficient amounts of a substance called dopamine in the brain. Caffeine may interact with brain cells that produce dopamine and help maintain a steady supply. The role of caffeine in Alzheimer's disease, which damages the brain and causes memory loss and confusion, may be related to a problem in the blood–brain barrier, possibly a contributor in Alzheimer's, if not the major cause. Caffeine has been found to protect the barrier against disruption resulting from high levels of cholesterol.

Habitual coffee and tea drinkers had long been observed to have a lower incidence of non-melanoma skin cancers, although no one knew why. A recent study found that caffeine affects skin cells damaged by ultraviolet radiation, a main cause of skin cancer. Caffeine interferes with a protein that cancerous cells need to survive, leaving the damaged cells to die before they become cancerous. Drinking caffeinated coffee has also been associated with a decreased incidence of endometrial cancer—that is, cancer of the cells lining the uterus. The strongest effect appears to be in overweight women, who are at greatest risk for the disease. Researchers believe blood sugar, fat cells, and estrogen may play a role. Although the mechanism remains unknown, people who drink more than two cups of coffee or tea a day reportedly have about half the risk of developing chronic liver disease as those who drink less than one cup of coffee daily; caffeinated coffee has also been associated with lowered risk of cirrhosis and liver cancer.

While many of caffeine's undesirable effects, such as elevated heart rate and blood pressure, are brief, some short-term benefits, including pain relief, increased alertness, and increased physical endurance, have also been attributed to caffeine. As a component of numerous over-the-counter diet pills and pain relievers, caffeine increases their effectiveness and helps the body absorb them more quickly. By constricting blood vessels in the brain, it can alleviate headaches—even migraines—and can help counter the drowsiness caused by antihistamines.

Caffeine does not alter the need for sleep, but it does offer a temporary solution to fatigue for people who need to stay alert. Research has shown that sleep-deprived individuals who consumed caffeine had improved memory and reasoning abilities, at least in the short term. Studies of runners and cyclists have shown that caffeine can improve their stamina—hence its addition to energy-boosting sports drinks.

People who consume a lot of caffeine regularly may develop temporary withdrawal symptoms, headache being the most common, if they quit or cut back on it abruptly. Fortunately, these symptoms last only a day or two in most cases. Individuals who are more sensitive to the stimulatory side effects of caffeine may want to avoid it, but most doctors agree that the equivalent of three cups of coffee a day does not harm healthy people. There is no medical basis to give up daily caffeine and many reasons to include a moderate amount in one's diet.

Questions 15–23

Do the following statements agree with the information given in the passage? On lines 15–23 on your answer sheet, write

TRUE	if the statement agrees with the information
FALSE	if the statement contradicts the information
NOT GIVEN	if there is no information on this

15 Before 200 years ago, people did not drink coffee regularly.

16 Children generally do not consume caffeine.

17 The nervous system is affected by caffeine.

18 Caffeine causes the heart to beat faster.

19 Caffeine can be addictive.

20 Alzheimer's disease may be caused in part by caffeine consumption.

21 Drinking coffee can help protect against some skin cancers.

22 Caffeine may increase the incidence of endometrial cancer.

23 Caffeine can help some medications work faster.

Questions 24–27

*Write the correct letter, **A**, **B**, or **C**, on lines 24–27 on your answer sheet.*

24 Caffeine is used to treat

    A high blood pressure.
    B liver cancer.
    C headaches.

25 Some athletes use caffeine to

    A increase their endurance.
    B improve their speed.
    C maintain their alertness.

26 Symptoms of caffeine withdrawal

    A can become an ongoing problem.
    B may last as long as a week.
    C are usually short-lived.

27 Drinking three cups of coffee a day

    A may be recommended by a doctor.
    B will probably not cause problems.
    C is harmful to the health.

READING PASSAGE 3

Animal Camouflage

The theory of natural selection, proposed by Charles Darwin almost 150 years ago, hypothesizes[1] that organisms with traits that give them a survival advantage tend to live longer and produce more offspring. Over many thousands of years of evolution, those beneficial characteristics dominate the gene pool. Animals that use camouflage to conceal themselves from their enemies, predator and prey alike, provide a classic example of natural selection at work. Creatures with some type of protective coloring pass along the genes responsible, with each generation fine-tuning them along the way, eventually providing the most effective coloring for their environment and lifestyle. Scientists have described four types of camouflage that animals use: background matching, disruptive coloration, counter-shading, and mimicry.

From dirt-colored chipmunks and gophers to leaf-green praying mantises and tree frogs to ocean-gray mackerel and sharks, all sorts of wildlife use background matching, also known as *crypsis*, to blend in with their surroundings. Some animals have the ability to alter their coloring as their environment changes seasonally or as they change locations. The arctic fox and the snowshoe hare both have white winter fur that matches the snow and ice around them, but a brown pelt in warmer weather blends in with their woodland environs. Some reptiles and fish can alter their surface appearance instantly as they move from place to place. The green anole lizard changes from green to brown as it travels among leaves and branches, whereas the flounder and other types of flatfish are able to match not just the color but also the silty or mottled sandy texture of the ocean floor beneath them.

Most animals, though, cannot change their appearance so easily. Because background matching works only for a specific setting and often requires animals to remain motionless for long periods, a somewhat more effective strategy involves having a camouflage that works on many backgrounds, blending in with all, but not perfectly matching any of them.

Disruptive coloration uses a pattern such as stripes or spots to disrupt the body's outline. The pattern breaks up the contour of the animal's body, confusing observers and making it difficult to distinguish an individual shape. Colors with more contrast, like a tiger's stripes, tend to increase the disruptive effect. This type of camouflage works well for animals that travel in herds. It helps zebras blend in not so much with their background as with each other. Their major predator, the lion, sees a mass of moving stripes and has trouble targeting

---

[1] *British: hypothesises*

a specific animal. A single zebra, on the other hand, may use background matching when hiding in tall grass, where its black and white stripes merge with the green and yellow stalks. The different colors of the grasses and zebra are no help to a lion, which is color-blind.[1]

Animals with countershading typically have a dark backside and a light belly, which affect an onlooker's perception of their three-dimensional appearance and help decrease their visibility in sunlight. Countershading also can create a more uniformly dark appearance, presenting an apparent lack of depth. Caterpillars make good use of this effect, which gives them a flat look that blends in with tree bark.

Countershading is useful to birds and marine animals that are typically seen against a light environment from below and against dark surroundings from above. Predatory birds like hawks take advantage of it to conceal themselves from the small birds and rodents they hunt. While in flight, a dark back absorbs the sunlight above them and a light underside reflects the light below, diminishing telltale shadows that might give them away. On the ground or in a tree, their mottled brown feathers blend in with branches and leaves. Penguins also use countershading. Their white chests and black backs stand out on land but disappear in water where penguins spend most of their time. They are almost invisible to an observer looking down into dark water, while a creature in deeper water looking up sees a splash of white that looks like a beam of sunlight.

Mimicry, or masquerading, works not by hiding a creature but by making it appear to be something else. Walking stick insects are virtually indistinguishable from twigs, and katydids look so much like green leaves that leaf-eating insects have been observed trying to chew on them.

A type of mimicry known as *aposematism* involves masquerading as an animal that is undesirable or even dangerous. Predators bypass the foul-tasting monarch butterfly, but they also avoid the tasty look-alike viceroy butterfly. Coral snake impersonators, like the harmless scarlet snake, have the same red, black, and yellow bands but in a different order: black, yellow, red, yellow on the coral snake and red, black, yellow, black on the scarlet snake. Different types of moths use aposematism to scare off predators; some species have a big spot on each wing to mimic the eyes of a large animal, while the hawk moth caterpillar has a pattern on its rear that looks like a snake head.

Some predators use what is known as aggressive mimicry to disguise themselves as something harmless so they can catch prey off guard. Small animals are not afraid of turkey vultures, which are scavengers, not predators. So when the similar zone-tailed hawk flies with a group of turkey vultures, it has an easy time locating and zeroing in on its living prey.

No single type of camouflage works best in all situations, and many animals use more than one technique to enhance their ability to avoid detection by predator and prey alike.

---

[1] *British: colour-blind*

Questions 28–36

Complete the summary below. Choose **NO MORE THAN THREE WORDS**
from the passage for each answer.
Write your answers on lines 28–36 on your answer sheet.

Camouflage helps animals hide from both **28** _____ .
Animals pass on their **29** _____ through their genes.
There are four different types of camouflage. In background matching, an
animal's appearance helps it **30** _____ with its environment.
The arctic fox and snowshoe hare are examples of animals that
31 _____ with the seasons. However, not all animals can
easily change their appearance. Many use a different strategy, having camouflage
that helps them disguise themselves **32** _____. Animals with
disruptive coloration have marking such as **33** _____ that
make it difficult for a predator to discern the shape of the body. Therefore, the
predator has a hard time targeting one animal out of a group. Although zebras
are black and white, they can hide in tall grass because their major predator is
34 _____. **35** _____ is a type of
camouflage that helps hide animals that are seen from above or below. Penguins,
for example, have **36** _____, which help them blend in
with the dark water from the point of view of an observer standing above.

Questions 37–40

*Do the following statements agree with the information in the passage? On lines
37–40 on your answer sheet, write:*

TRUE	if the statement agrees with the information
FALSE	if the statement contradicts the information
NOT GIVEN	if there is no information on this

37 The walking stick insect looks like a small stick.

38 The viceroy butterfly is similar in appearance to the monarch butterfly.

39 The scarlet snake is extremely poisonous.

40 The hawk moth caterpillar is brightly colored.

Academic Module
Practice Test 5

Candidate Name and Number: _____

INTERNATIONAL ENGLISH LANGUAGE TESTING SYSTEM

ACADEMIC WRITING

TIME 1 HOUR

Instructions to Candidates

Do not open this booklet until you are told to do so.

Write your name and candidate number in the space at the top of this page.

All answers must be written on the separate answer booklet provided. (The answer sheets can be found beginning on page 183.)

Do not remove the booklet from the examination room.

Information for Candidates

There are **2** tasks on this question paper.

You must do **both** tasks.

Under-length answers will be penalized.[1]

---

[1] *British: penalised*

WRITING TASK 1

You should spend about 20 minutes on this task. Write at least 150 words.

The chart below shows the cost-of-living averages in two different cities as compared to the national cost-of-living average.

Summarize[1] the information by selecting and reporting the main features, and make comparisons where relevant.

Cost-of-Living Percentage Averages Above and Below the National Average

	Riverdale	Cape Alicia
Groceries	4.7%	0.5%
Housing	19%	−12.5%
Utilities	4.5%	1.2%
Transportation	4%	−3.8%
Health care	7%	0.8%
Clothing	5.5%	1%

WRITING TASK 2

You should spend about 40 minutes on this task. Write at least 250 words.

Write about the following topic:

Life now is better than it was 100 years ago.

To what extent do you agree or disagree with this statement? Give reasons for your answer and include any relevant examples from your own knowledge or experience.

---

[1] *British: Summarise*

SPEAKING

Examiner questions:

Part 1

How much time do you spend using a computer?

Do you use a computer more for work, study, or personal reasons?

What different kinds of things do you do on the computer?

What are some things you like and dislike about using computers?

How often do you use the Internet?

What are some things you do on the Internet?

Do you prefer shopping online or in real stores? Why?

Part 2

Tell about your favorite[1] subject you studied in school.

You should say:

What the subject was

In which grade or grades you studied it

What kinds of things you learned about it and explain what you liked it about it

> You will have one to two minutes to talk about this topic.
>
> You will have one minute to prepare what you are going to say.

Part 3

What subjects should be required in school?

Do you think math and science are more important subjects than literature and art? Why or why not?

At what age should students be allowed to choose their own subjects?

What subjects should schools offer in the future that they don't offer now?

---

[1] *British: favourite*

Practice Test 5—Academic Module
IELTS LISTENING ANSWER SHEET

1. _____
2. _____
3. _____
4. _____
5. _____
6. _____
7. _____
8. _____
9. _____
10. _____
11. _____
12. _____
13. _____
14. _____
15. _____
16. _____
17. _____
18. _____
19. _____
20. _____

21. _____
22. _____
23. _____
24. _____
25. _____
26. _____
27. _____
28. _____
29. _____
30. _____
31. _____
32. _____
33. _____
34. _____
35. _____
36. _____
37. _____
38. _____
39. _____
40. _____

Practice Test 5—Answer Sheet

Practice Test 5–Academic Module
IELTS READING ANSWER SHEET

1. _____
2. _____
3. _____
4. _____
5. _____
6. _____
7. _____
8. _____
9. _____
10. _____
11. _____
12. _____
13. _____
14. _____
15. _____
16. _____
17. _____
18. _____
19. _____
20. _____

21. _____
22. _____
23. _____
24. _____
25. _____
26. _____
27. _____
28. _____
29. _____
30. _____
31. _____
32. _____
33. _____
34. _____
35. _____
36. _____
37. _____
38. _____
39. _____
40. _____

Practice Test 5–Academic Module
WRITING TASK 1

Writing Task 1 *continued*

Practice Test 5–Academic Module
WRITING TASK 2

Writing Task 2 *continued*

_____

_____

_____

_____

_____

_____

_____

_____

_____

_____

_____

_____

_____

_____

_____

_____

_____

_____

_____

_____

_____

_____

Writing Task 2 *continued*

_____

_____

_____

_____

_____

_____

_____

_____

_____

_____

_____

_____

_____

_____

_____

_____

_____

_____

_____

_____

_____

Practice Test 5—Answer Sheet

Answer Key

PRACTICE TEST 5—ACADEMIC MODULE

Listening

1. June	12. E	23. F	33. B
2. Karla	13. A	24. G	34. A
3. 257	14. F	25. I	35. A
4. vegetarian	15. C	26. 1895	36. a (gardener's) calendar
5. B	16. swimming lessons	27. new wing	37. served tomatoes
6. A	17. tennis competition	28. local artists	38. in public
7. C	18. party/club party	29. art history	39. tomato recipe/recipes
8. A	19. B	30. concerts/concert series	40. raw tomatoes
9. D	20. C	31. C	
10. E	21. B	32. C	
11. B	22. C		

Reading

1. A	12. D	23. True	33. stripes or spots
2. C	13. D	24. C	34. color-blind
3. C	14. B	25. A	35. countershading
4. C	15. Not Given	26. C	36. black backs
5. D	16. False	27. B	37. True
6. C	17. True	28. predators and prey	38. True
7. A	18. True	29. protective coloring	39. False
8. B	19. True	30. blend in	40. Not Given
9. C	20. False	31. alter their coloring	
10. D	21. True	32. on many backgrounds	
11. B	22. False		

Practice Test 5—Answer Key

Answer Explanations

ACADEMIC MODULE—PRACTICE TEST 5

Listening

1. *June.* The speakers discuss the month of the River Valley tour, and the man says, "It actually takes place the first week of June."

2. *Karla.* The woman spells her first name, "That's Karla with a K, not a C. K-A-R-L-A."

3. *257.* The woman gives her P.O. box number, "It's P. O. Box 257, Manchester."

4. *vegetarian.* The speakers discuss dietary restrictions, and the woman says, "Well, yes, I'm a vegetarian."

5. **(B)** The man says he needs a 30 percent deposit. Choice (A) is the size of the recommended tip. Choice (C) sounds similar to $750, the total cost of the trip.

6. **(A)** The man explains that Karla will need to pay the deposit in two weeks. Choice (B) is confused with how long before a tour the deposit must be paid. Choice (C) is when the tour begins.

7. **(C)** The man explains that a van will carry the luggage from hotel to hotel. Choice (A) is not mentioned. Choice (B) is what the woman asks.

8. **(A)** The man recommends, "so you should bring a raincoat. . . ."

9. **(D)** The man says, "you should definitely have a water bottle."

10. **(E)** The man says, "A camera would be a good idea, too. . . ."

11. **(B)** The guide points out the new paint and says, "Both of the pools needed painting. . . ."

12. **(E)** The guide says, "We've expanded both the men's and women's locker rooms. . . ." *Expanded* means the same as *enlarged.*

13. **(A)** The guide says, "Here you'll notice the new floor."

14. **(F)** The guide says, "We replaced all the nets and the ball-throwing machine." Nets and a ball-throwing machine are types of *equipment.*

15. **(C)** The guide says, "here we are at the club store in its new location."

16. *swimming lessons.* The guide says, "Now that the pools are ready for use again, swimming lessons will begin tomorrow, for both adults and children."

17. *tennis competition.* The guide says, "If you're a tennis player, you'll be interested to hear about the tennis competition coming up on Wednesday."

18. *party/club party.* The guide says, "you're invited to our club party, coming up next weekend."

19. **(B)** The guide says, "The entire renovation project was finished in just nine months." Choice (A) is confused with the fact that the work took three months less than planned. Choice (C) is the number of months originally planned for the work.

20. **(C)** The guide says, "next year we plan to install an outdoor pool. . . ." Choices (A) and (B) are things the club already has.

21. **(B)** Dr. Johnson explains, "You'll spend some time working in here so you can learn what the administrative duties involve. . . ."

22. **(C)** Dr. Johnson says, "you'll all have a chance to lead some tours. . . ." *Lead* means the same as *guide*.

23. **(F)** Dr. Johnson tells the students that they will spend some time working in the Research Department.

24. **(G)** Dr. Johnson says, "Also, as an extension of your research work, you'll probably contribute to some of the museum's brochures." In this context, *contribute* means *do some writing*.

25. **(I)** Dr. Johnson says, "We've planned a reception for the first day of your internship, and you'll have the chance to meet several local artists then."

26. *1895.* Dr. Johnson explains, "The main part of the museum was built in 1895 with a combination of public and private funds."

27. *new wing.* Dr. Johnson says, "The new wing was built sixty years later with a donation from the Rhinebeck family."

28. *local artists.* Dr. Johnson describes the museum's collections, "In the main part of the museum, we have a gallery devoted to works by local artists, our sculpture collection, and a small collection of classical European art."

29. *art history.* Dr. Johnson says, "In our Adult Education program, we offer a series of art history classes. . . ."

30. *concerts/concert series.* Dr. Johnson says, "We offer a weekly concert series during the fall and winter. . . ."

31. **(C)** The speaker says, "The tomato originated in the highlands of Peru." Choice (A) is mentioned as a place where tomatoes were later cultivated. Choice (B) is confused with the mention of Spanish explorers.

32. **(C)** The speaker says, "The Aztec tomato was not the large red vegetable we know today. Rather, it was small and yellow." Choice (A) is the color of tomatoes today. Choice (B) is plausible but is not mentioned.

33. **(B)** The speaker says, "The actual word *tomato* comes from the Aztec name for the vegetable, meaning "plump thing.'" Choice (A) is the meaning of the Italian name for *tomato*. Choice (C) is the way the speaker describes tomatoes.

34. **(A)** The speaker says, "The tomato arrived in Europe in the 1500s and quickly became a popular food in Spain and Italy." Choice (B) is what the British did with tomatoes. Choice (C) is not mentioned.

35. **(A)** The speaker says, "It was grown as an ornamental plant in Britain in the 1600s, but it wasn't eaten because it was thought to be poisonous." Choice (B) is what the Italians did. Choice (C) is not mentioned and would have happened later.

36. *a (gardener's) calendar.* The speaker says, "In 1806, a gardener's calendar mentioned that tomatoes could be used to improve the flavor of soups and other foods."

37. *served tomatoes.* The speaker says, "Thomas Jefferson. . . .first served tomatoes to visitors at his home in Virginia in 1809."

38. *in public.* The speaker says, "To prove his point, he ate one kilo of ripe red tomatoes in public."

39. *tomato recipes/recipes.* The speaker says, "By the 1830s, American newspapers and magazines were publishing thousands of tomato recipes."

40. *raw tomatoes.* The speaker says, "It wasn't until a century later, in the 1930s, that it became popular for people to eat raw tomatoes."

Reading

PASSAGE 1

1. **(A)** Paragraph 1: "paraffin wax, which is derived from petroleum." This means it is a by-product of petroleum. Choice (B) is where crude oil is found, not parrafin. Choice (C) is confused with the explanation of the wax coming from decayed vegetable matter.

2. **(C)** Paragraph 2: "At that time, paraffin was derived by a process of distilling bituminous schist, now known as shale oil." Choice (A) is what paraffin is derived from now. Choice (B) is confused with the explanation of petroleum coming from "decayed vegetable matter."

3. **(C)** According to paragraph 2, James Young was an industrial chemist, a type of scientist. Choice (A) is confused with a use for paraffin. Choice (B) is confused with the material James Young worked with.

4. **(C)** According to paragraph 6, tallow was made from the fat of cattle and sheep.

5. **(D)** According to paragraph 7, the "Bayberry shrubs. . .grow. . .in salt-laden, coastal soil unsuitable for other horticulture. . . ." A *shrub* is a bush, and *coastal* means "near the sea."

6. **(C)** According to paragraph 6, tallow was melted and then strained, or filtered, to remove impurities.

7. **(A)** Paragraph 2: "Paraffin, however, was not discovered until the early 1800s." The 1800s are the nineteenth century.

8. **(B)** Paragraph 3: "beeswax candles emit no smoke when burning. . . ."

9. **(C)** Paragraph 6: "Tallow candles needed to be stored in tightly closed containers, usually made of tin or wood, to keep out rodents and other animals that might eat them." Mice and rats are types of rodents.

10. **(D)** Paragraph 7: "In winter, the female plants bear clusters of blue–gray berries, which lend their color to the wax."

11. **(B)** Paragraph 5: "Many of the early settlers brought honeybee hives with them from Europe."

12. **(D)** According to paragraph 8, bayberry candles "were often saved for special occasions, particularly Christmas and New Year's Eve."

13. **(D)** According to paragraph 7, bayberry candles have "a pleasing scent." *Scent* means the same as *aroma*.

14. **(B)** According to paragraph 5, honey and beeswax were used for bartering. *Bartering* means the same as *trading*.

PASSAGE 2

15. *Not Given.* The passage does not mention when people began drinking coffee.

16. *False.* Paragraph 2: "Many of the world's people, including children, ingest it in some form daily."

17. *True.* Paragraph 4 discusses the effect of caffeine on nerve cells.

18. *True.* Paragraph 4 explains how caffeine contributes to increased heart rate.

19. *True.* Paragraph 5: "Caffeine. . . .is, after all, a mildly habit-forming stimulant. . . ." *Habit-forming* means the same as *addictive.*

20. *False.* Paragraph 6 explains how caffeine may help lower the incidence of Alzheimer's disease.

21. *True.* Paragraph 7 explains how caffeine may help lower the incidence of non-melanoma skin cancers.

22. *False.* Paragraph 7 explains how caffeine may help decrease, not increase, the incidence of endometrial cancer.

23. *True.* Paragraph 8: "As a component of numerous over-the-counter diet pills and pain relievers, caffeine increases their effectiveness and helps the body absorb them more quickly."

24. **(C)** Paragraph 8: "By constricting blood vessels in the brain, it can alleviate headaches. . . ." Choice (A) refers to a disease that caffeine can make worse. Choice (B) is a condition that caffeine may help to prevent, but caffeine is not mentioned as a treatment for it.

25. **(A)** Paragraph 9: "Studies of runners and cyclists have shown that caffeine can improve their stamina. . . ." *Endurance* means the same as *stamina.* Choice (B) is plausible but is not mentioned. Choice (C) is mentioned in the paragraph but not in reference to athletes.

26. **(C)** According to paragraph 10, withdrawal symptoms last only one or two days. Choices (A) and (B) are plausible but not mentioned.

27. **(B)** Paragraph 10: "most doctors agree that the equivalent of three cups of coffee a day does not harm healthy people." Choice (A) is incorrect because there is no recommendation by doctors mentioned. Choice (C) contradicts the information given.

PASSAGE 3

28. *predators and prey.* Paragraph 1: "Animals that use camouflage to conceal themselves from their enemies, predator and prey alike, provide a classic example of natural selection at work."

29. *protective coloring.* Paragraph 1: "Creatures with some type of protective coloring pass along the genes responsible. . . ."

30. *blend in.* Paragraph 2: "all sorts of wildlife use background matching. . .to blend in with their surroundings."

31. *alter their coloring.* Paragraph 2: "Some have the ability to alter their coloring as their environment changes seasonally. . . ."

32. *on many backgrounds.* Paragraph 3: "a somewhat more effective strategy involves having a camouflage that works on many backgrounds. . . ."

33. *stripes or spots.* Paragraph 4: "Disruptive coloration uses a pattern such as stripes or spots to disrupt the body's outline."

34. *color-blind.* Paragraph 4: "The different colors of the grasses and zebra are no help to the lion, which is color-blind."

35. *countershading.* Paragraph 6: "Countershading is useful to birds and marine animals that are typically seen against a light environment from below and against dark surroundings from above."

36. *black backs.* Paragraph 6: "Their white chests and black backs stand out on land but disappear in water where penguins spend most of their time. They are almost invisible to an observer looking down into dark water. . . ."

37. *True.* Paragraph 7: "Walking stick insects are virtually indistinguishable from twigs. . . ."

38. *True.* "Paragraph 8: "Predators bypass the foul-tasting monarch butterfly, but they also avoid the tasty look-alike viceroy butterfly."

39. *False.* Paragraph 8: "Coral snake impersonators, like the harmless scarlet snake, have the same red, black, and yellow bands but in a different order. . . ."

40. *Not Given.* Paragraph 8 mentions the shape of a pattern on the hawk moth caterpillar but does not mention its coloring.

Writing

These are models. Your answers will vary. See page vi in the Introduction to see the criteria for scoring.

WRITING TASK 1

The chart shows how the cost of living in two different cities, Riverdale and Cape Alicia, compares with the national average cost of living. The average costs of several different types of living expenses are shown.

The cost of living in the city of Riverdale is higher than the national average in all the areas shown. The highest is housing, with an average cost 19 percent higher than the national average. The lowest is transportation, but that is still 4 percent higher than the national average. Groceries, utilities, health care, and clothing all have average costs between 4 and 7 percent higher than the national average.

The cost of living in Cape Alicia is close to the national average for most types of expenses. The expense that differs most from the national average is housing, with an average cost 12.5 percent lower than the national average. Transportation costs average 3.8 percent lower than the national average. The other expenses listed range from .5 to 1.2 percent higher than the national average. The cost of living in Cape Alicia appears to be significantly lower than it is in Riverdale, and it is probably also lower than many other cities in the nation.

WRITING TASK 2

The way we live now is different in many aspects from the way people lived 100 years ago. Technology has changed how we earn our livings and carry out our daily lives. Our lives have improved in many important ways over the past 100 years. At the same time, there are certain positive things that have been lost.

Technology has improved our lives in many ways. We have machinery, electronic devices, and appliances that make our work and daily chores easier. Advances in communications technology make it easier to be in contact with colleagues, personal friends, and relatives everywhere. We have many types of transportation that make it easy to travel anywhere, even around the world, for both business and personal reasons. Finally, because of advances in medicine, fewer people die of common diseases that were fatal not long ago. For all these reasons, we can say that life now is better than it was a century ago.

On the other hand, there are other, less material, aspects of our lives that have not necessarily improved. For example, while it is true that technology makes communication with distant loved ones easier, at the same time families are breaking up. Family members no longer tend to live near one another as was common in the past. This means a loss of important social and emotional support. In addition, because we have so many electronic devices, such as personal computers, cell phones, and so on, people tend to pay more attention to these devices than they do to their actual face-to-face personal relationships.

It is easy to see that in a material sense, life is much better for many people now than it was just 100 years ago. However, even though our material existence has greatly improved, our social and emotional lives have suffered. This is a challenge for people living in the twenty-first century.

Speaking

These are models. Your answers will vary. See page vi in the Introduction to see the criteria for scoring.

PART 1

How much time do you spend using a computer?
I spend several hours every day using a computer because it's an important part of my work. I try to stay away from the computer on weekends, but I'm not always successful at that because there are always so many things I want to do with it. Maybe I spend too much time on the computer. I don't know. It's a little bit addictive.

Do you use a computer more for work, study, or personal reasons?

The reason I'm on the computer so much is because I use it at work. Most of my work involves creating documents for the company. Because of that, the computer has become a habit for me, so I also end up using it a lot for personal reasons. So, I guess I could say the main reason I use it is for work, but it's a big part of my personal life, too.

What different kinds of things do you do on the computer?

Besides creating documents at work, I use e-mail a lot to communicate with my work colleagues and also with my friends and relatives. I also keep a lot of personal records on the computer, like the family budget, photographs, and things like that. And I have to admit that I spend a lot of time playing computer games. That helps me relax when I'm working on a big project.

What are some things you like and dislike about using computers?

Nobody can deny that computers make so many things convenient. I couldn't do my job without a computer, and e-mail makes communications so much easier. Everything I do on the computer is a lot easier than it would be without the computer. On the other hand, as I said before, a computer can be addictive. Sometimes I end up spending an entire Saturday afternoon doing things on the computer, instead of spending time with my family or going outside and getting exercise. It takes some discipline, I think, to keep from overusing the computer.

How often do you use the Internet?

I use the Internet quite frequently. I use it in the course of my work every day. For example, I frequently use e-mail to discuss things with my colleagues. I often have to look for information online, for both work and personal reasons. So, I'd have to say I use the Internet several times a day.

What are some things you do on the Internet?

Besides e-mailing my colleagues and my friends and relatives, I use the Internet for a number of other things. I often use it to find information I need for my work. I also use it to research products before I make a big purchase; I mean something expensive. Last year I had to buy a new refrigerator, so I did some research online to figure out what kind I wanted and what it should cost. I often read the news online, and I find out about movies I want to see and books I want to buy. I do a lot on the Internet.

Do you prefer shopping online or in real stores? Why?

As I mentioned, I like to research products online before I make a major purchase, but usually I prefer to buy things in a regular store. Especially if I'm buying something expensive, I like to see it before I buy it. Also, shipping costs can be very high, and you don't have to pay them if you buy from a store. Sometimes it's hard to find things locally, and sometimes you can find a really, really good price online, so sometimes I buy things that way. But usually I go to stores.

PART 2

When I was in school, my favorite subject was history. I liked all kinds of history, and I still do. I studied it every year I was in high school, from ninth through twelfth grade. I learned a lot of things. I learned about the important events in the history of my country and about the important people. I learned about all kinds of people—politicians, inventors, soldiers, and even common everyday people who contributed to our history. I learned these things about other countries, too. I like history a lot because I like to imagine and understand what life was like at different times. People have lived under different conditions during different periods of history, and they've had different kinds of interests, motivations, and needs. In each period of history, the conditions of that time shaped the events. I think it's interesting to learn about these things and important to understand them. We are who we are today because of what our ancestors did. I'm still interested in history, and I still read about it often.

PART 3

What subjects should be required in school?
I think everyone agrees what the basic primary and secondary school curriculum should be. Everyone needs to study math, science, literature, and history, and probably art and music too. In addition to these things, I think every student should be required to study foreign languages because international relations are so important in the modern world. In addition to that, students should study the history and culture of countries around the world.

Do you think math and science are more important subjects than literature and art? Why or why not?
I suppose many people think math and science are very important because we have a lot of emphasis on technology in the modern world. But technology isn't everything. For one thing, not everyone has talents in math or science. But even for mathematicians and scientists, literature and art are important. They give us a different perspective on things, and they also help us develop our creativity, no matter what field of specialty we pursue.

At what age should students be allowed to choose their own subjects?
I think high school students should be allowed to choose some of their own subjects. They shouldn't choose all their own subjects, of course, because there are certain things that are the foundations of a good education, but they can choose some. For example, they can be given a choice among different kinds of literature classes or they could choose certain aspects of history to study. So, I think that beginning in high school, students should be given some choices about what they study. Before high school, I think they're too young to make wise choices.

What subjects should schools offer in the future that they don't offer now?
Schools in the future may have to put even more emphasis on using computers since we're now doing practically everything on computer. Computer skills will be just as important, or more important, than reading and writing skills. So students will have to become skilled at using the computers and the software they'll need for different tasks.

ACADEMIC MODULE
PRACTICE TEST 6

Academic Module
Practice Test 6

Candidate Name and Number: _____

INTERNATIONAL ENGLISH LANGUAGE TESTING SYSTEM

LISTENING

TIME APPROX. 30 MINUTES

Instructions to Candidates

Do not open this booklet until you are told to do so.

Write your name and candidate number in the space at the top of this page.

You should answer all questions.

All the recordings will be played ONCE only.

Write all your answers on the test pages.

At the end of the test, you will be given ten minutes to transfer your answers to an Answer Sheet. (The answer sheet can be found on page 221.)

Do not remove the booklet from the examination room.

Information for Candidates

There are **40** questions on this question paper.

The test is divided as follows:

Section 1	Questions 1–10
Section 2	Questions 11–20
Section 3	Questions 21–30
Section 4	Questions 31–40

SECTION 1　QUESTIONS 1–10

Note

If you do not have access to an audio CD player, refer to the audioscripts starting on page 432 when prompted to listen to an audio passage.

Questions 1–5

Complete the information below.
Write **NO MORE THAN TWO WORDS AND/OR A NUMBER**
for each answer.

City Library

Head Librarian　　Example: *Mrs. Phillips*

<u>Hours</u>　**1** _____ to 4:30

<u>Books</u>

Ground floor[1]　**2** _____

Second floor　Adult collection

Third floor　**3** _____

<u>Book carts</u>

Brown cart　　books to re-shelve

Black cart　　books to **4** _____

White cart　　books to **5** _____

Questions 6–10

Complete the library schedule below.
Write **NO MORE THAN ONE WORD AND/OR A NUMBER** *for each answer.*

Activity	Location	Day and Time
Story Time	Children's Room	**6** _____ at 11:00
7 _____	Reference Room	Saturday at **8** _____
Lecture Series	**9** _____ Room	Friday at **10** _____

---

[1] *In the United States the ground floor is considered the first floor; the next floor up is the second floor.*

SECTION 2   *QUESTIONS 11–20*

Questions 11–15

Choose FIVE letters, A–I.
Which FIVE activities are available at Golden Lake Resort?

A swimming

B boating

C waterskiing

D fishing

E tennis

F golf

G horseback riding

H hiking

I arts and crafts

Questions 16–20

Complete the schedule below.
Write NO MORE THAN ONE WORD for each answer.

Night	Activity
Sunday	16 _____
Monday	Dessert Night
Tuesday	17 _____ Night
Wednesday	18 _____
Thursday	19 _____
Friday	Talent Show
Saturday	20 _____

CD 2 Track 11 **SECTION 3   QUESTIONS 21–30**

Questions 21–23

Choose **THREE** *letters, A–F.*
Which **THREE** *things are the students required to submit to their professor?*

A   a written summary

B   maps

C   a case study

D   charts and graphs

E   a list of resources used

F   a video

Questions 24 and 25

Answer the questions below.
Write **NO MORE THAN THREE WORDS** *for each answer.*

24   What two sources of information will the students use when preparing their presentation?

_____

25   What will the students show during their presentation?

_____

Academic Module–Practice Test 6

26 Only rescue birds that are

   A all alone.
   B obviously hurt.
   C sitting on the ground.

27 Protect yourself by wearing

   A gloves.
   B a hat.
   C protective glasses.

28 Put the bird in a

   A cage.
   B box.
   C bag.

29 Keep the bird calm by

   A petting it.
   B talking to it.
   C leaving it alone.

30 When transporting the bird,

   A speak quietly.
   B play music.
   C drive very slowly.

 CD 2 Track 12

SECTION 4   QUESTIONS 31–40

The Great Barrier Reef is made up of 3,000 **31** _____ and

600 **32** _____ . Over 400 kinds of **33** _____ can

be found there.

Questions 34–38

Choose **FIVE** *letters, A–I.*
Which **FIVE** *of these kinds of animals inhabiting the Great Barrier Reef are mentioned?*

A sharks

B starfish

C seahorses

D clams

E whales

F dolphins

G sea turtles

H crocodiles

I frogs

Questions 39 and 40

Answer the questions below.
Write **NO MORE THAN THREE WORDS** *for each answer.*

39 What causes coral bleaching?

_____

40 What has been one response to this problem?

_____

Take ten minutes to transfer your answers onto the Answer Sheet on page 221.

Academic Module
Practice Test 6

Candidate Name and Number: _____

INTERNATIONAL ENGLISH LANGUAGE TESTING SYSTEM

ACADEMIC READING

TIME 1 HOUR

Instructions to Candidates

Do not open this booklet until you are told to do so.

Write your name and candidate number in the space at the top of this page.

Start at the beginning of the test and work through it.

You should answer all questions.

If you cannot do a particular question, leave it and go on to the next. You can return to it later.

All answers must be written on the Answer Sheet. (The answer sheet can be found on page 222.)

Do not remove the booklet from the examination room.

Information for Candidates

There are **40** questions on this question paper.

The test is divided as follows:

Reading Passage 1	Questions 1–14
Reading Passage 2	Questions 15–27
Reading Passage 3	Questions 28–40

READING PASSAGE 1

*You should spend about 20 minutes on **Questions 1–14**, which are based on Reading Passage 1 below.*

Pollination

Plants have evolved a wide variety of methods to reproduce themselves. Some plants reproduce asexually by splitting off new roots or bulbs (e.g., garlic, lilies) or even branches, stems, or leaves (e.g., mangroves, spider plants). Plants that reproduce asexually are essentially reproducing clones of themselves. This is a simple and direct method of reproduction, producing new plants more quickly and with less energy than plants using sexual reproduction. The majority of plants, however, reproduce sexually. The advantages from an evolutionary perspective include more genetic variety and better dispersal than the colonies of clones formed by asexual reproduction. In flowering plants, pollen (male) grains are moved from the anther to the stigma, where the pollen fertilizes[1] the ovaries (female), resulting in seeds.

A few flowering plants such as peas, beans, and tomatoes pollinate themselves, but more commonly, pollination occurs between separate plants, either through pollen being borne by the wind (most conifers and many grasses) or by pollinators, animal species that plants rely on to help move the pollen from one plant to the ovaries of another. Most pollinators are insects, but some species of bird and bats also play an important role.

Plants have evolved a variety of methods to entice pollinators to do their work. Many produce nectar, a sugary substance that pollinators use as food. A well-known example is the honeybee, which collects nectar as well as pollen for food. When a bee enters one flower, it brushes against the anther, and pollen grains are picked up by the surface of its body. When the bee enters a second flower and brushes against the stigma, some of that pollen comes in contact with the ovaries of the second plant, thus fertilizing it, resulting in seeds that contain genetic material from the male gametes of the first plant combined with the female reproductive organs of the second plant. Most bees, butterflies, and moths, as well as certain species of bats and birds, are attracted to nectar-producing flowers.

Flowering plants have evolved a variety of methods for signaling[2] their usefulness to pollinators or for otherwise making their work easier. Butterflies are attracted to flowers that are open during the day, are bright—typically red, yellow, or orange—and have a "landing platform." In contrast, many moths are active at night and thus are attracted to flowers that are pale or white, have a strong fragrance, but also have broad areas to land on. Both butterflies and moths have long tongues and have co-evolved with plants that have developed deep sources of nectar that are available only to certain species. Hummingbirds are also attracted by color[3] especially by bright reds, and flowers that attract these tiny birds also have strong stems and are designed for pollen to be brushed on the hummingbirds' heads as they sip nectar.

---

[1] *British: fertilises*
[2] *British: signalling*
[3] *British: colour*

Bees do not see red; thus, flowers that attract bees tend to be blue, yellow, purple, or other colors. Many bee attractors also have nectar guides, which are spots near the center[1] of each flower that reflect ultraviolet light, making it easier for the bees to find the nectar. Bees are also attracted to flowers with a mintlike or sweet smell. Snapdragons not only attract bees visually, they are adapted to appeal to certain bee species: snapdragons have a landing platform that, if the bee is the correct weight, opens—allowing access to the nectar and pollen.

Pollinators play a major role in agriculture. While many staple crops such as rice, corn, canola, and wheat are self-pollinating or pollinated by the wind, farmers are dependent on pollinator species for many fruit, vegetable, nut, and seed crops. Over 30 percent of the world's crops require the work of pollinator species. Bees are the most common agricultural pollinators, with crops including fruit trees such as apples and cherries; vegetables such as squash, beans, tomatoes, and eggplant; flowering shrubs and annual and perennial flowers; forage crops such as clover and alfalfa; and fiber[2] crops such as cotton. Other pollinators include midges (cocoa), wasps (figs), moths (yucca, papaya), butterflies (asters, daisies, marigolds), and even a few species of bats (agave, palms, durians) and hummingbirds (fuchsia).

Recent declines in honeybees and in other pollinator species around the world have raised concerns about future food production, and many scientists have called for increased study of the role of pollinators, the agricultural and environmental changes involved in the declines, as well as the economic and environmental effects and ways to prevent further declines.

---

[1] *British: centre*

[2] *British: fibre*

Questions 1–5

Complete the summary using the list of words and phrases below.
Write the correct letter, A–I, on lines 1–5 on your answer sheet.

The reproduction of plants occurs in different ways. Some plants send out new parts such as **1** _____ or bulbs. These grow into new plants, which are actually **2** _____ of the original plant. The advantage of this form of reproduction is that it does not require a lot of **3** _____ or energy. Many **4** _____ reproduce themselves by forming seeds through the process of pollination. Some plants pollinate themselves. Others rely on the **5** _____ or animals to carry the pollen from plant to plant.

A	pollen
B	flowering plants
C	roots
D	grains
E	spider plants
F	air
G	copies
H	fertilization
I	time

Questions 6–14

Do the following statements agree with the information given in the passage? On lines 6–14 on your answer sheet, write:

TRUE	if the statement agrees with the information
FALSE	if the statement contradicts the information
NOT GIVEN	if there is no information on this

6 Honeybees eat both nectar and pollen.

7 If an attractive flower is very small, a butterfly will land on its leaves.

8 Moths are attracted by both color and scent.

9 Certain flowers have evolved to be pollinated by hummingbirds.

10 Special markings on a flower help bees to locate the nectar.

11 Bees rarely respond to scent.

12 Most grain crops are pollinated by insects.

13 Close to one third of the world's harvest depends on animals for pollination.

14 Farmers in certain parts of the world have suffered economically because of the decline in the honeybee population.

READING PASSAGE 2

Paleolithic[1] Cave Art

Students of art history tend to be familiar with the images of horses and bison discovered in the famous cave art site in Lascaux, France, in 1940. Less well known but vitally important to understanding Ice Age art and culture is the art discovered by three cave explorers in the Chauvet Cave near Vallon-Pont-d'Arc in southern France in 1994.

The Chauvet Cave hosts one of the largest group of Paleolithic drawings yet discovered on one site, as well as the fossilized[2] remains of a number of now-extinct animals. The art found in the Chauvet Cave differs from that found in most other European cave art sites, which primarily feature prey animals such as horses, bison, wild cattle, and reindeer. The Chauvet paintings include many animals that humans would have feared—panthers, bears, lions, hyenas, and rhinoceroses. While the Chauvet paintings also include many species that would have been hunted by the artists—horses, aurochs, bison, and extinct species of moose and deer—the presence of non-prey animals calls into question a common theory that the primary purpose of cave art was to magically ensure plentiful game. Perhaps the discovery of the Chauvet art points to a shift in emphasis from the hunters' predators to the hunters' prey over time, but more evidence is needed.

Carbon-14 dating has established three of the paintings (one bison and two rhinoceroses) as being 31,000 years old. This discovery pushes the common understanding of the date range for European cave art much further back than what had been assumed. It has also clearly disproved theories that earlier cave art was cruder and more primitive because these older images are equally sophisticated in execution.

In addition to the hundreds of animal paintings, the Chauvet Cave also has an image of a being, referred to as the Sorcerer, with the body of a human and the head of a bison. There is also part of an image of a woman. In addition, explorers found the skull of a cave bear placed on a squared-off altarlike rock. The cave had been untouched for thousands of years due to a rock slide that had sealed off the cave; the floor of the cave contains the footprints of humans and cave bears, and fire pits, stone tools, remnants of torches, and bones from meals. After scientists collected data and recorded images, the site was placed off-limits to prevent the damage that has occurred at many other caves known for their rock art.

---

[1] *British: Palaeolithic*
[2] *British: fossilised*

Ice Age paintings in certain European caves have been extremely well preserved and have reached iconic status because of their beauty and the artists' skill in execution. As a result, many people assume that the art of early hunters and gathers was limited to cave paintings. While the artwork in the deep caves has been the best preserved, artwork was also done on the walls of rock shelters and on rock faces out in open light. Paleolithic artists not only painted with pigments but also created engravings by scratching designs into rock with pointed tools, as well as creating low-relief sculptures. Often the artists seemed to have seen a suggestion of an animal's shape in a rock, and then added detail through incising lines, incorporating clay, or applying pigment. In addition to animal images, most sites also have geometrical designs, including dots and quadrangles. Archeologists[1] have also discovered small sculpted figures from the same time period.

Images of hands, created either by wetting the palm of the hand with paint and pressing the hand onto rock or by applying paint around the hand, perhaps by spitting pigment from the mouth, are common. However, full images of humans are rare in the European caves. Images combining human and animal elements such as the Chauvet Cave Sorcerer have been found in various sites as have partial images of women, but portrayals of a full human are few and far between, and they tend to be simple abstract depictions. Most of the animal images, on the other hand, are detailed, realistic portrayals of an individual animal species, not simply an abstract symbol meant to depict an animal such as a horse or bison.

[1] *British: Archaeologists*

Questions 15–21

*Choose the correct letter. Write the correct letter **A**, **B**, or **C**, on lines 15–21 on your answer sheet.*

15 As compared with the Chauvet Cave, the cave art site in Lascaux is

    A more well known.
    B less important.
    C more difficult to explore.

16 The art discovered in the Chauvet Cave differs from other European cave art because

    A it does not include images of horses and bison.
    B it shows images of now-extinct animals.
    C it includes images of predatory animals.

17 According to the passage, a common belief about the function of cave art is that

    A it was meant to bring animals to be hunted.
    B it was intended to drive away predatory animals.
    C it was used to warn others about the presence of fearsome animals.

18 As compared with other European cave art sites, the art in the Chauvet Cave is

    A cruder and more primitive.
    B significantly older.
    C more sophisticated in subject matter.

19 Images found in the Chauvet Cave include

    A a crude map.
    B a part-human, part-animal being.
    C a complete drawing of a woman.

20 In addition to art, other discoveries in the Chauvet Cave include

    A implements made of stone.
    B human bones.
    C bison pelts.

21 No humans had visited the Chauvet Cave for thousands of years because

    A cave bears lived inside it.
    B it was declared off limits.
    C the entrance was blocked by rocks.

Questions 22–27

Complete the sentences below.
*Choose **NO MORE THAN TWO WORDS** from the passage for each answer.*
Write your answers on lines 22–27 on your answer sheet.

22   People often believe that Paleolithic art consisted only of _____

23   Ice Age artists used pointed tools to make _____ and sculptures on rocks.

24   As well as pictures of animals, _____ are common in most sites.

25   Pictures of _____ were sometimes made by wetting the palm with paint.

26   It is unusual to see an image of a _____ in European cave art.

27   Rather than being symbolic, paintings of animals are _____ images.

READING PASSAGE 3

*You should spend about 20 minutes on **Questions 28–40**, which are based on Reading Passage 3 below.*

The Braille System

A

About 200 years ago, a curious three-year-old boy playing in his father's shop had an accident that ended up changing the lives of hundreds of thousands of people. The little boy was Louis Braille, and his father was a harness maker in Coupvray, France, a small town near Paris. Louis poked his eye with one of the sharp tools on his father's workbench. The injury and the ensuing infection, which spread through both eyes, caused him to lose his vision. Only a dozen years later, at the age of fifteen, Braille developed a system of raised dots on paper that made it possible for blind people to read and write. While he was not the first person to toy with the idea of tactile reading—that is, reading by feeling shapes on a flat surface—his system surpassed others thanks to its simplicity, ease of use, and adaptability.

B

During the first few years after his accident, Braille attended a local school with sighted children, where he learned by the only means available to him—listening and memorizing,[1] He was a gifted student and at the age of ten earned a scholarship to attend the Royal Institution for Blind Youth in Paris. He later became a teacher at the Institution and remained there until his death in 1852 at the age of forty-three. The Institution relied largely on oral instruction, but pupils had access to a few books specially designed for blind students by Valentin Haüy, the school's founder. Haüy had developed a method for pressing shapes of letters onto wet paper and then letting them dry, providing pages with raised characters that students could "read" by running their fingertips across the thick paper. The books were big and cumbersome and took a long time to produce—and to read. In addition, they addressed only part of the blind students' communication dilemma—the ability to read. For full literacy, students also needed to be able to write.

C

A man named Charles Barbier, who had invented a system known as night writing for soldiers to send messages in the dark, provided the inspiration Braille needed for his reading method. Barbier visited the Royal Institution for Blind Youth in 1821 to demonstrate his technique, which used rectangular cells with raised dots. The cells, thirty-six in all, represented sounds rather than individual letters of the alphabet and consisted of a template of twelve dots in six rows of two. Braille saw the system's benefits right away and then zeroed in on its drawbacks. He thought it should be based on the alphabet—the way sighted people read—and not on phonetics. It also needed a way to designate punctuation marks, accents, numbers, and other symbols; and, for the user to be able to read with ease, a cell had to be small enough to fit beneath one's fingertip.

D

For the next three years, Braille fine-tuned his system and in 1824 came up with a version that worked to his satisfaction: a six-dot cell (three rows of two) that allowed for sixty-three possible combinations of dots, enough for all twenty-six letters of the Roman alphabet plus accents, capital letters, punctuation marks, and numbers. For example, a cell with one dot at the top left (position one) represents the letter *a*, whereas a cell with one dot at the bottom right (position six) means the next symbol is a capital letter. The numbers zero to nine are coded the same as the letters *a* to *j*, except they are preceded by a cell with dots in positions three through six (bottom left dot and all three dots in the right column). Users could read an individual cell with a single touch of the fingertip, and they scanned dots from left to right as in normal reading. What's more, the Braille system made it possible to write by punching dots into paper (from right to left because the reverse side is read).

---

[1]*British: memorising*

E

Originally, Braille symbols were written with a slate and stylus—the equivalent of paper-and-pencil writing, using the slate to hold the paper and the stylus to prick holes in it. In 1892, a Braille writing machine was invented; used like a typewriter, it has six keys and a space bar. Today, writing Braille is no more difficult or time-consuming than producing a printed document. You need only to hook up a standard computer to a machine that will emboss the text in Braille. Braille's fellow students quickly learned his system; for the first time, they could take notes in class and write papers, not to mention pass notes back and forth to one another. Yet the system was not widely used in Braille's lifetime. It did not become the official communication system for blind people in France until 1854, two years after he died.

F

The system remains in use today, only slightly altered from the original version. It has incorporated symbols for math, science, and music and has been adapted to dozens of languages, including many with non-Roman alphabets, such as Chinese and Japanese. Braille symbols often show up in public places, such as on elevator buttons, and their helpfulness in labeling household items like canned goods is undisputed. Nevertheless, knowledge of Braille has declined in recent years as technology has provided innovations, such as recorded books and computers with synthetic speech, that make it less necessary to read the old-fashioned way. Many now deem Braille an obsolete system, but its devotees still consider it a form of literacy as basic as the three R's.

Questions 28–36

*Reading Passage 3 has six paragraphs, **A–F**. Which paragraph contains the following information? Write the correct letter, **A–F**, on lines **28–36** on your answer sheet. You may use any letter more than once.*

28 a description of the Braille system of representing letters and numbers

29 Louis Braille's early education

30 how people write in Braille

31 when Louis Braille first developed his system

32 when the Braille system was officially accepted in France

33 a reading system for the blind used when Louis Braille was a child

34 how Braille is read

35 the reason why Louis Braille was blind

36 a description of the method on which Louis Braille based his system

Questions 37–40

Do the following statements agree with the information given in the passage? On lines 37–40 on your answer sheet, write:

TRUE	if the statement agrees with the information
FALSE	if the statement contradicts the information
NOT GIVEN	if there is no information on this

37 Braille symbols represent letters and numbers only.

38 Braille is used in a variety of languages.

39 Braille readers can read faster than sighted readers.

40 Modern technology has made Braille less important.

Academic Module
Practice Test 6

Candidate Name and Number: _____

INTERNATIONAL ENGLISH LANGUAGE TESTING SYSTEM

ACADEMIC WRITING

TIME 1 HOUR

Instructions to Candidates

Do not open this booklet until you are told to do so.

Write your name and candidate number in the space at the top of this page.

All answers must be written on the separate answer booklet provided. (The answer sheets can be found on page 223.)

Do not remove the booklet from the examination room.

Information for Candidates

There are **2** tasks on this question paper.

You must do **both** tasks.

Under-length answers will be penalized.[1]

---

[1] *British: penalised*

WRITING TASK 1

> You should spend about 20 minutes on this task. Write at least 150 words.

The graphs below show unemployment rates and average earnings according to level of education.

Summarize[1] the information by selecting and reporting the main features, and make comparisons where relevant.

Unemployment and Average Earnings by Educational Level—2008

Unemployment Rate by Education Level

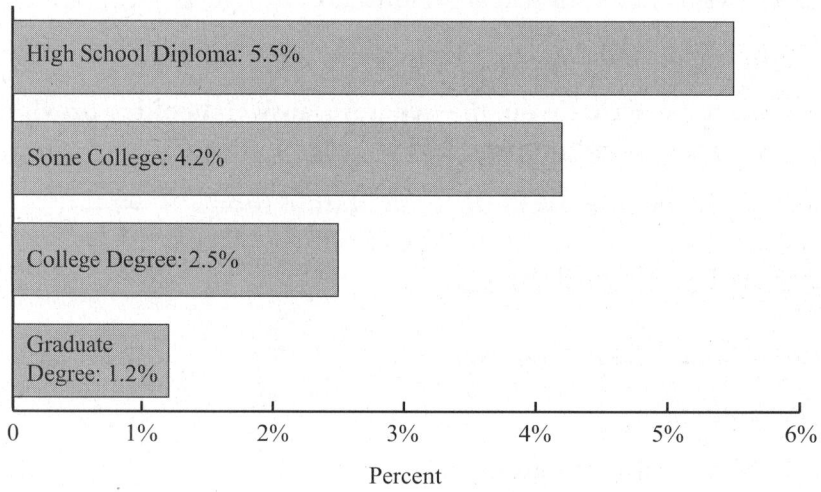

Average Weekly Earning by Education Level

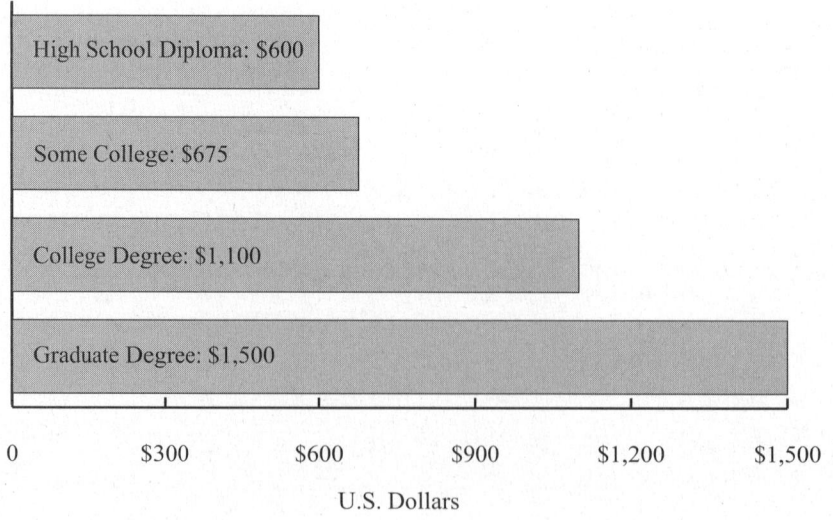

---

[1] *British: Summarise*

WRITING TASK 2

You should spend about 40 minutes on this task. Write at least 250 words.

Write about the following topic:

In your opinion, should young people choose their professions, or should their parents choose for them?

Give reasons for your answer and include any relevant examples from your own knowledge or experience.

SPEAKING

Examiner questions:

Part 1

How often do you go shopping?

What kinds of shops are there in your neighborhood[1]?

What kinds of things do you usually shop for?

Do you enjoy shopping? Why or why not?

What are some of your favorite[2] foods?

Who does the cooking at your house?

Do you prefer eating at home or in restaurants? Why?

What kinds of restaurants do you enjoy eating in?

Part 2

Tell about a place you would like to visit.

You should say:

The name of the place and where it is

What kind of a place it is

What things you would do there and explain why you want to go there

> You will have one to two minutes to talk about this topic.
>
> You will have one minute to prepare what you are going to say.

Part 3

What are some popular places to visit in your country? Why are they popular?

Why do people travel?

Do you think parents should make a point of taking their children to see a variety of different places? Why or why not?

How do you think travel will be different in the future?

---

[1] *British: neighbourhood*

[2] *British: favourite*

Practice Test 6–Academic Module
IELTS LISTENING ANSWER SHEET

1. _____	21. _____
2. _____	22. _____
3. _____	23. _____
4. _____	24. _____
5. _____	25. _____
6. _____	26. _____
7. _____	27. _____
8. _____	28. _____
9. _____	29. _____
10. _____	30. _____
11. _____	31. _____
12. _____	32. _____
13. _____	33. _____
14. _____	34. _____
15. _____	35. _____
16. _____	36. _____
17. _____	37. _____
18. _____	38. _____
19. _____	39. _____
20. _____	40. _____

Practice Test 6–Answer Sheet

Practice Test 6—Academic Module
IELTS READING ANSWER SHEET

1. _____	21. _____
2. _____	22. _____
3. _____	23. _____
4. _____	24. _____
5. _____	25. _____
6. _____	26. _____
7. _____	27. _____
8. _____	28. _____
9. _____	29. _____
10. _____	30. _____
11. _____	31. _____
12. _____	32. _____
13. _____	33. _____
14. _____	34. _____
15. _____	35. _____
16. _____	36. _____
17. _____	37. _____
18. _____	38. _____
19. _____	39. _____
20. _____	40. _____

Practice Test 6–Academic Module
WRITING TASK 1

Writing Task 1 *continued*

Practice Test 6—Academic Module
WRITING TASK 2

Writing Task 2 *continued*

_____

_____

_____

_____

_____

_____

_____

_____

_____

_____

_____

_____

_____

_____

_____

_____

_____

_____

_____

_____

Writing Task 2 *continued*

Answer Key

PRACTICE TEST 6—ACADEMIC MODULE

Listening

1. 8:30	11. A	21. A	31. individual reefs/coral reefs
2. reference books	12. B	22. C	32. islands
3. children's books	13. D	23. E	33. coral(s)
4. be repaired/repair	14. G	24. interviews, journal articles	34. A
5. be sold/sell	15. I	25. photos (of birds)	35. D
6. Thursday	16. film/movie	26. B	36. E
7. (family) movies	17. discussion	27. A	37. H
8. 2:30	18. lectures	28. B	38. I
9. meeting	19. games	29. C	39. rising sea temperatures
10. 6:30	20. dance	30. A	40. shading the reef/shading certain areas

Reading

1. C	11. False	21. C	31. A
2. G	12. False	22. cave paintings	32. E
3. I	13. True	23. engravings	33. B
4. B	14. Not Given	24. geometrical designs	34. D
5. F	15. A	25. hands	35. A
6. True	16. C	26. (full) human	36. C
7. Not Given	17. A	27. detailed, realistic	37. False
8. True	18. B	28. D	38. True
9. True	19. B	29. B	39. Not Given
10. True	20. A	30. E	40. True

Answer Explanations

ACADEMIC MODULE—PRACTICE TEST 6

Listening

1. *8:30.* The librarian says, "the library opens at eight-thirty in the morning. . . ."

2. *reference books.* The man says, "It looks like here on the ground floor is where the reference books are," and on the next line the librarian agrees with him.

3. *children's books.* The librarian says, "Children's books are up one more flight on the third floor."

4. *be repaired/repair.* The speakers discuss the books in the black cart, and the librarian says, "They're all books that need to be repaired."

5. *be sold/sell.* The speakers discuss the books in the white cart. The man asks, "So they're all ready to sell?" and the librarian says "Yes".

6. *Thursday.* The librarian says, "Story Time. . . takes place in the Children's Room on Thursday mornings at eleven."

7. *(family) movies.* The librarian explains, "we had to switch Family Movies to the weekend—Saturday afternoon."

8. *2:30.* The librarian says, "The movie always starts at two thirty in the Reference Room."

9. *meeting.* The librarian tells the man, "one of your duties will be to set up the Meeting Room on the first floor for the lecture."

10. *6:30.* The librarian says, "The lecture starts at 6:30. . . ."

11. **(A)** The man says, "We have a pleasant beach for swimming."

12. **(B)** The man says, "We also have canoes and sailboats available, and many of our guests enjoy boating on the lake."

13. **(D)** The man says, "you'll often see guests fishing from our dock or from the canoes."

14. **(G)** The man says, "We've made an arrangement with a local stable, so now we're going to have horseback riding available for our guests. We've created several riding trails around the lake."

15. **(I)** The man says, "some of our very talented staff members offer arts and crafts classes, for all ages."

16. *film/movie.* The man says, "Every Sunday we show a film. . . ."

17. *discussion.* The man says, "Our discussion night is on Tuesday."

18. *lectures.* The man says, "Then on Wednesdays we have lectures."

19. *games.* The man says, "Thursday nights are totally different because that's when we play games."

20. *dance.* The man says, "And we end every week with big fun, with a dance on Saturday night."

21. **(A)** Student 2 says, "We have to give the professor a written summary of the information we've gathered on our topic. . . ."

22. **(C)** Student 1 says, "The other written thing we have to turn in is a case study of the rehabilitation of one bird."

23. **(E)** Student 1 says, "But we do have to turn in a list of the resources we used."

24. *interviews, journal articles.* In discussing the sources, Student 2 mentions interviews with wildlife rehabilitators and Student 1 mentions journal articles.

25. *photos (of birds).* Student 1 says, "But we have lots of photos of rehabilitated birds. We can show those."

26. **(B)** Student 2 says, "we should emphasize that people should only attempt to rescue a bird that's clearly injured." Choices (A) and (C) refer to how people might find a bird that does not need rescuing.

27. **(A)** Student 1 says, "the rescuer needs to wear protective gloves. . . ." Choices (B) and (C) are both plausible but are not mentioned.

28. **(B)** Student 2 says, "let's tell people to put the injured bird in a box . . . with good air circulation." Choice (A) is something that is not necessary. Choice (C) is something that should not be used.

29. **(C)** Student 1 says, "the best way to help the bird stay calm is not by petting it or talking to it, but by leaving it completely alone." Choices (A) and (B) are the things that people should not do.

30. **(A)** Student 1 says, "Yes, it's better just to speak quietly while you have the bird in the car." Choice (B) is something that people should not do. Choice (C) is not mentioned.

31. *individual reefs/coral reefs.* The speaker says, "The Great Barrier Reef is composed of approximately 3,000 individual reefs. . . ."

32. *islands.* The speaker says, "In addition, around 600 islands are scattered throughout the area. . . ."

33. *coral(s).* The speaker says, "The reefs themselves are composed of over 400 different kinds of coral. . . ."

34. **(A)** The speaker says, "All together, approximately 1,500 species of fish inhabit the reef area, including a number of different kinds of sharks."

35. **(D)** The speaker says, "One of the more interesting mollusks to be found in the reefs is the giant clam."

36. **(E)** The speaker says, "Sea mammals abound in the area, which serves as the breeding ground for certain types of whales, many of which are endangered."

37. **(H)** The speaker says, "Saltwater crocodiles, for example, inhabit the marshes along coastal areas."

38. **(I)** The speaker says, "Amphibians include at least seven species of frogs inhabiting the islands of the reef."

39. *rising sea temperatures.* The speaker says, "Rising sea temperatures have led to an effect called coral bleaching. . . ."

40. *shading the reef/shading certain areas.* The speaker says, "One proposed solution involves shading the reef in certain areas to help keep the surrounding water temperatures down."

Reading

PASSAGE 1

1. **(C)** Paragraph 1: "Some plants reproduce asexually by splitting off new roots or bulbs . . . or even branches, stems, or leaves."

2. **(G)** According to paragraph 1, these plants make clones, or copies, of themselves.

3. **(I)** Paragraph 1: "This is a simple and direct method of reproduction, producing new plants more quickly and with less energy than plants using sexual reproduction."

4. **(B)** Paragraph 1: "In flowering plants, pollen . . . fertilizes the ovaries . . . resulting in seeds."

5. **(F)** Paragraph 2: "more commonly, pollination occurs between separate plants, either through pollen being borne by the wind . . . or by pollinators. . . ."

6. *True.* Paragraph 3: "the honeybee, which collects nectar as well as pollen for food."

7. *Not Given.* Paragraph 4 mentions a butterfly's need for a "landing platform" but does not mention what a butterfly does if there is no place to land on a flower.

8. *True.* Paragraph 4: "many moths are active at night and thus are attracted to flowers that are pale or white, have a strong fragrance. . . ."

9. *True.* Paragraph 4: "flowers that attract these tiny birds also have strong stems and are designed for pollen to be brushed on the hummingbirds' heads as they sip nectar."

10. *True.* Paragraph 5: "Many bee attractors also have nectar guides, which are spots near the center of each flower that reflect ultraviolet light, making it easier for the bees to find the nectar."

11. *False.* Paragraph 5: "Bees are also attracted to flowers with a mintlike or sweet smell."

12. *False.* Paragraph 6: "While many staple crops such as rice, corn, canola, and wheat are self-pollinating or pollinated by the wind. . . ."

13. *True.* Paragraph 6: "Over 30 percent of the world's crops require the work of pollinator species."

14. *Not Given.* Paragraph 7 mentions the decline of the honeybee population and concern for effects that may have, but it does not mention any specific economic effects.

PASSAGE 2

15. **(A)** Paragraph 1 explains that the Chauvet Cave is less well known than the cave art site in Lascaux. Choices (B) and (C) are plausible but incorrect.

16. **(C)** Paragraph 2 explains that most European cave art sites show images of prey animals but that the Chauvet Cave also has images of animals that people feared. Choice (A) is contradicted by the information in the passage. Choice (B) refers to animal remains found in the cave.

17. **(A)** Paragraph 2: "a common theory that the primary purpose of cave art was to magically ensure plentiful game." Choice (B) is the opposite of the correct answer. Choice (C) refers to images found in the cave art, but these are not mentioned as the function of cave art.

18. **(B)** Paragraph 3 explains that some of the images in the Chauvet Cave are much older than people had assumed most European cave art is. Choice (A) refers to a theory about cave art that has been disproved. Choice (C) confuses the meaning of the last sentence of the paragraph.

19. **(B)** Paragraph 4: "the Chauvet Cave also has an image of a being, referred to as the Sorcerer, with the body of a human and the head of a bison." Choice (A) is not mentioned. Choice (C) is incorrect because only an incomplete image of a woman's body is mentioned.

20. **(A)** Paragraph 4: "the floor of the cave contains the footprints of humans and cave bears, and fire pits, stone tools. . . ." *Implements made of stone* means "stone tools." Choice (B) is confused with the "bones from meals," which must have been animal bones. Choice (C) is confused with the image of the bison's head.

21. **(C)** Paragraph 4: "The cave had been untouched for thousands of years due to a rock slide which had sealed off the cave. . . ." Choice (A) is confused with the evidence of cave bears found when scientists visited the cave. Choice (B) occurred after humans had visited the cave.

22. *cave paintings.* Paragraph 5: "many people assume that the art of early hunters and gathers was limited to cave paintings."

23. *engravings.* Paragraph 5: Paleolithic artists not only painted with pigments but also created engravings by scratching designs into rock with pointed tools, as well as creating low-relief sculptures."

24. *geometrical designs.* Paragraph 5: "In addition to animal images, most sites also have geometrical designs, including dots and quadrangles."

25. *hands.* Paragraph 6: "Images of hands, created . . . by wetting the palm of the hand with paint . . . are common."

26. *(full) human.* Paragraph 6: "full images of humans are rare in the European caves."

27. *detailed, realistic.* Paragraph 6: "Most of the animal images, on the other hand, are detailed, realistic portrayals of an individual animal species. . . ."

PASSAGE 3

28. **(D)** This paragraph gives some examples of how letters and numbers are represented by dots in the Braille system.

29. **(B)** This paragraph briefly describes Braille's experiences at his local school up to age ten.

30. **(E)** This paragraph describes the Braille slate and stylus and the Braille writing machine, as well as the use of a computer.

31. **(A)** This paragraph noted that at the age of fifteen, Braille developed a system of raised dots on paper that made it possible for blind people to read and write.

32. **(E)** This paragraph says that it did not become the official communication system for blind people in France until 1854, two years after Braille died.

33. **(B)** This paragraph describes the system developed by Valentin Haüy, which was used at the institution where Braille studied as a child.

34. **(D)** This paragraph describes how the Braille system of raised dots is read.

35. **(A)** This paragraph describes the injury to Braille's eyes when he was three years old.

36. **(C)** This paragraph describes the system developed by Charles Barbier, which inspired Braille's system.

37. *False.* Paragraph F: "The system . . . has incorporated symbols for math, science, and music."

38. *True.* Paragraph F: "has been adapted to dozens of languages, including many with non-Roman alphabets, such as Chinese and Japanese."

39. *Not Given.* There is no comparison made between the reading speed of Braille readers and sighted readers.

40. *True.* Paragraph F: "knowledge of Braille has declined in recent years as technology has provided innovations, such as recorded books and computers with synthetic speech."

WRITING

These are models. Your answers will vary. See page vi in the Introduction to see the criteria for scoring.

WRITING TASK 1

The graph compares unemployment rates and average weekly earnings across different educational levels in the year 2008. The information clearly illustrates that people with higher educational levels were better off economically than those with lower educational levels.

The first graph shows unemployment rates. There was a significant gap between those with the lowest educational level and those with the highest. In 2008, unemployment for workers with a high school diploma only was at 5.5 percent. This rate gradually decreased with each succeeding educational level. It was lowest among those with a graduate degree—only 1.2 percent.

The second graph shows average weekly earnings. Again, the differences between the lower and higher educational levels are significant. In 2008, workers with a high school diploma earned an average of just $600 a week. The level of earnings increased with each educational level. Workers with a college degree earned an average of $1,100 weekly, almost twice as much as the high school graduates. The workers with graduate degrees earned almost half again as much as the workers with college degrees. These graphs show that it pays to get an education.

WRITING TASK 2

In many families it has been traditional for parents to choose their children's professions. In other families, the children themselves decide what professions they are interested in pursuing. I can see the advantages to both situations. However, I think it is best to let the children decide for themselves.

Many parents around the world still follow the tradition of choosing their children's professions for them. Some parents want their children to follow in their footsteps. Other parents choose professions for their children that they believe will enable a comfortable lifestyle. Parents are, of course, older and more experienced than their children, and they know their children well. It is reasonable to expect that they can make good choices for their children.

On the other hand, by the time someone is old enough to start thinking about college and preparing for a profession, he or she is no longer really a child. He or she is old enough to know something about him- or herself, what things interest him or her, and what his or her strengths are. His or her future is his or her own to live, so he or she should be the one to make important decisions about it. In addition, the modern world changes rapidly. By the time a young person is ready to prepare for a profession, things are probably very different from the way they were when his or her parents were young. Because of this, in a certain sense, a young person may understand the world better than his or her parents do and so make better decisions for his or her future.

The tradition of parents choosing professions for their children is just that—a tradition. Young people of today are more independent. Of course, it is never a bad idea for a young person to ask his or her parents for advice, but the final decision about a profession should be made by the young person.

SPEAKING

These are models. Your answers will vary. See page vi in the Introduction to see the criteria for scoring.

PART 1

How often do you go shopping?
I don't go shopping very often. Well, I generally stop at a store a few times a week to pick up something small, pens, maybe, or something like that, my everyday needs. But I don't make major shopping trips very often, maybe once a month, maybe even less than that. I just don't need to buy very many things.

What kinds of shops are there in your neighborhood?
My neighborhood is residential, so there are very few businesses. We have a small grocery store. It has a limited assortment of things for sale, and they're more expensive than at a supermarket, so we really just use that store for convenience. We use it when we need only one or two things and don't want to go all the way to the supermarket, which is farther away. We also have a drugstore and a small bookstore that sells newspapers and magazines as well as books. Those are all the shops we have. We usually have to go to another part of the city to go shopping.

What kinds of things do you usually shop for?
I don't have to shop for groceries or anything for the house because my mother does that, so I just have to buy the things I need. Once or twice a year I buy the clothes I need for school. Besides that, I like to buy CDs and DVDs and things for my computer, and I have to buy the things I need for school, books and pens and things like that.

Do you enjoy shopping? Why or why not?
I don't think shopping is very interesting. If I need something, I buy it. If I don't need anything, there's no reason to go to the store. I know some people think of shopping like a hobby or a sport, but I don't. I just think of it as a necessity. Well, sometimes I like to go to the store and look through the music and movies that are for sale, just because I like to look at them. Then sometimes I'll buy a movie that maybe I hadn't been planning on buying. But most of the time I never think about shopping unless there's something I particularly need.

What are some of your favorite foods?
I like all different kinds of foods. I especially like to try foods from different countries. I like dishes that are served with rice and noodles and that have a lot of vegetables. I don't like meat very much. I almost never eat it. I don't like sweet things too much either.

Who does the cooking at your house?
My mother does almost all the cooking at my house. She's a very good cook, and I always enjoy the meals she prepares. Sometimes I do some of the cooking, or one of my brothers or sisters might cook a meal occasionally. My mother has taught all of us to cook, so we help her out in the kitchen from time to time. But she does most of the cooking.

Do you prefer eating at home or in restaurants? Why?
I like eating at home because, as I said, my mother always prepares delicious meals. And usually it's more convenient to eat at home. But I like eating in restaurants, too. The food is different, and it's really fun to get together with my friends at a restaurant. But it's also expensive to eat out, so I don't do it very often.

What kinds of restaurants do you enjoy eating in?
I like eating in restaurants that specialize in food from other countries. I like to try all different kinds of foods. My favorite thing to do is to go to a restaurant that has a style of cooking I haven't tried before and just choose something from the menu. Most of the time I end up with a dish I really like. It's a fun adventure to try different kinds of food. We have a lot of different restaurants in my city, so I have a lot of opportunities to try new kinds of foods.

PART 2

I've always wanted to go to the Great Barrier Reef, off the coast of Australia. It's a natural place, a place where you can see and learn about the natural world, specifically, about ocean life. I think it might be considered one of the wonders of the natural world. I would really like to have the opportunity to go diving there. I think it would be really fun and really interesting to go swimming among the coral reefs and see all the different kinds of animals that live there. There are thousands of species of animals and fish living there, as well as different kinds of coral. I'd like to go there because I'm interested in marine biology. I'm interested in learning about ocean life, and the Great Barrier Reef is one of the best places to observe it. Also, I've never been diving, and I would really like to learn how. I'm thinking about getting a degree in marine biology, so learning to dive at the Great Barrier Reef would probably be a good way to start!

PART 3

What are some popular places to visit in your country? Why are they popular?
There are a lot of popular places to visit in my country. We have a lot of natural places that are interesting to see, we have historical sites, and we have some very nice beaches. One of my favorite places to visit is Mountain National Park. It's a popular place for tourists to visit, mostly because it's very beautiful. Also, it has something for everybody. There are some great hiking trails, there's fishing in the rivers, there's camping, and for people who like to take things easy, there's a road to the top of the mountain. You can drive to the top and see the spectacular views, or take a tour by bus. Then you can ride back to your hotel and be comfortable.

Why do people travel?
I think the biggest reason people travel is that change is relaxing. If you follow the same routine at school or at work every day, then when you have a vacation, you want to do something different. Being in a different place can take your mind off the problems or boredom of your daily life. You can empty your mind of all those things and just relax. People like to take all different kinds of vacations. Some people like to go to other countries and see a different way of life. Some like outdoor adventures. Some like to relax on the beach or at a resort. But the one thing all these different ways of traveling have in common is that they all involve a change of scene from the traveler's usual daily life.

Do you think parents should make a point of taking their children to see a variety of different places? Why or why not?
I think it's very important for parents to take their children traveling. Children should learn from an early age that life everywhere isn't the same as the life they know at home. That's one thing that's important to learn. The other thing is that traveling gives children the opportunity for different kinds of experiences. They can learn how to go camping, they can learn about art and history in museums, they can go on a boat and experience the ocean. Having different experiences like these is an important part of learning and growing up.

How do you think travel will be different in the future?
Sometimes I think people will have fewer opportunities to travel in the future. That's because it seems that people are working longer and harder all the time and it seems that their vacation time is becoming shorter and shorter. In the future, I don't think people will have the time to take long trips exploring other countries, or long hiking trips, or any kind of traveling that involves a lot of time. So maybe they'll go to resorts more often, since that's an easier way to travel.

PART 2

GENERAL TRAINING MODULE

PRACTICE TEST 1

PRACTICE TEST 2

PRACTICE TEST 3

PRACTICE TEST 4

PRACTICE TEST 5

PRACTICE TEST 6

The following practice tests include only the Reading and Writing sections for the General Training Module.

For the Listening and Speaking sections, go to the Academic Module, Practice Tests 1–6. The Listening and Speaking sections are the same for all test takers. See the charts on page v for page numbers.

GENERAL TRAINING MODULE
READING
WRITING
PRACTICE TEST 1

General Training Module
Practice Test 1

Candidate Name and Number: _____

INTERNATIONAL ENGLISH LANGUAGE TESTING SYSTEM

GENERAL TRAINING READING

TIME 1 HOUR

Instructions to Candidates

Do not open this booklet until you are told to do so.

Write your name and candidate number in the space at the top of this page.

Start at the beginning of the test and work through it.

You should answer all questions.

If you cannot do a particular question, leave it and go on to the next. You can return to it later.

All answers must be written on the Answer Sheet. (The answer sheet can be found on page 255.)

Do not remove the booklet from the examination room.

Information for Candidates

There are **40** questions on this question paper.

The test is divided as follows:

Section 1	Questions 1–14
Section 2	Questions 15–27
Section 3	Questions 28–40

SECTION 1   *QUESTIONS 1–14*

*You are advised to spend 20 minutes on **Questions 1–14**.*
Read the text below and answer Questions 1–7.

Barchester Office Towers
Visitor Information

Welcome to Barchester Office Towers. Visitors must register with the Security Desk in order to obtain a visitor's badge and be allowed entrance to the building. The Security Desk is located on the ground[1] floor lobby near the main entrance. The security officer on duty will direct you to the office you are visiting. In addition, a map of the building is displayed near the main elevators,[2] located behind the Security Desk.

To reach the rooftop parking area, take the elevator to the fourth floor, then follow the signs. Also located on that floor is the City View Restaurant, serving three meals a day, Tuesday–Sunday.

Barchester Office Towers offers a number of business services for the convenience of tenants and visitors. The Copy Center[3] is located on the second floor. Photocopy and fax services are available here. Computers with Internet access are also available. The Copy Center is open twenty-four hours a day. You must show your visitor's badge when requesting services.

A small branch post office is located down the hall from the Copy Center. Envelopes and stamps are sold here. Mail pickup is twice a day, at 7:30 A.M. and 5:00 P.M. On the third floor, you will find a branch of the National Bank. All basic banking services are offered. Next to the bank is the Barchester Coffee Shop. Coffee, tea, and snacks are sold here, and most major daily newspapers and business magazines are available for perusal. The coffee shop is open from 7:00 A.M. until 4:30 P.M. Monday–Saturday.

---

[1] *In the United States., the ground floor is considered the first floor; the next floor up is the second floor, and so on.*
[2] *British: lifts*
[3] *British: Centre*

Questions 1–7

On which floor of the office complex can you do each of the following activities?
On lines 1–7 on your answer sheet, write:

A   if you can do this on the ground floor

B   if you can do this on the second floor

C   if you can do this on the third floor

D   if you can do this on the fourth floor

---

1   have lunch

2   cash a check

3   mail a letter

4   get a pass to enter the building

5   read a newspaper

6   fax a document

7   look at a map of the building

Questions 8–14

Read the text below and answer Questions 8–14.

Spring Willow Farm Museum and Education Center

Spring Willow Farm is a fully operating farm designed to educate the public about farm operation, farming history, and issues facing farmers today.

Schedule

We are open to the public year-round, with reduced hours during the winter months. Closed Mondays and holidays.

Visiting the Farm

Visitors are free to tour the farm on their own. Please note that children must be accompanied by an adult at all times. Maps are available at the information desk in the Main Building. Guided tours are included in the cost of admission. Tours leave from the Main Building front entrance at 10:00 A.M. and 2:00 P.M. daily.

The ground floor of the Main Building is open to visitors. It contains exhibits explaining daily farm life in different periods of history, with displays showing farm implements, kitchen and other household utensils, photographs, and more. The information desk is also located here, as well as the Farm Museum Gift Shop.

Classes

The museum offers classes on various aspects of farming and farm history two evenings a week throughout the year. Ask at the information desk for a schedule of upcoming classes. In addition, classes on special subjects related to farming can be arranged for your club or group. Please contact the Education Office for further information. All classes take place in the classrooms located on the second floor of the Main Building.

Do the following statements agree with the information given in the text about the Spring Willow Farm Museum and Education Center? On lines 8–14 on your answer sheet, write:

TRUE	if the statement agrees with the information
FALSE	if the statement contradicts the information
NOT GIVEN	if there is no information on this

8 Spring Willow Farm is closed during the winter months.

9 Children are not allowed to visit the farm.

10 Spring Willow Farm charges visitors an admission fee.

11 The guided tours last two hours.

12 The museum has gifts for sale.

13 Farmers are offered a special discount on classes.

14 The museum buildings are open in the evening.

SECTION 2   *QUESTIONS 15–27*

*You are advised to spend 20 minutes on **Questions 15–27**.*

Questions 15–20

*The following reading passage has six sections **A–F**. Choose the correct heading for sections **A–F** from the list of headings below. Write the correct number, **i–viii**, on lines 15–20 on your answer sheet. There are more headings than sections, so you will not use them all.*

15   Section A

16   Section B

17   Section C

18   Section D

19   Section E

20   Section F

LIST OF HEADINGS

i	Feeling Confident
ii	Solving Problems
iii	Room Arrangement
iv	Equipment
v	Defining Your Purpose
vi	Using Visuals
vii	Your Audience
viii	Speaking Well

How to Give an Effective Presentation

When planning an effective presentation, there are a number of things to keep in mind.

A

First ask yourself, "Why am I giving this presentation?" The point of your presentation may be to outline a project plan, report on work that has been done, solve a problem, provide training, or generate support for an idea. Once you are clear on the reason for your presentation, it will be easier to organize[1] your information.

---

[1] *British: organise*

B

If you are not used to giving presentations, you may feel nervous. There are a few things you can do to counteract this. The most important thing is to rehearse your presentation several times until you feel comfortable with it. Before you begin speaking, take a few deep breaths. This will help you relax. Stand up straight and look your audience in the eye. Most of all, don't try to be perfect. This is an impossible goal.

C

Even though you may be using a microphone, you still need to pay attention to your voice. Talk slowly and clearly. Pause often to give your audience time to absorb the information. Do not garble your words or talk so quickly that no one can follow you.

D

There is no better way to lose your audience than to stand at the front of the room and talk on and on but give them nothing to look at. Plan to use presentation software to show charts and graphs, photographs, maps, or other graphics that will make your ideas clearer. This is particularly important for numbers, but it is also useful for other kinds of information.

E

Before you begin your presentation, remember to check the microphone, computer, and any other special tools you may be using. Make sure everything is in working order before you start talking so that there will be no interruptions due to breakdowns.

F

Something that is often overlooked but that is very important for an effective presentation is the location setup. Make sure that the seating is placed so that it allows everyone to see your slides and hear your voice. The chairs should be comfortable, too.

Questions 21–27

Read the text below and answer Questions 21–27.

The Marcy Corporation
Information for New Employees

All new employees at the Marcy Corporation are required to attend an orientation session during their first month of employment. The next orientation session will be held on <u>March 21</u> in the company conference room. Employee benefits, payment policies, employee responsibilities, and other personnel matters will be discussed. Employees are requested to read the employee manual and submit the signed statement prior to attending the orientation.

The Marcy Corporation Employee Manual has been provided to inform our employees about the company's procedures and policies. We ask each employee to take the time to read the manual carefully. After a thorough review of the manual, the statement below should be signed and returned to the employee's supervisor by the date noted below. Every effort has been made to present the information in the manual in a clear and concise manner. If there are any questions regarding the content of the manual, they should be submitted in writing to Human Resources.

. . . .

Statement

I, _____, have read a copy of the Marcy Corporation Employee Manual and am familiar with its contents. By signing below, I certify that I understand and accept the information contained in the Marcy Corporation Employee Manual and agree to abide by the Marcy Corporation's policies.

_____

(Employee signature)

Please submit by: <u>March 15</u>

Questions 21–27

Complete the sentences below.
*Choose **NO MORE THAN THREE WORDS** from the text for each answer.*
Write your answers on lines 21–27 on your answer sheet.

21 All _____ must participate in an orientation session.

22 The _____ will take place in the company conference room.

23 The manual should be read before _____.

24 The employee manual contains information about the company's _____.

25 The signed statement should be submitted to _____.

26 _____ will answer questions about the content of the manual.

27 The due date for the signed statement is _____.

SECTION 3 *QUESTIONS 28–40*

*You should spend 20 minutes on **Questions 28–40**, which are based on the reading passage below.*

Canoes Around the World

Many cultures throughout the world have developed some form of canoe—a long, slender, open boat powered by handheld paddles. In each case, the technologies and materials used to construct the canoe reflect the resources available to that particular culture. There are three basic types of canoe: the frame-and-bark canoe, the dugout, and the plank canoe. Developed by cultures on every continent since prehistoric times, canoes continue to be used today both for survival and for recreation.

The birch-bark canoe, an example of the frame-and-bark type of construction, was developed in the region that is now the northeastern United States and eastern Canada. Native Americans constructed birch-bark canoes by building a frame from spruce wood and then using roots to stitch pieces of birch bark over the frame. In areas where birch was not available, bark from elm or spruce trees was used instead. After the bark was sewn to the frame, the canoes were then sealed with a mixture of spruce gum and bear grease. These substances worked very well to make the boat watertight. Birch-bark canoes were lightweight and thus easily portaged around waterfalls or from lake to lake. Most were designed to hold no more than two or three people and were used for lake and river travel. When Europeans opened up the fur trade in North America in the seventeenth century, the French traders used larger versions (30 to 40 feet in length) to transport furs in large quantities across the Great Lakes for shipment back to Europe.

The dugout—a canoe created from a single tree trunk—has been used in many areas throughout the world. Simple versions of hollowed-out logs were used by native peoples throughout much of North America. Coastal groups such as the Haida and Tlinglit in the Pacific Northwest developed large dugout crafts 60 feet or longer that could carry large numbers of people on the ocean for trade, warfare, fishing, whaling, and travel to ceremonial gatherings. First, the outer and inner bark around the entire circumference of a tall, straight tree, often a cedar or redwood, was removed. This process, called girdling, cuts off the flow of sap, thus killing the tree and making it easier to chop down. Then the tree was felled and cut to the appropriate length. The opening of the dugout was created by repeatedly burning the wood, then carving it out with tools. In early times, stone tools were used, but later metal tools came into use. Once the canoe was carved out, the boat builders filled it with water and brought the water to a boil using stones heated on a fire. This softened the wood and the weight of the water caused the walls of the canoe to bow outward, giving it more width than the original girth of the tree.

The ocean-going Chumash people of what is now southern California developed the *tomol,* or plank canoe. They created their canoes by cutting planks from redwood trees, carving and shaping them into a canoe without any frame. They lashed the planks together by drilling holes and tying them with cords. Pitch from pine trees and tar, also found locally, were used between the planks and over the entire hull for waterproofing.

The canoe played a major role in the spread of all the Pacific Island cultures. These cultures developed outrigger and double-hulled dugout canoes. Outriggers have one or more parallel floats attached to a dugout canoe with poles for increased stability in ocean waves. Double-hulled canoes have a platform between two parallel dugouts. These highly stable designs, combined with sails, enabled the Polynesians to go on epic ocean journeys and to inhabit far-flung islands. Several families (or as many as 200 people in the largest vessels), could sail in each of these double-hulled canoes with food, water, and domesticated plants and animals across huge expanses of ocean, and in this way the Polynesian people spread throughout the Pacific, establishing new communities on previously uninhabited islands.

In areas of dense rain forest throughout the world, including the Amazon basin, and parts of Africa and Asia, river travel with dugouts was, and in many cases still is, the primary means of transportation. In West Africa, large war canoes capable of transporting many fighters were carved from single trees.

Descendants of the ancient canoes are still widely used today. Traditional cultures around the world still use dugout canoes for fishing and transportation. Today's modern recreational canoes, while now often constructed with aluminum,[1] fiberglass,[2] wood, and canvas, plastic, and other synthetic materials, still retain the shape and basic design of the birch-bark canoes developed in the distant past. The catamaran sailboat, widely used in racing, is a direct descendant of the double-hulled sailing canoe used thousands of years ago by the Polynesian cultures.

[1] *British: aluminium*
[2] *British: fibreglass*

Questions 28–34

Look at the following descriptions, Questions 28–34, of the different types of canoes.
*Match each description with the correct canoe, **A**, **B**, or **C**.*
*Write the correct letter, **A**, **B**, or **C**, on lines 28–34 on your answer sheet.*

28 held together with rope

29 made from a hollowed-out log

30 made waterproof with gum and grease

31 constructed with the use of both fire and water

32 easy to carry over land

33 sealed with pitch and tar

34 made to carry just a few people

TYPES OF CANOES

A birch-bark

B dugout

C plank

Questions 35–40

Complete the summary below.
*Choose **NO MORE THAN TWO WORDS** from the text for each answer.*
Write your answers on lines 35–40 on your answer sheet.

Polynesians turned dugout canoes into outrigger canoes by attaching

35 _____ to them. Double-hulled canoes were made by

connecting two outrigger canoes with **36** _____. Because

they could travel over **37** _____ of ocean in these canoes,

Polynesians were able to inhabit islands all across the Pacific Ocean. In West

Africa, large war canoes were used to carry **38** _____. Today,

39 _____ canoes are made of modern materials such as

aluminum, fiberglass, and plastic. These modern canoes are similar in form to

40 _____ canoes.

General Training Module
Practice Test 1

Candidate Name and Number _____

INTERNATIONAL ENGLISH LANGUAGE TESTING SYSTEM

GENERAL TRAINING WRITING

TIME 1 HOUR

Instructions to Candidates

Do not open this booklet until you are told to do so.

Write your name and candidate number in the space at the top of this page.

All answers must be written on the separate answer booklet provided. (The answer sheet can be found beginning on page 256.)

Do not remove the booklet from the examination room.

Information for Candidates

There are **2** tasks on this question paper.

You must do **both** tasks.

Under-length answers will be penalized.[1]

---

[1] *British: penalised*

WRITING TASK 1

You should spend about 20 minutes on this task. Write at least 150 words. You do NOT need to write any addresses. Begin your letter as follows:

Dear _____,

You have been offered a job that will require you to move to a city that you have never visited before. You have an acquaintance who lives there.

Write a letter to the acquaintance. In your letter

- explain your situation
- say why you feel unsure about living in the city
- ask some questions about life in the city

WRITING TASK 2

You should spend about 40 minutes on this task. Write at least 250 words.

Write about the following topic:

In some countries, employees are generally given two weeks of paid vacation[1] time each year. In other countries, employees are given four or six weeks of paid vacation time.

Considering the needs of both employee and employer, what do you think is a reasonable amount of paid vacation time for employees to have? Give reasons for your answer and include any relevant examples from your own knowledge or experience.

---

[1] *British: holiday; in the United States, holiday refers to a specific date on which a special event, such as Thanksgiving, is observed*

Practice Test 1–General Training Module
IELTS READING ANSWER SHEET

1. _____

2. _____

3. _____

4. _____

5. _____

6. _____

7. _____

8. _____

9. _____

10. _____

11. _____

12. _____

13. _____

14. _____

15. _____

16. _____

17. _____

18. _____

19. _____

20. _____

21. _____

22. _____

23. _____

24. _____

25. _____

26. _____

27. _____

28. _____

29. _____

30. _____

31. _____

32. _____

33. _____

34. _____

35. _____

36. _____

37. _____

38. _____

39. _____

40. _____

Practice Test 1–General Training Module
WRITING TASK 1

Writing Task 1 *continued*

Practice Test 1–General Training Module
WRITING TASK 2

Writing Task 2 *continued*

Writing Task 2 *continued*

Answer Key
PRACTICE TEST 1–GENERAL TRAINING MODULE

Reading

1. D	11. Not Given	21. new employees	31. B
2. C	12. True	22. next orientation session	32. A
3. B	13. Not Given	23. (attending) the orientation	33. C
4. A	14. True	24. procedures and policies	34. A
5. C	15. v	25. the employee's supervisor	35. parallel floats
6. B	16. i	26. Human Resources	36. a platform
7. A	17. viii	27. March 15	37. huge expanses
8. False	18. vi	28. C	38. many fighters
9. False	19. iv	29. B	39. (modern) recreational
10. True	20. iii	30. A	40. birch-bark

Answer Explanations

GENERAL TRAINING MODULE—PRACTICE TEST 1
Reading

1. **(D)** The City View Restaurant is on the fourth floor and serves three meals a day.

2. **(C)** The National Bank is located on the third floor.

3. **(B)** The post office is down the hall from the Copy Center, which is on the second floor.

4. **(A)** The Security Desk, where visitor's badges are issued, is located on the ground floor.

5. **(C)** Newspapers are available in the Barchester Coffee Shop, located next to the bank on the third floor.

6. **(B)** Fax services are available in the Copy Center, located on the second floor.

7. **(A)** The map is behind the Security Desk, which is on the ground floor.

8. *False.* Paragraph 2: The museum has reduced hours during the winter months.

9. *False.* Paragraph 3: We know that children are allowed because it is stated that they must be accompanied by an adult.

10. *True.* Paragraph 3: "Guided tours are included in the cost of admission."

11. *Not Given.* Guided tours are mentioned in the third paragraph, but their length is not mentioned.

12. *True.* Paragraph 4 mentions the Farm Museum Gift Shop.

13. *Not Given.* Classes are discussed in the fifth paragraph, but no discount is mentioned.

14. *True.* Paragraph 5 mentions that classes are offered in the evenings and that they take place in the Main Building.

15. *v.* Section A lists the different reasons, or purposes, for a presentation.

16. *i.* Section B discusses ways to relax and overcome nervousness, that is, ways to feel confident when giving a presentation.

17. *viii.* Section C discusses talking and voice.

18. *vi.* Section D talks about using presentation software to give the audience something to look at.

19. *iv.* Section E talks about computers and microphones, that is, equipment.

20. *iii.* Section F talks about the seating arrangement.

21. *new employees.* Paragraph 1: "All new employees at the Marcy Corporation are required to attend an orientation session . . . ."

22. *next orientation session.* Paragraph 1: "The next orientation session will be held . . . in the company conference room."

23. *(attending) the orientation.* Paragraph 1: "Employees are requested to read the employee manual . . . prior to attending the orientation."

24. *procedures and policies.* Paragraph 2: "The Marcy Corporation Employee Manual has been provided to inform our employees about the company's procedures and policies."

25. *the employee's supervisor.* Paragraph 2: "the statement below should be signed and returned to the employee's supervisor . . . ."

26. *Human Resources.* Paragraph 2: "If there are any questions regarding the content of the manual, they should be submitted in writing to Human Resources."

27. *March 15.* The bottom of the form shows March 15 as the date to submit the statement.

28. **(C)** Paragraph 4: "They lashed the planks together by drilling holes and tying them with cords."

29. **(B)** Paragraph 3 describes how the dugout canoe is made from a single tree trunk, or log.

30. **(A)** Paragraph 2 explains that birch-bark canoes were: "sealed with a mixture of spruce gum and bear grease."

31. **(B)** Paragraph 3: "The opening of the dugout was created by repeatedly burning the wood, then carving it out with tools . . . the boat builders filled it with water and brought the water to a boil using stones heated on a fire . . . ."

32. **(A)** Paragraph 2: "Birch-bark canoes were lightweight and . . . easily portaged around waterfalls or from lake to lake." *Portaged* means the same as *carried.*

33. **(C)** Paragraph 4 says of plank canoes: "Pitch from pine trees and tar . . . were used between the planks and over the entire hull for waterproofing."

34. **(A)** Paragraph 2 says of birch-bark canoes: "Most were designed to hold no more than two or three people . . . ."

35. *parallel floats.* Paragraph 5: "Outriggers have one or more parallel floats attached to a dugout canoe with poles for increased stability in ocean waves."

36. *a platform.* Paragraph 5: "Double-hulled canoes have a platform between two parallel dugouts."

37. *huge expanses.* Paragraph 5: "across huge expanses of ocean . . . ."

38. *many fighters.* Paragraph 6: "capable of transporting many fighters . . . ."

39. *(modern) recreational.* Paragraph 7: "Today's modern recreational canoes, while now often constructed with aluminum, fiberglass, wood, and canvas, plastic, and other synthetic materials . . . ."

40. *birch-bark.* Paragraph 7: "still retain the shape and basic design of the birch-bark canoes developed in the distant past."

Writing

These are models. Your answers will vary. See page vi in the Introduction to see the criteria for scoring.

WRITING TASK 1

[NOTE: Even though this is an informal letter, you should not use contractions on the Writing tasks in the test.]

Dear Chris,

    I am writing to ask you for some information that will help me make a decision. I have recently been offered a job in Seattle. I am very much interested in the job, but, as you know, I have never even visited Seattle. I am not sure whether I would like living there. Since you have lived there for a while, I thought you could answer some questions for me.

    One thing I am worried about is the weather. I have heard that it rains in Seattle all the time. Is this true? It sounds very depressing. I have also heard that Seattle is a growing city, and I am afraid it would feel very crowded to me. I have never lived in a big city before. Another thing I wonder about is leisure activities. I like going out dancing a lot. Are there good places to go dancing in Seattle? What about music? I would not want to live in a place where I could not go to concerts frequently.

Another important issue is housing. I have heard that Seattle is very expensive. Is it hard to find a nice apartment at a reasonable rent? What neighborhoods would you recommend?

I appreciate your taking the time to answer my questions, and I look forward to hearing from you. If I decide to accept the job in Seattle, then I hope we will be able to get together frequently.

Best wishes,
Miranda

WRITING TASK 2

I believe that two weeks of annual vacation time is a good amount for a company to offer employees, at least when they are first hired. There are several reasons this is a good practice. It saves the employer money, it minimizes disruption to normal work routines, and the possibility of earning more vacation time in the future can act as an incentive to the employee.

When an employee uses paid vacation time, he or she is not contributing to the company but is still being paid. This means the employer is paying out money without getting work in return. The shorter the vacation, the less the employer has to pay out. Of course, we could say that the cost to the employer is repaid when the employee returns from vacation rested and with renewed energy. For longer vacations, however, the loss of work is probably greater than the benefit to be gained when the employee returns with greater energy. Of course, something like this is difficult to measure, and each employer must evaluate his or her own particular situation.

An employee takes a vacation, but in most cases his or her work does not. Other people must carry out the worker's responsibilities while he or she is away. In many cases, companies hire temporary workers to cover for employees who are on vacation. This is an extra expense and an inconvenience. The longer the vacation, the greater the disruption to the normal work routine.

At many companies, employees are offered more vacation time after they have worked there for a certain amount of time. This benefit can be an incentive, encouraging employees to do well in their positions and remain at the company.

Generally, I feel that all new employees should be given two weeks of annual vacation time initially, with the possibility of earning more after working with the company for some time. I think a system like this is fair to both the employer and the employee.

GENERAL TRAINING MODULE
READING
WRITING
PRACTICE TEST 2

General Training Module Practice Test 2

Candidate Name and Number: _____

INTERNATIONAL ENGLISH LANGUAGE TESTING SYSTEM

GENERAL TRAINING READING

TIME 1 HOUR

Instructions to Candidates

Do not open this booklet until you are told to do so.

Write your name and candidate number in the space at the top of this page.

Start at the beginning of the test and work through it.

You should answer all questions.

If you cannot do a particular question, leave it and go on to the next. You can return to it later.

All answers must be written on the Answer Sheet. (The answer sheet can be found on page 281.)

Do not remove the booklet from the examination room.

Information for Candidates

There are **40** questions on this question paper.

The test is divided as follows:

Section 1	Questions 1–14
Section 2	Questions 15–27
Section 3	Questions 28–40

SECTION 1 *QUESTIONS 1–14*

*You are advised to spend 20 minutes on **Questions 1–14**.*

Questions 1–4

*The following text has four sections **A–D**. Choose the correct heading for each section from the list of headings below. Write the correct number **i–vii** on lines 1–4 on your answer sheet. There are more headings than sections, so you will not use them all.*

> **LIST OF HEADINGS**
> i   Other Uses for Your Machine
> ii   Baking Bread
> iii   The Science of Bread Dough
> iv   Customer Assistance
> v   Ingredients for Bread
> vi   Caring for Your Machine
> vii   Equipment Included

1   Section A
2   Section B
3   Section C
4   Section D

Presto Bread Machine

Thank you for buying a Presto Bread Machine. You and your family will enjoy delicious homemade bread for years to come.

A

Please check the contents of the box to make sure they are complete. Your Presto Bread Machine comes with a removable baking pan, a measuring cup, a measuring spoon, and a recipe booklet. You may also wish to have on hand an extra measuring cup and several other measuring spoons in different sizes. Ingredients for the bread recipes are not included.

B

Choose a recipe from the enclosed recipe booklet. Each recipe lists the ingredients in the order they are to be added to the machine. Liquid ingredients should be added to the machine before dry ingredients. Place all the ingredients in the removable pan, place the pan inside the machine, and close the lid. Push the *menu* button and the type of bread you are making—white, whole wheat, or raisin. If you are making rolls, select *dough*. Push the *start* button. Your bread will be ready in three hours for white or raisin bread or four hours for whole wheat bread. Dough takes two hours.

C

It is important to clean the inside of the machine after each use. Small bits of dough may fall out of the pan and burn during baking. Over time this may build up and become hazardous. For cleaning, remove the bread pan from the machine and let the machine cool down. Wipe the inside of the machine with a damp sponge. To clean the bread pan, let it soak in warm, soapy water. Then wipe gently with a damp sponge. Do not use a brush or scouring pad as these may damage the stick-free coating.

D

If you have any questions or require help using your bread machine, please call our twenty-four-hour help line: 800-555-9845. A list of frequently asked questions and answers is available on the website: *www.prestobread.com.* Also available on the website is a variety of international bread recipes. If you are dissatisfied with your Presto Bread Machine for any reason, simply return it, in its original box, to the store where you purchased it. A complete refund will be sent to you within thirty days of purchase.

Questions 5–7

Answer the questions below. Choose **NO MORE THAN THREE WORDS** *from the text for each answer. Write your answers on lines 5–7 on your answer sheet.*

5   How long does it take to bake raisin bread? _____

6   How often should you clean the inside of the machine?

_____

7   According to these instructions, where can you find bread recipes from around the world? _____

Questions 8–14

Read the text below and answer **Questions 8–14**.

Regional Share-Your-Ride

Information for Commuters
Regional Share-Your-Ride is a free service offered to all commuters in our area. We help you save costs on commuting by matching you up with other commuters who travel the same route. When you share your daily ride to work with other commuters, you save on transportation costs and help reduce traffic congestion and air pollution.

Carpool

Share your ride to work with one or more other commuters. You can choose to carpool daily or just a few days a week, whatever suits your schedule best.

Vanpool

Using your van to share your ride with four or more people will save you even more on commuting costs. Regional Share-Your-Ride is available to help you keep your van running smoothly and filled with riders. According to state law, vanpools are permitted to travel in special high-occupancy vehicle (HOV) lanes located on highways in urban areas throughout the region.

Matching

Log on to our website at *www.rsyrp.net*. Type in your location, destination, and work schedule. Our system will generate a list of other commuters whose route and schedule match yours. The website also has maps of the region to help you plan the most efficient route for your commute. These are available for free download.

Contact

Contact the commuters on the list, and arrange a ride-sharing schedule and route with them. You can also discuss how you want to share the responsibility of driving. When you have arranged a carpool or vanpool group, return to our website and register your group with us.

Benefits

Registered participants in Regional Share-Your-Ride can sign up to receive daily traffic and weather reports by e-mail. As a participant, you are also eligible for the Urgent Ride service, which provides you with free transportation to your house in case you or your carpool or vanpool driver has an emergency.

*Complete each sentence with the correct ending, **A–M**, below.*
*Write the correct letter, **A–M**, on lines 8–14 on your answer sheet.*

8 Regional Share-Your-Ride provides

9 By using a carpool or vanpool, commuters can save

10 Commuters who travel by van receive

11 Commuters can get free maps by

12 Commuters should register with the program[1]

13 After signing up for the program, participants can receive by e-mail

14 In case of emergency, program participants can get

---

[1] *British: programme*

A money on traveling[1] costs.

B participating in the program for one month.

C a free ride home.

D a reduced-cost Regional Share-Your-Ride program membership.

E wear and tear on their cars.

F permission to use certain highway lanes.

G rentals of cars and vans for commuting purposes.

H after forming a carpool or vanpool group.

I if interested in learning more about carpools.

J information to commuters who want to share rides.

K daily information on road conditions.

L a trip to the hospital.

M visiting the website.

SECTION 2   QUESTIONS 15–27

You are advised to spend 20 minutes on **Questions 15–27.**

Questions 15–20

Read the text below and answer Questions 15–20.

Job Interview Success

When you apply for a job, the impression you create during the interview is just as important as the skills and background you bring to the table. The following suggestions will help you prepare for a successful interview.

Before You Leave Home

Dress appropriately. This means the attire you choose should be the same as what you would wear for work once you are hired. Conservative colors[2] and styles always convey a more trustworthy image.

Rehearse the interview at home. Think of questions that you will probably be asked, and prepare answers for them. This will help you be calm when you are at the actual interview.

Don't be late for your interview. The best way to avoid this problem is to decide ahead of time how you want to get there. If by bus or subway, check the schedules the day before. If by car, plan your route carefully and figure out how long it will take. Careful planning will ensure that you will make a good impression by arriving on time.

---

[1] *British: travelling*

[2] *British: colours*

During the Interview

Speak clearly. Look the interviewer in the eye when speaking and use clear, confident tones. Do not speak too quickly or nervously. Rather, pronounce your words carefully and pause when searching for ideas. Speaking with a firm, clear voice is one of the best ways to give an impression of self-assurance.

Ask questions. Do not be afraid to do this. It will not make you appear unprepared or stupid. On the contrary, asking the right questions shows that you are knowledgeable about the company and conveys the impression that you are interested and enthusiastic.

Complete the sentences below.

Choose **NO MORE THAN THREE WORDS** *from the text for each answer. Write your answers on lines 15–20 on your answer sheet.*

15 Wearing _____ clothes makes a better impression during the job interview.

16 Practice answering questions ahead of time so that you feel _____ during the interview.

17 If traveling to the interview by bus, make sure you know _____ ahead of time.

18 You will be _____ for the interview if you plan your trip beforehand.

19 Use your _____ to convey an attitude of confidence.

20 Show what you know by asking _____.

Questions 21–27

Read the text below and answer Questions 21–27.

Five Reasons Your Business Needs a Website

All businesses, large or small, need a website. Here are several reasons a website can help a company of any size improve its business.

A

A website is the most important tool a business has for maintaining contact with customers. The website gives customers a way to know what services or products you sell and how to contact you. By offering an e-newsletter sign-up on your website, customers can stay informed about events related to your business and your products, and you save on printing costs. A link to your blog keeps customers up-to-date on what is happening with your business, and keeps them coming back.

B

A website allows you to expand your customer base beyond your immediate community, and even to other countries. Anyone in the world can have access to your services and products through your website, at no extra cost.

C

No matter what the size of your business, it is not hard to afford a website. It is easy to set up, and it does not have to break your budget. There are templates available if you want to create a website yourself. Or, you can hire a Web designer for a more professional look. Depending on what you need, using the services of a professional does not necessarily cost huge amounts of money. The hosting fees you pay to keep your website up and running are minimal.

D

You can save on expenses by keeping your website simple. Even just a few pages can be enough to provide your customers with the necessary information to keep them interested in what your business has to offer. A large website with lots of pages is not always necessary. The most essential facts to include in any website—your business name and location, your products, and your contact information—can be contained on just one page.

E

Your website can be a place for your customers to buy your products. You may still do most of your selling at your physical place of business, but the website is another opportunity to sell, and you can reach more customers this way, too.

*The text contains five sections, **A–E**. In which section can information about the following be found? Write the correct letter, **A–E**, on lines 21–27 on your answer sheet. You may use any letter more than once.*

21 finding international customers

22 the cost of maintaining a website

23 ways to communicate with customers

24 selling your products online

25 the size of your website

26 website design

27 the most important information to include

SECTION 3 *QUESTIONS 28–40*

You are advised to spend 20 minutes on **Questions 28–40**, *which are based on the reading passage below.*

Phases of the Moon

Traveling a distance of approximately 382,400 kilometers, the moon takes just over twenty-nine days to complete its orbit around the Earth. During this lunar cycle, many different phases of the moon are visible from Earth, even though the moon itself never changes shape. The cyclic period of the moon is determined by the extent to which the sun illuminates the moon on the side that is facing Earth. Just like Earth, the moon is sphere shaped, and thus always half illuminated by the sun. However, because the moon and the Earth are in synchronous rotation, we can see only the near side of the moon. The side we do not see is called the far side, or the *dark side*, a term that is often misunderstood. The dark side refers to the mysteriousness of this unseen side, not the amount of light it receives. Both the near and the far sides of the moon receive approximately the same amount of sunlight. Though we see a slightly different moon from Earth each day, its repetitive cycle is both predictable and functional.

There are eight phases of the moon, each with a unique name that signifies how much of the moon is visible from Earth. In the early phases, the moon is said to be *waxing*, or gradually getting larger. The first phase is called *new moon*. In this phase, the moon is lined up between the Earth and the sun. The illuminated side of the moon is facing the sun, not the Earth, so from Earth, there appears to be no moon at all. As the moon begins to move slowly eastward away from the sun, it becomes slightly more visible.

After new moon, the *waxing crescent* phase begins. During this phase, the moon appears to be less than half illuminated. *First quarter* occurs when one-half of the moon is visible. It is called first quarter, not because of its size, but because it represents the end of the first quarter of the moon's cycle. The next phase is called *waxing gibbous* and represents a moon that is larger than half a sphere, but not quite a whole. This phase is followed by *full moon*, which occurs when the moon's illuminated side is directly facing Earth.

As the moon begins to get smaller again, it is said to be *waning*. The phases in the second half of the cycle appear the same as the first, except that the opposite half of the near side of the moon is illuminated, thus the moon appears to be shrinking rather than growing. *Waning gibbous* is followed by *last quarter*, when one-half of the moon is visible, and finally *waning crescent*. In the Northern Hemisphere, when the moon is waxing, the light of the moon increases from right to left. The opposite occurs in the Southern Hemisphere.

Like the sun, the moon is an accurate tool for measuring time. A complete cycle of the moon is called a *lunation*. A full cycle of the moon typically lasts just under one calendar month, therefore, the phase of the moon that starts a month usually repeats just before the month is through. When two full moons occur in one calendar month the second one is called a *blue moon*. This phenomenon occurs about once every 2.7 years. Within one cycle, the moon's "age" is calculated from the last day of the new moon. For example, the moon is approximately fifteen days old during the full moon phase.

The moon can also be used to calculate the time of day. Just like the sun, the moon rises and sets each day and is visible on the Earth's horizon. At new moon, the moon and sun rise and set at almost the same time. As the moon begins to wax, or move farther in its orbit, it rises approximately one hour later each day. By full moon, the moon rises at about the same time the sun sets and sets when the sun rises. Therefore, the moon is out in the daytime as often as it is at night even though it is not always as easy to see in the daylight. The Islamic calendar is based on the phases of the moon. The beginning of each new month in the Islamic calendar begins when the waxing crescent first appears in the night sky.

The primary phases of the moon, which include new moon, first quarter, full moon, and last quarter are published in almanacs for each month. The phases can also be found on many calendars in the Western world. Despite the world's fascination with the moon, its phases are not entirely unique. The planets Venus and Mercury have similar phases; however, unlike the moon, these planets can never be on the opposite side of the Earth from the sun. To see the equivalent of the "full moon" phase of these planets, we would need to have the capacity to see through the sun.

Questions 28 and 29

*Write the correct letter **A**, **B**, or **C**, on lines 28 and 29 on your answer sheet.*

28 It takes the moon approximately twenty-nine days to

  A orbit the sun.
  B travel 382,400 kilometers.
  C become fully illuminated.

29 The dark side of the moon

  A receives a lot of light.
  B faces the Earth during the day.
  C is never visible from the Earth.

Questions 30–33

Label the diagram below. Choose **NO MORE THAN TWO WORDS** *from the reading passage for each answer. Write your answers on lines 30–33 on your answer sheet.*

The Primary Phases of the Moon

1ˢᵗ of the month

30 _____   31 _____   32 _____   33 _____

Questions 34–40

Do the following statements agree with the information given in the passage? On lines 34–40 on your answer sheet, write:

YES	if the statement agrees with the information
NO	if the statement contradicts the information
NOT GIVEN	if there is no information on this

34 A lunation takes a little more than one month to complete.

35 The term *blue moon* refers to the color of the moon at certain times of the year.

36 It takes about fifteen days for the moon to move from new moon to full moon.

37 At certain times of the month, the moon rises at the same time as the sun.

38 There are twelve months on the Islamic calendar.

39 Some planets have phases similar to the moon's phases.

40 The moons of Venus and Mercury are visible from Earth.

General Training Module
Practice Test 2

Candidate Name and Number: _____

INTERNATIONAL ENGLISH LANGUAGE TESTING SYSTEM

GENERAL TRAINING WRITING

TIME 1 HOUR

Instructions to Candidates

Do not open this booklet until you are told to do so.

Write your name and candidate number in the space at the top of this page.

All answers must be written on the separate answer booklet provided. (Answer sheets can be found beginning on page 282.)

Do not remove the booklet from the examination room.

Information for Candidates

There are **2** tasks on this question paper.

You must do **both** tasks.

Under-length answers will be penalized.[1]

---

[1] *British: penalised*

WRITING TASK 1

You should spend about 20 minutes on this task. You should write at least 150 words. You do NOT need to write any addresses. Begin your letter as follows:

Dear _____,

Your next-door neighbor[1] likes to listen to music late at night. Because of the loud music, you often lose sleep.

Write a letter to your neighbor. In your letter

- describe the situation
- explain the problems it is causing you
- offer at least one solution

WRITING TASK 2

You should spend about 40 minutes on this task. Write at least 250 words.

Write about the following topic:

The use of cell phones (mobile phones) has grown rapidly in the past few years. People use them for both business and personal reasons.

What are the advantages and disadvantages of the widespread use of cell phones (mobile phones)? Give reasons for your answer and include any relevant examples from your own knowledge or experience.

---

[1] *British: neighbour*

Practice Test 2–General Training Module
IELTS READING ANSWER SHEET

1. _____
2. _____
3. _____
4. _____
5. _____
6. _____
7. _____
8. _____
9. _____
10. _____
11. _____
12. _____
13. _____
14. _____
15. _____
16. _____
17. _____
18. _____
19. _____
20. _____

21. _____
22. _____
23. _____
24. _____
25. _____
26. _____
27. _____
28. _____
29. _____
30. _____
31. _____
32. _____
33. _____
34. _____
35. _____
36. _____
37. _____
38. _____
39. _____
40. _____

Practice Test 2–Answer Sheet

Practice Test 2—General Training Module
WRITING TASK 1

Writing Task 1 *continued*

Practice Test 2–General Training Module
WRITING TASK 2

Writing Task 2 *continued*

Writing Task 2 *continued*

Answer Key

PRACTICE TEST 2—GENERAL TRAINING MODULE

Reading

1. vii	11. M	21. B	31. first quarter
2. ii	12. H	22. C	32. full moon
3. vi	13. K	23. A	33. last quarter
4. iv	14. C	24. E	34. No
5. three hours	15. conservative	25. D	35. No
6. after each use	16. calm	26. C	36. Yes
7. on the website	17. the schedule(s)	27. D	37. Yes
8. J	18. on time	28. B	38. Not Given
9. A	19. voice	29. C	39. Yes
10. F	20. (the right) questions	30. new moon	40. Not Given

Answer Explanations

GENERAL TRAINING MODULE—PRACTICE TEST 2
Reading

1. *vii.* Section A is about the items included in the box: baking pan, measuring cup, and measuring spoon, that is, the equipment needed for baking bread.

2. *ii.* Section B explains how to use the machine to bake bread.

3. *vi.* Section C is about cleaning, or caring for, the bread machine.

4. *iv.* Section D is about the help available to customers who have bought a bread machine.

5. *three hours.* Section B: "Your bread will be ready in three hours for white or raisin bread. . . ."

6. *after each use.* Section C: "It is important to clean the inside of the machine after each use."

7. *on the website.* Section D: "Also available on the website is a variety of international bread recipes."

8. **(J)** The program provides lists of commuters who are looking to share rides as well as maps to help plan efficient commuting routes.

9. **(A)** Paragraph 1: "When you share your daily ride to work with other commuters, you save on transportation costs and help reduce traffic congestion and air pollution."

10. **(F)** Paragraph 3: "According to state law, vanpools are permitted to travel in special high-occupancy vehicle (HOV) lanes. . . ."

11. **(M)** Paragraph 4: "The website also has maps. . .to help you plan the most efficient route for your commute. . .available for free download."

12. **(H)** Paragraph 5: "When you have arranged a carpool or vanpool group, return to our website and register your group with us."

13. **(K)** Paragraph 6: "Registered participants in Regional Share-Your-Ride can sign up to receive daily traffic and weather reports by e-mail."

14. **(C)** Paragraph 6: "As a participant, you are also eligible for the Urgent Ride service, which provides you with free transportation to your house in case you or your carpool or vanpool driver has an emergency."

15. *conservative.* Paragraph 2, about clothes to wear to the interview, suggests "conservative colors and styles."

16. *calm.* Paragraph 3 advises that rehearsing the interview at home "will help you be calm when you are at the actual interview."

17. *the schedule(s).* Paragraph 4: "check the schedules the day before."

18. *on time.* Paragraph 4: "Careful planning will ensure that you will make a good impression by arriving on time."

19. *voice.* Paragraph 5: "Speaking with a firm, clear voice is one of the best ways to give an impression of self-assurance."

20. *(the right) questions.* Paragraph 6: "asking the right questions shows that you are knowledgeable about the company and conveys the impression that you are interested and enthusiastic."

21. **(B)** "A website allows you to expand your customer base beyond your immediate community, and even to other countries."

22. **(C)** "The hosting fees you pay to keep your website up and running are minimal."

23. **(A)** This section talks about using newsletters and blogs to keep customers informed.

24. **(E)** This section talks about the website as a place where customers can buy products.

25. **(D)** This section mentions that a large website is not necessary and that just a few pages can be enough.

26. **(C)** This section talks about using either a template or a professional to design your website.

27. **(D)** This section mentions "the most essential facts to include in any website."

28. **(B)** Paragraph 1 explains that the moon travels 382,400 kilometers in its orbit around Earth. Choice (A) is incorrect because the moon orbits the Earth, not the sun. Choice (C) is incorrect because the moon only ever becomes half illuminated by the sun.

29. **(C)** Paragraph 1: "we can see only the near side of the moon. The side we do not see is called the far side, or the dark side. . . ." Choice (A) is incorrect because the dark side of the moon receives no light at all. Choice (B) is incorrect because the dark side of the moon is the side that we do not see.

30. *new moon.* Paragraph 2 explains that during the new moon phase there appears to be no moon at all.

31. *first quarter.* Paragraph 3: "First quarter occurs when one half of the moon is visible."

32. *full moon.* Paragraph 3: "This phase is followed by full moon, which occurs when the moon's illuminated side is directly facing Earth."

33. *last quarter.* Paragraph 4: "last quarter, when one half of the moon is visible."

34. *No.* Paragraph 5: "A full cycle of the moon typically lasts just under one calendar month. . . ."

35. *No.* Paragraph 5: "When two full moons occur in one calendar month the second one is called a blue moon."

36. *Yes.* Paragraph 5: "Within one cycle, the moon's "age" is calculated from the last day of the new moon. . .the moon is approximately fifteen days old during the full moon phase."

37. *Yes.* Paragraph 6: "At new moon, the moon and sun rise and set at almost the same time."

38. *Not Given.* The Islamic Calendar is mentioned, but the number of months in it is not.

39. *Yes.* Paragraph 7: "The planets Venus and Mercury have similar phases. . . ."

40. *Not Given.* The planets Venus and Mercury are mentioned, but their moons are not.

Writing

These are models. Your answers will vary. See page vi in the Introduction to see the criteria for scoring.

WRITING TASK 1

[NOTE: Even though this is a personal letter, you should not use contractions on the Writing tasks in the test.]

Dear Mr. Wilson,

I have enjoyed living next door to you for the past year and getting to know you as a neighbor. In the interest of maintaining a good neighborly relationship, I would like to bring a small problem to your attention.

I generally go to bed by ten o'clock in the evening. Recently, I have noticed that you enjoy listening to music at night, often as late as midnight or later. You may not be aware that the volume is high enough for me to hear the music in my bedroom. Often, I have trouble falling asleep because of the music. This is a problem for me since I have to get up at 5:30 A.M. in order to get to work on time.

I wonder if you would consider listening to the music at a lower volume. Or, you might enjoy your music in another room of your house that is farther away from my bedroom window. That way you could still play your music, and I could sleep better.

Please come over to my house anytime and we can discuss this matter more, if you would like.

Your neighbor,
Mark Jones

WRITING TASK 2

The use of cell phones has spread rapidly over the past decade or more. They are used for both business and personal reasons. Cell phones have many advantages because they have made communication much easier. However, they also have disadvantages in both professional and personal situations.

Cell phones make business communication much more convenient. Office workers, for example, are no longer tied to their desks. They can make and receive business calls from any place they happen to be. They do not have to worry about losing a client or missing out on a deal because they were not in the office at the right time. Cell phones also facilitate communication among family members. Parents no longer have to worry about where their children are because they can always reach them by cell phone. Spouses can call each other frequently throughout the day. Cell phones make it easy to keep in touch with relatives who are traveling or who live far away.

Even though cell phones make life easier in many ways, they also have some disadvantages. For one, they can make it difficult to leave work at the office. People often receive business calls on their cell phones when they are out with friends or relaxing at home. Cell phones can give parents a false sense of security. Many parents feel that their child is safe because he or she carries a cell phone, but there are many dangerous situations in which a cell phone cannot offer protection. Another disadvantage for families is that the monthly cell phone bill can be a large expense in the household budget.

As with everything, there are both advantages and disadvantages to cell phones. These days they are so commonly used that it seems people are more attentive to the advantages.

GENERAL TRAINING MODULE
READING
WRITING
PRACTICE TEST 3

General Training Module
Practice Test 3

Candidate Name and Number: _____

INTERNATIONAL ENGLISH LANGUAGE TESTING SYSTEM

GENERAL TRAINING READING

TIME 1 HOUR

Instructions to Candidates

Do not open this booklet until you are told to do so.

Write your name and candidate number in the space at the top of this page.

Start at the beginning of the test and work through it.

You should answer all questions.

If you cannot do a particular question, leave it and go on to the next. You can return to it later.

All answers must be written on the Answer Sheet. (The answer sheet can be found on page 309.)

Do not remove the booklet from the examination room.

Information for Candidates

There are **40** questions on this question paper.

The test is divided as follows:

Section 1	Questions 1–14
Section 2	Questions 15–27
Section 3	Questions 28–40

SECTION 1 *QUESTIONS 1–14*

*You are advised to spend 20 minutes on **Questions 1–14**.*
Read the text below and answer Questions 1–8.

AREA HOTELS

A

Rosewood Hotel. Spend your vacation with us. We offer luxury suites, an Olympic-sized pool, a state-of-the-art fitness center,[1] and a beauty spa. Leave business cares behind while you relax in luxury at the Rosewood. You'll never want to leave! Call 800-555-0942 for reservations.

B

The Woodside Motel is the place to stay while visiting our city. After a day of sightseeing, relax in the comfort of your luxury room. All our rooms have king-sized beds, free movies, and minibars. Our outdoor playground and indoor recreation room mean the little ones will never be bored. Babysitting service available. Enjoy your next family vacation at the Woodside Motel.

C

The Columbus Hotel is conveniently located in the heart of the city's theater[2] district and close to the city's finest restaurants and clubs. Enjoy the spectacular view of the city skyline from the Columbus Rooftop Restaurant. Host your next conference or banquet with us. We have a selection of reception rooms and banquet rooms suitable for conferences and parties. Call 245-555-0982 to speak to our banquet coordinator, 245-555-0987 for dinner reservations at the Rooftop Restaurant, and 245-555-0862 to reserve a room.

D

Next time you're in town, stay at the City View Suites. Whether you're here to shop, play, or work, City View's location can't be beat. We're close to all major bus lines and right next to the city's business district. All rooms include kitchenettes. Call 492-555-5932 for reservations. Don't forget to ask about our special weekly and monthly rates.

E

Sunflower Motel offers reasonable rates, a convenient location, and cable TV in every room. Pets are welcome (extra charge applies). Special weekend rates. Call 488-555-0821 for reservations.

---

[1]*British: centre*
[2]*British: theatre*

*Look at the five hotel advertisements, **A–E**. Which hotel is appropriate for each of the following people? Write the correct letter, **A–E**, on lines 1–8 on your answer sheet. You may use any letter more than once.*

Which hotel is most appropriate for a person who

  1 plans to stay for over a month?

  2 is traveling[1] with children?

  3 always travels with a dog?

  4 plans to go out for entertainment in the evenings?

  5 is on a business trip?

  6 likes to exercise every day?

  7 is looking for a place to hold a wedding reception?

  8 prefers cooking to eating in restaurants?

Questions 9–14

*The following reading passage has six sections, **A–F**. Choose the correct heading for each section from the list of headings below. Write the correct number, **i–ix**, on lines 9–14 on your answer sheet. There are more headings than sections, so you will not use them all.*

LIST OF HEADINGS

i	Pool User Fees
ii	Lifeguard Training
iii	Pool Schedule
iv	Equipment Rental
v	Pool Rules
vi	Individual Membership Benefits
vii	Food
viii	Parking
ix	Classes

  9 Section A

 10 Section B

 11 Section C

 12 Section D

 13 Section E

 14 Section F

---

[1] *British: travelling*

Welcome to the Riverdale City Pool

The following information is provided for your convenience.

A

The Riverdale City Pool is for everybody's enjoyment. To make sure that all pool users have a pleasant experience, please observe the following:

- All children under twelve must be accompanied by an adult.
- Running and shouting in the pool area are not allowed.
- Diving is permitted only in the designated area at the deep end of the adult pool.
- Please shower before entering the pool.

Thank you for your cooperation.

B

The pool is open for the summer season from May 15 through September 15. Hours are Monday–Thursday, noon until 7:30 P.M.; Friday, noon until 9:30 P.M.; Saturday and Sunday, 9:30 A.M. until 9:30 P.M. During the week, the pool will be open for classes only from 8:30 until 11:30 A.M. Three trained lifeguards will be on duty at all times that the pool is open.

C

The pool garage will be closed from June 1 to August 31 for renovations. We are sorry for any inconvenience this may cause. Pool users can leave their cars in the area behind the pool office during this time. A bicycle rack is also located there. There is no fee for using this area.

D

For Riverdale residents, charges for using the pool are $5 per individual per visit, $250 for an individual season pass, and $500 for a family season pass. For non-residents, the charge is $7 per individual per visit. Season passes are not available to pool users who are not residents of Riverdale.

E

This summer we are offering swimming lessons for children, teens, and adults, as well as diving lessons and water aerobics. Morning lessons are from 9:30 to 10:30 and afternoon lessons are from 2:00 to 4:00. Fees start at $75 a week. The Riverdale swim team will continue this season as well. Please visit the pool office for a complete schedule of this summer's lessons and swimming meets.

F

The new snack bar is now open. The hours are 11:30–5:00 daily. It serves a variety of inexpensive drinks and snacks, including cold and hot sandwiches, ice cream treats, and homemade cookies. All items purchased at the snack bar as well as snacks, drinks, and lunches brought from home must be consumed in the picnic area.

SECTION 2   QUESTIONS 15–27

Lakeville College
Employee Benefits

Vacations[1]

All employees are entitled to a minimum of two weeks paid vacation time annually. The actual days to be used as vacation are subject to approval by the individual employee's supervisor.

Insurance

All employees are eligible for any of the health insurance plans offered by the college. Information on the various plans are available from Human Resources. This benefit is extended to members of the employee's immediate family. Part-time employees may apply for this benefit but will pay a higher percentage of the premium.

Use of College Facilities

All employees, full and part time, may use any of the college facilities, including the library, gym, swimming pool, and tennis courts, free of charge. A faculty or staff ID card must be shown when requesting access to these facilities. Immediate family members are also entitled to this benefit, but must obtain an ID card from Human Resources before using college facilities.

Parking

Free parking is available on campus for all college employees; however, a parking sticker must be obtained from Human Resources. The sticker must be displayed on the windshield[2] at all times when parked on campus. The sticker is valid for parking in specially designated employee parking areas as well as in any parking space marked "Visitor." Student parking areas are reserved for student parking only.

Taking Classes

Employees may take classes in any department at the college. Show your faculty or staff ID when registering for the class. Employees may enroll[3] in up to three classes per year free of charge. Any additional classes beyond that must be paid for at the full tuition rate. In addition, any employee wishing to pursue a degree must apply for and be accepted into the program of his or her choice before being considered a degree candidate. In this case, student service fees will apply.

---

[1] British: holiday; in the United States, holiday *refers to a specific date on which a special event, such as Thanksgiving, is observed*
[2] British: windscreen
[3] British: enrol

15 How much annual vacation time are employees allowed?

    A No more than two weeks
    B Exactly two weeks
    C At least two weeks

16 Who is qualified for health insurance benefits?

    A Full-time employees only
    B All employees and their spouses and children
    C All employees, but not their family members

17 What must an employee's family member do in order to use the library?

    A Get an ID card
    B Apply for a job at Human Resources
    C Pay a fee

18 Where can employees park their cars?

    A In the employee parking areas only
    B Anywhere on campus
    C In both employee and visitor parking areas

19 If an employee takes one class in a year, how much will he or she have to pay?

    A Nothing
    B The full tuition rate
    C A student service fee

20 What is required of employees who want to study for a degree?

    A Permission of their supervisors
    B Application for admission into a program
    C Payment of full tuition

Questions 21–27

Read the text below and answer Questions 21–27.

Long Mountain Learning Center
Writing Courses

A

The Art of Correspondence

Have you always wished you could write more elegantly? This course will help you develop your own style when writing letters of friendship, condolence, congratulations, and so on.
Mondays, 5–7 P.M.

B

Client Communication

The success of any business depends on clear communications with clients. This course will show you the essentials of letter, e-mail, and fax writing to help you enhance those all-important business relationships with clients.
Tuesdays, 1–3 P.M.

C

Rules of Communication

Do you wonder where to place commas or when to use exclamation points? Do you know when it is appropriate to use apostrophes and when it is not? This course will clear up any confusion you may have about the rules for using commas, periods, semicolons, and so on, and it will help you to make your writing clear and correct.
Wednesdays, 9:30–10:30 A.M.

D

Fiction Workshop

This course is for writers who are currently working on a novel or short story. Class time will be spent reading and critiquing classmates' work.
Saturdays, 9:30–11:30 A.M.

E

What Do You Mean?

Finding the exact words to express your ideas is an art in itself. In this course, you will learn about words, what they mean, how to avoid confusing similar words, and how to choose just the right words in your writing.
Thursdays, 7:30–9:30 P.M.

F

Write It Right

Writing a research paper involves more than gathering information. Knowing how to organize[1] your information, express your ideas clearly, and document your sources are essential. This course is specifically designed for students preparing to enter college.
Tuesdays, 3:30–5:00 P.M.

---

[1]*British: organise*

G
Express Your Opinion

The Letters to the Editor column in your local paper is a public forum for expressing opinions on matters of interest to all citizens. In this course, you will learn how to develop and eloquently express your opinions and improve your chances of getting your letter published.
Fridays, 8:45–10:00 P.M.

H
Report It

Have you always dreamed[1] of being a correspondent for a newspaper or magazine? This course will cover the basics of gathering news and turning it into interesting newspaper and magazine articles.
Wednesdays, 1–3 P.M.

I
Retelling Old Favorites[2]

Do you remember the traditional folktales and fairy tales that you loved as a child? In this course, you will rewrite some of your favorite old tales in new ways that will delight the youngsters in your life.
Tuesdays, 5–7 P.M.

J
Writing to Sell

In this course, you will learn to write advertisements that will attract more clients to your product or business. Previous business writing experience is required.
Thursdays, 9:30–11:30 A.M.

K
Selling for Poets

Don't let anyone tell you there aren't any good markets for poetry. In fact, there are hundreds of places, both online and in print, that publish poetry and pay good money for it, too. Find out about how to sell your poetry in this course.

---

*Look at the descriptions of the writing courses, **A–K**. For which descriptions are the following statements true? Write the correct letter, **A–K**, on lines 21–27 on your answer sheet.*

21 This course helps you with academic writing.

22 This course shows you how to write personal letters.

23 This course helps you improve your vocabulary.

24 This course is about writing stories for children.

25 This course teaches you about journalism.

26 This course teaches you how to use punctuation.

27 This course is about business marketing.

---

[1] *British: dreamt*
[2] *British: Favourites*

SECTION 3   *QUESTIONS 28–40*

*You are advised to spend 20 minutes on **Questions 28–40**, which are based on the reading passage below.*

Questions 28–34

*The following passage has seven paragraphs, **A–G**. Choose the most suitable heading for each paragraph from the list of headings below. Write the correct numbers, **i–x**, on lines 28–34 on your answer sheet. There are more headings than paragraphs, so you will not use them all.*

LIST OF HEADINGS

i	The Neoclassical Architectural Style
ii	Choosing a Location
iii	Naming the President's House
iv	First Ladies and Interior Design
v	A Designer Is Chosen
vi	Reconstruction of the President's House
vii	The President's House Burns Down
viii	Funding the Construction
ix	Renovation and Modernization[1]
x	Completion of the First President's House

---

28 Paragraph A

29 Paragraph B

30 Paragraph C

31 Paragraph D

32 Paragraph E

33 Paragraph F

34 Paragraph G

The Construction of the White House

A

Lo cated at 1600 Pennsylvania Avenue in Washington, DC, the White House was originally designed by James Hoban, an Irish-born American architect. In 1792, after defeating eight other entrants, Hoban won a contest to design a

---

[1] *British: Modernisation*

mansion for the president of the United States. President George Washington oversaw the original construction, which began on October 13, 1792. Prior to the design contest, engineer Pierre Charles L'Enfant had worked with President Washington to design the capital city. L'Enfant's vision of the president's house was four times larger than the mansion Hoban built. Labor[1] and material expenses required Hoban to build the house on a much smaller scale, with only two main floors instead of three. In addition, rather than using the expensive imported stone of his original plan, the majority of the brick he used was made right on site. Hoban employed builders and craftsmen from overseas as well as local slaves and laborers. The total expenditure for the project was $232,372. This was just a fraction of what L'Enfant's proposed palace would have cost.

B

James Hoban's design was a near copy of a residence in James Gibbs's *Book of Architecture*, published in 1728. Neoclassicism, influenced by the Greco–Roman style, was the popular choice for architects throughout Europe during that time. When Napoleon became emperor, he employed the best architects he knew to transform Paris into a classical Roman capital. Roman triumphal arches and Corinthian columns adorned all of Paris's major structures. Architects in Germany built monuments, halls, and theaters inspired by classic Greek structures such as the Acropolis in Athens. The popularity of the neoclassical style grew internationally, spreading as far as America. Though the architectural styles were borrowed from classical designs, each country added a unique flair in order to achieve a sense of nationalism in its capital.

C

The house that James Hoban designed was not completed until after the second president of the United States took office. Despite the unfinished interior, President John Adams and his family moved from the temporary capital in Philadelphia, Pennsylvania, into the president's house on November 1, 1800. Throughout his term, Adams lived in the mansion with half-finished walls, no heating, and no running water. The interior of the building was completed in 1801 during Thomas Jefferson's term. Before Jefferson moved in, he hired architect Benjamin Latrobe to install coal-burning fireplaces and two water closets. Latrobe also created two terraces on the east and west sides of the building and installed a furnace that relied on kettles and pipes in the basement.

D

Just over twenty years after the construction of the president's house began, the building was burned down during the War of 1812. After British troops torched the house on August 25, 1814, rumors[2] surfaced as to whether the capital would be moved inland. However, the Battle of New Orleans, an encounter in which the Americans came out victorious over Britain, evoked a sense of nationalism in the country's heart. The victory inspired the rebuilding of the president's house, a task that was once again handed over to James Hoban.

---

[1] *British: Labour*
[2] *British: rumours*

E

Hoban worked on the rebuilding for two years before President James Monroe moved into the unfinished home and purchased a number of furnishings. Benjamin Latrobe, who later built the Capitol building, designed large porticos for the house with columns that supported the roof. In 1824, his south portico was completed with a double staircase leading up to the new porch. The north portico was completed in 1830 during the presidency of Andrew Jackson. Though these columns give the White House its distinguishing features today, there was some criticism at the time that they overshadowed the intricate stone carvings on the house. During Jackson's term, running water was installed, though a furnace and gas lighting were not introduced until the 1840s.

F

Major renovations on the president's house continued through the 1800s, including modern innovations such as the telephone and electric wiring. A hot water system, a greenhouse, a private bath, and a number of conservatories were also added. The conservatories, including the rose and orchid houses were removed in 1902, when construction began on the West Wing. The president's Oval Office was added to the West Wing at the order of President Taft in 1909. Each succeeding president and first lady contributed to the interior and its furnishings. Inspectors ordered a full renovation of the White House after the building almost collapsed while a balcony was being added for Harry Truman in the late 1940s. During the temporary closure, all of the modern conveniences, including central air conditioning were added. The last major modification to the White House was the removal of over forty layers of paint from the exterior walls in 1978.

G

For over 100 years, the White House was only a nickname associated with the presidents' home. This term was likely related to the whitewashed exterior that stonemasons completed in 1798. The home was either referred to as the "President's House" or the "Executive Mansion" until Theodore Roosevelt formally established it as the White House soon after taking office in 1901.

Questions 35–40

Choose the correct letters, **A–C,** *and write them on lines 35–40 on your answer sheet.*

35 Pierre Charles L'Enfant was

    A an importer of stone.
    B the designer of the capital city.
    C the winner of a contest to build the president's house.

36 The influential *Book of Architecture* was written by

    A James Hoban.
    B James Gibb.
    C Napoleon.

37 The first president to live in the original president's house was

    A John Adams.
    B Thomas Jefferson.
    C George Washington.

38 The White House burned down in

    A 1800.
    B 1812.
    C 1814.

39 The Oval Office was built during the presidency of

    A Taft.
    B Truman.
    C Jackson.

40 In 1901,

    A the White House was repainted.
    B the first lady bought new furniture.
    C Theodore Roosevelt became president.

General Training Module
Practice Test 3

Candidate Name and Number: _____

INTERNATIONAL ENGLISH LANGUAGE TESTING SYSTEM

GENERAL TRAINING WRITING

TIME 1 HOUR

Instructions to Candidates

Do not open this booklet until you are told to do so.

Write your name and candidate number in the space at the top of this page.

All answers must be written on the separate answer booklet provided. (The answer sheets can be found beginning on page 310.)

Do not remove the booklet from the examination room.

Information for Candidates

There are **2** tasks on this question paper.

You must do **both** tasks.

Under-length answers will be penalized.[1]

---

[1] *British: penalised*

WRITING TASK 1

You should spend about 20 minutes on this task. You should write at least 150 words. You do NOT need to write any addresses. Begin your letter as follows:

Dear _____,

While your friend was away on vacation, you stayed in his apartment. While you were there, you dropped an expensive bowl and broke it.

Write a letter to your friend. In your letter

- explain what happened
- apologize[1] for the accident
- tell your friend how you plan to make it up to him

WRITING TASK 2

You should spend about 40 minutes on this task. Write at least 250 words.

Write about the following topic:

Some people choose a career according to the social status and salary it will give them. Others choose a career according to whether they will enjoy the work.

Which do you think is the best way to choose a career? Give reasons for your answer and include any relevant examples from your own knowledge or experience.

---

[1] *British: apologise*

Practice Test 3—General Training Module
IELTS READING ANSWER SHEET

1. _____	21. _____
2. _____	22. _____
3. _____	23. _____
4. _____	24. _____
5. _____	25. _____
6. _____	26. _____
7. _____	27. _____
8. _____	28. _____
9. _____	29. _____
10. _____	30. _____
11. _____	31. _____
12. _____	32. _____
13. _____	33. _____
14. _____	34. _____
15. _____	35. _____
16. _____	36. _____
17. _____	37. _____
18. _____	38. _____
19. _____	39. _____
20. _____	40. _____

Practice Test 3–General Training Module
WRITING TASK 1

Writing Task 1 *continued*

Practice Test 3—General Training Module
WRITING TASK 2

Writing Task 2 *continued*

Writing Task 2 *continued*

Answer Key
PRACTICE TEST 3—GENERAL TRAINING MODULE

Reading

1. D	11. viii	21. F	31. vii
2. B	12. i	22. A	32. vi
3. E	13. ix	23. E	33. ix
4. C	14. vii	24. I	34. iii
5. D	15. C	25. H	35. B
6. A	16. B	26. C	36. B
7. C	17. A	27. J	37. A
8. D	18. C	28. v	38. C
9. v	19. A	29. i	39. A
10. iii	20. B	30. x	40. C

Answer Explanations

GENERAL TRAINING MODULE—PRACTICE TEST 3
Reading

1. **(D)** This hotel has suites with small kitchens and special weekly and monthly rates.

2. **(B)** This hotel has a playground, recreation room, and babysitting service.

3. **(E)** This hotel welcomes pets.

4. **(C)** This hotel is near theaters, restaurants, and clubs.

5. **(D)** This hotel is near the business district.

6. **(A)** This hotel has a large swimming pool and a fitness room.

7. **(C)** This hotel has reception and banquet rooms for rent.

8. **(D)** This hotel has suites with kitchenettes.

9. *v.* Section A explains what is and is not allowed, in other words, rules.

10. *iii.* Section B tells the months and the hours the pool is open.

11. *viii.* Section C talks about the garage and where to leave cars.

12. *i.* Section D explains how much it costs to use the pool.

13. *ix.* Section E talks about lessons, or classes, and swim meets.

14. *vii.* Section F explains what snacks are for sale and where the food can be eaten.

15. **(C)** Paragraph 1 explains that all employees have "a minimum of two weeks." *Minimum* means *at least.* Choices (A) and (B) are incorrect because they do not correctly interpret the meaning of *minimum.*

16. **(B)** Paragraph 2: "All employees are eligible for any of the health insurance plans offered by the college . . . . This benefit is extended to members of the employee's immediate family." Choice (A) is incorrect because the benefit is for "all employees." This includes part-time employees. Choice (C) is incorrect because the benefit is also for "members of the employee's immediate family."

17. **(A)** Paragraph 3: "Immediate family members are also entitled to this benefit, but must obtain an ID card from Human Resources . . . ." Choice (B) is confused with the mention of Human Resources, where the ID cards are available. Choice (C) is incorrect because use of college facilities is "free of charge."

18. **(C)** Paragraph 4 explains that the parking sticker is valid in employee and visitor parking areas but not in student parking areas. Choices (A) and (B) are contradicted by the information in the paragraph.

19. **(A)** Paragraph 5: "up to three classes per year free of charge." Choices (B) and (C) are contradicted by the information in the paragraph.

20. **(B)** Paragraph 5: "In addition, any employee wishing to pursue a degree must apply for and be accepted into the program of his or her . . . ." Choice (A) is not mentioned. Choice (C) is incorrect because an employee in a degree program might choose to take only three classes per year, which would be free of charge.

21. **(F)** Course F is about writing research papers and is for students who will enter college.

22. **(A)** Course A is about writing letters of friendship, condolence, and congratulations, which are examples of personal letters.

23. **(E)** Course E is about words, that is, vocabulary.

24. **(I)** Course I is about rewriting traditional tales (stories) for youngsters (children).

25. **(H)** Course H is about writing news articles for newspapers and magazines, which is journalism.

26. **(C)** Course C is about commas, periods, semicolons, and so on, that is, punctuation.

27. **(J)** Course J is about writing advertisements for businesses.

28. *v.* Paragraph A is about James Hoban, the man who won the design contest.

29. *i.* Paragraph B discusses the influence of neoclassical architecture on eighteenth-century design.

30. *x.* Paragraph C describes how the building was completed during the term of Thomas Jefferson.

31. *vii.* Paragraph D describes the burning of the president's house during the War of 1812.

32. *vi.* Paragraph E describes the rebuilding of the president's house.

33. *ix.* Paragraph F talks about improvements made to the building over the years.

34. *iii.* Paragraph G tells how the building came to be called the "White House."

35. **(B)** Paragraph A: "engineer Pierre Charles L'Enfant had worked with President Washington to design the capital city." Choice (A) refers to the material used to build the White House. Choice (C) is James Hoban, not Pierre L'Enfant.

36. **(B)** Paragraph B: "James Hoban's design was a near copy of a residence in James Gibbs's *Book of Architecture*, published in 1728." Choice (A) is the person who was inspired by the book. Choice (C) is mentioned as a person who influenced European architecture.

37. **(A)** Paragraph C: "The house that James Hoban designed was not completed until after the second president of the United States took office." Choice (B) is the man who was president when the interior of the building was completed. Choice (C) is the president who oversaw the original construction, but he did not live in the building.

38. **(C)** Paragraph D: "After British troops torched the house on August 25, 1814. . . ." Choice (A) is the year John Adams moved into the house. Choice (B) refers to the name of the war.

39. **(A)** Paragraph F: "The president's Oval office was added to the West Wing at the order of President Taft in 1909." Choices (B) and (C) refer to other presidents mentioned in the passage.

40. **(C)** Paragraph G: "Theodore Roosevelt formally established it as the White House soon after taking office in 1901." Choices (A) and (B) refer to improvements that were done at different times over the years.

Writing

These are models. Your answers will vary. See page vi in the Introduction to see the criteria for scoring.

WRITING TASK 1

[NOTE: Even though this is an informal letter, you should not use contractions on the Writing tasks in the test.]

Dear Diego,

Thank you very much for letting me use your apartment while you were away. I tried to leave everything just as I found it. You will, unfortunately, find one thing missing. I wanted to do you a favor by cleaning the living room. While I was dusting that beautiful bowl you keep on the coffee table, it fell out of my hands and broke.

I am terribly sorry about breaking your bowl. I know that it was a present from your grandmother and that it means a lot to you. Things like that are irreplaceable. I think, however, that the bowl can be fixed. It broke into just three large pieces. I have a friend who is an expert on valuable china, and I have given her the bowl to repair. You should have it back in a few days, and I think it will look as good as new.

I hope this solution is satisfactory to you. Again, I am so very sorry this happened. I will bring you the bowl soon.

Your friend,
Michael

WRITING TASK 2

If I had to choose between a high salary and a high level of enjoyment when deciding on a career, I think I would have to choose the high salary. Earning money is the major reason why we work. If we choose a career only on the basis of enjoyment, we might not earn enough money. Once we have a comfortable level of earning, then we can use our free time to pursue our personal interests.

We work to support ourselves and our families. We need to pay for a place to live, food to eat, and clothes to wear. If we have children or other relatives who depend on us, we need to provide these things for them, too. Even just the basic necessities of life cost money, and the prices are always going up.

If we do not make earning an adequate salary a top priority, we might not be able to afford to buy the things we need. We might not be able to provide our dependents with adequate food, clothing, and shelter. We might enjoy our work, but if we and our relatives cannot eat, that does not really matter.

When we earn enough money to support ourselves and our families, then we can pursue our own interests in our free time. If we are not earning enough money, we spend a lot of time and energy worrying about it. When we do earn enough money, we feel secure. We can focus our energy on playing sports, playing music, painting pictures, or whatever activities we enjoy.

Earning an adequate salary means that we can provide the necessities of life for ourselves and our relatives. It gives us the security we need to enjoy the other things that interest us.

GENERAL TRAINING MODULE
READING
WRITING
PRACTICE TEST 4

General Training Module
Practice Test 4

Candidate Name and Number: _____

INTERNATIONAL ENGLISH LANGUAGE TESTING SYSTEM

GENERAL TRAINING READING

TIME 1 HOUR

Instructions to Candidates

Do not open this booklet until you are told to do so.

Write your name and candidate number in the space at the top of this page.

Start at the beginning of the test and work through it.

You should answer all questions.

If you cannot do a particular question, leave it and go on to the next. You can return to it later.

All answers must be written on the Answer Sheet. (The answer sheet can be found on page 335.)

Do not remove the booklet from the examination room.

Information for Candidates

There are **40** questions on this question paper.

The test is divided as follows:

Section 1	Questions 1–14
Section 2	Questions 15–27
Section 3	Questions 28–40

SECTION 1 *QUESTIONS 1–14*

*You are advised to spend 20 minutes on **Questions 1–14**.*

Questions 1–7

Read the text below and answer Questions 1–7.

Volunteer Opportunities for Redux, Inc. Employees

You can give back to the community through the company's Volunteer Program. By signing up for the program, you can spend up to five hours a month of company time volunteering in an approved community program. This program is open to all Redux, Inc. employees. The following opportunities are currently available:

A

Nursing home residents are usually unable to get out to see plays, movies, and concerts. They count on your generosity to bring entertainment to them. Do you like to perform? Do you have a special talent that's just waiting for an audience? An appreciative audience is guaranteed if you can give just one afternoon a week to share your special talent with these special people.

B

The Citizen's Park Cleanup Committee needs more help. Committee members spend the last Saturday of each month at a different city park, picking up trash, repairing equipment, pulling weeds, and planting flowers.

C

Mayfield Elementary School needs people to help with their afterschool program. Volunteers will tutor children in reading and math. Must be able to commit to one afternoon a week for the entire school year.

D

The Mayfield Free Clinic is open every weekend and is looking for people willing to spend two days a month assisting the clinic staff. Volunteers will complete patient intake forms, educate the patients about clinic services, and provide assistance contacting other medical providers.

E

The Mayfield Shelter serves hot dinners to the homeless every evening. The shelter needs volunteers to help with preparing and serving meals. If you can volunteer one evening a week, the shelter needs you.

Look at the volunteer opportunities, **A–E**. Which volunteer opportunity is appropriate for each of the following people? Write the correct letter, **A–E**, on lines 1–7 on your answer sheet. You may use any letter more than once.

Which opportunity is most appropriate for a person who

1   is only free in the evening?

2   is interested in health care?

3   plays the guitar and sings?

4   enjoys spending time outdoors?

5   likes to cook?

6   only has one day a month free?

7   enjoys young children?

Questions 8–14

Read the text below and answer Questions 8–14.

Summer Classes at the Community Center[1]

The Community Center is offering adult summer classes again this year. The schedule includes classes in basic computer skills, martial arts, painting and drawing, and dance.

Registration

There are two ways to register for classes:

1. Go to our website: *www.cc.org/classes/winterschedule*. Click on "Class Descriptions" to see a full listing of the classes that are available this winter. Decide which class or classes you are interested in.

   Then click on "Register Now" and a registration form will appear.* Complete the form and calculate the amount of money you owe. This will include the cost of your classes plus a $15 registration fee. Any materials fees will be payable to the instructor on the first day of class. In addition, if your address is outside of the city, you will pay a nonresident fee of $25 per class.

   Fill in your credit card information and click "Send Now." You will receive registration confirmation by e-mail.

2. If you do not have access to a computer, you can call the Community Center at 872-555-5068 to request a class catalog[2] and registration form. Select your classes from the catalog, complete the form, and return it by mail with your check or credit card information.

---

[1] *British: Centre*

[2] *British: catalogue*

Withdrawal Policy

Full refunds, minus the $25 registration fee, will be given for any withdrawals made up to one week before the class begins. Withdrawals made before the start of the second class will receive a 50 percent refund, minus the registration fee. No refunds will be made after the start of the second class.

Classes offered by the Community Center are for adults only. You must be eighteen years of age or older to participate. Classes for children and teens are offered through the City Department of Recreation.

Do the following statements agree with the information given in the text? On lines 8–14 on your answer sheet, write:

TRUE	if the statement is true
FALSE	if the statement is false
NOT GIVEN	if the information is not given in the text

8 You must visit a website in order to sign up for classes.

9 A registration fee is required for all classes.

10 Dance classes cost less than computer classes.

11 People who live outside of the city pay an extra fee.

12 You are allowed to register for only two classes at a time.

13 You will not get your money back if you withdraw after the second class.

14 Classes at the Community Center are for people of all ages.

SECTION 2   *QUESTIONS 15–27*

You are advised to spend 20 minutes on **Questions 15–27***.*

Questions 15–20

Read the text below and answer Questions 15–20.

The Murgatroyde Corporation Employee Manual
Chapter 8: Professional Development Requirements

All employees of the Murgatroyde Corporation are required to attend fifteen hours of professional development workshops or classes in each calendar year. While there are many opportunities provided by the company, professional development hours can also be earned externally at local training centers, colleges, and other locations.

Listings of upcoming professional development opportunities offered by the company are posted on the company website and updated frequently. Employees can register for these workshops online. Before signing up for a particular workshop, employees should check with their supervisors to make sure they can be excused from their duties on the date of the workshop.

Employees who wish to receive professional development credit for attending workshops or courses offered elsewhere should provide their supervisor with materials describing the opportunity. The supervisor will determine whether the workshop or course is pertinent to the employee's work. After obtaining the supervisor's approval, the employee can apply to the Human Resources Office for tuition reimbursement if tuition is to be paid.

Employees attending any workshop offered by the company will receive a certificate of attendance. The number of professional development hours earned will be reported to the Human Resources Office by the workshop organizer.[1] In order to receive professional development credit for a course or workshop offered outside the company, the employee must have the workshop organizer complete a company Proof of Attendance form, and the employee must then submit the form to the Human Resources Office within one month of the end date of the course. Timely submission of this form is required in order for credit to be granted. There are will be no exceptions.

---

[1] *British: organiser*

Complete the sentences below.
*Choose **NO MORE THAN THREE WORDS** from the text for each answer.*
Write your answers on lines 15–20 on your answer sheet.

15 Employees can choose from professional development workshops and classes offered _____ or at local training centers or colleges.

16 Employees can find out which workshops will be offered by looking at

_____.

17 It is the responsibility of _____ to decide whether a workshop is relevant.

18 Employees who need help paying for a class or workshop can ask the Human Resources Office for _____.

19 The workshop presenter will let the Human Resources Office know how many _____ the employee should be credited with.

20 Professional development credit will be granted for workshops taken outside of the company if a special form is filled out by _____.

Questions 21–27

Read the text below and answer Questions 21–27.

Hampford College
Work–Study Program

   Certain students at Hampford College may be eligible for the college Work–Study Program. To determine eligibility and to apply for the program, read the information below.

   * The Hampford College Work–Study Program is open to all full-time Hampford College students, regardless of the particular study program in which they are enrolled. The program is not open to part-time students. Information on financial support programs for part-time students is available in the Counseling[1] Center.

   * Before applying for a work–study position, the student must demonstrate financial need. To do this, complete the Statement of Financial Need Form, available in the Counseling Center.

---

[1] *British: Counselling*

* To apply for a work–study position, submit a letter of interest to the Work–Study Program Office, describing your skills and interests. You may also, but are not required to, submit a résumé describing any previous jobs you may have held. Students both with and without an employment history are eligible for the program.

* Once you have been approved for the program, look at the help-wanted ads posted on the Counseling Center website. All of the jobs are located at the college. You may apply for any job that you are interested in. Please note that job placement is subject to job availability. While we make every effort to place all Work–Study Program students in a job, there are no guarantees.

* All work–study students must be students in good standing at the college; that is, they must receive passing grades in all their courses in order to continue in the program the following semester.

* Work–study positions are generally for one year. Students wishing to continue in the program after one year must resubmit their applications.

Questions 21–27

Do the following statements agree with the information given in the text about the Hampford College Work–Study Program? On lines 21–27 on your answer sheet, write:

TRUE	if the statement agrees with the information
FALSE	if the statement contradicts the information
NOT GIVEN	if there is no information on this

21 The Work–Study Program is available to all students at the college.

22 Work–study students must prove that they require monetary support.

23 Work–study students must choose a job that is related to their study program.

24 Previous work experience is required to participate in the Work–Study Program.

25 All students in the Work–Study Program will be given a job.

26 Work–study students cannot stay in the program if they receive failing grades.

27 Work–study students have to apply for the program every year.

SECTION 3 *QUESTIONS 28–40*

You are advised to spend 20 minutes on **Questions 28–40***, which are based on the reading passage below.*

Seasonal Affective Disorder

A

When fall[1] days shorten and winter is around the corner, many people start to feel sluggish, moody, antisocial, or irritable. Like bears, they may feel as though they want to hibernate for the winter. But these symptoms may be more than the winter blues; they could indicate seasonal affective disorder (SAD). This is a form of depression that appears in the early fall and lasts through the first month or so of spring. It is triggered by the shortened daylight of the colder months and then dissipates as the days get longer and the warmer months approach.

B

Because a decrease in the number of daylight hours is a significant contributor, geographic location is an important factor in the incidence of the disorder. Residents of Canada and the northern United States, for example, are eight times more likely to suffer from SAD than are residents of sunny regions of the southern United States and Mexico. SAD is also more common in countries in arctic latitudes, such as Finland, where the rate of SAD is nearly 10 percent. It is seldom found in countries within 30 degrees of the equator, where there are long, constant hours of sunlight throughout the year.

C

As with other forms of depression, serious SAD may be accompanied by suicidal thoughts. One study of suicides in Japan examined a multitude of variables for each suicide, including hours of sunlight in the latitude, temperature, and economic factors, among others. Researchers found that yearly total sunshine was the only individual variable that correlated to a significant difference in the suicide rate. Thus, the study suggested that one's latitude can have a significant effect on mental health and even on tendencies toward suicidal thoughts.

D

SAD usually begins in adults between the ages of eighteen and thirty, and it is four times more prevalent in women than men. The disorder also tends to run in families. Some people suffer debilitating symptoms that interfere with interpersonal relationships and careers. Others with SAD experience mild symptoms. For people with this milder version of SAD, the winter may bring increased sadness or irritability, but they remain fully functional.

---

[1] *British: autumn*

E

SAD's symptoms include many that are common in other forms of depression. SAD sufferers, like people who suffer from depression, experience fatigue, decreased levels of energy, and difficulty concentrating. Increased appetite, especially a craving for carbohydrates, and weight gain, as well as an increased need for sleep and a desire to be alone are other common symptoms of depression that are seen among SAD sufferers as well.

F

The exact mechanism causing SAD is not known, but some researchers theorize[1] that SAD is related to hormonal changes. One theory is that reduced sunlight during fall and winter leads to reduced production of serotonin, a neurotransmitter with a calming effect, in the brain. Low levels of serotonin are associated with many forms of depression and can manifest in symptoms such as fatigue, carbohydrate craving, and weight gain. Because high-carbohydrate foods, such as chips, pretzels, and cookies,[2] boost serotonin, experts believe they have a soothing effect on the body and mind.

G

Others believe SAD is caused by the hormone melatonin, which is related to the body's circadian rhythms and can cause drowsiness. Plentiful light decreases the secretion of melatonin in the brain. However, during shorter and darker days more melatonin is produced, causing lethargy and other symptoms of depression.

H

The most common treatment for SAD is light therapy, in which patients expose themselves to full-spectrum lights, usually twenty times brighter than normal room lights, for fifteen to sixty minutes a day. Light helps to decrease the amount of melatonin and boost the serotonin in the brain. Thus, light therapy has an antidepressant effect. Sometimes, light therapy is used in combination with antidepressant medication and individual psychotherapy.

I

Experts also recommend some lifestyle changes that help to prevent SAD. People who have a tendency to suffer from SAD are encouraged to go outside every day during the winter months and to exercise regularly. Eating a well-balanced diet with plenty of vitamins and minerals is also important. Social support is extremely important for those with depression, so maintaining an active social life and regular activities is also recommended. For patients who use a light box, it is recommended to start using it in the early fall, before SAD symptoms appear.

J

Although some aspects of SAD are still being researched, experts agree that people who think they are suffering from SAD should see a doctor immediately. They do not advise using light therapy or any other treatment without the supervision of a physician.

---

[1] *British: theorise*

[2] *British: biscuits*

Questions 28–31

*The text has ten paragraphs, **A–J**. Which paragraph contains the following information? Write the correct letter, **A–J**, on lines 28–31 on your answer sheet.*

28 a reason why certain types of food may alleviate the symptoms of SAD

29 types of people who tend to suffer from SAD

30 parts of the world where SAD is common

31 a study showing a relationship between sunlight and mental health

Questions 32–36

*Choose **FIVE** letters, **A–H**. Write the correct letter on lines 32–36 on your answer sheet.*
*Which **FIVE** of the following symptoms of SAD are mentioned in the passage?*

- **A**   uncontrollable crying
- **B**   feeling tired frequently
- **C**   eating more than usual
- **D**   thinking dark thoughts
- **E**   increased weight
- **F**   unhappy feelings
- **G**   frequent bad temper
- **H**   inability to sleep

Questions 37–40

*Choose **FOUR** letters, **A–G**. Write the correct letter on lines 37–40 on your answer sheet.*
*Which **FOUR** of the following treatments for SAD are mentioned in the passage?*

- **A**   taking drugs
- **B**   writing in a journal
- **C**   attending a support group
- **D**   using a light box
- **E**   spending time outdoors
- **F**   traveling[1] to a sunny location
- **G**   talking with a therapist

---

[1]*British: travelling*

General Training Module
Practice Test 4

Candidate Name and Number: _____

INTERNATIONAL ENGLISH LANGUAGE TESTING SYSTEM

GENERAL TRAINING WRITING

TIME 1 HOUR

Instructions to Candidates

Do not open this booklet until you are told to do so.

Write your name and candidate number in the space at the top of this page.

All answers must be written on the separate answer booklet provided. (The answer sheets can be found beginning on page 336.)

Do not remove the booklet from the examination room.

Information for Candidates

There are **2** tasks on this question paper.

You must do **both** tasks.

Under-length answers will be penalized.[1]

---

[1] *British: penalised*

WRITING TASK 1

You should spend about 20 minutes on this task. You should write at least 150 words. You do NOT need to write any addresses. Begin your letter as follows:

Dear _____,

You recently spent a vacation at the home of some friends who live in a different city.

Write a letter to your friends. In your letter

- thank your friends for letting you stay with them
- describe some things you enjoyed about your vacation
- invite your friends to visit you

WRITING TASK 2

You should spend about 40 minutes on this task. Write at least 250 words.

Write about the following topic:

Learning to play team sports is an important part of a child's education.

Do you agree or disagree? Give reasons for your answer and include any relevant examples from your own knowledge or experience.

Practice Test 4–General Training Module
IELTS READING ANSWER SHEET

1. _____
2. _____
3. _____
4. _____
5. _____
6. _____
7. _____
8. _____
9. _____
10. _____
11. _____
12. _____
13. _____
14. _____
15. _____
16. _____
17. _____
18. _____
19. _____
20. _____

21. _____
22. _____
23. _____
24. _____
25. _____
26. _____
27. _____
28. _____
29. _____
30. _____
31. _____
32. _____
33. _____
34. _____
35. _____
36. _____
37. _____
38. _____
39. _____
40. _____

Practice Test 4–Answer Sheet

Practice Test 4–General Training Module
WRITING TASK 1

Writing Task 1 *continued*

Practice Test 4–General Training Module
WRITING TASK 2

Writing Task 2 *continued*

Writing Task 2 *continued*

Answer Key

PRACTICE TEST 4—GENERAL TRAINING MODULE

Reading

1. E	15. by the company	28. F
2. D	16. the company website	29. D
3. A	17. the supervisor	30. B
4. B	18. tuition reimbursement	31. C
5. E	19. professional development hours	32. B
6. B		33. C
7. C	20. the workshop organizer	34. E
8. False	21. False	35. F
9. True	22. True	36. G
10. Not Given	23. Not Given	37. A
11. True	24. False	38. D
12. Not Given	25. False	39. E
13. True	26. True	40. G
14. False	27. True	

Answer Explanations

GENERAL TRAINING MODULE–PRACTICE TEST 4
Reading

1. **(E)** This opportunity asks for one evening a week.

2. **(D)** This opportunity is at a health clinic, assisting with patients.

3. **(A)** This opportunity is for people who can provide entertainment (for example, playing music and singing) for nursing home residents.

4. **(B)** This opportunity takes place outside in a park.

5. **(E)** This opportunity involves preparing food.

6. **(B)** This opportunity takes place once a month, on the last Saturday of the month.

7. **(C)** This opportunity involves working with elementary school children.

8. *False.* You may either visit the website or call the Community Center to register.

9. *True.* In Part 1: "calculate the amount of money you owe. This will include the cost of your classes plus a $15 registration fee."

10. *Not Given.* Differences in the costs of the different classes is not mentioned.

11. *True.* In Part 1: "In addition, if your address is outside of the city, you will have to pay a nonresident fee of $25 per class."

12. *Not Given.* There is no mention of a limit on classes.

13. *True.* In Part 2: "No refunds will be made after the start of the second class."

14. *False.* In Part 2: "Classes offered by the Community Center are for adults only."

15. *by the company.*

16. *the company website.*

17. *the supervisor.*

18. *tuition reimbursement.*

19. *professional development hours.*

20. *the workshop organizer.*

21. *False.* Paragraph 2 explains that the program is open to full-time students but not part-time students.

22. *True.* Paragraph 3 states, "Before applying for a work–study position, the student must demonstrate financial need."

23. *Not Given.* There is no mention of such a requirement.

24. *False.* Paragraph 4 states, "Students both with and without an employment history are eligible for the program."

25. *False.* Paragraph 5 states, "While we make every effort to place all Work–Study Program students in a job, there are no guarantees."

26. *True.* Paragraph 6 explains that work–study students must have passing grades in order to stay in the program.

27. *True.* Paragraph 7 states, "Students wishing to continue in the program after one year must resubmit their applications."

28. **(F)** Paragraph F: "Because high-carbohydrate foods, such as chips, pretzels, and cookies, boost serotonin, experts believe they have a soothing effect on the body and mind."

29. **(D)** Paragraph D: "SAD usually begins in adults between the ages of eighteen and thirty, and it is four times more prevalent in women than men. The disorder also tends to run in families."

30. **(B)** Paragraph B: "Residents of Canada and the northern United States, for example, are eight times more likely to suffer from SAD . . . ."

31. **(C)** Paragraph C: "One study of suicides in Japan examined a multitude of variables for each suicide, including hours of sunlight in the latitude, temperature, and economic factors, among others."

32. **(B)** Paragraph E: "SAD sufferers, like people who suffer from depression, experience fatigue, . . . as well as an increased need for sleep . . . ." *Fatigue* means *feeling tired frequently.*

33. **(C)** Paragraph E: "Increased appetite, especially a craving for carbohydrates, and weight gain . . . are seen among SAD sufferers as well."

34. **(E)** Paragraph E: "Increased appetite, especially a craving for carbohydrates, and weight gain . . . are seen among SAD sufferers as well."

35. **(F)** Paragraph F: "Low levels of serotonin are associated with many forms of depression . . . ."

36. **(G)** Paragraph D: "may bring increased sadness or irritability . . . ." *Irritability* means *bad temper.*

37. **(A)** Paragraph H: "Sometimes, light therapy is used in combination with antidepressant medication and individual psychotherapy."

38. **(D)** Paragraph H: "Sometimes, light therapy is used in combination with antidepressant medication and individual psychotherapy."

39. **(E)** Paragraph I: "People who have a tendency to suffer from SAD are encouraged to go outside every day during the winter months and to exercise regularly."

40. **(G)** Paragraph H: "Sometimes, light therapy is used in combination with antidepressant medication and individual psychotherapy." *Psychotherapy* means *talking with a therapist.*

Writing

These are models. Your answers will vary. See page vi in the Introduction to see the criteria for scoring.

WRITING TASK 1

[NOTE: Even though this is a personal letter, you should not use contractions on the Writing tasks in the test.]

Dear Fred and Mary,

   I am writing to thank you for your kind hospitality during my recent visit to your city. You made my vacation a really pleasant one. I thoroughly enjoyed the time we spent together, as well as seeing all the interesting sights in your city. I especially enjoyed the evening we went to the theater. The play was very interesting, and the actors were so talented. It was also very kind of you to provide the tickets. I also want to thank you for recommending that I visit the art museum and the gardens in Essex Park. I found so many things to interest me in both those places.

   I would like to return your hospitality and invite you to visit me sometime next summer. There are a lot of interesting things to see and do here that I know you would enjoy, and it would be great to spend more time with you. Just let me know what dates are convenient for you. I look forward to hearing from you.

Your friend,
Jonathan

WRITING TASK 2

Playing team sports offers many benefits to children. However, I do not believe that all children need to learn to play these sports. I feel that there are other ways to get the same benefits and that team sports do not offer advantages to children who do not enjoy playing them.

Team sports offer a lot of good things to children who enjoy playing them. In the first place, children get a lot of exercise, which is important for their physical and mental health. In addition, they learn important skills such as teamwork, dealing with defeat, and winning graciously. Last but not least, they can have a lot of fun. However, team sports are not the only way to gain these benefits. Many children enjoy individual activities such as hiking or biking. Sports such as these are as healthy and as much fun for children as team sports. Team sports are also not the only way to learn to work with others. Children have opportunities to work on teams at school and with clubs or organizations.

Not all children enjoy playing team sports. For these children, being forced to play such sports can be a very disagreeable experience. They learn to associate physical exercise and teamwork with unpleasantness. After having bad experiences with team sports, children can easily be discouraged from learning to enjoy any form of physical exercise or to value being part of a group or team.

Team sports have a lot to offer, but they are not for everybody. There is no point in forcing them on children who do not like them. Children should be encouraged to work hard at being the best they can be in whatever they enjoy. That is the most beneficial type of learning situation for any child.

GENERAL TRAINING MODULE
READING
WRITING
PRACTICE TEST 5

General Training Module
Practice Test 5

Candidate Name and Number: _____

INTERNATIONAL ENGLISH LANGUAGE TESTING SYSTEM

GENERAL TRAINING READING

TIME 1 HOUR

Instructions to Candidates

Do not open this booklet until you are told to do so.

Write your name and candidate number in the space at the top of this page.

Start at the beginning of the test and work through it.

You should answer all questions.

If you cannot do a particular question, leave it and go on to the next. You can return to it later.

All answers must be written on the Answer Sheet. (The answer sheet can be found on page 361.)

Do not remove the booklet from the examination room.

Information for Candidates

There are **40** questions on this question paper.

The test is divided as follows:

Section 1	Questions 1–14
Section 2	Questions 15–27
Section 3	Questions 28–40

SECTION 1   *QUESTIONS 1–14*

You are advised to spend 20 minutes on **Questions 1–14***.*

Questions 1–7

Read the text below and answer Questions 1–7.

Techno Institute of Training
Information for Students

Welcome to the Techno Institute of Training. Please read the following information carefully.

All texts and manuals required in our classes are available for sale in the Main Office, Room 105. Please see the receptionist to purchase your reading materials. You must have all materials when you arrive at your first class meeting, so please plan to get them ahead of time.

If for any reason you need to withdraw from a class that you are enrolled in, please note the following policies. Tuition will be fully refunded if you withdraw from the class before the second class meeting. Withdrawals made after the second class meeting but before the third will receive a refund of 50 percent of the tuition. Refunds cannot be made after the third class meeting. To withdraw from a class, please visit the Registrar's Office in Room 103.

Tickets to our Friday night lecture series are available to all students free of charge. If you are interested in attending a lecture, please get your ticket from the Student Activities Office, Room 107. Each student is allowed only one free ticket per lecture. Also, visit the Student Activities Office to see a schedule of local field trips, student social hours, and other upcoming events.

The Counseling[1] Office, Room 109 is open Monday through Thursday from 3:00 to 9:00 P.M. Assistance is available for choosing classes, making future educational plans, and searching for employment.

Changes in your class schedule may be made during the first week of the semester only. Class change forms are available in the Counseling Office. You must obtain the instructor's signature to change classes.

---

[1] *British: Counselling*

The passage mentions several different offices at the school. Which office would you visit in the following circumstances? You may use any office more than once.

On lines 14–20 on your answer sheet write:

A	if you would visit the office in Room 103.
B	if you would visit the office in Room 105.
C	if you would visit the office in Room 107.
D	if you would visit the office in Room 109.

1 You are looking for a job.

2 You want to attend a lecture.

3 You have decided not to take a class and you want your money back.

4 You have decided not to take a class and you want to take another class instead.

5 You need to buy books for your classes.

6 You want to visit a nearby museum with other students.

7 You are trying to decide which classes to take.

Questions 8–14

Read the text below and answer Questions 8–14.

Department of Motor Vehicles
Applying for a Driver's License[1]

The Department of Motor Vehicles (DMV) is located on the fourth floor of City Hall. Business hours are Monday through Thursday 9:00 A.M. to 5:30 P.M. and Friday 12 noon to 8:30 P.M. Closed on holidays.

New Drivers
The fee for a first-time driver's license is $100, payable by check or credit card. You must take both a written test and a road test. Study manuals for the written test are available at the General Information desk in Room 400. Call the General Information desk at 473-555-7839 to make an appointment to take your tests. When you arrive for your appointment, you will take the written test first and then the road test. If you fail the written test, a thirty-day wait is required before taking the test again. You will not be permitted to take the road test until you have passed the written test. If you fail the road test, you must show a certificate of completion of a driver's education course given by an accredited institution before retaking the test. Driving courses are offered by the DMV. Ask for a course schedule at the General Information desk.

---

[1]*British: Licence*

First-time applicants are required to present a valid form of identification with a photograph such as a passport, student identification card, work identification card, or military registration card when applying for a license. Citizens of other countries are asked to present a current visa in addition to one of the above-mentioned forms of identification.

License Renewals

You must renew a license no more than six months after the expiration date to avoid having to retake the written and road tests. You can renew your current driver's license in person or online. Bring your license and $65 cash or a check made out to the Department of Motor Vehicles to Room 405 during business hours. Credit cards are also accepted. License renewals can be made online at the DMV website. A credit card is required for online payment.

*Complete each sentence with the correct ending, **A–L**, from the box below. Write the correct letter, **A–L**, on lines 8–14 on your answer sheet.*

8 People who work during the day can

9 People who fail the written test must

10 People who fail the road test must

11 People from other countries have to

12 People who want to renew their license can

13 People who apply for their first license must

14 People whose license has been invalid for a year have to

A	present their passport.
B	wait a month before retaking the test.
C	sign up for a course at the DMV.
D	make an appointment before 9 A.M.
E	show a valid visa.
F	retake the written and road tests.
G	visit the office on Friday.
H	visit the DMV website.
I	show a work or student I.D. card.
J	take a driver's education course.
K	pay $100.
L	get a study manual from the DMV.

SECTION 2 QUESTIONS 15–27

*You are advised to spend 20 minutes on **Questions 15–27**.*

Questions 15–20

*The following reading passage has six sections, **A–F**. Choose the correct heading for each section from the list of headings below. Write the correct number, **i–viii**, on lines 15–20 on your answer sheet. There are more headings than sections, so you will not use them all.*

LIST OF HEADINGS

i	Find Places for Everything
ii	Organize[1] Your Mail
iii	Empty Your Desk
iv	Follow a Schedule
v	Maintain Your Files
vi	Why Is it Important?
vii	Categorize[2] Supplies and Papers
viii	Make It a Habit

15 Section A

16 Section B

17 Section C

18 Section D

19 Section E

20 Section F

Organizing Your Desk

Follow these easy steps to a clutter-free desk:

A

The best way to begin is with a clean slate. Remove everything from the top of the desk—office supplies, documents, computer, printer—everything. Then move on to the drawers. Take out everything, then wipe down all surfaces with a damp cloth. Now all is clean and you are ready to start anew.

B

Next, take all those supplies and materials and sort through them. Group similar items together. For example, you might have a pile for small supplies such as paper clips and rubber bands, one for filing materials such as folders and labels, one for

---

[1] *British: Organise*
[2] *British: Categorise*

paperwork pertaining to current projects and another for paperwork to be filed, and so on. Group the items in a way that makes sense to you and the way you work.

C

Now, create an appropriate place for each group of items. A few items can be kept on the desktop, such as a pencil holder or a mail tray, but try to keep the desktop as clear as possible. Office supply stores sell a variety of trays, boxes, and other containers that are handy for storing everything from paper clips to large documents. They will help you keep both the drawers and the desktop organized.

D

Now you have completed the most important steps. Everything on your desk is organized. How will you keep it that way? The best way is to follow a routine. After you have finished using the paper clips or the scissors, put them back in their place. As soon as mail arrives on your desk, attend to it instead of letting it pile up. By developing regular practices like these, you will find it much easier to keep your desk organized.

E

Even when you have become accustomed to the routine of putting everything back in its place after use, you may still find that over time the organization starts to break down. This is why it is a good idea to develop a schedule. If you spend a short while reorganizing your desk at the end of every week or every month, you can keep the clutter from becoming overwhelming.

F

It is worth the small amount of time and effort it takes to keep your desk organized. Why? Psychologists tell us that an organized work space leads to more efficient and productive work.

Questions 21–27

Read the text below and answer Questions 21–27.

Telecommuting

Telecommuting, defined as working from home at least part of the time, is an increasingly common way to work. It has many benefits for employees. The fact that a telecommuter does not have to spend time each day traveling[1] to and from work is one obvious advantage. Working from home can mean significant savings in time and money that was formerly spent on daily travel. The telecommuter no longer has to spend part of his or her salary just to get to work in order to earn that salary. Not having to deal with traffic, bus schedules, or other logistics of travel also saves the telecommuter a good deal of unnecessary stress. As a result, the telecommuter can approach work with more energy and more positive feelings. There can

---

[1] *British: travelling*

also be a similar positive effect on the telecommuter's personal life, as there will be more energy and time left to devote to family.

Telecommuting is not for everyone. It works best for people who are able to manage their own time and work independently. Unfortunately, even the most independent worker can start to feel isolated over time. This can be managed, however, by creating a schedule that balances work hours spent at home with work hours spent at the office. Many telecommuters, for example, go into the office periodically in order to attend staff meetings or work with colleagues. Another issue many telecommuters face is the distractions of home life. It can be hard to concentrate on work when family members are demanding attention. Therefore, it is important for telecommuters to establish a work plan that is satisfactory to all members of the family. In addition, some telecommuters find that spending their workday at home results in higher costs for electricity and heating. They may also have new expenses, such as paying for an Internet connection, that they did not have before.

Questions 21–24

*Choose **FOUR** letters, **A–G**. Write the correct letter on lines 21–24 on your answer sheet.*
*Which **FOUR** of the following advantages of telecommuting are mentioned in the passage?*

A reduced travel expenses

B salary increases

C a better employer–employee relationship

D more time to spend with the family

E a more relaxed life

F more time for personal business

G an improved attitude toward work

Questions 25–27

*Choose **THREE** letters, **A–E**. Write the correct letter on lines 25–27 on your answer sheet.*
*Which **THREE** of the following disadvantages of telecommuting are mentioned in the passage?*

A feeling lonely

B missed staff meetings

C interruptions of work

D problems with colleagues

E more expenses at home

SECTION 3   *QUESTIONS 28–40*

*You are advised to spend 20 minutes on Questions **28–40**, which are based on the reading passage below.*

The Power of Earthquakes

Earthquakes have inspired both fear and curiosity in people throughout history. While ancient peoples used myths to explain earthquakes, modern scientists have developed the theory of plate tectonics. According to this theory, the Earth's surface is broken into many pieces that can move against each other, causing tremors at the Earth's surface. To better understand these events, scientists have developed sophisticated equipment to measure, record, and even begin to predict future earthquakes. While the scientists of today may understand a great deal more than our ancestors did, they also recognize that there is still much to learn about the destructive powers held deep within the Earth.

Before scientific explanations were established, many cultures explained earthquakes by attributing them to the movements of mythical creatures, such as frogs, turtles, and even flea-infested dogs. Japanese mythology tells of a great catfish guarded by the deity Kashima. When Kashima let his guard down, the catfish thrashed about, causing the Earth to tremble. In India, myths tell of the Earth being held upon the shoulders of an elephant that shook its head when tired. The Greeks believed that the shaking of the Earth was the rumbling of the god Poseidon's horses traveling through the skies or across the Earth. Or it was caused by Poseidon pounding his trident on the ground. The number and variety of these mythological explanations for earthquakes show how important it has always been to people everywhere to understand what causes the mysterious shakings of the Earth.

Beginning in the early 1960s, many in the scientific community began espousing the theory of plate tectonics, which explains that the surface of the Earth, the crust, is broken into many pieces called tectonic plates. Some of these plates are extremely large, such as the Eurasian Plate, on which sits most of Europe and Asia. Others are smaller, such as the Caribbean Plate, which is mostly underwater in the Caribbean Sea. These plates float on the Earth's mantle, a bed of molten rock called magma. Deeper forces inside the Earth's core heat this magma and cause it to flow underneath the plates, pushing the plates. The tension created at the boundaries of opposing plates can often become strong enough to snap them past each other, sometimes with the violent force that we know as an earthquake.

Scientists describe the movement of the plates in relation to each other in three principal ways. First, when two plates are forced into each other, one plate slides below the other. This is known as a *convergent boundary*. As the lower plate goes down, the upper plate often rises, forming mountains. The Himalayas, for example, were formed by the Indian Plate crashing into the Eurasian Plate. The second type of boundary is where two plates move apart from each other. This is known as a *divergent boundary*. An example of this is the Mid-Atlantic Rift, found at the bottom of the Atlantic Ocean. At this boundary, the North American Plate and the Eurasian plate are being forced apart, at an average rate of 2.5 centimeters[1] per year. The third type is a *transform boundary*, where the edges of two plates slide in opposite directions parallel to each other. When the pressure between these plates is great enough, they snap violently past each other. This type of interaction between plates is the cause of many of the earthquakes felt in California.

Seismologists, the scientists who study earthquakes, use a device called a seismograph to measure the force of earthquakes and tremors. The most sophisticated of these are capable of measuring even the slightest tremor and locating its origin. The measuring system most commonly used is called the Richter Scale. It was invented in 1935 by a seismologist named Charles F. Richter. Because the difference in power between small and large earthquakes is so great, he developed a logarithmic scale in which an increase of one on the scale represents a tenfold increase in power. This means that an earthquake with a magnitude of 4.0, which would be easily felt at the Earth's surface, is ten times more powerful than a magnitude 3.0 quake and 100 times more powerful than a magnitude 2.0 quake, which often goes unnoticed. The data the scientists collect allow them not only to document past earthquakes, but to learn to predict future events.

While scientists today know much more about earthquakes than ever, there is still much to be learned. Seismologists have helped us understand more about how earthquakes happen and why they occur in some parts of the world but not others. All of this knowledge informs us about our Earth and protects us from some of the potential dangers. There are still, however, many forces in the Earth that we do not understand, with the potential to move, shake, and reshape the world.

---

[1] *British: centimetres*

Questions 28–33

*Choose the correct letter, **A**, **B**, or **C**.*

28 Modern scientists are

    A uncertain about the cause of earthquakes.
    B able to forecast some earthquakes.
    C more curious about earthquakes than their ancestors were.

29 In ancient times, people explained earthquakes by

    A telling stories.
    B developing scientific theories.
    C watching the reactions of animals.

30 Kashima was a

    A king.
    B catfish.
    C god.

31 The ancient Greeks believed that earthquakes were caused by a god's

    A horses.
    B elephants.
    C frogs.

32 The quantity and diversity of explanations for earthquakes from ancient cultures show that

    A ancient people were not capable of understanding natural forces.
    B people have always been interested in earthquakes.
    C earthquakes were more common in ancient times.

33 The Caribbean Plate

    A sits next to a convergent boundary.
    B forms part of the Mid-Atlantic Rift.
    C lies mostly beneath the ocean.

General Training Module–Practice Test 5

Questions 34–40

*Complete each sentence with the correct ending from the box. Write the correct letter, **A–K**, on lines 34–40 on your answer sheet.*

34 A place where two plates slide in opposite directions is called

35 Tectonic plates lie on

36 An earthquake measuring 4.0 is ten times more powerful than

37 The Himalayas were caused by

38 The Mid-Atlantic Rift is an example of

39 A tectonic plate is

40 The machine used to measure the strength of earthquakes is known as

A	a transform boundary.
B	a seismograph.
C	an unnoticed tremor.
D	an earthquake measuring 2.0.
E	a logarithmic scale.
F	a divergent boundary.
G	a magnitude 3.0 earthquake.
H	a layer of magma.
I	a collision between two plates.
J	a piece of the Earth's crust.
K	a convergent boundary.

General Training Module
Practice Test 5

Candidate Name and Number: _____

INTERNATIONAL ENGLISH LANGUAGE TESTING SYSTEM

GENERAL TRAINING WRITING

TIME 1 HOUR

Instructions to Candidates

Do not open this booklet until you are told to do so.

Write your name and candidate number in the space at the top of this page.

All answers must be written on the separate answer booklet provided. (The answer sheet can be found beginning on page 362.)

Do not remove the booklet from the examination room.

Information for Candidates

There are **2** tasks on this question paper.

You must do **both** tasks.

Under-length answers will be penalized.[1]

---

[1] *British: penalised*

WRITING TASK 1

You should spend about 20 minutes on this task. Write at least 150 words. You do NOT need to write any addresses. Begin your letter as follows:

Dear _____,

You have decided to leave your current job and look for a new one.

Write a letter to a friend. In your letter

- explain why you want to leave your current job
- what kind of job you are looking for
- ask for some help or advice

WRITING TASK 2

You should spend about 40 minutes on this task. Write at least 250 words.

Write about the following topic:

These days, many people are interested in buying organic food even though it is often more expensive than conventionally produced food.

What are some reasons that people prefer organic food? Do you think it is important to buy organic food despite the higher price? Give reasons for your answer and include any relevant examples from your own knowledge or experience.

Practice Test 5–General Training Module
IELTS READING ANSWER SHEET

1. _____

2. _____

3. _____

4. _____

5. _____

6. _____

7. _____

8. _____

9. _____

10. _____

11. _____

12. _____

13. _____

14. _____

15. _____

16. _____

17. _____

18. _____

19. _____

20. _____

21. _____

22. _____

23. _____

24. _____

25. _____

26. _____

27. _____

28. _____

29. _____

30. _____

31. _____

32. _____

33. _____

34. _____

35. _____

36. _____

37. _____

38. _____

39. _____

40. _____

Practice Test 5–Answer Sheet

Practice Test 5–General Training Module
WRITING TASK 1

Writing Task 1 *continued*

Practice Test 5–General Training Module
WRITING TASK 2

Writing Task 2 *continued*

Writing Task 2 *continued*

Answer Key

PRACTICE TEST 5–GENERAL TRAINING MODULE

Reading

1. D	11. E	21. A	31. A
2. C	12. H	22. D	32. B
3. A	13. K	23. E	33. C
4. D	14. F	24. G	34. A
5. B	15. iii	25. A	35. H
6. C	16. vii	26. C	36. G
7. D	17. i	27. E	37. I
8. G	18. viii	28. B	38. F
9. B	19. iv	29. A	39. J
10. J	20. vi	30. C	40. B

Answer Explanations

GENERAL TRAINING MODULE—PRACTICE TEST 5

Reading

1. **(D)** The Counseling Office is in Room 109 and has assistance for people searching for employment.

2. **(C)** Tickets for the Friday night lecture series are available in Room 107, the Student Activities Office.

3. **(A)** Students who want to withdraw from a class and get a tuition refund should visit the Registrar's Office in Room 103.

4. **(D)** Class change forms are available in the Counseling Office, Room 109.

5. **(B)** Books are for sale in the Main Office, Room 105.

6. **(C)** Information on field trips is available in the Student Activities Office, Room 107.

7. **(D)** The Counseling Office, Room 109, provides assistance with choosing classes.

8. **(G)** Paragraph 1: Friday is the one day of the week that the office is open until 8:30 in the evening.

9. **(B)** Paragraph 2: "If you fail the written test, a thirty-day wait is required before taking the test again."

10. **(J)** Paragraph 2: "If you fail the road test, you must show a certificate of completion of a driver's education course. . . ."

11. **(E)** Paragraph 3: "Citizens of other countries are asked to present a current visa. . . ."

12. **(H)** Paragraph 4: "License renewals can also be made online at the DMV website."

13. **(K)** Paragraph 2: "The fee for a first-time driver's license is $100. . . ."

14. **(F)** Paragraph 4: "You must renew a license no more than six months after the expiration date to avoid having to retake the written and road tests."

15. *iii.* Section A suggests removing everything from desktop and drawers.

16. *vii.* Section B discusses grouping, or categorizing, desk supplies and paperwork.

17. *i.* Section C discusses creating a place for each group of items.

18. *viii.* Section D discusses a "routine" and "regular practices," that is, habits.

19. *iv.* Section E discusses developing a schedule for reorganizing.

20. *vi.* Section F explains why it is worth the time and effort to keep an organized desk.

21. **(A)** Paragraph 1: "Working from home can mean significant savings in time and money that was formerly spent on daily travel."

22. **(D)** Paragraph 1: There can also be a similar positive effect on the telecommuter's personal life, as there will be more energy and time left to devote to family."

23. **(E)** Paragraph 1: "Not having to deal with traffic, bus schedules, or other logistics of travel also saves the telecommuter a good deal of unnecessary stress."

24. **(G)** Paragraph 1: "As a result, the telecommuter can approach work with more energy and more positive feelings."

25. **(A)** Paragraph 2: "Unfortunately, even the most independent worker can start to feel isolated over time."

26. **(C)** Paragraph 2: "It can be hard to concentrate on work when family members are demanding attention."

27. **(E)** Paragraph 2: "In addition, some telecommuters find that spending their workday at home results in higher costs for electricity and heating. They may also have new expenses, such as paying for an Internet connection. . . ."

28. **(B)** Paragraph 1: "scientists have developed sophisticated equipment to measure, record, and even begin to predict future earthquakes." Choice (A) is contradicted by the discussion of the theory of plate tectonics. Choice (C) is incorrect because there is nothing in the paragraph to suggest that any one group of people is more curious than another.

29. **(A)** Paragraph 1: "ancient peoples used myths to explain earthquakes." *Myths* are *stories*. Choice (B) is how earthquakes are explained in modern times. Choice (C) is not mentioned.

30. **(C)** According to paragraph 2, Kashima is a *deity*, that is, a god. Choice (A) is plausible but is not mentioned. Choice (B) is the animal that appears in the myth of Kashima.

31. **(A)** Paragraph 2: "The Greeks believed that the shaking of the Earth was the rumbling of the god Poseidon's horses. . . ." Choices (B) and (C) are other animals mentioned in the discussion of myths.

32. **(B)** Paragraph 2: "The number and variety of these mythological explanations. . .show how important it has always been to people everywhere to understand what causes the mysterious shakings of the Earth." Choices (A) and (C) are not mentioned.

33. **(C)** Paragraph 3: "the Caribbean Plate, which is mostly underwater in the Caribbean Sea." Choices (A) and (B) refer to other geological features mentioned in the passage.

34. **(A)** Paragraph 4: "The third type is a *transform boundary*, where the edges of two plates slide in opposite directions parallel to each other."

35. **(H)** Paragraph 3: "These plates float on the Earth's mantle, a bed of molten rock called magma."

36. **(G)** Paragraph 5: "an earthquake with a magnitude of 4.0, which would be easily felt at the Earth's surface, is ten times more powerful than a magnitude 3.0 quake. . . ."

37. **(I)** Paragraph 4: "The Himalayas, for example, were formed by the Indian Plate crashing into the Eurasian Plate."

38. **(F)** Paragraph 4: "The second type of boundary is where two plates move apart from each other. This is known as a *divergent boundary*. An example of this is the Mid-Atlantic Rift, found at the bottom of the Atlantic Ocean."

39. **(J)** Paragraph 3: "the surface of the Earth, the crust, is broken into many pieces, called tectonic plates"

40. **(B)** Paragraph 5: "Seismologists, the scientists who study earthquakes, use a device called a seismograph to measure the force of earthquakes and tremors."

Writing

These are models. Your answers will vary. See page vi in the Introduction to see the criteria for scoring.

WRITING TASK 1

[NOTE: Even though this is a personal letter, you should not use contractions on the Writing tasks in the test.]

Dear Sam,

I am writing to let you know about my current job situation, hoping that you can give me some advice. I have decided to leave my current position at the Acme Company. I have worked there for several years now, and I think I have advanced as far as possible in this company. I would like to work at a larger company where there are more opportunities for advancement.

As you know, my most recent position at Acme has been as an assistant in the Human Resources Department. I have learned a great deal about this type of work and am very interested in it. I am hoping to find a similar sort of position at a larger company. I do not mind starting at a new company at the same level as I am working at now, as long as I feel there are good opportunities to move up before too long. Since you have a lot of experience in this field, I was hoping that you could help me identify some companies that might be a good fit for me. I would also appreciate some help with my résumé, if you do not mind my asking. I hope to hear from you soon.

Your friend,
Jane

WRITING TASK 2

There are two main reasons people prefer organic food: Organic food is better for our health, and it is better for the environment. Certainly, organic food costs more than conventionally produced food, but considering its benefits, it is well worth the price.

People who buy organic food know how good it is for our health. Conventionally produced food has many additives. For example, fruits and vegetables are grown with the use of pesticides and herbicides. These poisons stay on our food, and we ingest them when we eat. Over the years, this can cause serious health problems such as cancer. Cows on conventional farms are fed hormones and antibiotics. We also ingest these things when we drink milk and eat beef. Organic food, on the other hand, does not contain any kind of poisons or additives. It is clean and fresh and good for our health.

In addition to being good for our health, organic food is good for the environment. The pesticides and herbicides that are used with conventionally produced food poison the environment as well as our bodies. These things can harm insects and other animals and deplete the soil of nutrients. Organic food, on the other hand, is produced in harmony with the environment. Organic farming methods help build up healthy soil and use natural controls for insects and weeds.

Organic food can be expensive. However, there is nothing more important than our health or the natural environment we live in. If we spend a little more money so we can eat organic food, then we just spend a little less money on other, less important things. Buying organic food is a good use of our money.

GENERAL TRAINING MODULE
READING
WRITING
PRACTICE TEST 6

General Training Module
Practice Test 6

Candidate Name and Number: _____

INTERNATIONAL ENGLISH LANGUAGE TESTING SYSTEM

GENERAL TRAINING READING

TIME 1 HOUR

Instructions to Candidates

Do not open this booklet until you are told to do so.

Write your name and candidate number in the space at the top of this page.

Start at the beginning of the test and work through it.

You should answer all questions.

If you cannot do a particular question, leave it and go on to the next. You can return to it later.

All answers must be written on the Answer Sheet. (The answer sheet can be found on page 389.)

Do not remove the booklet from the examination room.

Information for Candidates

There are **40** questions on this question paper.

The test is divided as follows:

Section 1	Questions 1–14
Section 2	Questions 15–27
Section 3	Questions 28–40

SECTION 1   *QUESTIONS 1–14*

You are advised to spend 20 minutes on **Questions 1–14**.

Questions 1–7

Read the text below and answer Questions 1–7.

A

Good Deal Car Rentals

Have we got a deal for you!

Compact cars only $375/week

We offer:

- The lowest rates in town
- Two convenient locations
- Payment by cash or credit card

To reserve your car, call us at:
   432-555-0943 (airport)
   432-555-7118 (train station)

Open from 7:30 A.M. to 9:30 P.M.
every day of the week

B

Fast 'n Frugal Car Rental

- Compact and mid-sized cars
- Vans
- Small trucks
- Rent by the day, week, or month

We have the best rates in town. Compact cars start at $350/week.

Special prices for National Car Club members—10 percent off our usual low prices!

Reserve your vehicle today by calling our convenient downtown location:
   921-555-9642

Open 6:30 A.M. to 10:30 P.M. every day.
Closed Sundays.

All major credit cards accepted. No cash, please.

C

Dollar Dan's Rent-a-Car

- Conveniently located next to the Hilltown Hotel
- Guaranteed lowest prices around. Compact cars only $35/day.

We have hundreds of compact, mid-sized, and luxury cars to choose from, all right on our lot. So come on down and pick out your car. There's no need to reserve a car at Dollar Dan's because we guarantee that we'll always have a car available for you.

- Visit us anytime. We're open twenty-four hours/day, seven days/week.
- Payment by credit card only.

---

*Look at the three advertisements for car rental agencies, **A–C**. Answer the questions by writing the letter of the appropriate car rental agency, **A–C**, on lines 1–7 on your answer sheet.*

Which car rental agency

1 has the lowest price for a compact car?

2 accepts payments in cash?

3 offers a discount?

4 is convenient for people arriving by plane?

5 is always open?

6 does not require a reservation?

7 has vehicles suitable for moving furniture?

Questions 8–11

Read the text below and answer Questions 8–11.
The following text has four sections A–D. Choose the correct heading for each section from the list of headings below. Write the appropriate numbers, i–vi, on lines 8–11 on your answer sheet. There are more headings than sections, so you won't need to use them all.

LIST OF HEADINGS

i	Instructor's Teaching Schedule
ii	Assignments
iii	Assistance Outside Class
iv	Using the Language Lab
v	Class Schedule
vi	Grading

8 Section A

9 Section B

10 Section C

11 Section D

Spanish for Health-care Workers
Instructor: Dr. Lucia Mendez

A
Classes are held in Room 203. The class meets twice weekly, Monday and Wednesday evenings from 6:30 to 8:15 P.M. You are expected to attend every class and to arrive on time. Please speak with the instructor about any unavoidable absences.

B
We will use the text *Spanish for Health-care Workers*. Students are required to read one or more chapters before each class (see reading schedule below). In addition, each student will prepare an oral presentation to give to the class before the end of the semester. The Language Laboratory, Room 302, is open Monday–Friday from 9:30 A.M. until 8:30 P.M. In addition to attending class, each student must complete a weekly exercise in the lab.

C
There will be four to five quizzes throughout the semester in addition to a midterm and a final exam. Missed quizzes or exams will count against your grade; there will be no make-ups. The breakdown for calculating each student's final mark is as follows: quizzes and exams—50 percent; oral presentation—30 percent; class participation—20 percent. A grade of B or higher is required to pass this class.

D

If you need extra help or would like to discuss anything with the instructor, my office hours (Room 320) are 5:00–6:30 on Mondays and Wednesdays. The Language Lab staff is also available to help you with your assignments. In addition, individual Spanish tutors are available. Please talk to the staff in the Language Lab for more information about tutors.

Questions 12–14

*Choose the correct answer. Write the correct letter, **A–C**, on lines 12–14 on your answer sheet.*

12 Which of the following people would be most interested in this class?

A A nurse
B A tourist
C A literature student

13 What is located in Room 302?

A The classroom
B The language lab
C The instructor's office

14 How many exams will there be?

A One
B Two
C Four or five

SECTION 2 QUESTIONS 15–27

*You are advised to spend 20 minutes on **Questions 15–27**.*

Questions 15–20

Read the text below and answer Questions 15–20.

Asking for a Raise

If you are thinking about asking for a raise in salary, there are several things to keep in mind. First, consider whether you deserve a higher salary. You probably do, but you should be able to explain exactly why to your boss. Sit down and make a list of your job accomplishments. Be as specific as possible. For example, think about important projects you have worked on, things you have done to improve the organization[1] of work in your department, or how your efforts have brought more money to the company. Also include any professional development opportunities you have taken advantage of recently and be ready to explain how they have improved your performance on the job. By going through the process of listing your accomplishments, not only will you be better prepared when you meet with your boss, you will also feel more confident that you deserve what you are asking for.

Bear in mind that salary levels are based not only on performance but also on the market for your particular skills. Before you ask for a raise, you will need to do some research. You should investigate the industry standards for salaries for people in similar positions with similar levels of experience. This will help you determine what would be a reasonable amount of money to ask for. Your initial request should actually be slightly higher than the amount you want in order to leave some room for negotiation. Then, if you have to go lower than this amount, you still end up with something close to what you want.

A crucial point is the timing of your request. If you have recently been given new responsibilities, it makes sense to ask for a higher level of compensation. On the other hand, if the company is going through financial difficulties, a request for more money will probably not be met with a favorable[2] response. It would be better to wait until the company is in a better financial position. Finally, there is one thing you should never do: Never give personal reasons for wanting a higher salary. Your need to pay your child's college tuition or buy a bigger house is of no concern to your boss. Your salary level should be based on professional considerations alone, and that is where you need to keep the conversation.

---

[1] *British: organisation*
[2] *British: favourable*

*Choose the correct answer. Write the correct letter, **A–C**, on lines 15–20 on your answer sheet.*

15 Before asking for a salary increase, you should

    A send your boss a list of your accomplishments.
    B take some professional development courses.
    C write down all the reasons you deserve a raise.

16 Preparing yourself before talking with your boss will help you

    A get the highest raise possible.
    B feel more self-assured.
    C improve your job performance.

17 You should find out

    A salaries of other people in your field.
    B how much money your boss can offer you.
    C what job openings are available in your company.

18 You should ask for

    A slightly more money than you want.
    B the exact amount of money that you want.
    C a little less money than you want.

19 A good time to ask for a salary raise is

    A when your boss is in a favorable mood.
    B before discussing financial records.
    C soon after you have taken on new duties.

20 While negotiating a salary raise, it is a good idea to

    A discuss professional topics only.
    B mention your financial needs.
    C ask your boss about his or her family.

Questions 21–27

Read the text below and answer Questions 21–27.

Hanson, Inc.   **Employee Manual**

Chapter V: Employee Benefits

Leave

All full-time employees are entitled to a minimum of two weeks of annual leave time. Employees who have completed five years at Hanson are entitled to three weeks of annual leave. After completing ten years at Hanson, employees may have four weeks of annual leave. In order to take advantage of annual leave time, the employee must complete the Request for Annual Leave Form and submit it to his or her supervisor a minimum of thirty days in advance. The supervisor has the final decision about whether to grant the leave as requested. Any annual leave days not used in a calendar year may be rolled over and added to the leave days for the following year. In addition to annual leave, all full-time employees are entitled to ten personal leave days per year. Personal leave days must be used within the calendar year, or they will be forfeited. Part-time employees are entitled to five personal leave days per year.

Health Insurance

Employees may choose to sign up for a company-sponsored health plan. Complete information on the available plans can be requested from the Human Resources Department. Health benefits are also provided for the employee's spouse and children. The company pays 50 percent of the monthly premiums, with the other 50 percent being deducted from each paycheck. Part-time employees are also eligible for the company-sponsored health plans; the company pays 25 percent of the premiums.

Retirement

Employees may determine how much they wish to contribute to the company retirement fund, up to 5 percent of their salary. Contributions will be deducted from each paycheck. The company will contribute an equal amount to each employee's retirement fund. This benefit is available to both full-time and part-time employees.

Do the following statements agree with the information given in the text about employee benefits? On lines 21–27 on your answer sheet, write:

TRUE	if the statement agrees with the information
FALSE	if the statement contradicts the information
NOT GIVEN	if there is no information on this

21 All full-time employees are entitled to three weeks of annual leave.

22 Annual leave must be requested a month in advance.

23 Annual leave for part-time employees is half that of full-time employees.

24 Personal leave days not used before the end of the year will be lost.

25 The company pays half the monthly insurance charges for full-time employees.

26 Part-time employees do not receive health benefits.

27 Employees must contribute 5 percent of their salary to the retirement fund.

SECTION 3   QUESTIONS 28–40

*You are advised to spend 20 minutes on **Questions 28–40**, which are based on the reading passage below.*

Green Energy

As energy prices rise and the effects of greenhouse gas emissions become more widespread, people everywhere are becoming increasingly concerned about using fossil fuels. More and more people are turning to so-called "green technologies" as a way to reduce dependence on nonrenewable fossil fuels. The ideal alternative energy source would be sustainable (the supply will not be exhausted), clean (no emissions), and reliable. The three most popular alternative energy sources are geothermal power, solar power, and wind power.

Since geothermal energy taps heat from the earth, its resources range from water found just below the surface of the earth, to hot water and hot rock found a few miles below the surface, to even deeper rock of extremely high temperatures. In a process similar to drilling for oil, wells as deep as a mile or more can be drilled into underground reservoirs to tap steam and hot water that are used to run turbines and create energy. Power companies can then transmit this energy over power lines.

Geothermal power on a smaller scale can be used for heating and cooling houses or commercial buildings. Geothermal heat pumps, also known as ground-source heat pumps, rely on the fact that the earth beneath the surface remains at a relatively constant temperature throughout the year. Like a cave, the ground is warmer than the air above it during the winter and cooler in the summer. The geothermal heat pump transfers the heat stored in the earth into the building during the winter, and transfers it out of the building and into the ground during the summer. The ground, in other words, acts as a heat source in winter and a heat sink in summer. While geothermal heat pumps are an emissions-free and reliable source of energy, the biggest disadvantage is that such systems are expensive to install.

Solar energy has come a long way from the clunky boxes of the 1970s. Today, solar energy is commonly collected by sleek and efficient photovoltaic (PV) panels. The photovoltaic cells convert sunlight directly into electricity and are made of semiconductors such as crystalline silicon or other thin-film materials. The benefits of solar power vary according to how much exposure a given building has to the sun. However, one does not need to live in the desert to take advantage of solar power. Cloudy Germany is the worldwide leader in the use of solar power.

Solar power is not as pricey as geothermal power, but having a panel professionally installed can still be costly. Some enterprising home-owners reduce the initial costs by purchasing inexpensive kits and setting up the system on their own. The biggest disadvantage of a solar power system is its dependence on the amount of sunlight collected, but some cutting-edge panels can generate energy even in the rain.

Wind power is created when wind is used to generate mechanical power or electricity. Most wind turbines convert the wind's kinetic energy into mechanical power. The wind turns the blades, which spin a shaft connected to a generator. A generator then converts this mechanical power into electricity. A group of wind turbines can produce electricity and feed it into the utility grid, where it is sent through transmission lines to homes and businesses. Like solar and geothermal energy, wind is a renewable resource that produces no emissions.

Small wind energy systems can be used by homes, farms, or communities. Such systems can be connected to the larger electrical grid or used for stand-alone energy generation—a particularly attractive option for anyone living far from power company lines. A grid-connected wind turbine can reduce one's reliance on the power company for electricity . If the turbine cannot deliver the needed energy, the power company then makes up the difference. However, in order to take advantage of wind energy, a turbine must be in an area with average wind speed of at least 10 miles an hour, and such systems can be very expensive.

Whether a given home or business uses wind, solar, or geothermal power depends on a variety of economic and environmental factors. However, experts agree that investing in alternative energy now—whether by individuals or power companies—will pay dividends in the future.

Questions 28–30

Complete the summary below. Choose **NO MORE THAN TWO WORDS** *from the passage for each answer.*

Write your answers on lines 28–30 on your answer sheet.

These days, people are interested in reducing their consumption of

28 _____. They are looking at sources of **29** _____

to supply their power needs. People want sources that are **30** _____,

do not cause pollution, and can be consistently depended on.

Questions 31–33

Which of the following facts about geothermal energy are mentioned in the passage? Choose **THREE** *answers from the list below and write the correct letters,* **A–E**, *on lines 31–33 on your answer sheet.*

A is easiest to use where there is a plentiful supply of groundwater

B is used to run power plants

C costs a good deal of money to set up

D requires electricity to power the heat pump

E is used for cooling as well as heating buildings

Questions 34–36

Which of the following facts about solar energy are mentioned in the passage? Choose **THREE** *answers from the list below and write the correct letters,* **A–E**, *on lines 34–36 on your answer sheet.*

A can be used even in areas without intense sunlight

B the panels are usually installed on the roof of the house

C does not have to be installed by a professional

D the amount of power generated fluctuates with the amount of exposure to the sun

E is often used by farmers to power electric fences

Questions 37–40

Which of the following facts about wind energy are mentioned in the passage? Choose **FOUR** *answers from the list below and write the correct letters,* **A–G**, *on lines 37–40 on your answer sheet.*

A wind turbines are considered unsightly by many people

B is used by individual home-owners as well as by power companies

C the energy that it generates cannot be stored for later use

D must be installed in an area that receives a certain amount of wind

E wind turbines create a lot of noise

F can be used in conjunction with electricity supplied by a power company

G is as clean a source of energy as geothermal and solar systems

General Training Module
Practice Test 6

Candidate Name and Number: _____

INTERNATIONAL ENGLISH LANGUAGE TESTING SYSTEM

GENERAL TRAINING WRITING

TIME 1 HOUR

Instructions to Candidates

Do not open this booklet until you are told to do so.

Write your name and candidate number in the space at the top of this page.

All answers must be written on the separate answer booklet provided. (The answer sheets can be found beginning on page 390.)

Do not remove the booklet from the examination room.

Information for Candidates

There are **2** tasks on this question paper.

You must do **both** tasks.

Under-length answers will be penalized.[1]

---

[1] *British: penalised*

WRITING TASK 1

You should spend about 20 minutes on this task. Write at least 150 words. You do NOT need to write any addresses. Begin your letter as follows:

Dear _____ *,*

You are planning a two-week vacation, and you need someone to take care of your house while you are away.

Write a letter to your neighbor.[1] In your letter

- tell your neighbor that you are going away
- ask your neighbor to take care of your house for you
- explain what tasks you would like your neighbor to do

WRITING TASK 2

You should spend about 40 minutes on this task. Write at least 250 words.

Write about the following topic:

Discuss the advantages and disadvantages of high school students having part-time jobs.

Give reasons for your answer and include any relevant examples from your own knowledge or experience.

---

[1]*British: neighbour*

Practice Test 6–General Training Module
IELTS READING ANSWER SHEET

1. _____
2. _____
3. _____
4. _____
5. _____
6. _____
7. _____
8. _____
9. _____
10. _____
11. _____
12. _____
13. _____
14. _____
15. _____
16. _____
17. _____
18. _____
19. _____
20. _____

21. _____
22. _____
23. _____
24. _____
25. _____
26. _____
27. _____
28. _____
29. _____
30. _____
31. _____
32. _____
33. _____
34. _____
35. _____
36. _____
37. _____
38. _____
39. _____
40. _____

Practice Test 6–Answer Sheet

Practice Test 6–General Training Module
WRITING TASK 1

Writing Task 1 *continued*

Practice Test 6–General Training Module
WRITING TASK 2

Writing Task 2 *continued*

Writing Task 2 *continued*

Answer Key

PRACTICE TEST 6—GENERAL TRAINING MODULE

Reading

1. C	12. A	23. Not Given	34. A
2. A	13. B	24. True	35. C
3. B	14. B	25. True	36. D
4. A	15. C	26. False	37. B
5. C	16. B	27. False	38. D
6. C	17. A	28. fossil fuels	39. F
7. B	18. A	29. alternative energy	40. G
8. v	19. C	30. sustainable	
9. ii	20. A	31. B	
10. vi	21. False	32. C	
11. iii	22. True	33. E	

Answer Explanations

GENERAL TRAINING MODULE–PRACTICE TEST 6

Reading

1. **(C)** This agency charges $35 per day, which is $245 per week.

2. **(A)** This agency accepts payment by credit card or cash. The others accept credit cards only.

3. **(B)** This agency offers a 10 percent discount to National Car Club members.

4. **(A)** This agency has a phone number listed for the airport, so we can assume they have an office at the airport.

5. **(C)** This agency is open twenty-four hours a day, seven days a week.

6. **(C)** This agency states: "There's no need to reserve a car . . . ."

7. **(B)** This agency rents vans and small trucks.

8. *v.* Section A explains the days and hours the class meets.

9. *ii.* Section B explains the reading, oral presentation, and language lab assignments.

10. *vi.* Section C explains how the grades are calculated.

11. *iii.* Section D talks about getting help outside of class from the instructor or at the Language Lab.

12. **(A)** The class is for health-care workers, so a nurse would be most interested. Choices (B) and (C) are people who might be interested in a language class, but this class is not intended for them.

13. **(B)** According to section B, the Language Lab is in Room 302. Choice (A) is in Room 203. Choice (C) is in Room 320.

14. **(B)** According to section C, there will be two exams—a midterm and a final. Choice (A) is contradicted by the paragraph. Choice (C) is the number of quizzes, not exams.

15. **(C)** Paragraph 1 mentions listing all your job accomplishments in order to show why you deserve a raise. Choice (A) is confused with the suggestion to make a list of accomplishments, but it is never suggested to share this list with your boss. Choice (B) is confused with the suggestion to include professional development courses taken in the list of accomplishments.

16. **(B)** Paragraph 1 suggests that going over your accomplishments will help you feel more confident. *Confident* means *self-assured.* Choices (A) and (C) use words mentioned in the paragraph, but they are not part of the reason given for preparing ahead of time.

17. **(A)** Paragraph 2: "You should investigate the industry standards for salaries for people in similar positions with similar levels of experience." Choices (B) and (C) are not mentioned.

18. **(A)** Paragraph 2: "Your initial request should actually be slightly higher than the amount you want in order to leave some room for negotiation." Choices (B) and (C) are contradicted by "slightly higher."

19. **(C)** Paragraph 3: "If you have recently been given new responsibilities, it makes sense to ask for a higher level of compensation." Choice (A) repeats the word *favorable.* Choice (B) repeats the word *financial.*

20. **(A)** Paragraph 3: "Your salary level should be based on professional considerations alone, and that is where you need to keep the conversation." Choices (B) and (C) are things that should not be discussed.

21. *False.* Paragraph 1: "All full-time employees are entitled to a minimum of two weeks of annual leave time."

22. *True.* Paragraph 1: "the employee must complete the Request for Annual Leave Form and submit it to his or her supervisor a minimum of thirty days in advance."

23. *Not Given.* There is no information on annual leave for part-time employees.

24. *True.* Paragraph 1: "Personal leave days must be used within the calendar year, or they will be forfeited."

25. *True.* Paragraph 2: "The company pays 50 percent of the monthly premiums . . . ."

26. *False.* Paragraph 2: "Part-time employees are also eligible for the company-sponsored health plans; the company pays 25 percent of the premiums."

27. *False.* Paragraph 3: "Employees may . . . contribute . . . up to 5 percent of their salary." This means they can choose any amount from zero up to 5 percent but no higher.

28. *fossil fuels.* Paragraph 1: "More and more people are turning to so-called 'green technologies' as a way to reduce dependence on nonrenewable fossil fuels."

29. *alternative energy.* Paragraph 1: "The ideal alternative energy source . . . ."

30. *sustainable.* Paragraph 1: "sustainable (the supply will not be exhausted), clean (no emissions), and reliable."

31. **(B)** Paragraph 2: "wells as deep as a mile or more can be drilled into underground reservoirs to tap steam and hot water that are used to run turbines and create energy."

32. **(C)** Paragraph 3: "the biggest disadvantage is that such systems are expensive to install."

33. **(E)** Paragraph 3: "Geothermal power on a smaller scale can be used for heating and cooling houses or commercial buildings."

34. **(A)** Paragraph 4: "However, one does not need to live in the desert to take advantage of solar power. Cloudy Germany is the worldwide leader in the use of solar power."

35. **(C)** Paragraph 5: "Some enterprising home owners reduce the initial costs by purchasing inexpensive kits and setting up the system on their own."

36. **(D)** Paragraph 4: "The benefits of solar power vary according to how much exposure a given building has to the sun."

37. **(B)** Paragraph 6 mentions wind power being used to generate power for the utility grid, and paragraph 7 discusses the use of wind power for individual homes and farms.

38. **(D)** Paragraph 7: "However, in order to take advantage of wind energy, a turbine must be in an area with average wind speed of at least 10 miles an hour . . . ."

39. **(F)** Paragraph 7: "If the turbine cannot deliver the needed energy, the power company then makes up the difference."

40. **(G)** Paragraph 6: "Like solar and geothermal energy, wind is a renewable resource that produces no emissions." This means it is a clean energy source.

Writing

These are models. Your answers will vary. See page vi in the Introduction to see the criteria for scoring.

WRITING TASK 1

[NOTE: Even though this is a personal letter, you should not use contractions on the Writing tasks in the test.]

Dear Joe,

I would like to ask you a big favor. Next Saturday I am leaving on vacation. I will be gone for two weeks. That is a long time to leave my house alone, and I was hoping that you would be able to take care of a few things for me.

The tasks I would like you to do are very simple. The most important thing is to keep an eye on the house and make sure no strangers enter it. If you could take the mail out of the box every day and put it inside the house, that would be very helpful. Also, if it is not too much trouble, I would like to ask you to water the garden if it does not rain. I would be happy to pay you a small amount of money in exchange for your help. Please let me know if you will be able to help me out. Thank you very much.

Your neighbor,
Pat

WRITING TASK 2

[Note: Be consistent with your pronoun choice in the essay. Here, the pronoun used consistently is she. *The writer could have used* he *alone or* he *or* she *to refer to both males and females, respectively.]*

Many families encourage their teenage children to get part-time jobs. Other families prefer their children to focus on schoolwork and friends. There are both benefits and drawbacks to teenagers working while they are still in school.

Having a job helps a teenager become an adult. In the first place, it helps her learn a sense of responsibility. She has to be at work at a certain time and do the job she was hired to do. If she does not, she could lose her job. Earning money also brings responsibility. A working teenager may have to pay for her own clothes, school supplies, and entertainment. She may be saving her money for college or even just to buy something fun that she wants for herself. Whatever she does with her money, earning it and learning to use it responsibly help her mature.

On the other hand, having a job can interfere with other important aspects of the teenage years. A job can distract a teenager's energy and attention from her schoolwork. It can leave her with little time to relax and be with friends. In addition, although learning to be responsible is important, teenagers are also still children. Soon enough they will have the responsibilities of college, a career, and a family to care for. The teenage years may be the last time they have the chance for a carefree life. A job could possibly add too much responsibility at too early an age.

Each family has a different situation, and each teenager is a different person. Teenagers and their families have to evaluate their individual circumstances when deciding whether having a job is a good idea.

AUDIOSCRIPTS for Listening Parts 1–4

PRACTICE TEST 1

Narrator: You will hear a number of different recordings, and you will have to answer questions on what you will hear. There will be time for you to read the instructions and questions, and you will have a chance to check your work. All the recordings will be played once only.

The test is in four sections. Write all of your answers on the test pages. At the end of the test you will be given ten minutes to transfer your answers to an answer sheet.

Now turn to Section 1 on page 5.

Section 1. You will hear a man asking for information about language classes over the phone.

First you have some time to look at Questions 1 to 4 on page 5.

You will see that there is an example that has been done for you. On this occasion only, the conversation relating to this will be played first.

Example

Woman: Good morning. Globetrotters Language School. How may I help you?
Man: Yes, I was wondering if you could give me some information on language classes.

Narrator: The woman answers the phone, "Globetrotters Language School," so the word *Globetrotters* has been written at the top of the form. Now we shall begin. You should answer the questions as you listen, because you will not hear the recording a second time. Listen carefully and answer Questions 1 to 4.

Questions 1 to 4

Woman:	Good morning. Globetrotters Language School. How may I help you?
Man:	Yes, I was wondering if you could give me some information on language classes.
Woman:	Certainly. What language are you interested in studying?
Man:	Well, that's the thing. I'm interested in learning Japanese, but I'd also like to improve my Chinese. I don't know which to study right now.
Woman:	Maybe the class schedule will help you decide. Did you want to study in the morning, afternoon, or evening?
Man:	I work in the evenings, so mornings or afternoons would be best.
Woman:	Then that decides it for you. We offer an advanced Chinese class, but it meets on Wednesday and Friday evenings.
Man:	I couldn't do that. When do the Japanese classes meet?
Woman:	We have beginning Japanese on Tuesday and Thursday mornings, no wait, that's intermediate Japanese. Which level do you want? Advanced?
Man:	No, beginning. Definitely. I know some Chinese and some French, but I'm a real beginner with Japanese.
Woman:	Well then, are you free Monday, Wednesday, and Friday mornings? That's when the beginning Japanese classes meet. We also have intermediate French on Friday mornings.
Man:	I could do those mornings, but I'd prefer afternoon. Don't you have anything in the afternoon?
Woman:	We have intermediate Japanese class on Wednesday and Friday afternoons.
Man:	I really need a beginner class. So I'll take the morning Japanese class. Could you give me an idea of the cost? What would be the tuition for the Japanese class?
Narrator:	Before you hear the rest of the conversation, you have some time to look at Questions 5 to 10 on page 5.
	Now listen and answer questions 5 to 10.

Questions 5 to 10

Woman:	The beginning-level classes meet three times a week, so they cost a bit more than the other levels. For a six-week course, the cost would be $175.
Man:	That's a bit steep.
Woman:	If it's hard for you to pay that much, you could sign up for just four weeks of class and pay $410. Or, you could pay for one week at a time, at $125 a week.
Man:	That comes out to be much more expensive once you add up all the weeks.
Woman:	That's true. You can save money by registering for two levels together. For example, pay for your beginning and intermediate classes now and you'll get twelve weeks of class for just $1,050.

Man:	That's not a bad deal, but I can't come up with that much money at once. I'll just pay for the six-week course.
Woman:	Fine. That class begins next week, so you need to register right away.
Man:	Can't I register over the phone?
Woman:	No, I'm sorry, we don't take phone registrations. What you'll need to do is visit the school office today or tomorrow. Bring a check for the tuition and a photo ID.
Man:	Is that all?
Woman:	Yes, we'll give you a registration form to complete, or you can save time by visiting our website and downloading the form there. Complete it and bring it into the office with your check.
Man:	Great. I'll stop by this afternoon.
Woman:	Fine. When you arrive, ask for Mr. Lindsay. He's in charge of student registration.
Man:	I'm sorry, Mr. who?
Woman:	Mr. Lindsay, spelled L-I-N-D-S-A-Y.
Man:	Thank you for your help.
Woman:	Thank you. We'll look forward to seeing you in class.
Narrator:	That is the end of Section 1. You now have half a minute to check your answers.
	Now turn to Section 2 on page 6.
	Section 2. You will hear a tour guide giving information about a shopping district.
	First, you have some time to look at Questions 11 to 15 on page 6.
	As you listen to the first part of the talk, answer Questions 11 to 15.

Questions 11 to 15

Tour guide:	This afternoon we'll visit the city's shopping district. Several blocks in the area are closed to car traffic, and I know you'll enjoy walking around there. I'd like to give you an overview of the district now since you'll be on your own once we get there.
	You'll see on this map here that the shopping district consists of two streets—Pear Street, which runs north and south, and Cherry Street, which crosses Pear Street right here. Let's start our tour here on Pear Street where the star is. This star marks the Harbor View Bookstore. It's very popular among locals as well as tourists. You can buy a range of books of local interest as well as a variety of magazines and newspapers. It's directly across the street from the City Library, which is also worth a visit. It's in one of the oldest buildings in the city and contains, among other things, an interesting collection of rare books.
	Now, moving up Pear from the bookstore toward Cherry, the next building on the left is the Pear Café. You'll notice it's right on the corner of Pear and Cherry streets. It's a great place to relax

while enjoying a delicious cup of coffee or tea. You can talk with friends or read quietly. They have a variety of books and magazines available.

From the windows of the café, you can look right across Cherry Street for a lovely view of City Gardens. It's a rather small garden, but it contains a variety of exotic plants and flowers.

Let's leave the café and cross Pear Street. On the opposite corner, we're at Caldwell's Clothing Store, which you might also want to visit. They sell both men's and women's fashions from countries around the world.

Continuing down Cherry Street, the next building on the right after Caldwell's is the souvenir shop. Stop in here to get maps and books about the local area, as well as T-shirts and postcards with pictures of the city. Now, we cross Cherry Street and we're at the art gallery, one building down from the corner. Here you can see and, of course, purchase many fine paintings and sculptures by local artists.

Let's keep going down Cherry Street toward the harbor. On the left, right after the gallery, is Harbor Park. It's a lovely place, and it's certainly worth spending some time there.

Narrator:	Before you hear the rest of the talk, you have some time to look at questions 16 to 20 on page 7.
	Now listen and answer questions 16 to 20.

Questions 16 to 20

Harbor Park was built on land donated to the city by Captain Jones, a lifelong resident of this city. Captain Jones designed the park himself, and it was built in 1876. Exactly in the center of the park a statue of Captain Jones was erected, and it's still standing there today. It shows Captain Jones on the bow of his ship.

After viewing the statue, you can follow the path that goes through the woods just behind. It will lead you to a lovely garden, in the middle of which is a fountain. This is a nice place to enjoy a few quiet moments.

If you still feel like walking, continue on to the far end of the garden. There, you'll find a wooden staircase, which will take you down to the harbor. You might enjoy the view of the boats from there. There's also a walking path along the water, which will eventually bring you back up to Cherry Street.

You can see that there's plenty to do in this part of the city. The bus leaves at 1:30.

Narrator:	That is the end of Section 2. You now have half a minute to check your answers.

Now turn to Section 3 on page 7.

Section 3. You will hear a conversation between a university student and a librarian about using the City Archives.

First, you have some time to look at Questions 21 to 24 on page 7.

As you listen to the first part of the conversation, answer Questions 21 to 24.

Questions 21 to 24

Student:	Hello. I was wondering if you could give me some information about using the archives.
Librarian:	I'd be happy to. Are you a resident of the city?
Student:	Actually, I live just outside the city, but I study at the university downtown.
Librarian:	That's fine. All you need to do is show your university identification card and you can use the archives at no charge, as long as your ID card is current, of course.
Student:	Yes, it's valid. So I don't have to pay anything?
Librarian:	No. City residents pay an annual fee, but students can use the archives for free. Everyone else needs to get special permission from the director, but that doesn't apply to you, of course.
Student:	Oh, good. I was also wondering about the schedule. I have classes every day, Monday through Friday, and I also have a part-time job, so I could really only use the archives on weekends.
Librarian.	That's not a problem at all. We're open all weekend; actually the only day we're closed is Monday. So you can come any day, Tuesday through Sunday.
Student:	Are you open in the evenings?
Librarian:	Yes, we're open from 9:30 in the morning until 8:30 in the evening.
Student:	That will fit my schedule well.
Narrator:	Before you hear the rest of the conversation, you have some time to look at Questions 25 to 30 on page 8.
	Now listen and answer Questions 25 to 30.

Questions 25 to 30

Librarian:	Is there something else I can help you with?
Student:	Yes. One thing I'll be needing to see for one of my class projects is old photographs. Do you have photographs of the city in the nineteenth century that I could look at?
Librarian:	Yes, we store all the photographs in the basement. Those stairs over there will take you down to the photography collection. Just tell the librarian there what you're interested in, and he'll help you.
Student:	Those would be nineteenth-century photographs?

Librarian:	Yes, the entire collection is there. Now, if you're interested in seeing documents from the nineteenth century, those are right here on the ground floor.
Student:	I would like to see some of those documents. Does that collection include newspapers, too?
Librarian:	No, all the newspapers from the earliest ones, in the eighteenth century, up to the current time, are on the second floor. Here, let me just give you this map of the archives, and you'll be able to find whatever it is you need.
Student:	Thank you. Oh, I see you have a whole room devoted to maps.
Librarian:	Yes, on the third floor.
Student:	That's great because one thing I need to do is look at how the city has developed over time.
Librarian:	I'm sure you'll find a lot of helpful information there. Of course, some of the maps are several centuries old, so generally visitors are only allowed to see photographic reproductions of them.
Student:	That shouldn't be a problem. What's this on the fourth floor—Ogden's Woolen Mill?
Librarian:	As I'm sure you know, Ogden's Woolen Mill was the major entity responsible for the growth of this city in the nineteenth century. The Ogden heirs gave money for the archives to devote an entire floor to information about the history of the mill.
Student:	Will I be able to find information about the Ogden family there—photographs, personal papers, things like that?
Librarian:	Probably the family photographs are stored downstairs in the photography collection. The personal papers would be on the fifth floor, where we keep all the personal papers of famous residents of our city.
Student:	Thank you so much for your help. I'll be able to do a lot of my research here.
Narrator:	That is the end of Section 3. You now have half a minute to check your answers.
	Now turn to Section 4 on page 8.
	Section 4. You will hear a lecture about wind energy.
	First, you have some time to look at Questions 31 to 33 on page 8.
	Now listen carefully and answer Questions 31 to 33.

Questions 31 to 33

Lecturer:	With the rising cost of fossil fuels, there's a great deal of interest these days in developing alternative sources of energy. Today, I'd like to talk about one of these—wind power. In the past couple of decades, there's been an upsurge of interest in using the wind as a source of energy, but the idea isn't new at all. People have been harnessing the power of the wind for centuries, ever since ancient

peoples first used sailboats. In ancient China, farmers used a rudimentary sort of windmill to pump water. Wind power was used in other parts of the ancient world, as well. In Persia, for example, farmers used wind-powered mills to grind their grain. During the Middle Ages in the Netherlands, people went back to the ancient idea of using the power of the wind to move water. They used windmills to drain lakes, thereby creating more land for farming.

Narrator: Before you hear the rest of the talk, you have some time to look at Questions 34 to 40 on page 9.

Now listen carefully and answer Questions 34 to 40.

Questions 34 to 40

Lecturer: At present, people around the world are using the wind to generate electricity, some old methods, some new. Is this the solution to our modern energy problems? Well, as with anything, there are both advantages and disadvantages to using wind power. Let's take a look at some of the reasons to use wind power. One of the biggest problems with using fuels such as oil and coal is pollution. Wind power, on the other hand, is clean. It causes no pollution and therefore doesn't contribute to global warming. Another great advantage of wind power is that it's a renewable resource. Oil and coal reserves are limited, but we'll never run out of wind. Economics is another reason to use wind power. Using the wind to generate electricity costs less, much less, than running other types of generators. In addition, since wind turbines don't take up much land, the land around them can be used for other purposes, such as farming.

There are disadvantages, however. Even though generating electricity with wind is relatively inexpensive, the technology isn't cheap. The initial costs of setting up wind turbines can be quite high. Another issue is reliability. Wind doesn't blow at a constant strength. Therefore, at times, a lot of electricity can be produced while at others there may be little or none. Wind turbines usually have to be located in rural areas where the land is open. Their distance from cities, where the most electricity is needed, is another issue. Although wind is considered to be a clean source of energy, wind turbines cause their own sort of pollution. Wind turbines are usually placed in high, open areas, where they're easy to be seen. Rural residents often feel that the beautiful local scenery is spoiled by the sight of the wind turbines. In addition, wind turbines aren't quiet. In fact, one wind turbine can produce as much noise as a car traveling at highway speeds.

Narrator: That is the end of Section 4. You now have half a minute to check your answers.

You will now have ten minutes to transfer your answers to the listening answer sheet.

PRACTICE TEST 2

Narrator:	You will hear a number of different recordings, and you will have to answer questions on what you will hear. There will be time for you to read the instructions and questions, and you will have a chance to check your work. All the recordings will be played once only.
	The test is in four sections. Write all of your answers on the test pages. At the end of the test you will be given ten minutes to transfer your answers to an answer sheet.
	Now turn to Section 1 on page 45.
	Section 1. You will hear a woman asking for information over the phone.
	First you have some time to look at questions 1 to 5 on page 45.
	You will see that there is an example that has been done for you. On this occasion only, the conversation relating to this will be played first.

Example

Man:	Good afternoon. Plainfield Community Center.
Woman:	Yes, hi. I'm new in town, and I was curious about the services the Community Center has to offer.
Narrator:	The man answers the phone, "Plainfield Community Center," so the words "Community Center" have been written at the top of the form. Now we shall begin. You should answer the questions as you listen, because you will not hear the recording a second time. Listen carefully and answer Questions 1 to 5.

Questions 1 to 5

Man:	Good afternoon. Plainfield Community Center.
Woman:	Yes, hi. I'm new in town, and I was curious about the services the Community Center has to offer.
Man:	We offer a variety of recreational activities. What were you interested in, in particular?
Woman:	Well, everything, I guess. OK, let's start with kids. I have a teenage son. What activities do you have for teens?
Man:	Right now, during the school year, we have tutoring sessions for children and teens, in all subjects.
Woman:	That would be good. He needs help with algebra.
Man:	We can certainly help with that. Just have him come by any Wednesday or Saturday afternoon. That's when the tutoring sessions are scheduled.
Woman:	Fantastic. What about sports? Do you have sports activities for teens?

Man:	We have tennis lessons on Sunday mornings for teens and Sunday afternoons for adults.
Woman:	Hmmm, I don't think my son would like that, but my husband might. For myself, I'd be more interested in yoga. Do you offer yoga classes?
Man:	We do. Our yoga classes take place on Tuesday and Thursday evenings. We divide it up into several groups, so there's one class for younger children, one for teens, and one for adults.
Woman:	Really? I doubt my husband and son would be interested, but I'd like to sign up for yoga. I also like reading. Do you have any book clubs?
Man:	We have one just about to start. The first meeting will be next Friday morning. It will focus on early twentieth-century novels.
Woman:	Too bad it's Friday morning. I think my son would enjoy it, but of course he's in school at that time.
Man:	Well, actually, that book club is for adults only. We may start one up for teens next summer, but we have nothing for that age group right now.
Woman:	Oh, well. I suppose he has enough to keep him busy for now. Now, what about fees? Do these classes and activities cost anything?
Narrator:	Before you hear the rest of the conversation, you have some time to look at Questions 6 to 10 on page 45.
	Now listen and answer Questions 6 to 10.

Questions 6 to 10

Man:	There's a small charge for non-members for each class. However, they're all free to members. Would you be interested in becoming a member?
Woman:	How much does the membership cost?
Man:	Not much at all. The yearly fee is $75 for individuals and $225 for families.
Woman:	What do I get with the membership?
Man:	You get free access to all classes and activities, and you can use our facilities, like the tennis court, the exercise room, and the meeting room.
Woman:	It's not a bad deal, really. Could you tell me exactly where the center is located?
Man:	It's at 107 [one-oh-seven] Eliot Street.
Woman:	Is that Eliot with two Ls or one L?
Man:	One L. E-L-I-O-T. It's right downtown.
Woman:	I think I know where it is. Do you have free parking?
Man:	Yes. You can park just across the street. There's a garage there.
Woman:	That sounds easy enough. Maybe I'll come in one day next week and sign up for some classes.
Man:	That would be fine, but don't come on Monday because we're closed that day. We're open Tuesday through Sunday.

Woman:	Oh. Thanks for telling me. Maybe I'll stop in on Tuesday then. Can I pay for the classes with a personal check?
Man:	We accept checks and credit cards.
Woman:	OK. Thank you very much. You've been very helpful.
Narrator:	That is the end of Section 1. You now have half a minute to check your answers.

Now turn to Section 2 on page 45.

Section 2. You will hear a hike leader giving information about an upcoming hiking trip.

First, you have some time to look at Questions 11 to 15 on page 45.

As you listen to the first part of the talk, answer Questions 11 to 15.

Questions 11 to 15

Hike leader:	Good evening, everyone. As you know, this is our last meeting before we set off on our annual week-long hiking trip, so tonight I'll be telling you everything you'll need to know to be ready for the trip. Let's talk about equipment first. Having the right equipment is essential for your comfort and safety. First, you'll need a warm and comfortable sleeping bag. However, you won't need to worry about carrying a tent since we'll be sleeping in shelters along the way. Also, part of the fee you've paid for the trip goes toward food, so you won't need to put that on your packing list either. We've found, though, that it's more efficient for each person to bring his or her own dishes, so be sure to pack a plastic bowl, a cup, and a fork, knife, and spoon. That's all you'll need in the way of dishes.
	Perhaps the most important item to put on your list is a comfortable pair of hiking boots. Nothing ruins a hike more than getting blisters and sores from ill-fitting boots. So make sure your boots fit you right. Shoes and sneakers aren't adequate for the type of hiking we'll be doing. Of course, a backpack is necessary for carrying your equipment. Make sure you have one that's lightweight and comfortable to carry. Walking poles have become popular among hikers recently, but we don't recommend them. They can get in the way when too many hikers are using them at once, and some serious injuries have been caused, so it's best to leave those at home.
	Let's see…What else? Oh, yes. Some people have asked me about trail maps. They're available, but you really don't need them, as your hike leaders have scouted out the trail and will be guiding you along the way. And don't forget to bring a warm jacket. You may think you won't need one in this warm summer weather, but remember that

evenings in the mountains can get quite cold. Is there anything else I need to tell you? Oh, yes, your guides will each be carrying a first-aid kit, so that's one less thing for you to pack yourself. Remember, you'll be carrying your backpack all day, so keep your load light and don't overpack.

Narrator: Before you hear the rest of the talk, you have some time to look at Questions 16 to 20 on page 46.

Now listen and answer Questions 16 to 20.

Questions 16 to 20

I know you're all experienced hikers, but it's always worth repeating the rules of the trail since they're so important. These rules are in place for the safety of everyone on the trip. As you know, there'll be a hike leader walking at the head of the line, who will show the group the way. At the end of the line will be the rear leader, or sweep. It's important to always stay ahead of this person while we're on the trail. There are several different trails on the mountain where we'll be hiking, and they cross each other at some points. When you come to any intersection of trails, stop and wait for the rest of the group to catch up. This way we can be sure that no one goes off on the wrong trail. Let me emphasize here how important it is to stay on the trail. We'll be climbing through some steep and rocky areas. Don't be tempted to go off on your own and try to climb some rocks. That can be quite dangerous. Also, it's not likely, but it is possible that we'll encounter some large wild animals along the way. The last thing you want to do is try to feed any of them. That will just encourage them to follow us, which could lead to some dangerous situations. One last thing: Before we set off hiking each morning, be sure to fill up your water bottle. This is perhaps the most important safety rule. Dehydration can be a serious problem when you're out in the wilderness, so you must always be sure to carry an adequate supply of water with you.

I think that covers just about everything. Are there any questions?

Narrator: That is the end of Section 2. You now have half a minute to check your answers.

Now turn to Section 3 on page 46.

Narrator: Section 3. You will hear a conversation between a university student and a faculty advisor about the requirements for the student teaching semester.

First, you have some time to look at Questions 21 to 24 on page 46.

As you listen to the first part of the conversation, answer Questions 21 to 24.

Questions 21 to 24

Advisor:	I'd like to go over with you today some of the requirements for your student teaching, which you'll be undertaking next semester.
Student:	I'm really looking forward to working in a real classroom and teaching children, but I'm nervous about it, too.
Advisor:	One of my roles is to provide you with whatever support you may require. One thing that helps me do that is to know what you're doing in the classroom, so I require all my students to keep a journal about their teaching experience.
Student:	That sounds like a lot of work. Will I have to write in it every day?
Advisor:	Yes, if you can. You'll give it to me at the end of each week. Another thing I'll want from you is a few sample lesson plans. I'll let you know ahead of time exactly how I want you to do them.
Student:	Several of us from the university will be student teaching at the same school. Are we supposed to get together regularly to discuss our work?
Advisor:	I'll meet with each student teacher individually, but you aren't required to meet with each other. Of course, you can talk together as much as you want. You will, however, have to observe some of the other teachers in the school, besides the teacher you'll be working with.
Student:	Then will I get an evaluation from my supervising teacher at the end of the semester?
Advisor:	Actually, no. I'll do your evaluation, and I'll base it on several things. One is your required portfolio, which should contain samples of your class activities and your students' work. Another important thing is your term paper.
Student:	Then there won't be a final exam?
Advisor:	No, we don't feel that's necessary for student teaching.
Narrator:	Before you hear the rest of the conversation, you have some time to look at Questions 25 to 30 on page 46.
	Now listen and answer Questions 25 to 30.

Questions 25 to 30

Student:	I know I have to get an agreement form signed. Since you're my advisor, are you the one to do that?
Advisor:	No, that form is for your supervising teacher to sign, to document that he or she agrees to have you in the classroom as a student teacher.
Student:	Oh, I see. I'm concerned about the term paper I'll have to do, and the evaluation process. I'm not sure I understand what I'm supposed to do.
Advisor:	Regarding the term paper, the first thing is to choose a topic. It should be related to your teaching work. You should let me know your term paper topic by the end of the first week of the semester.
Student:	Will you be observing me regularly in the classroom?

Advisor:	Yes, and during the fourth week of the semester, we'll have our first evaluation meeting to discuss my observations.
Student:	One thing I'm really looking forward to is the student teacher conference that the university puts on every year.
Advisor:	I'm glad you're looking forward to it. Of course, everyone in the program is required to attend. The conference takes place, let me check, yes, the seventh week of the semester.
Student:	When will I have to turn in my term paper?
Advisor:	The term paper is due by the end of the fourteenth week of the semester. Then during the fifteenth and final week, we'll get together one last time for a semester review.
Student:	Wow. It looks like I have a busy semester ahead of me.
Narrator:	That is the end of Section 3. You now have half a minute to check your answers.
	Now turn to Section 4 on page 47.
	Section 4. You will hear a lecture about customer psychology.
	First, you have some time to look at Questions 31 to 35 on page 47.
	Now listen carefully and answer Questions 31 to 35.

Questions 31 to 35

Lecturer:	An understanding of customer psychology is an invaluable aid for retailers looking for ways to increase sales. Much can be done to the store environment to encourage shoppers to linger longer and spend more money. The first aspect to consider is the physical organization of the store. Placement of merchandise has a great deal of influence on what customers buy. For example, a common practice among retailers is to place the store's best-selling merchandise near the back of the store. In order to get to these popular items from the front entrance, customers have to walk down aisles filled with merchandise that they might not see otherwise. Carpets are also used to direct customers through particular areas of the store. Retailers choose carpets not only for their decorative or comfort value, but also because lines or other types of patterns in the carpets can subtly guide shoppers in certain directions. Besides encouraging shoppers to go to certain areas of the store, retailers also want to keep them in the store longer. One way to do this is to provide comfortable seating throughout the store, but not too close to the doors. This gives customers a chance to rest and then continue shopping.
	Retailers can do a number of things to create a pleasant atmosphere in the store, thereby encouraging more purchases. Music is commonly used, not as entertainment, but as a calming influence. It can slow the customers' pace through the store, making them spend more time shopping and, consequentially, making more purchases. Scent's

are also used in various ways. Everyone has had the experience of being drawn into a bakery by the smell of fresh bread. Experiments have been done with other types of scents, as well. For example, the scent of vanilla has been used to increase sales in clothing stores.

Narrator:	Before you hear the rest of the talk, you have some time to look at Questions 36 to 40 on page 48.
	Now listen carefully and answer Questions 36 to 40.

Questions 36 to 40

Lecturer:	Use of color is another important aspect of store environment. Certain colors can affect behavior as well as mood. Light purple, for example, has been found to have an interesting effect on customer behavior. People shopping in an environment where light purple is the predominating color seem to spend money more than shoppers in other environments. Orange is a color that's often used in fast-food restaurants. It encourages customers to leave faster, making room for the next group of diners. Blue, on the other hand, is a calming color. It gives customers a sense of security, so it's a good color for any business to use. In addition to using color to create mood and affect customer behavior, color can also be used to attract certain kinds of customers to a business. Stores that cater to a younger clientele should use bold, bright colors, which tend to be attractive to younger people. Stores that are interested in attracting an older clientele will have more success with soft, subtle colors, as older people find these colors more appealing.
Narrator:	That is the end of Section 4. You now have half a minute to check your answers.
	You will now have ten minutes to transfer your answers to the listening answer sheet.

PRACTICE TEST 3

Narrator:	You will hear a number of different recordings, and you will have to answer questions on what you will hear. There will be time for you to read the instructions and questions, and you will have a chance to check your work. All the recordings will be played once only.
	The test is in four sections. Write all of your answers on the test pages. At the end of the test you will be given ten minutes to transfer your answers to an answer sheet.
	Now turn to Section 1 on page 83.
	Section 1. You will hear a woman making a hotel reservation over the phone.
	First you have some time to look at questions 1 to 4 on page 83.

You will see that there is an example that has been done for you. On this occasion only, the conversation relating to this will be played first.

Example	
Man:	Good afternoon. Grandview Hotel.
Woman:	Yes, hello. I, uh, I'm planning to spend a few days in your city next week, and I'd like to, uh, make a reservation.

Narrator: The man answers the phone, "Grandview Hotel," so the word "Grandview" has been written at the top of the form. Now we shall begin. You should answer the questions as you listen, because you will not hear the recording a second time. Listen carefully and answer Questions 1 to 4.

Questions 1 to 4

Man: Good afternoon. Grandview Hotel.

Woman: Yes, hello. I, uh, I'm planning to spend a few days in your city next week, and I'd like to, uh, make a reservation.

Man: Of course. When did you want to stay here?

Woman: Next week. Wednesday night and Thursday night.

Man: So, that's February 13th and 14th.

Woman: Yes, that's right.

Man: And how many guests will there be?

Woman: Just me. So, do you have a room available?

Man: Yes, we do. I'll just need to take some of your information. May I have your name, please?

Woman: Oh, right, yes. It's Roxanne Wilson. W-i-l-s-o-n.

Man: Thank you, Ms. Wilson. And may I have your credit card number?

Woman: It's 2336189872.

Man: . . .9872. Got it. All right, Ms. Wilson, I have your reservation confirmed. Can I help you with anything else?

Narrator: Before you hear the rest of the conversation, you have some time to look at Questions 5 to 10 on page 83.

Now listen and answer Questions 5 to 10.

Questions 5 to 10

Woman: Well, yes. I was wondering, since I'll have a couple of free hours Friday morning before I leave, is there anything interesting to see close to the hotel?

Man: Do you like museums? The art museum's very close by.

Woman: I love museums, but not art. Can't stand it. I've heard your city has a very interesting science museum, though.

Man: Yes, but unfortunately it's closed in the winter. Are you interested in shopping?

Woman:	Sure, I love shopping. Are there any good stores nearby?
Man:	Yes. We have a large shopping mall just two bus stops away. You take the bus to Monument Square, and it's just half a block from there. Just look for the post office, and you'll see the mall entrance next to it.
Woman:	Fabulous. What about lunch? I hear your city has good restaurants.
Man:	Yes. There's a nice restaurant very near. It's just across the street from the park.
Woman:	Sounds good. I can have lunch, then walk in the park afterwards. I have one more question. What's the best way to get to the hotel from the airport?
Man:	Subway is the fastest, of course. There are buses, but they're quite slow.
Woman:	I'll be arriving quite late, after 10 P.M. I thought I might have to take a taxi.
Man:	The subway runs until midnight.
Woman:	Oh, good. Then I'll do that. Will there be someone at the hotel front desk that late?
Man:	Oh, yes. The front desk stays open until two.
Narrator:	That is the end of Section 1. You now have half a minute to check your answers.

Now turn to Section 2 on page 84.

Section 2. You will hear a tour leader giving information about a bus tour.

First, you have some time to look at Questions 11 to 15 on page 84.

As you listen to the first part of the talk, answer Questions 11 to 15. |

Questions 11 to 15

Tour leader:	Thank you for choosing City Tours. The reason so many people choose our tours when visiting this city is because you can design your tour to suit your own interests. Your all-day pass entitles you to board our bus at any stop and stay as long as you like at each place. The all-day bus pass costs $18 for adults. Children between the ages of five and twelve pay half the adult fare, and children under five ride for free. Our buses run every hour on the half hour, starting at 8:30 A.M.

Our most popular tour is the Center City Tour, which goes to all the major attractions in the center of the city. From the starting point here at the tour bus office, the bus goes to the first stop, Hill Park. As you may guess, this park is located at the top of a small hill. The next stop is the fishing docks. Following that, the bus goes on to the third stop, Bay Bridge, located at the foot of the bridge which crosses the bay. The fourth stop is in the shopping district, then the fifth and last stop is at Green Street. |

Narrator:	Before you hear the rest of the talk, you have some time to look at Questions 16 to 20 on page 85.
	Now listen and answer Questions 16 to 20.

Questions 16 to 20

Tour leader:	There are many interesting things to do and see on the Center City Tour. At the first stop, you can enjoy a spectacular view of the bay, the city, and especially of the fishing docks, which are located at the foot of the hill. At the second stop, you can walk around and look at the boats. Fresh fish from the bay is also for sale here, since this is the place where the fishermen bring in their catch. The next stop is where some of the city's finest seafood restaurants are located, so you might want to plan a lunch stop here. You can eat fresh fish here prepared in the traditional local way. The fourth stop is, of course, where you can do your shopping. Don't miss the opportunity to purchase some of our city's famous handmade baskets. You'll want to take several home as souvenirs of your visit to our city. Finally, at the last stop on the tour, you can visit one of the oldest buildings in our city, the theater. This building was built over 400 years ago and is still used today as a place to see plays, musicals, and other performances, as well as our annual film festival.
Narrator:	That is the end of Section 2. You now have half a minute to check your answers.
	Now turn to Section 3 on page 86.
Narrator:	Section 3. You will hear a conversation between two students planning a research project.
	First, you have some time to look at Questions 21 to 23 on page 86.
	As you listen to the first part of the conversation, answer Questions 21 to 23.

Questions 21 to 23

Student 1:	We'd better start planning our research project, because we don't have much time left before it's due.
Student 2:	I know, only three more weeks.
Student 1:	Is that all? I thought we had more time than that. Well, let's get to work, then.
Student 2:	OK, so we agreed we're going to interview shoppers about their spending habits. Did we decide to conduct our interviews at the department store?
Student 1:	We haven't decided anything definitely yet, but I think the shopping mall would be a better place. We'd get more of a variety of shoppers there.

Audioscripts

Student 2:	Yes, that's a good point. So, let's do that. How many interviews did the professor say we had to complete?
Student 1:	She said at least thirty. That sounds like a lot, doesn't it?
Student 2:	Yes, but if we divide it up between the two of us, that's just fifteen each. That's not so bad.
Narrator:	Before you hear the rest of the conversation, you have some time to look at Questions 24 to 30 on page 86.
	Now listen and answer Questions 24 to 30.

Questions 24 to 30

Student 1:	OK, so I guess we'd better start designing our questionnaire.
Student 2:	Well, we have to do some reading first, don't we? Didn't we say we were going to compare our results to the results of a government study?
Student 1:	Right, the government study about how the economic crisis has changed people's spending habits. We want to see if we get similar results.
Student 2:	Yes, so we'd better read that first and then design our questionnaire. Then I guess we'll be ready to go out and interview shoppers.
Student 1:	No. Don't you remember? The professor said she had to approve our questionnaire first, before we actually conducted the interviews.
Student 2:	Oh, right. So we'll get her approval and then conduct the interviews. I think a Saturday would be the best day for the interviews, because everyone's out shopping then.
Student 1:	Right. We'll do it on a Saturday, then.
Student 2:	And let's also plan to get together the next day to analyze the results. It's best to do that while everything's fresh in our minds. Don't you think?
Student 2:	Sure. That sounds like a good idea. OK, so then we're going to have to present our results to the class. Do you have any ideas for that? It's an important part of our grade, so I think we should plan it well.
Student 1:	Well, I think the obvious thing is to prepare some charts showing our results and how they compare with the government study. That will help make the information a lot clearer to the class.
Student 2:	Right. OK, so we'll draw up some charts of the results.
Student 1:	And then that's it. All that will be left to do is give the class presentation. Do you think we can be ready on time?
Student 2:	I sure hope so. Let's get started now.
Narrator:	That is the end of Section 3. You now have half a minute to check your answers.
	Now turn to Section 4 on page 87.
	Section 4. You will hear a professor give a lecture on Louisa May Alcott. First you have some time to look at the questions 31 to 40 on page 87.
	Now listen carefully and complete the timeline in Questions 31 to 40.

Questions 31 to 40

Lecturer: Good afternoon. Today, I'd like to continue our discussion of the lives of prominent American writers by talking about Louisa May Alcott, one of the best-known nineteenth-century writers. Alcott is known for her moralistic girl's novels, but she was a much more serious individual than those novels might lead one to believe. She was born in 1832, the daughter of Bronson Alcott, who was one of the founders of the Transcendentalist Movement. Bronson Alcott was a philosopher but not a provider, and the family lived close to poverty. From an early age, Louisa was determined to find a way to improve her family's economic situation. As a teenager, she worked to support her family by taking on a variety of low-paying jobs, including teacher, seamstress, and household servant. Alcott also started writing when she was young. She wrote her first novel when she was just seventeen years old; although, it wasn't published until many years after her death. It was called *The Inheritance.*

In 1861, the Civil War broke out. Alcott worked as a volunteer, sewing uniforms and bandages for soldiers. The following year, she enlisted as an army nurse. She spent the war years in Washington, nursing wounded soldiers at a military hospital. While working at the hospital, she wrote many letters to her family at home in Massachusetts. After the war, she turned the letters into a book, which was published under the title *Hospital Sketches.* She also wrote numerous romantic stories, which she sold to magazines.

Around this same time, she was offered the opportunity to travel to Europe as the companion to an invalid. When she returned home from Europe in 1866, she found her family still in financial difficulty and in need of money, so she went back to writing. Her big break came in 1868 with the publication of her first novel for girls, *Little Women.* The novel achieved instant success, and the public wanted more. From then on, Alcott supported herself and her family by writing novels for girls. It wasn't the writing she had dreamed of doing, but it earned her a good income.

Alcott took care of her family for the rest of her life. In 1878, her youngest sister, May, got married. A year later, May died after giving birth to a daughter. Louisa Alcott raised her sister's orphaned child. In 1882, Bronson Alcott suffered a stroke. Soon after that, Louisa Alcott set up a house for him, her niece, her sister Anna, and Anna's two sons in Boston. Her mother was no longer living by this time. Alcott was still writing novels for girls, including two sequels to *Little Women*: *Little Men* and *Jo's Boys.* The latter was published in 1886.

Louisa Alcott had suffered poor health ever since she contracted typhoid fever while working as a war nurse. She died in March of 1888 at the age of 55. She was buried in Concord, Massachusetts.

Narrator:	That is the end of Section 4. You now have half a minute to check your answers.
	You will now have ten minutes to transfer your answers to the listening answer sheet

PRACTICE TEST 4

Narrator:	You will hear a number of different recordings, and you will have to answer questions on what you will hear. There will be time for you to read the instructions and questions, and you will have a chance to check your work. All the recordings will be played once only.
	The test is in four sections. Write all of your answers on the test pages. At the end of the test you will be given ten minutes to transfer your answers to an answer sheet.
	Now turn to Section 1 on page 123.
	Section 1. You will hear a man arranging to get a telephone connection. First you have some time to look at Questions 1 to 4 on page 123.
	You will see that there is an example that has been done for you. On this occasion only, the conversation relating to this will be played first.

Example

Woman:	This is the ClearPoint Telephone Company customer service office. My name is Ms. Jones. How may I help you?
Man:	Yes. I'm moving, and I'd like to arrange to have a phone line installed.

Narrator:	The woman answers the phone, "This is the ClearPoint Telephone Company customer service office," so the words "Telephone Company" have been written at the top of the form. Now we shall begin. You should answer the questions as you listen, because you will not hear the recording a second time. Listen carefully and answer Questions 1 to 4.

Questions 1 to 4

Woman:	This is the ClearPoint Telephone Company customer service office. My name is Ms. Jones. How may I help you?
Man:	Yes. I'm moving, and I'd like to arrange to have a phone line installed.
Woman:	Of course. Let me get some information from you first. May I have your name, please?
Man:	It's Kramer. Harold Kramer.
Woman:	And would you spell your last name for me, please?
Man:	K-R-A-M-E-R.
Woman:	M-E-R. Got it. OK, could I have the address where you'd like to have the telephone connected?
Man:	That would be number 58 Fulton Avenue, apartment 12.

Woman:	Is that a business or a residence?
Man:	A residence. It's my new home address.
Woman:	Then the type of phone service you want is residential, not business?
Man:	Yes, yes. It's for my home.
Woman:	All right. Fine. Now let me get your employment information. Who is your current employer?
Man:	I work at the Wrightsville Medical Group.
Woman:	Then your occupation is doctor?
Man:	No, I work for the doctors. I'm the office manager.
Narrator:	Before you hear the rest of the conversation, you have some time to look at Questions 5 to 10 on page 123.
	Now listen and answer Questions 5 to 10.

Questions 5 to 10

Woman:	OK. And could I have your work phone number?
Man:	It's 637-555-9014.
Woman:	9014. Great. Just one more thing, I need to know how long you've been at your current job.
Man:	I've been working there for quite a while now, let me see, eight, no, nine, that's right, nine years.
Woman:	OK, good. You've been there long enough, so I don't need to ask about any other work history. Now, in addition to our basic phone service, we have several special services available.
Man:	Could you explain them to me?
Woman:	Most customers opt for unlimited long-distance service. It really saves you money if you make a lot of long-distance calls.
Man:	That sounds like a good idea.
Woman:	Then I'll put you down for long-distance service. Another popular service is voicemail. Voicemail takes all your messages electronically, and all it takes is one simple phone call to retrieve them.
Man:	Hmmm, voicemail. No, I don't think so. I have an answering machine to take my messages. It's old, but it still works fine.
Woman:	We also provide Internet service if you're interested in that.
Man:	I am. Please put me down for Internet as well as phone service.
Woman:	Right. OK, I think we're almost finished. I just need to schedule a time for the technician to go to your apartment and do the installation. Let me see…. What about next Tuesday? Would that work for you?
Man:	No, not Tuesday. I'll be at a conference all day. Wednesday would work, though.
Woman:	I'm afraid I won't have any technicians in your area on Wednesday. I could send someone on Friday.
Man:	That would be fine.
Woman:	What time of day works best for you? Morning or afternoon?
Man:	Morning would be best.
Woman:	All right then. It's on the schedule. Do you have any questions?
Man:	No, I don't think so.

Woman:	Thank you for calling ClearPoint.
Narrator:	That is the end of Section 1. You now have half a minute to check your answers.
	Now turn to Section 2 on page 124.
	Section 2. You will hear a radio interview about an upcoming fair.
	First, you have some time to look at Questions 11 to 14 on page 124.
	As you listen to the first part of the talk, answer Questions 11 to 14.

Questions 11 to 14

Man:	Good afternoon, and welcome to City Hour, the radio show that brings you all the latest information about events in and around our city. Today we have with us Cynthia Smith, who is heading up this year's City Fair. Cynthia, would you start by giving us some of the basic information about the fair? Where will it take place this year?
Woman:	I'm glad you asked that question, because I know most people will be expecting the fair to be at the fairgrounds as usual, but we've had to change the location this year due to some construction work. You know, they're building the new high school in that neighborhood, and they've been using the fairgrounds as a place to store construction materials. So we've moved the fair to City Park, which I think is a wonderful location.
Man:	Yes, that will be a great place for the fair. I understand that the fair begins on Friday morning with a special opening event.
Woman:	Actually, it won't begin until that evening, but you're right about the special event. Traditionally, we've begun with a parade, but this year our opening event will be a special dance performance, and the most exciting part is that the mayor will be one of the dancers.
Man:	The mayor is a woman of many talents. Cynthia, could you tell our listeners about the price of admission? What will it cost to attend the fair?
Woman:	We're trying to keep the price down as much as possible. A three-day pass is just $25. Or you can buy a Saturday- or Sunday-only pass for $15. The opening event on Friday, the dance performance, doesn't cost anything to attend, and we're hoping a lot of people will come watch that.
Narrator:	Before you hear the rest of the talk, you have some time to look at Questions 15 to 20 on page 124.
	Now listen and answer Questions 15 to 20.

Questions 15 to 20

Man:	Could you tell us about some of the events planned for Saturday and Sunday, the main days of the fair?
Woman:	We have a lot of exciting things planned. There are a number of events especially for children, including a clown show on Saturday

afternoon. On Saturday evening, we've got an event that can be enjoyed by the whole family—a concert by the lake.

Man: I'm sure that will be a popular event. Is there anything special planned for Sunday?

Woman: Yes, a really fun event, and we hope a lot of people will participate. There will be a singing contest in the afternoon. It's open to everyone, at no charge. It doesn't matter whether you're an experienced singer or not. If you've always dreamed of singing on stage, this is your chance.

Man: That sounds like a lot of fun.

Woman: I think it will be. I'd also like your listeners to know that besides the special events I've mentioned, there will be things taking place all weekend. For example, at the food court, international food will be served. You'll be able to sample dishes from all around the world. There will also be special games for children at different locations around the fair.

Man: Will there be things people can buy, souvenirs, anything like that?

Woman: We have a large area set aside where there will be crafts for sale. This will be an opportunity to buy many lovely handmade things, and to get to know some of our local artists and craftspeople, as well.

Man: It sounds like there will be a lot of fun for everyone at this year's fair. Thank you for sharing the information with us, Cynthia.

Woman: Thank you for inviting me.

Narrator: That is the end of Section 2. You now have half a minute to check your answers.

Now turn to Section 3 on page 125.

Narrator: Section 3. You will hear a conversation between a prospective student and a university advisor about applying to enter the university.

First, you have some time to look at Questions 21 to 23 on page 125.

As you listen to the first part of the conversation, answer Questions 21 to 23.

Questions 21 to 23

Student: I'm interested in entering your Business Administration program, and I'd like some information on how to apply. I'm a little concerned because I've been out of school for a number of years.

Advisor: That could actually work to your advantage. It's possible to get academic credit for work experience, if that experience is related to courses in our program.

Student: I've been working in business for several years. How would I get academic credit for that?

Advisor: First, you'll need to read the university catalog to see if any of the course descriptions match your specific job experience. For example, if you've worked in accounting, you may be able to get credit for an accounting course.

Student:	So then what would I do?
Advisor:	You would write a summary of your work experience, relating it to specific courses we offer. Submit that to the Admissions Office with a letter from your work supervisor confirming your experience.
Narrator:	Before you hear the rest of the conversation, you have some time to look at Questions 24 to 30 on page 125.
	Now listen and answer Questions 24 to 30.

Questions 24 to 30

Student:	Would I submit those things at the same time that I apply for admission?
Advisor:	That would be the best idea. Have you seen a copy of our university catalog?
Student:	Not the most recent one. I have a copy from last year.
Advisor:	You'll need to look at the latest one. Unfortunately, I've run out of copies, but you can get one from the library for now, and I'll send you your own copy as soon as I have more available.
Student.:	Thank you. How does the admissions process work?
Advisor:	Well, first you'll need to get an application for admission. Those are available in the Admissions Office. The application form contains all the instructions you'll need.
Student:	That sounds simple enough.
Advisor:	Of course, you'll need to make sure you meet all the admissions requirements.
Student:	How can I know what those are?
Advisor:	We have copies of the requirements lists for all university programs here in the Counseling Center. I'll give you one before you leave today.
Student:	Will I need to get recommendations from my employer or former teachers?
Advisor:	Yes, you will. The recommendation forms are available in the Admissions Office. Now, I don't know if you'll also be applying for a part-time job through the university work-study program.
Student:	I'm considering that. How can I find out what kinds of jobs are offered?
Advisor:	You can access the job listings from the computers in the library. Are you planning to study full time or part time?
Student:	I want to be a full-time student.
Advisor:	Good. Then you'll qualify for the work-study program. Part-time students aren't eligible.
Student:	As a full-time student, would I be eligible for a free buss pass?
Advisor:	No, unfortunately, we don't have those available for any of our students. However, you can apply for financial assistance to help pay for your books or for your tuition.
Student:	I'd like to look into that. Do I apply for that at the Admissions Office?

Advisor: No, that's through us. You'll need to make an appointment with a counselor.

Narrator: That is the end of Section 3. You now have half a minute to check your answers.

Now turn to Section 4 on page 126.

Section 4. You will hear a lecture about the black bear.

First, you have some time to look at Questions 31 to 35 on page 126.

Now listen carefully and answer questions 31 to 35.

Questions 31 to 35

Lecturer: The black bear, or *Ursus americanus*, has a wide range, inhabiting forested areas of North America, including Canada, the United States, and parts of northern Mexico. Black bears are omnivores, getting their nutrition from a wide variety of plants and animals. The particular foods any one bear eats depends on what's available in the area where that bear lives, as well as on the season of the year. Generally speaking, plant foods make up 90 percent of the bear's diet. The rest of its meals consist of animal foods such as insects and fish.

Bears have a relatively long gestation period. Mating takes place in the spring or early summer, but bear cubs aren't born until the following winter. Usually, two cubs are born at a time, although some litters may have as many as five cubs. Bear cubs are dependent on their mother and may stay with her for close to two years. Wild black bears can live as long as 25 years. They've lived for as long as 30 years or more in captivity.

Narrator: Before you hear the rest of the talk, you have some time to look at Questions 36 to 40 on page 126.

Now listen carefully and answer Questions 36 to 40.

Questions 36 to 40

Lecturer: Much of the black bear's range coincides with the range of its close cousin, the grizzly bear. Although these bears are somewhat similar in appearance and habits, it isn't difficult to tell the difference between them. Color isn't necessarily a distinguishing characteristic, as both species of bears occur in a range of colors from almost blonde to dark brown or black. Many black bears, however, have a patch of fur on their chests that's lighter in color than the rest of their fur. Grizzly bears don't have this patch. Size isn't always a distinguishing feature either, although grizzly bears are usually heavier, with an average weight of 225 kilos. Black bears average 140 kilos in weight. Grizzly bears spend time digging in the ground for roots and tubers that make up part of their diet. The large muscles they need for this give them a distinct shoulder hump. This hump is absent in black bears, which don't do the same kind of digging. The shape of the face and ears is also different in each species of bear. Grizzly bears have a depression between the eyes and nose and short, round ears. Black bears, on the other hand, have a straighter profile and longer, more pointed ears. Grizzly bears are known for their fearsome long, sharp claws. Black bears have shorter claws, which are better suited for climbing trees.

Narrator: That is the end of Section 4. You now have half a minute to check your answers.

You will now have ten minutes to transfer your answers to the listening answer sheet.

PRACTICE TEST 5

Narrator: You will hear a number of different recordings, and you will have to answer questions on what you will hear. There will be time for you to read the instructions and questions, and you will have a chance to check your work. All the recordings will be played once only.

The test is in four sections. Write all of your answers on the test pages. At the end of the test you will be given ten minutes to transfer your answers to an answer sheet.

Now turn to Section 1 on page 163.

Section 1. You will hear a woman booking a bicycle tour over the phone.

First you have some time to look at Questions 1 to 4 on page 163.

You will see that there is an example that has been done for you. On this occasion only, the conversation relating to this will be played first.

Example

Man: Global Bicycle Tours. May I help you?
Woman: Yes, thank you. I'd like to sign up for a bicycle tour.

Narrator: The man answers the phone, "Global Bicycle Tours," so the word "Global" has been written at the top of the form. Now we shall begin. You should answer the questions as you listen, because you will not hear the recording a second time. Listen carefully and answer Questions 1 to 4.

Questions 1 to 4

Man: Global Bicycle Tours. May I help you?
Woman: Yes, thank you. I'd like to sign up for a bicycle tour.

Man:	Which tour were you interested in? We have the River Valley tour coming up in June and the Mountain tour in July.
Woman:	The River Valley tour is in June? I thought it was in May.
Man:	It actually takes place the first week of June.
Woman:	Oh, I see. Well, I can still do that. The River Valley tour is the one I want.
Man:	Splendid. Just let me take your information. May I have your name please?
Woman:	Karla Schmidt. That's Karla with a K, not a C. K-A-R-L-A.
Man:	Thank you, Ms. Schmidt. Address?
Woman:	Do you need a street address, or can I give you my post office box?
Man:	A post office box is fine.
Woman:	It's P. O. Box 257 [two-five-seven], Manchester.
Man:	Thank you. OK, next. Will you be bringing your own bicycle, or do you want to rent one from us?
Woman:	I'll bring my own.
Man:	Excellent. Now, we provide all the meals, so we need to know if you have any dietary restrictions.
Woman:	I don't think so. What do you mean?
Man:	I mean if there's any food you can't eat. Some people have food allergies or are vegetarian or have to avoid dairy products, things like that.
Woman:	Oh, I see. Well, yes, I'm a vegetarian. I never eat meat.
Narrator:	Before you hear the rest of the conversation, you have some time to look at Questions 5 to 10 on page 163.
	Now listen and answer Questions 5 to 10.

Questions 5 to 10

Man:	All right. I'll make a note of that. Now, the total cost of the tour is $750.
Woman:	That much!
Man:	The price includes everything—food, hotel, transportation, everything.
Woman:	Everything?
Man:	Yes, everything. The only other thing is you'll want to tip the tour guide. We usually recommend five percent of the total tour cost.
Woman:	A five-percent tip. I guess that's reasonable.
Man:	In order to reserve your space on the tour I'll need a 30 percent deposit.
Woman:	Do you need that right away?
Man:	We generally ask for the deposit at least four weeks before the tour begins. The River Valley tour begins, let me see, six weeks from now. So you'll need to pay the deposit in two weeks.
Woman:	I think I can do that. I wonder if you could tell me something. How will our luggage be transported? Do we carry it on our bicycles?

Man:	No, you leave that to us. We have a van that carries your luggage from hotel to hotel each day, so you don't have to worry about it.
Woman:	Great! I have a luggage rack for my bike, but I guess I won't have to bring that.
Man:	No, you won't. But there are a few items we recommend that you bring. We can't control the weather, so you should bring a raincoat or raingear.
Woman:	Yes, that's a good idea. And I should have my own spare tire, too, shouldn't I?
Man:	Actually, you don't need that, as our guide always carries some. And, of course, you won't need maps either, since our guide has the route all planned.
Woman:	What about a water bottle? I'll need that, won't I?
Man:	Yes, you should definitely have a water bottle. A camera would be a good idea, too, since that tour goes through some very scenic areas.
Woman:	I have a guide book of that area. I wonder if I should bring it along.
Man:	We don't recommend guide books. It would just be extra weight, and the tour guide knows a great deal about the area.
Woman:	Yes, I see. Is there anything else I need to know?
Man:	I think we've covered the important points. I'll send you a tour brochure, and you can call again if you have any questions.
Woman:	Thank you very much.
Narrator:	That is the end of Section 1. You now have half a minute to check your answers.
	Now turn to Section 2 on page 164.
	Section 2. You will hear a tour of a newly renovated health club.
	First, you have some time to look at Questions 11 to 15 on page 164.
	As you listen to the first part of the talk, answer Questions 11 to 15.

Questions 11 to 15

Guide:	Thank you all for coming to see the new renovations to the Hartford Health Club. I know you'll be as pleased as I am to see the wonderful results of our months of hard work to improve the club and bring you the best facilities ever. We'll begin in here with the swimming pool. You'll notice the new color of the adult pool, a lovely, cool green. Now walk over here and look at the children's pool. It's the same green but, as you see, with brightly colored sea creatures painted everywhere. Both of the pools needed painting, not only for maintenance, but I think the new color greatly improves the atmosphere of this part of the club. Next, let's take a look at the locker rooms. Don't worry, there's no one using them just now. Doesn't it feel roomy in here? We've expanded both the men's and women's locker rooms, so now they'll be much more comfortable to use. There are bigger lockers, a good deal more room in the dressing area, and more places to

store extra towels and equipment. Be careful as you walk through here. The floor has just been polished and may be a bit slippery.

Let's go up to the exercise room next. Here you'll notice the new floor. Walk on it. Doesn't that feel comfortable? It's a special material, softer than the old floor, an ideal surface for jogging and exercising. They had to move all the exercise equipment out while they were working on the floor, but don't worry, it will be brought back in before the end of today. Let's step outside now and look at the tennis courts. We haven't done a great deal here except to the equipment. We replaced all the nets and the ball-throwing machine. Otherwise, everything is the same as it was before. Let's walk down this hallway, and here we are at the club store in its new location. We thought here by the entrance was a better place for it than where it used to be by the swimming pool. But it still has all the same items for sale: sports equipment and clothes in the club colors.

Narrator:	Before you hear the rest of the talk, you have some time to look at Questions 16 to 20 on page 164.
	Now listen and answer Questions 16 to 20.

Questions 16 to 20

Guide:	We're excited about the upcoming activities and events to take place in our newly renovated club. Now that the pools are ready for use again, swimming lessons will begin tomorrow, for both adults and children. If you haven't signed up yet, you can stop by the office before you leave today and put your name on the list. If you're a tennis player, you'll be interested to hear about the tennis competition coming up on Wednesday. Players from different clubs all over the region will be participating. If you'd like to watch the event, tickets are available in the office.
	Also, I want to be sure you all know you're invited to our club party, coming up next weekend. We're celebrating the completion of the renovation work, and we have a lot to celebrate. The entire renovation project was finished in just nine months. That's three months less than the twelve months we had originally planned on. We're proud of that and proud that we came in under budget, too. Because we've had such good results with this project, we're already planning the next one. We already have two indoor pools, and next year we plan to install an outdoor pool right next to the tennis courts. Details of these plans will be made available to all club members soon.
	All right, I think we've covered just about everything. Are there any questions?
Narrator:	That is the end of Section 2. You now have half a minute to check your answers.

Now turn to Section 3 on page 165.

Section 3. You will hear a museum director talking to several student interns, explaining their internship duties at the museum.

First, you have some time to look at Questions 21 to 25 on page 165.

As you listen to the first part of the conversation, answer Questions 21 to 25.

Questions 21 to 25

Dr. Johnson:	Welcome to the City Museum of Art. I'm Dr. Shirley Johnson, the director of the museum's internship program. Today I'll be giving you an orientation to the museum and our museum administrator's internship program.
Student 1:	Will we get a chance to tour the museum today?
Dr. Johnson:	Yes. We'll start right now with a tour of the building. We'll skip the basement. Most of that part of the building is devoted to art conservation, which won't be part of your internship. Let's begin here on the ground floor with the museum offices.
Student 2:	I guess this is where we'll be spending most of our time, helping with the office work.
Dr. Johnson:	You'll spend some time working in here so you can learn what the administrative duties involve, but you'll also get a chance to experience all aspects of museum work. This room in here is the Museum Tours Office.
Student 3:	I'm interested in that. I'd really like to help out with the tours.
Dr. Johnson:	That's great because you'll all have a chance to lead some tours and maybe even to develop a tour of your own, too. Let's go up to the second floor now.
Student 1:	This is the board room in here, isn't it? Will we get to go to board meetings?
Dr. Johnson.	Only members of the Board of Directors attend those. Now, back here behind the galleries are the classrooms. You're all welcome to attend any class you want at no charge.
Student 2:	But we won't be teaching any, will we?
Dr. Johnson:	No, the staff of the Education Department is responsible for that. Let's move up to the third floor now and the Research Department. Each of you will spend some time working in here.
Student 3:	Great. I'd like to help with the research.
Dr. Johnson:	We're working on some very interesting research projects right now. Also, as an extension of your research work, you'll probably contribute to some of the museum's brochures.
Student 1:	I'm looking forward to that. I like writing about art. Another thing I've been hoping to be able to do is meet some artists.
Dr. Johnson:	You're in luck, then. We've planned a reception for the first day of your internship, and you'll have the chance to meet several local artists then.

Narrator:	Before you hear the rest of the conversation, you have some time to look at Questions 26 to 30 on page 165.
	Now listen and answer Questions 26 to 30.

Questions 26 to 30

Student 2:	Could you give us a little background of the museum? I mean, when it was built and some information about the collections and things like that?
Dr. Johnson:	Of course. The main part of the museum was built in 1895, with a combination of public and private funds. The new wing was built 60 years later, with a donation from the Rhinebeck family.
Student 3:	That part of the museum was built for the modern art collection, wasn't it?
Dr. Johnson:	Yes, it was. In the main part of the museum, we have a gallery devoted to works by local artists, our sculpture collection, and a small collection of classical European art.
Student 1:	You mentioned classes earlier. What kinds of classes does the museum offer?
Dr. Johnson:	In our Adult Education program, we offer a series of art history classes, and for children we have a program of arts and crafts workshops. You can get a brochure from the office that will give you more information.
Student 2:	I saw a lot of chairs set up in the main hall. What are those for?
Dr. Johnson:	Those are there for tonight's musical performance. We offer a weekly concert series during the fall and winter, and, of course, all of you are welcome to attend. Now, if there are no more questions, let's step into my office and I'll show you your schedules.
Narrator:	That is the end of Section 3. You now have half a minute to check your answers.
	Now turn to Section 4 on page 166.
	Section 4. You will hear a lecture about the history of the tomato.
	First, you have some time to look at Questions 31 to 35 on page 166.
	Now listen carefully and answer Questions 31 to 35.

Questions 31 to 35

Lecturer:	The tomato is a popular vegetable, which figures in the cuisine of many countries around the world. It is particularly prominent in Italian cooking, but it was unknown in Europe until Spanish explorers brought it back from the Americas. The tomato originated in the highlands of Peru. From there, it eventually found its way to Mexico, where it was cultivated by the Aztecs. The Aztec tomato wasn't the large red vegetable we know today. Rather, it was small and yellow. When this small, round fruit arrived in Italy, it was named "golden

apple" for its bright yellow color. You'll notice I just called it a fruit. That's because a tomato is botanically a fruit, even though most everyone calls it a vegetable. The actual word *tomato* comes from the Aztec name for the vegetable, meaning "plump thing."

The tomato arrived in Europe in the 1500s and quickly became a popular food in Spain and Italy. In the late 1600s, the Italians began publishing recipes that used tomatoes. The British, however, had a different attitude toward the vegetable. It was grown as an ornamental plant in Britain in the 1600s, but it wasn't eaten because it was thought to be poisonous. It wasn't until the 1700s that tomatoes became part of the daily diet in Britain.

Narrator:	Before you hear the rest of the talk, you have some time to look at Questions 36 to 40 on page 167.
	Now listen carefully and answer Questions 36 to 40.

Questions 36 to 40

Lecturer:	In the United States, tomatoes were also used as ornamental plants rather than as food for a long time. This attitude began to change in the 1800s. In 1806, a gardener's calendar mentioned that tomatoes could be used to improve the flavor of soups and other foods. Thomas Jefferson did much to enhance the tomato's reputation as a food. He first served tomatoes to visitors at his home in Virginia in 1809. Then, in 1820, a man named Robert Gibbon Johnson decided it was time to discard, once and for all, the idea that tomatoes were poisonous. To prove his point, he ate one kilo of ripe red tomatoes in public. Two thousand people gathered to watch this feat, which took place on the steps of the court house in Salem, Massachusetts. Amazingly enough, Johnson survived this stunt! The popularity of the tomato as a food began growing rapidly. Soon, people all around the country were eating tomatoes. By the 1830s, American newspapers and magazines were publishing thousands of tomato recipes. However, all those recipes involved using tomatoes in some cooked form. Tomato salads and sandwiches were still unknown. It wasn't until a century later, in the 1930s, that it became popular for people to eat raw tomatoes.
Narrator:	That is the end of Section 4. You now have half a minute to check your answers.
	You will now have ten minutes to transfer your answers to the listening answer sheet.

PRACTICE TEST 6

Narrator:	You will hear a number of different recordings, and you will have to answer questions on what you will hear. There will be time for you

to read the instructions and questions, and you will have a chance to check your work. All the recordings will be played once only.

The test is in four sections. Write all of your answers on the test pages. At the end of the test, you will be given ten minutes to transfer your answers to an answer sheet.

Now turn to Section 1 on page 201.

Section 1. You will hear a woman and a man talking about their work at a library.

First you have some time to look at Questions 1 to 5 on page 201.

You will see that there is an example that has been done for you. On this occasion only, the conversation relating to this will be played first.

Example	
Woman:	Hello. I'm Mrs. Phillips, the head librarian. You're the new library assistant, aren't you?
Man:	Yes, I'm Robert Haskell, but please call me Bob.
Narrator:	The woman introduces herself as the head librarian, Mrs. Phillips, so the name "Mrs. Phillips" has been written in. Now we shall begin. You should answer the questions as you listen, because you will not hear the recording a second time. Listen carefully and answer questions 1 to 5.

Questions 1 to 5

Woman:	Hello. I'm Mrs. Phillips, the head librarian. You're the new library assistant, aren't you?
Man:	Yes, I'm Robert Haskell, but please call me Bob.
Woman:	All right, Bob. Let me take a few minutes to explain how the library works and what your duties will be. First, the library opens at 8:30 in the morning, so, naturally, we expect you to be here and ready to work by then.
Man:	Of course.
Woman:	And you can go home at 4:30 when the library closes. Now, let me explain where everything's kept.
Man:	It looks like here on the ground floor is where the reference books are.
Woman:	Yes, that's right. Up on the second floor is where the Adult Collection is, both fiction and nonfiction.
Man:	And the children's books are there, too, aren't they? I thought I saw them in the room by the stairway.
Woman:	No, those are magazines and newspapers for adults. Children's books are up one more flight on the third floor. We'll take a look at them later. Let me show you how we organize our work. Do you see that brown book cart over there?
Man:	The one by the door?
Woman:	Yes, that one. Those books have been checked in and need to go back on the shelves.

Man: OK, so the brown book cart has books to re-shelve. What about this black cart by the desk?

Woman: Those books have torn pages or damaged covers. They're all books that need to be repaired.

Man: OK, I know how to do a lot of that. I'm pretty good at mending torn pages and covers.

Woman: That's great because we really need help with that.

Man: And that white cart in the corner? What are those books for?

Woman: Those are old books that we've taken off the shelves to make room for new ones. We sell them as used books to raise money for the library.

Man: So they're all ready to sell?

Woman: Yes, that's right. So, now you know what to do with the books in the carts. Lets talk about our activities schedule.

Narrator: Before you hear the rest of the conversation, you have some time to look at Questions 6 to 10 on page 201.

                    Now listen and answer Questions 6 to 10.

Questions 6 to 10

Man: I understand this library has a number of interesting activities every week.

Woman: Yes, our activities are quite popular. The most popular one is Story Time for the children.

Man: Do a lot of children show up for that?

Woman: Yes, a good many. It takes place in the Children's Room on Thursday mornings at eleven.

Man: Isn't there a family movie night, too?

Woman: Yes, but it's not at night anymore. We used to have Family Movies on Fridays when the library is open until nine, but now we have a different activity at that time, so we had to switch Family Movies to the weekend—Saturday afternoon.

Man: How much do you charge for the movies?

Woman: They're all free. The movie always starts at 2:30 in the Reference Room. But you don't have to worry about that since you don't work on weekends.

Man: And what takes place on Friday evenings?

Woman: We've just started a weekly Lecture Series. We have a different speaker every week, and the lectures cover all different kinds of topics.

Man: That sounds like something I'd be interested in attending.

Woman: Good, because we'll need your help with that. You'll be working Friday evenings, and one of your duties will be to set up the Meeting Room on the first floor for the lecture.

Man: What time will you need that done?

Woman: Let's say by 6:15. The lecture starts at 6:30, and the room needs to be ready well ahead of time. A lot of people arrive early.

Man: Maybe I should have the room ready by six?

Woman:	That wouldn't be a bad idea. OK, why don't I take you upstairs and show you the rest of the collection......... (voice fades out.)
Narrator:	That is the end of Section 1. You now have half a minute to check your answers.
	Now turn to Section 2 on page 202.
	Section 2. You will hear a radio interview about a lakeside resort.
	First, you have some time to look at Questions 11 to 15 on page 202.
	As you listen to the first part of the talk, answer Questions 11 to 15.

Questions 11 to 15

Woman:	Good afternoon, and welcome to today's show. The warm months are with us, and many of you are getting ready to plan vacation trips. To help you with that, we have a special guest today, Robert Sampson, director of the Golden Lake Resort. Robert, I understand Golden Lake is a popular place for families to spend their vacations.
Man:	Yes, families enjoy spending time at Golden Lake. Many come back year after year. We have a spectacular location and fun activities for both children and adults.
Woman:	Could you describe for us some of the activities available at Golden Lake?
Man:	We have a lot of water activities, of course, since we're right on the lake. We have a pleasant sandy beach for swimming. We also have canoes and sailboats available, and many of our guests enjoy boating on the lake.
Woman:	I imagine water skiing would be popular among your guests.
Man:	Actually, we don't permit waterskiing in the resort area. It can be dangerous for swimmers and for the canoeists, too. We do have a great location for fishing, though, and you'll often see guests fishing from our dock or from the canoes.
Woman:	That sounds very relaxing. What about activities on land? Do you have facilities for tennis?
Man:	We had tennis in the past, but the courts fell out of repair and since we found that most of our guests weren't interested in the game, we closed the courts down. So that's no longer an option. And, naturally, because of our location in the woods, we don't have an adequate area for a golf course. But I'd like to let your listeners know that we'll be adding a new activity this year. We've made an arrangement with a local stable, so now we're going to have horseback riding available for our guests. We've created several riding trails around the lake.
Woman:	That sounds lovely. Now, what about rainy days? What can your guests do when the weather's bad?
Man:	We have a games room and a crafts room. When the weather's rainy, some of our very talented staff members offer arts and crafts classes, for all ages.

Woman:	What fun. Do you offer any other classes or activities?
Narrator:	Before you hear the rest of the talk, you have some time to look at Questions 16 to 20 on page 220.
	Now listen and answer Questions 16 to 20.

Questions 16 to 20

Man:	We have a weekly schedule of evening activities, which anyone can attend if they choose. Every Sunday we show a film, always something that's suitable for the whole family. Monday's my favorite night because that's dessert night. Our cook prepares a variety of desserts, and we get to taste them all.
Woman:	Mmmmm. I'd like to be there for that.
Man:	Yes, it's great. We get more serious toward the middle of the week. Our discussion night is on Tuesday.
Woman:	Discussion night?
Man:	Yes, we discuss different current events, depending on what's happening that week in the news. Then on Wednesdays we have lectures. We invite different experts to talk about local history or nature topics. This is actually one of our most popular evening activities. We've found that our guests are really interested in learning about the local area.
Woman:	It sounds quite interesting.
Man:	Yes, we've had some excellent speakers. Thursday nights are totally different because that's when we play games. That's especially fun for the children. The children love Fridays, too, because that's talent show night. Everyone gets in on that, staff, guests, everyone.
Woman:	It looks like you have a lot of fun at Golden Lake Resort.
Man:	We do. And we end every week with big fun, with a dance on Saturday night.
Woman:	Now I understand a little more why Golden Lake is such a popular place for family vacations. With such a variety of activities, there's something for every member of the family there.
Man:	There is, and I hope your listeners will consider spending their next vacation with us.
Narrator:	That is the end of Section 2. You now have half a minute to check your answers.
	Now turn to Section 3 on page 203.
Narrator:	Section 3. You will hear two students talking about a class assignment about wild bird rescue and rehabilitation.
	First, you have some time to look at Questions 21 to 25 on page 203.
	As you listen to the first part of the conversation, answer Questions 21 to 25.

Questions 21 to 25

Student 1:	OK, let's go over the requirements and see what we have left to do.
Student 2:	Let's see…We have to give the professor a written summary of the information we've gathered on our topic: wild bird rescue and rehabilitation.
Student 1:	The other written thing we have to turn in is a case study of the rehabilitation of one bird. We've have the information on that already.
Student 2:	Right. All we have to do is write it up. What about charts and graphs? Do we need to include something like that?
Student 1:	I don't think so. They aren't really relevant. But we do have to turn in a list of the resources we used.
Student 2:	Naturally. What about videos? I heard some of the other students were doing that.
Student 1:	Well, I guess that must be optional, because I don't see it on the requirements list. OK. We should start planning our class presentation since that counts for half the grade.
Student 2:	We've looked at lots of sources of information, but I think our best source was the interviews we did with the wildlife rehabilitators.
Student 1:	Agreed. That and the journal articles. I think we have enough information from those two sources, for the presentation anyhow. The books we looked at weren't all that helpful.
Student 2:	I wonder if we should try to bring in some live birds for the presentation?
Student 1:	That would be too difficult, don't you think? But we have lots of photos of rehabilitated birds. We can show those.
Narrator:	Before you hear the rest of the conversation, you have some time to look at Questions 26 to 30 on page 204.
	Now listen and answer Questions 26 to 30.

Questions 26 to 30

Student 2:	Right. OK, I think we should start by talking about how to rescue a bird. Probably first we should help people understand which birds need rescuing.
Student 1:	Yeah, that's really important because a lot of times people see a baby bird that's all alone, or they find a bird sitting on the ground, and they think it needs to be rescued.
Student 2:	And usually those are just baby birds learning to fly, so we should emphasize that people should only attempt to rescue a bird that's clearly injured.
Student 1:	For certain kinds of birds, the rescuer needs to wear protective gloves, because some of those birds have sharp claws and can tear your shirt or, worse, injure your face or some other part of your body.
Student 2:	Yes. that's an important point. OK, next, let's tell people to put the injured bird in a box, a box with good air circulation. We should let

them know that a cage isn't necessary and a bag, especially a plastic one, could hurt the bird more.

Student 1: Another thing we need to say is that the best way to help the bird stay calm is not by petting it or talking to it, but by leaving it completely alone. Then people should take the bird to the bird rescue center as soon as possible.

Student 2: Right, and we should also point out that when they're driving the bird to the rescue center, it's better not to play music on the radio or talk loudly because those things just stress the bird.

Student 1: Yes, it's better just to speak quietly while you have the bird in the car. OK, we've got that part covered. Next, we should talk about what happens at the rescue center.....

Narrator: That is the end of Section 3. You now have half a minute to check your answers.

Now turn to Section 4 on page 204.

Section 4. You will hear a lecture about the Great Barrier Reef.

First, you have some time to look at Questions 31 to 33 on page 204.

Now listen carefully and answer Questions 31 to 33.

Questions 31 to 33

Lecturer: Despite its name, the Great Barrier Reef isn't just one large coral reef. Rather, it's a system of coral reefs that stretches along the east coast of Australia, covering an area of around three hundred thousand square kilometers. The Great Barrier Reef is composed of approximately three thousand individual reefs, which range in size from one hectare to more than ten thousand hectares each. In addition, around 600 islands are scattered throughout the area, particularly at the northern and southern ends. The reefs themselves are composed of over 400 different kinds of coral, the largest variety of corals found anywhere in the world.

Narrator: Before you hear the rest of the talk, you have some time to look at Questions 34 to 40 on page 205.

Now listen carefully and answer Questions 34 to 40.

Questions 34 to 40

Lecturer: Thousands of species of sea animals live in and around the reefs. All together, approximately fifteen hundred species of fish inhabit the reef area, including a number of different kinds of sharks. One of the more interesting mollusks to be found in the reefs is the giant clam. This huge shellfish can live for more than 100 years and can weigh as much as two hundred kilos. Sea mammals abound in the area, which serves as the breeding ground for certain types of whales, many of which are endangered. Over 200 species of sea and shore birds feed, roost, or nest among the reefs and islands. Many types of reptiles can also be found living among and near the reefs. Saltwater crocodiles, for example, inhabit the marshes along coastal areas. Amphibians include at least seven species of frogs inhabiting the islands of the reef.

Unfortunately, this wondrous area of the world is threatened by climate change. Rising sea temperatures have led to an effect called coral bleaching, that is, large numbers of corals dying off, especially in the shallower areas of the reef. The Great Barrier Reef Marine Park Authority is attempting to find effective ways to deal with this issue that threatens the reef. One proposed solution involves shading the reef in certain areas to help keep the surrounding water temperatures down.

Narrator: That is the end of Section 4. You now have half a minute to check your answers.

You will now have ten minutes to transfer your answers to the listening answer sheet.

If you purchased the optional book and CD set, you may listen to the CDs on a CD player or on a computer. To play a CD on your computer, insert it into the CD-ROM drive, and choose an audio media program if one doesn't launch automatically.

CD1

Track	1	Introduction
Track	2	IELTS Practice Test 1—Section 1 (Questions 1–10)
Track	3	IELTS Practice Test 1—Section 2 (Questions 11–20)
Track	4	IELTS Practice Test 1—Section 3 (Questions 21–30)
Track	5	IELTS Practice Test 1—Section 4 (Questions 31–40)
Track	6	IELTS Practice Test 2—Section 1 (Questions 1–10)
Track	7	IELTS Practice Test 2—Section 2 (Questions 11–20)
Track	8	IELTS Practice Test 2—Section 3 (Questions 21–30)
Track	9	IELTS Practice Test 2—Section 4 (Questions 31–40)
Track	10	IELTS Practice Test 3—Section 1 (Questions 1–10)
Track	11	IELTS Practice Test 3—Section 2 (Questions 11–20)
Track	12	IELTS Practice Test 3—Section 3 (Questions 21–30)
Track	13	IELTS Practice Test 3—Section 4 (Questions 31–40)

CD2

Track	1	IELTS Practice Test 4—Section 1 (Questions 1–10)
Track	2	IELTS Practice Test 4—Section 2 (Questions 11–20)
Track	3	IELTS Practice Test 4—Section 3 (Questions 21–30)
Track	4	IELTS Practice Test 4—Section 4 (Questions 31–40)
Track	5	IELTS Practice Test 5—Section 1 (Questions 1–10)
Track	6	IELTS Practice Test 5—Section 2 (Questions 11–20)
Track	7	IELTS Practice Test 5—Section 3 (Questions 21–30)
Track	8	IELTS Practice Test 5—Section 4 (Questions 31–40)
Track	9	IELTS Practice Test 6—Section 1 (Questions 1–10)
Track	10	IELTS Practice Test 6—Section 2 (Questions 11–20)
Track	11	IELTS Practice Test 6—Section 3 (Questions 21–30)
Track	12	IELTS Practice Test 6—Section 4 (Questions 31–40)